Lecture Notes in Computer Science

Vol. 117: Fundamentals of Computation Theory. Proceedings, 1981. Edited by F. Gécseg. XI, 471 pages. 1981.

Vol. 118: Mathematical Foundations of Computer Science 1981. Proceedings, 1981. Edited by J. Gruska and M. Chytil. XI, 589 pages. 1981.

Vol. 119: G. Hirst, Anaphora in Natural Language Understanding: A Survey. XIII, 128 pages. 1981.

Vol. 120: L. B. Rall, Automatic Differentiation: Techniques and Applications. VIII, 165 pages. 1981.

Vol. 121: Z. Zlatev, J. Wasniewski, and K. Schaumburg, Y12M Solution of Large and Sparse Systems of Linear Algebraic Equations. IX, 128 pages. 1981.

Vol. 122: Algorithms in Modern Mathematics and Computer Science. Proceedings, 1979. Edited by A. P. Ershov and D. E. Knuth. XI, 487 pages. 1981.

Vol. 123: Trends in Information Processing Systems. Proceedings, 1981. Edited by A. J. W. Duijvestijn and P. C. Lockemann. XI, 349 pages. 1981.

Vol. 124: W. Polak, Compiler Specification and Verification. XIII, 269 pages. 1981.

Vol. 125: Logic of Programs. Proceedings, 1979. Edited by E. Engeler. V, 245 pages. 1981.

Vol. 126: Microcomputer System Design. Proceedings, 1981. Edited by M. J. Flynn, N. R. Harris, and D. P. McCarthy. VII, 397 pages. 1982.

Voll. 127: Y. Wallach, Alternating Sequential/Parallel Processing. X, 329 pages. 1982.

Vol. 128: P. Branquart, G. Louis, P. Wodon, An Analytical Description of CHILL, the CCITT High Level Language. VI, 277 pages. 1982.

Vol. 129: B. T. Hailpern, Verifying Concurrent Processes Using Temporal Logic. VIII, 208 pages. 1982.

Vol. 130: R. Goldblatt, Axiomatising the Logic of Computer Programming. XI, 304 pages. 1982.

Vol. 131: Logics of Programs. Proceedings, 1981. Edited by D. Kozen. VI, 429 pages. 1982.

Vol. 132: Data Base Design Techniques I: Requirements and Logical Structures. Proceedings, 1978. Edited by S.B. Yao, S.B. Navathe, J.L. Weldon, and T.L. Kunii. V, 227 pages. 1982.

Vol. 133: Data Base Design Techniques II: Proceedings, 1979. Edited by S.B. Yao and T.L. Kunii. V, 229–399 pages. 1982.

Vol. 134: Program Specification. Proceedings, 1981. Edited by J. Staunstrup. IV, 426 pages. 1982.

Vol. 135: R.L. Constable, S.D. Johnson, and C.D. Eichenlaub, An Introduction to the PL/CV2 Programming Logic. X, 292 pages. 1982.

Vol. 136: Ch. M. Hoffmann, Group-Theoretic Algorithms and Graph Isomorphism. VIII, 311 pages. 1982.

Vol. 137: International Symposium on Programming. Proceedings, 1982. Edited by M. Dezani-Ciancaglini and M. Montanari. VI, 406 pages. 1982.

Vol. 138: 6th Conference on Automated Deduction. Proceedings, 1982. Edited by D.W. Loveland. VII, 389 pages. 1982.

Vol. 139: J. Uhl, S. Drossopoulou, G. Persch, G. Goos, M. Dausmann, G. Winterstein, W. Kirchgässner, An Attribute Grammar for the Semantic Analysis of Ada. IX, 511 pages. 1982.

Vol. 140: Automata, Languages and programming. Edited by M. Nielsen and E.M. Schmidt. VII, 614 pages. 1982.

Vol. 141: U. Kastens, B. Hutt, E. Zimmermann, GAG: A Practical Compiler Generator. IV, 156 pages. 1982.

Vol. 142: Problems and Methodologies in Ma... matical Software Production. Proceedings, 1980. Edited b... na and A. Murli. VII, 271 pages. 1982.

Vol. 143: Operatin... 1980. Edited by M. Maek...

Vol. ... J. Calmet. XIV, ...

Vol. 1... 1983. Edited by A.B. ... 1982.

Vol. 146 ... pment in Information Retrieval. Proceedi... by G. Salton and H.-J. Schneider. IX, 311 pages.

Vol. 147: RIMS Symposia on Software Science and Engineering. Proceedings, 1982. Edited by E. Goto, I. Nakata, K. Furukawa, R. Nakajima, and A. Yonezawa. V. 232 pages. 1983.

Vol. 148: Logics of Programs and Their Applications. Proceedings, 1980. Edited by A. Salwicki. VI, 324 pages. 1983.

Vol. 149: Cryptography. Proceedings, 1982. Edited by T. Beth. VIII, 402 pages. 1983.

Vol. 150: Enduser Systems and Their Human Factors. Proceedings, 1983. Edited by A. Blaser and M. Zoeppritz. III, 138 pages. 1983.

Vol. 151: R. Piloty, M. Barbacci, D. Borrione, D. Dietmeyer, F. Hill, and P. Skelly, CONLAN Report. XII, 174 pages. 1983.

Vol. 152: Specification and Design of Software Systems. Proceedings, 1982. Edited by E. Knuth and E. J. Neuhold. V, 152 pages. 1983.

Vol. 153: Graph-Grammars and Their Application to Computer Science. Proceedings, 1982. Edited by H. Ehrig, M. Nagl, and G. Rozenberg. VII, 452 pages. 1983.

Vol. 154: Automata, Languages and Programming. Proceedings, 1983. Edited by J. Díaz. VIII, 734 pages. 1983.

Vol. 155: The Programming Language Ada. Reference Manual. Approved 17 February 1983. American National Standards Institute, Inc. ANSI/MIL-STD-1815A-1983. IX, 331 pages. 1983.

Vol. 156: M.H. Overmars, The Design of Dynamic Data Structures. VII, 181 pages. 1983.

Vol. 157: O. Østerby, Z. Zlatev, Direct Methods for Sparse Matrices. VIII, 127 pages. 1983.

Vol. 158: Foundations of Computation Theory. Proceedings, 1983. Edited by M. Karpinski, XI, 517 pages. 1983.

Vol. 159: CAAP'83. Proceedings, 1983. Edited by G. Ausiello and M. Protasi. VI, 416 pages. 1983.

Vol. 160: The IOTA Programming System. Edited by R. Nakajima and T. Yuasa. VII, 217 pages. 1983.

Vol. 161: DIANA, An Intermediate Language for Ada. Edited by G. Goos, W.A. Wulf, A. Evans, Jr. and K.J. Butler. VII, 201 pages. 1983.

Vol. 162: Computer Algebra. Proceedings, 1983. Edited by J.A. van Hulzen. XIII, 305 pages. 1983.

Vol. 163: VLSI Engineering. Proceedings. Edited by T.L. Kunii. VIII, 308 pages. 1984.

Vol. 164: Logics of Programs. Proceedings, 1983. Edited by E. Clarke and D. Kozen. VI, 528 pages. 1984.

Vol. 165: T.F. Coleman, Large Sparse Numerical Optimization. V, 105 pages. 1984.

Vol. 166: STACS 84. Symposium of Theoretical Aspects of Computer Science. Proceedings, 1984. Edited by M. Fontet and K. Mehlhorn. VI, 338 pages. 1984.

Lecture Notes in Computer Science

Edited by G. Goos and J. Hartmanis

206

Foundations of Software Technology and Theoretical Computer Science

Fifth Conference, New Delhi, India
December 16–18, 1985
Proceedings

Edited by S. N. Maheshwari

Springer-Verlag
Berlin Heidelberg New York Tokyo

Editorial Board

D. Barstow W. Brauer P. Brinch Hansen D. Gries D. Luckham
C. Moler A. Pnueli G. Seegmüller J. Stoer N. Wirth

Editor

S. N. Maheshwari
Department of Computer Science and Engineering
Indian Institute of Technology Delhi
New Delhi 110 016, India

CR Subject Classifications (1985): B.7, D.1, D.2, F.1, F.2, F.3, F.4, H.1, H.2, I.1

ISBN 3-540-16042-6 Springer-Verlag Berlin Heidelberg New York Tokyo
ISBN 0-387-16042-6 Springer-Verlag New York Heidelberg Berlin Tokyo

This work is subject to copyright. All rights are reserved, whether the whole or part of the material is concerned, specifically those of translation, reprinting, re-use of illustrations, broadcasting, reproduction by photocopying machine or similar means, and storage in data banks. Under § 54 of the German Copyright Law where copies are made for other than private use, a fee is payable to "Verwertungsgesellschaft Wort", Munich.

© by Springer-Verlag Berlin Heidelberg 1985
Printed in Germany

Printing and binding: Beltz Offsetdruck, Hemsbach/Bergstr.
2145/3140-543210

PREFACE

The Conferences on Foundations of Software Technology and Theoretical Computer Science were conceived with the idea of creating a forum in India where Indian computer scientists working in theoretical and foundational areas could meet, present, and discuss problems of current interests with their counterparts elsewhere. The fifth conference in this series, FST&TCS 5, sponsored jointly by Indian Institute of Technology Delhi and Tata Institute of Fundamental Research, Bombay, has achieved a substantial degree of success in meeting these aims in that it has attracted 90 submissions from authors in 16 countries.

25 of these papers were selected for presentation and inclusion in the conference proceedings by the Programme Committee on the basis of reviews of each full paper by a panel of atleast three referees. The Programme Committee has always strived to provide each author with detailed comments on his/her paper. The success of this can, perhaps, be guaged by the number of authors who have acknowledged the help of the anonymous referees in improving the presentation of their papers.

Local arrangements have been overseen by the Conference Organising Committee consisting of R.K. Arora, P.C.P. Bhatt, K.K. Biswas, Anshul Kumar, A.K. Jain, S.N. Maheshwari, N. Sharma of the Department of Computer Science and Engineering at Indian Institute of Technology, Delhi, and R.K. Shyamasunder of TIFR, Bombay. The Organising Committee has been very ably assisted by Mr.M.S. Patwal and Mr.J.S. Kwatra of the Department of Computer Science and Engineering at Indian Institute of Technology, Delhi.

On behalf of the Organising Committee I gratefully acknowledge the financial support received from Indian Institute of Technology, Delhi, Tata Institute of Fundamental Research, Bombay, and Departments of Electronics and Science and Technology of Government of India.

Finally, I would like to thank all those who submitted papers and the many others who have helped in different ways.

S.N. Maheshwari

Conference Advisory Committee

A Chandra, IBM Res
B Chandrasekaran, Ohio State
S Crespi-Reghizzi, Milan
D Gries, Cornell
A Joshi, Pennsylvania
U Montanari, Pisa
A Nakamura, Hiroshima
R Narasimhan, NCSDCT/TIFR
J Nievergelt, North Carolina
M Nivat, Paris
R Parikh, New York
S Rao Kosaraju, Johns Hopkins
B Reusch, Dortmund
S Sahni, Minnesota
R Sethi, AT&T Bell Labs
P S Thiagarajan, Aarhus
W A Wulf, Tartan Labs

Programme Committee

M Joseph, TIFR/Warwick
K B Lakshmanan, IIT Madras
S N Maheshwari, IIT Delhi
S L Mehndiratta, IIT Bombay
K V Nori, Tata RDDC
S V Rangaswamy, IISc. Bangalore
R K Shyamasundar, TIFR
R Siromoney, Madras Christian College
C E Veni Madhavan, IISc. Bangalore

LIST OF REVIEWERS

The Programme Committee would like to thank the following reviewers for their comments on papers submitted for the Conference.

V Agarwal, McGill
A Aggarwal, IBM Yorktown Heights
S Aggarwal, AT&T Bell Labs
K R Apt, IBM Yorktown Heights
S Arun Kumar, IIT Bombay
S Arun-Kumar, TIFR
E Astesiano, Genova
R J Back, Abo Akademi
A Bagchi, IIM Calcutta
C Bajaj, Purdue
G Barua, IIT Kanpur
A Bernstein, SUNY at Stony Brook
E Best, GMD, St Augustin
M Beynon, Warwick
B B Bhattacharya, Nebraska
G P Bhattacherjee, IIT Kharagpur
J Cheriyan, IIT Delhi
G Costa, Genova
S Crespi-Reghizzi, Milan PolyTech
D Crookes, Queens U of Belfast
S K Debray, SUNY at Stony Brook
N Deo, Washington State
R G Dromey, Wollongong
P Dublish, IIT Delhi
A Finkel, Paris-Sud
N Francez, Technion, Haifa
G Frederickson, Purdue
C Frougny, LITP, Paris
Z Galil, Columbia
J H Gallier, Pennsylvania
J von zur Gathen, Toronto
S K Ghosh, TIFR
G Goos, GMD, Karlsruhe
P Gupta, SAC, Ahmedabad
M C Henson, Essex
S Jajodia, Naval Res Lab
A K Joshi, Pennsylvania
G Kahn, INRIA Sophia Antipolis
K Kakehi, Rikkyo
N C Kalra, IIT Delhi
R Kannan, Carnegie-Mellon
S Kapoor, Illinois
D Kapur, GE Research Labs
J Karhumaki, Waterloo
C Kintala, AT&T Bell Labs
S Rao Kosaraju, Johns Hopkins
M S Krishnamoorthy, RPI, Troy
C Kruskal, Illinois
M Kudlek, Hamburg
R Kuiper, Manchester
A Kumar, IIT Delhi
S Kumar, IIT Delhi
S Lakshmivarahan, Oklahoma
C Levcopoulos, Linkoping
A Lingas, Linkoping
K Lodaya, TIFR
V M Malhotra, IIT Kanpur
A D McGettrick, Strathclyde
R M McKeag, Queens U of Belfast
A Moitra, Cornell
U Montanari, Pisa
S P Mudur, NCSDCT, Bombay
B N S Murthy, IIT Delhi
C R Muthukrishnan, IIT Madras
A Nakamura, Hiroshima
K T Narayana, Pennsylvania State
F Nielson, Aalborg
J F Nilsson, Tech U of Denmark
R Parikh, City U of New York
L M Patnaik, IISc, Banglore
R H Perrott, CERN, Geneva
G Persch, GMD, Karlsruhe
A Pnueli, Weizmann Inst
B Poizat, P&M Curie
V Ramachandran, Illinois
A Ravichandran, TIFR
A P Ravn, Tech U of Denmark
M Regnier, INRIA, Rocquencourt
R Sangal, IIT Kanpur
F de Santis, Salerno
P Shankar, IISc, Banglore
K Sikdar, ISI, Calcutta
M K Sinha, NCSDCT, Bombay
J L A van de Snepscheut, Groningen
K G Subramanian, Madras Chr. Coll.
P S Thiagarajan, Arhus
V G Tikekar, IISc, Banglore
P Tiwari, Illinois
H Vahia, INRIA, Rocquencourt
P M Vaidya, Illinois
V Vaishnavi, Georgia State
P J Varman, Rice
V V Vazirani, Cornell
P A S Veloso, PUC, Rio de Jeneiro
T M Vijayaraman, NCSDCT, Bombay
P R Vishnubhotla, Ohio State
P J L Wallis, Bath

TABLE OF CONTENTS

*Short Presentation

THE MATHEMATICS OF PROGRAMMING

C.A.R. Hoare

Summary

I hold the principle that the construction of computer programs is a mathematical activity like the solution of differential equations. Programs can be derived from their specifications by mathematical insight calculation and proof, using algebraic laws as simple and elegant as those of elementary arithmetic.

1. Principles

I start with four basic principles;

1. Computers are mathematical machines. Every aspect of their behaviour can be defined with mathematical precision, and every detail can be deduced from this definition with mathematical certainty by the laws of pure logic.

2. Computer programs are mathematical expressions. They describe with unprecedented precision and in every minutest detail the behaviour, intended or unintended, of the computer on which they are executed.

3. A programming language is a mathematical theory. It includes concepts, notations, definitions, axioms and theorems, which help a programmer to develop a program which meets its specification, and to prove that it does so.

4. Programming is a mathematical activity. Like other branches of applied mathematics and engineering, its successful practice requires determined and meticulous application of traditional methods of mathematical understanding and proof.

These are general philosophical and moral principles, and I hold them to be self-evident - which is just as well, because all the real evidence is against them. Nothing seems actually as I have described it, neither computers nor programs nor programming languages nor even programmers.

Digital computers of the present day are very complicated and rather poorly defined. As a result, it is usually impractical to reason logically about their behaviour. Sometimes the only way of finding out what they will do is by experiment. Such experiments are certainly not mathematics. Unfortunately, they are not even science, because it is impossible to generalise from their results or to publish them for the benefit of other scientists.

Many computer programs of the present day are of inordinate size - many thousands of pages of closely printed text. Mathematics has no tradition of dealing with expressions on this scale. Normal methods of calculation and proof seem wholly impractical to conduct by hand; and fifteen years of experience suggest that computer assistance can only make matters worse.

Programming languages of the present day are even more complicated than the programs which they are used to write and the computers on which they are intended to run. Valiant research has been directed to formulate mathematical definitions of these standard languages. But the size and complexity of the definitions make it impractical to derive useful theorems, or to prove relevant properties of programs.

Finally, many programmers of the present day have been educated in ignorance and fear of mathematics. Of course, there are many programmers who are mathematical graduates, and have acquired a good grasp of topology, calculus and group theory. But it never occurs to them to take advantage of their mathematical skills to define a programming problem and search for its solution.

Our present failure to recognise and use mathematics as the basis for a discipline of programming has a number of notorious consequences. They are the same consequences as would result from a similar neglect of mathematics in the drawing of maps, marine navigation, bridge building, air traffic control, and the exploration of space. In the older branches of science and engineering, the relevant physical and mathematical knowledge is embodied in a number of equations, formulae and laws, many of which are simple enough to be taught to children at school. The practicing scientist or engineer will be intimately familiar with the laws, and will use them explicitly or even instinctively to find solutions to otherwise intractable problems.

What then are the laws of programming, which help the programmer to control the complexity of his tasks? Many programmers would be hard pressed to name a single law. Those who have suffered from bad programs might claim that programmers are such an undisciplined crew that even if they know any laws, they would instantly violate them.

2. Arithmetic

To refute this malicious accusation, I shall now show by example that the laws of programming are as simple and as obvious and as useful as the laws you find in any other branch of mathematics, for example, in elementary arithmentic. Consider multiplication of numbers. Figure 1 shows some of the relevant algebraic laus; multiplication is associative, its identity (or unit) is the number 1, it has the number 0 as its zero or fixed point, and finally it distributes through addition. Figure 2 gives the defining properties of an ordering relation like comparison of the magnitude of numbers. Such an order is reflexive, antisymmetric and transitive. These laws hold also for a partial ordering such as the inclusion relation between sets.

Figure 3 describes the properties of the least upper bound or lub of an ordering, denoted by the traditional cup notation. These laws are equally valid, whether the lub is the union of two sets or the greater of two numbers. The first law states the fundamental property that the lub is an upper bound on both its operands, and it is the least of all such bounds. The remaining laws are derived from the fundamental law by the properties of ordering. They state that the lub operator is idempotent, symmetric and associative. Finally, the partial ordering can itself be defined in terms of lub.

Laws of multiplication

$$x \times (y \times z) = (x \times y) \times z$$

$$x \times 1 = 1 \times x = x$$

$$x \times 0 = 0 \times x = 0$$

$$(x + y) \times z = (x \times z) + (y \times z)$$

FIGURE 1

Partial Ordering

$$x \subseteq x$$

$$x \subseteq y \wedge y \subseteq x \Rightarrow x = y$$

$$x \subseteq y \wedge y \subseteq z \Rightarrow x \subseteq z$$

Figure 2

Least upper bound (lub)

$$(x \cup y) \subseteq z \Leftrightarrow x \subseteq z \wedge y \subseteq z$$

$$x \cup x = x$$

$$x \cup y = y \cup x$$

$$x \cup (y \cup z) = (x \cup y) \cup z$$

$$x \subseteq y \Leftrightarrow x \cup y = y$$

Figure 3

Figure 4 shows some additonal laws which hold for natural numbers or non-negative integers. Here, the least upper bound of two numbers is simply the greater of them. If you multiply the greater of x or y by z, you get the same result as multiplying both x and y by z, and then choosing the greater of the products. This fact is clearly and conveniently stated in the laws of distribution of multiplication through the least upper bound. An immediate consequence of these laws is that multiplication is a monotonic operator, in the sense that it preserves the ordering of its operands. If you decrease either factor the product can only decrease too, as stated in the last law of Figure 4.

In the arithmetic of natural numbers, multiplication does not in general have an exact inverse. Instead, we commonly use a quotient operator - which approximates the true result from below. It is obtained from normal integer division by just ignoring the remainder. Thus the result of dividing y by non-zero z is the largest number such that when you multiply it back by z the result still does not exceed y. This fact is clearly stated in the first law of Figure 5. The same fact is stated in the second law, which I will call the fundamental law of division.

Other properties of division can be easily proved from the fundamental law. For example, the third law of Figure 5 is proved by substituting y divided by z for x in the first law. The last law states that division by a product is the same as successive division by its two factors. A proof is given in Figure 6. The proof shows that any w which is bounded by the left hand side of the equation is bounded also by the right hand side, and vice versa; it follows by the properties of partial ordering that the two sides are equal. The only laws used in the main part of the proof are the associativity of muliplication and the funadmental law of division, which is used three times to move a divisor from one side of the inequality to the other.

3. Programs

This selection of the laws of elementary arithmetic has been made to ensure that computer programs satisfy exactly the same laws. I will write programs in a mathematical notation first introduced by Edsger W. Dijkstra, and summarised in Figure 7. The SKIP command terminates, but does nothing else. In particular, it leaves the values of all variables unchanged.

The ABORT command is at the other extreme. It may do anything whatsoever, or it may fail to do anything whatsoever. In particular it may fail to terminate. It describes the behaviour of a computer that has gone wrong or a program that has run wild, perhaps by corrupting its own code. ABORT is not a command you would ever wantto write; in fact you should take pains to prove that you have not done so by accident. In such proofs, and in the general mathematics of programming, the ABORT command plays a valuable role. However much we dislike it, there is also abundant empirical evidence for its existence.

The sequential composition of two commands x and y is written (x;y). This starts behaving as x. If and when x terminates, y starts in an initial state equal to the

Natural Numbers

$x \cup y$ = the greater of x and y

$$(x \cup y) \times z = (x \times z) \cup (y \times z)$$

$$z \times (x \cup y) = (z \times x) \cup (z \times y)$$

$$w \subseteq y \wedge x \subseteq z \Longrightarrow w \times x \subseteq y \times z$$

Figure 4

Quotient of Natural Numbers

if $z \neq 0$

$$y \div z = \max \{x \mid x \times z \subseteq y\}$$

$$x \subseteq (y \div z) \Longleftrightarrow (x \times z) \subseteq y$$

$$(y \div z) \times z \subseteq y$$

$$x \div (y \times z) = (x \div z) \div y$$

Figure 5

A Proof

given $y \neq 0$ and $z \neq 0$

$w \subseteq \boldsymbol{x} \div (y \times z)$

$\Leftrightarrow \quad w \times (y \times z) \subseteq \boldsymbol{x}$

$\Leftrightarrow \quad (w \times y) \times z \subseteq \boldsymbol{x}$

$\Leftrightarrow \quad w \times y \subseteq \boldsymbol{x} \div z$

$\Leftrightarrow \quad w \subseteq (\boldsymbol{x} \div z) \div y$

Figure 6

Commands

SKIP

does nothing, but terminates

ABORT

does anything, and may fail to terminate

$\boldsymbol{x}\ ;\ y$

does $\boldsymbol{x}$ first; when $\boldsymbol{x}$ terminates it does y

Figure 7

final state of x. (x;y) terminates when y terminates, but fails to terminate if either x or y fails.

The basic algebraic laws for sequential composition are given in Figure 8. The first law is an associative law, stating that if three commands are combined sequentially, it does not matter in which way they are bracketed. The second law gives SKIP as the unit of composition. It states that a command x remains unchanged when it is either preceded or followed by SKIP. The third law gives ABORT as a zero for composition. You cannot recover from abortion by preceding it or following it by any other command. Note that the algebraic laws for composition are the same as those for multiplication of numbers.

The next important feature of programming is the conditional. Let b be a logical expression which in all circumstances evaluates to a logical value true or false. If x and y are commands, I introduce the notation

$x \triangleleft b \triangleright y$ (x if b else y)

to denote the conditional command. It is obeyed by first evaluating the logical expression b. If the result is true, then the command x is obeyed and y is omitted. If the result is false, then y is obeyed an x is omitted. This informal description is summarised in the first law of Figure 9.

I now regard the if symbol $\triangleleft$ and the else symbol $\triangleright$ as brackets surrounding the logical expression b, so that the notation

$\triangleleft b \triangleright$

appears as an infix operator between two commands. The reason for this novel notation is that it simplifies expression and use of the relevant algebraic laws. For example, the conditional $\triangleleft b \triangleright$ is idempotent, and associative, and it distributes through c for any logical expression c. Finally, sequential composition distributes leftward (but not rightward) through a conditional.

Figure 10 shows a picture of the conditional as a structured flowchart. Such pictures are useful in first presenting a new idea, and in committing it to memory. Their role is similar to that of the picture of an apple or a zebra in a child's alphabet book. But excessive reliance on pictures continued into later life would not be regarded as a good qualification for one seeking a career as a professional author.

Unfortunately there exist problems which are so widespread and so severe that even flowcharts must be recommended and actually welcomed as their solution. Figure 11 shows how we have taught a generation of schoolchildren to express the structure of a conditional in BASIC. Programming in BASIC is like doing arithmetic with Roman numerals. To start with, for simple tasks like addition and subtraction, Roman numerals are much easier than Arabic, because you do not first have to learn one hundred facts about addition and subtraction of the ten digits, and you avoid the complications of carry and borrow. Roman numerals have another advantage - they are easier to carve on stone.

The disadvantages of Roman numerals become apparent only in more complex tasks

Laws for composition

$$x;(y;z) = (x;y);z$$

$$\mathrm{SKIP};x = x = x;\mathrm{SKIP}$$

$$\mathrm{ABORT};x = \mathrm{ABORT} = x;\mathrm{ABORT}$$

Figure 8

Conditional

$$(x \triangleleft \mathrm{true} \triangleright y) = x = (y \triangleleft \mathrm{false} \triangleright x)$$

$$(x \triangleleft b \triangleright x) = x$$

$$x \triangleleft b \triangleright (y \triangleleft b \triangleright z) = (x \triangleleft b \triangleright y) \triangleleft b \triangleright z$$

$$= x \triangleleft b \triangleright z$$

$$x \triangleleft b \triangleright (y \triangleleft c \triangleright z) = (x \triangleleft b \triangleright y) \triangleleft c \triangleright (x \triangleleft b \triangleright z)$$

$$(x \triangleleft b \triangleright y);z = (x;z) \triangleleft b \triangleright (y;z)$$

Figure 9

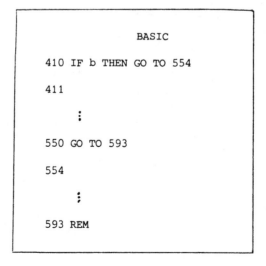

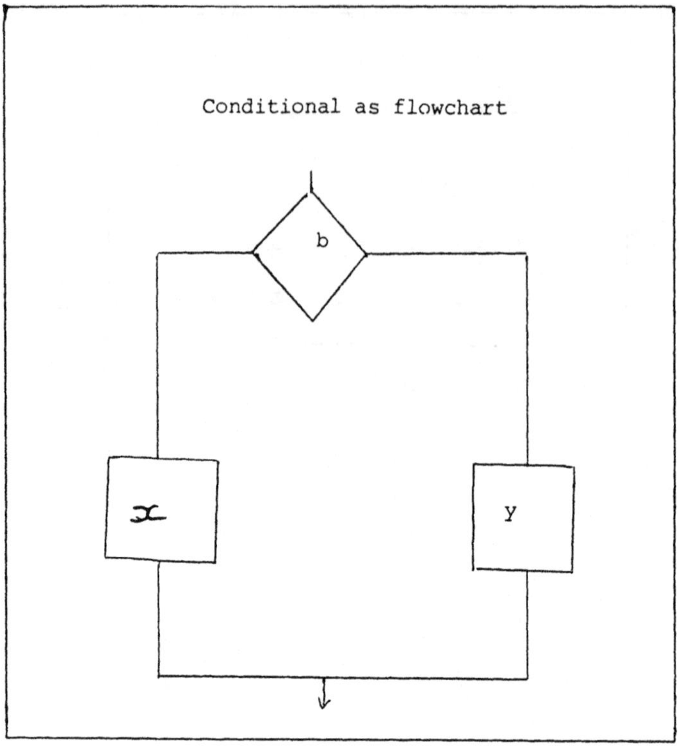

Figure 10

BASIC

```
410 IF b THEN GO TO 554
411
      ⋮
550 GO TO 593
554
      ⋮
593 REM
```

Figure 11

such as multiplication. Even worse is the division of Roman numerals, for which the only known technique is trial and error. You have to guess the solution, test it by multiplying it by the divisor and comparing the dividend, and make a new guess if it was wrong. This is exactly the way we teach schoolchildren to write and debug their Basic programs. Compared with that, division of Roman numerals is much easier, because the fundamental law of division tells you whether the new guess should be smaller or greater than the last.

Thankfully, Arabic numerals have displaced Roman ones, and the effective algorithm for long division has replaced the Roman method of trial and error by an orderly process of calculation; when carefully executed, it leads invariably to the correct solution. In cases of doubt, the answer can be checked by multiplication; but if this discovers an error, you do not try to debug the digits of your answer by trial and error. You go back over the steps of the calculation, and correct them - or else start again.

4. Abstraction

I now have great pleasure in introducing the concept of an abstract command. An abstract command is one that specifies general properties of the desired behaviour of a computer, without prescribing exactly how it is to be achieved. A simple example of an abstract command is the union $(x \cup y)$ of two commands x and y, which may themselves be abstract or concrete. The union command may be obeyed by obeying either of its operands. The choice between them is left open, and may be made later by the programmer, by a compiler, or even by some device in a machine executing the program. For this reason, abstract programs are sometimes called non-deterministic.

The properties of the union operator (Figure 12) are exactly what you would expect. A command to do x or x leaves you no choice but to do x. To do x or y gives you the same choice as y or x. And in a choice between three alternatives, it does not matter in what order you choose between one of them and a subsequent choice between the other two. And finally ABORT is the abstract program which allows any behaviour whatsoever. Thus to allow further choice does not alter the range of options permitted by ABORT.

The introduction of abstraction permits the definition of a useful ordering relation between concrete and abstract commands. If y is an abstract command specifying some desired effect, and x is a concrete command which achieves that effect, we say that x satisfies y, or

$$x \subseteq y$$

The command x may also be abstract, in which case the ordering relation means that x is the same as y, or it is more specific, concrete or deterministic than y. In either case, x meets the specification y, because every possible execution of x is described and therefore allowed by y. As stated in Figure 13, the satisfaction relation is a partial order, and the union is its least upper bound.

Abstraction

$x \cup y$ behaves like x or y

$x \cup x = x$

$x \cup y = y \cup x$

$x \cup (y \cup z) = (x \cup y) \cup z$

$x \cup \text{ABORT} = \text{ABORT}$

Figure 12

Satisfaction

$x \subseteq y \Leftrightarrow x \cup y = y$

$\Leftrightarrow x$ satisfies specification y

$x \subseteq x$

$x \subseteq y \wedge y \subseteq x \Rightarrow x = y$

$x \subseteq y \wedge y \subseteq z \Rightarrow x \subseteq z$

$(x \cup y) \subseteq z \Rightarrow x \subseteq z \wedge y \subseteq z$

Figure 13

Abstract commands may be combined by all the same operators as concrete commands. Figure 14 shows that sequential composition distributes through abstract choice in both directions. It follows that composition is monotonic in both its arguments. In fact all the operators of a programming language are monotonic in this sense. There are good theoretical reasons for this; and there are also very beneficial consequences for practical solution of programming problems, as shown in the next section.

5. Refinement

The task of a programmer can now be described as a problem in mathematics. We start with an abstract description of what we want the computer to do, carefully checking that it is an accurate description of the right problem. This is often the most difficult part of our task, and requires the most powerful tools. So in the specification y, we take advantage of the full range of concepts and notations of mathematics, including even concepts which cannot be represented on a computer and operations which could never be implemented in a programming language.

Turning now to the second part of the programmers task, we must find some program x which solves the inequation

$$x \subseteq y$$

where y is the specification of the program.Mathematics provides many formulae and methods for the solution of equations and inequations, form linear and quadratic to differential and integral. In all cases, the derivation of a solution may use the full power of mathematics, but the solution itself must be expressed as a formula in some more restricted notation. And so it is in programming, where the eventual solution must be expressed in the restricted notations of an implemented programming language.

The most powerful general method of solving a complicated problem is to split it into simpler subproblems, which can then be solved independently. The same method can be applied again to the subproblems until they are simple enough to solve directly by some other more direct method. In the case of computer programming, this is often called top-down development or stepwise refinement; and it is illustrated in Figure 15. We start with the problem of finding some command x which meets the specification y. The first step requires the insight to split this into two subproblems, and the skill to specify them as abstract programs v and w. Before proceeding further, we prove the correctness of our design so far by showing that the sequential composition of v and w meets the original specification y, or more formally

$$v;w \subseteq y$$

Now these two subproblems v and w may be solved sequentially or concurrently by a single programmer or by two teams of programmers, according to the size of the task. When both subproblems are solved, we will have two commands t and u, expressed in the restricted notations of our chosen programming language, each meeting their respective specifications.

$$t \subseteq v$$

$$\text{and } u \subseteq w$$

Sequential Composition

$$(x \cup y);z = (x;z) \cup (y;z)$$

$$z;(x \cup y) = (z;x) \cup (z;y)$$

$$w \subseteq y \wedge x \subseteq z \Rightarrow w;x \subseteq y;z$$

Figure 14

Topdown Development

Problem: find x such that $x \subseteq y$

Step 1: find v,w such that $v;w \subseteq y$

Step 2a: find t such that $t \subseteq v$

Step 2b: find u such that $u \subseteq w$

Step 3: deliver t;u

Proof: $t;u \subseteq v;w$; monotonic,(2)

$\therefore$ $t;u \subseteq y$ $\subseteq$ transitive,(1)

Figure 15

Now all that remains is to deliver their sequential composition (t;u) as a solution to the original problem y. Correctness of the solution has been established not by the traditional laborious and ultimately unsound method of integration testing and debugging after the components have been constructed; but rather by a mathematical proof, which was completed even before their construction began.

The validity of the general method of top-down development depends on transitivity of the abstraction ordering and monotonicity of the composition operator. The method can therefore be applied to any other operator of a concrete programming language. The method has justifiably been treated at length in many learned articles and books. It is characteristic of the simplifying power of mathematics that the whole method can be described, together with a proof of its validity, within the seven short lines of Figure 15.

I have drawn an analogy between multiplication of natural numbers and sequential composition in programming. This analogy extends even to division. As with division of natural numbers, the quotient of two commands is not an exact inverse. However, it is defined by the same fundamental law, as shown in Figure 16. The quotient of y by z is the most abstract specification of a program x, which when followed by z is sure to meet the specification y. As a consequence, the quotient itself, when followed by z meets the original specification. And finally, when the divisor is the composition of two commands, the quotient may be calculated by successive division by these two commands in the reverse order.

In factorisation of large numbers, division obviously saves a lot of effort, because you only have to guess one of the factors, and obtain the other one by a mere calculation. The division of commands offers the same advantages in the factorisation of programming problems. It replaces the guesswork required in discovering two simpler subtasks by the discovery of only the second of them, as shown in Figure 17. Furthermore the proof obligation in step 1 has been eliminated It is replaced by a formal calculation of the weakest specification which must be met by the first operand of the composition. Reduction of guesswork and proof to mere calculation is the way in which a mathematician simplifies his own tasks, as well as those of the user of mathematics - the scientist, the engineer, and now also the programmer.

The quotient operator for commands was discovered in a slightly restricted form by Edsger W. Dijkstra, who called it the weakest precondition. It is one of the most effective known methods for the design and development of correct algorithms as shown in numerous examples by David Gries. The relevant references are given in Figure 18.

6. Program maintenance

In my description of the task of a programmer, I have concentrated on the more glamorous part of that task, that of specifying, designing and writing new programs. But a significant proportion of a programmer's professional life is spent on making changes to old programs. Some of these changes are necessitated by the discovery of errors, and some by changes in the specification of the desired behaviour of the

Quotient of commands

$$(x\,;z) \subseteq y \iff x \subseteq (y \div z)$$

$$(y \div z);z \subseteq y$$

$$x \div (y;z) = (x \div z) \div y$$

Figure 16

Development by Quotient

Problem: find x such that $x \subseteq y$

Step 1: choose suitable z

Step 2a: find t such that $t \subseteq y \div z$

Step 2b: find u such that $u \subseteq z$

Step 3: deliver t;u

Proof: $t;u \subseteq (y \div z);z$;monotonic

$(y \div z);z \subseteq y$ property of $\div$

$\therefore\ t;u \subseteq y$ $\subseteq$ transitive

Figure 17

program. The program and the specification are so large that it is not practical to write a new program from scratch; so when only a small part of the specification is changed, it is hoped that only a small part of the program will need changing to meet the changed specification

Of course, such a hope is not always justified. Consider the analogy of the division of numbers. A small change in the least significant digits of the dividend results in a small change in the least significant digits of the quotient, and can be achieved by a small amount of recalculation. But a small change in the most significant digit of either operand requires the calculation to be started again, and leads to a completely different result. In the case of programs it is often very difficult to know which small changes in a large specification will require major changes to the program.

It is therefore one of the most important duties of the original programmer to determine which parts of a specification are most likely to be changed, and choose a program design in which a change to one part of the specification requires a change to only one part of the program. The programmer should then document the program with instructions on how to carry out the change. This too can be done in a rigorous mathematical fashion (Figure 19). Let y be that part of a complete specification g(y) which is liable to change. Let x be that command in a big program f(x) which is designed to change when y changes. To make this change easy, we need to define how the specification of x changes as a function of the changeable y.

The problem of program maintenance is most easily solved when the structure of the program f is the same as the structure of the specification g, because in this case, it is sufficient to ensure that the modified component meets the modified specification.

But it is not always possible to preserve the structure of a specification in the design of a program. This is because a specification is often most clearly structured with the aid of such operators as negation and conjunction, which are not available in an implemented programming language. Nevertheless, mathematics can often help. If the program f has an approximate inverse, (f^{-1}), defined in the same way as for the quotient, it is possible to calculate the proof obligation of the modified program as

$$x \subseteq f^{-1}(g(y'))$$

Of course, if f is a program of a million lines, a blind calculation of its inverse may well be impractical. This is a problem that should be considered when the program is first designed.

7. Conclusion

I have given only a very small selection of the laws which govern the commands of a computer programming language. I have shown two ways in which these laws can be used to derive solutions for practical programming problems. I have also pointed out how little use is made of mathematics in current programming practice. It is

References

$y \div z \simeq wp(z,y)$

A Discipline of Programming

E.W. Dijkstra Prentice Hall 1976

The Science of Programming

D. Gries Springer 1981

Figure 18

Maintenance

Given: $f(x) \subseteq g(y)$

Problem: find x' such that $f(x') \subseteq g(y')$

Case 1: $f = g$

solve $x' \subseteq y'$

Case 2: f has approximate inverse f^{-1}

solve $x' \subseteq f^{-1}(g(y'))$

Figure 19

likely that a more mathematical aproach will mitigate some of the notorious outstanding deficiencies in computer programs. There remains a substantial research obligation to find new and simple mathematical methods, and an educational obligation to teach programmers how to use them.

Concurrent Programming Using Actors: Exploiting Large-Scale Parallelism

Gul Agha

Carl Hewitt

The Artificial Intelligence Laboratory

Massachusetts Institute of Technology

Cambridge, Massachusetts 02139

August 16, 1985

Abstract

We argue that the ability to model shared objects with changing local states, dynamic reconfigurability, and inherent parallelism are desirable properties of any model of concurrency. The *actor model* addresses these issues in a uniform framework. This paper briefly describes the concurrent programming language *Act3* and the principles that have guided its development. *Act3* advances the state of the art in programming languages by combining the advantages of object-oriented programming with those of functional programming. We also discuss considerations relevant to large-scale parallelism in the context of *open systems*, and define an abstract model which establishes the equivalence of systems defined by actor programs.

---

*The authors acknowledge helpful comments from Carl Manning and Tom Reinhardt. The work described in this paper was supported by a grant from the System Development Foundation.

1 Background

The theory of concurrent programming languages has been an exciting area of research in the last decade. Although no consensus has emerged on a single model of concurrency, many advances have been made in the development of various contending models. There have also been some consistent paradigm shifts in the approach to concurrency; an interesting discussion of such paradigm shifts may be found in [Pratt 83].

The actor model of computation has developed contemporaneously in the last decade along with other models based on Petri Nets, the λ-calculus, and communicating sequential processes. There has been a great deal of useful cross fertilization between the various schools of thought in addressing the very difficult issues of concurrent systems. Over the years Hoare, Kahn, MacQueen, Milner, Petri, Plotkin, and Pratt, have provided fruitful interaction on the development of the actor model.

Landin [65] first showed how *Algol 60* programs could be represented in applicative-order λ-calculus. Kahn-MacQueen [77] developed this area further by expanding on the construct of *streams* which captured functional systems. Brock-Ackerman [77] extended the Kahn-MacQueen model with the addition of inter-stream ordering information in order to make it more suitable for concurrent computation. Pratt [82] generalizes the functional model by developing a theory of processes in terms of sets of partially ordered multisets (*pomsets*) of events. Each pomset in Pratt's *Process Model* represents a *trace* of events. Pratt's model satisfies several properties desirable in any model of concurrent computation. For example, the model does not assume the existence of global states: a trace is only a partial order of events. Thus the model is compatible with the laws of parallel processing formulated in [Hewitt and Baker 77] and shown to be consistent in [Clinger 81].

On the practical side, McCarthy [59] first made functional programming available by developing Lisp. The standard dialect of Lisp now incorporates lexical scoping and upward closures which makes the semantics simpler and programming modular [Steele, *et al* 84]. *Act3* generalizes the lexical scoping and upward closures of Lisp and in the context of parallel systems.

Hoare [78] proposed a language for concurrency, called *CSP*, based on sequential processes. *CSP*, like *Act3*, enhances modularity by not permitting any shared variable between processes; instead, communication is the primitive by which processes may affect each other. At a more theoretical level, Milner [80] has proposed the *Calculus of Concurrent Systems (CCS)*. One of the nice properties of *CCS* is its elegant algebraic operations. In both *CSP* and *CCS* communication is synchronous and resembles a handshake. In contradistinction, the actor model postulates the existence of a mail system which buffers communication.

The plan of this paper is as follows: the first section outlines the actor model. The second section describes the *Act3* language. The final section discusses the general principles of open systems and there relation to the actor model.

2 The Actor Model

In this section we motivate the primitives of the actor model. We will outline the basic issues and describe a set of minimal constructs necessary for an actor language.

2.1 Foundational Issues

A number of difficult open problems and foundational issues in the design of programming languages for concurrent systems merit attention. We consider the following three significant:

1. **Shared Resources.** The programming model must deal with the problem of shared resources which may change their internal state. A simple example of such an object in a concurrent environment is a shared bank

account. Purely functional systems are incapable of implementing such objects [Hewitt, *et al* 84].

2. **Dynamic Reconfigurability.** The programming model must deal with the creation of new objects in the evolution of the system. In particular, to accommodate the creation of new objects, there must be a mechanism for communicating the existence of such new objects (or processes) to already existing ones. Thus when a bank creates a new account, it should be able to inform its book-keeping process of the existence of such an account. This requirement is violated in systems such as *CSP* and *dataflow* [Brock 83] where interconnection topology of processes is static.

3. **Inherent Parallelism.** The programming model should exhibit inherent parallelism in the sense that the amount of available concurrency should be determined as much as possible from the structure of programs written. It should not be necessary to do extensive reasoning to uncover implicit parallelism that is hidden by inappropriate language constructs. In particular, the assignment command is a bottleneck inherited from the von Neumann architecture. Assignment commands tie the statements in the body of a code in such a way that only through flow analysis is it possible to determine which statements can be executed concurrently. Functional Programming has the advantage of being inherently parallel because it allows the possibility of concurrent execution of all subexpressions in a program [Backus 78].

The object-based and functional, λ-calculus-based languages represent two of the most important schools of thought in programming language theory today. As the above discussion suggests, both have a certain advantages. *Act3* attempts to integrate both in a manner that preserves some of their attractive features.

2.2 Basic Constructs

The actor abstraction has been developed to exploit message-passing as a basis for concurrent computation [Hewitt 77; Hewitt and Baker 77]. The actor construct has been formalized by providing a mathematical definition for the behavior of an actor systems [Agha 85]. Essentially, an actor is a computational agent which carries out its actions in response to accepting a communication. The actions it may carry out are:

- Send communications to itself or to other actors.
- Create more actors.
- Specify the *replacement behavior*.

In order to send a communication, the sender must specify a mail address, called the *target*. The *mail system* buffers the communication until it can be delivered to the target. However, the order in which the communications are delivered is nondeterministic. The buffering of communications has the consequence that actor languages support recursion. In languages relying on synchronous communication, any recursive procedure immediately leads to *deadlock*.

All actors have their own (unique) mail addresses which may be communicated to other actors just as any other value. Thus mail addresses provide a simple mechanism for *dynamically reconfiguring* a system of actors. The only way to affect the behavior of an actor is to send it a communication. When an actor accepts a communication, it carries out the actions specified by its behavior; one of these actions is to specify a *replacement actor* which will then accept the next communication received at the mail address.

Two important observations need to be made about replacement. First, replacement implements local state change while preserving *referential transparency* of the identifiers used in a program. An identifier for an object always denotes that object although the behavior associated with the object may be subject to change. In particular, the code for an actor does not contain spurious variables to which different values are assigned (see [Stoy 77] for a thorough discussion of referential transparency). Second, since the computation of a replacement actor is an action which may be carried out concurrently with other actions performed by an actor, the replacement process is intrinsically concurrent. The replacement actor cannot affect the behavior of the replaced actor by changing the local state of that actor.

The net result of these properties of replacement actors is that computation in actor systems can be speeded-up by *pipelining* the actions to be performed. As soon as the replacement actor has been computed, the next communication can be processed even as other actions implied by the current communication are still being carried out. In actor-based architectures, the only constraints on the speed of execution stem from the logical dependencies in the computation and the limitations imposed by the hardware resources. In von Neumann architectures, the data dependencies caused by assignments to a global store restrict the degree of pipelining (in the form of instruction pre-fetching) that can be realized [Hwang and Briggs 84].

All actors in a system carry out their actions concurrently. In particular, this has the implication that message-passing can be used to spawn concurrency: An actor, in response to a communication, may send several communications to other actors. The creation of new actors also increases the amount of parallelism feasible in a system. Specifically, *continuations*, in the sense of the semantics of λ-calculus, can be incorporated as first-class objects. The dynamic creation of *customers* in actor systems (discussed later) provides a parallel analogue to such continuations.

2.3 Transitions on Configurations

To describe an actor system, we must specify the behaviors associated with the mail addresses internal to the system. This is done by specifying a *local states function* which basically gives us the behavior of each mail address (i.e., its response to the next communication it receives). We must also specify the communications that have been sent but not accepted. Such communications are contained in *tasks* that simultaneously specify the target of the communication. A *configuration* is an instantaneous snapshot of an actor system from some viewpoint. Each configuration has the following parts:

- A *local states function* which basically gives us the behavior of a mail address. The actors whose behaviors are specified by the local states function are elements of the *population*.
- A set of *unprocessed tasks* for communications which have been sent but not yet accepted.
- A subset of the population, called *receptionist* actors, which may receive communications from actors outside the configuration. The set of receptionists can not be mechanically determined from the local states function of a configuration: they must be specified based on our knowledge of the larger environment.
- A set of *external actors* whose behavior is not specified by the local states function, but to whom communications may be sent.

A fundamental transition relation on configurations can be defined by applying the behavior function of the target of some unprocessed task to the communication contained in that task. Given the nondeterminism in the *arrival order* of communications, this transition relation represents the different possible paths a computation may take. The processing of communications may, of course, overlap in time. We represent only the acceptance of a communication as an event. Different transition paths may be observed by different view-points, provided that these paths are consistent with each other (i.e. do not violate constraints such as causality).

Definition: Possible Transition. *Let c_1 and c_2 be two configurations. c_1 is said to have a possible transition to c_2 by processing a task τ, symbolically, $c_1 \xrightarrow{\tau} c_2$ if $\tau \in tasks(c_1)$, and furthermore, if α is the target of the of the task then the tasks in c_2 are*

$$tasks(c_2) = (tasks(c_1) - \{\tau\}) \cup T$$

where T is the set of tasks created by α in response to τ, and the actors in c_2 are

$$actors(c_2) = (actors(c_1) - \{\alpha\}) \cup A \cup \{\alpha'\}$$

where A are the actors created by α in response to τ and α' is the replacement specified by α. Note that α and α' have the same mail address.

In the actor model, the delivery of all communications is guaranteed. This form of fairness can be expressed by defining a second transition relation which is based on processing finite sets of tasks until a particular task is processed, instead of simply processing a single task [Agha 84]. A denotational semantics for actors can be defined in terms of the transition relations; this semantics maps actor programs into the initial configuration they define [Agha 85].

3 The Act3 Language

Act3 is an actor-based programming language which has been implemented on the *Apiary architecture*. The Apiary is a network architecture based on a group of Lisp machines and supports features such as dynamic load balancing, real-time garbage collection, and the mail system abstraction [Hewitt 80]. *Act3* is a descendant of *Act2* [Theriault 83] and is written in a Lisp-based interface language called *Scripter*.

A program in *Act3* is a collection of behavior definitions and commands to create actors and send communications to them. A behavior definition consists of an identifier (by which the actor may be known), a list of the names of acquaintances, and a script (which defines the behavior of the actor in response to the communication it accepts). When an actor is created its acquaintances must be specified. For example, a bank-account actor may have an acquaintance representing its current balance.

When a communication is accepted by an actor, an environment is defined in which the script of the actor is to be executed. The commands in the script of an actor can be executed in parallel. Thus *Act3* differs fundamentally from programming languages based on communicating sequential processes where the commands in the body of a process must be executed sequentially.

We will first provide the syntax for a kernel language, *Act*, and use it to explain the basic concepts of message-passing. We then discuss some extensions to *Act* which are provided in *Act3*. Finally, we illustrate these extensions by means of examples.

3.1 The Kernel Language Act

The language *Act* is a sufficient kernel for the *Act3* language: all constructs in the *Act3* language can be translated into *Act* [Agha 85]. Since there are so few constructs in *Act*, it will be easier to understand the primitives involved. The acquaintance list in *Act* is specified by using identifiers which match a pattern. The pattern provides for freedom from *positional* correspondence when new actors are created. Patterns are used in pattern matching to bind identifiers, and authenticate and extract information from data structures. The simplest pattern is a *bind pattern* which literally binds the value of an identifier to the value of an expression in the current environment. We will not concern ourselves with other patterns here.

When an actor accepts a communication it is *pattern-matched* with the *communication handlers* in the actor's code and dispatched to the handler of the pattern it satisfies. The bindings for the communication list are extracted by the pattern matching as well. The syntax of behavior definitions in *Act* programs is given below.

```
⟨behavior definition⟩ ::=
    (define (id {(with identifier ⟨pattern⟩)}*)
              ⟨communication handler⟩*)
⟨communication handler⟩ ::=
    (Is-Communication ⟨pattern⟩ do ⟨command⟩*)
```

The syntax of commands to create actors and send communications is the same in actor definitions as their syntax at the program level. There are four kinds of commands: we describe these in turn. ***send commands*** are used to send communications. The syntax of the ***send command*** is the keyword send-to followed by two expressions: The two expressions are evaluated; the first expression must evaluate to a mail address while the second may have an arbitrary value. The result of the send command is to send the value of the second expression to the target specified by the first expression. ***let commands*** bind expressions to identifiers in the body of commands nested within their scope. In particular, ***let commands*** are used to bind the mail addresses of newly created actors. ***new expressions*** create new actors and return their mail address. A ***new expression*** is given by the keyword new followed by an identifier representing a behavior definition, and a list of acquaintances.

The ***conditional command*** provides a mechanism for branching, and the ***become command*** specifies the replacement actor. The expression in the ***become command*** may be a ***new expressions*** in which case the actor becomes a forwarding actor to the actor created by the ***new expression***; in this case the two actors are equivalent in a very strong sense. The expression can also be the mail address of an existing actor, in which case all communications sent to the actor replaced are forwarded to the existing actor.

```
⟨command⟩ ::= ⟨let command⟩ | ⟨conditional command⟩ |
              ⟨send command⟩ | ⟨become command⟩
```

```
⟨let command⟩ (let (⟨let binding⟩ ) do ⟨command⟩*)

⟨conditional command⟩ ::= (if ⟨expression⟩
                              (then do ⟨command⟩*)
                              (else do ⟨command⟩*))

⟨send command⟩ ::= (send-to ⟨expression⟩ ⟨expression⟩)

⟨become command⟩ ::= (become ⟨expression⟩)
```

A Recursive Factorial. We first provide a simple factorial example to illustrate the use of message-passing in actors to implement control structures. The code makes the low level detail in the execution of an actor language explicit. We will subsequently provide some higher-level constructs which will make the expression of programs easier. The factorial actor creates *customers*, called FactCust, whose behavior is also given below. Note that the behavior of a factorial is *unserialized*, i.e, it is not history sensitive. Hence, no acquaintances have been specified in the script for a factorial actor.

```
(define (Factorial( ))
  (Is-Communication (a do (with customer ≡m)
                          (with number ≡n))
      (become Factorial)
      (if (NOT (= n 0))
        (then (send-to m 1))
        (else (let (x = (new FactCust (with customer m)
                                      (with number n)))
                (send-to Factorial (a do (with customer x)
                                         (with number n-1))))))))

(define (FactCust (with customer ≡m)
                  (with number ≡n))
    (Is-Communication (a number k)
        (send-to m n*k)))
```

The acceptance of a communication containing an integer by `Factorial` causes `n` to be bound to the integer and concurrently for factorial to become "itself" so that it can immediately process another integer without any interaction with the processing of the integer it has just received. When the factorial actor processes a communication with a non-zero integer, n, it will:

- Create an actor whose behavior will be to multiply n with an integer it receives and send the reply to the mail address to which the factorial of n was to be sent.
- Send itself the "request" to evaluate the factorial of $n - 1$ and send the value to the customer it created.

The customer created by the factorial actor is also an independent actor. The work done to compute a factorial is conceptually distributed by the creation of the customer. In particular, this implies that computation can be speeded-up if several factorials are to be evaluated concurrently. In the case of the factorial, the same result can be obtained by multiple activations of a given function. However, the solution using multiple activations does not work if the behavior of an actor is serialized.

3.2 Functional Constructs

In this section we will develop some notation for representing expressions at a higher-level. *Act3* provides many such constructs which make *Act3* far more expressive than *Act*, although the two languages have the same expressive power. To allow functional programming without forcing the programmer to explicitly create the customers, *Act3* provides *call expressions* which automatically create a customer and include its mail address in the communication sent; The value of the *expression* is returned (in a message) to the customer created at the time of the call. The code below specifies a factorial actor in expressional terms. By comparing the code to that in the previous section, one can see how it is executed in an actor-based environment.

```
(define (call Factorial (with number ≡n))
    (if (= n 0)
        (then 1)
        (else (* n (call Factorial (with number n-1))))))
```

Parallel control structures can also be specified quite easily. For example, a parallel algorithm for evaluating the factorial function of *n* is by recursively subdividing the problem of computing the range product from 1 to *n*. We define an actor, called **RangeProduct** for recursively computing the range product in the above manner. The code for **Rangeproduct** is given below. Note that the One-Of construct provides a generalized conditional command: it dispatches on the value of the expressions (cf. the guarded command [Dijkstra 76]).

```
(define (call RangeProduct (with low ≡lo)
                           (with High ≡hi))
  (One-Of
    (if (= lo hi) lo)
    (if (> lo hi) 1)
    (if (< lo hi)
        (Let ((mid = (/ (+ lo hi) 2)))
           (* (call Rangeproduct (with low lo)
                                 (with high mid))
              (call Rangeproduct (with low (+ mid 1))
                                 (with high hi)))))))
```

The pipelining of the replacement actors implies that two calls to the **Range-Product** actor are in fact equivalent to creating two actors which function concurrently. This equivalence follows from the unserialized nature of the behavior. In case the behavior is unserialized, the behavior of the replacement is known immediately and thus its computation is immediate; in particular, it can be computed even before a communication is received.

Act3 provides a number of other expressional constructs, such as delayed expressions and allows one to require *lazy* or *eager* evaluation strategies for expressions. Such evaluation strategies have been used in extensions of pure functional programming to model *history-sensitive* behavior [Henderson 80]. However, because these systems lack a mail address abstraction, the inter-connection network topology of processes is entirely static.

3.3 Modelling Local-State Change

A problem with functional programming is the difficulty of dealing with shared objects which have changing local states. Some constructs, such as *delayed expressions* have been defined to model changing local states. However, the problem with these techniques is that they create expressional forms totally local to the caller and thus can not be used to represent shared objects. Actors permit a graceful implementation of shared objects with a changing local state. The example below shows the implementation of a bank account in *Act3*. A bank account is a canonical example of a shared object with a changing local state.

We use the keyword Is-Request to indicate a request communication is expected. A *request* communication comes with the mail address of the *customer* to which the *reply* is to be sent. The customer is used as the target of the reply. A *request* also specifies a mail address to which a *complaint* can be sent, should the request be unsuccessful. From a software point of view, providing independent targets for the complaint messages is extremely useful because it allows the error-handling to be separated from successfully completed transactions.

```
(define (Account (with Balance ≡b))
   (Is-Request (a Balance) do (reply b))
   (Is-Request (a Deposit (with Amount ≡a)) do
       (become (Account (with Balance (+ b a))))
       (reply (a Deposit-Receipt (with Amount a))))
   (Is-Request (a Withdrawal (with Amount ≡a)) do
       (if (> a b)
        (then do (complain (an Overdraft)))
        (else do
          (become (Account (with Balance (- b a))))
          (reply (a Withdrawal-Receipt (with Amount a)))))))
```

Note that the become command is pipelined so that a replacement is available as soon as the *become command* is executed. The commands for other actions are executed concurrently and do not affect the replacement actor which will be free to accept further communications.

3.4 Transactional Constructs

Analyzing the behavior of a typical program in terms of all the transitions it makes is not very feasible. In particular, the development of *debugging tools* and *resource management* techniques requires us to preserve the abstractions in the source programs. Because actors may represent shared objects, it is often critical that transitions relevant to independent computations be kept separate. For example, if the factorial actor we defined is asked to evaluate the factorial of -1, it will create an "infinite loop." Two observations should be made about such potentially infinite computations. First, any other requests to the factorial will not be affected because the guarantee of delivery means that communications related to those requests will be interleaved with the "infinite loop" generated by the -1 message. Second, in order to keep the performance of the system from degrading, we must assess costs for each "computation" independently: we can then cut-off those computations that we do not want to support indefinitely.

To formalize the notion of a "computation," we define the concept of *transactions*. Transactions are delineated using two specific kinds of communications, namely, *requests* and *replies*. A request, r_1, may trigger another request, say r_2; if the reply to r_2 also precedes the reply to r_1, then the second transaction is said to be *nested* within the first. Proper nesting of transactions allows simpler resource management schemes since resources can be allocated dynamically for the sub-transaction directly from the triggering transaction.

Transactions also permit the development of *debugging* tools that allow one to examine a computation at different levels of granularity [Manning 84]. Various constructs in *Act3* permit proper nesting of transactions; for example, requests may be buffered while simultaneously preserving the current state of a server using *enqueue*. The request is subsequently processed, when the server is free to do so, using a *dequeue* operation. Enqueue and dequeue are useful for programming servers such as those controlling a hard copy device; they guarantee continuous availability [Hewitt *et al* 1984].

Independent transactions may affect each other; requests may be sent to the same actor whose behavior is history-sensitive thus creating events which are shared between different transactions. Such intersection of events creates interesting problems for the dynamic allocation of resources and for debugging tools. Dynamic transaction delimitation remains an exciting area of research in the actor paradigm.

4 Open Systems

It is reasonable to expect that large-scale parallel systems will be composed of independently developed and maintained modules. Such systems will be open-ended and continually undergoing change [Hewitt and de Jong 85]. Actor languages are intended to provide linguistic support for such *open systems*. We will briefly outline some characteristics of open systems and describe how the actor model is relevant to the problem of open systems. A calculus of configurations can be developed to satisfy the constraints of open systems modelling.

4.1 Characteristics of Open Systems

We list three important considerations which are relevant to any architecture supporting large-scale parallelism in open systems [Hewitt 85]. These considerations have model theoretic implications for an algebra used to characterize the behavior of actors.

- *Continuous Availability*: A system may receive communications from the external environment at any point in time. There is no closed-world hypothesis.
- *Modularity*: The inner workings of one subsystem are not available to the any other system; there is an arms-length relationship between subsystems. The behavior of a system must be characterized only in terms of its interaction with the outside.
- *Extensibility*: It is possible for a system to grow. In particular, it is possible to compose different systems in order to define larger systems.

4.2 A Calculus of Configurations

We have described two transition relations on configurations (see §2.3). These relations are, however, operational rather than extensional in nature. The requirements of modularity imply that an abstract characterization of the behavior of an actor system must be in terms of communications received from outside the system and those sent to the external actors. All communications sent by actors within a population, to other actors also within the population, are not observable from the outside.

In the denotational semantics of sequential programming languages, it is sufficient to represent a program by its input-output behavior, or more completely, as a map from an initial state to a final state (the so-called *history relation*). However, in any program involving concurrency and nondeterminism, the history relation is not a sufficient characterization. Specifically, when two systems with identical history relations are each composed with an identical system, the two resulting systems have different history relations (Brock and Ackerman 81) The reason for this anomaly is the closed-world assumption inherent in the history relation: It ignores the possible interactions of the output with the input [Agha 85].

Instead we represent the behavior of a system taking into account the fact that communications may be accepted from the outside at any point. There are three kinds of derivations from a configuration:

1. A configuration c is said to have a derivation to c' given an *input* τ, symbolically, $c \stackrel{+\tau}{\Longrightarrow} c'$, if

$$\begin{aligned} states(c') &= states(c) \\ tasks(c') &= tasks(c) \cup \tau \ \wedge \ target(\tau) \in population(c) \end{aligned}$$

   where *states* represents the local states function (see §2.3), and *tasks* represents the tasks in a configuration. The receptionists remain the same but the external actors may now include any actors whose mail addresses have been communicated by the communication accepted.

2. A configuration c is said to have a derivation to c' producing an *output* τ, symbolically, $c \stackrel{-\tau}{\Longrightarrow} c'$, if

$$\begin{aligned} states(c') &= states(c) \\ tasks(c') &= tasks(c') - \tau \ \wedge \ target(\tau) \notin population(c) \end{aligned}$$

   where the *states* and the *tasks* are as above, and "−" represents set theoretic difference. The external actors of c' are the same as those of c. The receptionists may now include all actors whose mail addresses have been communicated to the outside.

3. A configuration c has a *internal* or silent derivation to a configuration c', symbolically, $c \stackrel{\varrho}{\Longrightarrow} c'$, if it has a possible transition to c' for some task τ in c.

We can now build a calculus of configurations by defining operations such as composition, relabeling (which changes the mail addresses), restriction (which removes a receptionist), etc. We give the axioms of compositionality to illustrate the calculus of configurations.

Definition: Composition. *Let $c_1 \parallel c_2$ represent the (concurrent) composition of c_1 and c_2. Then we have the following rules of derivation about the composition:*

1. (a) *Let τ be a task whose target is in c_1, then*

$$\frac{c_1 \stackrel{+\tau}{\Longrightarrow} c_1' \, , \; c_2 \stackrel{-\tau}{\Longrightarrow} c_2'}{c_1 \parallel c_2 \stackrel{\varrho}{\Longrightarrow} c_1' \parallel c_2'}$$

   (b) *Let λ be any derivation $(\tau, \tau', or \varrho)$, provided that if λ is an input or output derivation then its sender or target, respectively, are not actors in c_2, then*

$$\frac{c_1 \stackrel{\lambda}{\Longrightarrow} c_1'}{c_1 \parallel c_2 \stackrel{\lambda}{\Longrightarrow} c_1' \parallel c_2}$$

2. *The above rules hold,* mutatis mutandis, *for $c_2 \parallel c_1$.*

The only behavior that can be observed in a system is represented by the "labels" on the derivations from its configurations. These represent the communications between a system and its external environment. Following Milner [80] we can define an *observation equivalence* relation on configurations. The definition relies on equality of all possible finite sequences of communications sent to or received from the external environment (ignoring all internal derivations). One way of formalizing observation equivalence is inductively:

Definition: Observation Equivalence. *Let c_1 and c_2 be any two tasks, μ be either an input or an output task, ϱ^* represent any arbitrary (finite) number of* *internal transitions, and* $\overset{\varrho^{*}\mu}{\Longrightarrow}$ *represent a sequence of internal transitions followed by a* μ *transition, and furthermore* $\approx_k$ *be defined inductively as:*

1. $c_1 \approx_0 c_2$

2. $c_1 \approx_{k+1} c_2$ *if*

   (a) $\forall \mu (if\ c_1 \overset{\varrho^{*}\mu}{\Longrightarrow} c_1'\ then\ \exists c_2' (c_2 \overset{\varrho^{*}\mu}{\Longrightarrow} c_2') \wedge c_1' \approx_k c_2')$

   (b) $\forall \mu (if\ c_2 \overset{\varrho^{*}\mu}{\Longrightarrow} c_2'\ then\ \exists c_1' (c_1 \overset{\varrho^{*}\mu}{\Longrightarrow} c_1') \wedge c_1' \approx_k c_2')$

Then c_1 *is said to be observationally equivalent to* c_2*, symbolically,* $c_1 \approx c_2$*, if* $\forall k (c_1 \approx_k c_2)$.

The notion of observation equivalence is weaker than that of the history relation— it creates fewer equivalence classes and thus distinguishes between more configurations. Specifically, it allows for distinguishing between systems that behave differently in response to new tasks, after having sent some communication to an external actor.

We can characterize actor programs by the equivalence classes of initial configurations they define. Properties of actor system can be established in a framework not relying on a closed-world assumption, while at the same time providing an abstract representation of actor systems that does not rely on the internal details of a systems behavior.

5 Conclusions

Actor languages uniformly use message-passing to spawn concurrency and are inherently parallel. The mail system abstraction permits a high-level mechanism for achieving dynamic reconfigurability. The problem of shared resources with changing local state is dealt with by providing an object-oriented environment without the sequential bottle-neck caused by assignment commands. The behavior of an actor is defined in *Act3* by a script which can be abstractly represented as a mathematical function. It is our claim that *Act3* has the major advantages of object-based programming languages together with those of functional and applicative programming languages.

An actor language also provides a suitable basis for large-scale parallelism. Besides the ability to distribute the work required in the course of a computation, actor systems can be composed simply by passing messages between them. The internal workings of an actor system are not available to any other system. A suitable model to support the composition of different systems is obtained by composing the configurations they may be in.

References

[Agha 84] Agha, G. Semantic Considerations in the Actor Paradigm of Concurrent Computation. Proceedings of the NSF/SERC Seminar on Concurrency, Springer-Verlag, 1984. Forthcoming

[Agha 85] Agha, G. Actors: A Model of Concurrent Computation in Distributed Systems. Ph.D. Th., University of Michigan, 1985.

[Backus 78] Backus, J. Can Programming be Liberated from the von Neumann Style? A Functional Style and Its Algebra of Programs. *Communications of the ACM 21*, 8 (August 1978), 613-641.

[Brock 83] Brock, J. D. A Formal Model of Non-determinate Dataflow Computation. LCS Tech Report 309, MIT, Aug, 1983.

[Brock and Ackerman 81] Brock J.D. and Ackerman, W.B. Scenarios: A Model of Non-Determinate Computation. In *107: Formalization of Programming Concepts*, Springer-Verlag, 1981, pp. 252-259.

[Clinger 81] Clinger, W. D. Foundations of Actor Semantics. AI-TR- 633, MIT Artificial Intelligence Laboratory, May, 1981.

[Dijkstra 77] Dijkstra, E. W. *A Discipline of Programming*. Prentice-Hall, 1977.

[Henderson 80] Henderson, P. *Functional Programming: Applications and Implementation*. Prentice-Hall International, 1980.

[Hewitt 77] Hewitt, C.E. Viewing Control Structures as Patterns of Passing Messages. *Journal of Artificial Intelligence 8-3* (June 1977), 323-364.

[Hewitt 80] Hewitt, C.E. Apiary Multiprocessor Architecture Knowledge System. Proceedings of the Joint SRC/University of Newcastle upon Tyne Workshop on VLSI, Machine Architecture, and Very High Level Languages, University of Newcastle upon Tyne Computing Laboratory Technical Report, October, 1980, pp. 67-69.

[Hewitt 85] Hewitt, C. The Challenge of Open Systems. *Byte 10*, 4 (April 1985), 223-242.

[Hewitt and Baker 77] Hewitt, C. and Baker, H. Laws for Communicating Parallel Processes. 1977 IFIP Congress Proceedings, IFIP, August, 1977, pp. 987-992.

[Hewitt and de Jong 82] Hewitt, C., de Jong, P. Open Systems. A.I. Memo 692, MIT Artificial Intelligence Laboratory, 1982.

[Hewitt, et al 84] Hewitt, C., Reinhardt, T., Agha, G. and Attardi, G. Linguistic Support of Receptionists for Shared Resources. Proceedings of the NSF/SERC Seminar on Concurrency. Springer-Verlag, 1984. Forthcoming

[Hoare 78] Hoare. C. A. R. Communicating Sequential Processes. *CACM 21*, 8 (August 1978), 666-677.

[Hwang and Briggs 84] Hwang, K. and Briggs, F. *Computer Architecture and Parallel Processing.* McGraw Hill, 1984.

[Kahn and MacQueen 78] Kahn, K. and MacQueen, D. Coroutines and Networks of Parallel Processes. Information Processing 77: Proceedings of the IFIP Congress, IFIP, Academic Press, 1978, pp. 993-998.

[Landin 65] Landin, P. A Correspondence Between ALGOL 60 and Church's Lambda Notation. *Communication of the ACM 8*, 2 (February 1965).

[Manning 85] Manning, C. A Debugging System for the Apiary. M.I.T. Message-Passing Semantics Group Memo, January, 1985.

[McCarthy 59] McCarthy, John. Recursive Functions of Symbolic Expressions and their Computation by Machine. Memo 8, MIT, March, 1959.

[Milner 80] Milner, R. *Lecture Notes in Computer Science. Vol. 92: A Calculus of Communicating Systems.* Springer-Verlag, 1980.

[Pratt 82] Pratt, V. R. On the Composition of Processes. Proceedings of the Ninth Annual ACM Conf. on Principles of Programming Languages. 1982.

[Pratt 83] Pratt, V. R. Five Paradigm Shifts in Programming Language Design and their Realization in Viron, a Dataflow Programming Environment. Proceedings of the Tenth Annual ACM Conf. on Principles of Programming Languages, 1983.

[Steele, Fahlman, Gabriel, Moon, Weinreb 84] Steele Jr., Guy L.,. *Common Lisp Reference Manual.* Mary Poppins Edition edition, Department of Computer Science, Carnegie-Mellon University, Pittsburgh, Pa., 1984.

[Stoy 77] Stoy, Joseph E. *Denotational Semantics: The Scott-Strachey Approach to Programming Language Theory.* The MIT Press, Cambridge, MA, 1977.

[Theriault 83] Theriault, D. Issues in the Design and Implementation of Act2. Technical Report 728, MIT Artificial Intelligence Laboratory, June, 1983.

A NEW CLASS OF HIGH LEVEL PROGRAMS FOR DISTRIBUTED COMPUTING SYSTEMS

S. Ramesh and S. L.Mehndiratta
Department of Computer Science and Engineering
Indian Institute of Technology
Powai, Bombay 400 076, India

1. INTRODUCTION

A distributed computing system, in general, possesses the following four important features : (i) Non-determinism, (ii) Concurrency, (iii) Asynchronism and (iv) Decentralization. These features endow distributed systems with certain useful properties such as low susceptibility to failures, absence of centralized control etc. But these have rendered the task of programming a distributed system a difficult one as can be seen from [2, 8, 15]. In order to lessen this difficulty, many suggestions have recently been put forward [3, 12, 17, 19]. According to these, distributed programs can be developed via certain classes of intermediate high level programs which can be easily developed and do not possess one or more of the aforementioned features. Centralized action systems [3], layered programs [12] and sequential programs [17, 19] are the different classes of intermediate programs which have been proposed.

This paper presents an alternate class of intermediate high level programs called PPSAs (acronym for Programs with Processes that interact via Shared Actions). Some of the characteristic features of the PPSAs are (i) they possess all the important properties of distributed programs (namely, nondeterminism, concurrency, asynchronism and decentralization), (ii) they allow specification of arbitrary degree of asynchronism and decentralization, i.e., they allow any number of processes to get synchronized and communicate with each other through shared actions and (iii) they are process oriented and model terminating programs. These features have been found to be useful in the systematic development of highly decentralized and asynchronous programs from specifications that include process structure information (process structure information gives number of processes, their input-output variables and optionally the topology of the underlying network); the reason for including process structure specifications is that, like Chandy [8], we believe that process structures of distributed programs are dependent upon physical considerations such as distribution of data and resources. Feature (ii) mentioned above enables adoption of a transformational approach – that starts with centralized and synchronous programs and refines them gradually by increasing the degree of asynchrony and decentralization – for developing distributed programs, while feature (i) helps in perceiving the degree of asynchrony and decentralization of any program, thereby enabling application of appropriate transformation to increase the degree. Such a transformational approach has been found to make the process of developing distributed programs systematic [20].

PPSAs are different from other intermediate programs used for developing distributed programs. In layered programs [12], only two process communication and global synchronization at layer boundaries are possible. Furthermore, the methodology outlined in [12] is informal and less systematic. The centralized action systems [3] are centralized, action oriented and model nonterminating/deadlocking programs. However, shared actions, similar to joint actions, involve variables of more than one process. Sequential programs [17, 19] are completely centralized and the method that uses them decides process structures based on efficiency considerations and does not assume process structures to be specified a priori.

Shared actions are essentially generalization of two process communication mechanisms like CSP I/O commands and ADA rendezvous. The idea of generalizing two-process mechanisms to multiprocess mechanisms is not new and already two such mechanisms have been proposed. They are Script [13] and Joint Actions [4]. The difference between Scripts and Shared Actions is that the script is not a communication primitive but a procedure facility that utilizes existing primitives like CSP I/O commands; on the other hand, shared actions are communication primitives and processes using them communicate only through them. Joint actions [4] are, however, like shared actions synchronous communication primitives. But joint action systems are different from PPSAs; they are action oriented, do not specify explicitly the control structure of processes and model nonterminating/deadlocking programs, whereas PPSAs are process oriented, specify explicitly the control structure and model terminating programs.

The use of PPSAs in the systematic development of distributed programs and their difference with the existing proposals prompts a formal study of PPSAs, which we attempt in this paper. Specifically, this paper is concerned with an informal and a formal description of PPSAs and the verification of correctness of PPSAs with respect to their specifications. For the purpose of formal description, an operational semantics of PPSAs, in the style of Plotkin [18], is discussed. Using this operational semantics, correctness notions for PPSAs are formally defined and a verification method that is proved to be sufficient is presented. Other formal semantics like denotational and WP-semantics can also be defined for PPSAs. But we have chosen an operational semantics because it has been found to be useful in the methodology for developing distributed programs using PPSAs. We do not discuss in this paper this methodology as it has been dealt in a separate paper [20], which can be referred also for the usefulness of operational semantics.

The organization of this paper is as follows. The next section introduces PPSAs. In Section 3, the operational semantics is discussed. Section 4 is concerned with the verification of PPSAs. Section 5 contains an illustration that illustrates the various notions discussed in the previous sections. The paper concludes with Section 6.

2. PPSAs

A PPSA is a highlevel distributed program consisting of a fixed number of processes. Each process has its own set of variables (disjoint from those of other processes) and a process code. The process code may involve four kinds of actions : <u>simple shared actions</u>, <u>boolean shared actions</u>, <u>alternate actions</u> and <u>iterative actions</u>. A simple shared action involves a command in GCL (except for the command <u>abort</u>), while a boolean shared action involves a quantifier-free predicate expression. A shared action (simple/boolean) occurs <u>at most once</u> in the process code of a process and may occur in the process codes of more than one process. It is said to be <u>shared by</u> all those processes in whose process codes it occurs; trivially the set of processes sharing an action could be a singleton. A shared action may <u>involve</u> the variables of a process that shares it. Also whenever a variable of a process occurs in a shared action, the action should be shared by that process.

An alternate action (iterative action) is of the form **if** $ga_1 \, \square \ldots \ldots \square \, ga_k$ **fi** (**do** $ga_1 \, \square \ldots \square \, ga_k$ **od**), where for each $i \in \{1,\ldots,k\}$, ga_i is a <u>guarded action</u> of the form $g \rightarrow S$; g is a guard and S is a sequence of actions involving simple shared/alternate/iterative actions. The general form of g is b;b', where b is a boolean shared action shared by <u>only one process</u> and b' is a boolean shared action shared by <u>more than one</u> process. The actions b and b' are respectively called the <u>local</u> and <u>nonlocal components</u> of g. The guard g can have only a local or nonlocal component and must have at least one such component.

Syntactically, a PPSA consists of a declaration followed by a list of shared actions and a list of processes. The declaration defines a set of variables of the PPSA. Each shared action, in the shared action list, has a name, a list of names of processes that share it and a body which is either a GCL command or a predicate expression. Similarly, each process in the process list has a name, a list of its variables and a process code; the process code is an action list consisting of names of simple shared actions, alternate actions or iterative actions.

The execution of a PPSA is similar in many respects to that of a CSP program. It involves concurrent execution of their process codes by the processes. The execution of an action (in a process code) succeeds or fails (for the sake of simplicity, we ignore trivial modes of failures like arithmetic overflow, division by zero etc.). Shared actions, like I/O commands of CSP, bring about synchronization among all processes that share them. Any process ready to execute a shared action is delayed until all the processes sharing that action become ready to execute the action in their respective process codes. The action is then collectively executed by all these processes.

In the case of a simple shared action, such a collective execution may result in a change of values of the variables involved in the action. This change is same as that would be produced when the body of the shared action is executed as per GCL semantics. On the other hand, such a collective execution of a boolean shared action makes the processes know the value of the body, which is nothing but a boolean expression.

The collective execution of a simple shared action succeeds iff the execution of its body, as per GCL semantics, succeeds, whereas that of a boolean shared action succeeds iff the body evaluates to true.

The execution of an alternate action consists of selecting (the selection is nondeterministic) a guarded action, with a successfully executable guard, and executing it. The execution of a guarded action consists of executing its guard first and then the action list following the guard. A guard is executed by executing its constituent components from left to right. The guard succeeds iff the execution of its constituent component(s) succeed(s). The execution of an iterative action similarly consists of repeatedly performing the following : select nondeterministically a guarded action, with a successfully executable guard and execute it. The termination (failure) of an iterative (alternate) action is different from that of the corresponding CSP commands and is more elaborate. An iterative (alternate) action a terminates (fails) if there exists a set A of iterative/alternate actions such that (i) A contains a, (ii) all the guards of each of the actions in A fail and (iii) whenever the failure of a guard (of an action in A) is due to its nonlocal component evaluating to false, then the following holds : each process, sharing the nonlocal component, finds that it is executing an action in the set A (in the sequel, any such set is referred to as a <u>closed set of actions</u>). Thus, in general, the termination of an iterative action in a process requires termination of a host of actions in other processes. However, local components, like boolean guards in CSP, provide an option to terminate an iterative action locally.

The execution of a PPSA terminates successfully when all its processes have successfully completed their executions. It fails whenever the execution of at least one of its processes fails or a deadlock occurs. A deadlock occurs when there is a set of processes, each of which is ready to execute a shared action but is waiting for one or more processes, in the set, to reach the stage of executing the shared action.

Illustration

Consider the remote adder problem [12] in which there is an array P(1...n) of processes. Each process P(i), 1 < i < n, is connected to its left and right neighbors P(i-1) and P(i+1); P(1) is connected to P(2) alone while P(n) to P(n-1) alone. The process P(1) has a constant local array **M**[1...N], N $\geq$ 1 of integers which are propagated one by one through processes P(2),...,P(n-1) to P(n). In P(n), these values are summed up and stored in a local variable.

We give three different solutions to this problem, each differing in the degree of asynchronism and decentralization.

<u>Solution 1</u> :

```
PP:: i : int; x(j:1...n) : int;
     init1 : shared by P(1) :
             i : = 1
     end;
     initn : shared by P(n) :
```

```
            x(n) := 0
        end;
        sum : shared by P(j:1...n);
              do i ≤ N → x(2) := M[i];
                         x(3) := x(2);
                               :
                         x(n-1) := x(n-2);
                         x(n) := x(n) + x(n-1);
                         i := i + 1
              od
        end;
        [P(1) :: i,x(1) : int;
                 init1; sum
       ||P(j:2...n-1) :: x(j) : int; sum
       ||P(n) :: x(n) : int;
                 initn; sum
        ]
```

It can be easily seen that this solution is a PPSA, PP that has n-processes P(1),...,P(n) whose process codes involve the three simple shared actions init1, initn and sum. Furthermore, this solution is highly synchronous and centralized as the incrementation of i and propagation of subsequent values to P(n) are done only after the sum of all the previous values has been computed. Another version could be as follows.

Solution 2 :

```
    PP:: i : int; x(j:1...n) : int; b(j:1...n-1) : bool;
         not_send_right(j:1...n-1) : shared by P(j),P(j+1) :
                                          b(j)
         end;
         send_right(1) : shared by P(1),P(2) :
                         x(2) := M[i]
         end;
         send_right(j:2...n-2) : shared by P(j),P(j+1) :
                                 x(j+1) := x(j)
         end;
         send_right(n-1) : shared by P(n-1),P(n) :
                           x(n) := x(n-1) + x(n)
         end;
         [P(1) :: i,x(1) : int; b(1) : bool;
                  i := 1; b(1) := (i ≤ N);
                  do not_send_right(1) → send_right(1);
```

```
                                     i : = i+1; b(1) : = (i ≤ N)
            od
       ||
       P(j:2...n-1) :: x(j) : int; b(j) : bool;
                       b(j) : = false;
                       do ¬ b(j); not_send_right(j-1)→
                                   send_right(j-1); b(j) : = true
                       [] not_send_right(j) → send_right(j);
                                              b(j) : = false
                       od
       ||
       P(n) :: x(n) : int;
               do not_send_right(n-1) → send_right(n-1) od
       ]
```

In Solution 2, for ease of readability, shared actions shared by only one process are not declared and they appear explicitly as a sequence of GCL commands in process codes. Other shared actions are indexed by the indices of processes, and their definitions are parametrized; the use of the arrays of variables x(j:1...n) and b(j:1...n-1) is essentially to enable such a parametric definition.

It can be easily seen that Solution 2 is more asynchronous than Solution 1; here propagation of subsequent values at the 'left end' can take place concurrently with the propagation of previous values at the 'right end'. For more improvement, let us examine the following solution.

<u>Solution 3</u> :

This solution requires two additional boolean arrays b'(j:1...n) and b''(j:1...n-1). Each process P(j) owns b'(j) and b''(j). The following are the new shared actions needed :

not_send_end(j:1...n-1): **shared by** P(j), P(j+1) : b''(j) **end**

The processes are given by

```
    P(1) :: i, x(2) : int; b(1),b'(1),b''(1) : bool;
            i : = 1; b(1),b'(1),b''(1) : = (i ≤ N), false, false;
            do ¬ b'(1) ∧ b(1); not_send_right(1) → send_right(1);
                                               i : = i+1; b(1) : = (i ≤ N);
                                               if ¬ b(1) → b''(1) : = true
                                               [] b(1) → skip
                                               fi
```

```
        [] ¬ b'(1) /\ b''(1); not_send_end(1) → b'(1) := true
        od
P(j:2...n-1) :: x(j) : int; b(j), b'(j), b''(j) : bool;
                b(j),b'(j),b''(j) := false, false, false;
                do ¬ b'(j) /\ ¬ b(j); not_send_right(j-1) →
                                       send_right(j-1); b(j) := true
                 [] ¬ b'(j) /\ b(j); not_send_right(j) →
                                       send_right(j); b(j) := false
                 [] ¬ b'(j); not_send_end(j-1) → b''(j) := true
                 [] ¬ b'(j) /\ b''(j); not_send_end(j) → b'(j) := true
                od
P(n) :: x(n) : int; b'(n) : bool;
        b'(n) := false;
        do ¬ b'(n); not_send_right(n-1) → send_right(n-1)
         [] ¬ b'(n); not_send_end(n-1) → b'(n) := true
        od
```

It may be noted that Solution 3 is the most asynchronous solution among all the three solutions. The difference between Solution 2 and Solution 3 is that in Solution 3 the processes terminate locally.

The power of PPSAs, to allow specification of arbitrary degree of asynchrony and decentralization, should be evident from the above illustration. Solution 1 is highly synchronous and easy to develop while Solution 3 is highly asynchronous and difficult to derive directly from the problem specification. However, Solution 3 can be derived from Solution 1 via Solution 2 by applying correctness preserving transformation rules. Such a transformational approach for developing highly asynchronous and decentralized programs is discussed in [21].

Implementation of PPSAs

The execution of PPSAs as stated above is abstract, and it is necessary to furnish a concrete distributed model of computation that can implement PPSAs. A brief discussion of such an implementation is given in this section; more details can be found in [21].

The implementation of a PPSA, say, PP, requires a network of nodes, each of which houses one or more processors. Each node has a unique index, which is a natural number, identifying the node. Furthermore, each node is connected via communication channels to few other nodes. The processors of different nodes do not share any memory space but can communicate by passing messages via the channels. The channels are bidirectional and they neither corrupt, lose nor change the order in which messages are communicated.

Furthermore, the implementation involves associating a process in PP with each node in the network. One of the processors in each node has a memory location for every variable of the associated process. This processor executes the process code of the associated process. Recall that the execution of a simple shared action involves collective execution by all the processes (processors actually) sharing that action. The effect of collective execution can be achieved by making each of the processes (sharing the action) execute a distinct piece of code that involves only local computation and exchange of messages. These codes are similar to the process codes of the processes of the CSP program obtained by translating the body of shared action, using the method suggested in [17].

The execution of an iterative (alternate) action (by a process) involves selection of guarded actions with successfully executable guards. This selection process requires that (i) local and nonlocal components of the selected guarded action evaluate to false and (ii) all other processes, sharing the nonlocal component, are ready to select guarded actions having the same nonlocal component. It can be seen that such a selection process is essentially the multi-process generalization of the guard selection problem in the implementation of CSP with output guards [5, 6]. Hence, the protocols employed for this problem, especially the one suggested in [22], can be generalized and used for the present purpose. The termination (failure) of an iterative (alternate) action also requires execution of an elaborate protocol. Recall that the termination (failure) of an iterative (alternate) action requires termination (failure) of each action in a closed set of alternate/iterative actions. Checking whether there exists such a set is essentially similar to the detection of deadlocks in communication networks [7] and hence the protocol used for this problem can be employed for termination/failure detection.

3. FORMAL DESCRIPTION OF PPSAs

The tool used for this purpose is operational semantics [18]. In this semantics, an abstract machine state is defined, the notion of execution is formalized and the meaning of a program is given in terms of the effect of executing the program on the machine state. PPSAs are simple programs and hence we take the simplest machine state which is just a mapping that maps variables of programs into their values. We follow Plotkin [18] and Apt [1] in formalizing the execution of PPSAs. That is, we model execution of a program in terms of the transition relation, a binary relation over the set of configurations. A configuration is an ordered pair consisting of a program segment and a state. A pair of configurations $\langle PP_1, \sigma_1 \rangle$ and $\langle PP_2, \sigma_2 \rangle$, where PP_1 and PP_2 are program segments and σ_1 and σ_2 are states, is related by the transition relation, denoted by $\langle PP_1, \sigma_1 \rangle \longrightarrow \langle PP_2, \sigma_2 \rangle$ if executing PP_1 in a state σ_1 leads in a single step of execution to a state σ_2 with PP_2 being the remainder of PP_1 to be executed.

The rest of this section is devoted to the definition of $\longrightarrow$. In the definition of $\longrightarrow$ we prefer the approach adopted by Apt [1] to the axiomatic definition due to Plotkin [18].

We start with some preliminaries. The following notations are with respect to a PPSA, PP :

n	Total number of processes in PP
$P_1, \ldots, P_n$	Processes in PP
A	Set of (names of) shared actions of PP
A_S	Set of simple shared actions in PP
A_{LC}	Set of boolean shared actions that are local components of guards in PP
A'_{LC}	Set of those elements of A_{LC} that occur in guards whose nonlocal components are absent
A_{NC}	Set of boolean shared actions that are non-local components of guards in PP

(Clearly, $A = A_S \cup A_{LC} \cup A_{NC}$ and $A'_{LC} \subseteq A_{LC}$.)

C, R	Sets of alternate and iterative actions in PP, respectively
x, x', y, y' with possible sub- and superscripts	Variables of PP
e, e' with possible sub- and superscripts	Expressions that may involve the variables, operations and the names of shared actions in PP
a, a' with possible sub- and superscripts	Actions in $A_S \cup C \cup R$
b, b' with possible sub- and superscripts	Members of $A_{LC} \cup A_{NC}$
E	Empty sequence of actions/commands

S, S' with possible sub- and superscripts	Sequences of actions that are segments of process codes of PP
SS, SS' with possible sub- and superscripts	PPSA segments of the form $[S_1 \| \ldots \| S_n]$
$\underline{n}$	The set $\{1,\ldots,n\}$
I	Any subset of $\underline{n}$
I^C	Complement of I with respect to $\underline{n}$
a_I	$\{a_j \mid j \in I\}$
σ, τ with possible subscripts	States that map variables of PP into values in appropriate domains
$e(\sigma)$	Value of the expression e in state σ
<u>failure</u>	Configuration that denotes the failure of execution of PP.

In addition to these notations conventional logical and set-theoretic notations will also be used. Furthermore, in what follows any $a_i \in C$ is

$$\textbf{if} \mathop{\square}_{j \in \underline{m(i)}} b_{i,j};\ b'_{i,j} \rightarrow S_{i,j}\ \textbf{fi}$$

for some $m(i) \geq 1$, $b_{i,j} \in A_{LC} \cup \{\textbf{true}\}$, $b'_{i,j} \in A_{NC} \cup \{\textbf{true}\}$ and $S_{i,j}$ a sequence of actions; $b_{i,j} = \textbf{true}$ ($b'_{i,j} = \textbf{true}$) when the corresponding guard does not have the local (nonlocal) component. $\textbf{true}(\sigma)$ is taken to be true in any state σ. Similarly, any $a_i \in R$ is

$$\textbf{do} \mathop{\square}_{j \in \underline{m(i)}} b_{i,j};\ b'_{i,j} \rightarrow S_{i,j}\ \textbf{od}.$$

Assumptions

(1) PP makes use of a finite number of variables ranging over any one of a set of predefined data types.

(2) Each of these predefined data types has a finite number of operations using which the expressions in PP are constructed.

(3) These operations are <u>deterministic</u> and <u>total</u>.

(4) All state functions are <u>total</u>.

Functions and Predicates

<u>IND</u> : For a variable x, IND(x) is the index of the process that owns x. For a shared action a, IND(a) is the set of all indices of processes that share a.

<u>NEIGHBOR</u> : For $b \in (A_{LC} \cup A_{NC})$, $b' \in (A_{LC} \cup A_{NC} \cup \{\textbf{true}\})$ is a neighbor of b in P_i, denoted by b' = NEIGHBOR(b,i), if $b;b' \rightarrow S$ or

b';b → S occur in the process code of P_i for some S.

Clearly, if b' ≠ **true**, then

$$b' = \text{NEIGHBOR}(b,i) \equiv b = \text{NEIGHBOR}(b',i).$$

<u>OCCURS</u> : For a_I, a set of actions in $\mathcal{C} \cup \mathcal{R}$ and $b \in A_{LC} \cup A_{NC}$

$$\text{OCCURS}(b, a_I) \equiv \bigwedge_{j \in I} \bigvee_{\ell \in \underline{m(j)}} [(b_{j,\ell} = b) \vee (b'_{j,\ell} = b)],$$

i.e., OCCURS(b,a_I) holds iff b is a local or nonlocal component of one of the guarded actions of each $a_j, j \in I$. For b = **true**, OCCURS(b, a_I) is taken to be false.

<u>OCCURS_ONLY</u> : For $b \in (A_{LC} \cup A_{NC})$ and a collection of actions a_j, $j \in I$, in $\mathcal{C} \cup \mathcal{R}$ occurring respectively in the process codes of $P_j, j \in I$,

$$\text{OCCURS\_ONLY}(b,a_I) \equiv (\text{IND}(b) \subseteq I) \wedge \text{OCCURS}(b, a_{\text{IND}(b)}),$$

i.e., OCCURS_ONLY(b,a_I) holds iff all occurrences of b, in PP, are in the guarded actions of $a_j, j \in I$. For b = **true**, OCCURS_ONLY(b,a_I) is taken to be **false**.

<u>CLOSED</u> : For a set of actions $a_j, j \in I$, in $\mathcal{C} \cup \mathcal{R}$, occurring respectively in the process codes of $P_j, j \in I$,

$$\text{CLOSED}(a_I) \equiv \bigwedge_{j \in I} \bigwedge_{\ell \in \underline{m(j)}} [(b_{j,\ell} = \textbf{true}) \Rightarrow \text{OCCURS\_ONLY}(b'_{j,\ell},a_j)] \wedge$$
$$[(|I| = 1) \vee (\bigwedge_{j \in I} \bigvee_{\ell \in \underline{m(j)}} \text{OCCURS\_ONLY}(b'_{j,\ell},a_j))].$$

a_I is a closed set of actions iff CLOSED(a_I) is true. It may be noted that there may be more than one closed sets that contain a particular action.

<u>FAIL</u> : For $b \in A_{LC}$,

$$\text{FAIL}(b) \equiv \neg b.$$

For $b \in A_{NC}$,

$$\text{FAIL}(b) \equiv \neg b \wedge \bigwedge_{j \in \text{IND}(b)} \text{NEIGHBOR}(b,j).$$

For b = **true**,

$$\text{FAIL}(b) \equiv \textbf{false}.$$

For $a_j, j \in I$, in $\mathcal{C} \cup \mathcal{R}$, occurring respectively in the process codes of $P_j, j \in I$,

$$FAIL(a_I) \equiv CLOSED(a_I) \wedge \bigwedge_{j \in I} \bigwedge_{\ell \in \underline{m(j)}} [(OCCURS\_ONLY(b'_{j,\ell}, a_I) \wedge FAIL(b'_{j,\ell})) \vee FAIL(b_{j,\ell})].$$

Recall that a guard fails iff either its local component evaluates to false or its nonlocal component evaluates to false with all the neighbors of the nonlocal component evaluating to true. FAIL(b) and FAIL(b') hence characterize these two conditions under which the guard b;b' fails. $FAIL(a_I)(\sigma)$ characterizes the situation in which all the guards of $a_j, j \in I$ evaluate to false; as $a_j, j \in I$ form a closed set, when $FAIL(a_I)(\sigma)$ holds execution of the iterative actions (alternate actions) in a_I terminate (fail).

The definition of $\longrightarrow$ requires the definition of $\longrightarrow$ for GCL programs. A variant of $\longrightarrow$ for GCL programs defined in [1] is given below :

(1) $<$**skip**$,\sigma> \longrightarrow <E, \sigma>$.

(2) $<x := e, \sigma> \longrightarrow <E, \sigma[e(\sigma)/x]>$,
where $\sigma[v/x]$ represents the state σ' such that $\sigma'(y) = \sigma(y)$ for any $y \neq x$ and $\sigma'(x) = e(\sigma)$.

(3) $<$**if** $\square_{j \in \underline{m}}\ b_j \to S_j$ **fi**$, \sigma> \longrightarrow <S_k, \sigma>$,
if $b_k(\sigma)$, for each $k \in \underline{m}$.

(4) $<$**if** $\square_{j \in \underline{m}}\ b_j \to S_j$ **fi**$, \sigma> \longrightarrow$ **failure**,
if $\neg b_k(\sigma)$ for all $k \in \underline{m}$.

(5) $<$**do** $\square_{j \in \underline{m}}\ b_j \to S_j$ **od**$, \sigma> \longrightarrow <S_k;$ **do** $\square_{j \in \underline{m}}\ b_j \to S_j$ **od**$, \sigma>$,
if $b_k(\sigma)$, for each $k \in \underline{m}$.

(6) $<$**do** $\square_{j \in \underline{m}}\ b_j \to S_j$ **od**$, \sigma> \longrightarrow <E, \sigma>$,
if $\neg b_k(\sigma)$ for all $k \in \underline{m}$.

Remarks : (i) Because of our assumptions (3) and (4), $e(\sigma)$ is always defined and no failure configuration is possible as a result of ill-definedness of expression evaluation; these assumptions are made only to have such a simplified definition of $\longrightarrow$.

(ii) What Dijkstra [10] calls as abortion is called failure.

Given this definition of $\longrightarrow$, we can define the input-output behavior of GCL programs as a function M_{GCL} :

$M_{GCL}(a)(\sigma) = \{\tau \mid \langle a,\sigma\rangle \xrightarrow{*} \langle E,\tau\rangle\} \cup \{\textbf{failure} \mid \langle a,\sigma\rangle \xrightarrow{*} \textbf{failure}\}$,

where $\xrightarrow{*}$ is the reflexive transitive closure of $\longrightarrow$.

Semantics of PPSAs

We shall now proceed to extend $\longrightarrow$ to segments of PPSAs. This extension requires a centralized model of execution of PPSAs. In this model, execution of PP progresses by executing its constituent actions one at a time. At any instant of the execution, each of its processes has a segment of the process code, called the rest of the process, that remains to be executed. One of the executable actions heading one or more of the rests of the processes, at that instant, is nondeterministically selected for execution. This execution results in a new state and in the alteration of one or more of the rests of processes. As execution progresses, the rests of the processes are reduced and a stage may be reached when all the rests of the processes are empty. When such a stage is reached, the execution terminates and the current state is the final state of the execution. It may be noted that such an execution deadlocks when at least one of the rests of processes is not empty and none of the actions heading the lists is executable. It can be easily seen that the centralized execution of PP is essentially an interleaved execution and is equivalent to the informal execution model discussed in Section 2.

At any instance of (centralized) execution of PP, the rests of the processes of PP are given by $S_i = E$ or $S_i = a_i;\ S_i'$ for some action a_i and action list S_i' for $i \in \underline{n}$; $a_i \in (A_s \cup C \cup R)$.

An action $a \in A_s$ can be executed if it heads the rests of all those processes that share a, i.e., if the following predicate holds :

$$PROG1(SS, a) \equiv \bigwedge_{i \in IND(a)} [(S_i \neq E) \wedge (a_i = a)].$$

Guarded actions that have b as their local/nonlocal components can be selected in an execution of SS, if PROG2(SS, b) holds, where PROG2 is given as follows :

$$PROG2(SS, b) \equiv (S_i \neq E) \wedge (a_i \in C \cup R) \wedge OCCURS(b, \{a_i\}) \wedge b,$$

where $i \in IND(b)$ for $b \in A'_{LC}$; for $b \in A_{NC}$,

$$PROG2(SS, b) \equiv b \wedge \bigwedge_{i \in IND(b)} [(a_i \in C \cup R) \wedge OCCURS(b, \{a_i\}) \wedge NEIGHBOR(b, i)].$$

If the predicate PROG3(SS, I) given by

$$PROG3(SS, I) \equiv \bigwedge_{i \in I} [(S_i \neq E) \wedge (a_i \in \mathcal{R}) \wedge FAIL(a_I)]$$

holds, then all the iterative actions in a_I can be terminated. The execution of SS fails when

$$FAIL(SS, I) \equiv \bigwedge_{i \in I} (S_i \neq E) \wedge \bigvee_{i \in I} (a_i \in \mathcal{C}) \wedge FAIL(a_I)$$

is true for some $I \subseteq \underline{n}$.

Thus the execution of SS can progress iff

$$PROG(SS) \equiv \bigvee_{a \in A_S} PROG1(SS, a) \vee \bigvee_{b \in A_{NC} \cup A'_{LC}} PROG2(SS, b) \vee \bigvee_{I \subseteq \underline{n}} PROG3(SS, I)$$

holds. The different PPSA segments that result in one step of execution of SS are SS_1, SS_2 and SS_3 given as follows :

$$SS_1 = [\ \|_{i \in IND(a)} S'_i \ \| \ \|_{i \in IND(a)^c} S_i\ ],$$

when PROG1(SS, a)(σ) holds and a is executed, for some $a \in A_S$.

$$SS_2 = \textbf{if}\ b \in A'_{LC}\ \textbf{then}\ [\ \|_{j \neq i} S_j \ \| \ a'_i; S_i\ ]$$

$$\textbf{else}\ [\ \|_{i \in IND(b)} a'_i ; S_i \ \| \ \|_{j \in IND(b)^c} S_j\ ]$$

on selecting the guarded actions (action) with $b \in A_{NC}$ ($b \in A'_{LC}$) as their nonlocal (local) component such that PROG2(SS, b)(σ) holds, where

$$a'_i = \textbf{if}\ a_i \in \mathcal{C}\ \textbf{then}\ S\ \textbf{else}\ S; a_i,$$

for i such that $i \in IND(b)$ and $b_i;b \rightarrow S$ ($b \rightarrow S$) is a guarded action of a_i, for some local component b_i.

$$SS_3 = [\ \|_{i \in I} S'_i \ \| \ \|_{i \in I^c} S_i\ ]$$

when PROG3(SS, I)(σ) holds and all the iterative actions in a_I are terminated.

Using these predicates and program segments, $\longrightarrow$ can be defined by the following six clauses :

(1) $\langle SS, \sigma \rangle \longrightarrow \langle SS_1, \tau \rangle$
if PROG1(SS, a)(σ) is true and $\tau(\neq \textbf{failure}) \in M_{GCL}(a)(\sigma)$.

(2) $< SS, \sigma > \longrightarrow$ **failure**
if PROG1(SS, a)(σ) holds and **failure** $\in M_{GCL}(a)(\sigma)$.

(3) $< SS, \sigma > \longrightarrow < SS_2, \sigma >$
if PROG2(SS, b)(σ) and $b \in (A'_{LC} \cup A_{NC})$.

(4) $< SS, \sigma > \longrightarrow$ **failure**
if FAIL(SS, I)(σ), for some $I \subseteq \underline{n}$.

(5) $< SS, \sigma > \longrightarrow < SS_3, \sigma >$
if PROG3(SS, I)(σ), for some $I \subseteq \underline{n}$.

(6) $< SS, \sigma > \longrightarrow$ **failure**
if $\neg$ PROG(SS)(σ) and $\neg$ FAIL(SS, I), for any $I \subseteq \underline{n}$.

Given the above definition of $\longrightarrow$, as in the case of GCL programs, input-output behavior of PP can be defined as follows :

$$M_{PPSA}(PP)(\sigma) = \{ \tau \mid < SS,\sigma > \xrightarrow{*} < [\underbrace{E \| \ldots \| E}_{n\text{-times}}],\tau > \} \cup \{ \textbf{failure} \mid < SS, \sigma > \xrightarrow{*} \textbf{failure} \},$$

where $SS = [S_1 \| \ldots \| S_n]$ and S_i is the process code of P_i, $i \in \underline{n}$.

<u>Remarks</u> : (1) The above definition of $\longrightarrow$ does not represent a realistic model of execution of PP as it may not be possible to carry out, in a single step, the transitions specified by some of the clauses. We are satisfied with this definition rather than with the one that corresponds more closely to reality because of its simplicity; as we shall see in the next section, this gives rise to relatively simpler verification conditions.

(ii) Three situations under which execution of PP can fail are distinguished. They are :

(a) When execution of a simple shared action fails (Clause 2).
(b) When an alternate action fails (Clause 4).
(c) When PP deadlocks (Clause 6).

4. CORRECTNESS VERIFICATION OF PPSAs

We make use of the conventional notions like partial correctness, total correctness and nontermination. These notions can be formally defined using the operational semantics given in the previous section.

<u>Definition 1</u> : A PPSA is partially correct with respect to a pair of predicates $< Q, R >$, if for all σ, τ,

$$[(Q(\sigma) \wedge (\tau \in M_{PPSA}(PP)(\sigma)) \wedge (\tau \neq \textbf{failure})) \Rightarrow R(\tau)].$$

Definition 2 : PP can fail with respect to Q, if there exist states σ, τ and a PPSA segment SS' such that any one of the following three conditions holds :

(i) $Q(\sigma) \wedge (<SS,\sigma> \xrightarrow{*} <SS',\tau>) \wedge PROG1(SS', a)(\tau) \wedge \textbf{failure} \in M_{GCL}(a)(\tau)$,

for some $a \in A_{s'}$,

(ii) $Q(\sigma) \wedge (<SS,\sigma> \xrightarrow{*} <SS',\tau>) \wedge FAIL(SS', I)(\tau)$,

for some $I \subseteq \underline{n}$ and

(iii) $Q(\sigma) \wedge (<SS,\sigma> \xrightarrow{*} <SS',\tau>) \wedge \neg PROG(SS')(\tau) \wedge \bigwedge_{I \subseteq \underline{n}} \neg FAIL(SS', I)(\tau)$,

where $SS = [S_1 || \ldots || S_n]$, S_i being the process code of P_i for all $i \in \underline{n}$.

It can be easily seen that the above three conditions correspond to three kinds of failures mentioned in the previous section.

Definition 3 : PP can be nonterminating with respect to Q, if there exist a state σ and an infinite sequence of configurations $<SS_i, \tau_i>$, $i = 1,2,\ldots$ such that

$$Q(\sigma) \wedge [<SS,\sigma> \xrightarrow{*} <SS, \tau_1> \xrightarrow{*} <SS_2, \tau_2> \xrightarrow{*} \ldots],$$

where SS is as mentioned above.

Definition 4 : PP is totally correct with respect to $<Q,R>$ if it is partially correct with respect to $<Q,R>$ and it can neither fail nor can nonterminate with respect to Q.

In what follows, we describe a method of verifying the total correctness of PPSAs. This method is based on Levin-Gries method of verifying CSP programs [15], from which it borrows the following three important ideas : (1) Association of predicates with actions in each process to specify the local states, (2) Use of auxiliary variables to relate local states of different processes and (3) Use of information about the states of all the processes involved in a communication to validate the annotation of the corresponding communication command (i.e., use of satisfaction tests). This method, however differs from Levin-Gries approach in the following aspects : (i) Since PPSAs involve multiprocess synchronization, two-process-satisfaction proofs have been generalized to multiprocess-satisfaction proofs, (ii) Auxiliary variables do not occur explicitly in the text of the program being verified but occur in separate program segments that are associated with the actions in the PPSA, (iii) Process proofs and satisfaction proofs have been integrated into a single proof for actions that consists of verifying the validity of the annotation of each action in the PPSA and (iv) A proof method like Manna's approach [16] rather than a formal axiomatic system is used. The changes (i) and (ii) are required because of the inherent differences between PPSAs and CSP programs, while the other two changes make the proof method more natural to PPSAs. The idea of generalizing the satisfaction proofs for multiprocess synchronization constructs has already been employed in the verification of Scripts [23]. The method proposed in [23] is different from our method and cannot be used for verifying PPSAs as PPSAs are different from programs that use scripts. Another important difference is that the method of verification of Scripts has been obtained by generalizing the proof system due to Apt et al. [2], while our method is based on Levin-Gries approach.

The Verification Method

Given a PPSA, PP and a pair of pre- and post-conditions $\langle Q, R\rangle$ the first step of the method consists of annotating PP with a collection of predicates and actions in the following manner :

- Associate with each action $a \in \mathcal{A} \cup \mathcal{C} \cup \mathcal{R}$, in process P_i, a pair of predicates Pre(a, i) and Post(a, i) called the pre- and post-conditions of a in P_i for each $i \in \underline{n}$.
- Associate with each $a \in \mathcal{R}$ in P_i. a predicate Inv(a, i) (the invariant condition) and an integer valued expression t(a,i) (the decreasing function).
- For every $i \in \underline{n}$ and $a \in \mathcal{A} \cup \mathcal{C} \cup \mathcal{R}$, Pre(a, i), Post(a, i), Inv(a, i) and t(a, i) involve <u>only</u> the variables of P_i and certain new variables called auxiliary variables.
- The auxiliary variables include a distinct integer variable for each iterative action in PP and <u>do not occur</u> anywhere in the program text of PP; their initial values are characterized by a predicate INIT.
- For every $a \in \mathcal{R}$, in P_i given by

$$a = \textbf{do} \ \underset{j \in \underline{m}}{\square} \ b_j \ ; \ b_j' \rightarrow S_j \ \textbf{od},$$

(i) each of Pre(a, i) and $Pre(b_j, i)$ ($Pre(b'_j, i)$, if b_j = **true**) for $j \in \underline{m}$ is identical to Inv(a, i), (ii) $Pre(S_j, i)$ for each $j \in \underline{m}$ is of the form $W \wedge (t(a, i) = T)$ for some predicate W, where T is the integer auxiliary variable associated with a and (iii) $Post(S_j, i)$ is identical to $Inv(a, i) \wedge (t(a, i) < T)$ for each $j \in \underline{m}$.

- For every $a \in C$, in P_i, given by

$$a = \textbf{if} \underset{j \in \underline{m}}{\Box} b_j ; b'_j \rightarrow S_j \textbf{ fi},$$

Pre(a, i) is same as $Pre(b_j, i)$ ($Pre(b'_j, i)$, if b_j = **true**), while $Post(S_j, i)$ is identical to Post(a, i) for each $j \in \underline{m}$.

- For every pair of actions $a, a' \in A \cup C \cup R$ such that a occurs immediately before a', Post(a, i) is same as Pre(a, i).
- Associate with each $a \in (A_S \cup A'_{LC} \cup A_{NC} \cup R)$, a distinct GCL segment called an auxiliary action.
- Auxiliary actions involve the auxiliary variables and program variables of PP; they do not update but may access the program variables.

Once PP has been annotated as mentioned above, the next and the final step in the verification method is to check that the annotation satisfies the following conditions.

1. Input-Output Verification Conditions :

$$(Q \wedge INIT) \Rightarrow \bigwedge_{i \in \underline{n}} Pre(S_i, i)$$

$$\bigwedge_{i \in \underline{n}} Post(S_i, i) \Rightarrow R ,$$

where S_i is the process code of P_i, $Pre(S_i, i)$ and $Post(S_i, i)$ are the pre- and post-condition predicates associated respectively with the first and the last actions of S_i for each $i \in \underline{n}$.

2. Action Verification Conditions :

Shared Action Verification Conditions :

(SA1) For every $a \in A_S$,

$$\bigwedge_{j \in IND(a)} Pre(a, j) \Rightarrow WP(a; a', \bigwedge_{j \in IND(a)} Post(a, j)),$$

where a' is the auxiliary action corresponding to a.

(SA2) For every $b \in A'_{LC}$, occurring in P_i,

$$Pre(b, i) \wedge b \Rightarrow WP(b', Post(b, i)),$$

where b' is the auxiliary action corresponding to b.

(SA3) For every $b \in A_{NC}$,

$$COND(b) \Rightarrow WP(b', \bigwedge_{j \in IND(b)} Post(b, j)),$$

where

$$COND(b) \equiv \bigwedge_{\substack{j \in IND(b) \\ b_j \neq \mathbf{true}}} [Pre(b_j, j) \wedge b_j] \wedge \bigwedge_{\substack{j \in IND(b) \\ b_j = \mathbf{true}}} Pre(b, j) \wedge b$$

b_j = NEIGHBOR(b, j) for each $j \in IND(b)$

and b' = auxiliary action corresponding to b.

Alternate Action Verification Condition (ALT) : For every $a_j, j \in I$ occurring respectively in the process codes of $P_j, j \in I$ such that $a_i \in C$ for some $i \in I$,

$$\bigwedge_{j \in I} Pre(a_j, j) \wedge FAIL(a_I) \Rightarrow \mathbf{false}.$$

Iterative Action Verification Conditions :

(ITR1) For every guarded action, in $a_i \in R$ (in P_i), whose nonlocal component is $b \neq \mathbf{true}$,

$$COND(b) \Rightarrow t(a_i, i) > 0$$

and for every guarded action in a_i whose nonlocal and local components are **true** and b respectively,

$$Pre(b, j) \wedge b \Rightarrow t(a, i) > 0.$$

(ITR2) For every $a_j \in R$ occurring in P_j, for all $j \in I \subseteq \underline{n}$,

$$\bigwedge_{j \in I} Pre(a_j, j) \wedge FAIL(a_I) \Rightarrow WP(\mathop{\mathbf{S}}_{j \in I} a'_j, \bigwedge_{j \in I} Post(a_j, j)),$$

where $\mathop{\mathbf{S}}_{j \in I} a'_j$ is an arbitrary sequence involving the auxiliary actions $a'_j, j \in I$.

3. Deadlock Freedom :

For every PPSA segment SS of PP given by $SS = [S_1 || \ldots || S_n]$ for some $S_1, \ldots, S_n$,

$$(BLOCKED(SS) \wedge \bigwedge_{i \in \underline{n}} [\mathbf{if}\ S_i = E\ \mathbf{then}\ Post(S'_i, i)\ \mathbf{else}\ Pre(S_i, i)]) \Rightarrow \mathbf{false},$$

where S_i' is the process code of P_i and

$$BLOCKED(SS) \equiv \neg PROG(SS) \wedge \bigwedge_{I \subseteq \underline{n}} \neg FAIL(SS, I).$$

4. Interference Freedom :

(IF1) For every action a' in P_i and $a \in A_s$ such that $i \notin IND(a)$,

$$(Pre(a', i) \wedge \bigwedge_{j \in IND(a)} Pre(a, j)) \Rightarrow WP(a; a'', Pre(a', i)),$$

where a" is the auxiliary action corresponding to a.

(IF2) For every action a' in P_i and $b_j \in A'_{LC}$ in P_j such that $j \neq i$,

$$(Pre(a', i) \wedge Pre(b_j, j)) \Rightarrow WP(b_j', Pre(a', i))$$

and for every action a' in P_i and $b \in A_{NC}$ such that $i \notin IND(b)$,

$$(Pre(a', i) \wedge COND(b)) \Rightarrow WP(b', Pre(a', i)),$$

where b_j' and b' are the auxiliary actions corresponding to b_j and b respectively.

(IF3) For every action a' in P_i and a set of iterative actions $a_j, j \in I$ occurring respectively in P_j, $j \in I$ with $i \notin I$,

$$[Pre(a', i) \wedge \bigwedge_{j \in I} Pre(a_j, j) \wedge FAIL(a_I)]$$
$$\Rightarrow WP(\underset{j \in I}{\mathbf{S}} a_j', Pre(a', i)).$$

As we shall prove below that these four verification conditions guarantee that during an execution of PP in an initial state satisfying Q, whenever a process P_i is ready to execute an action a, Pre(a, i) holds, while Post(a, i) holds after the execution of a; these four conditions also ensure that PP cannot fail nor nonterminate with respect to Q. The proof of these facts makes use of the operational semantics of PPSAs. The semantics discussed in the previous section does not consider auxiliary actions and variables and hence has to be modified for the purpose of this proof. The required modifications are : (i) Execution of each shared action is to be followed by the execution of the corresponding auxiliary action, (ii) Selection of guarded actions should involve the execution of the auxiliary action corresponding to the boolean shared action that is local/nonlocal component of the actions selected and (iii) Termination of every closed set of iterative actions should involve the execution of the corresponding auxiliary actions. Accordingly, the definition of $\longrightarrow$ given earlier should be modified as follows :

(1) The domains of all states are enlarged to include auxiliary variables.

(2) In Clause (1), τ should be an element of $M_{GCL}(a;\ a')(\sigma)$.

(3) In Clause (2), the condition **failure** $\in M_{GCL}(a)(\sigma)$ should be modified to **failure** $\in M_{GCL}(a;\ a')(\sigma)$.

(4) Clause (3) is replaced by the following two clauses :

(3.1) $$\langle SS, \sigma \rangle \longrightarrow \langle SS_2, \tau \rangle$$

if PROG2(SS, b)(σ) and τ ($\neq$ **failure**) $\in M_{GCL}(b')(\sigma)$ and

(3.2) $$\langle SS, \sigma \rangle \longrightarrow \textbf{failure}$$

if PROG2(SS, b)(σ) and **failure** $\in M_{GCL}(b')(\sigma)$ for $b \in (A'_{LC} \cup A_{NC})$, where b' is the auxiliary action corresponding to b.

(5) Clause (5) is also replaced by two clauses given by

(5.1) $$\langle SS, \sigma \rangle \longrightarrow \langle SS_3, \tau \rangle$$

if PROG3(SS, I)(σ) for some $I \subseteq \underline{n}$, where τ ($\neq$ **failure**) $\in M_{GCL}(\mathop{\textbf{S}}_{j \in I} a'_j)(\sigma)$ and

(5.2) $$\langle SS, \sigma \rangle \longrightarrow \textbf{failure}$$

if SS is as before and **failure** $\in M_{GCL}(\mathop{\textbf{S}}_{j \in I} a'_j)(\sigma)$.

With this modified semantics, the four verification conditions can be explained as follows :

- Condition (1) is simple to understand.
- An action $a \in A_S$ is executed only when all processes sharing a are ready to execute it. Furthermore, execution of a is followed by execution of the corresponding auxiliary action a'. Accordingly, Post(a, j) need hold only after the execution of a followed by a', if Pre(a, j) holds for all P_j's sharing a before the execution of a. This essentially is condition (SA1).
- It can be easily seen that COND(b) in (SA3) characterizes the situation in which all processes P_j, $j \in$ IND(b) are ready to select the guarded actions that have b as the nonlocal component. As per the modified semantics of PP, such a selection involves the execution of auxiliary actions corresponding to the local/nonlocal component. Hence (SA3) requires that Post(b, j) holds for $j \in$ IND(b) after executing the auxiliary action b', in a state satisfying COND(b). The meaning of (SA2) is same as that

of (SA3) with the difference that it considers the selection of a guarded action whose nonlocal component is absent.

- The similarity of conditions (SA1)-(SA3) and the satisfaction rule [15] may be noted.

- Execution of an alternate action a_i fails if there is a closed set of alternate/iterative actions such that the set includes a_i and all actions in the set fail/terminate. Condition (ALT) forbids such a situation.

- (ITR1) guarantees that the value of the decreasing function $t(a_i, i)$ is a nonzero positive integer whenever a_i has a guarded action that can be selected; the conditions for selecting the guarded actions with and without nonlocal components are different and hence (ITR1) considers two cases. The value of the decreasing function decreases with the execution of each guarded action since $t(a_i, i) < T$ is a conjunct of the post conditions of the guarded action and the value of T is equal to $t(a_i, i)$ before the execution of the guarded action. The termination of a_i requires and is accompanied by the termination of a closed set of actions. Furthermore, it involves execution of all the auxiliary actions corresponding to the actions in the closed set. Hence to guarantee $Post(a_i, i)$ holds after the termination of a_i, it is required to show that for every closed set of iterative actions that includes a_i, $Post(a_i, i)$ holds after the execution of the relevant auxiliary actions in a state in which all the concerned processes are ready to execute the actions in the set but the guards of all these actions fail. This essentially is condition (ITR2).

- Condition (3) is the familiar deadlock freedom test that refutes the reachability of a 'blocked' situation in any execution of PP.

- As the predicates involve auxiliary variables which can be referred in predicates associated with any process, the interference freedom condition (4) is required. A noteworthy point about this condition is that it considers, as 'atomic', (i) the execution of simple shared actions, (ii) selection of guarded actions and (iii) termination of iterative actions. The conditions (IF1), (IF2) and (IF3) guarantee that $Pre(a', i)$ is not affected under the execution of a simple shared action, selection of guarded actions and termination of iterative actions respectively.

We shall now prove a theorem that establishes the sufficiency of the method.

Theorem : PP is totally correct with respect to $<Q, R>$ if there exists an annotation of PP satisfying the four verification conditions, for some appropriate predicate INIT.

We shall prove the above theorem with the help of the following lemmas.

Lemma 1 : Whenever $<[S_1 \| \ldots \| S_n], \sigma> \xrightarrow{*} <[S'_1 \| \ldots \| S'_n], \tau>$ for some σ, τ, $S_1, \ldots, S_n$ and $S'_1, \ldots, S'_n$ such that $(Q \wedge INIT)(\sigma)$ and $S_1, \ldots, S_n$ are the process codes of $P_1, \ldots, P_n$ respectively, then $Pre(S'_i, i)(\tau)$ holds for each $i \in \underline{n}$.

Lemma 2 : PP can neither fail nor nonterminate with respect to Q.

It is obvious from verification condition (1) that these two lemmas imply the theorem.

Proof of Lemma 1 : Consider the relation $\xrightarrow{k}$, $k \geq 0$, defined as follows :

$$\xrightarrow{0} \; \equiv \text{Identity relation}$$

$$\xrightarrow{1} \; \equiv \; \longrightarrow$$

$$\xrightarrow{k+1} \; \equiv \; \xrightarrow{k} \cdot \xrightarrow{1},$$

where '.' is the relational composition operator. We have from the definition of $\xrightarrow{*}$,

$$<[S_1 \| \ldots \| S_n], \sigma> \xrightarrow{k} <[S'_1 \| \ldots \| S'_n], \tau>$$

for some $k \geq 0$. We prove the required result by induction on k.

Base $k = 0$: We have $S'_i = S_i$ for $i \in \underline{n}$ and $\tau = \sigma$. The lemma follows directly from condition (1) which states that

$$[Q \wedge INIT] \Rightarrow \bigwedge_{i \in \underline{n}} Pre(S_i, i).$$

Induction $k > 0$: Assume that the lemma holds for all $k' < k$. Then we have

$$<[S_1 \| \ldots \| S_n], \sigma> \xrightarrow{k-1} <[S''_1 \| \ldots \| S''_n], \tau'>$$

$$\longrightarrow <[S'_1 \| \ldots \| S'_n], \tau>$$

for some $S''_1, \ldots, S''_n$. Because of the inductive assumption, $Pre(S''_i, i)(\tau')$ for $i \in \underline{n}$. We shall now prove that this implies $Pre(S'_i, i)(\tau)$ for $i \in \underline{n}$. The definition of $\longrightarrow$ suggests that there are three cases (i), (ii) and (iii) to consider corresponding to the three clauses (1), (3.1) and (5.1), respectively.

Case (iii) : $PROG3(SS'', I)(\tau')$ holds for some $I \subseteq \underline{n}$. Then $S''_i = a_i; S'_i$, where $a_i \in \mathcal{R}$, for each $i \in I$, $S''_i = S'_i$ for $i \notin I$ and $\tau = M_{GCL}(\underset{i \in I}{\mathbf{S}} a'_i)(\tau')$. Further, because of condition (ITR2),

$$[\bigwedge_{i \in I} Pre(a_i, i) \wedge FAIL(a_I)] \Rightarrow WP(\underset{i \in I}{\mathbf{S}} a'_i, Post(a_j, j))$$

for each $j \in I$. Since $PROG3(SS'', I)(\tau')$, the antecedent of the above condition holds. This together with the fact that $Post(a_j, j)$ is identical to $Pre(S'_j, j)$ implies that $Pre(S'_j, j)(\tau)$ holds for all $j \in I$. Condition (IF3) and the fact that $Pre(S''_i, i)(\tau')$ holds for $i \notin I$ guarantee that $Pre(S''_i, i)$ is true in state τ, for $i \notin I$. Since $S''_i = S'_i$ for $i \notin I$, we have for all $i \in \underline{n}$, $Pre(S'_i, i)(\tau)$ is true.

The proofs for Cases (i) and (ii) are similar and hence omitted.

Proof of Lemma 2 : It is obvious from conditions (SA1), (SA2), (SA3), (ALT) and (DF) that PP cannot fail. We shall prove by contradiction that PP is also terminating. If PP is nonterminating with respect to Q, then there exist σ_i and $SS_i = [S^i_1 \| \ldots \| S^i_n]$ for $i = 1,2,\ldots,$ such that

$$<SS, \sigma> \longrightarrow <SS_1, \sigma_1> \longrightarrow <SS_2, \sigma_2> \longrightarrow \ldots .$$

It follows then from the fact that there are only a finite number of distinct segments of any process code that there exist $k_i > 0$, $i = 1,2,\ldots,$ and an iterative action a such that for $i,j = 1,2,\ldots,$

(i) $SS_{k_i} = SS_{k_j}$,

(ii) $S^{k_i}_\ell = a; S'_\ell$

for some $\ell \in \underline{n}$ and S'_ℓ,

(iii) $S^{k'_i}_\ell = S ; a ; S'_\ell$

for some $k'_i : k_i < k'_i < k_{i+1}$ and S, the sequence of actions following one of the guards of a, and

(iv) $S^i_\ell = S'_\ell$

for no $i > k_1$. It can be easily seen that condition (iii) states that one of the guarded actions of a is selected between k_i and k_{i+1}-th steps of execution, while condition (iv) is that in no step after k_1 steps of execution, is a terminated. The annotation of PP is such that $t(a,\ell) = T$ and $t(a,\ell) < T$ are conjuncts of Pre(S,ℓ) and Post(S,ℓ) respectively. Hence from Lemma 1 and (ITR1), it follows that there is an infinitely decreasing sequence of positive integers

$$\sigma_{k_1'}(t(a,\ell)) < \sigma_{k_2'}(t(a,\ell)) < \ldots$$

which is impossible. Hence there is a contradiction.

The above theorem establishes only the soundness of the verification method. The completeness of the method, which is nothing but the converse of the theorem, is yet to be proved.

5. ILLUSTRATION

Consider the following PPSA that corresponds to the parallel sorting problem [2] :

```
PP :: x(i:1...n) : int;
      init(i:1...n) : shared by P(i) :
                          x(i) : = K(i)
      end;
      less(i:2...n) : shared by P(i), P(i-1) :
                          x(i) < x(i-1)
      end;
      exchange(i:2...n) : shared by P(i), P(i-1) :
                              x(i-1), x(i) : = x(i), x(i-1)
      end;
      [P(1) :: x(i) : int;
                init(1); do less(2) → exchange(2) od
      ||
      P(i:2...n-1) :: x(i) : int;
                          init(i); do less(i) → exchange(i)
                                   □ less(i+1) → exchange(i+1)
                                   od
      ||
      P(n) :: x(n) : int;
              init(n); do less(n) → exchange(n) od
      ]
```

Let $S_1,\ldots,S_n$ denote the process codes of P(1),...,P(n) respectively. Then, it can be easily shown that, for a state σ that assigns unique integers to each K(i), $i \in \underline{n}$, any execution sequence of PP, starting in σ, is of the form

$$<SS,\sigma> \xrightarrow{*} <SS',\sigma_1> \xrightarrow{*} <SS',\sigma_2> \xrightarrow{*} \cdots \xrightarrow{*} <[\underbrace{E\| \ldots \|E}_{n\text{-times}}],\sigma_k>,$$

where $SS = [S_1 \| \ldots \| S_n]$
$SS' = [a_1 \| \ldots \| a_n]$
a_i = iterative action in S_i, $i \in \underline{n}$
and $\sigma_1,\ldots,\sigma_k$ are the states satisfying the following :

(1) $x(i)(\sigma_1) = K(i)(\sigma_1)$, $i \in \underline{n}$

(2) $< x(1)(\sigma_j),\ldots,x(n)(\sigma_j) >$ is a permutation of $< K(1)(\sigma_1),\ldots,K(n)(\sigma_n) >$ for every $j \in \underline{k}$, and

(3) $x(1)(\sigma_k) < \ldots < x(n)(\sigma_k)$.

That is, executing SS in the state σ results in a final state in which x(1),...,x(n) is the sorted sequence of K(1),...,K(n). We shall now formally verify this fact using the verification method discussed in the previous section. The following is the specification with respect to which PP is verified :

Q ≡ K(1),...,K(n) are distinct integers.
R ≡ <x(1),...,x(n)> is a permutation of <K(1),...,K(n)> **and** x(1) < ... < x(n).

For the purpose of verification, every shared action in PP is associated with an auxiliary action; furthermore, each action in PP is annotated with a pair of predicates. Let

DISTINCT ≡ K(1),...,K(n) are distinct integers.
PERM(y(1),...,y(n)) ≡ <y(1),...,y(n)> is a permutation of <K(1),...,K(n)> .

Then the annotation of the various actions is given as follows :

$\text{Pre}(\text{init}(i),i) \equiv \text{DISTINCT} \wedge \text{PERM}(y(1),\ldots,y(n)) \wedge (y(i) = K(i))$

$\text{Inv}(a_i, i) \equiv \text{DISTINCT} \wedge \text{PERM}(y(1),\ldots,y(n)) \wedge (x(i) = y(i)) \wedge (z(i) = 0)$

$t(a_i, i) = f(y(1),\ldots,y(n))$,

where

$$f(x_1,\ldots,x_n) = \sum_{\substack{i,j=1 \\ i<j}}^{n} g(x_i, x_j)$$

$$g(x_i, x_j) \quad = \textbf{ if } x_i > x_j \textbf{ then } 1 \textbf{ else } 0.$$

The function f is essentially the number of exchanges required to sort $x_1, \ldots, x_n$.

$$\begin{aligned}
&\mathrm{Post}(\mathrm{init}(i), i) && \equiv \mathrm{Pre}(a_i, i) \equiv \mathrm{Inv}(a_i, i)\\
&\mathrm{Pre}(\mathrm{less}(i), i) && \equiv \mathrm{Pre}(\mathrm{less}(i+1) \equiv \mathrm{Inv}(a_i, i)\\
&\mathrm{Pre}(\mathrm{exchange}(i), i) && \equiv \mathrm{PERM}(y(1),\ldots,y(n)) \wedge (x(i) = y(i)) \wedge\\
& && \quad (x(i) < y(i-1)) \wedge (z(i) = 1) \wedge\\
& && \quad (x(i-1) = 2) \wedge (t(a_i, i) = T(i))\\
&\mathrm{Post}(\mathrm{less}(i), i) && \equiv \mathrm{Pre}(\mathrm{exchange}(i), i)\\
&\mathrm{Pre}(\mathrm{exchange}(i+1), i) && \equiv \mathrm{PERM}(y(1),\ldots,y(n)) \wedge (y(i) = x(i)) \wedge\\
& && \quad (x(i) > y(i+1)) \wedge (z(i) = 2) \wedge\\
& && \quad (z(i+1) = 1) \wedge (t(a_i, i) = T(i))\\
&\mathrm{Post}(\mathrm{less}(i+1), i) && \equiv \mathrm{Pre}(\mathrm{exchange}(i+1), i)\\
&\mathrm{Post}(\mathrm{exchange}(i), i) && \equiv \mathrm{Post}(\mathrm{exchange}(i+1), i)\\
& && \equiv \mathrm{Inv}(a_i, i) \wedge (t(a_i, i) < T(i))\\
&\mathrm{Post}(a_i, i) && \equiv \mathrm{PERM}(y(1),\ldots,y(n)) \wedge (y(i) = x(i)) \wedge\\
& && \quad (y(i-1) < x(i) < y(i+1)) \wedge\\
& && \quad (z(1) = \ldots = z(n) = 3)
\end{aligned}$$

$y(i)$, $z(i)$ and $T(i)$, $i \in \underline{n}$ are the auxiliary variables which are updated in the following actions :

$$\begin{aligned}
&\mathrm{init}'(i) && = z(i) := 0\\
&\mathrm{less}'(i) && = z(i) := 1;\ z(i-1) := 2;\\
& && \quad T(i) := t(a_i, i);\ T(i-1) := t(a_{i-1}, i-1)\\
&\mathrm{exchange}'(i) && = y(i), y(i-1) := x(i), x(i-1);\ z(i), z(i-1) := 0,0\\
&a_i' && = z(i) := 3
\end{aligned}$$

The initial values of these auxiliary variables are characterized by

$$\mathrm{INIT} \equiv \bigwedge_{i \in \underline{n}} (y(i) = K(i)).$$

The meaning of these auxiliary variables should be clear : $y(i)$ is a copy of $x(i)$; $T(i)$ is the integer variable associated with a_i. The value of $z(i)$ indicates the control point of $P(i) : z(i) = 0,1,2$ and 3 respectively when $P(i)$ is at a_i, in the first guarded action of a_i, in the second guarded action of a_i and after a_i.

It can be easily seen that the verification conditions (1)-(4) are satisfied for this annotation. For instance, consider the annotation of a_i. For this action (ITR1) is given by

$$[\mathrm{Inv}(a_i, i) \wedge \mathrm{Inv}(a_{i-1}, i-1) \wedge (x(i) < x(i-1))] \Rightarrow (t(a_i, i) > 0)$$

<u>and</u>

$$[\mathrm{Inv}(a_{i+1}, i+1) \wedge \mathrm{Inv}(a_i, i) \wedge (x(i+1) < x(i))] \Rightarrow (t(a_i, i) > 0).$$

These two implications follow directly from the definition of t. Since CLOSED (a_I) holds only for $I = \underline{n}$, (ITR2) for a_i is

$$[\bigwedge_{i \in \underline{n}} \mathrm{Inv}(a_i, i) \wedge (x(1) < x(2)) \wedge \ldots \wedge (x(n-1) < x(n))]$$
$$\Rightarrow \mathrm{WP}(\underset{i \in I}{\mathbf{S}} a_i', \mathrm{Post}(a_j, j))$$

for every $j \in \underline{n}$, which is obviously true.

6. CONCLUSION

A new class of high level programs for describing the behavior of distributed systems has been proposed. Two important features of these programs are : (i) They possess all the fundamental properties of distributed systems and (ii) They specify arbitrary degree of asynchrony and decentralization. These features have been found to be useful in the systematic development of distributed programs from specifications that include process structure specifications. A transformational approach has been proposed for the systematic development in [20, 21] which makes use of a number of correctness preserving transformation rules. Using the operational semantics given here, the validity of these rules can be proved by showing that these rules preserve the meanings of the programs being transformed. The verification method proposed here is also useful in the systematic development, as some of the transformation rules require a correct annotation for the program being transformed. The correctness and the verification method assume the specifications to consist of pre- and post-condition pairs. As the methodology discussed in [21] assumes specifications to include process structure information, another notion of correctness, called process structure correctness, is also required for PPSAs. Precise definition of this notion and a method of verifying the corrctness of PPSAs with respect to process structure specifications are discussed in [21].

We have furnished the operational semantics of PPSAs based on the centralized execution model. In the centralized execution of a PPSA, at an instant, any action among the possible executable actions, can be executed without considering fairness in selection. It would be interesting to study the behavior of PPSAs under different types of fairness as has been done for joint action systems [4].

Acknowledgements : We wish to thank the referees for their

constructive comments and suggestions which have improved this paper considerably. We also thank the Department of Mathematics, I.I.T., Bombay, for the help offered in typing this paper.

REFERENCES

1. Apt, K. R., Formal justification of a proof system for communicating sequential processes, Journal of the ACM, Vol. 30, No. 1 (1983).
2. Apt, K. R., Francez, N. and de Rover, W. P., A proof system for communicating sequential processes, ACM TOPLAS, Vol. 2, No. 3 (1980).
3. Back, R. J. R. and Kurki-Suonio, R., Decentralization of process nets with centralized control, Proc. of 2nd ACM Conf. on PODC, Montreal, August 1983.
4. Back, R. J. R. and Kurki-Suonio, R., Cooperation in Distributed Systems Using Symmetric Multi-Process Handshaking, Technical Report, Ser. A, No. 34, Abo Akademi, Finland, 1984.
5. Back, R. J. R., Ekulund, P. and Kurki-Suonio, R., A Fair and Efficient Implementation of CSP with Output Guards, Technical Report, Ser. A, No. 38, Abo Akademi, Finland, 1984.
6. Buckley, G. N. and Silberschatz, A., An effective implementation for the generalized input-output construct of CSP, ACM TOPLAS, Vol. 5, No. 2 (1983).
7. Chandy, K. M., Misra, J. and Hass, L. M., Distributed deadlock detection, ACM TOPLAS, Vol.1, No. 2 (1983).
8. Chandy, K. M., Paradigm for distributed computing, Rec. of 3rd Conf. on FST-TCS, Bangalore, December 1983.
9. Chang, E. J. H., Echo algorithms: Depth parallel operations on general graphs, IEEE-TSE, Vol. SE-8, No. 4 (1980).
10. Dijkstra, E. W. D., A Discipline of Programming, Prentice-Hall, Englewood Cliffs, 1976.
11. Donahue, J. E., Complementary Definition of Programming Language Semantics – LNCS 42, Springer-Verlag, Berlin, 1976.
12. Elrad, Tz. and Francez, N., Decomposition of distributed programs into communication closed layers, Science of Computer Programming, Vol. 2 (1982).
13. Francez, N. and Hailpern, B., Script : A communication abstraction mechanism, Proc. of 2nd ACM Conf. on PODC, Montreal, August 1983.
14. Hoare, C. A. R., Communicating sequential processes, Communication of the ACM, Vol. 21, No. 8 (1978).
15. Levin, G. and Gries, D. Proof techniques for communicating sequential processes, Acta Informatica, Vol.15 (1981).
16. Manna, Z., A Mathematical Theory of Computation, McGraw-Hill, Kogakusha Ltd., Tokyo, 1974.
17. Moitra, A., Synthesis of communicating processes, Proc. of 2nd ACM Conf. on PODC, Montreal, August 1983.
18. Plotkin, G. D., An operational semantics of CSP, In : D. Bjorner (Ed.), Proc. of IFIP Conf. on Formal Description of Programming Concepts - II, North Holland Pub. Co., Amsterdam, 1983.

19. Prasad, V. R., Derivation of Distributed Programs from Sequential Programs, Technical Report, TR 87, T.I.F.R., Bombay, August 1983.

20. Ramesh, S. and Mehndiratta, S. L., A methodology for developing distributed programs, Submitted for publication.

21. Ramesh, S., Programming with Shared Actions : A Methodology for Developing Distributed Programs, Ph.D. Thesis to be submitted to I. I. T., Bombay.

22. Schwartz, J. S., Distributed Synchronization of Communicating Sequential Processes, Technical Report, DAI TR 56, Department of A. I., University of Edinburgh.

23. Taubenfeld, G. and Francez, N., Proof rules for communication abstraction, Proc. of 4th Conf. on FST-TCS, LNCS 181, Springer-Verlag, Berlin, 1984.

A Class of Termination Detection Algorithms For Distributed Computations[1]

Devendra Kumar
Department of Computer Sciences, University of Texas at Austin

Abstract

We present a class of efficient algorithms for termination detection in a distributed system. These algorithms do not require the FIFO property for the communication channels. Assumptions regarding the connectivity of the processes are simple. Messages for termination detection are processed and sent out from a process only when it is idle. Thus it is expected that these messages would not interfere much with the underlying computation, i.e., the computation not related to termination detection. The messages have a fixed, short length. After termination has occurred, it is detected within a small number of message communications.

The algorithms use markers for termination detection. By varying assumptions regarding connectivity of the processes, and the number of markers used, a spectrum of algorithms can be derived, changing their character from a distributed one to a centralized one. The number of message communications required to detect termination after its occurrence depends on the particular algorithm – under reasonable connectivity assumptions it varies from order N (where N is the number of processes) to a constant.

This paper introduces message counting as a novel and effective technique in designing termination detection algorithms. The algorithms are incrementally derived, i.e., a succession of algorithms are presented leading to the final algorithms. Proofs of correctness are presented. We compare our algorithms with other work on termination detection.

1. Introduction

We develop a class of efficient algorithms for termination detection in a distributed system. We do not require the FIFO property for the communication channels, which is usually assumed in other works. (The FIFO property for a communication channel means that messages in the channel are received in the same order as they were sent.) Our assumptions regarding connectivity of processes are simple. We have categorized our algorithms in three classes. Algorithms in classes 1 and 2 assume that there exists a cycle involving all processes in the network. This cycle need not be an elementary cycle, i.e., a process may be arrived at several times in a traversal of the cycle. Moreover, the edges of the

[1]This work was supported by Air Force Grant AFOSR 81-0205.

cycle need not be *primary edges*, i.e., the edges involved in the underlying computation; *secondary edges* may be introduced in the network to facilitate termination detection. (We use the terms *edges*, *lines*, and *channels* interchangeably.) Normally the length of this cycle would affect performance of the algorithms; by using secondary edges, if necessary, the length of this cycle may be kept to a minimum. Algorithms in class 3 assume the existence of cycles in several parts of the networks.

In these algorithms, messages for termination detection are processed and sent out from a process only when it is idle. Thus it is expected that these messages would not interfere much with the underlying network computation, i.e., the computation whose termination is to be detected.

Except for algorithms in class 1, the messages for termination detection in these algorithms have a fixed, short length (a pair of integers). In all algorithms presented, termination is detected within a small number of message communications after its occurrence.

In devising an algorithm for detecting termination, deadlock, or some other stable property [Chandy 85a, Chandy 85b], one important issue is how to determine if there are no primary messages in transit (*primary messages* are those transmitted in the underlying computation; *secondary messages* are those related to termination detection). Several approaches have been developed to handle this issue – acknowledgement messages [Chandy 85a], using a marker to "flush out" any messages in transit (with the assumption of FIFO property) [Misra 83, Chandy 85a], etc. One contribution of this paper is to suggest a new approach – counting the number of primary messages sent and received. As shown in this paper, this approach has several desirable features – it results in simple and flexible connectivity requirements, it does not require the FIFO property for the communication channels, and it does not generate too much overhead in terms of the number of secondary messages after the occurrence of termination. Moreover, we show that it is not necessary to count and transmit information regarding number of primary messages on *individual lines* – it is sufficient to count and transmit information about the total number of primary messages received and the total number of primary messages sent by individual processes.

Classification of Our Algorithms

Algorithms in class 1 are based on counting primary messages on every line. Each process keeps a count of the number of primary messages it has received or sent on each adjacent line (i.e., input line or output line respectively). As mentioned above, algorithms in class 1 assume that there exists a cycle C including every process of the network at least once. A marker traverses the cycle, and uses these counts in detecting termination. After termination has occurred, it will be detected within $|C|-1$ communications of the marker. ($|C|$ refers to the length of the cycle C, i.e., the number of edge traversals required to complete the cycle.) The problem with this algorithm is that each message is long – it consists of E number of integers where E is the total number of primary lines in the network.

Algorithms in class 2 reduce the message length. In these algorithms, each process counts the total number of primary messages received by it, and the total number of primary messages sent by it. Here counts are not being kept for individual adjacent lines. A marker traverses the cycle C, and collects this information to detect termination. In this case the message length is short (two integers). After the occurrence of termination, it will be detected within $2 \cdot |C| - 2$ message communications. Note that if C is an elementary cycle then

$|C| = N$, where N is the number of processes in the distributed system.

Next, class 3 of our algorithms improve the performance of the algorithms in class 2, by using multiple markers which traverse different parts of the system. We make simple connectivity assumptions to permit these traversals. Using two markers, under reasonable assumptions the number of message communications after the occurrence of termination is reduced to approximately 3N/2, each message carrying an integer and a boolean. As the number of markers is increased, this number reduces further and the algorithm tends to change its character to a centralized one. Finally, using N markers, this number is reduced to the constant 4, and the algorithm becomes a purely centralized one.

On the Nature of This Presentation

A number of excellent papers on deadlock and termination detection for distributed systems have appeared in recent years. These papers usually discuss how the algorithm executes, i.e, what are the key data or execution steps in the algorithms. Proofs of correctness are usually provided to convince the reader that the given algorithm works. However, certain other important questions are usually left unanswered. How was the algorithm developed in the first place? Why were certain decisions (conventions, assumptions, major data, major execution steps) in the design of the algorithm taken – are they critical to the correctness, or are they present simply to enhance performance, or understandability, etc.? How would a simple variation of these decisions affect either correctness or performance? For the algorithms discussed here, our presentation attempts to answer some of these questions to a certain extent. We discuss a succession of algorithms, each algorithm differing from the previous ones in a simple manner. Several simple variations of the algorithms are considered. As would be noted in the discussion, some of these "algorithms" are not even correct; they are discussed simply to enhance understandability of later algorithms. Moreover, specific details, for instance initial conditions, are derived from more general considerations. It is hoped that with this method of presentation, the reader can develop a better insight as to how various decisions were arrived at. Since the relationships among various algorithms are explicitly discussed, this approach would also help keep a clear and organized view of the class of algorithms presented.

Related Work

Termination detection in distributed systems has been a subject of much study in recent years. One of the earliest works in this area is the elegant algorithm of [Dijkstra 80]. This is one of the few algorithms that do not assume the FIFO property for the communication channels. However, this algorithm requires that for any primary line from a process i to a process j, there must be a line from j to i. Termination is detected within N message communications after its occurrence, where N is the number of processes in the system. However, depending on the nature of the underlying computation, *in the entire computation* the total number of secondary messages generated in this algorithm may be too much. (The total number of secondary messages in this algorithm is equal to the total number of primary messages.) This may severely affect performance. Moreover, secondary messages are processed and sent out from a process even when it is active. This may slow down the underlying computation itself.

The above algorithm was extended in [Misra 82a] to CSP [Hoare 78] environment. The basic idea of the algorithm has been used in several distributed algorithms in many application areas [Cohen 82, Misra 82b, Chandy 82b, Chandy 81].

Marker based algorithms usually do not suffer from the drawbacks mentioned above for the algorithm in [Dijkstra 80]. A marker is sent from a process only when it is idle. Therefore normally the secondary computation would not significantly slow down the underlying computation. (*Secondary computation* is that related to termination detection; the underlying computation is also called the *primary computation*.) Moreover, usually the total number of secondary messages would also be small. Roughly speaking, if the primary computation becomes more intense (i.e., primary messages are being generated at a higher rate), then the recipient processes are likely to be active more of the time (i.e., idle for lesser time). Hence the marker is likely to move less frequently since it has to wait till the process has become idle. However, this is not to say that marker based algorithms always result in better performance; in fact many such algorithms require more than N message communications after the occurrence of termination.

Earlier works on distributed termination detection using a marker are by Gouda [Gouda 81] and Francez et. al. [Francez 80, Francez 81, Francez 82]. These approaches were improved upon, removing some of their restrictions, in another marker based algorithm [Misra 83]. In this algorithm a marker traverses a cycle C' that includes every edge of the network at least once. The algorithm requires the FIFO property for the communication channels. Termination is detected, after its occurrence, within two rounds of this cycle. Note that, in principle, assuming the existence of a cycle traversing every edge is equivalent to assuming the existence of a cycle traversing every process (as in our approach). However, the performance resulting from the two approaches would normally be different. The cycle C' in general may be quite large – usually it would be longer than the total number of primary edges in the network, and the number of primary edges can be $O(N^2)$. In contrast, in our approach we can always define an elementary cycle (whose length will be N), introducing secondary edges if necessary. Defining an optimal or near optimal cycle in our approach is much simpler, since we don't require the cycle to involve every primary edge. If the network is evolving over time (e.g., new primary lines or processes being added to the network) our approach would normally require simpler changes in the data stored at the processes regarding this cycle.

In several recent works [Chandy 85a, Chandy 85b) the notion of termination and deadlock has been generalized and elegant schemes have been presented to solve these general problems. [Chandy 85a] shows how the general scheme presented there can be applied in many ways to solve the specific problems of termination and deadlock detection. The termination detection algorithm described there assumes the FIFO property for the communication channels. A marker traverses a cycle that includes every process of the network at least once. Termination is detected, after its occurrence, within two rounds of this cycle. The marker is a short message, containing only one integer. However, before the marker is sent out from a process, another message (containing no data) is sent out on output lines of this process. This effectively doubles the number of message communications after occurrence of termination. Since our algorithms in class 2 involve two rounds of the same cycle, with each secondary message having two integers, we expect comparable performance between the above algorithm and our algorithms in class 2. However, our schemes in class 3 improve the performance even further. As indicated in [Chandy 85a], the FIFO requirement for the communication channels may be removed, leading to another algorithm. But that algorithm would involve too many acknowledgement messages (equal to the number of primary messages).

One nice property that the two algorithms above ([Misra 83] and the algorithm in [Chandy 85a] using the FIFO property) enjoy is that the termination detection algorithm may be initiated with the underlying computation of the network in an arbitrary state, i.e., there may be an arbitrary number of primary messages in transit and the processes may be in arbitrary states. Our algorithms and most of the other algorithms published require special initializations for the secondary computation before the underlying computation starts.

As mentioned earlier, termination detection has been used in designing several other distributed algorithms. Many distributed algorithms can be devised as multiphase algorithms, where a new phase is started after the termination detection of the previous phase. Distributed simulation schemes have been devised using this approach [Chandy 81, Kumar 85]. [Francez 81] suggests a methodology for devising distributed programs using termination detection.

A problem of considerable importance that is closely related to termination detection, is the problem of deadlock detection in distributed systems. Several important pieces of works have appeared in this area [Gligor 80, Beeri 81, Obermarck 82, Chandy 82a, Chandy 83, Bracha 83, Haas 83].

Synopsis of the Rest of the Paper

Section 2 defines the model of computation and defines the termination detection problem. Criteria used for comparing termination detection algorithms may vary widely – performance, storage requirements, communication cost, simplicity of implementation, etc. In this paper we concern ourselves only with performance. In section 3 we discuss our performance criteria. Sections 4, 5, and 6 discuss our algorithms in classes 1, 2, and 3 respectively (we have commented on these classes earlier in the introduction). Finally section 7 gives concluding remarks.

2. Problem Definition

First we describe a basic model of a distributed system. For ease of exposition, we discuss our algorithms in terms of this basic model. Our algorithms are applicable to more general distributed systems; we briefly mention these systems later in this section.

The Basic Model

A distributed system consists of a finite set of processes, and a set of unidirectional *communication channels* (or *lines*, or *edges*). Each communication channel connects two distinct processes. Given two processes i and j, there is at most one communication channel from i to j, denoted by the ordered pair (i, j).

In addition to their local computations, processes may send or receive messages. Process i can send a message to process j only if the line (i, j) exists. Process i does so by depositing the message in the channel (i, j). This message arrives at process j after an arbitrary but finite (possibly zero) delay. Process j receives the message by removing it from the channel, within a finite time (possibly zero) of its arrival. The channels are error-free, except that they need not be FIFO channels.

The "Underlying" Computation

Now we describe the nature of the computation (called the *underlying computation* or the *primary computation*) whose termination is to be detected. The messages sent or received in this computation are called *primary messages*. Later other computation (called *secondary computation*) would be superimposed on this computation for the purpose of termination detection.

From the point of view of the underlying computation, at any moment a process is in one of two states:

1. *Active state:* In this state, a process may send primary messages on its outgoing lines. It may become idle at any time.

2. *Idle state:* In this state, a process can not send any primary messages. On receiving a primary message, it may remain idle or switch its state to active.

A process in any of the two states may receive primary messages or do any local computations. It is assumed that initially, (i.e., when the primary computation starts) there are no primary messages in transit; though the processes may be in arbitrary states.

The Termination Detection Problem

A message in the distributed system is said to be a *transient message* if it has been sent, but has not been received yet. We say that at a moment t the distributed computation is terminated iff:

1. all the processes are idle at time t, and

2. there are no transient primary messages at time t.

It is obvious that if the network computation is terminated at a time instant t, then it would remain terminated for all times after t (unless forced otherwise by some outside agent). The problem is to detect the state of termination within a finite time after its occurrence. To this end, we will devise an algorithm to be superimposed on the underlying computation; this algorithm must satisfy the following properties:

1. Termination is reported, to some process in the network, within a finite time after termination of the underlying computation, and

2. if termination is reported at some time t, the network must be terminated at time t (i.e., no "false detection" of termination is allowed).

Messages related to termination detection are called *secondary messages.* It may be noted that an idle process may send secondary messages, even though it can not send primary ones.

Other Models

We briefly mention here other features that could be incorporated in our model of computation, without affecting the applicability of our algorithms (possibly with some minor modifications).

1. We may allow multiple communication channels from a process i to a process j. Also, a process could be allowed to send a message to itself. These extensions may be useful if a process consists of a set of interacting subprocesses.

2. A process may *broadcast* a message to a set of processes. This is equivalent to sending the same message via communication lines to each process in the set.

3. There may be a third state for a process – a *terminated state.* A process enters this state when it is guaranteed that it will not send out any primary messages in

future, and no more primary messages would arrive at its input lines.

3. Performance Criteria

There are two major criteria for performance evaluation of termination detection algorithms:

1. The effect of secondary computation on the primary computation itself, i.e., how the primary computation gets slowed down and

2. How long it takes to detect termination after its occurrence.

In general, the two criteria above would be assigned different weights, depending on the objectives of the primary computation and its termination detection. One has to consider not only the time delays involved, but also how *time critical* the two delays are. Depending on application, one of these may carry a higher weight than the other. The following examples illustrate this:

1. Consider a distributed system that monitors a physical system. The primary computation is triggered by an extreme state in the physical system and its objective is to bring the system to a steady state. The primary computation terminates after the system returns to the steady state. Here the former criterion would be more significant.

2. Consider a secondary computation whose objective is to detect the termination of a token in a token ring [Misra 83]. Suppose the loss of the token represents an extreme state that must be corrected immediately. Here the second criterion would be more significant.

3. Consider a multiphase distributed simulation [Chandy 81, Kumar´ 85]. Here the objective is to reduce the *total* simulation time. In this case none of the two delays above are time critical and both affect the overall objective in the same way; thus both criteria would have equal weights here.

In this paper we will focus on the second criterion. (As mentioned above, in a particular application this may or may not be a good criterion for performance measurement.) Let I denote the time interval between the occurrence of termination and its detection.

How should one estimate I? Obviously, the value of I depends on characteristics of the system that supports the primary computation. We use the number of (secondary) message communications during the interval I and the lengths of these messages as a measure of I. Knowing the characteristics of communication delays, one may establish either I or an upper bound on it. For simplicity of discussion, we assume that any communication delay in the system is a linear function of message length. We mention below a few details about our performance evaluation:

1. Note that the value of I (and the associated measures mentioned above) would depend on where the marker is at the time when termination occurs, etc. For simplicity, we would normally consider only the worst case values.

2. Message communications at the same time on different lines will be taking place *in parallel* – this must be taken into account in determining the number of messages, i.e., during any overlapping period, only one message is considered being

communicated. In general, any two independent events will be assumed to take place in parallel.

3. During the interval I, the number of messages received may be different (slightly) from the number of messages sent. We consider the latter one as the number of message communications. (This would be more reasonable in situations where the time involved in the act of sending a message, i.e., the *transmission time*, is longer than the propagation delay of the message.)

4. By message length we mean the total length of data in it. It is assumed that even for a message of length zero, there would be a non-zero communication delay.

4. Class 1 of Algorithms: Counting Primary Messages on Each Line

In these algorithms, a marker traverses a cycle C that includes every process of the network at least once (discussed in section 1). Information as to how many messages are in transit is kept by counting the number of primary messages sent, and received, for each line. Each process i has two local arrays $SNTP_i$ and $RECP_i$. (For simplicity of discussion, we assume here that primary lines in the network are globally numbered 1, 2, ..., E and each array $SNTP_i$ and $RECP_i$ has E elements. We will discuss more appropriate data structures later.) At any time, $SNTP_i(e)$ = the number of primary messages sent by process i on line e after the last visit of marker at i (or since the initial time, if the marker has not visited i yet). $RECP_i(e)$ is similarly defined for messages received. Each process i increments $SNTP_i(e)$ or $RECP_i(e)$, respectively, on sending or receiving a primary message on line e.

The marker has two arrays *SNTM* and *RECM*, where it keeps its knowledge as to how many primary messages have been sent or received on each line.

(For convenience, in this paper we use the obvious notation for *array assignments*, *array equality*, etc. Also, we often use a time argument in a variable to refer to its value at that time.)

An Algorithm-Skeleton

The following basic algorithm-skeleton is followed by the marker.

(* marker *arrives* at process i, i.e. it is received by i. *)
  The marker waits till process i becomes idle;

(* Process i is idle now. Marker starts its *visit* at i. *)
  $SNTM := SNTM + SNTP_i$;
  $SNTP_i := 0$;
  $RECM := RECM + RECP_i$;
  $RECP_i := 0$;
(* The visit at process i is completed. *)

(* *Declare termination* or *depart* from process i. *)
  Under an appropriate condition (to be discussed) the marker
  declares termination. If this condition does not hold,
  the marker leaves process i along the next line on cycle C.

We discuss later (under the heading "some improvements and details") the algorithm and data structures required to facilitate the repeated traversal of the cycle C by the marker.

A process does not receive any messages during the interval between the start of marker's visit and its departure. In other words, the underlying computation at a process is carried out only before the marker's visit and after its departure. As mentioned earlier, the variables $SNTP_i$ and $RECP_i$ are incremented on sending or receiving (respectively) a primary message.

The variables related to termination detection are initialized before the primary computation starts. Initially, a value of zero is assigned to all elements of *SNTM*, *RECM*, $SNTP_i$, and $RECP_i$. (This initialization will be changed later in the discussion.) Also, the marker is initially at an arbitrary process, and visits it when the process becomes idle.

The above is only a skeleton of an algorithm; we have not yet discussed when the marker declares termination. We address this issue now. Suppose the primary computation terminates at time T_f. Then within a finite time after T_f the system would reach a state where the condition *SNTM* = *RECM* is true (i.e., the corresponding elements of the two arrays are equal) and would remain true forever. (After T_f this condition may become true or false several times, but definitely after one complete traversal of the cycle C by the marker it will remain true forever.) This is stated as theorem 1 below. This suggests a way of detecting termination, but we still have to avoid the possibility of detecting "false termination". Note that the condition *SNTM* = *RECM* being true at a point in computation does not guarantee that termination has occurred. For example, initially this condition holds, but the system may have active processes. We ask the question – suppose in a sequence of visits along the cycle C, the marker continuously finds that *SNTM* = *RECM*. Can it conclude termination after a (predefined) finite number V of such visits? Theorem 2 looks at this question in a 'brute force' manner, and answers it in the affirmative with $V = 2.|C|$. Using this theorem one can complete the algorithm. Thereafter we consider the question of efficiency. Theorem 3 improves the efficiency of this algorithm by reducing V to $|C|$. Theorem 4 provides a way of reducing V to 1 if an additional condition is guaranteed before announcing termination. Later we discuss how to ensure this condition in an efficient way. (It will be observed that as we progress from theorem 2 towards theorem 4, the results become less obvious and the proofs of correctness more complex.) Let us first discuss some intermediate results that will be used in the proofs of these theorems.

For convenience, in this paper we will be implicitly using the convention that events are totally ordered, e.g., as in [Misra 81]. The events of interest are – sending a primary message, receiving a primary message, a process changing its state, and the marker arriving at a process, starting a visit, completing a visit, and departing the process. All time instants mentioned in this paper correspond to a point in the trace of events in the system, unless otherwise specified. In particular, normally no time instant refers to a moment in between the start and completion of a visit. (Otherwise many of our lemmas will become incorrect!)

Let *tsnt*(e, t) = the total number of messages sent on line e up to (including) time t.

trec(e, t) is similarly defined for messages received.

Let r(e, t) = the number of transient messages on line e at time t.

Lemma 1: For any line e and any time t:

$$tsnt(e, t) = trec(e, t) + r(e, t) \tag{1}$$

and $tsnt(e, t) \geq trec(e, t)$ (2)

Proof: Follows from the definitions.

Lemma 2: For any line e and any two time instants t, t' such that t < t':

$$tsnt(e, t) \leq tsnt(e, t') \tag{3}$$

and $trec(e, t) \leq trec(e, t')$ (4)

Proof: Follows from the definitions.

Lemma 3: For any line e = (i, j) and for any time t:

$$tsnt(e, t) = SNTM(e, t) + SNTP_i(e, t) \tag{5}$$

and $trec(e, t) = RECM(e, t) + RECP_j(e, t)$ (6)

Proof: The proof is by induction on the number of events in the system [Misra 81]. Initially, (5) and (6) are true. Also, each event leaves any of them invariant.

Lemma 4: For any line e = (i, j) and for any time t:

$$r(e, t) = SNTM(e, t) - RECM(e, t) + SNTP_i(e, t) - RECP_j(e, t) \tag{7}$$

Proof: Follows from (1), (5), and (6).

Lemma 5: Consider a "current" moment T in computation. For a line e = (i, j), suppose both processes i and j have been visited by the marker at least once. Let t_i and t_j, respectively, be the last times at which visits at processes i and j were completed. Then,

$$SNTM(e, T) - RECM(e, T) = tsnt(e, t_i) - trec(e, t_j) \tag{8}$$

Proof: Obviously $SNTM(e, T) = SNTM(e, t_i)$, $RECM(e, T) = RECM(e, t_j)$, $SNTP_i(e, t_i) = 0$, and $RECP_j(e, t_j) = 0$. The result follows from lemma 3.

Note: Later we will make certain changes that will make lemma 2 incorrect. However, lemmas 1, 3-5 will not be affected. Proofs of theorems 1-6 below will rest only on lemmas 1, 3-5 – they will not use lemma 2 directly.

Theorem 1: If the underlying computation terminates at a time T_f, then within a finite time after T_f the system would reach a state where the condition *SNTM* = *RECM* is true and would remain true forever thereafter (until termination is declared and possibly a new primary computation is started).

Proof: After T_f, all processes remain idle forever; therefore the marker does not wait indefinitely after its arrival at a process. Hence, within a finite time after T_f (say at a time T, $T \geq T_f$), the marker would have made a complete traversal of the cycle C, i.e., it would have visited every process at least once after time T_f (unless it has declared termination earlier). Let $T' \geq T$ be any "current" time. For any line e = (i, j) let t_i and t_j, respectively, be the last times at which processes i and j were visited. Obviously, $t_i \geq T_f$ and $t_j \geq T_f$. From lemma 5,

$$SNTM(e, T') - RECM(e, T') = tsnt(e, t_i) - trec(e, t_j)$$

But $tsnt(e, t_i) = tsnt(e, T_f)$, $trec(e, t_j) = trec(e, T_f)$, and $tsnt(e, T_f) = trec(e, T_f)$. The result follows.

∎

Theorem 2: Suppose in a sequence of V = 2.|C| visits, the marker continuously finds the condition *SNTM* = *RECM* to be true after each visit in the sequence. Then at the end of this sequence it can conclude that the underlying computation has terminated.

Proof: Let T_0 be the time when the marker has completed |C| number of visits in the above sequence. We will show that at time T_0 the primary computation is terminated. Let t_{i0} be the time at which the marker completed its last visit at process i up to (including) time T_0. Also, let t_{i1} and t_i be the times at which the marker started and finished, respectively, its fist visit at process i after time T_0 (here we are considering the start and completion of a visit as two distinct events in the history of events in the system). Obviously, for all i $t_{i0} \leq T_0 < t_{i1} < t_i$.

We first show that at time T_0, for all primary lines e = (i, j), $SNTP_i(e, T_0) = 0$. In a similar manner it can be shown that $RECP_j(e, T_0) = 0$. Suppose for some e = (i, j), $SNTP_i(e, T_0) > 0$. Obviously $SNTP_i(e, t_{i1}) \geq SNTP_i(e, T_0) > 0$. Hence $SNTM(e, t_i) = SNTM(e, t_{i1}) + SNTP_i(e, t_{i1}) > SNTM(e, t_{i1})$. But $SNTM(e, t_{i1}) = RECM(e, t_{i1})$ and $RECM(e, t_{i1}) = RECM(e, t_i)$. Therefore $SNTM(e, t_i) > RECM(e, t_i)$. This contradicts the hypothesis of the theorem.

Since for every line e = (i, j), $SNTP_i(e, T_0) = RECP_j(e, T_0) = 0$ and $SNTM(e, T_0) = RECM(e, T_0)$, it follows from lemma 4 that $r(e, T_0) = 0$. In other words there are no transient primary messages at time T_0.

Now we show that every process i is idle at time T_0. Obviously i is idle at time t_{i0}. Also, i did not receive any primary messages during the interval $[t_{i0}, T_0]$, otherwise we will have $RECP_i(e, T_0) > 0$ for the corresponding input line e, which will contradict the above result that $RECP_i(e, T_0) = 0$. Thus i is idle at time T_0. This completes the proof.

∎

Theorem 3: Theorem 2 remains valid if the requirement $V = 2.|C|$ in it is changed to $V = |C|$.

Proof: Let T_0 and T, respectively, be the times when the first and the last visits in the sequence are completed. For any process i, choose any particular visit that was completed in the interval $[T_0, T]$ and let t_{i1} and t_i, respectively, be the times at which this visit was started and finished. Claim (A) below can be shown easily (if i is the first process visited in the sequence and $t_i = T_0$, then (A) follows readily; for other cases it follows as in the proof of theorem 2):

(A) At any time t during the interval $[T_0, t_i]$, process i has $SNTP_i(e, t) = RECP_i(e, t) = 0$ for any adjacent primary line e.

Since $SNTM = RECM$ after each visit in the sequence, from (A) we conclude that:

(B) At time T_0 there are no transient primary messages, and

(C) Process i did not send or receive a primary message in the interval $[T_0, t_i]$.

Note that a process i may be active at time T_0. We will show that after time t_i, process i will never receive a primary message. Since any message in transit will be received after a finite time, this proves that there are no transient messages at time T when the above sequence of visits is completed. Moreover, since process i is idle at time t_i and does not receive any primary messages after time t_i, it will be idle at time T.

We say that a primary message is a *bad* message if it is received at a process i after time t_i. We will prove by contradiction that there can be no bad messages in the system. Suppose there are bad messages in the system. Let m be the bad message with the earliest time of reception (say t_r). Suppose m was sent on a line $e = (i, j)$ at time t_s. Obviously, $t_r > t_s$ and $t_r > t_j$. Consider the following two cases.

Case 1: $t_s > t_i$, i.e., m was sent out after the marker's last visit at i. Then process i must have received a bad message after t_i and before t_s (hence before t_r). this contradicts the assumption that m is the bad message with the earliest time of reception.

Case 2: $t_s < t_i$. We have shown above (C) that process i does not send any primary messages in the interval $[T_0, t_i]$. Therefore m must have been sent before T_0. Hence m is in transit at time T_0. This contradicts (B) above. This completes the proof.

[]

Now we attempt to reduce further the length of the sequence of visits required with the condition $SNTM = RECM$ before the marker can conclude termination. Note that in order to detect termination, the marker must visit every process at least once after the start of the secondary computation; since in our scheme the state (idle or active) of a process can not be deduced from the information available at the other processes. We show below in theorem 4 that if every process has been visited at least once, then the condition $SNTM = RECM$ after visiting a process guarantees that termination has indeed occurred.

Theorem 4: Suppose, after visiting a process, the marker finds that *SNTM* = *RECM*. Also, suppose the marker has visited every process at least once by this time. Then at this time T the underlying computation is in the terminated state.

Proof: Let t_i be the last time that the marker completed its visit at process i up to time T (i.e., $t_i \leq T$). We will show that after time t_i, process i would never receive a primary message. As argued in the proof of theorem 3, this leads to the conclusion.

With the above definition of t_i, we define *bad messages* in the same way as in the proof of theorem 3. The argument continues as before and case 1 is the same. Case 2 is different now and we consider it below.

Case 2: $t_s < t_i$, i.e., m was sent before the marker last visited process i. Since *SNTM*(e, T) = *RECM*(e, T), from lemma 5 we get *tsnt*(e, t_i) = *trec*(e, t_j). Consider the following two subcases.

Case 2.1: $t_i < t_j$. By definition of m, process i did not receive any primary messages in the interval $[t_i, t_j]$. Therefore process i did not send any primary messages in this interval. Therefore, *tsnt*(e, t_i) = *tsnt*(e, t_j). Hence *tsnt*(e, t_j) = *trec*(e, t_j). But there is at least one transient message, namely m, on line e at time t_j (since m was sent before t_i and received after t_j). This contradicts (1).

Case 2.2: $t_j < t_i$. Since *tsnt*(e, t_i) = *trec*(e, t_j), using (2) and (3) we conclude in this case that *tsnt*(e, t_i) = *tsnt*(e, t_j) = *trec*(e, t_j). In other words, no primary messages were sent on line e during $[t_j, t_i]$ and there are no transient messages on line e at time t_j. Hence m was sent before t_j and received by the time t_j. This contradicts with the definition of m.

∎

Note: The proof of case 2 will be simpler if one assumes the FIFO property for the communication channels. Informally, since m has been counted in *tsnt*(e, t_i) and has not been counted in *trec*(e, t_j), by the FIFO property we will get *tsnt*(e, t_i) > *trec*(e, t_j). Therefore we won't have to consider the cases 2.1 and 2.2.

Completion of the Algorithm

It may be noted that if the hypothesis of theorem 2 or theorem 3 is true then the hypothesis of theorem 4 is true as well, but not vice versa. Therefore the method suggested by theorem 4 would be more efficient. Hence we use theorem 4 to complete the algorithm. How would the marker decide that it has visited every process at least once? One brute force method would be to have a counter in the marker that counts how many visits have been completed. When this counter becomes |C|, obviously every process has been visited at least once. (Alternatively, the marker could count how many *distinct* processes it has visited, by marking a process "visited" after visiting it.)

We use a more efficient strategy – the initial values of the variables *SNTM*, *RECM*, $SNTP_i$, $RECP_i$ are assigned in a different way than mentioned earlier. This assignment guarantees the following two conditions:

1. As long as there is at least one process that has not been visited yet, the condition *SNTM* = *RECM* will remain false, i.e., at least one pair of corresponding elements in the two arrays will not match. (We will be assuming that each process has at least one adjacent primary line. Otherwise we have isolated processes in the system. If needed, such cases can be incorporated in the scheme in obvious ways.) This is stated as lemma 6 below.

2. Moreover, this assignment does not affect the correctness of theorems 1 and 4. (In fact, all of lemmas 1, 3-5 and theorem 1-4 remain valid.) This is stated as lemma 7 below.

Obviously, this strategy is more efficient since the additional counter in the marker is avoided, reducing its length. An infinite set of assignments guaranteeing the above conditions exist; here we consider one specific assignment.

Corresponding to every primary line e = (i, j), we initialize $SNTM(e) = 1$, $RECM(e) = 0$, $SNTP_i(e) = 1$, and $RECP_j(e) = 2$. The marker declares termination after a visit if it finds that $SNTM = RECM$. The rest of the algorithm remains the same as before. Theorems 5 and 6 below prove the correctness of the algorithm.

Lemma 6: With the above initialization, suppose after visiting a process the marker finds that $SNTM = RECM$. Then, the marker has visited every process at least once by this time (say T).

Proof: For any line (i, j), we show that the marker has visited both i and j by the time T. (Since every process has at least one adjacent line, this establishes the result.) Suppose, to the contrary, this is not true for a line e = (i, j). Consider the following cases.

Case 1: The marker has not visited the process j by the time T. Obviously, in this case $SNTM(e, T) \geq 1$ and $RECM(e, T) = 0$. This contradicts the assumption that $SNTM = RECM$ at time T.

Case 2: The marker has visited process j, but not i, by the time T. Obviously, in this case $SNTM(e, T) = 1$, and $RECM(e, T) \geq 2$. Again, this leads to a contradiction. This completes the proof.

Lemma 7: With the new initial values lemmas 1 and 3-5, and theorems 1-4 remain valid.

Proof: Note that with the new initial values, lemmas 1 and 2 remain valid. The results (5) and (6) in lemma 3 become slightly incorrect – the corrected versions of these results are:

$$tsnt(e, t) = SNTM(e, t) + SNTP_i(e, t) - 2 \qquad (5')$$

$$trec(e, t) = RECM(e, t) + RECP_j(e, t) - 2 \qquad (6')$$

The proofs of (5') and (6') are similar to the proofs of (5) and (6) before. From (5') and (6') it follows that lemmas 4 and 5 remain valid.

The previous proofs of theorems 1-4 do not directly rest on lemma 2 or the initial values of the program variables (so long as lemmas 1 and 3-5 remain valid). Therefore their correctness is not affected. This completes the proof.

Theorem 5: If the underlying computation is terminated at a time T_f, then the marker would declare termination within a finite time after T_f.

Proof: Follows from lemma 7 and theorem 1.

▯▯

Theorem 6: Suppose at a moment T, the marker declares termination. Then at this moment, the underlying computation is, indeed, in the terminated state.

Proof: The theorem follows from lemmas 6 and 7 and theorem 4.

▯▯

Some Improvements and Details

We briefly mention below some simple performance improvements to the algorithm. We also discuss a few details related to implementation.

1. Instead of keeping the two arrays *SNTM* and *RECM* in the marker, it is sufficient to keep a single array, say *SRM*, which would equal *SNTM* - *RECM*. This would reduce the secondary message length. Also, this reduces the chances of an overflow. (Elements of arrays *SNTM* and *RECM* are non-decreasing with time.)

2. In our description of the algorithm, the arrays $SNTP_i$ and $RECP_i$ have an element for every primary line of the network. Usually a process is connected to only a few other processes; in such cases, with this data structure updating *SNTM* or *RECM* or *SRM* may be quite inefficient. It may be more efficient to assign contiguous local line ids to the adjacent lines at each process, keep elements only for the adjacent lines in arrays $SNTP_i$ and $RECP_i$, and keep an array that maps from local line ids to global line ids.

3. How does the marker determine the next line to be traversed? If C is an elementary cycle, then obviously just keeping the successor's id at each process is sufficient. Otherwise, one may keep a circular list of outgoing lines at each process (a line may be repeated several times in this list) and a local pointer that points to the next line to be followed by the marker. These circular lists can be initialized by considering a single traversal of the cycle C "by hand". The pointers can be initialized by defining the starting point of the marker on the cycle. Note that the marker itself does not carry any information about its path of traversal; otherwise the secondary messages would become even longer.

Performance of the Algorithm

In the worst case, the number of message communications after the occurrence of termination is |C|-1. C can be chosen to be an elementary cycle, in which case this equals N-1, where N is the total number of processes in the system. Each message has a length of E integers, where E is the number of primary lines in the system. If communication delays depend significantly on the length of the messages, then this would be quite inefficient. On the other hand, if the message length does not significantly affect communication delays then this scheme would give a reasonable performance. One nice feature of this scheme is that in the *best* case, the number of message communications after termination is zero. Normally marker based algorithms [Misra 83, Chandy85a] require at least one complete cycle between the occurrence of termination and its detection.

5. Class 2 of Algorithms: Counting Total Number of Primary Messages Sent and Received in the System

Our motivation for devising algorithms in this class is to reduce the length of secondary messages. Here the marker has two *scalar* variables *SNTM2* and *RECM2* where it keeps its knowledge regarding the total number of primary messages sent and received, respectively, in the system. This differs from algorithms in class 1 where information about *individual lines* was being kept. Each process i has two scalar variables $SNTP2_i$ and $RECP2_i$. At any time $SNTP2_i$ = the total number of primary messages sent out by process i after the last visit of the marker at i (or since the initial time, if the marker has not visited i yet). $RECP2_i$ is similarly defined for messages received. The algorithm-skeleton of class 1 remains the same for this class, except that the variables *SNTM*, *RECM*, $SNTP_i$, and $RECP_i$ are replaced by *SNTM2*, *RECM2*, $SNTP2_i$, and $RECP2_i$ respectively. These variables are initialized to be zero, before the primary computation starts. (Unlike the discussion in class 1, we won't find a need to change this initialization later.) As in class 1, a process does not receive any messages during the interval between the start of the marker's visit and its departure. As before, the variables $SNTP2_i$ and $RECP2_i$ are incremented on sending or receiving (respectively) a primary message.

Now we consider the issue of when the marker declares termination. Theorem 7 below states that if the primary computation terminates at time T_f then within a finite time after T_f the system would reach a state where the condition *SNTM2* = *RECM2* will be true and will remain true forever afterwards. As before, we have to avoid the possibility of detecting "false termination". Again we ask the question – suppose in a sequence of visits along the cycle C, the marker continuously finds that *SNTM2* = *RECM2*. Can it conclude termination after a (predefined) finite number V of such visits? Unfortunately, the answer in this case is in the negative, as shown in example 1 below. Theorem 8 below gives a method to complete the algorithm. Theorem 9 considers simple variations of the method given by theorem 8. These variations reduce the computational requirements at the processes; they do not improve communication requirements. Theorem 10 improves the performance of the algorithm by reducing the number of message communications after termination. After proving theorem 10, we show that certain simple and obvious variations of theorem 10 do not work. First let us discuss some intermediate results that will be used in the proofs.

Note that the variables *SNTM*, *RECM*, $SNTP_i$, and $RECP_i$ of class 1 can be used as "auxiliary" or "ghost" variables in our proofs. The notion of auxiliary variables is discussed, for example, in [Owicki 76]. The use of these auxiliary variables in our proofs is not essential; we use them only to simplify our proofs by exploiting the results in section 4. We assume that these variables are initialized to be zero at the start of primary computation.

Lemma 8: Lemmas 1-5 and theorems 1-4 of section 4 remain valid for the present algorithm-skeleton (when the variables *SNTM*, *RECM*, $SNTP_i$, and $RECP_i$ are interpreted as auxiliary variables).

Proof: In the algorithm-skeleton of section 4, let us introduce variables *SNTM2*, *RECM2*, $SNTP2_i$, and $RECP2_i$ in the same way as they are used in the present algorithm-skeleton. Obviously, the previous results of section 4 hold for this new algorithm-skeleton. Now in this algorithm-skeleton, let us treat variables *SNTM*, *RECM*, $SNTP_i$, and $RECP_i$ as auxiliary variables. Obviously, the results would still hold.

Lemma 9: At any time t,

$$SNTM2(t) = \text{sum } \{SNTM(e,\ t), \text{ over all primary lines e}\} \tag{9}$$

$$RECM2(t) = \text{sum } \{RECM(e,\ t), \text{ over all primary lines e}\} \tag{10}$$

$$SNTP2_i(t) = \text{sum } \{SNTP_i(e,\ t), \text{ over all outgoing primary lines e of process i}\} \tag{11}$$

$$RECP2_i(t) = \text{sum } \{RECP_i(e,\ t), \text{ over all incoming primary lines e of process i}\} \tag{12}$$

Proof: Obvious, by induction on the number of events in the system.

Lemma 10: At any time t,

$$tr(t) = SNTM2(t) - RECM2(t) + \text{sum } \{SNTP2_i(t), \text{ over all processes i}\} - \text{sum } \{RECP2_i(t), \text{ over all processes i}\} \tag{13}$$

where $tr(t)$ = the total number of primary messages in transit at time t.

Proof: Let us take the sum of each side of (7) over e, e ranging over all primary lines in the system. The result follows from lemmas 9 and 8.

Theorem 7: Theorem 1 of section 4 remains valid if *SNTM* and *RECM* in that theorem are replaced by *SNTM2* and *RECM2* respectively.

Proof: Follows from lemma 8 and the results (9) and (10) in lemma 9.

[]

Example 1: To show that there exist computations (following the algorithm-skeleton) where in an infinite sequence of visits, the marker continuously finds that *SNTM2* = *RECM2*, and yet the primary computation never terminates.

Consider a network of 10 processes. The cycle C is the elementary cycle 1, 2, ..., 10, 1. Initially the marker is at process 1, process 5 is active, and process 10 is idle. Processes 1-4 and 6-9 never send or receive a primary message and are always idle. Consider the following sequence of events at processes 5 and 10:

1. 5 sends a primary message to 10, 10 receives it, 10 sends a primary message to 5, 5 receives it. At this point 5 becomes idle and 10 remains active.

2. The marker visits 5, and departs.

3. 10 sends a primary message to 5, 5 receives it, 5 sends a primary message to 10, 10 receives it. At this point 10 becomes idle and 5 remains active.

4. The marker visits 10, and departs.

5. The above steps 1-4 are repeated indefinitely.

Obviously, after every visit the marker will find that *SNTM2* = *RECM2*. But the primary computation would never terminate!

The above example illustrates why after a finite number of visits with *SNTM2* = *RECM2* after each visit, the marker can not in general announce termination. Roughly speaking, a process i may have sent and received messages in between two successive visits by the marker. Theorem 8 is based on this observation.

Theorem 8: Suppose in a sequence of V = |C| visits, the marker continuously finds that $SNTP2_i = RECP2_i = 0$ before each visit (except possibly the first visit in the sequence) and *SNTM2* = *RECM2* after each visit. Then, at the end of this sequence of visits it can conclude that the underlying computation has terminated.

Proof: We show by induction on the number of visits in the sequence that after each visit *SNTM* = *RECM*. The result follows by theorem 3.

Base Case: Consider the first visit. Let T_0 be the time when the first visit in the sequence is completed. Obviously, $SNTP2_i(T_0) = RECP2_i(T_0) = 0$ for each process in the system. Therefore from (11) and (12) in lemma 9, $SNTP_i(e, T_0) = RECP_j(e, T_0) = 0$ for each primary line e = (i, j). Hence from lemmas 4 and 1, $SNTM(e, T_0) \geq RECM(e, T_0)$ for any e. But $SNTM2(T_0) = RECM2(T_0)$. Therefore from (9) and (10) in lemma 9, we get $SNTM(e, T_0) = RECM(e, T_0)$ for every primary line e. Therefore *SNTM* = *RECM* at time T_0.

Inductive Case: Inductively, suppose *SNTM* = *RECM* after the kth visit. By the hypothesis of the theorem, at the start of the $(k+1)^{st}$ visit $SNTP2_i = RECP2_i = 0$ where i is the process being visited. Using (11) and (12) in lemma 9 it follows that *SNTM* = *RECM* at the end of the visit.

∎

Note: The above proof shows that if in a computation the hypothesis of theorem 8 is true then so is the hypothesis of theorem 3. The converse also follows, in an obvious way. Hence the two algorithms will require the same number of secondary message communications after and before the occurrence of termination. (Since the computation time in a visit in the two algorithms is different, the sequence of events in the two algorithms may be different. The above remark ignores any such differences.)

We state below some simple variations of theorem 8. These variations reduce only the processing requirements during a visit by the marker. Theorems 8 and 9 require the same number of secondary message communications after and before termination (again, this assumes that different processing requirements during a visit won't affect the sequence of events).

Theorem 9: Theorem 8 remains valid under any one of the following modifications (note: we are *not* considering here a combination of these modifications):

1. The requirement $SNTP2_i = RECP2_i = 0$ is replaced by $SNTP2_i = 0$.

2. The requirement $SNTP2_i = RECP2_i = 0$ is replaced by $RECP2_i = 0$.

3. The requirement "$SNTM2 = RECM2$ after each visit" is replaced by "$SNTM2 = RECM2$ at the end of the last visit of the sequence".

Proof: It is easy to see that any variation stated in theorem 9 is equivalent to theorem 8, in the sense that if the hypothesis of one is true then so is the hypothesis of the other.

∎

Now we consider a stronger modification to theorem 8. The algorithm suggested by theorem 10 below is *more* efficient than the one suggested by theorem 8, in terms of the number of message communications required after termination. We will discuss this after proving the theorem.

Theorem 10: Suppose in a sequence of $V = |C|$ visits, the marker continuously finds that $RECP2_i = 0$ before each visit (except possibly the first visit in the sequence) and $SNTM2 = RECM2$ at the completion of the last visit of the sequence. Then at the end of this sequence of visits it can be concluded that the underlying computation is terminated.

Proof: Let T_0 and T, respectively, be the times when the first and the last visits of the sequence were completed. Let t_i be the time when the marker completed its last visit at process i up to (including) time T. From (10),

$RECM2(T)$ = sum {$RECM(e, T)$, over all primary lines e}

= sum {$trec(e, t_j)$, over all primary lines e = (i, j)} by (6).

= sum {$trec(e, T_0)$, over all primary lines e = (i, j)} since, obviously, in the interval $[T_0, t_i]$ process i did not receive any primary messages.

Similarly,

$SNTM2(T)$ = sum {$tsnt(e, t_i)$, over all primary lines e = (i, j)} by (9) and (5)

= sum {$tsnt(e, T_0)$, over e} + sum {$r'(e)$, over e}

where $r'(e)$ = the number of primary messages sent on the line e = (i, j) during the interval $[T_0, t_i]$.

Since $SNTM2(T) = RECM2(T)$, using (2) we get $tsnt(e, T_0) = trec(e, T_0)$ and $r'(e) = 0$ for every primary line e. This is the same as conditions (B) and (C) in the proof of theorem 3. The rest of the proof is the same as the proof of theorem 3 after observation (C). (Alternatively, for any primary line e = (i, j), *tsnt*(e, t_i) - *trec*(e, t_j) = *tsnt*(e, T_0) + *r'*(e) - *trec*(e, T_0) = 0. Hence by (8), *SNTM*(e, T) = *RECM*(e, T). The result follows from theorem 4.)

Now we show that theorem 10 suggests a more efficient algorithm than theorem 8. Obviously, if the hypothesis of theorem 8 holds at a point in computation, then the hypothesis of theorem 10 holds as well. Example 2 below shows that the converse is not true. (However, for a given network topology, the worst case number of message communications after occurrence of termination is the same in both cases.)

Example 2: Consider the network of example 1 with the same initial conditions, except that the marker is initially at process 9. As before , processes 1-4 and 6-9 always remain idle. Consider the following sequence of events at processes 5 and 10:

1. 5 sends a message to 10, 10 receives it. At this point both processes are idle.

2. The marker arrives at process 10.

In the algorithm given by theorem 10, the marker will visit processes 10, 1, ..., 9 and then declare termination. Using the algorithm given by theorem 8, the marker will visit processes 10, ..., 5, ..., 10, ..., 4 and then declare termination.

One may be tempted to consider the following variation of theorem 10 – replace the requirement $RECP2_i = 0$ by $SNTP2_i = 0$. Example 3 below shows that this won't work.

Example 3: Consider the network of example 1 with the same initial conditions and the same behavior of processes 1-4 and 6-9. Consider the following sequence of events on processes 5 and 10:

1. 5 sends a primary message to 10 and becomes idle. (10 has not received it yet.)

2. Marker visits 5. It "restarts" a new sequence since $SNTP_5 \neq 0$ at the start of the visit.

3. Marker visits 10 and departs.

4. 10 receives the primary message sent by 5. It sends a primary message to 5 and remains active. 5 receives this message and remains idle.

5. Marker visits 5 and declares termination.

But process 10 is still active!

Since the above variation of theorem 10 doesn't work, it follows that the following variation will also not work – replace the requirement $RECP2_i = 0$ by ($RECP2_i = 0$ or $SNTP2_i = 0$). (If this variation had worked, obviously it would have been more efficient than theorem 10.)

We complete the algorithm-skeleton for class 2 by using theorem 10. Along the lines of the proof of theorem 1, it can be shown that if the primary computation terminates, say at time T_f, then the hypothesis of theorem 10 will become true within a finite time after T_f. The correctness of the algorithm follows from this observation and theorem 10.

Some Improvements and Details

1. As in class 1 (see "some improvements and details" in section 4), instead of keeping the two variables *SNTM2* and *RECM2* in the marker, it is sufficient to keep only a single variable *SRM2* which would equal *SNTM2 - RECM2*. This has the same advantages as before.

2. Also, at a process i instead of keeping $SNTP2_i$ and $RECP2_i$, one may keep a variable $SRP2_i$ which would equal $SNTP2_i$ - $RECP2_i$, and a boolean variable to indicate if $RECP2_i = 0$. This, of course, does not improve the efficiency regarding message communications; it only reduces the processing time involved in a visit.

3. Same as 3 in our discussion under "some improvements and details" for class 1.

4. How does the marker detect that the first condition of theorem 10 holds for the entire sequence? We roughly sketch a few possible ways of doing this:

   a. Sequence Length Counter: The marker carries a counter for this purpose. Initially this counter is 0. On visiting a process i, if $RECP2_i$ is zero at the start of the visit then the counter is incremented; else it is reset to 1. After the visit if the counter is $\geq |C|$, then the condition $SNTM2 = RECM2$ is checked.

   What if the counter has become $\geq |C|$ and the condition $SNTM2 = RECM2$ is not met? If the counter keeps getting incremented indefinitely, it may overflow. To avoid this, one may reset the counter to 1 during a visit if it is $\geq |C|$ at the start of the visit. This raises the following issue: there seems to be a possibility that termination may be detected after "too many" visits. For example, what if the condition $RECP2_i = 0$ is true before every visit, but the condition $SNTM2 = RECM2$ becomes true after $|C|+1$ visits and the counter was reset to 1 (to avoid overflow) during the visit $|C|+1$? It can be shown that such cases can not arise. In other words, at the start of a visit if the counter is $\geq |C|$, then it can be reset to 1 without loss of efficiency. At any such point T it can be asserted that the marker will definitely visit (either in future or in current visit) a process i such that $RECP2_i \neq 0$ at the start of the visit. To prove this, suppose this is not true. Then there are two possibilities: (i) There is a finite sequence of visits made after time T such that $RECP2_i = 0$ before each such visit at the process i being visited and $SNTM2 = RECM2$ at the completion of the last visit of the sequence. (ii) There is an infinite sequence of visits made after time T such that $RECP2_i = 0$ before each visit and $SNTM2 \neq RECM2$ after each visit.
   Note that after time T, for any visit at a process i if $RECP2_i = 0$ before the visit then $SNTP2_i = 0$ before the visit as well. Since $SNTM2(T) \neq RECM2(T)$, (i) above is impossible. In case (ii), obviously we

have primary messages in transit at time T. Within a finite time one of these messages will be received at a process i, making $RECP2_i$ nonzero. Hence (ii) above is impossible. This completes the proof.

b. Round Number: For simplicity, first let us assume that C is an elementary cycle. The marker contains a round number. At the start of a visit (say at process i) if $RECP2_i \neq 0$ then a new round is started, i.e., marker's round number is incremented. During any visit at a process i, the marker's round number is stored in a local variable at i. If at the start of a visit, the round number of the marker equals that of the current process i, it means that the marker has previously made a sequence of at least $|C|$ visits such that before each visit (except possibly the first one) $RECP2_j = 0$ at the corresponding process j. Therefore in this case if $RECP2_i = 0$ at the start of the visit, the condition $SNTM2 = RECM2$ is checked for termination after completion of the visit. (Alternatively, the termination check could be made at the start of a visit if the round numbers match.) At the start of secondary computation, round numbers of the marker and the processes are initialized to 1 and 0 respectively.

If the round number of the marker keeps getting incremented indefinitely, it may overflow. To solve this problem one may increment the round number as 1+ [(round number) mod $|C|$]. The new round number generated would obviously be different from local round numbers of all processes (except possibly the one being visited).

(As a side note, using this method the number of message communications after occurrence of termination is increased by 1.)

If C is not an elementary cycle, a counter may be kept at each process that counts the number of times the process has been visited in the current round.

c. Initial Process Id: Again let us first assume that C is an elementary cycle. In this method the marker keeps a pointer that points to the process id of the first process in the current sequence of visits such that before each visit (except possibly the first one) $RECP2_i = 0$. At the start of a visit (say at process i) if $RECP2_i \neq 0$ then this pointer is set to i. If at the start of a visit, this pointer is pointing to the current process i, this means that the marker has previously made a sequence of at least $|C|$ visits such that before each visit (except possibly the first one) $RECP2_j = 0$ at the corresponding process j. Therefore in this case if $RECP2_i = 0$ at the start of the visit, then the condition $SNTM2 = RECM2$ is checked for termination after completion of the visit. Similar to our discussion in (a) above (using sequence length counter), if the condition $SNTM2 = RECM2$ is false in this check, we need not reset the pointer.

Obviously, there is no overflow problem in this approach. As in the method using round numbers, the number of messages after termination in this method is increased by 1. If C is not an elementary cycle, one may keep local counters at the processes to count the number of times the process currently pointed to by the marker has been visited in the current sequence.

5. Suppose we designate a specific process where the decision regarding termination would be taken. In this case the marker needs to carry only an integer (the value of *SNTM2 - RECM2*) and a boolean (instead of an integer as in 4 above) which remembers whether in the current round the first condition of theorem 10 has been true so far. Since message length has decreased, this improves the performance in the worst case. However, in the average case the number of message communications after termination will increase.

Performance of the Algorithm

The worst case occurs when the marker departs a process i and before it reaches the next process, process i receives a primary message and the primary computation terminates at this point. The number of secondary messages sent after the termination of primary computation in this case is $2.|C| - 2$. Each secondary message contains two integers – one integer containing the value *SNTM2 - RECM2*, and the other used to check the first condition of theorem 10, as discussed in 4 above under "some improvements and details".

6. Class 3 of Algorithms: Using Multiple Markers

In classes 1 and 2 we have a *single* marker that sequentially traverses the system. In this section we will use multiple markers to enhance performance. First we observe that the *sequential* traversal of the system by a marker in the previous algorithms is not essential. If several processes could be visited in parallel, even then these results will hold. The following theorem is obtained from theorem 10 by an abstraction of the proof of that theorem (i.e., by avoiding details regarding sequential nature of the traversals). The proof of this theorem is essentially the same as that for theorem 10.

Theorem 11: Let $[T_0, T]$ be a time interval during which several visits have been completed, possibly in parallel. Suppose these visits satisfy the following:

1. At least one visit is completed at each process during this interval (the start times of these visits need not be in the interval).

2. At the start of each visit, say at process i, $RECP2_i = 0$, and

3. At time T $SNTM2 = RECM2$.

Then, at time T the primary computation is terminated.

Notes:

1. The values of *SNTM2* and *RECM2* at time T are defined in the obvious way – the results of various visits have to be accumulated.

2. Theorem 10 follows as a special case of theorem 11. On first sight this might not be so obvious, since theorem 10 allows the value of $RECP2_i$ for the first visit to be nonzero. However, after the very first visit in the sequence, one may consider an imaginary visit to the same process – theorem 10 would then readily follow from theorem 11.

Using theorem 11, one may devise schemes using several markers. The markers would check the values of $RECP2_i$, and accumulate values for *SNTM2* and *RECM2* in different parts of the system (these parts need not be disjoint).

A. Using Two Markers

Let us assume that we have two paths P_1 and P_2 from a given process I to a given process J. Also assume that these paths together cover all the processes in the system. Initially both markers are kept at process I. Then they traverse the two paths respectively. After both have visited J, a check for termination is made as follows. The values *SNTM2* and *RECM2* are computed by adding the corresponding values in the two markers. Each marker i also has a boolean variable $NZREC_i$ which is set to true if at the start of some visit at a process j in the current traversal of the path, $RECP2_j$ was found to be nonzero. At J, if $SNTM2 = RECM2$ and both booleans are false then termination is announced. Otherwise a new traversal is to be started. To start a new traversal, both markers may be sent back to I via a line (J, I). Alternatively, the markers may traverse the paths P_1 and P_2 in the reverse direction in which case the next check for termination would be made at process I.

Now we make a simple modification to the above scheme that would lead to an obvious generalization for the case of more than two markers. A new process, called a *central process* (*CP*), is introduced in the system where the check for termination would be made. (This process may be *implemented* as part of some existing process in the system.) Paths P_1 and P_2 now need not share their initial and final processes. Initially both markers are at the CP. A traversal of the system is started by the CP, by sending the markers to the initial processes of the respective paths. After traversing the paths, the markers arrive at the CP where the decision regarding termination is made in the same way as before.

Now we consider an erroneous variation of this scheme which supposedly attempts to improve its efficiency. Suppose a marker i has arrived at the CP after traversing its path and $NZREC_i$ is true. Suppose the other marker has not yet arrived at the CP. One might be tempted to consider the following. Since marker i knows that termination can not be announced after this traversal, it doesn't wait for the other marker to arrive; instead it goes back to traverse P_i. Equivalently, a marker i would traverse its path P_i repeatedly until the value of $NZREC_i$ is false at the end of a traversal, and then it would go to CP and wait for a termination check to be made. The following simple example shows that this scheme won't work:

Example 4: Let P_1 and P_2 consist of single processes, processes 1 and 2 respectively. Initially process 2 is idle and process 1 is active. Consider the following sequence of events:

1. Marker 2 visits process 2. It departs from process 2 (but hasn't arrived at the CP yet).

2. Process 1 sends a primary message to process 2. Process 2 receives this message and sends another one to process 1. Process 1 receives it and becomes idle. Process 2 remains active.

3. Marker 1 visits process 1. Since the value of $NZREC_1$ is true after this visit, it visits process 1 again (equivalently, after the first visit it goes to CP, then goes back and visits process 1). Now it arrives at the CP.

4. Marker 2 arrives at CP. Obviously both booleans $NZREC_i$ are false and $SNTM2 = RECM2$ at this point. Hence termination is declared. But process 2 is still active!

Performance of the Scheme

Let us assume that the length of each path P_1 or P_2 is approximately N/2. For worst case, consider the following scenario. Marker 1 visits and departs from the first process (say i) on its path. Now process i receives a primary message and at this point the primary computation is terminated. Obviously termination won't be detected after the current traversal. Again, it won't be detected in the next traversal since $RECP2_i$ would be nonzero at the start of the next visit to i (let us assume that i appears only once on P_1, and doesn't appear on P_2; otherwise this won't be strictly true). So the number of secondary message communications after termination is $\approx$ 3N/2. Each such message consists of an integer and a boolean.

B. Using More Markers

One may similarly use a CP, K paths, and K markers in general. Let L be the length of the longest of these paths. By considering a scenario similar to the above, we have the worst case number of message communications = 3L + 4. If each path has N/K processes then this equals 3N/K + 1. Note that as K is increased, the scheme tends to become more centralized. With K = N it is a purely centralized scheme (i.e., each process interacts only with the central processor for termination detection) with worst case number of message communications after termination = 4.

7. Conclusion

We have presented a class of efficient algorithms for termination detection in distributed systems. Our assumptions regarding the underlying computation are simple. In particular we do not require the FIFO property for the communication channels. Also, the topological requirements about communication paths are simple and flexible, both from the correctness and performance points of view. We discussed the correctness and performance of our algorithms. Depending upon the application, the nature of the chosen algorithm can be varied incrementally from a distributed one to a centralized one.

We introduced message counting as an effective technique in designing termination detection algorithms. We showed how one can avoid counting messages for *each and every line*, normally resulting in better performance. Our presentation involves deriving algorithms via a sequence of simple modifications. Several correct as well as incorrect variations have been considered. We hope that this approach of presentation has resulted in better understandability of the algorithms.

Acknowledgments

I am indebted to Professors J. Misra and K. M. Chandy for their masterful teaching of several courses at UT Austin which have significantly influenced me. Their financial support for this work is greatly appreciated. The idea of counting messages on the lines was inspired by a similar thought of Professor K. M. Chandy. I am thankful to Professor J. Misra for his encouragement and for his thoughts on performance of termination detection algorithms. Professor M. Gouda's encouragement and his positive influences on my writing style are greatly appreciated. I would like to extend my special thanks to Ted Briggs and Pradeep Jain for their comments on earlier drafts of this paper.

References

[Beeri 81] C. Beeri and R. Obermarck, "A Resource Class Independent Deadlock Detection Algorithm", *Research Report RJ3077*, IBM Research Laboratory, San Jose, California, May 1981.

[Bracha 83] G. Bracha and S. Toueg, "A Distributed Algorithm For Generalized Deadlock Detection", *Technical Report TR 83-558*, Cornell University, June 1983.

[Chandy 81] K. M. Chandy and J. Misra, "Asynchronous Distributed Simulation Via a Sequence of Parallel Computations", *Communications of the ACM*, Vol. 24, No. 4, pp.198-205, April 1981.

[Chandy 82a] K. M. Chandy and J. Misra, "A Distributed Algorithm for Detecting Resource Deadlocks in Distributed Systems", *ACM SIGACT-SIGOPS Symposium on Principles of Distributed Computing*, Ottawa, Canada, August 1982.

[Chandy 82b] K. M. Chandy and J. Misra, "A Computation on Graphs: Shortest Path Algorithms", *Communications of the ACM*, Vol. 25, No. 11, pp.833-837, November 1982.

[Chandy 83] K. M. Chandy, J. Misra, and L. Haas, "Distributed Deadlock Detection", *ACM Transactions on Computing Systems*, Vol. 1, No. 2, pp. 144-156, May 1983.

[Chandy 85a] K. M. Chandy and J. Misra, "A Paradigm for Detecting Quiescent Properties in Distributed Computations", working paper, Department of Computer Sciences, University of Texas, Austin, Texas 78712, January 9, 1985.

[Chandy 85b] K. M. Chandy and L. Lamport, "Distributed Snapshots: Determining Global States of Distributed Systems", to appear in *ACM Transactions on Computing Systems*.

[Chang 82] E. Chang, "Echo Algorithms: Depth Parallel Operations on General Graphs", *IEEE Transactions on Software Engineering*, Vol. SE-8, No. 4, pp.391-401, July 1982.

[Cohen 82] S. Cohen and D. Lehmann, "Dynamic Systems and Their Distributed Termination", *ACM SIGACT-SIGOPS Symposium on Principles of Distributed Computing*, pp. 29-33, Ottawa, Canada, August 18-20, 1982.

[Dijkstra 80] E. W. Dijkstra and C. S. Scholten, "Termination Detection for Diffusing Computations", *Information Processing Letters*, Vol. 11, No. 1, August 1980.

[Dijkstra] E. W. Dijkstra, "Distributed Termination Detection Revisited", EWD 828, Plataanstraat 5, 5671 AL Nuenen, The Netherlands.

[Francez 80] N. Francez, "Distributed Termination", *ACM Transactions on Programming Languages and Systems*, Vol. 2, No. 1, pp. 42-55, January 1980.

[Francez 81] N. Francez, M. Rodeh, and M. Sintzoff, "Distributed Termination with Interval Assertions", *Proceedings of Formalization of Programming Concepts*, Peninusla, Spain, April 1981. Lecture Notes in Computer Science 107, (Springer-Verlag).

[Francez 82] N. Francez and M. Rodeh, "Achieving Distributed Termination Without Freezing", *IEEE-TSE*, Vol. SE-8, No. 3, pp.287-292, May 1982.

[Gligor 80] V. Gligor and S. Shattuck, "On Deadlock Detection in Distributed Data Bases", *IEEE-TSE*, Vol. SE-6, No. 5, September 1980.

[Gouda 81] M. Gouda, "Distributed State Exploration For Protocol Validation", *Technical Report TR 185*, Department of Computer Sciences, University of Texas, Austin, 78712, October 1981.

[Haas 83] L. Haas and C. Mohan, "A Distributed Deadlock Detection Algorithm for a Resource Based System", *Research Report RJ3765*, IBM Research Laboratory, San Jose, California, January 1983.

[Herman 83] T. Herman and K. M. Chandy, "A Distributed Procedure to Detect AND/OR Deadlock", Department of Computer Sciences, University of Texas, Austin, 78712, February 1983.

[Hoare 78] C. A. R. Hoare, "Communicating Sequential Processes", *Communications of the ACM*, Vol. 21, No. 8, pp. 666-677, August 1978.

[Holt 72] T. Holt, "Some Deadlock Properties of Computer Systems", *Computing Surveys*, Vol. 4, No. 3, pp. 179-196, September 1972.

[Kumar 85] D. Kumar, "Distributed Simulation", Ph.D. Thesis (in preparation), Department of Computer Sciences, University of Texas, Austin, Texas 78712.

[Lamport 78] L. Lamport, "Time, Clocks, and the Ordering of Events in a Distributed System", *Communications of the ACM*, Vol. 21, No. 7, July 1978.

[Misra 81] J. Misra and K. M. Chandy, "Proofs of Networks of Processes", *IEEE Transactions on Softaware Engineering*, Vol. SE-7, No. 4, pp. 417-426, July 1981.

[Misra 82a] J. Misra and K. M. Chandy, "Termination Detection of Diffusing Computations in Communicating Sequential Processes", *ACM Transactions on Programming Languages and Systems*, Vol. 4, No. 1, pp. 37-43, January 1982.

[Misra 82b] J. Misra and K. M. Chandy, "A Distributed Graph Algorithm: Knot

Detection", *ACM Transactions on Programming Languages and Systems*, Vol. 4, No. 4, pp. 678-688, October 1982.

[Misra 83] J. Misra, "Detecting Termination of Distributed Computations Using Markers", *Proceedings of the ACM SIGACT-SIGOPS Symposium on Principles of Distributed Computing*, Montreal Canada, August 17-19, 1983.

[Obermarck 80] R. Obermarck, "Deadlock Detection For All Resource Classes", *Research Report RJ2955*, IBM Research Laboratory, San Jose, California, October 1980.

[Obermarck 82] R. Obermarck, "Distributed Deadlock Detection Algorithm", *ACM Transactions on Database Systems*, Vol. 7, No. 2, pp.187-208, June 1982.

[Owicki 76] S. Owicki and D. Gries, "An Axiomatic Proof Technique for Parallel Programs I", *Acta Informatica*, Vol. 6, pp.319-340, 1976.

NEW PROTOCOLS FOR THE ELECTION OF A LEADER IN A RING

A.Marchetti-Spaccamela
Dip. Informatica e Sistemistica
Universita' di Roma
via Eudossiana 18,
00185 Roma, Italy.

ABSTRACT In this paper we investigate the impact of time for the election of a leader in a distributed environment. We propose a new protocol schema that can be specialized to obtain several protocols with different communication-time characteristics when the network is ring shaped and the communications between processors are synchronous.

1. INTRODUCTION

In recent years great attention has been devoted to the computational resources required to solve problems in a distributed environment. In this paper we consider the problem of electing a leader in a synchronous ring-shaped network. There are n processors, but this is not known to the processors. The processors have only local information of the network and are identical except that each one has its own identifier. At various points in time one or more processors "wake up" and initiate their participation in an election to decide on an unique leader among the participating processors. We assume that the ring is unidirectional (i.e. each

---

work supported by project MPI Analisi e Progetto di Algoritmi

processor receives messages from one of its neighbour and send messages to the other one). The interesting resources are the total number of messages used and the time.

This problem is important not only because it occurs in practical situations (i.e. crash recoveries), but also because the communication costs (both upper and lower bounds) required in order to achieve any agreement in a decentralized network seems to be of the same order of the costs for the election of a leader.
The problem has received attention by a number of researchers (A), (B), (DKR), (FL), (GHS), (HS), (P), (V). In the case of a ring-shaped asynchronous network O(n logn) messages and O(n) time are sufficient (DKR) and (P); furthermore it has been proved that Ω(n logn) messages are necessary, even if all processors know the size of the ring (B). Since the lower bound proof does not apply to the case of synchronous networks it is interesting to study the impact of synchronization on the number of messages used.

A first important step in this direction has been performed by Frederickson and Lynch, (FL) and, independently, by Vitanyi (V). They found a protocol that uses O(n) messages and exponential time. Namely the protocol assumes that the identities of the processors are numbers and requires $O(n\ 2^{i_{min}})$ time units, where i_{min} is the identity of the leader. Furthermore it has been shown that both the use of time and of the identity number is essential if we want to use less than O(n logn) messages. In fact Frederickson and Lynch (FL) proved that in the synchronous case
i) if we consider algorithms that use only comparisons then Ω(n logn) messages are necessary;
ii) there is a (fast increasing) function f(n,t) such that if we allow identities to be chosen between 1 and f(n,t) then any protocol that finds a leader in less than t time units needs O(n logn) messages.

As a consequence of these results it is quite natural to investigate the tradeoff between time and number of messages required for the election of a leader in a synchronous ring.In this paper we address the question whether it is possible to obtain protocols that use less than exponential time and between O(n) and

O(n log n) messages. We positively answer this question by showing a protocol schema based on a new technique that can be specialized in order to obtain several protocols with different communication-time characteristics.

In paragraph 2 we present the main idea of the protocol schema that will be presented in paragraph 3. In paragraph 4 we analyse the resources required by the schema and in paragraph 5 we will obtain a number of different protocols. If i_{min} is the number representing the identity of the leader we can obtain protocols with the following characteristics:

P1) for any $c>0$ $O(n \log_c n)$ messages and $O(c\ n\ i_{min})$ time;

P2) $O(n \log\log n)$ messages and $O(n^2\ i_{min})$ time;

P3) $O(n \log\log\log n)$ messages and $O(n^{\log n}\ i_{min})$ time;

P4) $O(n \log^* n)$ messages and $O(2^n\ i_{min})$ time.

For the rest of the paper we assume, without loss of generality, that the identities of the processors are numbers and that the leader will be the participating processor with the smallest identity.

2 A (TOO MUCH) SIMPLIFIED PROTOCOL

In this paragraph we present a simple and efficient protocol based on relaxing some of the assumptions of the problem. The simple protocol we obtain is a good starting point in order to present how time is used in the protocol schema presented in paragraph 3. We make the following assumptions:

a) each processor knows n, the size of the ring;

b) all processors start the election at the same time $t=0$.

If assumptions a) and b) hold and processor 1 takes part at the election then it is the winner; hence the only thing it has to do is to broadcast to all processors the message "1 elected". If processor 1 does not participate at the election then there is no message in the ring for the first n time units. This implies that if processor 2 participates at the election and does not receive the message "1 elected", it knows at time n+1 that it is the winner and broadcast the message "2 elected". Analougously if processor i is participating at the election it waits for $n(i-1)+1$ time units.

If it has not received any message it is the winner and sends the message "i elected".
Clearly the protocol is correct and requires n+1 message and time $O(i_{min}n)$ where i_{min} is the identity of the winner.
If we know an upper bound N on n the protocol can be easily modified and its time complexity is $O(i_{min}N)$. It is possible to obtain a modified protocol when assumption b) does not hold but in order to eliminate assumption a) we need major modifications because the knowledge on n (or an upper bound on n) is essential in this protocol.

The main idea in order to circumvent the problem of knowing n is based on guessing its value.
Roughly speaking the new protocol will use hypotheses $h_1, h_2, \ldots$ of increasing value on the length of the ring. When hypothesis h_m holds the processors are in phase m and will behave according to the protocol introduced in this paragraph as the length of the ring would be h_m. If n is greater than h_m a new hypothesis h_{m+1} will be formulated. The protocol will proceed in this way until a hypothesis $h_r > n$ will be formulated; at the end of this phase the election is terminated.
We will obtain different protocols depending on the way we pass from hypothesis h_m to hypothesis h_{m+1} as we will see in paragraph 5.

3 THE PROTOCOL SCHEMA

The first problem that we face in order to formalize the ideas sketched at the end of the preceding paragraph is that not all the processors wake up at the same time.
In order to solve this problem we use an idea introduced by Frederickson and Lynch (FL) and Vitanyi (V). Namely, we have a preliminary phase 0; when a processor decides to participate at the election it spawns the message "election started" to its neighbour. The message is transmitted along the ring until it meets a processor that has already sent this message. When a processor receives the message "election started" it decides if it wants to take part at the election; in this case its identity enters phase 1. A processor cannot decide to participate at the election after

it has received the first message. Not all identities start phase 1 at the same time; we define t(i) the time identity i starts phase 1.

In the following phases of the protocol we focus on the identities of the participating processors. At the beginning all participating identities are "alive"; during the election they will travel along the ring, increasing their phase number, and will eventually "die" as soon as they are aware that there is a smaller identity participating at the election. At the end the smallest identity will be the only alive identity and the corresponding processor will be the leader.
At each moment the identities will travel along the ring at different speeds depending on their value and on their phase number and each processor will memorize the smallest participating identity it is aware of. When a processor receives identity i in phase m it decides one of the following actions:
a) if it is aware of a smaller participating identity it will kill i because i cannot be the leader any more;
b) if i is the lowest identity the processor has seen and i has not completed phase m then the processor sends i to its neighbour;
c) if i is the lowest identity the processor has seen and i has completed phase m then the processor delays i for a time proportional to the value of i. At the end of this period if no better value is arrived the processor sends i to its neighbour otherwise i dies;
d) if i is the identity of the processor itself then the processor is the winner of the election and sends the message "i elected".

In this way the number of alive messages will decrease as the election proceed and the elected processor will be the only one whose identity will be back home (i.e. the only identity that will walk for all the ring).

The stop and go schema is implemented as follows: at the beginning of phase 1 each participating processor formulates an hypothesis h_1 on the length of the ring and will delay its identity for $2ih_1$ time units. If in the meantime no better identity is arrived the processor forms the message $\langle i, h_1, 1\rangle$ (identity, hypothesis, distance walked) and sends it to its neighbour that will either kill it or will send the message $\langle i, h_1, 2\rangle$ to its neighbour that will either kill it or will send the message $\langle i, h_1, 3\rangle$. The identity will walk in this way for h_1 processors. When a processor p receives the message $\langle i, h_1, h_1\rangle$ identity i has performed at time $t(i) + h_1(2i+1)$ phase 1.

The processor p will formulate for i a new hypothesis h_2, $h_2 > h_1$, on the length of the ring and will delay identity i for $2i(h_2-h_1)$ time units. If, at the end of this period, no better identity is arrived identity i will start its second phase and the message $\langle i,h_2,h_1+1\rangle$ will be sent. During the phase identity i will walk for h_2-h_1 processors in the same way as before.

The phase will be completed when identity i has walked for h_2 processors or it is back at its starting point. In the former case a new hypothesis will be formulated in the latter case i is the winner. The identity i will proceed formulating new hypotheses on the length of the ring until it dies or it is back at its starting point.

The protocol schema for processor i.

```
/phase 0/ if awaken then
              begin
              send "election started";
              receive message;
              /the processor waits till it
              receives a message from its neighbour/
              start phase 1
              end
          else
              begin
              receive message;
              send "election started";
              if  willing to participate
                   then start phase 1
              end;
```

```
/following phases/
    form message = <i,h0,1> and
    insert it in the waiting list for 2h0 time units;
    bestid := i;
    loop
    if there is a message in the waiting list that
      has finished to wait then send it;
      if a message is arrived
      then begin
            receive  <j,hm,w>;
            if j = i
            then "proclaim elected"
            else if j < bestid
                       then begin
                              bestid := j;
                              if there is a waiting message
                              then kill it;
                              if w < hm
                              then /phase m is not finished/
                                  send <i,hm,w+1>;
                              else /phase m is finished/
                                  form message
                                  =<j,hm+1,w+1> and
                                  delay it for 2j(hm+1-hm)
                                  time units
                              end
      end
      endloop.
```

4 ANALYSIS OF THE PROTOCOL SCHEMA

The correctness of the algorithm follows from the following observations:

1) for each participating identity there is at most one message in the ring;

2) at the end of phase m an alive identity either has walked for h_m steps or it is back at its starting point;

3) for all m we have $h_{m+1} > h_m$;

4) there is only one identity, the identity of the leader, that arrives at the processor it started from.

Theorem 1 The protocol finishes in a finite amount of time and at the end a leader has been elected.

Proof The proof follows from observations 1 through 4.

The rest of this paragraph will be devoted to the analysis of the requirements of the protocol schema.
The proof of the following theorem is trivial and is omitted.

Theorem 2 Phase 0 requires n+1 messages and there are at most n time units between the time the first processor wakes up and the time the last identity enters phase 1.

The evaluation of the number of messages required in phase 1 is complicated by the fact that not all the identities start the phase at the same time. Furthermore the analysis of the following phases is more difficult because the time at which identity i will start phase m, m=2,3.... depends on the time at which i starts phase 1 and on the value of the identitiy itself.
The following theorem allows to bound the number of messages sent for each phase.

Theorem 3 For any set I of participating processors the total number of messages sent in phase m, m > 0, (i.e. the total number of messages of the form $\langle i,h_m,w\rangle$, $i\in I$, $h_{m-1}<w<h_m$) is less than 2n+1.

In order to prove the theorem we need some preliminary observations. First of all note that, during the execution of the algorithm, the relative order in the ring among alive identities does not change, because an identity that is passed by a faster one dies.
This allows to define a cyclic order on any set S of alive identities. We say that S=(id(1),id(2), ...,id(n)) is ordered if

a) id(i-1) is the immediate predecessor of id(i) (in clockwise order), i=2,3,....
b) id(n) is the immediate predecessor of id(1) (in clockwise order).

Given two identities i and j, let dist(i,j) be the clockwise distance between processors i and j; observe that

$$dist(i,j) + dist(j,i) = n + 1$$

$$t(j) \leq t(i) + dist\ (i,j)$$

The next lemma gives a bound on the maximum total delay that we can have for any ordered set of identities.

Lemma 1 For any ordered set of identities $S=\{id(1),\ i=1,2,\ldots,k\}$, we have

$$\sum_{i=2}^{h} \max\left[t(id(i))-t(id(i-1),0\right]+\max\left[t(id(1)-t(id(n)),0\right] \leq n$$

Proof of Lemma 1 It is sufficient to observe that a phase 0 message takes at most n time units to visit the ring.

Proof of Theorem 1 We colour the set of alive identities at phase m as follows:

- an identity i is white if there is some other identity j such that the segment walked by i during phase m is completely contained in the segment walked by j;

we say that an identity is dark if it is not white; we divide the class of dark identities in two subclasses:

- a dark identity i is black if there is not a processor that, during phase m, sends i and, after i, another dark identity $j < i$;

- an identity is red if it is neither white nor black.

It is not difficult to prove the following facts:

1) there is at least one black message: the winner;

2) a red identity is higher than the first dark identity that follows it;

3) the segments walked by black identities are non overlapping;

4) if all processors start phase 1 at the same time t, then there are only black messages.

Observation 3 implies that the number of messages used for black identities is no more than n + 1.
In order to bound the number of messages used for red and white identities we identify pairs of identities ⟨id(1),k(1)⟩, ⟨id(2),k(2)⟩, ..., such that:
1) id(1), k(1), id(2), ... are clockwise ordered
2) k(i) is different from id(i) (but it may happen that k(i)=id(i+1))

and we show that the total number of messages used for white and red identities is less than

$$\sum_{\forall i} t(id(i)) - t(k(i))$$

Applying lemma 1 we obtain the thesis.

Let us consider a black identity i and let us define

id(1) = i

B(id(1))= $\{j \mid$ there is a processor that sends both id(1) and j during phase m$\}$

Note that if j belongs to B(id(1)) then j > id(1) and j is not black. We distinguish two cases:

<u>case</u> <u>1)</u> there is a not a red identity in B(id(1))
Let us define

$k(1)= \max(j, j \in B(id(1)))$ $\qquad k(1) > |B(i)| + id(1)$

Note that k(l) starts phase m before id(l) does; this implies that the total number of messages sent with identities belonging to B(l) is no more than

$$|B(1)|\ h_m < h_m\ (k(1) - id(1)) < t(id(1)) - t(k(1))$$

Let id(2) be the first black identity that follows id(l).

<u>case 2)</u> there is a red identity in B(l)
Now let id(2) be the furthest red identity belonging to B(l) and let us define

$$B' = \{ i \mid i \in B \text{ and } i \text{ is between } id(1) \text{ and } id(2),\ i \neq id(2) \}$$

$$k(1) = \max\{(j \in B'(id(1))), id(2)\},\quad k(1) > id(1) + |B'(id(1))| + 1$$

Note that k(l) enters phase m before id(l) does; this implies that the total number of messages sent with identity id(2) and identities belonging to B'(l) is no more than

$$(\ B'(1) + 1)\ h_m < h_m\ (k(1) - id(1)) < t(id(1)) - t(k(1))$$

In both cases a) and b) we have defined two identities id(l) and id(2) and we have bound the total number of messages sent with identities between id(l) and id(2).
Having defined id(2) we continue in a similar way by defining

$$B(id(2)) = \{ j \mid \text{there is a processor that sends both } id(2) \text{ and } j \text{ during phase } m \}$$

and we distinguish two cases a) and b) depending on whether there is a red identity in B(2) or not. In both cases we proceed as before by defining k(2) as the largest identity belonging to B(2) (B'(2)) and by bounding the total number of messages used for identities in B(2) (B'(2)). We proceed in a similar way defining id(3), k(3), id(4),... until we have considered all alive identities.
The sequence of identities id(l), k(l), id(2),.... is an ordered set of identity and applying lemma 1 we have that the total number

of messages used for red and white identities during phase m is no more than n. This completes the proof of theorem 3.

5 FOUR DIFFERENT PROTOCOL FOR THE RING

Theorem 3 is the key theorem in the analysis of the different protocols that we can obtain from the protocl schema presented in paragraph 3. If a protocol uses $h_1, h_2, ..$ as hypotheses it terminates when the winning identity has completed phase h_t, where h_t is such that $h_{t-1} < n \leq h_t$. Hence the number of messages used is $O(t\ n)$ and the time required is $O(i_{min} h_t)$.
At this point the tradeoff between time and total number of messages used is clear: in order to diminish the total number of messages sent we want to have the number of phases as minimum as possible, but in this case we will have a rough approximation on the value of n, that will affect the time required by the protocol.

Finally we show four different protocols based on four different ways of passing from one hypothesis to the following one.

P1) $h_1 = c \quad c > 2,\ h_m = c\ h_{m-1};$

P2) $h_1 = 2,\ h_m = (h_{m-1})^2;$

P3) $h_1 = c,\ c>2,\quad h_m = (h_{m-1})^{\log h}$

P4) $h_1 = c,\ c>10,\ h_m = 2^{h^{\varepsilon}_{m-1}},\ \varepsilon > 0.$

<u>Theorem</u> <u>4</u> The number of messages and the time required by protocol i, i=1,2,3,4 are
P1) the time required is $O(c\ n\ i_{min})$ and the number of messages is $O(n \log_c n)$.

P2) the time required is $O(n^2\ i_{min})$ and the number of messages is $O(n \log\log n)$.

P3) the time required is $O(n^{\log n} i_{min})$ and the number of messages is $O(n \log\log\log n)$.

P4) the time required is $O(2^n i_{min})$ and the number of messages is $O(n \log^* n)$.

Proof

P1) We have

$n \leq h_t = c^t < c\,n$, $t < \log_c n + 1$

hence the time required is $O(c\,n\,i_{min})$ and the number of messages is $O(n \log_c n)$.

P2) We have

$n \leq h_t = 2^{2^t} < n^2$

$t \leq \log\log n + 1$

hence the time required is $O(n^2 i_{min})$ and the number of messages is $O(n \log\log n)$.

P3) We have

$n \leq h_t < n^{\log n}$

$t < \log\log\log n + 1$

hence the time required is $O(n^{\log n} i_{min})$ and the number of messages is $O(n \log\log\log n)$.

P4) We have

$n < h_t < 2^{n^t}$

$t = O(\log^* n)$

hence the time required is $O(2^n i_{min})$ and the number of messages is $O(n \log^* n)$.

6 CONCLUSIONS

The main result of this paper is to prove that it is possible to use less than O(n logn) messages and exponential time for the election of a leader in a ring. The result is mainly of theoretical interest because the time bounds of the proposed protocol are not practical in most cases. Nevertheless we think that the ideas presented in the paper can be used for further improvements.

For example, when the size of the ring of is known, it is possible

to modify the simple protocol presented in paragraph 2 to obtain the following result: for any $\varepsilon > 0$, the election of a leader in a synchronous ring can be achieved in O(n) messages and $O(n^{1+\varepsilon} i_{min})$ time, when the size of the ring is known.
The above result compares favourably with the Ω(n logn) lower bound on the number of messages required in the asynchronous case, even if the size of the ring is known.

The second possibility of investigations is to generalize the results to the case of networks with any shape. For example it is possible to prove that the election of a leader in a synchronous network can be achieved with O(n) messages and exponential time.
The proofs of the above results will appear in a forthcoming paper.

I knew from a referee of this paper, that similar ideas have been used by Gafni (G); unfortunately I did not suceed in having his paper ; hence I can give only the reference.

REFERENCES

(A) D.Angluin, "Local and Global Properties in Network of Processors" Proceedings of the 12th Annual Symposium on Theory of Computing (1980).

(B) J.E.Burns, "A formal model for message passing systems, TR91", Indiana University (September 1980).

(DKR) D.Dolev, M.Klawe, M.Rodeh, "An O(n log n) unidirectional distributed algorithm for extrema finding in a circle" J.Algorithms 3,3 (1982).

(FL) G.Frederickson, N.Lynch, "The impact of synchronous communication on the problem of electing a leader in a ring", Proceedings of the 16th Annual ACM Symposium on Theory of Computing (1984).

(G) E.Gafni, "Imprvements in the timme complexity of two message-optimal election algorithms", Proceedings of the 4th ACM Symposium on Principles of Distributed Computing (1985).

(HS)D.S.Hirschberg, J.B.Sinclair, "Decentralized extremafinding in circular configurations of processes, Communications ACM 23, (1980).

(P) G.L.Peterson, "An O(n log n) Unidirectional algorithm for the circular extrema problem", Trans.Prog. Lang.Sys. 4,4, (1982).

(V) P.Vitanyi, "Distributed elections in archimedean ring of processors", Proceedings of the 16th Annual ACM Symposium on Theory of Computing, (1984).

PROGRAM SIMPLIFICATION VIA SYMBOLIC INTERPRETATION

Carlo Ghezzi, Dino Mandrioli, Antonio Tecchio
Dipartimento di Elettronica, Politecnico di Milano, P.za L. da Vinci 32
ITALY

This work has been supported by ESPRIT, Project METEOR, the Italian Research Council (CNR) and by MPI 40%.

ABSTRACT

We investigate a specific program transformation technique, called simplification, which is a generalization of the "mixed computation" technique due to Ershov. Our technique allows one to develop truly generalized programs to be reused several times, for particular cases of their expected inputs.
Given a subset D' of an input domain D, specified via predicates on program variables, and a generalized program P, simplification yields a program P' which implements the same transformation as P on input data restriced to D', but is considerably more efficient than P.
We give examples and outline the structure of a prototype implementation, which is built on top of a symbolic intepreter for Pascal.

1. INTRODUCTION

Programs need to be transformed for many reasons /Bauer and Wossner 1982/ /Partsch and Steinbruggen 1983/. One of them is improving their efficiency. Some transformations are performed by hand by the programmer using ingenuity; others are performed automatically, for example by the compiler.

In some cases, transformations can be applied to given programs in order to improve their efficiency when their input data are restricted to a particular subset of the input domain. Consider, for instance, the configuration of an operating system designed for a family of different hardware: Efficiency can be highly improved by specializing the software for a particular hardware configuration. For instance, buffers and scheduling policies can be optimized.

In this paper we suggest that interesting program transformations can be obtained through specialization of existing programs by using interactive tools based on symbolic intepretation /King 1976/. For instance, suppose a given program P has an input domain D and the user wishes to run P on a particular subdomain D'<=D for which a predicate PR hodls. A symbolic interpreter, for example, may deduce that if PR holds on input variables, then some other predicate PR* holds at the statement *if C then S1 else S2*. If PR* implies C, P could be simplified by substituting the entire conditional statement with its *then* branch, *S1*.

The existence of such a tool would encourage design of general programs solving rather large classes of problems instead of a wide class of programs solving particular cases. Generalized programs should pay little or no prior attention at all to particular cases, thanks to a subsequent "specialization" phase. Thus, we could maintain libraries of long-lived, carefully designed and implemented, generalized programs for which it may be even worth investing in costly correctness proofs. Reusing such programs in less general cases does not cause any loss of efficiency, because the generalized program undergoes a suitable simplification phase. In addition, the resulting program is guaranteed correct by the simplifier.

This idea was first suggested by Ershov /Ershov 1977, 1982/. For instance, in this theory of "mixed computation" he showed how a compiler-compiler can be specialized to a particular language by deriving an actual compiler for that language.

In this paper, we consider the possibility of specializing programs by restricting their input in a fairly general way through predicates, whereas Ershov only allows the freezing of the value of some input variables. Furthermore, efficiency is a major concern for us.

Section 2 describes the very general lines of a tool for simplifying Pascal programs, based on symbolic interpretation.

Section 3 presents two examples in some detail. The first shows how a program designed to compute minimal points in a a multidimensional space can be naturally reduced to a program computing the minimum in a linear space. The secon example shows how a sorting algorithm can be transformed into an algorithms which reverses the contents of an array by providing an input predicate stating that the array to be sorted is actually sorted, but in reverse order. Furthermore, in both cases the resulting simplified program has lower computational complexity than the original program.

Finally, Section 4 briefly describes the state of a prototype implementation and the results of early experiences with such a tool.

2. STRUCTURE OF THE SIMPLIFIER

In this section we outline the essential features of a program simplifier based on symbolic execution. It embodies three major functional blocks :

1. A symbolic interpreter-simplifier;
2. An optimizer;
3. A folder-generalizer.

2.1 The symbolic interpreter-simplifier (SIS).

SIS is the core of the system. It is provided with logic deduction facilities. SIS can be described as a pair of functions having the same arguments (a programming language construct and a program state description) whose ranges are a modification of the construct and an update of the state description, respectively. The sequence of modified statements produced by SIS is the simplified program. Precisely, let *stat* denote a language statement and let *sd* be a state description given, say, by means of first-order formulae. At any given point of the program, *sd* can be either computed by SIS or (partially) directly supplied by the user. Thus SIS is the pair of functions *<NStat(stat,sd), NSd(stat,sd)>*, where the first component denotes a modification of the statement and the second component denotes a modification of the state. Some essential properties of SIS are now sketched using a semi-formal recursive notation, under the assumption that programs do not provide side-effects.

(a) Consider first expression *exp*. The function *eval(exp,sd)* computes the value of *exp* on the basis of the contents of *sd*. Such a value can be either a constant of a symbolic expression, depending on the deductions made possible by *sd*. For instance, if $sd = \{x>=0,\ y=3\}$ and

$exp = (z+y)*2$

then

$eval(exp,sd)=z*2+6$

(b) Let *stat* be the assignment statement *var:=exp*. SIS provides a new statement of the type *var:=eval(exp,sd)* and updates *sd* in the natural way. For instance, if *sd* is as above and *stat* is *z:=x+y*, the value computed by *NStat* is *z:=x+3* and the value computed by *NSd* is {*x>=0, y=3, z>=3*}.

(c) Let *stat* be the conditional statement *if cond then stat1 else stat2*. Then SIS is defined as follows:

case 1: *eval(cond,sd)=true*
In such case, *stat* is replaced by *NStat(stat1,sd)* and the new state is *NSd(stat1,sd)*

case 2: *eval(cond,sd)=false*
In such case, *stat* is replaced by *NStat(stat2,sd)* and the new state is *NSd(stat2,sd)*

case 3: *eval(cond,sd)* is a symbolic expression
In such a case, let *sd1=sd and eval(cond,sd)*, *sd2=sd and not eval(cond,sd)*.
Then the conditional statement is replaced by
if eval(cond,sd) then NStat(stat1,sd1)
else NStat(stat2,sd2)
and the new state is *NSd(stat1,sd1) or NSd(stat2,sd2)*

For instance, if *stat* is *if x>=0 then y:=z+x else y:=y-1* and *sd* is {*x>=y, y>=3*} we obtain the new statement *y:=z+x* and the new state {*y>=z+3*}.

(d) Let *stat* be the statment: *while cond do stat1*.
In such a case, if possible, SIS "unfolds" the loop in the following way.

case 1: *eval(cond,sd)=true*
In this case the iteration is replaced by the following sequence of applications of *NStat*.
NStat(stat1,sd);NStat(while cond do stat1, NSd(stat1,sd)),
and the new state is given by *NSd(while cond do stat1, NSd(stat1, sd))*.

case 2: *eval(cond,sd)=false*
In this case the iteration is replaced by the empty statement and the state remains unchanged.

case 3: *eval(cond,sd)* is a symbolic expression
In this case the original loop is replaced by
while cond do NStat(stat1, cond and I)*
and the new state after the loop is *(not cond) and I**
where *I** is an invariant part of *sd*(loop invariant). As

usual, the invariant may be either synthesized by SIS on the basis of *sd* and *stat1*, or it may be suggested interactively by the user.

In practice, unfolding the loop may not always be useful, even when possible. In such a case, the user may decide to select case 3, no matter what the value of *eval(cond,sd)* is.

The definition of SIS for other statements, such as *for* loops, *repeat*... *until*, etc. is omitted, as it is fairly obvious.

2.2 The optimizer

The optimizer is a program transformation module performing classical optimization on program code based on data-flow techniques. For instance, it can transform a straight code sequence of the type:

x:=y+1;

a:=x+2;

x:=b;

into the code:

a:=y+3;

x:=b;

Note that function *eval* of SIS already embodies some typical features of program optimization.

The literature includes accounts of a large number of optimizing techniques which may be of significant use in our environment /Aho and Ullman 1977/.

2.3 The folder-generalizer.

In some cases, program simplification through steps 2.1, 2.2 may produce an unacceptable unfolding of the source program. Thus it may be useful, or necessary, to perform some refolding by re-synthesizing loops. This action is performed by the folder-generalizer module. Typically, this module must be implemented as an interactive tool, since it requires inductive ingenuity, inasmuch as the SIS module requires deductive ingenuity.

The examples in the next section will show that a typical pattern of program simplification consists of :

i) symbolically executing and simplifying the program through SIS. The result is a partial execution of the program and a simplification thereof:

ii) applying optimization techniques;

iii) re-synthesizing possible unfolded loops.

3. EXAMPLES

3.1 Example 1

Let *PSET* be a set of m-tuples of integer numbers. Consider the problem of computing the subset *MIN* of *PSET*, consisting of minimal points of *PSET*, i.e. *MIN=(x* _in_ *PSET* _such that there is no_ *y* _in_ *PSET*, y=/=,y_h<=x_h _for all_ *1<=h<=m)*.

The Pascal progral *MINSET* shown in Fig. 1 computes the subset *MIN* of any given *PSET*. Its data elements have the following meaning:

- an element of *PSET* is represented by an array *POINT* of *MAXDIM* integers, where *MAXDIM* is the maximum number of coordinates of elements of *PSET*.
- *PSET* is represented as an array of *N POINTs*, *N* being the maximum cardinality of *PSET*.
- *MIND* is an array storing the indexes of the minimals of *PSET*. Clearly, *MIND* must be dimensioned with *N* elements.
- *m<=MAXDIM* is the actual number of coordinates of each points (the program works for *m*-dimensional spaces, where *m<=MAXDIM)*.
- *n<=N* is the actual cardinality of *PSET*.
  k<=n is the number of (index of) *POINTs* stored in *MIND*.
- *i,j,ii,jj* are integer variables used as indexes.
- *dom, subst, c1, c2* are logical variables.

The rationale of the program consists of a nested scanning of elements of *PSET* and *MIND*. *MIND* is initialized with the first element of *PSET*. For each point *x* in *PSET* starting from the second element, *MIND* is scanned to chek if

a. *x* "dominates" one element *y* (i.e. y_h<=x_h _for all_ *1<=h <=m)* whose index is in *MIND*.
   In such a case *MIND* remains unaffected.

b. *x* is dominated by
   b1. one element *y* whose index is in *MIND*. In such a case the index of *x* must replace the inedex of *y* in *MIND*.
   b2. p elements (p>1) $y^1,\dots,y^p$ whose indexes are in *MIND* . In such a case the indexes of $y^1,\dots,y^p$ must be removed from *MIND* and the index of *x* must be inserted; *k* must be decreased of *p-1*.

c. *x* neither dominates nor is dominated by an element of *MIND*.

In such a case, the index of x must be inserted into *MIND* and k increment.

If the elements of *PSET* represent points in a linear space, i.e. $m=1$, the problem of computing the set of minimals becomes the problem of computing the minimum element of a set of scalars. For such a problem, simpler and more efficient solutions than the *MINSET* program of Fig. 1 can be easily found. Let us show how, using our simplifier, one can (semi)automatically derive from *MINSET* a simplified program which computes the minimum integer of a set. In particular, we wish to simplify the program in a way that does not depend on the value of constants, such as N.

Assume the user supplies to the system the information that $m=1$ (i.e. the predicate $m=1$ is inserted into the state description sd of SIS). Let us outline how SIS operates on *MINSET* when sd initially is $m=1$. These are snapshots of the behavior of SIS, specified through the integer label of the program statement currently processed by SIS.

°1 After the reading phase, sd is $m=1$. All remaining program variables are set to symbolic values. Notice that $m=1$ allows SIS to unfold the inner reading loop, transforming it into

jj:=1; read(PSET[ii,jj])

which can be further optimized into

read(PSET[ii,1]).

°2 After the two assignments at line °2, sd contains $\{m = 1,\ MIND[1]=1,\ k=1\}$

°3 Since n is not known, the loop at line °3 is not unfolded. Thus SIS must operate on the body of the loop starting with an invariant part of sd, possibly enriched by the path condition $2<=i<=n$. That $m=1$ is a loop invariant can easily be realized even mechanically. Instead, asserting $k>=1$ invariant requires more insight. We assume that the user uses ingenuity to derive this fact, which is supplied to the system for further simplification. Thus, the simplifier proceeds with $sd=\{m=1,\ k>=1\}$.

°4 After the initialization statements at line 4, sd is $\{m=1,\ k>=1,\ j=1,\ subst=false,\ dom=false\}$.

°5 The condition of the <u>*while*</u> loop is evaluated to *true* for the first iteration. Thus the loop is unfolded and symbolic execution of its body is started.

°6-7 SIS transforms these lines into

c1:=true; ii:=1;

c1:=PSET[MIND[j],ii]<=PSET[i,ii]

which is easily optimized into

c1:=PSET[MIND[1],1]<=PSET[i,1]

Since the variables occurring in *sd* in °4 are not affected by execution of instruction °5-7, the new *sd* simply adds the clause *c1=(PSET[MIND[1],1]<=PSET[i,1])* to the previous one.

°8-10 SIS transforms these lines into

<u>*if*</u> *c1* <u>*then*</u> *dom:=true*

<u>*else*</u> <u>*begin*</u> *c2:=PSET[i,1]<=PSET[MIND[1],1]*

At this point, *sd* contains *c1=PSET[MIND[1],1]<=PSET[i,1],dom=false, c1=false*, since SIS is in the *else* branch of the conditional. Note that the conditional has not been reduced to a single branch, since at its entry there was not enough information to deduce whether *c1=true* or *c1=false*.

°11-19 SIS deduces that *c2* is true, since *c1* is false and the following facts are stored in *sd* :

c1=PSET[MIND[1],1]<=PSET[i,1],

c2=PSET[i,1]<=PSET[MIND[1],1]

Thus, the <u>*then*</u> branch is automatically selected and the <u>*else*</u> branch is erased from the simplified program. Similarly, *subset=false* enables a simplification of the inner conditional statement. As a result, lines °11-19 are simplified into :

MIND[1]:=1;

subst:=true

Before entering statement °20, *sd* contains the following predicate:

<u>*if*</u> *PSET [MIND.[1],1]<=PSET[i,1]* <u>*then*</u> *dom=true*

<u>*else*</u> *subst=true, MIND[1]=1*

°20 Here j is set to 2. Since the value of *k* is not modified within the <u>*for*</u> loop at line °3 and the initial value of *k* was 1, the <u>*while*</u> loop at line °5 is not iterated.

As a result, the main <u>*for*</u> loop is transformed into :

```
for i:=2 to n do
    begin j:=1; subst:=false; dom:=false;
        c1:=PSET[MIND[1],1]<=PSET[i,1];
        if c1 then dom:=true
        else begin c2:=PSET[i,1]<=PSET[MIND[1],1];
                  MIND[1]:=i;
```

```
                        subst:=true
                    end;j:=j+1
                end;
```

°21 The remaining writing loop is processed in a trivial way.

At this point, a simple optimization phase, which is easily realized on the basis of the usual compiling techniques, can discover that :

j. The second index of *PSET* is always equal to one, so that *MAXDIM* can be chosen exactly equal to one.

jj. The index of *MIND* is always equal to one, so that *MIND* can be reduced to a single variable instead of an array. (Notice that, while reduction j can be trivially foreseen at the very beginning, this reduction has been deduced from program transformation, and has a benificial effect on the amount of used memory).

jjj.The main loop can be further transformed into

```
for i:=2 to n do
    begin  c1:=PSET[MIND]<=PSET[i];
           if not c1 then MIND:=1
    end
```

3.2 Example 2

Consider the classical sorting algorithm "by straight insertion", coded by the Pascal program of Fig. 2 (the program use two array with the only purpose of simplifying our discussion). Also, consider the particular case where the input array *b* is ordered, but in reverse order! That is, for each $1<=i<=n$, $b/i/>=b/i+1/$. In this case, the approach of Example 1 would not prove very useful. Instead, we decide to give constant *n* a fixed value, say 3. This information, along with the previous predicate, allows SIS to completely unfold both loops, producing the following program:

```
begin read(b[1]);a[1]:=b[1];
      read(b[2]) ; a[2]:=b[2];
      read(b[3]);a[3]:=b[3];
      x:=a[2];a[0]:=x; a[2]:=a[1]; a[1]:=x;
      x:=a[3]; a[0]:=x,a[3]:=a[2]; a[2]=a[1];a[1]:=x
end
```

Now, byapplying straightforward optimization techniques, we obtain:

```
begin read(b[1]); read(b[2]); read(b[3]);
      a[3]:=b[1];a[2]:=b[2];a[1]:=b[3]
end
```

At this point, a brief inspection of the above result of simplification, maybe supported by a further run of SIS with n=4, suggests to refold the program into a simple loop :

```
begin for i:=1 to n do read (b[i]);
      for i:=1 to n do a[n-i+1]:=b[i]
end
```

This induction is certainly easy for the user, and in simple cases could be even automatically synthesized.

As a result, a simple algorithm which reverses the contents of an array has been derived semi-automatically from a sorting algorithm, by restricting its input domain. The reader is invited to verify that Example 1 could have been handled in the same way as Example 2 by assigning a specific value to the number of points. In such a case, SIS would unfold both loops completely without the user's suggestion that $k>=1$ is an invariant. A subsequent re-folding activity should be necessary to re-synthesize the main loop.

4. IMPLEMENTATION AND CONCLUDING REMARKS

A prototype implementation of SIS has been realized /Colombo et al. 1985/. It is built on top of a symbolic interpreter for Pascal, UNISEX (/Kemmerer and Eckmann 1983/), developed at the University of California, Santa Barbara, and running on a VAX 11 under the Berkeley UNIX(*) operating system.

The symbolic interpreter has no theorem proving capabilities, so that deductions must be performed by the user. State description is based on historical values of variables. This frees the user from the need for inserting dummy historical variables into programs, as we did in Example 2. A small optimizing capability is in the system, but sophisticated features typical of some optimizing compilers have not been included yet.No automatic loop-folder has been realized so far. All features not supported automatically by the system are substituted by interaction with the user.

The prototype implementation os SIS has been tested on several examples, including those presented in Section 3. In the above examples, the behavior of the system has been as described in Section 3, except for mathematical inductions and loop re-folding which are performed interactively by the user.

(*) UNIX is a trademark of AT&T.

In conclusion, early experience with program simplification seems to be encouraging enough to motivate further development of the present prototype and broader experimentation with real cases. Perhaps it is worth mentioning that while Example 1 exhibited expected results, others were somewhat surprising for the authors themselves.

```
program MINSET(input, output);
const N=...; MAXDIM=...;
type POINT=array[1.. MAXDIM]of integer;
var PSET:array[1.. N] of POINT;
    MIND:array[1.. N] of 1..N;
    m,k:1.. MAXDIM; n:1.. N;
    i,j,ii,jj:integer; subst,dom,c1,c2:boolean;
begin read(m,n);
(1)   for ii:=1 to n do for jj:=1 to m do read PSET[ii,jj];
(2)   MIND[1]:=1; k:=1;
(3)   for i:=2 to n do
(4)       begin j=1; subst:=false; dom:=false;
            {j is used as an index to scan MIND--subst becomes true
            if the value of i substitutes a value which was previous-
            ly stored in MIND--dom becomes true if PSET[i] dominates
            some element whose index is in MIND}
(5)   while j<=k and not dom do
(6)       begin c1:=true;
(7)           for ii=1 to m do c1:=c1 and
                        PSET[MIND[j], ii]<=PSET[i,ii];
                {C1 is true iff the i-th element of PSET
                 dominates the MIND[j]-th}
(8)           if c1 then dom:=true
(9)           else begin c2:=true;
(10)                   for ii:=1 to m do c2:=c2 and
                           (PSET[i,ii]<=PSET[MIND[j],ii]);
                       {c2 is true iff the i-th element of PSET
                        ia dominated by the MIND[j]-th}
(11)                         if c2 then
(12)                            if subst then
                                 {subst=true means that the i-th
                                 point has already substituted
                                 some point represented in MIND.
                                 Thus we must erase the current
                                 index from MIND}
(13)                             begin k:=k-1;
```

```
(14)                                      for jj:=j to k do
                                            MIND[jj]:=MIND[jj+1]
                                    end
                                else
                                {here i substitutes the index of
                                 the point of MIND dominating
                                 PSET [i]}
(15)                             begin MIND [j] := i;
(16)                                   subst := true
                                 end
(17)                          else if j=k and not subst then
                                        {i is added to MIND}
(18)                                     begin k:=k+1; j:=k
(19)                                           MIND[k]:=i
                                         end
                         end;
(20)                     j:=j+1
                 end
             end;
(21)   for ii:=1 to k do
          begin for jj:=1 to m do write(PSET [MIND [ii],jj]);
                writeln
          end
end
```

FIG. 1

```
program sort_by_straight_insertion (input, output);
const n = ...;
var   i, j, x: integer;
      a, b: array [0.. n] of integer;
begin for i:=1 to n do
            begin read (b[i]);a[i]:=b[i] end;
      for i:=2 to n do
            begin x:=a[i];a[0]:=x;j:=i-1;
                  while x < a[j] do
                        begin a[j+1]:=a[j]; j:=j-1 end
                  a[j+1]:=x
            end
end
```

FIG. 2

REFERENCES

/Aho and Ullman 1977/
Aho, A.V. and J.D. Ullman <u>Principles of CompilerDesign</u> Addison Wesley, Reading, MA 1977.

/Colombo et al. 1985/
Colombo, M., F. Furlani, G. Geretto "Un Semplificatore di Programmi Pascal Basato su Esecutore Simbolico", Dip. Elettronica, Politecnico di Milano, Tesi di Laurea 1985.

/Ershov 1977/
Ershov, A.P. "On The Partial Computation Principle", Information Processing Letters, 6,2, 1977.

/Ershov 1982/
Ershov, A.P., "Mixed Computation Potential Applications and Problems for Study", Theoretical Computer Science, 18, 1982.

/Kemmerer and Eckmann 1983/
Kemmerer, R.A., and S.T. Eckmann A User's Manual for the UNISEX System", UCSB, Dept. of Computer Science, TRCS83-05, Dec. 1983.

/King 1976/
King, J.C. "Symbolic Execution and Program Testing", Comm. ACM, 19, 7, pp 385-394, July 1976.

/Bauer and Wossner 1982/
Bauer, F. and Wossner, H. "Algoritmic Languadge and Program Development", Springer Verlag, New York 1982.

/Partsch and Steinbruggen 1983/
Partsch, H. and R. Steinbruggen, "Program Transformation Systems", ACM Computing Surveys, 15, 3, pp 199-236, Sept. 1983.

PROLOG-Based Inductive Theorem Proving

Jieh Hsiang
Mandayam Srivas

Department of Computer Science
State University of New York at Stony Brook
Stony Brook, NY 11794

Abstract

Although PROLOG is a programming language based on techniques from theorem proving its use as a base for a theorem prover has not been explored until recently ([Sti84]). In this paper, we introduce a PROLOG-based deductive theorem proving method for proving first order inductive theory representable in Horn clauses. The method has the following characteristics: (1) It automatically partitions the domains over which the variables range into subdomains according to the manner in which the predicate symbols in the theorem are defined. (2) For each subdomain of the domain the prover returns a lemma. If the lemma is *true*, then the target theorem is true for this subdomain. The lemma could also be an induction hypothesis for the theorem. (3) The method does not explicitly use any inductive inference rule. The induction hypothesis, if needed for a certain subdomain, will sometimes be generated from a (limited) forward chaining mechanism in the prover and not from employing any particular inference rule.

In addition to the backward chaining and backtracking facilities of PROLOG, our method introduces three new mechanisms - *skolemization by need, suspended evaluation,* and *limited forward chaining*. These new mechanisms are simple enough to be easily implemented or even incorporated into PROLOG. We demonstrate the use of the theorem prover for verifying PROLOG programs and proving properties of data types.

1. Introduction

PROLOG is a powerful and versatile programming language based on theorem proving techniques such as unification and resolution. Many of its implementations perform inferences at a much higher speed than general purpose theorem provers. Despite this fact PROLOG has not been successfully used as a theorem prover. Some of the reasons for this are that PROLOG is restricted in expressive power (Horn clause based), and has other obstacles such as the lack of occurs check and the inability to prove properties in which variables are universally quantified to range over recursively constructed domain. In [Sti84] an approach for using PROLOG as a general theorem prover was discussed. It included a general inference rule which provides PROLOG the ability of dealing with non-Horn clauses (and, consequently, does not need the closed world assumption [Rei]), as well as mechanisms for occurs check.[1] The universal quantification problem was handled in [Sti84] in a standard way -- by skolemizing (i.e., treating the variables as arbitrary constants) all of the universally quantified variables in the query before the resolution proof process began. However, this method does not work satisfactorily if the domains of the variables are defined inductively (such as lists) or if the predicate is defined in a conditional way. In such a case it might be necessary to use induction to prove a theorem.

In this paper we introduce an inductive theorem proving method to provide a more satisfactory answer to the universal quantification problem. This is done by supplementing the backward chaining mechanism of PROLOG with three new mechanisms - *skolemization by need*, *suspended evaluation*, and *limited forward chaining*. The new mechanisms introduced are simple enough to be easily implemented or even incorporated into PROLOG. We demonstrate the use of the theorem prover for verifying PROLOG programs and proving properties of data types.

---

[1] The occurs check problem was discussed in detail in [Pla84].

Our theorem proving method has the following characteristics.

(1) It can be used for proving properties in which the variables are universally quantified and range over recursively constructed domains.

(2) It automatically divides the domain(s) of the universally quantified variable(s) into a finite number of subdomains. Each subdomain is characterized by the instantiations (for the quantified variables) that the theorem prover returns.

(3) It proves the validity of the proposition for each subdomain separately. For each subdomain, it returns a *Lemma* the validity of which guarantees the validity of the proposition for that subdomain. The *Lemma* could be the literal *true*, or the induction hypothesis for the subdomain, or an arbitrary (Horn clause) formula. In the first two cases the *Lemma* is already proved, in the third case the *Lemma* can be fed back (by the user) to the prover again. Thus, the method does not use any explicit inductive inference rule.

(4) Also, since the method is based on subgoal reduction, the prover *always terminates*.

The main restriction of the method is that the proposition to be proved has to be in the form of a Horn clause. A secondary restriction imposed mainly for convenience is that every $n+1$-ary predicate $P(x_1, \cdots, x_{n+1})$ that appears in the proposition be defined as a total n-ary function with respect to its last argument.

One way of building the theorem prover is to integrate it into the environment provided by PROLOG. The extended environment, besides inheriting the normal features of PROLOG, will incorporate all the new mechanisms proposed in the paper. In such an environment a universally quantified proposition $prop(\overline{X})$ is proved by typing it in as a query, and indicating which of the variables in $\overline{X}$ are universally quantified. A simpler way of building the theorem prover is to implement it as a predicate on top of a PROLOG interpreter. In such a case a property is proved by defining it as a set of PROLOG clauses, and then invoking the theorem proving predicate. A preliminary implementation of our method has been completed using the second approach. We maintain the second perspective in describing the method in this paper, as well.

1.1. Organization of The Paper

The rest of the introduction provides an overview of the theorem proving method. Section 2 gives a formal functional description of the theorem prover. Section 3 describes in detail all the new mechanisms used by the theorem proving method. Section 4 gives an algorithm for implementing the method. Section 5 provides a discussion of how the output produced by the prover is to be interpreted, and a comparison of our method with other inductive theorem proving methods. The Appendix gives an illustration of the method on a couple of examples.

1.2. An Overview

We begin by describing the problems encountered in using PROLOG for proving a universally quantified property by typing the property as a query into a PROLOG interpreter. We introduce the new mechanisms by describing how they alleviate these problems, and then present the method informally.

1.2.1. The Problem of Unbounded Depth-First Search Strategy

PROLOG, which uses a query-respond paradigm to communicate with its users, is capable of proving only existentially quantified properties. For example, consider proving the associativity property of the *append* of two lists:

$$\forall X,Y,Z\,[(\forall L1,L2,L3)\; append(X,Y,L1), append(L1,Z,L2),$$
$$append(Y,Z,L3),\; append(X,L3,L4) \supset L2 = L4]$$

Append is defined as a predicate which checks if its third argument is the concatenation of its first two arguments. The property is expressed as a PROLOG clause defining a predicate $prop(X,Y,Z)$ as follows:[2]

$append([\,],L,L).$
$append([A \mid L1],L2,[A \mid L3])$:- $append(L1,L2,L3).$

$prop(X,Y,Z)$:- $append(X,Y,L1), append(L1,Z,L2),$
$append(Y,Z,L3), append(X,L3,L4),\ L2 = L4.$

The property cannot be proved by executing the query:

:- $prop(X,Y,Z).$

since PROLOG will only provide an instance (not necessarily the most general one) of the *input* variables X, Y, and Z which satisfies the property. In some interpreters of PROLOG, such as CPROLOG ([ClM81]), it is possible to request another instantiation (if any) which also satisfies $prop(X,Y,Z)$. Such a feature will not help in general when the domains of the variables are infinite.

The conventional method of dealing with universal quantification in a refutational theorem prover (such as PROLOG) is to treat them as skolem constants (e.g. [Sti84]). Such a method does not work satisfactorily if the domain of the variables are defined inductively (such as *List*) since skolem constants cannot be unified with any of the functors. For instance, consider the execution of the skolemized query shown below. (Henceforth a *hatted variable*, such as $\hat{X}$, will be used to denote a skolem constant. A skolem constant is like a meta-variable since it can denote an arbitrary value belonging to the domain under consideration.)

:- $prop(\hat{X}, \hat{Y}, \hat{Z}).$

This will not lead to a proof since the first subgoal, $append(\hat{X}, \hat{Y}, L1)$ does not match with any clause head. Thus, we are faced with a dilemma: by leaving the variables free we can prove the property true for only one instance, while skolemizing them may yield no proof at all.

To solve the above problem we introduce a new concept called *Ω-satisfiability*, which is weaker than the standard notion of satisfiability of a goal in PROLOG. Ω-satisfiability gives us a way of handling unsatisfiable goals whose unsatisfiability is due to the appearance of skolem constants. For instance, consider the goal $append(\hat{Y}, \hat{Z}, L3)$. The goal $append(\hat{Y}, \hat{Z}, L3)$ is not satisfiable since $\hat{Y}$ unifies with neither $[\,]$ nor $[A \mid L]$. However, we know that this goal *should* be satisfiable since $\hat{Y}$, being a list, has to be either $[\,]$ or $[A \mid L]$ for some A and L. Therefore, we *suspend the evaluation* of this goal by treating it as having been satisfied. The suspended state of the goal is recorded by binding $L3$ to a closure, called an *Ω-binding*[3]. The Ω-binding contains the constraint that $L3$ has to meet for the goal to succeed. In our notation, $L3$ is bound to a term of the form $\Omega(l3{:}append(\hat{Y}, \hat{Z}, l3))$, where $append(\hat{Y}, \hat{Z}, l3)$ is called the *Ω-constraint* of $L3$, and $l3$ is called the (bound) Ω-variable. A goal which can be satisfied in this way is called *Ω-satisfiable*.

To fully characterize the notion of Ω-satisfiability, we need to take into consideration two other situations in which a goal that would normally fail (under PROLOG satisfiability) would have to succeed for our purpose. Both these situations occur when the failure of a goal is because some of its arguments have Ω-bindings. To see the first situation, consider the goal $append(L1, \hat{Z}, L2)$, where $L1$ is bound to $\Omega(l1{:}append(\hat{X}, \hat{Y}, l1))$. We make this goal succeed by once again suspending the evaluation of this goal, and generating an Ω-binding for $L2$. Note that this goal has to be added as a new constraint to the currently existing Ω-bindings in the goal, and all the constraints in the currently existing Ω-bindings should be *propogated* to the new bindings generated. Thus, $L1$ is bound to $\Omega(l1{:}append(\hat{X}, \hat{Y}, l1), append(l1, \hat{Z}, l2))$ and $L2$ is bound to $\Omega(l2{:}append(\hat{X}, \hat{Y}, l1), append(l1, \hat{Z}, l2))$. The second situation is illustrated by the following example. Consider the goal $append([\,], L3, L2)$, where

[2]The clause defining *prop* and the property to be proved are not logically equivalent. However, the manner in which the goals are processed by our method makes this descripancy inconsequential. More about this is discussed in Section 2.1.

[3]A similar notion has also been used by Kornfeld ([Kor83]) for enriching the unification to include equational axioms.

$L3$ is bound to $\Omega(l3{:}append(\hat{Y}, \hat{Z}, l3))$, and $L2$ is bound to $\Omega(l2{:}append(\hat{Y}, \hat{Z}, l2))$. We would want this goal to succeed (although it would normally fail) because the bindings of $L2$ and $L3$ although different structurally impose the same constraint on the variables. We fix this problem by using *Ω-equivalence* instead of PROLOG equivalence (which is just structural identity) while comparing terms. Two Ω-terms are Ω-equivalent if they can be made identical upon renaming of the Ω-variables. On all other terms Ω-equivalence behaves just as PROLOG equivalence.

By using Ω-satisfiability instead of ordinary PROLOG satiafiablity the query:

$$:- prop([\,], \hat{Y}, \hat{Z}). \qquad (*)$$

can be executed successfully. The constraint (in the Ω bindings generated during the execution of *prop*) on which the success of the query depends is $append(\hat{Y}, \hat{Z}, l)$. This constraint is guaranteed to be satisfied because (by our totality assumption about the predicates) there always exists such an l for arbitrary lists that $\hat{Y}$ and $\hat{Z}$ denote. Thus, the successful execution of the above query proves the associativity property of *append* for the case where X is $[\,]$.

1.2.2. The Problem of Induction

As illustrated above, if we use the notion of suspended evaluation in executing an appropriately skolemized goal, we would, in general, be left with an Ω-constraint at the end of a successful execution of the goal. The Ω-constraint thus generated is sometimes obviously true, as was the case in the situation shown above. But, sometimes it might denote a conjunction of goals that is implied by a smaller instance of the original goal that we were trying to satisfy. It is extremely useful to detect this situation since it could give us the induction hypothesis needed to complete the inductive step in the proof of the original goal. PROLOG cannot detect such an implication since it uses only *backward chaining* (deducing subgoals from a goal), but not *forward chaining* (deducing a goal from a set of subgoals). It is not hard, in principle, to incorporate general forward chaining into PROLOG by constantly checking the remaining of the subgoals to see if some of them satisfy a clause. But this is undesirable since it would be extremely inefficient. We deal with the problem by introducing a *limited* forward chaining mechanism. This consists of (1) using only the clause that describes the proposition to be proved for forward chaining, and (2) only attempting to perform forward chaining on the Ω-constraint obtained at the end of Ω-satisfying all the goals in the body of the proposition clause.

For instance, consider the execution of the query:

$$:- prop([\hat{A} \mid \hat{L}], \hat{Y}, \hat{Z}). \qquad (**)$$

Assuming we are using Ω-satisfiability, the above query can be successfully executed. At the end of the execution the Ω-bindings generated will have the following constraint:

$$append(\hat{L}, \hat{Y}, l1),\ append(l1, \hat{Z}, l2),\ append(\hat{Y}, \hat{Z}, l3),\ append(\hat{L}, l3, l4),\ l2 = l4.$$

By performing forward chaining on the above set of goals using the clause defining *prop*, we have $prop(\hat{L}, \hat{Y}, \hat{Z})$ as the constraint on which the validity of $prop([\hat{A} \mid \hat{L}], \hat{Y}, \hat{Z})$ is dependent. Combining the execution of the queries (*) and (**), we have established the validity of the following formulas which completes the proof of $\forall X, Y, Z\ prop(X, Y, Z)$:

(1) $\forall Y, Z\ prop([\,], Y, Z)$

(2) $\forall A, L, Y, Z\ (prop(L, Y, Z) \supset prop([A \mid L], Y, Z))$.

Note that it might not always be possible to perform forward chaining on the Ω-constraint generated. In such a case the constraint is merely returned as a *Lemma* that has to be proved for establishing the validity of the proposition.

1.2.3. The Problem of Skolemization

In completing the proof of *prop* (shown above) the skolem constants with which the variables X, Y, and Z were instantiated were chosen *a priori*. In the first case it was chosen to be $([\,], \hat{Y}, \hat{Z})$, and in the second case it was $([\hat{A} \mid \hat{L}], \hat{Y}, \hat{Z})$. Together they form a *complete* set of skolemizations because they completely span the domain under consideration, namely the triple product of *Lists*. While completeness of the set of skolemizations is certainly necessary, it is also equally important that the skolemizations partition the domain appropriately. For instance, the naive skolemization, such as $(\hat{X}, \hat{Y}, \hat{Z})$ in the above example, in which every universally quantified variable is skolemized to a distinct unstructured constant is obviously complete but rarely leads to an inductive proof. For instance, execution of the query:

$$:- \ prop(\hat{X}, \hat{Y}, \hat{Z}). \qquad (***)$$

will give back $prop(\hat{X}, \hat{Y}, \hat{Z})$ as the *Lemma* leading us back to where we began.

The skolemization that is likely to lead to a proof is dependent on the inductive structure of the definition of the predicates in the proposition, and on the structre of the terms constructing the domain. To automate the generation of skolem constants in a way that takes into account the inductive structure of the predicates we introduce a mechanism called *skolemization by need*. In our theorem proving method bindings for the universally quantifed variables are generated using the skolemization by need mechanism.

Under this method, the universally quantified variables in a query start out as free variables (like any other variables in PROLOG) instead of being replaced by skolem constants (as was done in the proof of *prop* shown above). This allows PROLOG unification to keep instantiating them until they are skolemized. A variable gets *skolemized* only (and immediately) after a *decision* about the value to be bound for that variable is made. We consider a *decision* to have been made when

(1) the variable is unified with a non-variable term, or

(2) the variable appears in a goal whose execution does not lead to any new subgoals.

Note that the second situation may happen either because the goal was successfully matched with a fact, or because its evaluation was suspended by generating Ω-bindings. The fact that a variable X is skolemized is indicated by replacing every free variable in the term currently bound to X by its corresponding hatted skolem constant.

For instance, the goal $append(X, Y, L1)$, where X and Y are universally quantified, would succeed when unified with the fact in the *append* program; X would be bound to [ ] and Y (and hence also $L1$) would be bound to a skolem constant $\hat{Y}$ (rather than a variable) since the goal does not generate any new subgoals. On the other hand if $append(X, Y, L1)$ were unified with the head of the second clause in the specification of *append*, then X would get instantiated to $[A \mid L]$. X would then immediately get skolemized to $[\hat{A} \mid \hat{L}]$ since $[A \mid L]$ is a nonvariable term. The variable Y is not skolemized at this point since no decision is made about its value; neither is $L1$, since it is not an input variable.

When skolemization by need is used in conjunction with Ω-satisfiablity in executing a query the response will not only be a *Lemma* (constructed from the Ω-constraint), but also the skolemization that was responsible for the *Lemma*. To obtain a complete set of skolemizations and the corresponding *Lemmas*, we use the backtracking facility of PROLOG by forcing a failure after an execution of the query. The totality restriction we impose on the definition of predicates guarantees that a complete set of skolemizations will be produced after a finite number of forced failure attempts of the query. For instance, the first execution of the query

$$:- \ prop(X, Y, Z).$$

would yield the skolemization $([\,], \hat{Y}, \hat{Z})$ and the lemma *true*. A forced failure would yield, after backtracking, the skolemization $([\hat{A} \mid \hat{L}], \hat{Y}, \hat{Z})$ and the lemma $prop(\hat{L}, \hat{Y}, \hat{Z})$.

1.2.4. An Outline of The Method

The properties $(\forall \overline{X}\, \phi(\overline{X}))$ that our method is capable of proving have the general form of Horn clauses:

$$\phi(\overline{X}) : \forall \overline{Z}\,(P_1(\overline{X}, \overline{Z}) \wedge \cdots \wedge P_n(\overline{X}, \overline{Z}) \supset Q(\overline{X}, \overline{Z})).$$

where P_i's (the *antecedents*) and Q (the *consequent*) are predicates and $\overline{X}$ and $\overline{Z}$ (lists of variables) are the only variables in the predicates. We assume that all variables in $\overline{Z}$ appear in at least one of the antecedents P_i.

The method consists of Ω-satisfying every P_i subjecting the variables in $\overline{X}$ to skolemization by need in the process. If any of the P_i's cannot be Ω-satisfied then the proposition is vacuously true because one of the antecedents is false. The mechanisms of Ω-satisfaction and skolemization by need (and the fact that every variable in $\overline{Z}$ appears in at least one of the antecedents) guarantee that no variable in $\overline{X}$ or $\overline{Z}$ remains free at the end of Ω-satisfying all the antecedents. More specifically, the following conditions are guaranteed: (i) Every variable in $\overline{X}$ is skolemized. (ii) No variable in $\overline{Z}$ is free; it is either bound to an Ω-term, or to a term that contains skolemized variables.

After processing the antecedents, an attempt is made to Ω-satisfy the consequent $Q(\overline{X}, \overline{Z})$. Since none of the variables in Q is free the outcome of such an attempt can be one of the following:

(1) Q is satisfied under PROLOG satisfiability (with PROLOG equality extended to Ω-equivalence.). In this case no new Ω-bindings are generated, nor any of the existing Ω-bindings are altered.

(2) Q is Ω-satisfied by adding new constraints to the existing Ω-bindings. This happens when Q cannot be satisfied as in (1). In this case, according to the Ω-satisfiability mechanism, all the constraints in the current bindings will be merged, and Q will be included into the Ω-bindings as a new constraint. Thus, when Q cannot be satisfied as in (1) it will always become a part of the Ω-constraint generated.

In the former case the proposition is proved for the present skolemization because the validity of the consequent was shown despite the constraints on which the validity of the antecedents is based. Hence, the literal *true* is returned as the *Lemma*. In the latter case, the validity of the proposition is dependent on the Ω-constraint. Note that the eventual Ω-constraint, although represented as a list of goals, itself denotes a Horn clause formula with the constraints generated from the P_i's forming the antecedents and the constraint generated from Q forming the consequent. This formula is returned as the *Lemma* to be proved after checking if it is an instance of ϕ.

In either case, the skolemization generated for the variables in $\overline{X}$ is returned along with the *Lemma*. This takes care of the proof for the partition of the domain (of $\overline{X}$) that is characterized by the skolemization. To complete the proof for the remaining parts of the domain it is necessary to backtrack (*undoing* the skolemizataions in the process), and re-Ω-satisfy the goals in the proposition. The bactracking needed here is much like the one used by PROLOG, and will be explained in detail later in the paper.

2. Functional Description of The Prover

2.1. Representation of the Proposition

The PROLOG data base that *ind_prove* will operate on should include a description of the proposition to be proved, and a complete definition of all the predicates used in the proposition. In our formalism the proposition $\phi(\overline{X})$

$$\phi(\overline{X}) : \forall \overline{Z} (P_1(\overline{X}, \overline{Z}) \wedge \cdots \wedge P_n(\overline{X}, \overline{Z}) \supset Q(\overline{X}, \overline{Z})).$$

to be proved is represented as a predicate $prop(\overline{X})$ defined by the following PROLOG clause:

$$prop(\overline{X}) \text{:-} P_1(\overline{X}, \overline{Z}), \cdots, P_n(\overline{X}, \overline{Z}), Q(\overline{X}, \overline{Z}).$$

As a convention we refer to the variables in $\overline{X}$ as *input variable*. Note that ϕ is not logically equivalent to the PROLOG clause. However, this descripancy does not have any deliterious effect because *prop* is only used as a means of representing the property to be proved, but not as a predicate in any other clauses. Also, our method requires the antecedents to be processed before the consequent. The left-to-right strategy used by PROLOG for processing *and* goals accomplishes this automatically when ϕ is represented as *prop*. *Prop* thus defined also makes it convenient to check if the Ω-constraint generated is the induction hypothesis by using the clause to perform forward chaining.

2.2. Description of the Arguments

For ease of presentation, we introduce a new predicate *ind_prove*(*Theorem*, *Premise*, *Lemma*) to serve as the prover. To prove a proposition $prop(\overline{X})$, the prover would be invoked by $ind\_prove(prop(\overline{X}),P,L)$. This would result in a single skolemization (in the form of instantiations for the variables in $\overline{X}$), and a value for P and L. The rest of the skolemizations, and their corresponding premises and lemmas are obtained by using bactracking a finite number of times.

The arguments of *ind_prove* are described below:

Theorem
is the proposition to be proved.

Premise:
This is a list of conditions (predicates) on the skolem constants appearing in the skolemization generated for $\overline{X}$. When the list is empty, the *Premise* is considered to be *true*, otherwise, it is considered as the conjunction of all the predicates in the list. A nontrivial *Premise* appears mostly when some predicate is defined conditionally.

Lemma
is also a list of conditions (or *true*) like a *Premise*. These conditions determine the validity of the proposition being proved for the corresponding skolemization. The conditions in a *Lemma* are also interpreted in a way different from the ones in a *Premise*. If the list of conditions in a *Lemma* is $\{A_1, \cdots, A_m, Q'\}$, then its logical meaning is $A_1 \wedge \cdots \wedge A_m \supset Q'$.

Suppose $\{\overline{X}_1, \cdots, \overline{X}_k\}$ is the set of all instantiations generated for $\overline{X}$ by repeated invocations of $Ind\_prove(prop(\overline{X}),Premise,Lemma)$. For each $\overline{X}_j$, let $Pr_j(\overline{X}_j)$ be the premise, and $Lem_j(\overline{X}_j)$ be the lemma produced by *ind_prove*. Let D_X denote the domain of values, i.e., ground terms, over which X ranges. Then, the output produced by *ind_prove* automatically satisfies the following conditions:

(1) *Well-Spannedness*
For every $\overline{d} \epsilon D_{\overline{X}}$, there is some j such that $\overline{d}$ is an instance of $\overline{X}_j$ and $Pr_j(\overline{d})$ is true. In other words, the set of instantiations *well-span* (c.f. [Sri82], [HuH80]) domain $D_{\overline{X}}$. The use of *Premise* is for the possible splitting of cases in the domain. For example, given a proposition with two inputs A and L where A is an atom and L is a list, the set of instantiations may be $(A,[])$, $(A,[B \mid L])$, and $(A,[B \mid L])$, with premises, respectively, *true*, $A=B$, and $A \neq B$.

(2) *Problem Reduction*
For each $\overline{d} \epsilon D_{\overline{X}}$ which is an instance of some skolemization $\overline{X}_j$ we have the property: if $Lem_j(\overline{d})$, then $prop(\overline{X}_0)$.

Property (1) above describes a proper set of instantiations and property (2) indicates that for a particular instance $\overline{X}_0$, $Lem_j(\overline{X}_0)$ has to be proved for $prop(\overline{X}_0)$ to be true. For the *append* example, *ind_prove* would generate the following set of instantiations with the corresponding lemmas:

Instantiation	*Premise*	*Lemma*
$([\,], Y, Z)$	*true*	*true*
$([A \mid L], Y, Z)$	*true*	$prop(L, Y, Z)$

This means that

(1) $\forall Y,Z \; prop([\,],Y,Z)$

(2) $\forall A,L,Y,Z \; (prop(L,Y,Z) \supset prop([A \mid L],Y,Z))$.

Since $prop(L,Y,Z)$ is the induction hypothesis of $prop([A \mid L],Y,Z)$, we have proved $\forall X,Y,Z \; prop(X,Y,Z)$, and therefore *append* is associative.

3. The New Mechanisms

This section gives a detailed description of all the newly introduced mechanisms which form the building blocks for our theorem proving method.

3.1. Skolemization by Need

This mechanism provides a systematic way of skolemizing the input variables in the proposition. This method of skolemization is distinguished from the conventional methods in that the variables are not skolemized at the start of the resolution process. Instead, every input variable is left unskolemized (so that it could get instantiated by the unification of PROLOG) until a *decision* about its value has to be made. At this point the input variable is skolemized by simply *hatting* every variable occuring in the term currently bound to the input variable. We consider such a *decision* about an input variable to have been made when

(1) the variable is unified with a non-variable term, or

(2) the variable appears in a goal whose execution does not lead to any new subgoals. Note that this situation may occur either because the goal was successfully matched with a fact, or because its evaluation was suspended for generating Ω-bindings.

As an example, if the first subgoal $append(X, Y, L1)$, where X and Y are input variables, is unified with the head of the second clause in the definition of *append* (Section 1.2.1), $append([A \mid L1], L2, [A \mid L3])$, then the variable X will be instantiated to $[A \mid L]$. Then, X would be immediately skolemized to $[\hat{A} \mid \hat{L}]$ by hatting the variables A and L. The variable Y is not skolemized yet because no decision about its value is made. On the other hand, let us suppose the input variable Y appears in a goal $append(L2, Y, L3)$, in which $L2$ has an Ω-binding (see next section). Then this goal would be Ω-satisfied without creating any subgoals, and hence Y would be skolemized to $\hat{Y}$.

3.2. Ω-Satisfiability and Ω-Binding

Ω-satisfiability is a notion of satisfiability that is weaker than the notion of satisfiability used in PROLOG. It is used primarily to handle the failure of a goal that arises because some of the variables in the goal are skolemized variables. We define Ω-satisfiability so that a goal would succeed in such a situation by generating a special kind of binding, called an *Ω-binding*, for the free variables in the goal. Before describing how the Ω-bindings are generated we need to introduce some definitions.

An *Ω-term* is a term of the form $\Omega(x:P)$ where x is a variable, called the *Ω-variable*, and P is a (conjunction of) predicate(s), called the *Ω-constraint*. A variable X is *Ω-bound* to t if t is an Ω-term or it is a term containing *one* Ω-term as a subterm. If a variable X is bound to $[a \mid \Omega(l:P(\hat{Y}, l), Q(l, z))]$, it means that X is bound to the list $[a \mid L]$ where L is a list satisfying $P(\hat{Y}, L) \wedge Q(L, Z)$ for some Z. (Note that in our method an input variable will never be Ω-bound. It is always either instantiated, or skolemized.)

The essential idea of Ω-binding is to treat certain unsatisfiable goals as constraints which may eventually become part of the *Lemma* or the *Premise*. From now on we use the word *Ω-term* loosely to mean either an Ω-term as defined above or any term that contains an Ω-term.

Definition Two Ω-terms t_1 and t_2 are *Ω-equivalent* (denoted as $t_1 =_\Omega t_2$) if they are identical upon renaming of the Ω-variables.

For example, $1+\Omega(n:P(\hat{Y}, n))$ and $1+\Omega(m:P(\hat{Y}, m))$ are Ω-equivalent while $1+\Omega(n:P(\hat{Y}, n))$ and $1+\Omega(m:Q(\hat{Y}, m))$ are not (even if P and Q can be proven equivalent by other means), nor are $1+\Omega(n:P(\hat{X}, n))$ and $1+\Omega(m:P(\hat{Y}, m))$.

Definition A goal $P(t_1, \cdots, t_n)$, where the t_i's are either Ω-terms, constants, skolem constants, or free variables is *Ω-satisfiable* if one of the following conditions holds.

(1) It can be satisfied as in PROLOG with the PROLOG equality extended to include Ω-equivalence.

(2) The goal cannot be satisfied as in (1), and at least one of the variables in P is skolemized or Ω-bound.

For example, if "$G(X, [a \mid X])$." is a PROLOG fact, then the goal $G(\Omega(m:P(\hat{Y}, m)), [a \mid \Omega(n:P(\hat{Y}, n))])$ is Ω-satisfiable since the goal and the fact match and $\Omega(m:P(\hat{Y}, m)) =_\Omega \Omega(n:P(\hat{Y}, n))$.

Ω-binding Generation

Ω-binding generation will occur as a "side-effect" when a goal gets Ω-satisfied as per the second condition in the definition above. In such a case, the binding of every non-input variable in a goal $P(t_1, \cdots, t_n)$ that is being Ω-satisfied will be changed according to the following rules. (Note that skolemization by need requires all unskolemized input variables to be skolemized at such a juncture.) Then the non-input variables in P are bound to Ω-terms generated as described below.

Case 1: *At least one argument of $P(t_1, \cdots, t_n)$ is a non-input free variable.*

There are two subcases. Without loss of generality, let us assume that t_n is a free non-input variable X.

Case 1(a): *None of the arguments of $P(t_1, \cdots, t_{n-1}, X)$ is Ω-bound.*

In this case we consider the goal $P(t_1, \cdots, t_{n-1}, X)$ satisfied by simply binding X to the Ω-term $\Omega(x : P(t_1, \cdots, t_{n-1}, x))$. Every non-input free variable in P should be bound to an Ω-term in a similar way. It is not hard to see that these Ω-terms will have the same Ω-constraints, but different Ω-variables.

Case 1(b): *Some arguments of P are already Ω-bound.*

For simplicity we consider an example $P(\Omega(u : R(u, \hat{Y})), [\hat{A} \mid \Omega(l : Q(\hat{Z}, l))], X)$ (that is, a predicate $P(U, [\hat{A} \mid L], X)$ with U and L bound to Ω-terms). The general case follows in a similar way. P can be satisfied by performing an *Ω-merging*: Merging the constraints of all the existing Ω-terms, and adding the goal P as an additional constraint. In other words, X should be bound to an x which satisfies $P(u, [\hat{A} \mid l], x)$, where the variables u and l satisfy the constraints $R(u, \hat{Y})$ and $Q(\hat{Z}, l)$, respectively. So, X is bound to $\Omega(x : R(u, \hat{Y}), Q(\hat{Z}, l), P(u, [\hat{A} \mid l], x))$. As in case 1(a) every free non-input variable should be Ω-bound similarly.

Case 2: *There is no non-input free variable in the arguments of $P(t_1, \cdots, t_n)$.*

Case 2(a): *None of the arguments of P is Ω-bound.*

This can happen only when all the arguments of P are either constants or skolem constants from the input variables. This means that P is a condition which this particular instantiation of the input variables must satisfy. There are two cases which we need to consider separately. If P is a subgoal deduced from one of the antecedents of the original goal (i.e., from one of the P_i's), then put this subgoal into the list of *Premise*. If P is the consequent (i.e. the subgoal Q), then this subgoal is the *Lemma*.

Case 2(b): *Some arguments are Ω-bound.*

In this case an Ω-merging, as described in Case 1(b), needs to be performed, and all the Ω-bound variables should have their Ω-constraints changed accordingly. Once again we describe this process by an example. Suppose the Ω-unsatisfiable goal is $G(M, N)$ where $M \leftarrow \Omega(m : P(\hat{Y}, m))$ and $N \leftarrow [a \mid \Omega(n : Q(\hat{Y}, n))]$. In order to prevent this goal from failing, we re-bind the values of M and N and add G as part of the new constraints. That is, M should be Ω-bound to $\Omega(m : P(\hat{Y}, m), Q(\hat{Y}, n), G(m, [a \mid n]))$ and N to $[a \mid \Omega(n : P(\hat{Y}, n), Q(\hat{Y}, m), G(m, [a \mid n]))]$. Note that, in addition to the new constraint G, both of the Ω-constraints of the original bindings of M and N are now a part of the new Ω-constraints. Also note that $G(m, [a \mid n])$, instead of $G(m, n)$, is part of the new constraint, since N was originally bound to $[a \mid \Omega(n : \cdots)]$.

We now apply this Ω-binding mechanism to the second subgoal, *append*$(\hat{Y}, Z, L2)$ of the *append* example. *Append*$(\hat{Y}, Z, L2)$ is not Ω-satisfiable since $\hat{Y}$ can unify with neither $[\,]$ nor $[A \mid L]$. When invoking the Ω-binding procedure, Z is automatically hatted and becomes $\hat{Z}$. It is clear that Case 1(a) applies here since $L2$ is a free variable. Therefore to "satisfy" this goal, we assign $\Omega(l_2 : append(\hat{Y}, \hat{Z}, l_2))$ to $L2$.

3.3. Premise and Lemma Generations

Both premise and lemma are lists of constraints arising out of suspension of subgoals while the goals in *prop* are Ω-satisfied. Note that suspended goals are all converted into constraints via the Ω-binding generation mechanism. Every constraint so generated will end up exclusively as a part of either the premise or the lemma.

A premise is constructed by collecting all (sub)goals that fall under Case 2(a) during Ω-binding generation while the antecedents are being Ω-satisfied. A goal will fall under Case 2(a) only if every variablein it is already skolemized. Hence, a premise represents conditions to be assumed on the skolemization of the input variables. An empty premise is considered to be *true*.

A lemma is intended to denote the formula on which the validity of the proposition being proved depends. Hence it is constructed after Ω-satisfying the consequent as follows. The outcome of Ω-satisfying the consequent can be one of the following.

(i) The consequent was Ω-satisfied without having to employ Ω-binding generation.

(ii) The consequent was Ω-satisfied after going through Ω-binding generation.

In the first case the lemma constructed is the literal *true* because this means that the consequent could be satisfied regardless of the constraints upon which the validity of the antecedents depended. If the second were applicable then the consequent should have fallen under Case 2(a) or 2(b) during Ω-binding generation. In this case the lemma is either an instance of the consequent (produced by Case 2(a)), or returns the Ω-constraint of an Ω-bound variable of the consequent subgoal (produced by Case 2(b)). Note that since the Ω-constraints produced from Case 2(b) are the same for all the Ω-bound variables (the only difference being the Ω-variables), the lemma produced is unique.

Getting back to the *append* example, there are two instantiations for the variables (X, Y, Z), namely, $([], \hat{Y}, \hat{Z})$ and $([\hat{A} \mid \hat{X}], \hat{Y}, \hat{Z})$. Neither of them produces any premise (i.e. every subgoal from the antecedents can be satisfied by Ω-binding). So what remains is to satisfy the consequent, $L2 = L4$.

In the first case determined by the instantiation $([], \hat{Y}, \hat{Z})$, $L2$ is bound to $\Omega(l_2{:}append(\hat{Y}, \hat{Z}, l_2))$ and $L4$ to $\Omega(l_4{:}append(\hat{Y}, \hat{Z}, l_4))$. Since $\Omega(l_2{:}append(\hat{Y}, \hat{Z}, l_2)) =_\Omega \Omega(l_4{:}append(\hat{Y}, \hat{Z}, l_4))$, the goal $L2 = L4$ is Ω-satisfied. Therefore the lemma is *true*.

In the second instantiation $([\hat{A} \mid \hat{X}], \hat{Y}, \hat{Z})$, $L2$ is bound to $[\hat{A} \mid \Omega(l_2{:}append(\hat{X}, \hat{Y}, l_1), append(l_1, \hat{Z}, l_2))]$ and $L4$ to $[\hat{A} \mid \Omega(l_4{:}append(\hat{Y}, \hat{Z}, l_3), append(\hat{X}, l_3, l_4))]$. The consequent $L2 = L4$ is not Ω-satisfiable since

$\Omega(l_2{:}append(\hat{X}, \hat{Y}, l_1), append(l_1, \hat{Z}, l_2)) \neq_\Omega \Omega(l_4{:}append(\hat{Y}, \hat{Z}, l_3), append(\hat{X}, l_3, l_4))$.

Therefore Case 2(b) applies and the bindings of $L2$ and $L4$ now become

$$L_2 \leftarrow [\hat{A} \mid \Omega(l_2{:}\ append(\hat{X}, \hat{Y}, l_1), append(l_1, \hat{Z}, l_2),\ append(\hat{Y}, \hat{Z}, l_3), append(\hat{X}, l_3, l_4), l_2 = l_4)]$$
$$L_4 \leftarrow [\hat{A} \mid \Omega(l_4{:}\ append(\hat{X}, \hat{Y}, l_1), append(l_1, \hat{Z}, l_2),\ append(\hat{Y}, \hat{Z}, l_3), append(\hat{X}, l_3, l_4), l_2 = l_4)].$$

The lemma should, therefore, be

$$(append(\hat{X}, \hat{Y}, L1) \wedge append(L1, \hat{Z}, L2) \wedge append(\hat{Y}, \hat{Z}, L3) \wedge append(\hat{X}, L3, L4)) \supset L2 = L4,$$

produced from the Ω-constraint of either $L2$ or $L4$.

3.4. Limited Forward Chaining

The only purpose of using forward chaining in our method is to produce possible induction hypotheses of the original proposition. Therefore the forward chaining facility in our prover is very restricted. The idea is the following: Suppose the *Premise* and the *Lemma* for some instantiation $\overline{X}_0$ are $\{C_1, \cdots, C_k\}$ and $\{D_1, \cdots, D_m, Q\}$, where Q is an instance of the original consequent[4]. The set $\{C_1, \cdots, C_k, D_1, \cdots, D_m, Q\}$ is checked against the body of the PROLOG clause which defines the original proposition (*prop* in the *append* example). If it is an instantiation of a superset of the clause

[4] It is easy to see, from the construction of *Lemma*, that an instance of the consequent must be in the lemma if the lemma is not the literal *true*.

body, then the clause head of the proposition (with the corresponding instantiation) is returned as the new *Lemma*. (The *Premise* remains the same.) For instance in the second instantiation, $([\hat{A} \mid \hat{X}], \hat{Y}, \hat{Z})$, of the *append* example, the lemma

$$\{(append(\hat{X}, \hat{Y}, L1), append(L1, \hat{Z}, L2), append(\hat{Y}, \hat{Z}, L3), append(\hat{X}, L3, L4), L2{=}L4\}$$

matches with the body of the clause for $prop(X,Y,Z)$ with X bound to $\hat{X}$, Y to $\hat{Y}$, and Z to $\hat{Z}$. Therefore $prop(\hat{X}, \hat{Y}, \hat{Z})$ is returned as the new *Lemma*, replacing the previous one. Since this lemma $prop(\hat{X}, \hat{Y}, \hat{Z})$ is produced when trying to satisfy the goal $prop([\hat{A} \mid \hat{X}], \hat{Y}, \hat{Z})$, it is the induction hypothesis in the obvious structural induction of lists.

3.5. Generating A Well-Spanned Set of Instantiations

The concepts described above will guarantee that all the initial subgoals (the goals in the clause body of $prop(X,Y,Z)$) will be successfully processed and *one* instantiation will be generated for each of the input variables. However, our goal is to show that the proposition is true for *all* possible instances of the input variables. Therefore we need a mechanism to find more instantiations (and reprocess the initial set of subgoals) until the domains of the input variables are completely covered. This is done by backtracking to selected choice points.

First we call a choice point (i.e., the point where the PROLOG execution does an *or*-split) a *marked choice point* if either (1) some of the input variables are instantiated when matching the clause head or one of the subgoals in the clause body, or (2) one of the goals of the clause body becomes a premise. In other words, a marked choice point is a backtracking point at which a diffrerent choice of the clause to match may result in different instantiations (skolemizations) for the input variables.

As mentioned before, an instantiation along with a premise and lemma is generated when we finish processing all the initial subgoals in the proposition. Then our method of generating another instantiation is to force a failure at this point and re-evaluate the input predicate *ind_prove* again. Our *failure forcing* mechanism is similar to the one in PROLOG for generating a second solution. The difference, however, is that in our case the theorem prover backtracks to the last *marked* choice point, but not to the last choice point as in PROLOG. The well-spannedness of the set of instantiations thus generated can be checked using the method of Thiel ([Thi84]). The well-spannedness property is guaranteed in the case of abstract data types if the operations which the predicates represent are totally defined. It is because of the way the marked choice points are generated. A rigorous proof of the above statement will be given elsewhere.

In the Appendix we illustrate how the theorem proving method works on two examples.

4. An Algorithmic Description

The algorithm given below shows the generation of a single instantiation for the input (i.e., the universally quantified) variables in the proposition, a *Lemma* and a *Premise* for that particular instantiation. To generate a well-spanned set of instantiations, it is necessary to backtrack, as described in section 3.6, the algorithm to the latest marked choice point, and reexecute the algorithm by choosing a different clause/fact to unify a (sub)goal.

We have used an algorithmic notation (rather than a PROLOG notation) to keep it free of PROLOG idiosyncracies. The text within braces is intended to be treated as comments. The symbol $\leftarrow$ should be treated as an operation that binds the value of the expression on the right hand side to the variable on the left hand side.

```
Ind_Prove(Prop(X̄), Premise, Lemma)
        Body  ←  body of the clause that unifies with Prop(X̄)
        Antecedents  ←  all but the last element of Body
        Consequent  ←  the last element of Body
        Premise  ←  empty list
        Lemma  ←  empty list
        Processgoals(Antecedents, Premise)
        Processconseq(Consequent, Lemma)
end {Ind_Prove}

Processgoals(Goals, Constraints)
   {Goals is a list of goals to be processed.}
   {Constraints is a list of constraints on input variables.    }
   {Processgoals processes every goal in Goals, skolemizing      }
   {the input variables when necessary, and generating constraints}
   {or Ω-bindings when a goal is not satisfiable.              }
   {The constraints generated are also asserted in the data base. }

        if not empty(Goals) then

                G  ←  first(Goals)
                Goals  ←  rest(Goals)
                case G is
                  a successfully evaluable built-in predicate:
                        Evaluate G
                        Skolemize all free input variables in G
                        Processgoals(Goals, Premise)
                  unifiable with a fact:
                        Unify G
                        Skolemize all free input variables in G
                        Processgoals(Goals, Premise)
                  unifiable with the head of a clause:
                        Unify G with the clause head
                        Skolemize all variables that appear in terms that got
                          bound (due to unification) to the input variables in G
                        Goals  ←  append(body of the clause G was unified with, Goals)
                        Processgoals(Goals, Premise)
                  otherwise:
                        {Generation of premises and their assertion into the }
                        {data base are done inside Generate_Ω_bindings.}
                        Generate_Ω_bindings(G, Premise)
                        Processgoals(Goals, Premise)
                end case
        fi
end {Processgoals}

Processconseq(Consequent, Lemma)
        if Consequent is Ω_satisfiable without altering bindings
            then Lemma  ←  true
            else
                Generate_Ω_bindings(Consequent, Lemma)
                Add to Lemma the Ω-constraint of an Ω-binding (if any) in Consequent
        fi
end {Processconseq}
```

Generate_Ω_bindings($G(t_1, \ldots, t_n)$, *Constraints*)
Skolemize all free input variables in $G(t_1, \ldots, t_n)$
case $G(t_1, \ldots, t_n)$ **is such that**
at least one of its arguments is a free non-input variable:
case $G(t_1, \ldots, t_n)$ **is such that**
none of its arguments is Ω-bound:
Bind every free non-input variable in $G(t_1, \ldots, t_n)$
to an Ω-term generated as described in section 3.3
some of its arguments are Ω-bound:
Modify all Ω-bindings in the goal by performing
Ω-merging as described in section 3.3
end case
there is no free non-input variable in its arguments:
case $G(t_1, \ldots, t_n)$ **is such that**
none of its arguments is Ω-bound:
Add $G(t_1, \ldots, t_n)$ to the list currently bound to *Constraints*
Assert $G(t_1, \ldots, t_n)$ as a new fact in the data base
some of its arguments are Ω-bound:
Modify all Ω-bindings in the goal by performing
Ω-merging and adding the goal to the Ω-constraint
end case
end case
end {Generate_Ω_bindings}

5. Discussion

5.1. Interpreting the Outcome

Let $\overline{X}_0$ be an instantiation returned by the theorem prover, with the corresponding *Premise*

$$Prem(\overline{X}_0) : A_1, \cdots, A_k$$

and *Lemma*

$$Lem(\overline{X}_0) : B_1, \cdots, B_l, Q$$

where Q is (an instance of) the original consequent. Then the logical meaning of the outcome is

$$(A_1(\overline{X}_0) \wedge \cdots \wedge A_k(\overline{X}_0) \supset ((B_1(\overline{X}_0, \overline{Z}) \wedge \cdots \wedge B_l(\overline{X}_0, \overline{Z}) \supset Q(\overline{X}_0, \overline{Z}))$$

where all free variables in the predicates are universally quantified.

One of the following cases is applicable to the outcome:

(1) If *Lem* is *true* or if $Prem \supset Lem$, then $prop(\overline{X}_0)$ is true for those $\overline{X}_0$ which satisfy $Prem(\overline{X}_0)$.

(2) If *Lem* is the induction hypothesis for $prop(\overline{X}_0)$, then $prop(\overline{X}_0)$ is considered true for those $\overline{X}_0$ which satisfy $Prem(\overline{X}_0)$.

(3) If *Lem* is a false sentence then we cannot come to any conclusion about $prop(\overline{X}_0)$. Note that the procedure *ind_prove* never fails for any input proposition. We shall discuss the situation of having false lemmas later.

(4) Otherwise, a new proposition

$$newprop(\overline{X}_0) \text{:-} Prem(\overline{X}_0), Lem(\overline{X}_0, \overline{Z})$$

is created and can be fed into *ind_prove* as a new proposition to be proved. Note that the input variables for *newprop* should include all the free variables in $\overline{X}_0$, which may be different from those in $\overline{X}$. Also, the consequent subgoal of *newprop* is the last subgoal of $Lem(\overline{X}_0, \overline{Z})$.

Cases (1) and (2) are done automatically by the procedure *ind_prove*. Case (4) is described below, and Case (3) will be discussed in the next subsection.

Case (4) deals with the situation when the lemma generated from an instantation is neither (obviously) true nor in the form of some induction hypothesis. In this case we produce a new proposition and try to prove its correctness by invoking *ind_prove* on this new proposition. In our current system this is done manually. This process can be automated by treating the theorem prover as a problem reduction theorem prover and treat each invocation of *ind_prove* as one level of the problem reduction mechanism. In other words, for each level *ind_prove* reduces the present proposition to (a set of) lemmas, which in turn become new propositions for the next level. This can be done indefinitely until all lemmas are either obviously true, false, or are inductive hypotheses of some kind. In order to reduce the number of levels needed, we may incorporate some "linear" substrategies, such as the Boolean reduction strategy in [HsD83], for quickly checking tautologies.

5.2. Dealing with False Premises and Lemmas

A lemma which is false may be generated even if the proposition is true. Such a phenomenon arises naturally in theorems which have presumptions about the input variables. For example, let the theorem to be proved be $Z=f(X,Y) \wedge X=Y \supset p(X,Y,Z)$ (or, equivalently, $prop(X,Y)$:- $f(X,Y,Z), X=Y, p(X,Y,Z)$), where X, Y, and Z range over lists. For convenience of presentation, we let f denote both a function and a predicate. It is possible that *ind_prove* generates an instantiation $([\,], [\hat{A} \mid \hat{Y}])$, which leads to false premise $[\,]=[\hat{A} \mid \hat{Y}]$ and a lemma derived in attempting to fulfill the goal $p([\,], [\hat{A} \mid \hat{Y}], f([\,], [\hat{A} \mid \hat{Y}]))$. The lemma is likely to be false since the predicate $p(X,Y,Z)$ may not even be defined when X and Y are two different lists. However in this example, the falsity of the lemma does not imply the falsity of the proposition since the cause for the lemma being false is the false premise $[\,]=[\hat{A} \mid \hat{Y}]$. Therefore we cannot claim that the proposition is false even if we can prove that the lemma is false. (Incidentally, an instantiation such as $([\,],[\hat{A} \mid \hat{Y}])$ will not be generated in this particular example if the order of the goals in the proposition is rearranged as $prop(X,Y)$:- $X=Y, f(X,Y,Z), p(X,Y,Z)$ because X and Y will be bound to the same list by PROLOG.)

As another example, consider the following false statement:

$$prop(X,Y,A) \text{ :- } append(X,Y,L1), append(X,[A \mid Y],L2), L1=L2.$$

The first instantiation the prover produces is $([\,], \hat{Y}, \hat{A})$, with premise *true* and lemma $\hat{Y}=[\hat{A} \mid \hat{Y}]$. The lemma is false since $\forall A, Y (Y=[A \mid Y])$ is clearly not true. Unfortunately we cannot conclude, at this point, that the proposition is false since such a conclusion is not logically consistent with our system.

In general we deal with false lemmas in the following way:

(1) If the premise is false, such as the case in the first example ($[\,]=[\hat{A} \mid \hat{Y}]$), the whole instantiation can be discarded since such an instantiation actually does not exist.

(2) If the premise is not false, but the lemma is false, then we cannot come to any conclusion about the validity of the proposition with respect to this particular instantiation.

Nevertheless in the second case, the proposition may still be true for those instantiations which have provably true lemmas. Caution should be used, however, if some of these lemmas are in the form of induction hypotheses. Because if the unproved cases happen to be the inductive bases, the whole proof argument may collapse.

The fact that our theorem prover can find those instantiations which make the proposition true has a somewhat interesting consequence. That is, it may be possible to use the theorem prover as a unification algorithm for certain problems. To be more precise, given a theory whose axioms can be represented as PROLOG clauses, the unification problem between two terms s and t can be effectively transformed into a proposition

$$unif(\overline{X}) \text{:-} S(\overline{X}, Z1), T(\overline{X}, Z2), Z1=Z2.$$

where S and T represent the processes of constructing s and t in the correpsonding PROLOG clauses for the theory, and $\overline{X}$ are the free variables in s or t. Then those instantiations with provably true lemmas will be legitimate unifiers between s and t.

5.3. A Remark on Ω-satisfiability

In PROLOG, a goal is satisfied if it can be deduced to nothing but facts in the data base. The notion of Ω-satisfiability is different from PROLOG satisfiability in that we extended PROLOG equality between terms to Ω-equivalence. In order to construct more effective lemmas, we also include the list of premises in the data base as PROLOG facts (as shown in the algorithm in Section 4). This will not change the validity of the method since:

(1) The premises do not contain any variables. They contain only constants and skolem constants (hatted variables). Therefore no new bindings will be created from using these premises.

(2) By the logical meaning of the lemma generated, the condition *Premise* ⊃ *Lemma* needs to be verified for the proposition to be true. Since the premise is already part of the antecedent of the condition, using them as assertions (or say PROLOG facts) for generating the lemma do not have the effect of adding new axioms.

5.4. More on Generating Lemmas

As mentioned before, the marked choice points are used while backtracking for finding new instantiations of the input variables. The choice points that are left unmarked, however, are not used in our current system. Backtracking through some of these unmarked choice points (those that occur after the last marked choice point) may result in different lemmas for the same instantiation. Although this feature is not yet in our system, it is not hard to incorporate it and produce a lemma which is a disjunction of all the lemmas produced from these unmarked choice points. The lemma so produced is weaker than the one from our original system (and thus pressumably easier to verify). The disadvantage is that it may no longer be in Horn clause form.

5.5. Comparison

Proving inductive properties is considered one of the most difficult problems in automated theorem proving. To the authors' knowledge, two of the more successful methods that deal with this problem are the Boyer-Moore method ([BoM79]) and the inductive term rewriting method ([Mus80], [Gog80], [HuH80]).

A major difference between our method and that of Boyer-Moore is that our method is PROLOG-based as opposed to being LISP-based. Another significant difference is that we use unification on clause heads to find proper instantiations, as opposed to an artificial split of *nil* and *cons*. Therefore our method is also applicable to data types other than lists (see [HsS85] for examples), Nor do we explicitly use an EVAL operator. Our methods of generating lemmas (as well as the seperation of *premise* and *lemma*) are also different.

The term rewriting method was first developed to solve equational problems in universal algebra ([KnB70]). In the mid 70's, the method was employed by researchers in abstract data types and became a useful tool that linked the programming language community and the theorem proving community. (PROLOG is an example of another application of theorem proving to programming language design.) In recent years the term rewriting method has been extended to prove (equational) inductive properties of data types without using induction implicitly by building the inductive step into the Knuth-Bendix completion procedure. Although the inductive reasoning ability of the inductive rewriting method is less powerful than the Boyer-Moore method, it is much more efficient when it is applicable, and it also provides a uniform environment for program developement as well as verification (eg. OBJ [GoT79]). The rewriting method has also been generalized to richer theories ([JoK84]) and to first order theories in general ([Lan75], [HsD83]) and, thus, is no longer restricted to proving just equations. However, despite these extensions and more recent developments in conditional term rewriting methods ([Rem83], [Lan79]), the term rewriting approach still cannot handle conditional definitions of data types (or, non-unit equations in first order theory with equality) completely. The following is a simple example ([BDJ79]):

$$Define:\ f(x,y) = \textbf{if}\ x=y\ \textbf{then}\ g(x,y)\ \textbf{else}\ g(x,x).$$

$$Prove:\ f(x,y) = g(x,x).$$

The conditional rewriting methods of Remy and others (eg. Lankford [Lan79]) cannot prove the above statement even if the domain of x and y has a canonical term rewriting system (Remy's method gives a complete solution to the ground case).

Our inductive theorem proving method, being based on PROLOG, can also be used as a programming environment for program development and verification ([HsS85]). Compared to the rewriting approach, our method can handle conditions more effectively since it is not equation-based. We illustrate this point by solving the above example using our method: We use F and G for the relations corresponding to f and g. The program for F is:

$F(X,Y,Z)$:- $X=Y, G(X,Y,Z)$.[5]
$F(X,Y,Z)$:- $X \neq Y, G(X,X,Z)$.

and the proposition to be proved is:

$prop(X,Y)$:- $F(X,Y,Z1), G(X,X,Z2), Z1=Z2$.

The prover yields

Instantiation	*Premise*	*Lemma*
(X,X)	*true*	*true*
(X,Y)	$X \neq Y$	*true*

Since the instantiations well-span the domain of X and Y, the proposition is correct.

[5] This program is more complicated than what a PROLOG programmer will actually do.

6. References

[BoM79] R. Boyer and J. S. Moore, in *A Computational Logic*, Academic Press, New York, 1979.

[BDJ79] D. Brand, J. A. Darringer and W. H. Joyner, "Completeness of Conditional Reductions", in *Proc. 4th Conference on Automated Deduction*, 1979, 36-42.

[ClM81] W. F. Clocksin and C. S. Mellish, in *Programming in Prolog*, Springer-Verlag, Berlin, Heidelberg, New York, 1981.

[GoT79] J. A. Goguen and J. J. Tardo, "An Introduction to OBJ: A Language for Writing and Testing Formal Algebraic Program Specifications", in *Proceedings of the Conference on Specification of Reliable Software*, Cambridge, MA 02139, 1979.

[Gog80] J. A. Goguen, "How to Prove Algebraic Inductive Hypothesis Without Induction", in *Proc. 5th Conf. on Automated Deduction*, 1980, 356-372.

[HsD83] J. Hsiang and N. Dershowitz, "Rewrite Methods for Clausal and Nonclausal Theorem Proving", *Proc. 10th ICALP*, July 1983, 331-346.

[HsS85] J. Hsiang and M. K. Srivas, "A PROLOG Environment for Developing and Reasoning about Data Types", *Tech. Rep. 84/74, Dept. of CS, SUNY/Stony Brook, Stony Brook, NY 11794*, Berlin, March 25-29, 1985.

[HuH80] G. Huet and J. M. Hullot, "Proofs by Induction in Equational Theories with Constructors", in *21st IEEE Symposium on Foundations of Computer Science*, 1980, 797-821.

[JoK84] J. Jouannaud and H. Kirchner, "Completion of a Set of Rules Modulo a Set of Equations", in *11th Symposium on Principles of Programming Languages*, Salt Lake City, Utah, January, 1984.

[KnB70] D. E. Knuth and P. B. Bendix, "Simple Word Problems in Universal Algebras", in *Computational Algebra*, J. Leach, (ed.), Pergamon Press, 1970, 263-297.

[Kor83] W. A. Kornfeld, "Equality in Prolog", in *Proc. 8th IJCAI*, Karlsruhe, Germany, August 1983, 514-519.

[Lan75] D. S. Lankford, "Canonical Inference", Report ATP-32, Univ. of Texas at Austin, 1975.

[Lan79] D. S. Lankford, "Some New Approaches to the Theory and Application of Conditional Term Rewriting Systems", Report, Louisiana Tech Univ., 1979.

[Mus80] D. R. Musser, "On Proving Inductive Properties of Abstract Data Types", in *Conference Record of the Seventh Annual ACM Symposium on Principles of Programming Languages*, Las Vegas, Nevada, January 1980, 154-162.

[Pla84] D. A. Plaisted, "The Occur-Check Problem in Prolog", in *1984 International Symposium on Logic Programming*, Atlantic City, New Jersey, Feb. 6-9, 1984, 272-280.

[Rei] R. Reiter, "On Closed World Data Bases", in *Logic and Data Bases*, H. G. J. Minker, (ed.), Plenum Press,, New York, , 55-76.

[Rem83] J. L. Remy, "Conditional Term rewriting System for Abstract Data Types", in *Submitted for Publication*, University of Nancy, France, June 1983.

[Sri82] M. K. Srivas, "Automatic Synthesis of Implementations for Abstract Data Types from Algebraic Specifications", in *MIT/LCS/Tech. Rep.-276*, Laboratory for Computer Science, MIT, June 1982.

[Sti84] M. E. Stickel, "A Prolog Technology Theorem Prover", in *1984 International Symposium on Logic Programming*, Atlantic City, New Jersey, Feb. 6-9, 1984, 212-219.

[Thi84] J. Thiel, "Stop Losing Sleep over Uncomplete Data Type Specifications", in *11th Symposium on Principles of Programming Languages*, Salt Lake City, Utah, January, 1984.

Appendix: Examples

(I) Illustration of the Append Example

In the following we show how the theorem proving method produces a lemma and a premise for one of the instantiation, $([\hat{A} \mid \hat{X}], \hat{Y}, \hat{Z})$, of the input variables by providing a step by step illustration of the method on the proof of the associativity property of *append* for the inductive case. The other instantiation, $([], \hat{Y}, \hat{Z})$ is considerably easier to handle and will not be done here. We illustrate the processing of every goal that is considered during the proof process with one step corresponding to a single goal. At each step we indicate (as appropriate) the list of goals (the first of which is the current goal) remaining to be satisfied, a brief description of the action taken, the case applicable (section 3.3) within the Ω-binding generation conditions and any change that occurs in the bindings of the variables.

(1) $append([\,], L, L)$.
(2) $append([A \mid L1], L2, [A \mid L3])$:- $append(L1, L2, L3)$.

$prop(X, Y, Z)$:- $append(X, Y, L1)$, $append(L1, Z, L2)$
$append(Y, Z, L3)$, $append(X, L3, L4)$, $L2 = L4$.

Initialization

Antecedents $\leftarrow$ $[append(X, Y, L1), append(L1, Z, L2), append(Y, Z, L3), append(X, L3, L4)]$
Consequent $\leftarrow$ $L2 = L4$

Processing of the Antecedents

Goals: $[append(X, Y, L1), append(L1, Z, L2), append(Y, Z, L3), append(X, L3, L4)]$
How the current goal is processed: Unifies with clause (2)
Bindings of Variables:
$X \leftarrow [\hat{A} \mid \hat{X}], \quad L1 \leftarrow [\hat{A} \mid L5]$

Goals: $[append(\hat{X}, Y, L5), append(L1, Z, L2), append(Y, Z, L3), append(X, L3, L4)]$
How the current goal is processed: fails to unify
Case Applicable for Ω-binding generation: 1(a)
Bindings of Variables
$Y \leftarrow \hat{Y}, \quad L5 \leftarrow \Omega(l5{:}append(\hat{X}, \hat{Y}, l5))$

Goals: $[append(L1, Z, L2), append(Y, Z, L3), append(X, L3, L4)]$
How the current goal is processed: Unifies with clause (2)
Bindings of Variables:
$L2 \leftarrow [\hat{A} \mid L6]$

Goals: $[append(L5, Z, L6), append(Y, Z, L3), append(X, L3, L4)]$
How the current goal is processed: fails to unify

Case Applicable for Ω-binding generation: 1(b)
Bindings of Variables:
$Z \leftarrow \hat{Z}, \quad L5 \leftarrow \Omega(l5{:}append(\hat{X}, \hat{Y}, l5), append(l5, \hat{Z}, l6)),$
$L6 \leftarrow \Omega(l6{:}append(\hat{X}, \hat{Y}, l5), append(l5, \hat{Z}, l6))$

Goals: $[append(Y, Z, L3), append(X, L3, L4)]$
How the current goal is processed: fails to unify
Case Applicable for Ω-binding generation: 1(a)
Bindings of Variables:
$L3 \leftarrow \Omega(l3{:}append(\hat{Y}, \hat{Z}, l3))$

Goals: [*append* $(X, L3, L4)$]
How the current goal is processed: unifies with clause (2)
Bindings of Variables:

$L4 \leftarrow [\hat{A} \mid L7]$

Goals: [*append* $(\hat{X}, L3, L7)$]
How the current goal is processed: fails to unify
Case Applicable for Ω-binding generation: 1(b)
Bindings of Variables:

$L7 \leftarrow \Omega(l7{:}append(\hat{Y}, \hat{Z}, l3),\ append(\hat{X}, l3, l7))$
$L3 \leftarrow \Omega(l3{:}append(\hat{Y}, \hat{Z}, l3),\ append(\hat{X}, l3, l7))$

Processing the consequent
Goals: [$L2 = L4$]
How the current goal is processed: not Ω-satisfiable
Case Applicable for Ω-binding generation: 2(b)
Bindings of Variables:

$L7 \leftarrow \Omega(l7{:}append(\hat{X}, \hat{Y}, l5),\ append(l5, \hat{Z}, l6),\ append(\hat{Y}, \hat{Z}, l3),\ append(\hat{X}, l3, l7),\ l6 = l7)$
$L6 \leftarrow \Omega(l6{:}append(\hat{X}, \hat{Y}, l5),\ append(l5, \hat{Z}, l6),\ append(\hat{Y}, \hat{Z}, l3),\ append(\hat{X}, l3, l7),\ l6 = l7)$

Premise $\leftarrow$ *true*
Lemma $\leftarrow append(\hat{X}, \hat{Y}, l5),\ append(l5, \hat{Z}, l6),\ append(\hat{Y}, \hat{Z}, l3),\ append(\hat{X}, l3, l7),\ l6 = l7)$
$\leftarrow prop(\hat{X}, \hat{Y}, \hat{Z})$

(II) A Tree Example

In this example we present two versions of the membership relation of a tree (*isin*). The first one treats a tree as an abstract object constructed from two constructors *emptytree* and *mktree*. The second one treats a tree as a flat list. *Isin* takes a tree and an element as arguments and determines if the element is in the tree.

The Abstract Tree

isin (*emptytree*, *E*, *false*).
isin (*tree* (*L*, *N*, *R*), *N*, *true*).
isin (*tree* (*L*, *N*, *R*), *E*, *B*) :- $N \neq E$, *isin* (*L*, *E*, *B*1), *isin* (*R*, *E*, *B*2), *B* = *or* (*B*1, *B*2).

The List Tree

EMPTYTREE ([], []).
MKTREE ([], *N*, *R*, [*N* | *R*]).
MKTREE ([*X* | *L*], *N*, *R*, [*X* | *T*]) :- *MKTREE* (*L*, *N*, *R*, *T*).

ISIN ([], *X*, *false*).
ISIN ([*X* | *L*], *X*, *true*).
ISIN ([*X* | *L*], *Y*, *B*) :- $X \neq Y$, *ISIN* (*L*, *Y*, *B*).

The first tree can be considered as an *abstraction* of *isin* in the data type *Tree*, and the second one can be considered as an *implementation*. Both of them are executable PROLOG programs, nevertheless.

We want to show that the *ISIN* described in the second tree is the same as the *isin* in the first tree.

To put it informally, we want to prove that:

If *isin* $(tree(L,N,R),E,B1)$ **and**
$MKTREE(L,N,R,T)$ **and** $ISIN(T,E,B2)$,
then $B1 = B2$.

First note that the above description does indeed fit into the Horn clause formalism required for the propositions to be proved. Since *MKTREE* is defined in three different clauses, one proposition need to be established for each. They are:

$prop\,0(T,E)$:- $EMPTYTREE([],T)$, $ISIN(T,E,B)$, $B = false$.
$prop\,1(L,N,R,N)$:- $MKTREE(L,N,R,T)$, $ISIN(T,N,B)$, $B = true$.
$prop\,2(L,N,R,E)$:- $N \neq E$, $ISIN(L,E,B1)$, $ISIN(R,E,B2)$, $B = or(B1,B2)$,
$MKTREE(L,N,R,T)$, $ISIN(T,C)$,
$B = C$.

The more interesting case is *prop* 2, and the set of instantiations, with premises and lemmas, generated by *ind_prove* is the following:

Instantiations

$L \leftarrow [\,],\ N \leftarrow \hat{N},\ E \leftarrow \hat{E}$

(a) $R \leftarrow [\,]$	$\hat{N} \neq \hat{E}$	true
(b) $R \leftarrow [\hat{E} \mid \hat{R}]$	$\hat{N} \neq \hat{E}$	true
(c) $R \leftarrow [\hat{Y} \mid \hat{R}]$	$\hat{N} \neq \hat{E}$, $\hat{Y} \neq \hat{E}$	true

$L \leftarrow [\hat{E} \mid \hat{L}],\ N \leftarrow \hat{N},\ E \leftarrow \hat{E}$

(a) $R \leftarrow [\,]$	$\hat{N} \neq \hat{E}$	true
(b) $R \leftarrow [\hat{E} \mid \hat{R}]$	$\hat{N} \neq \hat{E}$	true
(c) $R \leftarrow [\hat{Y} \mid \hat{R}]$	$\hat{N} \neq \hat{E}$	true

$L \leftarrow [\hat{X} \mid \hat{L}],\ N \leftarrow \hat{N},\ E \leftarrow \hat{E}$

(a) $R \leftarrow [\,]$	true	$prop\,2(\hat{L}, \hat{N}, [\,], \hat{E})$
(b) $R \leftarrow [\hat{Y} \mid \hat{R}]$	$\hat{X} \neq \hat{E}$	$prop\,2(\hat{L}, \hat{N}, [\hat{Y} \mid \hat{R}], \hat{E})$
(c) $R \leftarrow [\hat{E} \mid \hat{R}]$	$\hat{X} \neq \hat{E}$, $\hat{N} \neq \hat{E}$	$TREE(\hat{L}, \hat{N}, [\hat{E} \mid \hat{R}], L)$, $ISIN(L, \hat{E}, B)$,

The last instantiation has an unresolvable lemma. As described before, the lemma can be converted into a new proposition which will be further proved by the same method. In this particular problem, the new proposition is:

$newprop(L,N,R,E)$:- $N \neq E$, $TREE(L,N,[E \mid R],M)$, $ISIN(M,E,B)$, $B = true$.

The proof generated by *ind_prove* for it is:

Instantiations	Premise	Lemma
(1) $newprop([\,],\hat{N},\hat{R},\hat{E})$	true	true
(2) $newprop([\hat{X} \mid \hat{L}],\hat{N},\hat{R},\hat{E})$	ture	$newprop(\hat{L},\hat{N},\hat{R},\hat{E})$

Another interesting characteristic of our method can be seen from this example. Note that the prover partitions, automatically, the domain into *nine* parts:

$prop2([\,],N,[\,],E)$	$prop2([\,],N,[E \mid R],E)$	$prop2([\,],N,[Y \mid R],E)$
$prop2([E \mid L],N,[\,],E)$	$prop2([E \mid L],N,[E \mid R],E)$	$prop2([E \mid L],N,[Y \mid R],E)$
$prop2([X \mid L],N,[\,],E)$	$prop2([X \mid L],N,[E \mid R],E)$	$prop2([X \mid L],N,[Y \mid R],E)$

instead of the usual three-part partition. It is because our prover partitions domains according to how the predicates are defined, not simply according to the structure of the data type.

On the Calling Behaviour of Procedures

Dieter Armbruster
Institut für Informatik,
Universität Stuttgart
Azenbergstr. 12
D-7000 Stuttgart 1
West-Germany

Abstract.

If a procedure P is relatively nonrecursive with respect to a procedure Q, i.e., P is always preceded by Q in the calling graph of the program, then P does not need an activation record of its own - it can be integrated into that of Q. Thus, the efficiency of a call to P is between that of a strictly recursive and a nonrecursive one.

An algorithm is presented which classifies each procedure (or function) in a program as being either nonrecursive, relatively nonrecursive or strictly recursive (i.e., recursive but not relatively nonrecursive) and associates each relatively nonrecursive with a strictly recursive one.

The method is based on finding dominators in the (transformed) calling graph.

1. Motivation

The prevailing approach for implementing procedures (and functions) in high-level programming languages is to treat them uniformly as being recursive and leave it to the hardware to make procedure calls efficient. But if there were information available on the structure of the calling behaviour of the procedures, more efficient code could be produced.

It is well known but rarely applied that the storage for nonrecursive procedures can be allocated in the global (static) area, allowing a faster access to its local data and avoiding any manipulation on the run-time stack. For the category of relatively nonrecursive (rn-recursive, for short) procedures, the costs of executing a call are somewhere between those of nonrecursive and strictly recursive ones: instead of creating a new activation record on the stack, when a procedure is called, we use part of an older activation record into which the caller can directly store the arguments, return address etc. (dynamic data structures are not part of an activation record, only the pointers to them). Thus the administrative overhead for these procedures gets smaller in code and time.

2. Introduction

Our approach of analyzing the calling behaviour is based on the calling graph, a directed graph with procedures (subsuming functions) as nodes, the main program as root, and an edge from P to Q iff P potentially calls Q, i.e., the call relation $P\mathcal{C}Q$ holds. (Whether or not P actually calls Q is of course undecidable; therefore we neglect all conditions on procedure statements.)

In order to determine the "actual values" of a formal procedure parameter in a procedure statement, we simply replace the formal procedure parameters successively by all actual parameters on the corresponding formal parameter position. If formal procedure parameters can again have procedures as parameters (as in ALGOL60 or ISO-PASCAL, but not in Wirth's PASCAL), this process has to be iterated until all possible actual values for the formals are established. This construction is presented in detail for example in [WAL76].

The transitive closure $\mathcal{C}^+$ of this graph is then a simple means to determine all potentially recursive procedures (they have an edge to themselves resp. a '1' in the diagonal of the corresponding boolean matrix representation of $\mathcal{C}$).

The disadvantage of this practical method is, that it yields more call relations in the transitive closure than the more accurate method of inspecting the execution tree which simulates the execution of the program as far as procedure calling is concerned in order to determine the "formally" recursive procedures - a subset of the potentially recursive ones [WIN82,LAN73].

The following example (fig. 1) should clarify the notion of the calling graph, the resulting transitive closure and the execution tree. Here, the transitive closure of the calling graph characterizes P as being potentially recursive, but the execution tree reveals its non-recursiveness. However, every non-recursive procedure (as determined by the transitive closure) is also non-recursive in the execution tree and is even actually non-recursive (this is because the constraints for a procedure to be recursive are relaxed by going from the actual program via the execution tree to the transitive closure).

```
        .
        .
    proc N;
      begin end;
    proc P;
      begin R(N) end;
    proc R(x : proc);
      begin x end;
    begin R(P) end.
```

Fig. 1a: a program

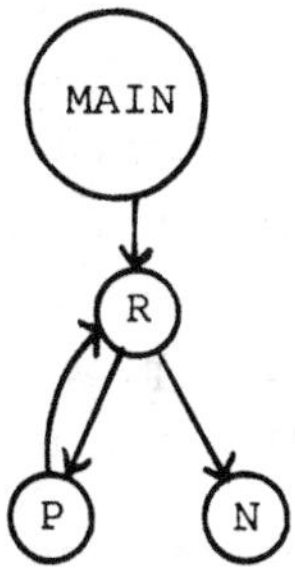

Fig. 1b: calling graph with N and P for x

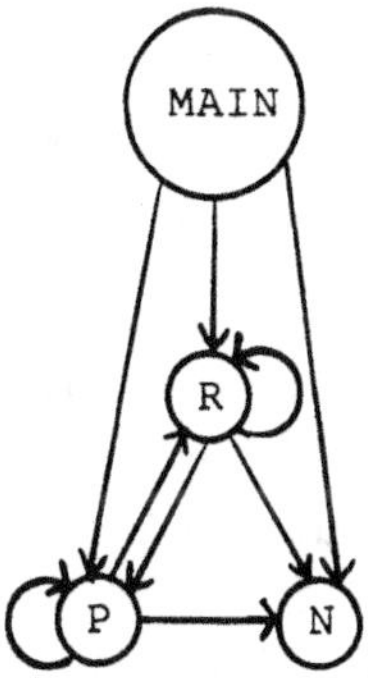

Fig. 1c: transitive closure

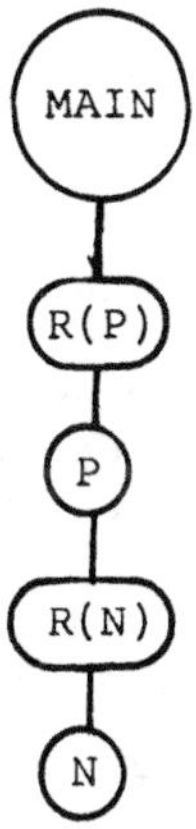

Fig. 1d: execution tree

The advantage of determining recursivity by the graph method is its practicability, whereas determination by inspection of the tree is at worst undecidable (for ALGOL 60 see [LAN73]) and at best much more expensive (for a finite mode language like Pascal see [WIN82]). For these reasons we chose the graph method as representation of the calling structure of a program and we always mean "potentially recursive" when we simply write "recursive".

Now, let's again look at fig. 1b. It is the simplest example to demonstrate the three different classes of procedures:

We see in fig. 1b that R and P are recursive and P is always preceded by R on any path from MAIN to P and from P to P. Therefore we can allocate the storage for P already at the time when R is called, i.e., the storage for P is located within R's activation record; when P is called, no new activation record is needed and P uses the already allocated area. That is why P is called rn-recursive and R is its associated strictly-recursive procedure (i.e., recursive but not rn-recursive), whereas N and MAIN are non-recursive.

In the following section 3 we give the necessary definitions and formulate the problem the solution of which is given in section 4, and its algorithm in section 5. The proofs of all theorems are combined in the concluding section 6.

3. Definitions

Let $\mathcal{P}$ = { P0, P1, ..., Pn}, n≥0, be the set of all procedures (and/or functions) of a program. P0 denotes the main program, a parameterless non-recursive procedure at the outermost level.

Let $\mathcal{C} \subseteq \mathcal{P}\times\mathcal{P}$ be a binary relation with the following meaning:
(Pi,Pj) $\in \mathcal{C}$ <=> Pi$\mathcal{C}$ Pj <=> Pi's body contains a procedure statement Pj(..) or x(..), where x is a formal with value Pj.

Definition 1: $\mathcal{G}$ = ($\mathcal{P}$, $\mathcal{C}$, P0) is a calling graph iff

a) P0 $\mathcal{C}^+$ Pi, i=1..n (all nodes are reachable);
b) ¬(Pi $\mathcal{C}$ P0), i=0..n (the root is never called).

Definition 2: Let $G = (P, C, P0)$ be a calling graph.
We say a procedure Pi ϵ P is

a) recursive iff Pi C^+ Pi,

b) relatively-nonrecursive (rn-recursive) iff Pi is recursive and there exists Pj, j≠i, such that on every path in G from P0 to Pi, Pj is visited at least as many often as Pi (this is equivalent to the previous informal definition: every path from P0 to Pi and from Pi to Pi goes through Pj),

c) strictly-recursive iff Pi is recursive but not relatively-nonrecursive,

d) non-recursive iff Pi is not recursive.

There are some immediate consequences of this definition:

1. The properties a) to c) partition P into three disjoint subsets S_N, S_{RN} and S_S respectively.

2. Procedure Pj in b) is recursive, since Pi is so, (actually Pj can be chosen to be strictly-recursive, as Theorem 1b will show) and it dominates Pi (see Def. 4).

Definition 3: Let $SAR \subseteq P \times P$ be a binary relation with
Pi SAR Pj (Pi uses a Sub-Activation-Record within Pj) iff (Pj = P0 or Pj strictly recursive) and (Pj is on every path in G from P0 to Pi and from Pi to Pi).

The following theorem reveals the relationship between the three categories and the relation SAR:

Theorem 1: a) Pi is non-recursive <=> Pi SAR P0.

b) Pi is rn-recursive <=> there exists a Pj, i≠j, such that Pi SAR Pj, with Pj strictly-recursive and Pi recursive.
(This assures that for each rn-recursive Pi there exists a strictly recursive Pj which can be associated with Pi.)

c) (Pi is strictly recursive or Pi = P0) <=> Pi SAR Pi <=> for all Pj, j≠i, $\neg$(Pi SAR Pj).
(For a strictly recursive procedure or the main program there is no associated Pj the activation record of which could be used).

Figure 2 gives an example of *SAR* :

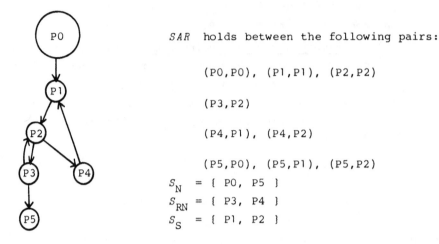

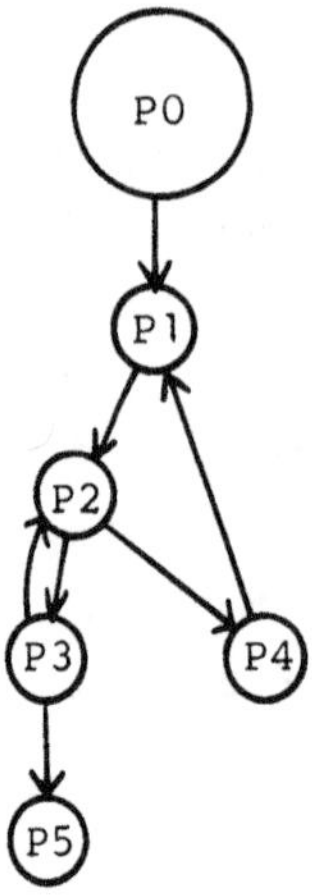

SAR holds between the following pairs:

(P0,P0), (P1,P1), (P2,P2)

(P3,P2)

(P4,P1), (P4,P2)

(P5,P0), (P5,P1), (P5,P2)

S_N = { P0, P5 }

S_{RN} = { P3, P4 }

S_S = { P1, P2 }

Fig. 2: *SAR* and the partition of *P*, found by inspection.

Now, we can state our problem more precisely:
Find all nonrecursive and rn-recursive procedures Pi and associate each of them with P0 resp. a strictly recursive Pj, such that Pi *SAR* Pj holds. But how can we get hold of *SAR*?

4. Solution

Obviously, the definition of *SAR* implicitly uses the notion of "dominance", as defined in [AU79]:

Definition 4: Let $G = (P, C, \text{P0})$ and Pi,Pj $\in P$.

a) Pj DOM_G Pi (Pj dominates Pi) iff every path in *G* from P0 to Pi goes through Pj.

b) $D_G(\text{Pi}) := \{ \text{Pj} \mid \text{Pj } DOM_G \text{ Pi} \}$ contains the dominators of Pi.

Theorem 2: a) DOM_G is a partial ordering on *P*.

b) $D_G(\text{Pi})$ is linearly ordered by DOM_G.

An algorithm to compute *DOM* with *G* as input is also described in [AU79].

Now we arrive at the crux:
As we see, $D_G(\mathrm{Pi})$ takes care of the dominators on all paths from P0 to Pi. However, according to our Definition 3 of *SAR* we are also interested in all paths from Pi to Pi. In order to integrate those, too, into one single computation of dominators, we transform G into a new graph $NG(\mathrm{Pi})$ by splitting node Pi into Pi and $\mathrm{Pi_r}$; $\mathrm{Pi_r}$ becomes the new root of NG with the same successors as Pi plus P0:

Definition 5: Let $\mathrm{Pi} \in P$ and $\mathrm{Pi_r} \neg\in P$.
$NG(\mathrm{Pi}) := (P \cup \{\mathrm{Pi_r}\},\ C \cup \{(\mathrm{Pi_r},\mathrm{Pj}) \mid (\mathrm{Pi},\mathrm{Pj}) \in C\} \cup \{(\mathrm{Pi_r},\mathrm{P0})\},\ \mathrm{Pi_r})$ is the new graph for Pi.

Consequences:

a) In any case, $\mathrm{Pi}, \mathrm{Pi_r} \in D_{NG(\mathrm{Pi})}(\mathrm{Pi})$ with $\mathrm{Pi_r}$ as the greatest and Pi as the smallest element with resp. to $DOM_{NG(\mathrm{Pi})}$ (Th. 2b).

b) Pj $DOM_{NG(\mathrm{Pi})}$ Pi <=> Pj DOM_G Pi and every path from Pi to Pi goes through Pj, with $\mathrm{Pi},\mathrm{Pj} \in P$.

$NG(\mathrm{P4})$:

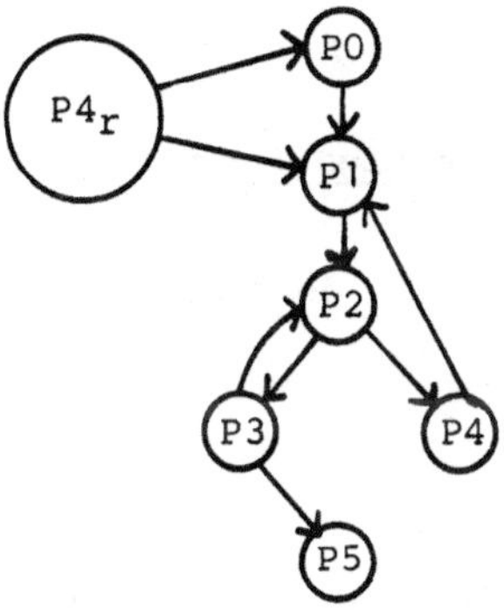

Fig. 3: The transformed graph of Fig. 2 for P4.

The next theorem shows, how close the relationship is between the notion of a nonrecursive, rn-recursive, or strictly recursive procedure Pi on one side and $NG(\mathrm{Pi})$ with the dominators for Pi on the other side:

Theorem 3: Let $D = D_{NG(\mathrm{Pi})}(\mathrm{Pi})$. Then

a) Pi is nonrecursive <=> $\mathrm{P0} \in D$ <=> P0 is the second greatest element in D with respect to $DOM_{NG(\mathrm{Pi})}$.

b) Pi is strictly rec. or Pi=P0 <=> $\{\mathrm{Pi_r},\mathrm{Pi}\} = D$.

c) Pi is rn-recursive <=> $\mathrm{P0} \neg\in D$ and there exists a Pj in D with $\mathrm{Pj} \neq \mathrm{Pi},\mathrm{Pi_r}$.

Now, we are able to state our main result:

<u>Theorem 4:</u> Let Pi ϵ P and let Pj be the second element in the linearly ordered set $D_{NG(\mathrm{Pi})}(\mathrm{Pi})$.
Then Pi *SAR* Pj.

For our example we get $D_{NG(\mathrm{P4})}(\mathrm{P4}) = \{ \mathrm{P4}_r, \mathrm{P1}, \mathrm{P2}, \mathrm{P4} \}$. According to Th. 3c, P4 is rn-recursive and Th. 4 asserts P4 *SAR* P1 thereby neglecting P4 *SAR* P2, which is allright, since only a dynamic analysis of the program flow could decide upon the best choice. However, only by choosing the second largest element as Pj, we can accomplish the desired association of non-recursive procedures with P0 (Th. 3a).

Furthermore, for the second element, Pi *SAR* Pj always holds, whereas this need not be the case for any other element (because this could be a rn-recursive procedure).

In case Pi is strictly recursive, Th. 4 yields Pi *SAR* Pi, according to Th. 3b or Th. 1c.

5. The Algorithm

We now present the algorithm that determines the three categories and the relation *SAR*.

<u>Input</u>: $G = (P, C, \mathrm{P0})$.
<u>Output</u>: 1. The three sets
S_N: the set of all nonrecursive procedures,
S_{RN}: the set of all relatively nonrecursive procedures,
S_S: the set of all strictly recursive procedures.
2. For all Pi ϵ P : Pj of Theorem 4, with Pi *SAR* Pj.

<u>Step 0:</u> Initialize S_N, S_{RN} and S_S to be the empty set.

<u>Step 1:</u> For all Pi ϵ P :

<u>Step 1.1:</u> Calculate $NG(\mathrm{Pi})$.

<u>Step 1.2:</u> Calculate $DOM_{NG(\mathrm{Pi})}$ and thus $D_{NG(\mathrm{Pi})}(\mathrm{Pi})$ (e.g. by using the algorithm from [AU79] or [TAR74]).

<u>Step 1.3:</u> Pj := the second largest element (with respect to $DOM_{NG(\mathrm{Pi})}$) of $D_{NG(\mathrm{Pi})}(\mathrm{Pi})$.

<u>Step 1.4:</u> Pi *SAR* Pj (according to Theorem 4).

$S_{RN} := S_{RN} \cup \{ Pi \mid j \neq i \}$ (according to Theorem 1b).

$S_S := S_S \cup \{ Pi \mid j = i \}$ (according to Theorem 1c).

$S_N := S_N \cup \{ Pi \mid j = 0 \}$ (according to Theorem 1a).

The complexity of the algorithm depends on how step 1.2 is implemented: if we use the calculation of dominators in [AU79] the complexity of which is $O(n^4)$ provided a depth-first ordering is used as sequence for the inner loop, then our overall complexity is $O(n^5)$, since step 1.2 is within a loop of O(n).

However, there is a dominator calculating algorithm with O(n log n + e) (e is the number of edges, i.e. calls) [TAR74] which yields an overall complexity of O(n(nlogn+e)). But since this algorithm is much more elaborate it is open whether it will be faster in practice.

Improvements on the algorithm:
The following optimizations refer to the above (high) level solution - not considering any lower level implementation aspects.

1. Instead of calculating S_N by constructing *NG*(Pi) also for non-recursive Pi's and then determine its dominators to calculate S_N by Pi *SAR* P0 (step 1.4), we could compute S_N directly by means of C^+ and then eliminate the non-recursive nodes in *G*. This will speed up the algorithm considerably, since most procedures of a program are likely to be non-recursive. A node of such a procedure is deleted from the graph by circumventing it, i.e. each incoming edge is connected to each outgoing one.

2. For the transformation of the remaining graph into *NG*(Pi) for each Pi, we can drop all edges (Pi,Pk), since the dominators for Pi are on all paths from Pi_r to Pi. Thus, while Pi_r has only outgoing edges, Pi has only incoming ones. Note that this reduced transformed graph remains a calling graph (Def. 1), since all nodes remain reachable from Pi_r.

6. Proofs

<u>Theorem 1:</u>

a) 1. We show: Pi is non-recursive => Pi *SAR* P0. Since Pi is nonrecursive, Pj=P0 and Pi are both visited once on every path from P0 to P1.

2. We show: Pi *SAR* P0 => Pi is non-recursive.
   If Pi were recursive, the number of visits of Pi were greater than that of visits of P0 (=1), i.e., ¬(Pi *SAR* P0).

b) 1. We show: Pi is rn-recursive => there exists Pj, j≠i, such that Pi *SAR* Pj, with Pj strictly-recursive and Pi recursive.
   It remains to show that Pj is strictly-recursive, then, by Def. 3 and 2b, the above follows. By the consequence of Def. 2b, Pj is recursive. Now assume that all such Pj are rn-recursive; but since Pj DOM_G Pi (again consequence of Def. 2b and Def. 4), there exists a Pjmax which is only dominated by P0 (Th. 2b). Thus, not all such Pj can be rn-recursive. Contradiction!

   2. The converse follows immediately from Defs. 3 and 2b.

c) First equivalence: immediately by Def. 3.
   Second equivalence:
   1. We show: Pi is strictly-recursive or Pi=P0 =>
      for all Pj, j≠i, ~(Pi *SAR* Pj).

      Case I: Pi is strictly-recursive. Then for all Pj, j≠i, there exists a path from P0 to Pi such that Pj is visited less often than Pi (negation of Def. 2b). This gives us the righthand side by Def. 3.

      Case II: Pi = P0. On every path from P0 to Pi=P0, P0 is visited once and Pj≠Pi is never visited. With the help of Def. 3, we get the righthand side.

   2. We show: For all Pj, j≠i, ~(Pi *SAR* Pj) =>
      Pi is strictly-recursive or Pi=P0.
      Contraposition, deMorgan, and distribution yield the equivalent statement:
      (Pi≠P0 and Pi non-recursive) or (Pi rn-recursive) => there exists a Pj, j≠i, such that Pi *SAR* Pj.

      Case I: Pi≠P0 and Pi non-recursive. Then there exists such a Pj, namely P0, such that Pi *SAR* Pj (Th. 1a).
      Case II: Pi is rn-recursive. See proof of Th. 1b, part 1.

Theorem 2: see [AU79]

Theorem 3:

a) First equivalence: Pi is non-recursive <=> in *NG*(Pi), Pi is only reachable from Pi_r via P0.

Second equivalence:

1. =>: If P0 ϵ $D_{NG(Pi)}(Pi)$, then it is the second element, since P0 is an immediate successor of Pi_r.
2. <=: Trivial.

b) 1. =>: Contraposition: Let Pj be different from Pi and Pi_r, and Pj ϵ $D_{NG(Pi)}(Pi)$. But then Pj is on every path from Pi_r to Pi and thus on every path from P0 to Pi and (if it exists) from Pi to Pi. Therefore Pi is not strictly-recursive and it cannot be P0.

2. <=: Contraposition: Pi is not strictly-recursive and Pi≠P0. Then Pi is either non-recursive or rn-recursive.

Case I: Then P0 ϵ $D_{NG(Pi)}(Pi)$ by a).

Case II: Then there exists Pj, j≠i, with Pi *SAR* Pj by Th. 1b. But then Pj ϵ $D_{NG(Pi)}(Pi)$.

c) follows from a) and b).

Theorem 4:

Case I: Pi non-recursive. By Th. 3a, Pj=P0 and by Th. 1a Pi *SAR* P0.

Case II: Pi strictly-recursive. By Th. 3b, Pj=Pi and by Th. 1c Pi *SAR* Pi.

Case III: Pi rn-recursive. Th. 3c guarantees the existence of a second element Pj in *D* with Pj≠Pi and Pj≠P0. Thus, Pj $DOM_{NG(Pi)}$ Pi and therefore (by consequence c of Def. 5) Pj DOM_G Pi and every path from Pi to Pi goes through Pj.

It remains to show that Pj is strictly-recursive; then by Def. 3, we have Pi *SAR* Pj. Pj must be recursive, otherwise it could not dominate Pi.

Now, assume Pj is rn-recursive. Then by Th. 1b, there exists a strictly-recursive Q≠Pj, such that Q DOM_G Pj and every path from Pj to Pj goes through Q; hence every path from Pi to Pi goes through Q, too. This fact together with Q DOM_G Pi (transitivity) yields Q $DOM_{NG(Pi)}$ Pi => Q is also in *D* and Pj $DOM_{NG(Pi)}$ Q since Q ≠ Pj,Pi_r. But then Pj DOM_G Q. Contradiction!

7. References

[AU79] Alfred V. Aho, Jeffrey D. Ullman:
Principles of Compiler Design, Chapter 13, Addison-Wesley Publishing Company, third Printing, April 1979

[LAN73] Hans Langmaack:
On Correct Procedure Parameter Passing in Higher Programming Languages
Acta Informatica 2, 110 - 142 (1973)

[TAR74] R. Tarjan:
Finding Dominators in Directed Graphs
SIAM Journal of Comp., Vol.3, No.1, 62 - 89, March 1974

[WAL76] Kenneth G. Walter:
Recursion Analysis for Compiler Optimization
Communications of the ACM, September 1976, Volume 19, Number 9, 514 - 516

[WIN82] Karl Winklmann:
On the Complexity of Some Problems Concerning the Use of Procedures. I.
Acta Informatica 18, 299 - 318 (1982)

Approximation Algorithms for Planar Matching*

Shankar M. Venkatesan
Department of Computer Science
University of Minnesota, USA

1. Introduction

Approximation algorithms for NP-Complete optimization problems have been widely studied, but rarely for problems in P. Given an optimization problem in P, a question one asks is whether known approximations for NP-Complete problems can be used as subroutines in *approximately* solving this problem. In any attempt at approximating problems in P, we can require (i) that the algorithm be almost linear or run in $O(n(\log n)^k)$ time, and (ii) that the relative error of the approximation be vanishingly small. Condition (i) facilitates approximate solution of much larger instances using currently available computers, as opposed to, say, a $\Theta(n^2)$ exact algorithm. Condition (ii) helps specify arbitrarily small relative errors, say, 1%.

Here we exhibit two approximation algorithms for the problem of finding a maximum weighted matching in a planar graph, for which the best exact algorithm runs in $O(n^{3/2}\log n)$ time [3].

One runs in $O(nf(n)(\log n)^2)$ time, and uses divide-and-conquer based on the separation of $f(n)$-outerplanar graphs as defined in [1]. Here $1/f(n)$ is the relative error demanded of the approximation, and hence this is a fully polynomial time approximation. For instance, setting $f(n) = \log n$, we get relative error asymptotically tending to zero.

Another approximation algorithm runs in $O(nc^{f(n)})$ time. Here c is a constant [1]. For instance, setting $f(n)$ equal to $\log^* n$, we get an almost-linear-time approximation with vanishing relative error.

---

*Research supported by NSF grant DCR-8402045

2. Weighted Matching is As Easy As Bounded-degree Weighted Matching

First, we show that the problem of finding a maximum weighted matching (hereafter called MWM's) in graphs of bounded degree is as hard as finding MWM's in general graphs; that is, we show how, given an instance G of the MWM problem, how to construct a graph G' of degree ≤ 3, such that a MWM in G' can be transformed in linear (in size of G and G') time to a MWM in G. Thus bounded degree does not help. For a similar reduction for the vertex cover problem, see [2].

The reduction takes each vertex v of degree $d_v \geq 2$ in G and replaces it by a cycle C_v of length $2d_v + 1$, where the edges on the cycle are given a weight M larger than the maximum edge in G, and where the original d_v edges connected to v in G are now connected to d_v mutually non-adjacent vertices in the cycle (if the graph is planar, we will later insist that the cyclic order of the edges be the same when reconnection of edges to the cycle occurs). See figure 1.

Lemma 1: Let X' be a MWM in G'. Let X'_v be the edges of X' incident on vertices of C_v. Then $|X'_v \cap E(G)| = 0$ *or* 1.

Proof: Let $m_v = |X'_v \cap E(G)|$. If $m_v = 0$, then clearly $|X'_v| = d_v$. If $m_v = 1$, then clearly $|X'_v| = d_v + 1$. Suppose it were true that $m_v \geq 2$; clearly, $|X'_v| \leq d_v + 1$; however, we can get a better matching by simply omitting all but the maximum edge from $X'_v \cap E(G)$ and augmenting the same number of edges (each of larger weight) from the cycle C_v itself, contradicting the fact that X' is maximum; Therefore, m_v cannot exceed 1. □

Lemma 2: A MWM X in G can be directly obtained from a MWM X' in G' by contracting the cycles introduced in obtaining G' from G. That is, $X' \cap E(G)$ is a MWM in G.

Proof: (Here we will speak of the edges of the original graph as the preimage of the corresponding edges in G' .) See figure 2 for this contracted matching; Suppose that $X = X' \cap E(G)$ is not a MWM in G; that is there exists a weighted augmenting path $P = (v = v_1, v_2, \cdots, v_s = w)$ from vertex v to w in G with respect to X. Our goal is to exhibit an augmenting path P' with respect to X' contradicting the fact that X' is a MWM in G'.

Suppose v is exposed. Then, by lemma 1 and because X' is a MWM, $|X'_v| = d_v$; Then the large weight matched edges in C_v can always be rearranged so that the image of the first edge in P is incident to an exposed vertex in G' without changing the value of the matching; Hence, whenever v is exposed in G, we can assume that the first edge in P is incident to an exposed vertex in G'; the same argument works for w and the last edge in P; See figure 3.

Note that, in each cycle C_{v_i}, $1<i<s$, by lemma 1, there is an even length alternating path P_i between the two vertices where the images of (v_{i-1}, v_i) and (v_i, v_{i+1}) are incident on C_{v_i}; See figure 4.

Since all edges on this subpath are of equally large weight, switching this alternating subpath will not change the total matched weight; Now consider switching the augmenting path $P' = (v_1, v_2) \mid P_2 \mid (v_2, v_3) \mid P_3 \mid (v_3, v_4) \mid \cdots \mid P_{s-1} \mid (v_{s-1}, v_s)$ in X' with respect to G'; the contribution from this switch must exactly equal the contribution from switching P in X with respect to G since switching the P_i's contributes zero change. Hence, P' is an augmenting path with respect to X' in G', contradicting the fact that X' is maximum in G'. □

This shows that if we want a MWM in G, we can convert it to G' as before, find a MWM in G', and contract it to a matching in G; the above lemma assures us that the resultant matching is a MWM in G. This shows that bounding the degree does not help in finding MWM's, just as it does not help in network flows, spanning tres, or shortest paths.

3. Approximate Maximum Weighted Matchings in Planar Graphs

Lemma 3: Let G be a k-outerplanar graph [1]; Then G' obtained as in the previous section is l-outerplanar, where $l \leq 2k + 1$.

Proof: By simple induction on the levels of G; First note that if *any* vertex x in C_v is at level p, then *every* vertex in C_v must be at level $\leq p+1$ (imagine the existence of edges from x that triangulate C_v).

Basis: Let V_0 be the set of level-0 vertices of G; It is clear that all vertices in $\bigcup_{v \in V_0} C_v$ are at levels either 0 or 1.

Step: Let V_i be the set of level-i vertices in G; Then all vertices in $\bigcup_{v \in V_i} C_v$ are at levels $\leq 2i + 1$ by hypothesis; Therefore *some* vertex in C_w for a level-(i+1) vertex w must be at level $\leq 2i + 2$; So *every* vertex in C_w for level-(i+1) vertices w must be at level $\leq (2i+2+1)$. □

It helps to imagine the construction of C_v's proceeding level by level, and to imagine the existence an edge between every level-(i+1) vertex and some level-i vertex.

Lemma 4 [6] : Let G' be planar graph of degree ≤ 3. Then the line graph of G', denoted $L(G')$, is also planar, and a maximum weighted matching in G' corresponds to a maximum weighted independent set in $L(G')$.□

Lemma 5: Let G' be a l-outerplanar graph of degree ≤ 3. Then $L(G')$ is $\leq 2l$-outerplanar.□

The approximation technique closely follows that of Baker [1], where $f(n)$-outerplanar graphs are used: The idea is to find such a k ($k \leq f(n)$) that we minimize the weight contributed to an optimum matching by the set U_k of all edges extending between levels i and $i+1$ for all i such that $i \equiv k$ modulo $f(n)$.

For each possible k, the following is done: U_k is removed from the graph to expose many $f(n)$-outerplanar graphs, in each of which a maximum weighted matching is found as explained in the next paragraph. Next, for this k, the union of the optimum matchings from all the induced $f(n)$-outerplanar graphs (which are of course edge-disjoint because of removal of U_k) is found as an approximate maximum matching; Finally, as in [1], the maximum over all k of these approximate solutions is reported as the approximate maximum matching in the original graph.

Each $f(n)$-outerplanar graph G gotten above is converted into a $2 \cdot f(n)+1$-outerplanar graph G' as in lemma 3. Then, by lemmas 4 and 5, $L(G')$ is $4 \cdot f(n)+2$-outerplanar. A maximum weighted independent set in $L(G')$ can be found in $O(n\ c^{f(n)})$ time [1], from which a maximum weighted matching in G' and a maximum weighted matching in G are obtained by contraction as in section 2.

Therefore, for each k, the time to report the union of the maximum weighted matchings in the induced $f(n)$-outerplanar graphs is $O(n\ c^{f(n)})$, and the total time is $O(n\ f(n)\ c^{f(n)})$. Since one of the U_k's has to contribute less than $OPT/f(n)$ to a MWM, this k will be eventually found, and the corresponding approximate solution, and hence our solution, will be no farther from the optimum value OPT by this amount.

In summary then, we first transform each induced $f(n)$-outerplanar graph into a bounded-degree graph as in previous section, where a MWM is found by applying Baker's method on its line graph. Once a MWM is found in this graph, it is converted back to a MWM in the original $f(n)$-outerplanar graph by contraction. Note that we do not convert the *original* graph into a bounded-degree graph, because then the set U_k might contain the large-weighted C_v-edges, and hence the approximation error may be very much larger; We *only* convert each individual induced $f(n)$-outerplanar graph into a bounded-degree graph, which ensures that the edges in U_k are always original edges , and hence the approximation error is as small as claimed.

There is also a second method, on which we do not elaborate here, of finding an approximate maximum matching in the same time and with the same error performance, by applying a Baker-like enumeration and slice aggregating procedure on the degree bounded $2 \cdot f(n)+1$-outerplanar graph directly to obtain a MWM.

Lemma 6: There exists an approximation algorithm for planar graphs that runs in $O(f(n) nc^{f(n)})$ time, and produces an approximate maximum weighted matching, with relative error of $O(1/f(n))$. □

4. A Weighted Matching Approximation in Time Polynomial in f(n)

Lemma 7: Let G be a k-outerplanar graph. In linear time, a set C of vertices can be identified and removed from G to partition G into two graphs G_1 and G_2, such that $|G_1|,|G_2| \leq 2/3|G|$, $|C| \leq 2k+1$, and the two resultant graphs are also $\leq k$-outerplanar.

Proof: We can always add dummy edges maximally to G so that every level-(i+1) vertex in G is adjacent to at least one level-(i) vertex. Also imagine the existence of a new root vertex s inside the level-0 face connecting to all level-0 vertices: then there exists a spanning tree of radius k for this modified graph rooted at s; then invoking a result from [4], there is a cycle C of length $2k+1$ defined by a non-tree edge that, on removal, partitions G into two graphs G_1 and G_2 with the required properties. Clearly the resultant graphs will be $\leq k$-outerplanar. □

Note that G_1 and G_2 themselves then admit k-separators; Hence G can be recursively partitioned by such k-separators. Note also that k is a constant here and has no relation to $|G|$.

Lemma 8: Let G be a k-outerplanar graph. Then a maximum weighted matching X_G in

G can be found in $O(k\ n\ (\log n)^2)$ time where $n = |G|$.

Proof: Let G_1 and G_2 be the k-outerplanar graphs induced by separation of G by C as in lemma 7. Let X_1 and X_2 be the maximum weighted matchings found recursively in them. A maximum matching in G can be found from $X_1 \bigcup X_2$ by repeatedly inserting back one more of the vertices from C, and in $O(n \log n)$ time reoptimize the matching as suggested in [3]. Hence the running time of our divide-and-conquer scheme is given by

$T(n) \leq T(n_1) + T(n_2) + O(n) + O(kn \log n)$, where $n_1, n_2 \leq 2/3n$, $n_1 + n_2 \leq n$.

The running time therefore follows.□

Lemma 9: Let G be a planar graph. Then an approximate maximum matching, with relative error of $O(1/f(n))$, can be found in $O((f(n))^2\ n\ (logn)^2)$ time.

Proof: The basic method is the same as in section 3; Only we apply here the algorithm from lemma 8 to find maximum weighted matchings in $f(n)$-outerplanar graphs, instead of using a Baker-like method. The sum of running times over all $f(n)$-outerplanar graphs in a single computation is $O(f(n)\ n\ (logn)^2)$, by lemma 8, picking $k = f(n)$. There are $f(n)$ such computations, one for each residue modulo $f(n)$. Hence the running time follows.□

Note that in the previous section, the running time is $O(f(n)\ n\ c^{f(n)})$. In this section, however there is a $(f(n)(logn)^2)$ additional factor replacing the $(c^{f(n)})$ factor. Clearly, the algorithm in this section is superior for $f(n) \geq c'\ loglogn$. Note that $f(n) = 1/\epsilon$, where ϵ is the specified relative error (compare with fully polynomial approximations for NP-Complete problems). This is especially nice when we want relative error to be much better than $O(1/loglogn)$: for instance, for the very attractive relative error of $O(1/logn)$, we need only $O(n(\log n)^4)$ time.

In summary, this section has employed the fact that k-outerplanar graphs are k-separable in order to find maximum weighted matchings in such graphs quickly.

In fact k-separability seems almost (except for a log$n$ factor) as widely applicable to k-outerplanar graphs as $\sqrt{n}$ -separability is to general planar graphs. For instance, we can find maximum flows in k-outerplanar graphs in $O(nk(logn)^2)$ time; we can find shortest path trees (negative edges allowed), find circulations, construct flows of a given value in $O(nk(logn)^2)$ time. Unfortunately, there seems to be no way to use these results as subroutines to speed up general planar graph solutions, as Baker does [1].

5. A Cardinality Matching Approximation that is Linear in f(n)

In this section, most of which was reported in [6], we outline an algorithm that runs in time linear in $f(n)$ but works only for maximum cardinality matching. It was while pursuing the ideas in this section that the ideas of section 6 and the sharpest results in this paper were found. This section is not needed for understanding section 6,7.

5.1 Finding a Subgraph with a Large Matching

First, we want to transform our given planar graph G into a planar subgraph G^1 such that (i) a maximum matching in G^1 is a maximum matching in G, and (ii) the size of a maximum matching in G^1 is $\Omega(|G^1|)$. That is, we want to judiciously 'chop' off parts of the original graph that do not 'contribute' to a maximum matching. The reason we do this, as we shall see, is to keep the relative error small.

By a result due to Papadimitriou and Yannakakis [5], we know that if the planar graph has minimum degree 3, then the graph admits a maximum cardinality matching of size at least $n/3$. Hence we only need to transform planar graphs with minimum degree less than 3, and in particular, look at only those vertices with degree 1 and 2.

To do this, we look at the problematic subgraphs of G:

Step 1: At every vertex, delete all degree-1 vertices incident to it *except one*.

Step 2: Look at subgraphs of G as in figure 5 and remove *all but two* connections.

If graph is connected, then the steps preserve connectedness. Matching size is clearly preserved after performing steps 1 and 2 on all appropriate vertices. Let G^1 be the graph obtained after performing the above two steps maximally on G.

Lemma 10: G^1 can be found in linear time from G, and G^1 admits a matching of size $\Omega(|G^1|)$.

Proof: Note first that a planar graph of minimum degree 3 admits a large sized matching [5]. Then see that step 1 deletes all 'bad' degree-1 vertices. So if number of degree-1 vertices is, say, $\geq n/10$, then we can directly show a matching of large size. Otherwise, connect these degree-1 vertices suitably (using new edges) without destroying planarity so as to make it a minimum degree=2 graph, and finally ignore any of these new edges that come into the matching.

Now look at the minimum degree=2 case and consider the graph after step-2 is maximally performed. If the number of degree-2 vertices is small, say $< n/5$, then we can directly conclude there are a large number of matched edges in the homeomorph, and hence in the original graph, using the result from [5]. If the number of degree-2 vertices is large, consider the subgraph induced by the edges incident to the degree-2 vertices: If its homeomorph is large in size, we are done; otherwise, we can argue that there are many matched edges incident on degree-2 vertices. Also it is quite easy to show the linear time.

□

5.2 Degree Reduction

We now convert G^1 into graph G^2 of degree ≤ 3 exactly as in the first section, but then the C_v edges are of weight ≥ 2. Here, we show that if edges of *weight 1* are used in C_v, we still can convert a maximum matching in G^2 to a maximum matching in G^1 in linear time as follows.

Let (v, w) be a matched edge of G^1. If m_v and m_w are both >1, then clearly we can get a better matching by deleting this edge and augmenting in C_v and C_w. If $m_v = 1$ and $m_w \geq 2$, we can get a matching of the same cardinality again by deleting this edge. In this case, adjust the matched edges 'around' C_v and C_w after deleting (v, w) from the matching: This can be done in a total of linear time, by looking at the vertex cycles in a clockwise direction, say. By repeating this, we arrive at a matching for which all $m_v \leq 1$. Now contraction can be performed as in section 2 to get a maximum matching in G^1.

5.3 Approximate Matchings in G^2

Lemma 11: Suppose we have a matching X^2 in G^2 which is no more than k away from the optimum in G^2. Then, in linear time, we can transform this into a matching in G^1 which is also no more than k away from the optimum in G^1.

Proof: Apply a transformation on X^2 as before to get $m_i \leq 1$, and augment maximally around the cycles C_v. This could actually increase the number of matched edges which is even better. Now we have at least as large a matching X^2 in G^2 as before with $m_i \leq 1$ for all i. Most importantly, every block C_i with $m_i = 1$ has no exposed vertices, and every block C_i with $m_i = 0$ has one exposed vertex.

We claim that the matching X^1 in G^1 obtained by contracting the C_v's in the resulting matching X^2 is *also* no more than k away from maximum cardinality in G^1. In proof, it is easy to show that every augmenting path in X^2 (note $m_i \leq 1$), when it crosses from block C_i to block C_j, *alternately* uses matched and unmatched edges in X^1. This means $|X^1|$ increases exactly by 1 for each augmentation of X^2. and over k augmentations of X^2, only increases by k. This means, by our contraction-proof, that we now have a contracted maximum matching in G^1 which has only k edges more than what we had in the original contraction of X^2 (before any augmentation of X^2). Hence the original contraction is no more than k away from maximum.□

Therefore, we now need only to find a matching in G^2 that is no more than $k = OPT(G^2)/f(n)$ away from optimal in G^2. But this is easy: since G^2 has maximum degree=3 and planar, use the independent set reduction with Baker's algorithm on its line graph. By results from section 5.1, $OPT(G) = \Omega(OPT(G^2))$. Hence, the approximation error is also $O(OPT(G)/f(n))$, and the running time is $O(f(n)\, n\, c^{f(n)})$. However we can compute faster by a factor of $f(n)$ as shown in section 5.4.

5.4 An Approximation That Runs Linearly in f(n)

We now apply the divide and conquer technique from Section 4, to find an approximate maximum cardinality matching in $O(f(n)\, n\, (\log n)^2)$ time, which is linear and not quadratic in $f(n)$. This is done by elimination of the $f(n)$ computations corresponding to the residues modulo $f(n)$, and substituting them with just one computation.

Lemma 12: An approximate maximum cardinality matching with relative error of $1/f(n)$ can be found in a planar graph in $O(\min\{n\, c^{f(n)}, f(n)\, n\, (logn)^2\})$ time.

Proof: First we obtain G^1 as in section 5.1. Next identify that U_k that has $O(|G^1|/f(n))$ edges. Such k must exist in any nontrivial case. Then remove this U_k to expose $f(n)$-outerplanar graphs. Find an optimum matching in their union.

Note that the maximum approximation error is $O(|G^1|/f(n))$. Now, by section 5.1, $OPT(G) = \Omega(|G^1|)$; Hence, the error due to deletion of U_k is $O(OPT(G)/f(n))$. So the relative error is $O(1/f(n))$. Thus one computation is sufficient for us. This avoids $f(n)$ computations for the $f(n)$ residues.

An optimum matching can be found in the union either by the techniques from section 3, or by using the divide-and-conquer technique from section 4. One application of the divide and conquer technique takes $O(f(n)\, n\, (logn)^2)$ time. One application of a Baker-like algorithm from section 3 takes $O(n\, c^{f(n)})$. Hence the running time.□

6. On Baker's Approximate Planar Maximum Independent Set Algorithm

Baker's approximation takes $O(f(n)\, n\, c^{f(n)})$ time. Here we make an observation on this method.

Let V_k, $k \leq f(n)$, be the set of all vertices at levels k *modulo* $f(n)$. We find a maximum independent set of value $OPT(V_k)$ in each V_k, in time $O(|V_k|)$, for a total time linear in $O(|V|)$. (note each V_k is a union of 1-outerplanar graphs, *not* $f(n)$-outerplanar).

Pick a value $k = k_{\min}$ which has the minimum $OPT(V_k)$. Say, $k_{\min}$ is even (odd case is similar). There are $f(n)/2$ V_k's for which k is even, and these V_k's are vertex-disjoint, being separated by the odd levels. Clearly $EVEN = \sum_{even\ k} OPT(V_k)$ is less than $OPT(G)$. But $OPT(V_{k_{\min}}) \leq EVEN \cdot 2/f(n)$. Hence $OPT(V_{k_{\min}}) \leq 2 \cdot OPT(G)/f(n)$. This $k_{\min}$ is precisely the k that we want (see section 3). Once the $k_{\min}$ has been identified in linear time, we strip $V_{k_{\min}}$ from G to expose a set of $f(n)$-outerplanar graphs in which Baker's algorithm is used to find a maximum independent set of value $APPROX_{k_{\min}}$ in $O(n\, c^{f(n)})$ time.

But $APPROX_{k_{\min}} + OPT(V_{k_{\min}}) \geq OPT(G)$. Hence by the above observation, $APPROX_{k_{\min}}$ is already no more than $2 \cdot OPT(G)/f(n)$ away from $OPT(G)$. Therefore we do not have to compute for each residue modulo $f(n)$ as Baker does, but only for one residue $k_{\min}$.

Therefore an approximate maximum weighted independent set, with relative error $2/f(n)$, can be computed in a planar graph in $O(n\, c^{f(n)})$ time. The same observation applies to many of the other problems mentioned in [1]. What we have done here is to absorb the 2 into the exponent, and the same even-odd arguments are crucial in speeding up the algorithm from section 4, as shown below.

7. A Fast Approximation for Planar Matching

Lemma 13: An approximate maximum weighted matching, with relative error of $2/f(n)$, can be computed in a planar graph in $O(\min\{f(n)\,n\,(\log n)^2,\ n\,c^{f(n)}\})$ time.

Proof: An even-odd argument similar to above is used to show that maximum weighted matching approximations in planar graphs can also be computed a factor $f(n)$ faster. Instead of looking at the sets V_k as above, we will now be looking at the sets U_k. First recall that U_k is the set of all edges extending between levels i and $(i+1)$ for all i, such that i *modulo* $f(n) = k$.

For each value of k, $k \leq f(n)$, we find an exact maximum weighted matching in U_k of value $OPT(U_k)$, in a total of linear time (note U_k is disjoint union of 2-outerplanar graphs); Let $OPT(U_{k_{\min}})$ be the minimum among these matchings; Then we delete $U_{k_{\min}}$ from the original graph to expose $f(n)$-outerplanar graphs, where an optimum matching is found using either our divide-and-conquer from section 4, or a Baker-like method from section 3, resulting in the running times stated.

Suppose $k_{\min}$ is even (the odd case is similar). Then, as before, we can show that $ERROR \leq OPT(U_{k_{\min}}) \leq EVEN \cdot 2/f(n) \leq 2 \cdot OPT(G)/f(n)$.□

8. References

1. Baker, B., Approximate Algorithms for NP-Complete Problems on Planar Graphs, 1983 FOCS Symposium.

2. Garey, M., Johnson, D.S., The Rectilinear Steiner Tree Problem is NP-Complete, SIAM J. Appl. Math., 1977.

3. Lipton and Tarjan, Applications of a Planar Separator Theorem, 1977 FOCS Symposium,

4. Lipton and Tarjan, A Separator Theorem for Planar Graphs, Conference on Theoretical Computer Science, Univ. of Waterloo, 1977.

5. Papadimitriou, C., Yannakakis, M., Worst Case Ratios for Planar Graphs, 1981 FOCS Symposium.

6. Venkatesan, S., Matchings and Independent Sets in Planar graphs, December 1983.

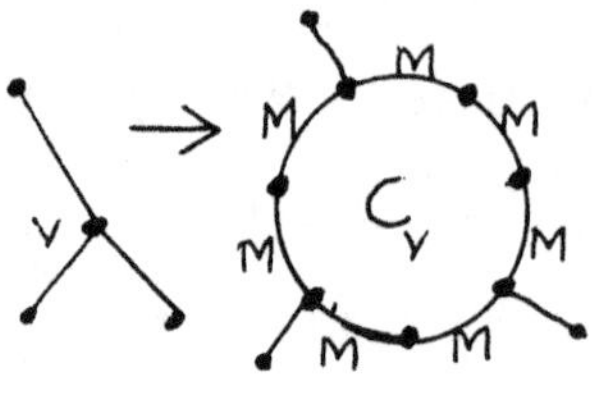

FIGURE 1

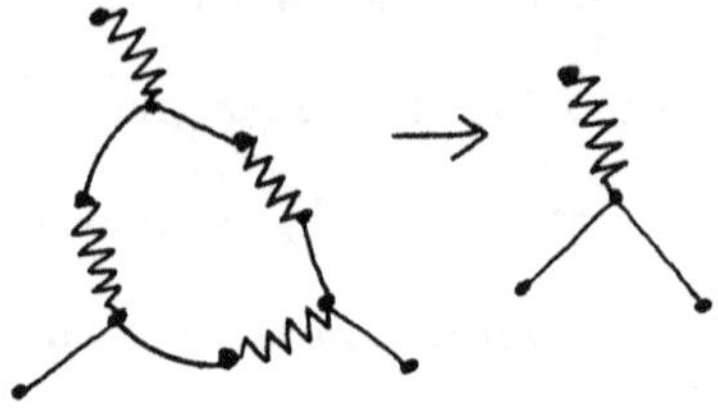

FIGURE 2

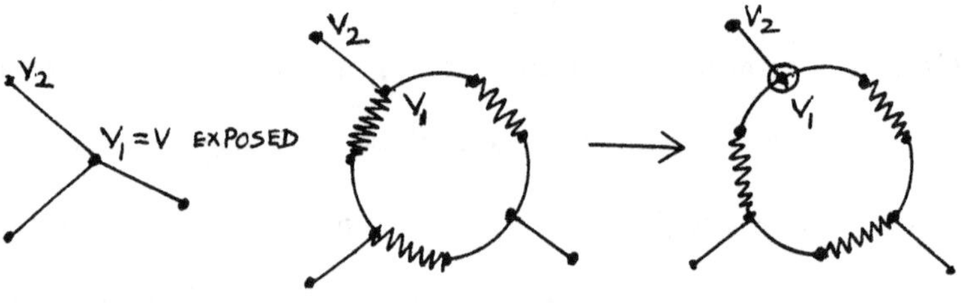

FIGURE 3

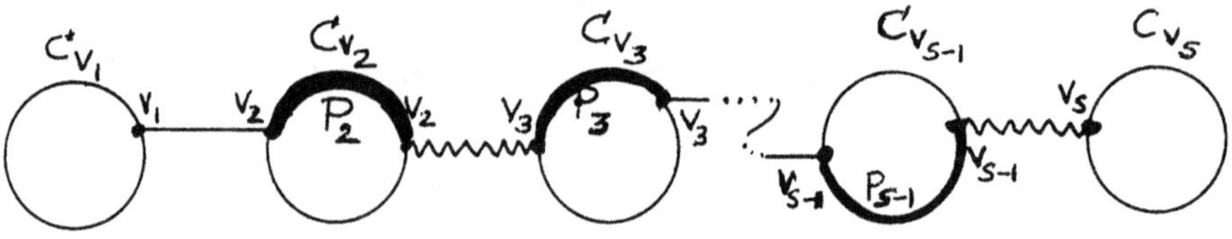

FIGURE 4

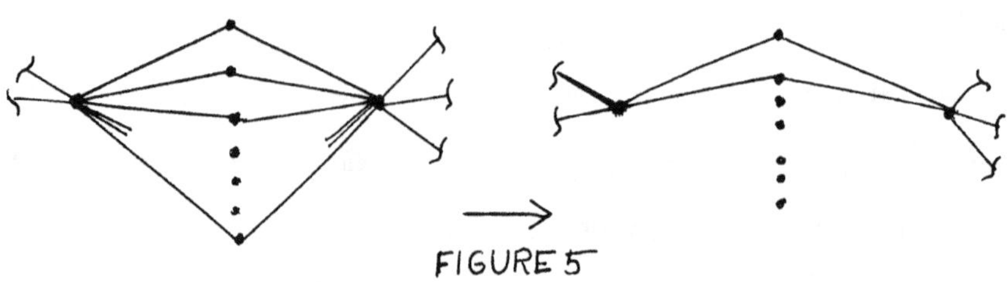

FIGURE 5

GEOMETRIC OPTIMIZATION AND THE POLYNOMIAL HIERARCHY

Chanderjit Bajaj
Department of Computer Science
Purdue University
West Lafayette, IN 47907

ABSTRACT

We illustrate two different techniques of accurately classifying geometric optimization problems in the polynomial hierarchy. We show that if NP≠Co-NP then there are interesting natural geometric optimization problems (location-allocation problems under *minsum*) in Δ_2^P that are in neither NP nor Co-NP. Hence, all these problems are shown to belong *properly* to Δ_2^P, the second level of the polynomial hierarchy. We also show that if NP≠Co-NP then there are again some interesting geometric optimization problems (location-allocation problems under *minmax*), *properly* in Δ_2^P and furthermore they are *complete* for a class D^P (which is contained in Δ_2^P and contains NP Co-NP).

1. Introduction

Geometric optimization problems are inherently not pure combinatorial problems since the optimal solution often belongs to an infinite feasible set, the entire real (Euclidean) plane. Such problems frequently arise in computer application areas such as robotics and cad/cam. It has thus become increasingly important to devise appropriate methods to analyze the complexity of such problems and to classify them accurately in the polynomial hierarchy. The adaptation of combinatorial analysis methods to these inherently not pure combinatorial problems, provides added significance.

Several of the algorithmic techniques that have been proposed for location and path planning problems in robotics use the idea of representing the problem in such a way that the object to be placed or moved is a point, in what has come to be known as configuration space, (C-space) [LP83]. For example, the position and orientation of a rigid object in the plane can be represented by a point (x,y,o) in a 3-dimensional parameter C-space where x,y represent the position of a reference point on the object and o represents the orientation of a reference line on the object, (say its angle with the positive x axis). Some points in C-space will correspond to placements of the object where it collides with obstacles in the physical space of the problem; such positions could be called illegal locations. In this paper we consider a number of natural geometric optimization multiple location problems in the plane (2-dimensional C-space) and illustrate two different techniques of accurately classifying their computational complexity. The C-space approach adapts directly for the case of homogeneous multiple objects (all of the same type) since the physical obstacles are all 'grown' identically into configuration space obstacles. For the more complicated case of locating multiple objects of different types, the allocation of the objects to the obstacles nearest them must also be determined. In the optimal solution under the above minsum and minmax criteria the costs due to the distances are minimized by an allocation of the obstacles to their closest located objects. In locating point objects amongst polygonal obstacles in 2-dimensional-C-space, we initially consider distances between the object and the vertices of the polygonal obstacles. We show that even with such simplifications the multiple location problems are quite difficult. These problems also arise as geometric reductions from various classes of location-allocation optimization problems [Co63], under standard ℓ_p metrics as well as more general arbitrary metrics.

In section 2, we show that if NP≠Co-NP then there are interesting natural geometric optimization problems (location-allocation problems under *minsum* in Δ_2^P that are in neither NP nor Co-NP. Hence, all these problems are shown to belong *properly* to Δ_2^P, the second level of the polynomial hierarchy. Next in section 3, we show that if NP≠Co-NP then there are again some interesting geometric optimization problems (location-allocation problems under *minmax*), *properly* in Δ_2^P and furthermore they are *complete* for a class D^P. The class of D^P was defined in [PY82] as follows: L is in D^P *if* L is an intersection of L_1 and L_2 such that L_1 is in NP and L_2 is in Co-NP. The class D^P contains both NP and Co-NP and is contained in $\Delta_2^P = P^{NP}$.

Many geometric optimization problems such as the Euclidean Traveling Salesman problem, the Euclidean Steiner Tree problem and the Euclidean Minimum Spanning Tree problem, can be thought of as *special* cases of well studied graph problems. Whereas the general problems deal with vertex points joined by edges having arbitrarily specified lengths, the corresponding geometric problems deal with points in the plane or in 3-space with the edge lengths being the actual interpoint distances under one of the standard ℓ_p metrics. Being special cases offers hope that although these problems are difficult for arbitrary graphs (networks), efficient algorithms could be possible for the corresponding geometric problems. However, it is at times possible to show that the geometric cases of these problems cannot be "any" easier than the general problems at least as far as the exact solution is concerned. In the past the recognition versions of the Euclidean Traveling Salesman and Euclidean Steiner Tree problems amongst other geometric problems have been shown to be NP-complete [GGJ76], [FPT81],[MS84],[Pa81]. Also there are certain fundamental geometric optimization problems whose recognition versions are not even known to be in the class NP and for some of these one can at times prove that there exists no exact algorithm under reasonable models of computation [Ba84]. However, such results have been few and far between. On the other hand efficient polynomial time algorithms have been discovered for a large number of simpler geometric optimization problems, [Sh78].

2. Geometric Optimization Location Problems shown Δ_2^P-*proper*

We consider three different classes of geometric optimization problems derived under a discrete *minsum* optimization criterion from certain location-allocation problems in the Euclidean plane. A *minsum* location objective is one which minimizes the sum of the costs resulting from a given location solution and is some measure of the average cost of serving the destinations. Various applications have been raised in the past under the discipline of location theory [FW74],[KP79]. A common real world example with a *minsum* objective that is cited there, is one of locating a water treatment plant so that the sum of the length of pipes required to serve water to the various households or industrial users is minimized. More recent examples are those of locating components on a VLSI chip so as to minimize the sum of the wire connections from the components or locating industrial robots so as to minimize the sum of their respective distances from work bins.

Under this minsum location objective it is possible to distinguish two basic approaches. The first suggests that location sites may be anywhere in the real Euclidean plane, giving an infinite number of possible location sites. The second approach considers only a finite number of known sites as feasible and models the constraints imposed on the possible location, ensuring that undesirable and impractical locations need not be considered. The various distance metrics[1] used, *Rectilinear* (ℓ_1), *Euclidean* (ℓ_2) and *Infinity* (ℓ_∞), reflect the appropriate problem restrictions.

Given a set $T=\{(x_i,y_i),\ i=1..n\}$, of n fixed destination points (*destinations*) in the plane and parameters k, m and L.

(O_1) Is L the *minimum sum* of the weighted distances of the n destinations and the closest of the k *locatable* sources.

(O_2) Is m the *maximum* number of destinations, $m \leq n$, for which the *sum* of the weighted distances of these destinations from the closest of the k *locatable* sources is $\leq L$.

(O_3) Is k the *minimum* number of *locatable* sources for which the *sum* of the weighted distances of the n destinations from the closest of these sources is $\leq L$.

In the case of locating multiple sources as above, the *allocation* of the destination to the sources must also be ascertained. In the *optimal* solution each destination is allocated to its closest located source. However this optimal allocation, is one of the exceedingly large number of possible allocations[2]. Not known a priori it needs

---

[1]Between two points $a=(a_x,a_y)$ and $b=(b_x,b_y)$ in the plane the ℓ_1 distance is $|a_x-b_x|+|a_y-b_y|$; the ℓ_2 distance is $\sqrt{(a_x-b_x)^2+(a_y-b_y)^2}$ and the ℓ_∞ distance is max $(|a_x-b_x|, |a_y-b_y|)$.

[2]The total number of possible assignments (allocations) of n destinations to k sources is $S(n,k)$, the Stirling number of the 2nd kind.

to be determined. It is also interesting to note that the capacitated versions of these geometric location-allocation optimization problems (with sources having finite capacities), turn out to be various cases of the more familiar transportation location problems and under discrete solution space constraints, to be the plant location and warehouse location problems [FW74].

We show that the above optimization problems, O's, under three different distance metrics, ℓ_1, ℓ_2 and ℓ_∞ as well as for feasible solutions sets which are both *finite* and *infinite*, all *properly* belong to the class Δ_2^P, the second level of the polynomial hierarchy. A problem P is a *proper*-Δ_2^P problem if (1) P is in Δ_2^P (2) P is not in Σ_1^P=NP, assuming NP≠Co-NP. (3) P is not in Π_1^P=Co-NP, assuming NP≠Co-NP. Let problems P_1, P_2 and P_3 correspond to problems which allow location of the sources to be anywhere in the plane. Let problems Q_1, Q_2 and Q_3 correspond to problems P_1, P_2 and P_3 respectively, with the location of the sources being constrained to a finite discrete set S of possible locations in the plane and of size polynomial in n. Further let problems R_1, R_2 and R_3 be *restricted* versions of problems Q_1, Q_2 and Q_3 respectively, with the location of the sources being a subset of T, the set of destination points.

To show that the above optimization problems are Δ_2^P-*proper* we first need to show the corresponding *recognition* versions of these optimization problems to be NP-complete To show the recognition versions of the above optimization problems to be NP-complete we must formulate them in a more suitable manner. We assume that the set of destinatic points T are given as a set of integer coordinate pairs. Furthermore we assume that the set $T=\{p_1,\ldots,p_n\}$ is a multiset with w_i points in T with exactly the same coordinat p_i conforming to a destination point p_i having an integer weight w_i. From the optimization problems P_i, we obtain the corresponding problems PP_i.

Given the multiset T of destination points as specified before and integers k, m and L

(PP_1) Is there a set $KS=\{s_1,\ldots,s_k\}$ of k sources in the plane such that the *sum* of the distances between the destinations in T and the sources closest to them is $\leq L$.

(PP_2) Is there a subset $T'\subseteq T$, $|T|'\geq m$, such that for a set $KS=\{s_1,\ldots,s_k\}$ of k sources in the plane, the *sum* of the distances between the destinations in T' and the sources closest to them is $\leq L$.

(PP_3) Is there a set KS, $|KS|\leq k$, of sources in the plane, such that the *sum* of the distances between the destinations in T and the sources closest to them is $\leq L$.

One can also formulate the corresponding problems QQ's and RR's with the location of sources restricted to finite sets, as specified before.

<u>Lemma</u> 2.1: PP_1 reduces to PP_2. Further, PP_1 reduces to PP_3. Similar results hold for the problems QQ's and problems RR's.

Proof: PP_1 reduces to PP_2, for $T'=T$ and $m=n$. Further, PP_1 directly reduces to PP_3 since if less than k sources satisfy the limit L, k sources would definitely do so. ■

The discrete problem, RR_1 was shown to be NP-complete for the (integerized)

Euclidean, ℓ_2 distance metric in [Pa81]. Since the *RR* problems are restricted versions of the corresponding *QQ* problems, it follows that the finite solution space problem, QQ_1 is also NP-complete for the $\ell_2$distance metric. In [MS84], the infinite solution space problem, PP_1 was shown to be NP-complete for the ℓ_1 and ℓ_2 distance metrics. We extend these results and show that for the ℓ_1 distance metric the infinite solution space problem, PP_1, reduces to the corresponding discrete RR_1 problem (and hence to the finite solution space problem, QQ_1) and thus these are all NP-complete. We complet the picture by showing that the PP_1, QQ_1 and RR_1 problems, for the ℓ_∞ distance metric, are also NP-complete. Using Lemma 2.1 it follows that the problems PP_2, PP_3 as well as the corresponding problems QQ_2, QQ_3 and RR_2, RR_3 are as difficult and also NP-complete for each of the three distance metrics. The NP-completeness of the above problems implies that the corresponding optimization problems, for both finite and infinite solution spaces and for the three distance metrics, are all NP-hard. Assuming NP≠Co-NP, one can **then** show that each of the above optimization problems belong properly in Δ_2^P.

The problems as formulated above are all in NP. We henceforth assume this fact in all the NP-completeness proofs.

Theorem 2.2: Problem RR_1, having a discrete feasible solution set, is NP-complete for the infinite (ℓ_∞), distance metric.

Proof: To prove it complete we show a polynomial-time reduction from the Exact Cover problem, a known NP-complete problem [GJ79]. The construction is exactly similar to the construction of [Pa81] with a few essential changes to correspond to the ℓ_∞ distance metric. We repeat the entire construction here only for the sake of completeness.

The configuration of points is as follows. A row *R* of *length* *m* has $6m+4$ points and the two extreme points *b*, *b´* have weight m^2, which implies that they have to be sources in any optimal solution. If we allocate $m+2$ *sources* to *R*, then the two best solutions are shown below, both having *b* and *b´* as sources. Solution 1 induces the

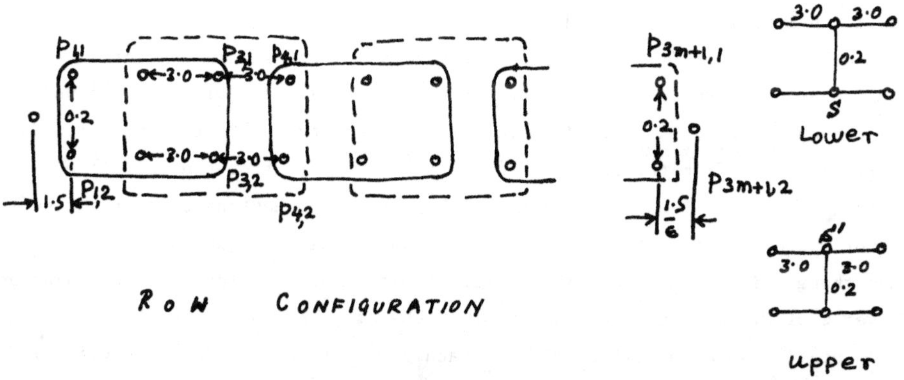

partition of R shown in solid lines while the broken lines conform to solution 2. Note that solution 1 is cheaper by 2ε, where $\varepsilon=m^{-4}$. Among each resulting group of 6 points the source can be chosen either as an *upper* source s or as a *lower* source s'.

For the reduction, given any instance $U=\{u_1,\ldots,u_{3n}\}$ and the family $F=\{S_1,\ldots,S_t\}$ of subsets of U, each of size 3, of the Exact Cover problem we construct a (weighted) point set T and integers k and L, such that T has k sources with cost L or less if there is an exact cover $C\subset F$ of U.

T consists of t rows $R_1,\ldots,R_t$, each of length $3n$, arranged parallel to each other. Thus the $3n$ columns of this formation, correspond to the elements of U.

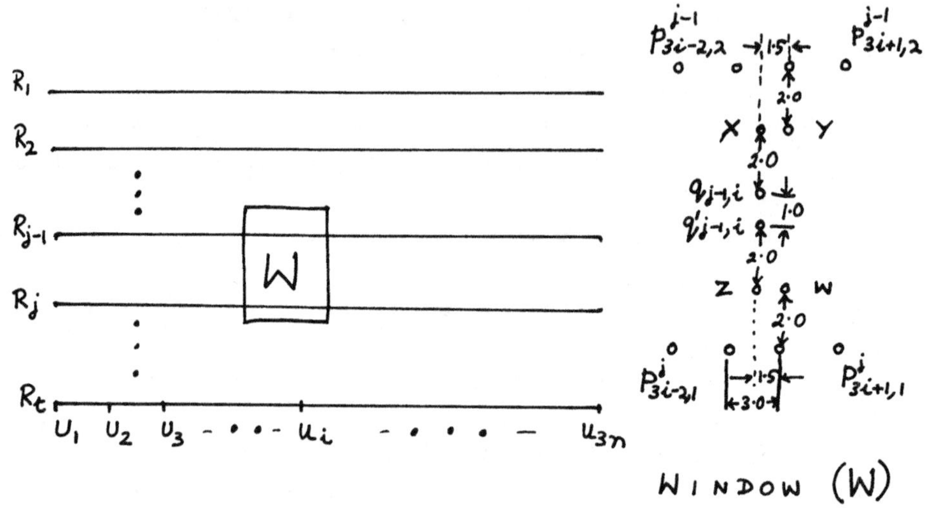

The window is shown above in detail. The spots x, y, w, z are not points of T but only possible positions of points. For each window, one of x, y and one of w, z positions is occupied with points of weight n^{-2}; x is occupied if $u_i\notin S_{j-1}$, y if $u_i\in S_{j-1}$. Similarly w if $u_i\in S_j$ and z if $u_i\notin S_j$. (We use fractional weights with the assumption that all coordinates as well as the limit L will eventually be multiplied by a sufficiently large integer and rounded).

Define $k=t(3n+2)+3n(t-1)$. The first term provides enough sources for all the t rows and the second term, one course for the q, q' pair in each window. L consists of three components $L_1+L_2+L_3$. $L_1=t(2*1.5+3n(4.6))-2n\varepsilon$ and comes from the t rows. $L_2=3n(t-1)$ and comes from the cost due to the q or q' pair, from the $3n(t-1)$ windows at a cost of 1 per pair. $L_3=12n(t-1)/n^2$ is the cost of connecting each of the $6n(t-1)$ points x or y and w or z to the closest q or q' point, always 2 away.

Then there exists a subset $KS\subset T$ of size k with cost L or less if F contains an exact cover C of U. Assume such a KS exists. Then for the cost to be L or less the optimal allocation is as specified above. Each row is then grouped by solution 1 or

2. Let row R_j grouped as solution 1 mean that $s_j \varepsilon C$ where C is the claimed exact cover. Again, for the cost to be at most L, at least n rows must be grouped by solution 1.

For R_j grouped by solution 1 consider the ith group where $u_i \varepsilon S_j$. Then both w (above) and y (below) positions are occupied by a point. Since positions w, x, y or z can charge only 2 to the cost in L_3 of L, the w and y must connect to their corresponding q sources. This further implies that the x or y point of $q_{j-1,i}$ must be picked up by their lower sources in R_{j-1} and w or z point of $q_{j,i}$ by their upper source. The same argument repeats and one notes that this change of upper to lower occurs only once per column, with the ith group of any row R_k, $k<j$, must have a lower source while for $k>j$, must have an upper source. Moreover R_j causes this change to all three collumns corresponding to the three elements $u_i \varepsilon S_j$. Also there are no overlaps in the sets S_j of C, since if $u_i \varepsilon S_j$, then by the crucial construction of the window, the positions w or y are 2 away just from the solution 2 source (appropriate upper or lower) and if linked up this way, implies R_j, is grouped as solution 2 which means that $S_j, \notin C$. Hence C contains n sets without overlap and so is an Exact Cover.

Conversely, assume there is an Exact Cover C, then there exists a solution KS having k sources of cost at most L, allocating $3n+2$ sources per row, 1 for each q-q' pair, with R_j grouped by solution 1 if $S_j \varepsilon C$ and solution 2 otherwise. Also for each (unique) $S_j \varepsilon C$ and $u_i \varepsilon S_j$, let the ith group of R_k for $k \leq j$ have a lower source and for $k>j$ have an upper source, giving the total cost of L. $\blacksquare$

Define the ℓ_∞ *grid points* of the set T of destination points to be the points shown in the figure below.

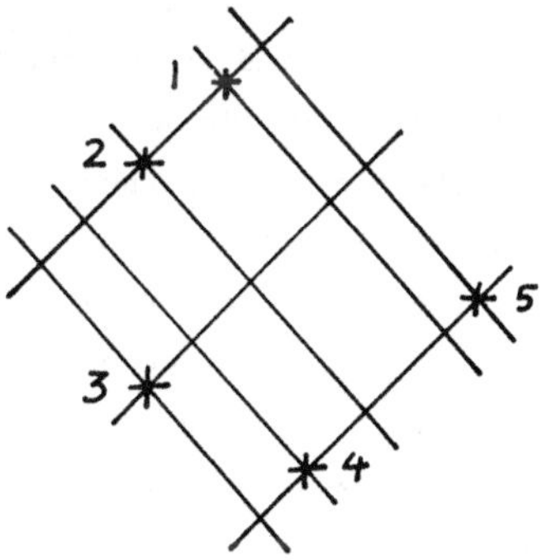

<u>Lemma</u> 2.3: In locating a source point in the plane to so that the sum of the ℓ_∞ distances from the destinations T is $\leq L$, one could as well let the source point be an element of the set S, the ℓ_∞ *grid points* of the set T.

Proof: Let us assume that for the source point p as shown in the figure below, the sum of the ℓ_∞ distances from the T destination points is $\leq L$. Then there must exist ℓ_∞ *grid lines* a, b, c and d, as above, such that they enclose point p, but the

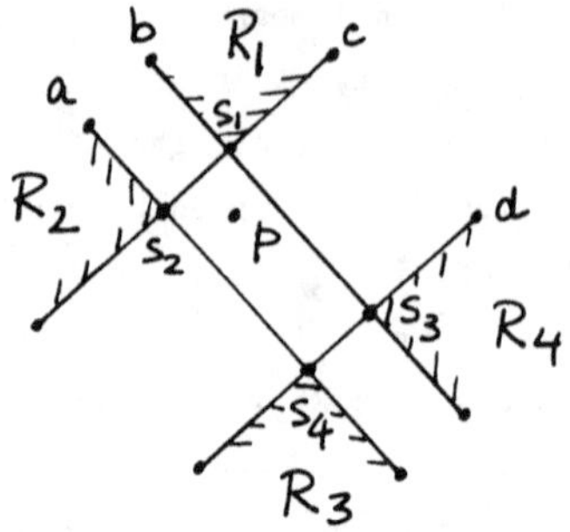

points of T are only in the regions R_1, R_2, R_3 and R_4. Let s_1, s_2, s_3 and s_4 be the ℓ_∞ *grid points* defined by these lines. With a little thought one can see that for the sum of the ℓ_∞ distances with respect to point p, the points in region R_1 and R_3 contribute their y-distances while points in regions R_2 and R_4 contribute their x-distances. Now if the number of T points in regions R_1 and R_2 are together greater than or equal to the number of points in regions R_3 and R_4, then one can move point p to the segment $s_1 s_2$, (otherwise move to segment $s_3 s_4$), in a direction parallel to line a or b and still keep the sum of the ℓ_∞ costs $\leq L$. By moving in this direction we decrease (or keep constant) the s and y distances equally with respect to p. Similarly, depending on whether the number of T points in regions R_2 and R_3 is $\geq$ (or $<$), than the number of T points in regions R_1 and R_4, one could move point p to either of the ℓ_∞ *grid points*, keeping the sum of the ℓ_∞ distances to the T points $\leq L$. ■

<u>Theorem</u> 2.4: The problem PP_1, having the entire Euclidean plane as a solution space, is NP-complete for the ℓ_∞ distance metric.

Proof: For the completeness, we use the same configuration of destination points T as in Theorem 2.2. For this T, we claim that there exists a set of k points, KS, in the plane with cost $\leq L$ *if* there exists a subset of k points of T with cost $\leq L$. The if-part is trivial. For the only-if part, assume there exists a set of k points KS in the plane. Note that for a known allocation the geometric location-allocation problem reduces to the location of k single source problems. The allocation for the above configuration is clearly determined by design; $(3n+2)$ sources per row and 1 per window. For each of the rows and windows, an application of Lemma 2.3 shows that there exists a corresponding subset of k points of cost $\leq T$. ■

We now prove a result similar to *Lemma* 2.3, for locating sources under the ℓ_1 distance metric. This result previously appears in [HPT80]. However, we provide a much simpler proof of this, in a way which suffices for our goal of proving QQ_1, for the ℓ_1 distance metric, to be NP-complete. Define the ℓ_1 *grid points* of the set T of destination points to be the points which have an x-coordinate equal to the x-

coordinate of any point $p \epsilon T$ and a y-coordinate equal to the y-coordinate of any point $q \epsilon T$, as in the figure below.

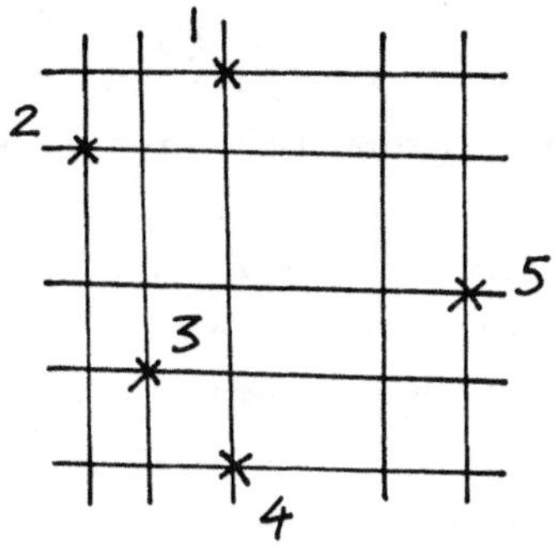

Lemma 2.5: In location a source point in the plane so that the sum of the ℓ_1 distances from the destinations T is $\leq L$, one could as well let the source point be an element of the set S, one of the ℓ_1 *grid points* of the set T.

Proof: Let us assume that for the source point p as shown in the figure below, the sum of the ℓ_1 distances from the T destination points is $\leq L$.

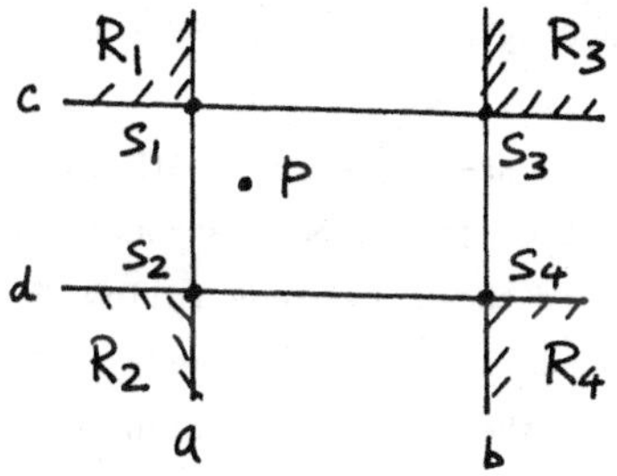

Then there must exist ℓ_1 *grid lines* a and b such that point p lies between them, but no points of T lie between them. Similarly for lines c and d. Let s_1, s_2, s_3 and s_4 be the ℓ_1 *grid points* defined by these lines. If the number of T points to the left of a is $\geq$ to the number of T points to the right of b, then one could move point p to the segment $s_1 s_2$ keeping the sum of the ℓ_1 distances to the T points $\leq L$. Otherwise move p to segment $s_3 s_4$. Similarly depending on whether the number of T points above line c is $\geq$ to (or <), than the number of T points below b, one could move point p to either of the ℓ_1 *grid points*, keeping the sum of the ℓ_1 distances to the T points $\leq L$. ■

Theorem 2.6: The discrete solution space problems RR's and QQ's for the ℓ_1 distance metric are all NP-complete.

Proof: The infinite solution space problem, PP_1, was shown to be NP-complete for the ℓ_1 distance metric in [MS84]. A simple reduction from this problem to the discrete solution space problem, RR_1, can be obtained by letting the destination set T' of RR_1 to be the ℓ_1 *grid points* of the discrete set PP_1. The proof of Lemma 2.5 suffices to show that there exists a solution for RR_1 *iff* there exists a solution for PP_1. The NP-completeness of QQ_1 again follows automatically from the NP-completeness of the RR_1 problem. ■

Theorem 2.7: All the problems PP's, QQ's and RR's, for each of the three distance metrics (ℓ_1, ℓ_2 and ℓ_∞), are *strongly* NP-complete.

Proof: The magnitude of the largest number occurring in any instance I of the problems PP_i's (similar for QQ_i's and RR_i's) for the ℓ_∞ distance metric, is determined by either the coordinate pairs of the destination set T or the parameters k, m or L. The parameters k and m are both integer values less than n. The constructions in Theorem 2.2 and Lemma 2.3, show the *strong* NP-completeness of PP_1, QQ_1 and RR_1, since what is exhibited is a *bounded polynomial transformation* from *Exact Cover* (a strong NP-complete problem [GJ79]. The lengths of the two problems are polynomially related and a polynomial of n. Further the function (the *iff* reduction mapping) is polynomial time computable. The integer coordinate pairs of the points of T are bounded by $O(n)$ and the value of L can be seen to be bounded by $O(n^3)$. Hence the maximum value occurring in the construction of the geometric location-allocation problems, is bounded by a polynomial in n and hence bounded by a polynomial of the maximum value and length of an instance of the Exact Cover problem.

The reduction of [MS81] for the NP-completeness of problem PP_1 for the ℓ_1 and ℓ_2 distances, is a bounded transformation from 3-*Sat* (strongly NP-complete [GJ79]) and hence the strong NP-completeness for these problems follows as above. The strong completeness of the problems QQ_1 and RR_1 for the ℓ_1 metric (Theorem 2.6) and for the ℓ_2 metric [Pa81] follows again from their transformation from the Exact Cover problem.

The problems PP_2 and PP_3 (similarly for the corresponding QQ and RR problems), have m and k, respectively, as their decision parameters and are actually number problems, consequently strongly NP-complete. The strong completeness of these problems also follow from the direct transformation from the above PP_1 problems, (Lemma 2.1). ■

We can now finally show that our (decision) optimization problems O_i's are Δ_2^P-*proper* for *infinite*, *finite* and *discrete* solution sets. [LM81] first showed how pure combinatorial optimization problems can be proven to be Δ_2^P-*proper*. We show that it applies to our case of geometric optimization problems in a similar fashion, based on our choice of decision problems and the strong NP-*completeness* result of Theorem 2.7. We repeat some of the constructions here only for the sake of completeness. Let $Length[I]$ = a measure of the size of the instance I of the problem and $Max[I]$ = magnitude of the largest number occurring in the instance I. For our problems we can have $Length[I]$ = any polynomial of n, where n is the number of given *destination* points.

Lemma 2.8: The optimization problems O_i's are in Δ_2^P.

Proof: A problem P is in Δ_2^P if $P\leq_T^P$ (*Turing* reduces) to Q, where Q is in NP. For each of the O_i's, where the sources are located in the entire plane, we show that a Turing reduction exists, to the corresponding recogniation NP-complete version PP_i's [AHU74]. (For those O_i's where the sources are located on a discrete set S or on the set of *destination* points T, the corresponding NP-complete versions QQ_i's and RR_i's are used respectively). For O_1, the value of parameter L in any instance I of the problem, lies in the range 0 to $c^{Length[I]}$, for some constant c. By a simple binary search one can find the optimum value of L in at most $\log c^{Length[I]} = O(Length[I])$ calls of the PP_1 oracle. Since $Length[I]$ is some polynomial in n, the reduction is polynomial time bound. For problems O_2 and O_3 with their respective parameters m and k, the parameter values range from 1 to n and so a sequential search suffices. ■

Lemma 2.9: If NP≠Co-NP, then the optimization problems O's are *not* in NP.

Proof: Each of the problems O_i, where the sources are located in the entire plane, is the optimization version of the corresponding NP-complete problem PP_i. Then the complement of PP_i, PP_i^c is a Co-NP-complete problem. Here one answers the question 'there does not exist a solution of (parameter) q or better' or 'the best is of size *worse* than q, (*worse* is either *less* or *greater* depending on whether PP_i is a *maximum* or a *minimum* optimization problem). Then if one can show that $PP_i^c\leq_m^{NP} O_i$, (a *non-deterministic polynomial-time* many-one reduction), then $O_i \varepsilon NP$ implies $PP_i^c \varepsilon NP$, since $\leq_m^{NP}$ preserves the class of NP [LLS75]. However, if NP≠co-NP, $PP_i^c \not\varepsilon NP$ implies $O_i \not\varepsilon NP$, that is, the optimization problems O_i's are *not* in NP.

For each of the O_i's the $\leq_m^{NP}$ reduction procedure guesses the optimal value of the parameter q, (L for O_1, m for O_2 and k for O_3), uses the O_i oracle to verify that q is the optimum and then checks to see if it is *worse* than the input q' to PP_i. Hence $PP_i^c\leq_m^{NP} O_i$ and the assertion follows. ■

Lemma 2.10: If NP≠Co-NP, then the optimizations problems O's are *not* in Co-NP.

Proof: The trick here is a double indirection [LM81], and is to show that $PP_i^c\leq_p^P O_i^c$, a *polynomial-time positive* reduction which uses only the 'yes' answers of an oracle, as opposed to a Turing reduction which uses both 'yes' and 'no' answers of the oracle. Now $O_i \varepsilon Co\text{-}NP$ if $O_i^c \varepsilon NP$. But $O_i^c \varepsilon NP$ implies $PP_i^c \varepsilon NP$, since $\leq_p^P$ preserves the class of NP. However, PP_i is NP-complete and so PP_i^c is Co-NP-complete and if NP≠Co-NP, $PP_i^c \not\varepsilon NP$ implies $O_i^c \not\varepsilon NP$ implies $O_i \not\varepsilon Co\text{-}NP$.

For O_i, the fact that the corresponding PP_i problem is *strongly* NP-complete guarantees that $PP_i^c\leq_p^P O_i^c$, since this requires at most $Max[I]$ 'yes' answers of the O_i^c oracle to answer any instance I of PP_i^c. Since $Max[I] \leq$ some polynomial of n (because of strong NP-completeness, Theorem 2.7), the reduction is polynomial time bounded. (For those O_i's where the sources are located on a discrete set S or on the set of *destination* points T, the corresponding NP-complete versions QQ_i's and RR_i's are used respectively). ■

The proof of the theorem below, follows from the above and Lemmas 2.8, 2.9 and 2.1

Theorem 2.11: The geometric location-allocation optimization problems, under MINSUM, for each of the three distance metrics as well as for *infinite* and *finite* feasible solution sets are all Δ_2^P-*proper*, assuming NP≠Co-NP.

3. Geometric Optimization Location Problems and D^P-*completeness*

We now consider geometric optimization problems derived under a discrete *minmax* optimization criterion from location-allocation problems. A *minmax* location objective is one which minimizes the maximum cost resulting from a given location solution.

Given the set T, as specified before, of n destinations in the plane

(P_1) Locate k points (sources) so as to *minimize* the *maximum* of the weighted distances between the destinations and the sources closest to them.

(P_2) Locate k points (sources) so that for a *maximum* number of destinations the weighted distances of these destinations from their closest sources does not exceed a prescribed limit R.

(P_3) Locate a *minimum* number of points (sources) so that the *maximum* of the weighted distances of the destinations and their closest sources does not exceed a prescribed limit R.

However in the following problems we assume that all weights are equal (similar to assuming that $w_j=1$, for $j=1..n$) and show that even for this restricted case the above problems are quite difficult.

Problems P_1, P_2 and P_3 allow location of the sources to be anywhere in the plane. Let problems Q_1, Q_2 and Q_3 correspond to problems P_1, P_2 and P_3 respectively, with the location of the sources being restricted to a finite discrete set S of possible locations in the plane and of size polynomial in n.

Under the *minimax* criterion with *Euclidean* ℓ_2 distance metrics each of the above location-allocation optimization problems reduces in a direct fashion to the placement of equal radius circular disks (*circles*) on the plane, with the *centers* of the circles corresponding to the location of the *sources*. Further all the destinations covered by the same circle correspond also in a direct fashion to an *allocation* of these destinations to the *source* (the center of the circle). Having equal weights for the above problems results in equal sized circles. Considering each of the above problems P's and Q's for equal sized *circles* which we call problems PC's and QC's we show that each of these problems are *complete* for the complexity class, D^P.

The geometric optimization problems turn out to be simple optimization questions concerning the size and number of geometric objects and are the natural questions that one may ask when dealing with the packing and covering of such geometrical objects. Initially versed in terms of circles we generalize them to other geometric figures in succeeding sections. In the following denote the Euclidean plane by E^2 and a circle *locatable* anywhere in E^2 to mean that the center of the circle can be any point in the Euclidean plane. Furthermore let an *R-circle* be a circle of radius R. Then given a set $T=\{(x_i,y_i),i=1..n\}$ of n fixed *points* in the plane, the set of optimization problems are

(PC_1) Is R the *minimum* radius of k equal sized *circles* locatable anywhere in E^2 to cover the n *points* of T?

(PC_2) Is m, $(m \leq n)$, the *maximum* number of *points* of T that k, R-*circles* locatable anywhere in E^2 can cover?

(PC_3) Is k the *minimum* number of R-*circles* locatable anywhere in E^2 to cover the n *points* of T?

Further consider the case where, besides the set T of n *points* in the plane, we are also given a finite discrete set of points S E^2 and the location of the *circles* are constrained to be from this set. Again a circle *locatable* anywhere in S means the center of the circle is a point of this set S.

(QC_1) Is R the *minimum* radius of k equal sized circles locatable anyshere in S to cover the n *points* of T?

(QC_2) Is m, $(m \leq n)$, the *maximum* number of *points* of T that k, R-*circles* locatable anywhere in S can cover?

(QC_3) Is k the *minimum* number of R-*circles* locatable anywhere in S to cover the n *points* of T?

For circles (circular disks) an alternate though similar set of optimization questions as above, may be asked. The *piercing* number for a set of circles is the number of 'needles' required to pierce all the circles of the system [HD64].

Given a set C of n fixed R-*circles* in the plane,

(DC_1) Is R the *minimum* radius of R-*circles* of C that k *needles* can pierce?

(DC_2) Is m the *maximum* number of R-*circles* of C that k *needles* can pierce?

(DC_3) Is k the *minimum* number of *needles* required to pierce all n R-*circles* of C?

Note that in these problems we optimally locate 'needles' (points), in order to tag each of the given circles.

We now show all the above geometric optimization problems to be complete for the complexity class D^P. We begin by first proving the following Theorem.

Theorem 3.1: The problems DC_1, DC_2 and DC_3 are *dual* problems of PC_1, PC_2 and PC_3 (respectively) and are *polynomial-time* transformable to each other.

Proof: The duality arises from the fact that if the k R-*circles* with centers $\{c_i\}$, $i=1..k$, have a common intersection point then they can all be pierced by a single *needle*. Furthermore, a single R-*circle* centered on any point of the common intersection can cover the k centers, $\{c_i\}$, $i=1..k$, (see [BL83] for further details of the duality).

For the problem DC_2 and similarly for the others, given the set $T=\{n$ points in the plane$\}$, obtain the set C of n circles of radius R with centers being the n points of T. Then m is the maximum number of R-*circles* of C that k needles can pierce *if* m is the maximum number of points of T that k R-*circles* can cover. The proof follows, since for each subset S of C of R-*circles* that a *needle* pierces, an R-*circle* centered on the piercing point of the needle can cover the centers (members of set T), of the *R-circles* of set S. Conversely, for each subset S of points, $S \subseteq T$, that are coverable by an *R-circle*, a *needle* pierces the subset of C of *R-circles* having S as their centers. ■

We now show that the problem PC_3 of locating the minimum number of *R-circles* in E^2 to cover all the n demand points is D^P *complete* by reducing (*Sat*, *UnSat*), a known D^P-complete problem [PY82], to it. To show membership in D^P we use the fact that D^P can be defined as the class of all predicates $R(x)$ that can be expressed as $R(x) = [\exists y\ P(x,y)] \wedge [\forall z\ Q(x,z)]$ for some polynomially balanced and polynomial-time checkable P and Q. Next we show the remaining problems to be D^P-complete by a similar reduction or a series of polynomial time reductions.

In [S82], it is proved that, similar to polynomial-time many-one reductions, polynomial-time positive reductions preserve the class of NP. That is if a language L_1 polynomial-time positive reduces (or polynomial-time many-one reduces) to a language L_2 then $L_2 \varepsilon NP ==> L_1 \varepsilon NP$. A similar fact is true for the class Co-NP. Therefore these positive reductions are *adequate* to separate the class of D^P *complete* languages from the classes of NP and Co-NP, (assuming NP≠Co-NP). A similar arguemnt is given when using polynomial-time Turing reductions as opposed to polynomial-time many-one reductions, in separating the class of NP-*complete* languages from the class of P, since both Turing reductions as well as many-one reductions preserve the class of P. Hence, they are both *adequate* to separate the classes NP-*complete* from P (assuming $P \neq NP$). Thus in our proofs we use both many-one and positive polynomial time reductions It is important to note that polynomial-time Turing reductions which do not preserve the class of NP, are not adequate in separating D^P languages from NP and Co-NP. Thus, for instance, it is possible to polynomial-time Turing reduce the D^P- *complete* language (*Sat*, *Unsat*), to (*Sat*), a known NP-*complete* problem. Also note that the special case of disjunctive, conjunctive positive reductions which we use here are by far the strongest of the various other positive and truth-table reductibilities known [LLS75]. In turn, any truth-table reduction is stronger than a Turing reduction.

Theorem 3.2: The problem PC_3 of locating the *minimum* number of *R-circles* in E^2 to cover the given n points is D^P *complete*.

Proof: The problem is in D^P since it can be rephrased as the conjunction of a predicate in NP and a predicate in Co-NP: $(\exists (p_1,\ldots,p_k) in E^2)$ [*R-circles* with centers at $p_1,\ldots,p_k$ cover n points] $\wedge$ $(\forall (q_1,\ldots,q_{k-1}) in E^2)$[*R-circles* with centers at $q_1,\ldots,q_{k-1}$ cover $<n$ points].

To prove the completeness we reduce (Sat, Unsat) to PC_3, using polynomial-time positive reductions. Starting from (F_1, F_2) and adapting a polynomial time construction in [FPT81], we construct two separate sets of points S_1 and S_2 in the plane such that for i=1,2, exactly k_i, *R-circles* are required to cover all the n_i points in S_i if F_i is satisfiable. Further if F_i is not satisfiable, at least k_i+1 and at most k_i+c_i,

R-*circles* are needed to cover all the n_i points of S_i, where c_i is the number of clauses in the CNF formula F_i.

Now construct c_2 additional copies of the set of points S_1. We how have (c_2+1) copies of sets of points S_1 and a single set of points S_2. It is important to note why (c_2+1) copies of S_1 are required. Let $(c_2\ \ )n_1+n_2$. It is not hard to see that k, the minimum number of circles of radius R needed to cover all the n points, satisfies $(c_2+1)k_1+k_2+1\leq k\leq(c_2+1)k_1+k_2+c_2$ *if* F_1 is satisfiable and F_2 is not satisfiable. Since this is a disjunction of at most c_2 calls of PC_3, problem PC_3 is D^P *complete* under a polynomial-time positive (disjunctive) reduction from (Sat, Unsat). ■

Theorem 3.3: The problem PC_2 of locating k R-*circles* in E^2, to cover a maximum number of the given points is D^P *complete*.

Proof: The problem is in D^P since it can be rephrased as before, as the conjunction of a predicate in NP and a predicate in Co-NP: $(\exists(p_1,\ldots,p_k) in E^2)$[R-*circles* with centers at $p_1,\ldots,p_k$ cover m points] $\wedge$ $(\forall(q_1,\ldots,q_k) in E^2)$[R-*circles* with centers at $q_1,\ldots,q_k$ cover $\leq m$ points].

To prove the completeness we again reduce (Sat, Unsat) to PC_3, using polynomial-time positive (disjunctive) reductions in a way very similar to Theorem 3.2. ■

Theorem 3.4: The problem PC_1 of locating k equal sized circles of minimum radius to cover all the given n points is D^P *complete*.

Proof: The problem is in D^P, when R is restricted to integers[3], since it can be rephrased as before, as the conjunction of a predicate in NP and a predicate in Co-NP: $(\exists(p_1,\ldots,p_k) in E^2)$[R-*circles* with centers at $p_1,\ldots,p_k$ cover n points] $\wedge$ $(\forall(q_\ell,\ldots,q_k) in E^2)$[(R-1)-*circles* with centers at $q_1,\ldots,q_k$ cover $<n$ points].

To prove it complete we show that PC_3 polynomial-time positive reduces to PC_1. We construct a set S of the radii of all possible circles which minimally cover n points in the plane. Since the minimum enclosing circle for a set of points is defined by exactly two or three of the points, the total size of S is at most $\binom{n}{2}+\binom{n}{3}$ which is $O(n^3)$. We claim that k is the minimum number of R-*circles* that cover all n points *if* for some $s\varepsilon S$, $s\leq R$, s is the minimum radius of k circles to cover all n points and for some $s\varepsilon S$, $s>R$, s is the minimum radius of k-1 circles to cover all n points. The proof is straightforward and follows from the definitions of the two problems PC_1 and PC_3. Again since we have a conjunction of two sets of disjunctive calls of PC_1, {at most $O(n^3)$ calls}, we have a polynomial-time positive reduction from PC_3 to PC_1.

Corollary: The dual problems DC_1, DC_2 and DC_3 are also D^P-*complete*. ■

Theorem 3.5: The finite solution set problem QC_3 is D^P *complete*.

Proof: The problem is in D^P since it can be rephrased as the conjunction of a predicate in NP and a predicate in Co-NP: $(\exists(p_1,\ldots,p_k) in S)$[R-*circles* with centers at $p_1,\ldots,p_k$ cover n points] $\wedge$ $(\forall(q_1,\ldots,q_{k-1}) in S)$[R-*circles* with centers at $q_1,\ldots,q_{k-1}$ cover $<n$ points].

---

[3]Otherwise the problem appears to be D^P *hard* when R is in general, a real number.

To prove it complete we prove that PC_3 polynomial-time many-one reduces to QC_3. It suffices to show that for any set T of n destination points in the plane there exists a finite set $S\subset E^2$, such that if a minimum of k, *R-circles* can cover T then these *R-circles* can be chosen to have their centers in S. Furthermore, S must be constructible in time polynomial in n.

We claim one can choose such an $S=T\cup\{$intersection points of *R-circles* centered at the points of $T\}$. For a proof of this claim let F be a (minimal) set of circles of radius R covering T and let circle $C\in F$. If C contains only a single point $p\in T$, replace C by an *R-circle* centered at $p\in T$ S. Otherwise, if C contains more than one point, move C without uncovering any point of T, until two points p, $q\in T$, lie on the boundary of the moved circle C'. Clearly the center c of C' lies at an intersection of the *R-circles* centered at p and q. Thus $c\in S$.

Finally note that S contains at most $O(n^2)$ points and can be constructed in $O(n^2)$ time. ■

Theorem 3.6: The finite feasible solution set problem QC_2 is D^P *complete.*

Proof: The problem is in D^P since it can be rephrased as before, as the conjunction of a predicate in NP and a predicate in Co-NP: $(\exists(p_1,\ldots,p_k)\,in S)$[*R-circles* with centers at $p_1,\ldots,p_k$ cover m points]$\wedge$ $(\forall(q_1,\ldots,q_k)\,in S)$[*R-circles* with centers at $q_1,\ldots,q_k$ cover $\leq m$ points].

To prove it complete we exhibit a polynomial-time reduction from PC_2 to QC_2 similar to the proof of Theorem c.5.

Theorem 3.7: The finite feasible solution set problem QC_1 is D^P *complete.*

Proof: The problem is in D^P, when R is restricted to integers, since it can be rephrased as before, as the conjunction of a predicate in NP and a predicate in Co-NP: $(\exists(p_1,\ldots,p_k)\,in S)$[*R-circles* with centers at $p_1,\ldots,p_k$ cover n points] $\wedge$ $(\forall(q_1,\ldots,q_k(in S)$[$(R-1)$*-circles* with centers at $q_1,\ldots,q_k$ cover $<n$ points].

To prove it complete we exhibit a polynomial time reduction from PC_1 to QC_1 similar to the proofs of Theorems 3.5 and 3.6. ■

The (ℓ_p, $1\leq p\leq\infty$) metrics

Between two points $p=(x_1,y_1)$ and $q=(x_2,y_2)$ in the plane the general ℓ_p distance for $1\leq p\leq\infty$, is $[|x_1-y_1|^p+|x_2-y_2|]^{1/p}$. Some of the more common distance metrics used are *Rectilinear* (ℓ_1), *Euclidean* (ℓ_2), and *Infinity* ℓ_∞. For the general ℓ_p metrics the *unit disks*[4] correspond to the following equal sized geometrical figures, all oriented the same way, and with the intersection points of their xx' and yy' axes.

For the *rectilinear* ℓ_1 distance metric the geometric figures involved in our above optimization problems *P's* and *Q's* are equal sized *diamonds* (squares rotated by 45°) of half-diagonal length R instead of *R-circles*. For the *infinity* ℓ_∞ distance metric the optimization problems reduce to placement optimization problems of equal sized squares of half-edge length R, having sides parallel to the respective

[4]The *unit disks* are given by $|x|^p + |y|^p = 1$.

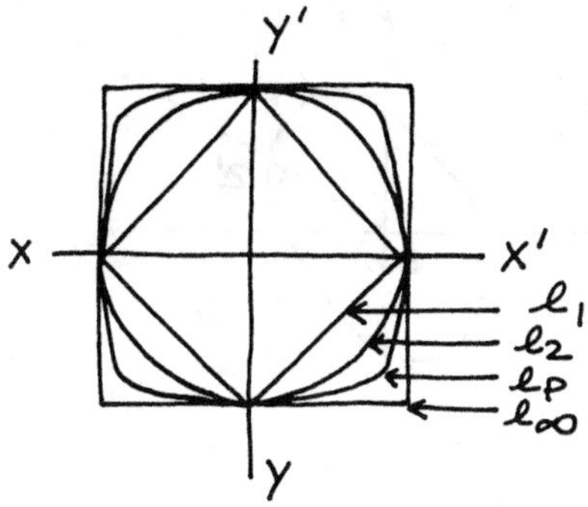

coordinate axes. Also a diamond (square) *locatable* anywhere in S or E^2 means the intersection point of the diagonals of the diamond (square) can be any point in the finite discrete set S or the Euclidean plane respectively.

For all these problems both membership and completeness for the class of D^P carry over in a fashion quite similar to the proofs of Theorems 3.2 to 3.7. Each of the constructions used here as well as the adapted constructions of [FPT81], can be modified in a direct fashion for these geometric figures with fixed orientations. Thus we have the following result,

Theorem 3.8: The above geometric optimization problems for the geometric figures corresponding to general ℓ_p metrics are all D^P-complete.

Arbitrary metrics

Between two points p and q in the plane, the various properties of a metric $d(p,q)$ are

(1) *translation invariance* - $d(p,q)$ is a function of the relative positions of p and q,
(2) *symmetry* - $d(p,q) = d(q,p)$,
(3) *triangle inequality* - $d(p,r) \leq d(p,q) + d(q,r)$,
(4) *positivity* - $d(p,q) \geq 0$,
(5) *homogeneity* - for $o=(0,0), p=(x,y)$ and $q=(ax,ay), d(o,q)=a^*d(o,p)$.

Each of the ℓ_p, $1 \leq p \leq \infty$, metrics satisfy the above properties. The Euclidean (ℓ_2) metric corresponding to the circle is the only metric which is also invariant under *rotation*. That is the reason why in the previous section, a specific fixed orientation was imposed on the geometric figures for the general ℓ_p metric.

A point set S is *symmetric* with respect to the origin if for each point (x,y) belonging to S, the point $(-x,-y)$ also belongs to S. A point set is *convex* if for each pair of points in S, the line segments joining these points is entirely in S.

Theorem 3.9: [BB61] If S is a point set containing the origin in its interior and S is *convex* and *symmetric* with respect to the origin, then there exists a distance function d for which S is the *unit disk*.

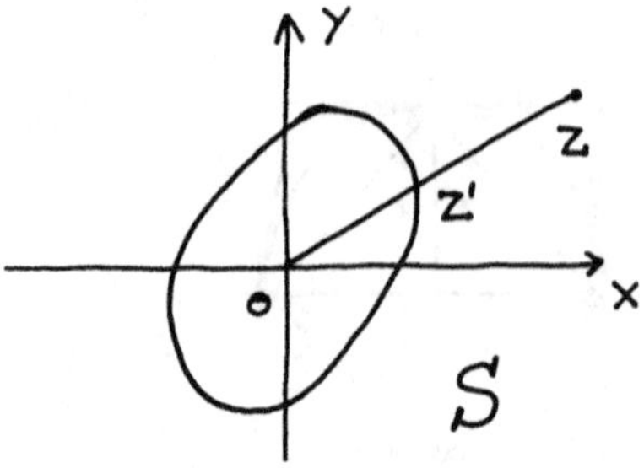

For the above *unit disk*, S, which is both *convex* and *symmetric*, define the distance from o to z to be $d(oz)=oz/oz'$. The distance $d(oz)$ is *less* than 1 if z is an interior point of S, *equal* to 1 if z is a boundary point of S and *greater* than 1 if z is an exterior point of S. For these unit disks we specify a certain fixed orientation, since they are not invariant under rotation. All the constructions can again be adapted as before, at times with closer tolerances, thereby providing reductions which show that the corresponding optimization problems for the placement of these *convex* and *symmetric* geometric figures to be D^P *complete*. Note that both the convexity and symmetric properties of these figures are essential in the reduction of the infinite solution set problems P'*s* to the finite solution set problems Q'*s* as in Theorems 3.5, 3.6 and 3.7. The duality used in these Theorems apply to all convex figures having a point of symmetry. Hence,

Theorem 3.10: The above geometric optimization problems for the geometric figures corresponding to arbitrary metrics are also D^P-complete.

4. Conclusion & Open Issues

We have shown a large number of natural geometric optimization problems concerning various types of geometric figures, to be *complete* for a class D^P. We believe these are the first set of geometric optimization problems to have been shown complete for this class D^P and the only other set of optimization problems, other than the list of problems in [PY82]. This result also proves the existence of natural geometric optimization problems that are *proper* in $\Delta_2^P = P^{NP}$. Further all of the above problems are *strongly* D^P-*complete* analogous to the similar concept for NP-*complete* languages, since all the above constructions hold even when the largest number occurring in any instance of the problems, that is parameter R and the coordinate points in set T, are restricted to be of size bounded by a polynomial in n.

There are a number of interesting open issues. First, is there a natural geometric optimization problem which is Δ_3^P-*proper*. This has been a persistent open problem in the context of combinatorial optimization. A problem Q is *proper* for Δ_3^P

if Q is in Δ_3^P and not in Σ_2^P or Π_2^P, assuming $\Sigma_2^P \neq \Pi_2^P$. Another open question is the precise complexity of the UNIQUE versions of the above geometric optimization problems. It is not too difficult to note that the optimization solution of the above problems is not unique. Furthermore the exact classification in the polynomial hierarchy of the 3-*dimension* versions of the above geometric optimization problems is an interesting open problem in its own right.

The structure of the class D^P as well as the existence of similar classes higher up in the polynomial hierarchy, are yet to be fully explored. We hope with the results of this paper, renewed interest for this class would surface.

Acknowledgments: I wish to thank Ming Li, Raimund Seidel and Yaacov Yesha for their corrections and suggestions.

5. References

[AHU74]

Aho, A., Hopcroft, J. and Ullman, J., *The Design and Analysis of Computer Algorithms*, Addison Wesley, 1974.

[Ba84]

Bajaj, C., *Geometric Optimization and Computational Complexity*, Computer Science Tech. Report, Cornell University, Ph.D. Thesis, TR84-629, 1984.

[BL83]

Bajaj, C. and Lim, M., *On the duality of intersections and closest points*, Computer Science Tech. report, Cornell University, TR83-568, 1983.

[BB61]

Beckenbach, E. and Bellman, R., *An Introduction to Inequalities*, Random House, 1961.

[Co63]

Cooper, L. *Location-Allocation Problems*, Operations Research Vol. 11, No. 3, pp 331-343, 1963.

[FPT]

Fowler, R., Paterson, M. and Tanimoto, S., *Optimal packing and covering in the plane are NP-complete*, Info. Proc. Letters, Vol. 12, no. 2, 1981.

[FW74]

Francis, R. and White J., *Facility layout and location - an analytic approach*, Prentice Hall, NJ, USA 1974.

[GGJ76]

Garey, M., Graham, R. and Johnson, D., *Some NP-complete geometric problems*, Proc. 8th STOC, p. 10-27, 1976.

[GJ79]

Garey, M. and Johnson, D., *Computers and Intractability: a guide to NP-completeness*, Freeman, San Francisco, 1979.

[HD64]

Hadwiger, H. and Debrunner, H., *Combinatorial geometry in the plane,* (Translated by Klee, V.), Holt, Rhinehart & Winston, 1964.

[HPT80]

Hansen, P., Perreur, J. and Thisse, J., *Location Theory, Dominance and Convexity: Some further results,* Opern. Res., vol. 28, p. 1241-1250, 1980.

[KP79]

Krarup, J. and Pruzan, P., *Selected families of discrete location problems,* Annals of Discrete Math. 5, North Holland, 1979.

[LLS75]

Ladner, R., Lynch, N. and Selman, A., *Comparison of Polynomial Time Reducibilities* Theoretical Computer Sci. 15, p. 279-289, 1981.

[LM81]

Leggett, E. W. and Moore, D. J., *Optimization Problems and the Polynomial Hierarchy,* Technical Computer Sci. 15, p. 279-289, 1981.

[LP83]

Lozano-Perez, T., *Spatial Planning: A Configuration Space Approach,* IEEE Trans. on Computers, V. C-32, p. 108-120, 1983.

[MS84]

Megiddo, N. and Supowit, K. J., *On the complexity of some common geometric location problems,* Siam J. on Computing, vol. 13, no. 1, p. 182-196, Feb. 1984.

[Pa81]

Papadimitriou, C., *Worst-case and Probabilistic analysis of a Geometric Location Proglem,* Siam J. of Computing, vol. 10, no. 3, 1981.

[PS82]

Papadimitriou, C. and Steiglitz, K., *Combinatorial Optimization, Algorithms and Complexity,* Prentice Hall, 1982.

[PY82]

Papadimitriou, C. and Yannakakis, M., *The Complexity of facets (and some facets of complexity),* 14th Annual STOC, May 1982, pp. 255-260.

[S82]

Selman, A. L., *Analogues of semirecursive sets and effective reducibilities to the study of NP completeness,* Information & Control, Vol. 52, Jan. 1982, pp36-51.

[Sh78]

Shamos, M. I., *Computational Geometry,* Yale University, Ph.D. Thesis, (Univ. Microfilms International), 1978.

[WH73]

Wendell, R. and Hurter, A., *Location Theory, Dominance and Convexity,* Opern. Res., vol. 21, p. 314-320, 1973.

DERIVING OBJECT OCTREE FROM IMAGES

Jack Veenstra
Narendra Ahuja

Coordinated Science Laboratory
University of Illinois
1101 W. Springfield Avenue
Urbana, Illinois 61801

Abstract

Octrees are used in many 3-D representation problems because they provide a compact data structure, allow rapid access to information, and implement efficient data manipulation algorithms. The initial acquisition of the 3-D information, however, is a common problem. This paper describes an algorithm to construct the octree representation of a 3-D object from silhouette images of the object. The images must be obtained from nine viewing directions corresponding to the three "face-on" and six "edge-on" views of an upright cube. The execution time is found to be linear in the number of nodes in the octree.

Introduction

Three-dimensional object representation is of crucial importance to robot vision. Part of the task lies in the generation and maintenance of a spatial occupancy map of the environment. The occupancy map describes the space occupied by objects. Some of the uses of such a representation include robot navigation and manipulation of objects on an assembly line. This paper is concerned with the construction of one representation of the occupancy map, namely, the octree representation, of an object from its silhouette images.

An octree [1, 5, 7] is a tree data structure. Starting with a cubical region of space, one recursively decomposes the space into eight smaller cubes called octants (see Figure 1). If an octant is completely inside the object, the corresponding node in the octree is marked black; if completely outside the object, the node is marked white. If the octant is partially contained in the object, the octant is decomposed into eight sub-octants each of which is again tested to determine if it is completely inside or completely outside the object. The decomposition continues until all octants are either inside or outside the object or until a desired level of resolution is reached. Those octants at the finest level of resolution that are only partially contained in the object are approximated as occupied or unoccupied by some criteria. The object in Figure

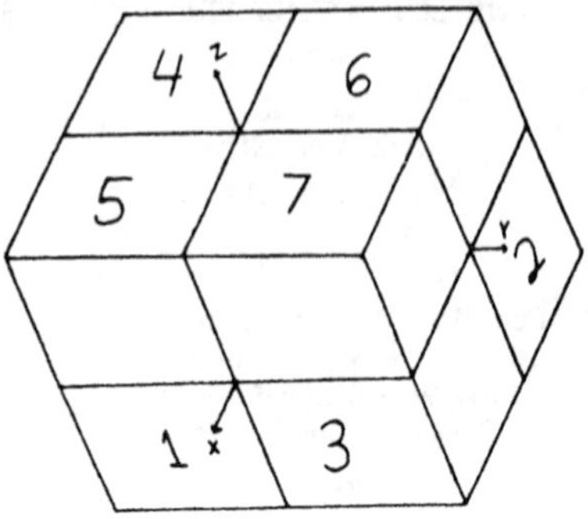

Figure 1

A cube and its decomposition into octants.

2(a), for example, would be represented by the octree in Figure 2(b).

In this paper we address the following problem: given a sequence of silhouette views of an object, construct the octree representing the object which gave rise to those views. A given silhouette constrains the object to lie in a cone (for perspective projection) or a cylinder (for orthographic projection) whose cross section is defined by the shape of the silhouette. In this paper, we will consider orthographic projection of an object onto a plane perpendicular to a viewing direction. We will call as "extended silhouette" the solid region of space defined by sweeping the silhouette along a line parallel to the viewing direction used in obtaining the silhouette. After several views, the object is constrained to lie in the intersection of all the extended silhouettes. As the number of silhouettes processed increases, the fit of the volume of intersection of the cylinders to the object volume becomes tighter. In our algorithm, we do not perform the intersection explicitly, but infer the octree nodes from silhouette images according to a predetermined table that

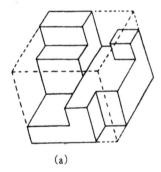

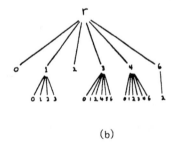

(a) (b)

Figure 2

An object (a), and the octree which represents it (b).

lists pairs of image regions and their corresponding octree nodes.

Another approach, by Shneier et al. [4, 8], to the problem of constructing the octree from silhouettes explicitly tests for the intersection between an octree node and the extended silhouette by projecting the nodes of the tree onto the silhouette image. The relative performance of algorithms based on their and our approach needs to be determined. Chien and Aggarwal [3] describe an efficient method for constructing an octree for an object from silhouettes of its three orthogonal views. Their method is similar to the method described here, though not as accurate since they only use three views. The accuracy of the octree describing the object is improved if, in addition to the three orthogonal views, information from six more views of the object is also used.

Octree generation

The method described in this paper constructs the octree without computing any projections or performing any intersection tests. The viewpoints, however, are restricted to be from one of the six face-on views or one of the twelve edge-on views. Although this allows only nine useful views (since silhouettes from two opposite faces or two opposite edges are identical), the views are distributed widely in space and together provide significant information to construct a good approximation of the object.

Restricting the viewpoints allows us to find a direct relationship between the pixels in the two-dimensional silhouette image and the octants in the three-dimensional space that define the octree. This relationship would be difficult to know for an arbitrary viewpoint. The relationship between pixels and octants for an orthographic face-on view is easily derived so it is described first. Then the relationship between pixels and octants for an orthographic edge-on view is presented.

Face-on view

A face-on view is the view obtained when the line of sight is perpendicular to one of the faces of the cubes of the octree space and passes through the origin. Thus a face x view is the orthographic projection of the object onto the yz plane. The digitized binary images for the three face-on views of the object in Figure 2(a) are given by the 4×4 square arrays of pixels in Figure 3. Pixels having a value of 1 denote the region onto which the object projects. Pixels having a value of zero represent the projection of free space.

The projection of the cube in Figure 1 along the x direction projects pairs of octants onto the same region in the image space. For example, octants 5 and 4 project onto the upper left quadrant, octants 7 and

1	1	0	0
1	1	0	1
1	1	1	1
1	1	1	1

(a)

0	0	0	1
0	0	1	1
1	1	1	1
1	1	1	1

(b)

1	1	1	1
1	1	1	1
1	1	1	1
1	1	1	0

(c)

Figure 3

Digitized silhouette images for face x, face y, and face z views of the object in Figure 2(a) are shown in (a), (b), and (c), respectively.

---

6 project onto the upper right quadrant, and so on. (See Figures 1, 4(a).) This simple relationship between octants and their projections allows the construction of the octree directly from the pixels in a digitized silhouette image.

Given a square array of pixels representing a face x silhouette image, its contribution to the octree can be obtained using the quadrant labels shown in Figure 4(a). The quadrants of the silhouette image are processed as if a quadtree were being constructed. A quadrant is recursively decomposed until it is either all ones or all zeroes. But instead of adding only one node per quadrant to the tree as is the case with quadtrees, two nodes are added. When a quadrant is decomposed, each sub-quadrant could add up to four nodes to the octree instead of one. Figure 4(b) shows the nodes assigned to the sub-quadrants. The object and the octree nodes resulting from the silhouette image of Figure 3(a) are shown in Figure 5.

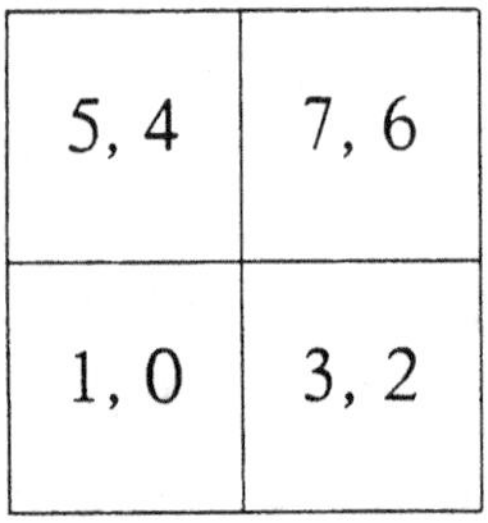

(a)

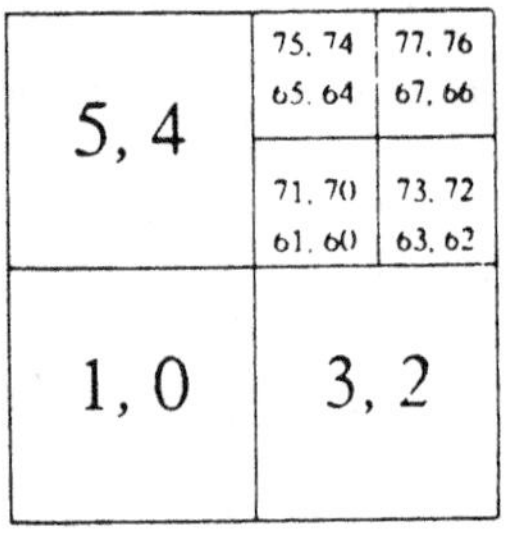

(b)

Figure 4

The labeling scheme for quadrants for the face x view. Each quadrant is assigned two labels (a) instead of the usual one. Each time a quadrant is sub-divided, the sub-quadrants have twice as many labels (b).

(a) (b)

Figure 5

The object (a) constructed from the digitized binary image in Figure 3(a) by extending the silhouette along the line of sight, and the octree (b) which represents this object.

A similar procedure is used for the other two face-on views. The objects generated by the face y and face z views are shown in Figure 6. The intersection of the objects generated from the three face-on views is shown in Figure 7. (Compare this with the original object in Figure 2(a).)

Edge-on view

An edge-on view of a cube is the view obtained when the line of sight bisects an edge of the cube and passes through the center of the cube. The edge-on views are labeled with the two adjacent octants which share the bisected edge. The octants of a cube viewed from edge 3-7 would appear as shown in Figure 8. The image in Figure 8 is longer by a factor of $\sqrt{2}$ in the horizontal direction. Since the octree generation algorithm requires a square array, the elongated image from an edge-on view must be compressed into a square array. This is accomplished by replacing rectangular regions of pixels, of aspect ratio $\sqrt{2}$, by single

(a) (b)

Figure 6

The objects (a) and (b) constructed from the digitized binary silhouette images of Figures 3(b) and 3(c), respectively.

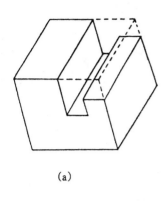

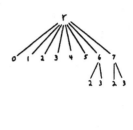

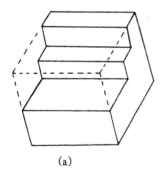

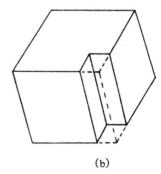

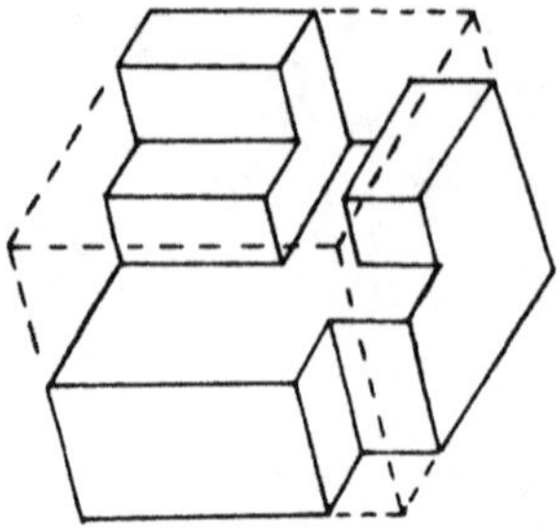

Figure 7

The intersection of the objects in Figures 5 and 6.

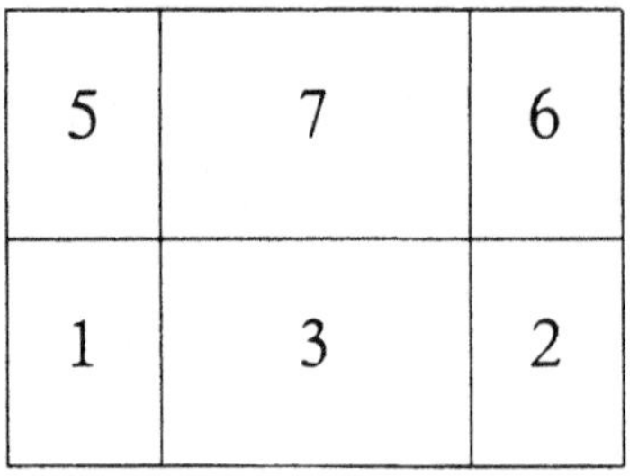

Figure 8

The cube in Figure 1 viewed from edge 3-7.

pixels (of aspect ratio 1). Uniform rectangular regions are replaced by their representative values. Rectangular regions containing both binary values can be replaced by 0 or 1 according to some criteria. The compressed binary image for the edge 3-7 view of the object in Figure 9 is the square array shown in Figure 10. The octree constructed from the edge-on silhouette in Figure 10 should, ideally, represent the object in Figure 11(a). Since the octree cannot represent this object exactly, it represents an approximation

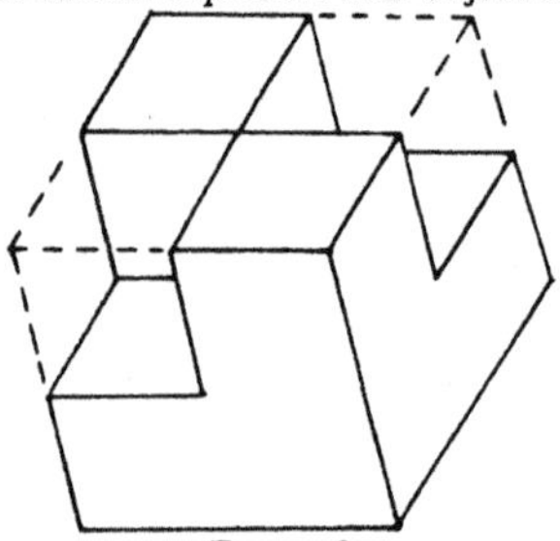

Figure 9

A cube with octants 5 and 6 missing.

0	1	1	0
0	1	1	0
1	1	1	1
1	1	1	1

Figure 10

The binary image of the object in Figure 9 viewed from edge 3-7 after compression into a square array.

---

of the object, shown in Figure 11(b). The approximation improves with an increase in resolution of the digitized image.

Figure 12 shows a side view of the projection of a cube onto an image plane. The cube is viewed edge-on. The area between two adjacent vertical lines extending from the image plane into the cube represents the region of space which projects, after compression, onto a pixel in the image plane. Since a

(a) (b)

Figure 11

Ideal construction (a) from image in Figure 10, and the actually constructed approximation (b).

(a) (b)

Figure 12

The geometry of an edge-on view of a cube.

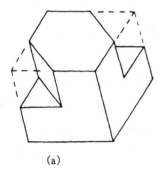

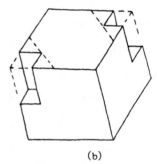

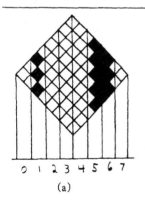

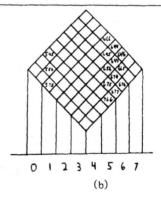

pixel value of zero indicates that the object does not exist in that region, octants which are completely contained in that region can be eliminated. For example, the shaded octants in Figure 12(a) would be removed from the octree if pixels 1, 5, and 6 had value zero.

Figure 12(b) shows the labels of the shaded octants from Figure 12(a) if the cube is viewed from edge 3-7. Figure 13 shows the labels of some of the octants on the outside of the cube.

The recursive procedure for constructing an octree from a square array of pixels representing an edge-on view is similar to procedures for constructing a quadtree. If the square array is all ones or all zeroes, then it is marked black or white, respectively. Otherwise it contains some ones and some zeroes and it is decomposed recursively in two different ways.

(1) It is decomposed into the usual four quadrants, each with one label. The labels depend on which edge is being viewed. The labels for the four quadrants for the edge 3-7 view are given in Figure 14(a). If a quadrant contains both zeroes and ones then it is recursively decomposed.

(2) It is decomposed into two center squares and two margins (see Figure 14(b)). The center squares are the same size as the quadrants in the first decomposition step. The margins are half the width of the squares and are not used. Each center square has two labels. These are treated in a manner similar to the way the quadrants with two labels for the face-on view were treated. Whenever a node with one of the two labels is added to the octree, another node with the other label is also added. If a center square contains both zeroes and ones, then it is recursively decomposed.

Each time a quadrant or center square is decomposed, it is decomposed using both methods described above, unless it is a 2×2 square in which case only the first method is used.

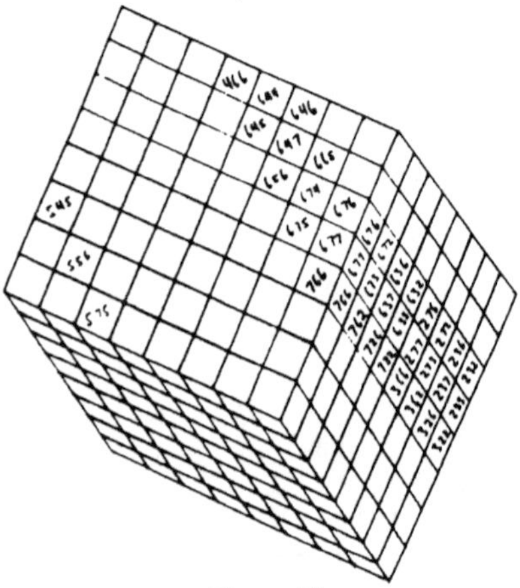

Figure 13

Labels of octants on the side of the cube shown in Figure 12.

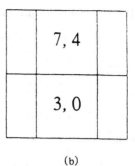

(a) (b)

Figure 14

The decomposition of the image array for the edge 3-7 view into 4 quadrants (a) and 2 center squares (b).

Figure 15 shows the center squares decomposed into four quadrants (each quadrant inherits two labels from the center square) and Figure 16 shows quadrant 6 decomposed into two center squares.

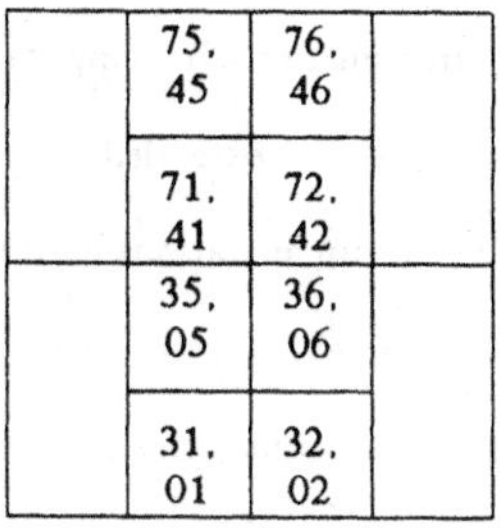

Figure 15

The further decomposition of center squares into quadrants.

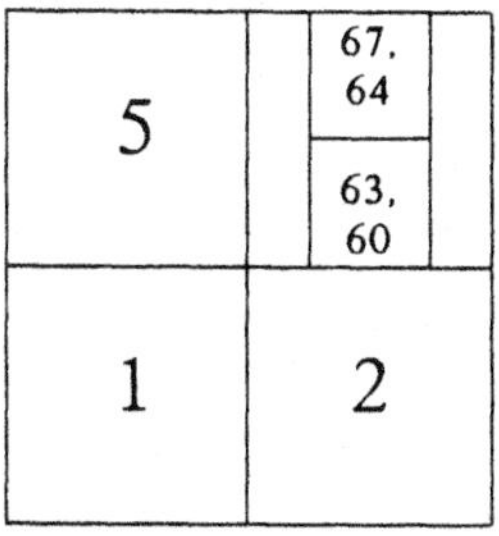

Figure 16

The further decomposition of the upper right quadrant into center squares.

This recursive procedure finds all the octants corresponding to the pixels in the image. Given the array of pixels in Figure 17(a), the octants corresponding to the zero pixels in the upper right quadrant are listed in Figure 17(b).

Some pixels in the array (especially those toward the middle) are examined several times by the recursive procedure since center squares overlap with quadrant squares. Some of these repeated pixel examinations can usually be avoided by exploiting the fact that, in practice, images contain relatively large regions of uniform pixel values. Thus, if two horizontally adjacent quadrants have pixel values which are all zeroes or all ones, then the overlapping center square need not be examined.

Performance

The algorithm described above makes use of up to nine views of an object to construct its octree. The directions chosen for these views allow the algorithm to take advantage of the simple relationship between image quadrants and octree space. Although an algorithm which allows an arbitrary viewpoint is obviously more general, this generality requires an explicit computation of the volume of intersection for determining the octree nodes corresponding to the extended silhouettes. The corresponding intersection tests may be more complex than the table look-up operations used in our approach. Since silhouette images taken from viewing directions which are widely spaced yield more information, in general, than do silhouette images taken from viewing directions which are close together, it needs to be determined how much more accuracy the general viewpoint provides than the nine widely spaced viewing directions used in our algorithm, and how the computational costs of the two algorithms compare. Towards this end, we plan to run both algorithms on a fixed set of objects and compare the accuracies of the volumes represented

1	0	1	1	1	0	0	1
1	0	1	1	1	0	0	1
1	0	1	1	1	0	0	1
1	0	1	1	1	0	0	1
1	0	1	1	1	0	0	1
1	0	1	1	1	0	0	1
1	0	1	1	1	0	0	1
1	0	1	1	1	0	0	1

(a)

612	656	64	726
616	661	67	462
621	665	422	466
625	60	426	762
652	63	722	766

(b)

Figure 17

The square array (a) representing the edge 3-7 silhouette of the cube in Figure 12 and the complete list of labels (b) for the octants corresponding to the zero pixels in the upper right quadrant.

by the octrees generated by the algorithms and the corresponding execution times.

Measures of Accuracy

In order to evaluate the performance of an arbitrary set of viewing directions it is necessary to define a method to measure the accuracy with which an object's volume can be approximated from silhouettes obtained from the given viewing directions. Defining a measure of accuracy is difficult since the approximation depends on the viewing directions, the shape of the object viewed, and the object's orientation with respect to the viewing directions.

The volume of the intersection of extended silhouettes of an object contains that object. Even if the object is convex, the volume of the object is probably smaller than the volume of intersection. One possible measure of accuracy for a set of viewing directions is the ratio of the volume of the smallest object which could give rise to a given set of silhouettes to the volume of intersection of the extended silhouettes. This worst-case definition means that if a given set of silhouettes has an accuracy measure of 90% then the volume of the actual object can be no less than 90% of the computed volume. Some restrictions must be placed on the object shape (like requiring it to be convex) to prevent the smallest object from having an arbitrarily small volume. Even with object restrictions, the accuracy measure can be very low if only a few views are used. For example, there exist convex objects smaller than a unit cube which have unit squares as silhouettes when viewed along three orthogonal directions. The projection of a tetrahedron oriented so that its four vertices coincide with four vertices of the unit cube is a unit square when viewed along a direction perpendicular to a face of the unit cube. The tetrahedron would be represented by the cube, even though the volume of the tetrahedron is one-third the volume of the cube. Since a tetrahedron inscribed in a unit cube is the smallest convex object whose three orthogonal silhouettes are unit squares, the accuracy measure for that set of three silhouettes is 33.3%.

While the above definition of accuracy may be of theoretical interest, the difficulty of finding the smallest object for each set of silhouettes makes this definition impractical. An alternate approach is to empirically measure the performance of a chosen set of viewing directions on a suitably selected set of objects. The measure of accuracy for a given object is the ratio of the volume of the object to the volume of the intersection of the extended silhouettes of the object. For example, a sphere would have an accuracy measure equal to the ratio of its volume to the volume of the intersection of circular cylinders containing it, where the axes of the cylinders coincide with the viewing directions. Using this measure of accuracy three orthogonal views of a sphere would yield an accuracy of 88.9%. The accuracy of the nine views described in this paper is approximately 98.7%.

Except for the sphere, the accuracy of a set of viewing directions for a given object is dependent on the object's orientation. In one orientation, the tetrahedron yields an accuracy of 33.3% for three orthogonal views; in another orientation, the accuracy is 100%. In fact, only two orthogonal views of the tetrahedron are necessary to exactly represent it. To obtain the average performance over all orientations, a Monte Carlo simulation experiment can be performed to measure the desired ratio of volumes over a large number of randomly chosen orientations. Then, for a given set of objects, the measure of accuracy for a set of viewing directions is the estimated expected value of the ratio of the object volume to the constructed volume for a randomly selected object at a randomly selected orientation.

How should the objects constituting the test set be chosen? One way to resolve this question is to use objects having shapes used as primitives for three-dimensional representations, e.g., generalized cones. A generalized cone is defined by a space curve spine and a planar cross section which is swept along the spine according to a sweeping rule. The sweeping rule determines how the cross section changes as it is translated along the spine. Figure 18 shows a sample of generalized cones used by Brooks [2] as primitive volume elements.

The measure of accuracy can then be computed as the average of the results of a large number of executions of the following three step procedure. First, an arbitrary object from the chosen set and a random orientation are selected. Second, the object is projected along each viewing direction to provide a set of silhouette images. Finally, the octree is constructed and the corresponding object volume computed. The ratio of the actual to the computed volume is the desired result for the chosen object and orientation. We plan to conduct the above mentioned Monte Carlo simulation experiments on the objects shown in Figure 18.

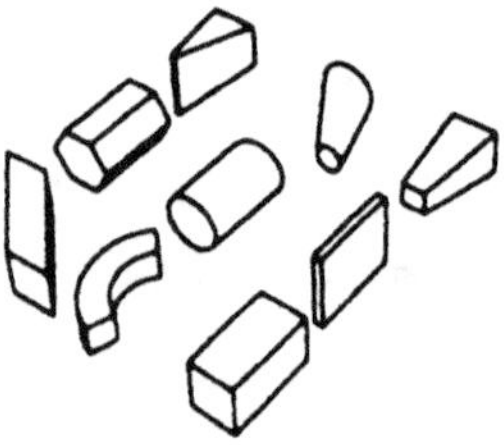

Figure 18

A selection of generalized cones.

Several common special cases of generalized cones, if favorably oriented, can be found exactly by taking the intersection of extended silhouettes:

(1) A straight spine, any cross section, and a constant sweeping rule. Example: circular cylinder, rectangular prism.

(2) A curved spine that lies in a plane, a rectangular cross section, and constant sweeping rule. Example: arc-shaped object in Figure 18.

(3) A straight spine, a rectangular or octagonal cross section, and a linear contraction sweeping rule (or contractions linear in two orthogonal directions). Example: pyramid, wedge.

The only object in Figure 18 which cannot be represented exactly by the intersection of extended silhouettes is the circular cone.

All but one of the objects in Figure 18 are convex, but the class of objects which can be represented exactly by the intersection of extended silhouettes includes many objects which are not convex. The following definition describes precisely which elements are in this class.

Definition. An object is ***representable*** if there is a finite set of viewing directions such that the intersection of the extended silhouettes obtained from the viewing directions is congruent to the object.

So, for example, a cube is representable; a sphere is not. The following theorem describes representable objects in terms of more elementary geometrical constructions such as points and lines.

Theorem. An object is representable if there is a finite set of viewing directions such that for every point P outside the object, there exists a line parallel to a viewing direction which contains P and does not intersect the object.

Proof. If a point P is outside the object and there exists a line containing P which is parallel to a viewing direction and does not intersect the object, then the silhouette for that viewing direction will not contain the projection of P. Hence the extended silhouette will not contain P, so the intersection of extended silhouettes will not contain P. Since this is true for every point P not contained in the object, the intersection of extended silhouettes does not contain any point which is outside the object. Since it is also true that the object is contained in the intersection of its extended silhouettes, it follows that the object is representable.

Theorem. If every planar face of a convex polyhedron is parallel to a viewing direction, then the intersection of extended silhouettes exactly represents the polyhedron.

Proof. A convex polyhedron is an object which lies entirely on one side of each of its faces. If a planar face F is parallel to a viewing direction, then that face projects onto a line segment and forms an outside edge of the silhouette. That edge becomes a planar section which contains face F when the silhouette is extended parallel to the viewing direction. Thus, any point contained in the extended silhouette must lie entirely on the object side of the plane containing face F. Consequently, if every face is parallel to some viewing direction, any point contained in the intersection of all the extended silhouettes must lie entirely on the object side of all the planes containing the faces of the polyhedron. Thus, every point which is contained in the intersection of the extended silhouettes is also contained in the convex polyhedron. Since the polyhedron is contained in the intersection of extended silhouettes, the polyhedron is represented exactly.

Execution time

The algorithm described above was implemented in the C programming language [6] on a VAX 11/780. The programs were timed using test data in the form of 64 × 64 arrays representing binary images of varying complexity. The average cpu time spent in the octree generation procedures was recorded and plotted as a function of the number of nodes in the octree. (See Figure 19.) The octree generation times for a single face-on view and a single edge-on view are plotted separately, where the data for the edge-on view

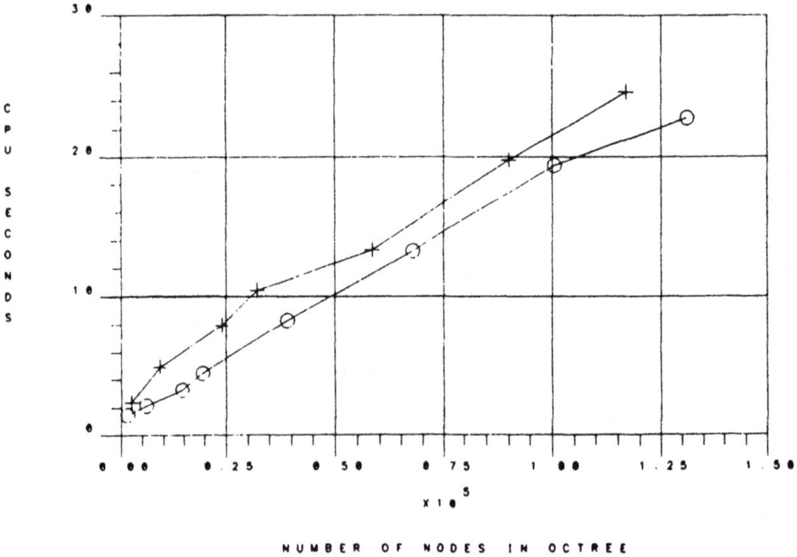

Figure 19

o represents the octree generation time for a face-on view
+ represents the octree generation time for an edge-on view

do not include the time required to compress the rectangular image into a square array. The graph shows that the execution time increases linearly with the number of nodes in the octree.

Summary

We have presented an algorithm to generate the octree representation of an object from silhouette images taken from a set of viewing directions. These viewing directions are parallel to three orthogonal faces and six face-diagonals of an upright cube. Each silhouette of an object is first extended into a cylinder parallel to the viewing direction, and the corresponding octree is constructed. An intersection is performed on the octrees generated from the silhouettes to obtain an octree representing the space occupied by the object. The octree for each silhouette image is computed efficiently by a recursive quadtree decomposition of the image and identification of the occupied octree nodes from a table listing corresponding pairs of image windows and octree nodes. We have also described briefly some ways of estimating the performance of the algorithm. We have outlined measures of the accuracy of the volume represented by the generated octree. We plan to obtain the performance of different numbers of viewing directions by a Monte Carlo simulation of the silhouettes for a set of objects and their corresponding octrees produced by the algorithm. We also plan to compare the performance of our algorithm with that of Shneier et al. [4, 8] which uses unrestricted viewing directions.

References

[1] N. Ahuja and C. Nash, Octree representations of moving objects, *Computer Vision, Graphics, and Image Processing*, *26*, 1984, 207-216.

[2] Rodney Brooks, Symbolic reasoning among models and 2-D images, *Artificial Intelligence*, *17*, (1981) 285-348.

[3] C. H. Chien and J. K. Aggarwal, A volume/surface octree representation, *Seventh International Conference on Pattern Recognition*, July 30 - August 2, 1984.

[4] T. H. Hong and M. Shneier, Describing a robot's workspace using a sequence of views from a moving camera, unpublished manuscript, National Bureau of Standards.

[5] C. L. Jackins and S. L. Tanimoto, Oct-trees and their use in representing three-dimensional objects, *Computer Graphics and Image Processing*, *14*, 1980, 249-270.

[6] B. W. Kernighan and D. M. Ritchie, *The C Programming Language*, Prentice-Hall, Englewood Cliffs, New Jersey (1978).

[7] W. Osse and N. Ahuja, Efficient octree representation of moving objects, *Proc. 7th Int. Conf. on Pattern Recognition*, Montreal, Canada, July 30 - August 2, 1984, 821-823.

[8] M. Shneier, E. Kent, and P. Mansbach, Representing workspace and model knowledge for a robot with mobile sensors, *Proc. Seventh Int. Conf. on Pattern Recognition*, Montreal, Canada, July, 1984, 199-202.

DEDUCTION WITH RELATION MATCHING

Zohar Manna
Computer Science Department
Stanford University

Richard Waldinger
Artificial Intelligence Center
SRI International

ABSTRACT

A new deduction rule is introduced to give streamlined treatment to relations of special importance in an automated theorem-proving system. This *relation matching* rule generalizes to an arbitrary binary relation the E-resolution and RUE-resolution rules for equality, and may operate within a nonclausal or clausal system. The new rule depends on an extension of the notion of *polarity* to apply to subterms as well as to subsentences, with respect to a given binary relation. It allows the system to draw a conclusion even if the unification algorithm fails to find a complete match, provided the polarities of the mismatched terms are auspicious. The rule allows us to eliminate troublesome axioms, such as transitivity and monotonicity, from the system; proofs are shorter and more comprehensible, and the search space is correspondingly deflated.

1. INTRODUCTION

In any theorem-proving system, the task of representing properties of objects is shared between axioms and rules of inference. The axioms of the system are easier to introduce and modify, because they are expressed in a logical language. However, because axioms are declarative rather than imperative, they are given no individual heuristic controls. The rules of inference, on the other hand, cannot be altered without reprogramming the system, and they are usually expressed in the system's programming language. However, the rules can be given individual heuristic controls and strategies.

It is customary to use rules of inference to express properties of the logical connectives, which are the same from one theory to the next, and to use axioms to express properties of constants, functions, and relations, which may vary. It is hazardous, however, to express certain properties of functions and relations by axioms. Some properties of the equality relation, for example, are rarely represented axiomatically. For one thing, in a first-order system indefinitely many axioms are necessary to represent the substitutivity property of this relation, depending on how many function and relation symbols are in the vocabulary of the theory. More importantly, axioms for equality are difficult to control strategically, because they have many irrelevant consequences.

In response to this problem, some theorem-proving researchers have paraphrased their theories to avoid explicit mention of the equality axiom (e.g., Kowalski [79]). Others have adopted special inference rules for dealing with equality. In resolution systems, two equality rules, paramodulation (Wos and Robinson [69]) and E-resolution (Morris [69]) have been found to be effective. Variations of these rules are used in many theorem provers today (e.g., Boyer and Moore [79], Digricoli [83]). By a single application of either of these rules, we can derive conclusions that would require several steps if the properties of equality were represented axiomatically. The proofs are markedly shorter, and the search spaces are even more dramatically compressed because the axioms and intermediate steps are not required. Within their limited domain of application, theorem-proving systems using these rules surpass most human beings in their capabilities.

This is an abbreviated version of a part of the paper "Special Relations in Automated Deduction" that will appear in the Journal of the ACM (1985). Another part of that paper appears in the proceedings of the Twelfth International Colloquium on Automata, Languages, and Programming (ICALP), Nafplion, Greece (July 1985), Springer-Verlag, Lecture Notes in Computer Science (W. Brauer, ed.), Vol. 194, pp. 413–423.

This research was supported in part by the National Science Foundation under grants MCS-82-14523 and MCS-81-05565, by the Defense Advanced Research Projects Agency under contract N00039-84-C-0211, by the United States Air Force Office of Scientific Research under contract AFOSR-81-0014, by the Office of Naval Research under contract N00014-84-C-0706, and by a contract from the International Business Machines Corporation.

Special Relations

The authors became involved in theorem proving because of its application to program synthesis, the derivation of a program to meet a given specification. We have been pursuing a deductive approach to this problem, under which computer programming is regarded as a theorem-proving task. In the proofs required for program synthesis, certain relations assume special importance. Again and again, proofs require us to reason not only about the equality relation, but also about the less-than relation $<$ (over the integers or reals), the subset relation $\subseteq$, the sublist relation $\preceq_{list}$, or the subtree relation $\preceq_{tree}$. To represent the transitivity and other properties of these relations axiomatically leads to many of the same problems that were faced in dealing with equality: the axioms apply almost everywhere, spawning innumerable consequences that swamp the system. Yet we would not want to implement a new inference rule for each of the relations we find important.

Both the paramodulation and the E-resolution rules are based on the *substitutivity* property of equality, that if two elements are equal they may be used interchangeably; i.e., for any sentence $\mathcal{P}\langle x, y\rangle$, the sentence

$$\begin{array}{l} \textit{if } x = y \\ \textit{then if } \mathcal{P}\langle x, y\rangle \textit{ then } \mathcal{P}\langle y, x\rangle \end{array}$$

is valid. Here $\mathcal{P}\langle y, x\rangle$ is the result of replacing in $\mathcal{P}\langle x, y\rangle$ certain (perhaps none) of the occurrences of x with y, and certain (perhaps none) of the occurrences of y with x. (The notations we use here informally will be defined systematically later on. We assume throughout that sentences are quantifier-free.)

We observe that many of the relations we regard as important exhibit substitutivity properties similar to the above property of equality, but under restricted circumstances. For example, over the nonnegative integers, we can show that

$$\begin{array}{l} \textit{if } x < y \\ \textit{then if } a \leq x \cdot b \textit{ then } a \leq y \cdot b \end{array}$$

and, over the lists, we can show that

$$\begin{array}{l} \textit{if } x \preceq_{list} y \\ \textit{then if } u \in x \textit{ then } u \in y. \end{array}$$

Knowing that $x < y$ or that $x \preceq_{list} y$ does not allow us to use x and y interchangeably, but it does allow us to replace certain occurrences of x with y, and vice versa.

Based on such substitutivity properties, we can introduce two deduction rules that generalize the paramodulation and E-resolution rules for equality to an arbitrary relation, under appropriate circumstances. Just as the equality rules enable us to drop the transitivity and substitutivity axioms for equality, the new relation rules enable us to drop the corresponding troublesome axioms for the relations of our theory.

Polarity

For the equality relation, knowing that $x = y$ allows us to replace in a given sentence any occurrence of x with y and any occurrence of y with x, obtaining a sentence that follows from the given one. For an arbitrary binary relation $\prec$, knowing that $x \prec y$ still may allow us to replace certain occurrences of x with y and certain occurrences of y with x. We describe a syntactic procedure that, for a given relation $\prec$, identifies which occurrences of x and y in a given sentence can be replaced, provided we know that $x \prec y$.

More precisely, we identify particular occurrences of subexpressions of a given sentence as being positive $(+)$, negative $(-)$, or both, or neither, with respect to $\prec$. If $x \prec y$, positive occurrences of x can be replaced with y, and negative occurrences of y can be replaced with x. In other words, we can establish the substitutivity property that, for any sentence $\mathcal{P}\langle x^+, y^-\rangle$, the sentence

$$\begin{array}{l} \textit{if } x \prec y \\ \textit{then if } \mathcal{P}\langle x^+, y^-\rangle \textit{ then } \mathcal{P}\langle y^+, x^-\rangle \end{array}$$

is valid (over the theory in question). Here $\mathcal{P}\langle y^+, x^-\rangle$ is the sentence obtained from $\mathcal{P}\langle x^+, y^-\rangle$ by replacing certain positive occurrences of x with y and certain negative occurrences of y with x. With respect to the equality relation, every subexpression is both positive and negative; therefore, if we take $\prec$ to be $=$, this property reduces to the substitutivity of equality.

The new rules, like the equality rules, allow us to perform in a single application inferences that would require many steps in a conventional system. Proofs are shorter and closer to an intuitive argument; the search space is condensed accordingly.

Nonclausal Deduction

The paramodulation and E-resolution rules are formulated for sentences in clausal form (a disjunction of atomic sentences and their negations); on the other hand, the two corresponding rules we introduce apply to free-form sentences, with a full set of logical connectives (cf. Manna and Waldinger [80], Murray [82], Stickel [82]). By adapting such a nonclausal system, we avoid the proliferation of sentences and the disintegration of intuition that accompany the translation to clausal form. Also, it is awkward to express the mathematical induction principle in a clausal system, because we must do induction on sentences that may require more than one clause to express. On the other hand, our rules are also immediately and directly applicable to clausal theorem-proving systems.

This is an abbreviated version of a full paper (Manna and Waldinger [85a]), from which we have omitted some results, all proofs, and many examples.

2. PRELIMINARIES

Before we can define our central notion, that of polarity of a subexpression with respect to a relation, we must introduce some concepts and notations. We will be brief and informal, because we believe that this material will be familiar to most readers.

Expressions

We consider ***terms*** composed (in the usual way) of constants, variables, and function symbols. (We reserve the symbols u, v, w, x, y, z, with optional subscripts, as variables.) The constants are identified with the 0-ary function symbols. We also consider ***propositions*** composed from terms, relation symbols, and the truth symbols (logical constants) ***true*** and ***false***, and ***sentences*** composed from propositions and logical connectives. (We regard logical connectives as relations over the truth values $\{T, F\}$.) Note that we do not include the quantifiers $\forall$ and $\exists$ in our language.

The ***operators*** consist of the function and the relation symbols. The ***expressions*** consist of the terms and the sentences; the ***ground*** expressions are those that contain no variables. The expressions that occur in a given expression are its ***subexpressions***. They are said to be ***proper*** if they are distinct from the entire expression.

Replacement

We introduce the operation of replacing subexpressions of a given expression with other expressions. We actually have two distinct notions of replacement, depending on whether or not every occurrence of the subexpression is to be replaced.

Suppose s, t, and e are expressions, where s and t are either both sentences or both terms. If we write e as $e[s]$, then $e[t]$ denotes the expression obtained by replacing every occurrence of s in $e[s]$ with t; we call this a ***total replacement***. If we write e as $e\langle s\rangle$, then $e\langle t\rangle$ denotes the expression obtained by replacing certain (perhaps none) of the occurrences of s in $e\langle s\rangle$ with t; we call this a ***partial replacement***. We do not require that $e[s]$ or $e\langle s\rangle$ actually contain any occurrences of s; if not, $e[t]$ and $e\langle t\rangle$ are the same as $e[s]$ and $e\langle s\rangle$, respectively. Also, while the result of a total replacement is unique, a partial replacement can produce any of several expressions. For example, if $e[s]$ is $p(s, s, b)$, then $e[t]$ is $p(t, t, b)$. On the other hand, if $e\langle s\rangle$ is $p(s, s, b)$, then $e\langle t\rangle$ could be any of $p(s, s, b)$, $p(t, s, b)$, $p(s, t, b)$, or $p(t, t, b)$. If we want to be more specific about which occurrences are replaced, we must do so in words.

We can extend the definition to allow the replacement of several subexpressions at once. Suppose $s_1, \ldots, s_n, t_1, \ldots, t_n$, and e are expressions, where the s_i are distinct and, for each i, s_i and t_i are either both sentences or both terms. If we write e as $e[s_1, \ldots, s_n]$, then $e[t_1, \ldots, t_n]$ denotes the expression obtained by replacing simultaneously every occurrence of each expression s_i in e with the corresponding expression t_i; we call this a ***multiple total replacement***. If we write e as $e\langle s_1, \ldots, s_n\rangle$, then $e\langle t_1, \ldots, t_n\rangle$ denotes any of the expressions obtained by replacing simultaneously certain (perhaps none) of the occurrences of some of the expressions s_i in e with the corresponding expression t_i; we call this a ***multiple partial replacement***.

Substitutions

We have a special notation for a substitution, indicating the total replacement of variables with terms. A theory of substitutions was developed by Robinson [65], in the paper in which the resolution principle was introduced. A fuller exposition of this theory appears in Manna and Waldinger [81].

For any distinct variables $x_1, x_2, \ldots, x_n$ and any terms $t_1, t_2, \ldots, t_n$, a *substitution*

$$\theta: \ \{x_1 \leftarrow t_1,\ x_2 \leftarrow t_2,\ \ldots,\ x_n \leftarrow t_n\}$$

is a set of replacement pairs $x_i \leftarrow t_i$. The ***empty substitution*** $\{\ \}$ is the set of no replacement pairs. For any substitution θ and expression e, we denote by $e\theta$ the expression obtained by ***applying*** θ ***to*** e, i.e., by simultaneously replacing every occurrence of the variable x_i in e with the expression t_i, for each replacement pair $x_i \leftarrow t_i$ in θ. We also say that $e\theta$ is an ***instance*** of e.

3. RELATIONAL POLARITY

We are now ready to define our key notion, the polarity of (an occurrence of) a subexpression with respect to a given binary relation. We actually define the polarity of a subexpression with respect to two binary relations, $\prec_1$ and $\prec_2$. This notion is to be defined so that, if the subexpression is positive, replacing that subexpression with a larger expression (with respect to $\prec_1$) will make the entire expression larger (with respect to $\prec_2$). Similarly, if the subexpression is negative, replacing that subexpression with a smaller expression (with respect to $\prec_1$) will make the entire expression larger (with respect to $\prec_2$).

Definition (polarity for the arguments of an operator):
Let f be an n-ary operator (i.e., function or relation) f and $\prec_1$ and $\prec_2$ binary relations. Then

- f is ***positive*** over its ith argument with respect to $\prec_1$ and $\prec_2$ if the sentence

$$\begin{array}{l} \textit{if } x \prec_1 y \\ \textit{then } f(z_1, \ldots, z_{i-1}, x, z_{i+1}, \ldots, z_n) \prec_2 f(z_1, \ldots, z_{i-1}, y, z_{i+1}, \ldots, z_n) \end{array}$$

is valid. In other words, replacing x with a larger element y makes $f(z_1, \ldots, z_{i-1}, x, z_{i+1}, \ldots, z_n)$ larger.

- f is to be ***negative*** over its ith argument with respect to $\prec_1$ and $\prec_2$ if the sentence

$$\begin{array}{l} \textit{if } x \prec_1 y \\ \textit{then } f(z_1, \ldots, z_{i-1}, y, z_{i+1}, \ldots, z_n) \prec_2 f(z_1, \ldots, z_{i-1}, x, z_{i+1}, \ldots, z_n) \end{array}$$

is valid. In other words, replacing y with a smaller element x makes $f(z_1, \ldots, z_{i-1}, y, z_{i+1}, \ldots, z_n)$ larger. ┘

When we say that a relation $p(z_1, \ldots, z_n)$ is positive or negative over its ith argument with respect to a single relation $\prec_1$, without mentioning a second relation $\prec_2$, we shall by convention take $\prec_2$ to be the *if-then* connective. Every relation is both positive and negative over each of its arguments with respect to the equality relation $=$. Also, every connective is both positive and negative over all its arguments with respect to $\equiv$. Note that a binary relation $\prec$ is transitive if and only if it is negative with respect to $\prec$ itself over its first argument, and $\prec$ is transitive if and only if it is positive with respect to $\prec$ over its second argument.

When we say that a connective is positive or negative over its ith argument, without mentioning any relations $\prec_1$ and $\prec_2$ at all, we shall by convention take both $\prec_1$ and $\prec_2$ to be the *if-then* connective. Polarity in this sense is close to its ordinary use in logic; for example, the negation connective *not* is negative in its first (and only) argument.

We are now ready to define polarity for the subexpressions of a given expression. The definition is inductive.

Definition (polarity of a subexpression):
Let $\prec_1$ and $\prec_2$ be binary relations. Then an expression s ***is positive*** [or ***negative***] ***in*** s itself with respect to $\prec_1$ and $\prec_2$ if the sentence

$$\textit{if } x \prec_1 y \textit{ then } x \prec_2 y \quad \left[\text{or} \quad \textit{if } x \prec_1 y \textit{ then } x \succ_2 y\right]$$

is valid.

Let f be an n-ary operator and $e_1, e_2, \ldots, e_n$ be expressions. Consider an occurrence of s in one of the expressions e_i. Then the occurrence of s is ***positive*** [or ***negative***] in $f(e_1, e_2, \ldots, e_n)$ with respect to $\prec_1$ and $\prec_2$ if there exists a binary relation $\prec$ such that the polarity of the occurrence of s in e_i with respect to $\prec_1$ and $\prec$ is the same as [is opposite to] the polarity of f over its ith argument with respect to $\prec$ and $\prec_2$. ┘

Note that if s has both polarities in e_i, or if f has both polarities over its ith argument, then s automatically has both polarities in $f(e_1, e_2, \ldots, e_n)$. We may indicate the polarity of a subexpression s by annotating it s^+, s^-, or $s^\pm$. For example, suppose our theory includes the theories of sets and nonnegative integers. The occurrence of s in the sentence $card(s^-) < m$ is negative with respect to the subset relation $\subseteq$ and the *if-then* connective. For note that *card* is positive over its argument with respect to $\subseteq$ and $\leq$ and that $<$ is negative over its first argument with respect to $\leq$ and *if-then*. Therefore, we know that s is positive in $card(s)$ with respect to $\subseteq$ and $\leq$ and that $card(s)$ is negative in $card(s) < m$ with respect to $\leq$ and *if-then*. By the definition, taking $\prec_1$ to be $\subseteq$, $\prec$ to be $\leq$, and $\prec_2$ to be *if-then*, we conclude that s is negative in $card(s) < m$ with respect to $\subseteq$ and *if-then*.

When we say that an occurrence of a subexpression is positive or negative in a sentence with respect to a single relation $\prec_1$, without mentioning a second relation $\prec_2$, we shall again take $\prec_2$ to be the *if-then* connective. When we say that an occurrence of a subsentence is positive or negative in a sentence, without mentioning any relation at all, we shall again take both $\prec_1$ and $\prec_2$ to be *if-then*.

We can now establish the fundamental property of polarity.

Proposition (polarity replacement):
For any binary relation $\prec$ and sentence $\mathcal{P}\langle x^+, y^-\rangle$, the sentence

$$\begin{array}{l} \textit{if } x \prec y \\ \textit{then if } \mathcal{P}\langle x^+, y^-\rangle \textit{ then } \mathcal{P}\langle y^+, x^-\rangle \end{array}$$

is valid. Here $\mathcal{P}\langle y^+, x^-\rangle$ is the result of replacing in $\mathcal{P}\langle x^+, y^-\rangle$ certain positive occurrences of x with y and certain negative occurrences of y with x, where polarity is taken in $\mathcal{P}\langle x^+, y^-\rangle$ with respect to $\prec$. ▟

The proposition allows us to replace occurrences of both x and y in the same sentence and (trivially) admits the possibility that no replacements are made.

Example:
Suppose our theory includes the theories of finite sets and integers. Take $\mathcal{P}\langle x^+, y^-\rangle$ to be the sentence

$$\mathcal{P}\langle x^+, y^-\rangle : \quad a < card(x^+ \sim y^-) \textit{ and } card(y^- \sim x^+) \leq b.$$

Take $\prec$ to be the subset relation $\subseteq$. Note that, with respect to $\subseteq$, both occurrences of x are positive and both occurrences of y are negative in $\mathcal{P}\langle x^+, y^-\rangle$, as indicated by the annotations. Therefore, according to the proposition, the following sentence (among others) is valid:

$$\begin{array}{l} \textit{if } x \subseteq y \\ \textit{then if } a < card(x \sim y) \textit{ and } card(y \sim x) \leq b \\ \qquad \textit{then } a < card(x \sim x) \textit{ and } card(y \sim y) \leq b, \end{array}$$

for which one occurrence of x and one occurrence of y in $\mathcal{P}\langle x^+, y^-\rangle$ has been replaced. ▟

4. NONCLAUSAL DEDUCTION

In this section we present a basic nonclausal deduction system, without any special-relation rules. This system bears some resemblance to those of Murray [82] and Stickel [82]; it is based on the system of Manna and Waldinger [80], but is simplified in several respects.

The Deduced Set

The deduction system we describe operates on a set, called the *deduced* set, of sentences in quantifier-free first-order logic. We attempt to show that a given deduced set is unsatisfiable, i.e., that there is nc interpretation under which all the sentences are true. We do not require that the sentences be in clausal form; indeed, they can use the full set of connectives of propositional logic, including equivalence ($\equiv$) and the conditional (*if-then-else*). If the truth symbol *false* belongs to the deduced set, the set is automatically unsatisfiable, because the sentence *false* is not true under any interpretation.

Because the variables of the sentences in the deduced set are tacitly quantified universally, we can systematically rename them without changing the unsatisfiability of the set; that is, the set is unsatisfiable before the renaming if and only if it is unsatisfiable afterwards. The variables of the sentences in the deduced set may therefore be *standardized apart*; in other words, we may rename the variables of the sentences sc that no two of them have variables in common.

For any sentence $\mathcal{F}$ in the deduced set and any substitution θ, we may add to the set the ***instance*** $\mathcal{F}\theta$ of $\mathcal{F}$, without changing the unsatisfiability of the set. In particular, if the deduced set is unsatisfiable after the addition of the new sentence, it was also unsatisfiable before. Note that in adding the new sentence $\mathcal{F}\theta$, we do not remove the original sentence $\mathcal{F}$.

The Deductive Process

In the deductive system we apply ***deduction rules***, which add new sentences to the deduced set without changing its unsatisfiability. Deduction rules are expressed as follows:

$$\mathcal{F}_1,\ \mathcal{F}_2,\ \ldots,\ \mathcal{F}_m \ \Rightarrow\ \mathcal{F}.$$

This means that, if the ***given*** sentences $\mathcal{F}_1, \mathcal{F}_2, \ldots, \mathcal{F}_m$ belong to the deduced set, the ***conclusion*** $\mathcal{F}$ may be added. Such a rule is said to be ***sound*** if the given sentences $\mathcal{F}_1, \mathcal{F}_2, \ldots, \mathcal{F}_m$ imply the sentence $\mathcal{F}$. If a deductive rule is sound, its application will preserve the unsatisfiability of the deduced set.

The deductive process terminates successfully if we introduce the truth symbol *false* into the deduced set. Because deduction rules preserve unsatisfiability, and because a set of sentences containing *false* is automatically unsatisfiable, this will imply that the original deduced set was also unsatisfiable.

In the basic systems, the only deduction rule is:

- The ***resolution*** rule, which performs a case analysis on the truth of matching subsentences.

This rule is described in this section. In later sections, we augment the basic system with a new class of rules:

- The ***matching*** rule, which introduces new conditions to be proved that enable subexpressions to be matched.

Resolution Rule

The resolution rule applies to two sentences of our set, and performs a case analysis on the truth of a common subsentence. Instances of the sentences can be formed, if necessary, to create a common subsentence; however, we present here only the ***ground version*** of the rule, which does not form instances of these sentences.

Rule (***resolution, ground version***):
For any ground sentences $\mathcal{P}$, $\mathcal{F}[\mathcal{P}]$, and $\mathcal{G}[\mathcal{P}]$, we have

$$\mathcal{F}[\mathcal{P}],\ \mathcal{G}[\mathcal{P}] \ \Rightarrow\ (\mathcal{F}[\mathit{false}] \ \mathit{or}\ \mathcal{G}[\mathit{true}]). \quad ⌟$$

In other words, if $\mathcal{F}[\mathcal{P}]$ and $\mathcal{G}[\mathcal{P}]$ are sentences in our deduced set with a common subsentence $\mathcal{P}$, we can add to the set the sentence $(\mathcal{F}[\mathit{false}]\ \mathit{or}\ \mathcal{G}[\mathit{true}])$ obtained by replacing every occurrence of $\mathcal{P}$ in $\mathcal{F}[\mathcal{P}]$ with *false*, replacing every occurrence of $\mathcal{P}$ in $\mathcal{G}[\mathcal{P}]$ with ***true***, and taking the disjunction of the results. We shall assume that $\mathcal{F}[\mathcal{P}]$ and $\mathcal{G}[\mathcal{P}]$ have at least one occurrence each of the subsentence $\mathcal{P}$. We do not require that $\mathcal{F}[\mathcal{P}]$ and $\mathcal{G}[\mathcal{P}]$ be distinct sentences. Because the resolution rule introduces new occurrences of the truth symbols ***true*** and *false*, it is always possible to simplify the resulting sentence immediately afterwards. These subsequent simplifications will be regarded as part of the resolution rule itself.

Murray's [82] ***polarity strategy*** allows us to consider only those applications of the resolution rule under which at least one occurrence of $\mathcal{P}$ is positive (or of no polarity) in $\mathcal{F}[\mathcal{P}]$ and at least one occurrence of $\mathcal{P}$ is negative (or of no polarity) in $\mathcal{G}[\mathcal{P}]$. In other words, not all the subsentences that are replaced with *false* are negative and not all the subsentences that are replaced with ***true*** are positive. This strategy blocks many useless applications of the rule and rarely interferes with a reasonable step. The intuitive rationale for the polarity strategy is that it is our goal to deduce the sentence *false*, which is falser than any other sentence. By replacing positive sentences with *false* and negative sentences with ***true***, we are moving in the right direction, making the entire sentence falser.

The general version of the rule, which we omit, allows us to instantiate the variables of the given sentences as necessary to create common subsentences.

The resolution rule presented here is an extension of the rule of Robinson [65] to the nonclausal case. Nonclausal resolution was developed independently by Manna and Waldinger [80] and Murray [82]. The resolution rule (with simplification) has been shown by Murray to provide a complete system for first-order logic. An implementation of a nonclausal resolution theorem prover by Stickel [82] employs a connection graph strategy.

We now begin to extend our nonclausal deduction system to give special treatment to a binary relation $\prec$. The new rule of the extension allows us to build into the system instances of the ***polarity replacement*** proposition, just as the E-resolution rule allows us to build in instances of the substitutivity of equality.

The resolution rule draws a conclusion when one subexpression in our proof unifies with another. The relation-matching rule allows this rule to apply even if the two expressions fail to unify, provided that certain conditions can be introduced into the conclusion.

5. RELATION MATCHING: GROUND VERSION

The ground version of the rule is as follows:

Rule (***resolution with relation matching, ground version***):
For any binary relation $\prec$, ground expressions s and t, and ground sentences $\mathcal{P}\langle s^+, t^+, s^-, t^-\rangle$, $\mathcal{F}[\mathcal{P}\langle s^+, s^+, t^-, t^-\rangle]$, and $\mathcal{G}[\mathcal{P}\langle t^+, t^+, s^-, s^-\rangle]$ we have

$$\frac{\begin{array}{l}\mathcal{F}[\mathcal{P}\langle s^+, s^+, t^-, t^-\rangle]\\ \mathcal{G}[\mathcal{P}\langle t^+, t^+, s^-, s^-\rangle]\end{array}}{\begin{array}{l}\textit{if } s \preceq t\\ \textit{then } \mathcal{F}[\textit{false}] \textit{ or } \mathcal{G}[\textit{true}]\end{array}}$$

Here

- $\mathcal{P}\langle s^+, t^+, s^-, t^-\rangle$ is an arbitrary sentence, called the ***intermediate*** sentence, which may have positive and negative occurrences of s and t; polarity is taken with respect to $\prec$.
- The sentence $\mathcal{F}$ may have several distinct subsentences $\mathcal{P}\langle s^+, s^+, t^-, t^-\rangle$, each obtained from the intermediate sentence $\mathcal{P}\langle s^+, t^+, s^-, t^-\rangle$ by replacing certain of the positive occurrences of t with s and certain of the negative occurrences of s with t.
- Similarly, $\mathcal{G}$ may have several distinct subsentences $\mathcal{P}\langle t^+, t^+, s^-, s^-\rangle$, each obtained from the intermediate sentence by replacing certain of the positive occurrences of s with t and certain of the negative occurrences of t with s. ◼

For a particular relation $\prec$, we shall refer to the above as the resolution rule with $\prec$-matching.

Note that if all the subsentences $\mathcal{P}\langle s^+, s^+, t^-, t^-\rangle$ and $\mathcal{P}\langle t^+, t^+, s^-, s^-\rangle$ were identical, we could apply the original resolution rule, obtaining the conclusion $(\mathcal{F}[\textit{false}] \textit{ or } \mathcal{G}[\textit{true}])$. The augmented rule allows us to derive the same conclusion even if the subsentences $\mathcal{P}$ do not match exactly, provided that the mismatches occur between terms s and t of restricted polarity and that the condition $s \preceq t$ is introduced.

The polarity strategy allows us to apply the rule only if an occurrence of one of the sentences $\mathcal{P}\langle s^+, s^+, t^-$ is positive or of no polarity in $\mathcal{F}$ and if an occurrence of one of the sentences $\mathcal{P}\langle t^+, t^+, s^-, s^-\rangle$ is negative or of no polarity in $\mathcal{G}$.

Note that the intermediate sentence $\mathcal{P}\langle s^+, t^+, s^-, t^-\rangle$ does not necessarily appear in either of the sentences of the deduced set and that the rule does not stipulate how to find such a sentence. We shall discuss the choice of the intermediate sentence in the subsection **Selection of Application Parameters**.

Example:
In the theory of lists, suppose that our deduced set includes the sentences

$$\mathcal{F}: \quad p(\ell) \textit{ or } \boxed{c \in (\textit{tail}(\ell))^+}^{+}$$

and

$$\mathcal{G}: \quad \textit{if } \boxed{c \in \ell^+}^{-} \textit{ then } q(\ell).$$

The two boxed subsentences are not identical. Let us take our intermediate sentence to be one of them, $\mathcal{P} : c \in \textit{tail}(\ell)$. The subterm $s^+ : \textit{tail}(\ell)$ is positive in $c \in \textit{tail}(\ell)$ with respect to the proper-sublist relation $\prec_{list}$. The other boxed subsentence $c \in \ell$ can be obtained by replacing this subterm with $t^+ : \ell$. Therefore we can apply the resolution rule with $\prec_{list}$-matching to obtain

$$\begin{array}{l} \textit{if } tail(\ell) \preceq_{list} \ell \\ \textit{then } p(\ell) \textit{ or } \textit{false} \\ \qquad \textit{or} \\ \qquad \textit{if } \textit{true} \textit{ then } q(\ell), \end{array}$$

which reduces under transformation to

$$\begin{array}{l} \textit{if } tail(\ell) \preceq_{list} \ell \\ \textit{then } p(\ell) \textit{ or } q(\ell). \end{array}$$ ■

We shall give some more complex examples of the application of the rule after we establish its soundness.

Justification (resolution with relation matching, ground version):
Note that (by the invertibility of partial replacement) the intermediate sentence $\mathcal{P}\langle s^+, t^+, s^-, t^-\rangle$ can be obtained from any of the subsentences $\mathcal{P}\langle s^+, s^+, t^-, t^-\rangle$ of $\mathcal{F}$ by replacing certain positive occurrences of s with t and certain negative occurrences of t with s, where polarity is taken in $\mathcal{P}$ with respect to $\prec$. Therefore (by the ***polarity replacement*** proposition) each of the sentences

$$(\dagger) \qquad \begin{array}{l} \textit{if } s \preceq t \\ \textit{then if } \mathcal{P}\langle s^+, s^+, t^-, t^-\rangle \\ \qquad \textit{then } \mathcal{P}\langle s^+, t^+, s^-, t^-\rangle \end{array}$$

is valid.

Also any of the subsentences $\mathcal{P}\langle t^+, t^+, s^-, s^-\rangle$ of $\mathcal{G}$ can be obtained from the intermediate sentence $\mathcal{P}\langle s^+, t^+, s^-, t^-\rangle$ by replacing certain positive occurrences of s with t and certain negative occurrences of t with s. Therefore (by the ***polarity replacement*** proposition again) each of the sentences

$$(\ddagger) \qquad \begin{array}{l} \textit{if } s \preceq t \\ \textit{then if } \mathcal{P}\langle s^+, t^+, s^-, t^-\rangle \\ \qquad \textit{then } \mathcal{P}\langle t^+, t^+, s^-, s^-\rangle \end{array}$$

is valid.

Suppose that the sentences $\mathcal{F}[\mathcal{P}\langle s^+, s^+, t^-, t^-\rangle]$ and $\mathcal{G}[\mathcal{P}\langle t^+, t^+, s^-, s^-\rangle]$ are true and that $s \preceq t$. We would like to show that then $(\mathcal{F}[\textit{false}] \textit{ or } \mathcal{G}[\textit{true}])$ is true. The proof distinguishes between two cases, depending on whether the intermediate sentence $\mathcal{P}\langle s^+, t^+, s^-, t^-\rangle$ is false or true. We show that in each case one of the two disjuncts, $\mathcal{F}[\textit{false}]$ or $\mathcal{G}[\textit{true}]$, is true.

Case: $\mathcal{P}\langle s^+, t^+, s^-, t^-\rangle$ is false.

Then by our previous conclusion (†), because $s \preceq t$, we know each of the subsentences $\mathcal{P}\langle s^+, s^+, t^-, t^-\rangle$ of $\mathcal{F}$ is false. Because $\mathcal{F}[\mathcal{P}\langle s^+, s^+, t^-, t^-\rangle]$ is true and because the subsentences $\mathcal{P}\langle s^+, s^+, t^-, t^-\rangle$ and *false* all have the same truth value, we know (by the ***value*** property) that the first disjunct, $\mathcal{F}[\textit{false}]$, is true.

Case: $\mathcal{P}\langle s^+, t^+, s^-, t^-\rangle$ is true.

Then by our previous conclusion (‡), because $s \preceq t$, we know each of the sentences $\mathcal{P}\langle t^+, t^+, s^-, s^-\rangle$ is true. Because $\mathcal{G}[\mathcal{P}\langle t^+, t^+, s^-, s^-\rangle]$ is true and because $\mathcal{P}\langle t^+, t^+, s^-, s^-\rangle$ and ***true*** have the same truth value, we know (by the ***value*** property again) that the second disjunct, $\mathcal{G}[\textit{true}]$, is true. ■

The resolution rule with relation matching must be regulated with strict heuristic controls; if the controls are too permissive, any two subsentences may be matched.

The following example is a bit contrived but illustrates some of the power of the rule.

Example:
In the theory of sets, suppose our deduced set includes the two sentences

$$\mathcal{F}: \quad \begin{array}{l} \boxed{e \in ((s^+ \sim a) \cup (b \sim t^-) \cup (t^+ \sim c) \cup (d \sim t^-))}^{+} \\ \quad \textit{or} \\ \boxed{e \in ((s^+ \sim a) \cup (b \sim s^-) \cup (s^+ \sim c) \cup (d \sim t^-))}^{+} \end{array}$$

and

$$\mathcal{G}: \quad not \left[\begin{array}{l} \boxed{e \in \big((t^+ \sim a) \cup (b \sim s^-) \cup (t^+ \sim c) \cup (d \sim t^-)\big)}^- \\ and \\ \boxed{e \in \big((s^+ \sim a) \cup (b \sim s^-) \cup (t^+ \sim c) \cup (d \sim s^-)\big)}^- \end{array} \right].$$

Let us take our intermediate sentence to be

$$\mathcal{P}: \quad e \in \big((s^+ \sim a) \cup (b \sim s^-) \cup (t^+ \sim c) \cup (d \sim t^-)\big).$$

The occurrences of s and t have been annotated with their polarities in $\mathcal{P}$ with respect to the proper-subset relation $\subset$. Note that each of the boxed sentences in $\mathcal{F}$ may be obtained from $\mathcal{P}$ by replacing certain of the positive occurrences of t with s and certain of the negative occurrences of s with t. Also, each of the boxed subsentences of $\mathcal{G}$ may be obtained from $\mathcal{P}$ by replacing certain of the positive occurrences of s with t and certain of the negative occurrences of t with s. Therefore we can apply the resolution rule with $\subset$-matching to obtain

if $s \subseteq t$
then false or false
or
not (true and true),

which reduces under transformation to the sentence

not $(s \subseteq t)$. ∎

Note that this conclusion, obtained by a single application of the rule, is not immediately evident to the human reader.

Special Case: Resolution with Equality Matching

In the case in which the relation $\prec$ is taken to be the equality relation $=$, the resolution rule with relation matching reduces to a nonclausal variant of the E-resolution rule. It may be expressed (in the ground version) as follows:

Rule (resolution with equality matching):
For any terms s and t and sentences $\mathcal{P}\langle s,t,s,t\rangle$, $\mathcal{F}[\mathcal{P}\langle s,s,t,t,\rangle]$, and $\mathcal{G}[\mathcal{P}\langle t,t,s,s\rangle]$, we have

$$\begin{array}{l} \mathcal{F}[\mathcal{P}\langle s,s,t,t\rangle] \\ \mathcal{G}[\mathcal{P}\langle t,t,s,s\rangle] \\ \hline \textit{if } s = t \\ \textit{then } \mathcal{F}[\textit{false}] \textit{ or } \mathcal{G}[\textit{true}]. \end{array}$$ ∎

Here $\mathcal{P}\langle s,s,t,t\rangle$ and $\mathcal{P}\langle t,t,s,s\rangle$ are obtained from $\mathcal{P}\langle s,t,s,t\rangle$ by replacing certain occurrences of s with t and certain occurrences of t with s. In other words, all the subsentences $\mathcal{P}\langle s,s,t,t\rangle$ and $\mathcal{P}\langle t,t,s,s\rangle$ are identical except that one may have occurrences of s where another has occurrences of t. We do not need to restrict the polarities, because every subterm of a sentence is both positive and negative with respect to the equality relation.

Multiple Mismatched Subsentences

The resolution rule with relation matching can be extended to allow several corresponding pairs of subexpressions $s_1, t_1, s_2, t_2, \ldots$ and s_n, t_n rather than a single pair s, t, and several binary relations $\prec_1, \prec_2, \ldots,$ and $\prec_n$ rather than a single binary relation $\prec$. To write the extended rule succinctly, we abbreviate $s_1, s_2, \ldots, s_n$ as $\hat{s}$, $t_1, t_2, \ldots, t_n$ as $\hat{t}$, $\prec_1, \prec_2, \ldots,$ and $\prec_n$ as $\hat{\prec}$, and

$$s_1 \preceq_1 t_1 \textit{ and } s_2 \preceq_2 t_2 \textit{ and } \ldots \textit{ and } s_n \preceq_n t_n \quad \text{as} \quad \hat{s} \mathrel{\hat{\preceq}} \hat{t}.$$

Then for any binary relations $\hat{\prec}$, expressions $\hat{s}$ and $\hat{t}$, and sentences $\mathcal{P}\langle \hat{s}^+, \hat{t}^+, \hat{s}^-, \hat{t}^-\rangle$, $\mathcal{F}[\mathcal{P}\langle \hat{s}^+, \hat{s}^+, \hat{t}^-, \hat{t}^-\rangle]$, and $\mathcal{G}[\mathcal{P}\langle \hat{t}^+, \hat{t}^+, \hat{s}^-, \hat{s}^-\rangle]$, we have

$$\begin{array}{l} \mathcal{F}[\mathcal{P}\langle \hat{s}^+, \hat{s}^+, \hat{t}^-, \hat{t}^-\rangle] \\ \mathcal{G}[\mathcal{P}\langle \hat{t}^+, \hat{t}^+, \hat{s}^-, \hat{s}^-\rangle] \\ \hline \textit{if } \hat{s} \mathrel{\hat{\preceq}} \hat{t} \\ \textit{then } \mathcal{F}[\textit{false}] \textit{ or } \mathcal{G}[\textit{true}]. \end{array}$$

The extended rule is easily justified, given the soundness of the original rule.

6. RELATION MATCHING: GENERAL VERSION

The general version of the rule allows us to instantiate the variables of the given sentences as necessary and then to apply the ground version. The precise statement, which we omit, is analogous to the precise statement of the general version of the resolution rule. We illustrate the application of the general rule with an example.

Example:
Suppose our deduced set contains the sentences

$$\mathcal{F}: \quad \begin{array}{l} \textit{if } q(u) \\ \textit{then } \boxed{p(u^+, u^+)}^{+} \end{array}$$

and

$$\mathcal{G}: \quad \textit{not}\boxed{p(\ell^+, f(\ell)^+)}^{-}.$$

Here the annotations of the subterms within the boxed subsentences indicate their polarity in these subsentences with respect to a binary relation $\prec$.

The substitution $\theta : \{u \leftarrow \ell\}$ fails to unify the boxed subsentences of $\mathcal{F}$ and $\mathcal{G}$; the results of applying θ to these subsentences are the sentences $p(\ell^+, \ell^+)$ and $p(\ell^+, f(\ell)^+)$, respectively. Note that the mismatched occurrences of ℓ and $f(\ell)$ are positive in these sentences with respect to $\prec$.

To apply the ground version of the rule to $\mathcal{F}\theta$ and $\mathcal{G}\theta$, let us take the intermediate sentence to be $p(\ell^+, \ell^+)$. We obtain

$$\begin{array}{l} \textit{if } \ell \preceq f(\ell) \\ \textit{then } \begin{bmatrix} \textit{if } q(\ell) \\ \textit{then false} \end{bmatrix} \quad \textit{or} \ (\textit{not true}), \end{array}$$

which reduces under *true-false* transformation to

$$\begin{array}{l} \textit{if } \ell \preceq f(\ell) \\ \textit{then not } q(\ell). \end{array}$$ ┘

7. SELECTION OF APPLICATION PARAMETERS

For each application of the resolution rule with relation matching, we must select the *application parameters*, i.e., the substitution θ, the intermediate sentence $\mathcal{P}$, and the subexpressions s and t. In fact, a satisfactory choice of application parameters is not straightforward: it depends on what other sentences are in the deductive set. Some considerations influencing the decision are illustrated in the next few sections.

Choice of Substitution

The substitution θ and the intermediate sentence $\mathcal{P}$ for applying the rule are not necessarily unique.

In the example above, consider again the boxed subsentences $p(u^+, u^+)$ and $p(\ell^+, f(\ell)^+)$ of $\mathcal{F}$ and $\mathcal{G}$. Instead of the substitution $\theta : \{u \leftarrow \ell\}$, consider the substitution $\theta' : \{u \leftarrow f(\ell)\}$. This substitution also fails to unify the boxed subsentences; the results of applying θ' to the boxed subsentences are the sentences $p(f(\ell)^+, f(\ell)^+)$ and $p(\ell^+, f(\ell)^+)$, respectively. Note that the mismatched occurrences of $f(\ell)$ and ℓ are positive in these sentences with respect to $\prec$.

To apply the ground version of the rule to $\mathcal{F}\theta'$ and $\mathcal{G}\theta'$, let us take the intermediate sentence to be $p(f(\ell)^+, f(\ell)^+)$. We obtain

$$\begin{array}{l} \textit{if } f(\ell) \preceq \ell \\ \textit{then } \begin{bmatrix} \textit{if } q(\ell) \\ \textit{then false} \end{bmatrix} \quad \textit{or} \ (\textit{not true}), \end{array}$$

which reduces under *true-false* transformation to

$$\textit{if } f(\ell) \preceq \ell \quad \textit{then not } q(\ell).$$

This is not equivalent to the sentence we obtained by applying the rule with the substitution θ,

$$\textit{if } \ell \preceq f(\ell) \quad \textit{then not } q(\ell).$$

In other words, we must consider both ways of applying the rule.

To Unify or Not to Unify

In previous examples, we have applied the resolution rule with relation matching only when it is illegal to apply the ordinary resolution rule because the matched subsentences fail to unify. In some cases, however, we must use relation matching to obtain a refutation even though the matched subsentences do unify and the resolution rule could be applied.

For example, suppose our deduced set consists of the sentences

1. $\boxed{p(x^{+})}$ *or* $q(x^{+})$
2. *not* $\boxed{p(a^{+})}^{-}$
3. *not* $\boxed{q(b^{+})}^{-}$
4. $c \preceq a$
5. $c \preceq b$,

where x is positive in the boxed subsentence $p(x)$ and in the subsentence $q(x)$ with respect to the relation $\prec$, as indicated by its annotation.

It is legal to apply the ordinary resolution rule to the first two sentences, taking the unifier to be $\{x \leftarrow a\}$, to deduce (after transformation)

$$q(a).$$

However, this sentence is of no use in a refutation.

If instead we apply the resolution rule with $\prec$-matching to the same boxed subsentences, taking the unifier to be the empty substitution $\{\ \}$, we obtain (after transformation)

6. *if* $x \preceq a$ *then* $\boxed{q(x^{+})}^{+}$.

We can then apply the resolution rule to sentences 6 and 3, taking the unifier to be the empty substitution $\{\ \}$, to obtain (after transformation)

7. *if* $x \preceq b$ *then not* $(x \preceq a)$.

We finally obtain a refutation by applying the resolution rule to this sentence and the last two sentences in turn; the unifier is $\{x \leftarrow c\}$.

In applying the ordinary resolution rule, we committed x to be a; this turned out to be a mistake. In applying the resolution rule with $\prec$-matching instead, we left x free to be any element such that $x \preceq a$; in particular, we could then take x to be c.

Choice of Mismatched Subexpressions

In the examples of resolution with relation matching we have seen, we have always taken the mismatched subexpressions s and t to be as small as possible. Sometimes this choice costs us a proof.

For instance, suppose our deduced set consists of the sentences

1. $\boxed{p(f(a))}^{+}$
2. *not* $\boxed{p(f(b))}^{-}$
3. $f(a) = f(b)$.

If we apply the resolution rule with equality matching to the first two sentences, taking s to be a and t to be b, we obtain

$$\textit{if } a = b \quad \textit{then false or not true},$$

which reduces under transformation to

$$\textit{not } (a = b).$$

This sentence is of no use in a refutation.

On the other hand, if instead we apply the same rule taking s to be $f(a)$ and t to be $f(b)$, we obtain

$$\textit{if } f(a) = f(b) \quad \textit{then false or not true},$$

which reduces under transformation to

$$\textit{not } \big(f(a) = f(b)\big).$$

A refutation can be obtained immediately by applying the resolution rule to the third sentence and this one.

In the preceding examples, we have seen that in applying the resolution rule with relation matching, the choice of appropriate application parameters, i.e., the substitution θ, the intermediate sentence $\mathcal{P}$, and the mismatched subexpressions s and t, are not unique and depend on the other sentences in the deduced set. Digricoli [83] provides an algorithm to generate all legal sets of application parameters. This algorithm is phrased in terms of his variant of the E-resolution rule but extends readily to the general, nonclausal case. Digricoli also suggests a heuristic ***viability criterion*** for selecting a single appropriate set of application parameters; this criterion appears to extend to the general case as well.

Another rule, the ***relation replacement*** rule, extends to an arbitrary relation the paramodulation rule for equality. It is described in the full version of this paper (Manna and Waldinger [85a]).

8. DISCUSSION

The theorem-proving system we have presented has been motivated by our work in program synthesis, and the best examples we have of its use are in this domain. We have used the system to write detailed derivations for programs over the integers and real numbers, the lists, the sets, and other structures. These derivations are concise and easy to follow: they reflect intuitive derivations of the same programs. A paper by Traugott [85] describes the application of this system to the derivation of several sorting programs. A paper by Manna and Waldinger [85b] describes the derivation of several binary-search programs. Our earlier informal derivation of the unification algorithm (Manna and Waldinger [81]) can be expressed formally in this system.

An interactive implementation of the basic nonclausal theorem-proving system was completed by Malachi and has been extended by Bronstein to include some of the relation rules. An entirely automatic implementation is being contemplated. The relation rules will also be valuable for proving purely mathematical theorems. For this purpose they may be incorporated into clausal as well as nonclausal theorem-proving systems.

Theorem provers have exhibited superhuman abilities in limited subject domains, but seem least competent in areas in which human intuition is best developed. One reason for this is that an axiomatic formalization obscures the simplicity of the subject area; facts that a person would consider too obvious to require saying in an intuitive argument must be stated explicitly and dealt with in the corresponding formal proof, lengthening the proof and cluttering the search space. A person who is easily able to conduct the argument informally may well be unable to understand the formal proof, let alone to produce it.

Our work in special relations is part of a continuing effort to make formal theorem proving resemble intuitive reasoning. In the kind of system we envision, proofs are shorter, the search space is compressed, and heuristics based on human intuition become applicable.

Acknowledgements: The authors would like to thank Alex Bronstein, Neil Murray, David Plaisted, Mark Stickel, and Jon Traugott for their suggestions and careful reading. Jon Traugott suggested extending the notion of polarity from one relation to two, making the rules more powerful and the exposition simpler. The manuscript was prepared by Evelyn Eldridge-Diaz with the TEX typesetting system.

7. REFERENCES

Anderson [70]
R. Anderson, Completeness results for E-resolution, *AFIPS Spring Joint Computer Conference*, 1970, pp. 652–656.

Boyer and Moore [79]
R. S. Boyer and J S. Moore, *A Computational Logic*, Academic Press, New York, N.Y., 1979.

Brand [75]
D. Brand, Proving theorems with the modification method, *SIAM Journal of Computing*, Vol. 4, No. 2, 1975, pp. 412–430.

Digricoli [83]
V. Digricoli, *Resolution By Unification and Equality*, Ph.D. thesis, New York University, New York, N.Y., 1983.

Kowalski [79]
R. Kowalski, *Logic for Problem Solving*, North Holland, New York, N.Y., 1979.

Manna and Waldinger [80]
Z. Manna and R. Waldinger, A deductive approach to program synthesis, *ACM Transactions on Programming Languages and Systems*, Vol. 2, No. 1, January 1980, pp. 90–121.

Manna and Waldinger [81]
Z. Manna and R. Waldinger, Deductive synthesis of the unification algorithm, *Science of Computer Programming*, Vol. 1, 1981, pp. 5–48.

Manna and Waldinger [82]
Z. Manna and R. Waldinger, Special relations in program-synthetic deduction, Technical Report, Computer Science Department, Stanford University, Stanford, Calif., March 1982.

Manna and Waldinger [85a]
Z. Manna and R. Waldinger, Special relations in automated deduction, Journal of the ACM (to appear).

Manna and Waldinger [85b]
Z. Manna and R. Waldinger, Origin of the binary search paradigm, in the Proceedings of IJCAI-85, Los Angeles, August 1985.

Morris [69]
J. B. Morris, E-resolution: extension of resolution to include the equality relation, *International Joint Conference on Artificial Intelligence*, Washington, D.C., May 1969, pp. 287–294.

Murray [82]
N. V. Murray, Completely nonclausal theorem proving, *Artificial Intelligence*, Vol. 18, No. 1, 1982, pp. 67–85.

Robinson [65]
J. A. Robinson, A machine-oriented logic based on the resolution principle, *Journal of the ACM*, Vol. 12, No. 1, January 1965, pp. 23–41.

Robinson [79]
J. A. Robinson, *Logic: Form and Function*, North-Holland, New York, N.Y., 1979.

Stickel [82]
M. E. Stickel, A nonclausal connection-graph resolution theorem-proving program. *National Conference on AI*, Pittsburgh, Pa., 1982, pp. 229–233.

Traugott [85]
J. Traugott, Deductive synthesis of sorting algorithms, Technical Report, Computer Science Department, Stanford University, Stanford, Calif. (forthcoming).

Wos and Robinson [69]
L. Wos and G. Robinson, Paramodulation and theorem proving in first order theories with equality, in *Machine Intelligence 4* (B. Meltzer and D. Michie, editors) American Elsevier, New York, N.Y., 1969, pp. 135–150.

RECURSIVELY DEFINED DOMAINS AND THEIR INDUCTION PRINCIPLES

Finn V. Jensen
Aalborg University Center
Strandvejen 19
Aalborg, Denmark.

Kim G. Larsen
University of Edinburgh
Department of Computer Science
Edinburgh, Scotland.

ABSTRACT: Recursion is one of the main tools in denotational semantics. This paper deals with the problem of establishing induction principles for domains defined by simultaneous recursion. We are particularly interested in induction principles supporting verification of properties of elements from (any) one of the domains defined by the simultaneous recursion. We offer two such principles, with the second principle being especially well-suited for implementation in a machine system such as LCF [5].

1. MOTIVATION

Recursion is a main tool in many areas of computer science and mathematics. Strongly connected to recursion is induction. In cases where an object is defined by a simple recursion equation, an analysis of this equation will provide a method for proving properties of the object by induction. In formalized systems this analysis can be carried out automatically and hence implemented into a computer system.

However, in the case of simulataneous recursion the situation is much more complicated. Suppose that the objects O_1 and O_2 are defined by two simultaneous recursion equations. Let the task be to prove that O_1 has property P_1. In order to give an induction proof an auxiliary property P_2 for the object O_2 will be needed. The problem is whether there is an automatic way of establishing P_2 by means of the recursion equations and P_1. This problem has so far not been dealt with successfully in any system.

In the present paper we deal with the above problem for systems of recursive *domain equations*. Recursive domain equations are heavily used in denotational semantics for specifying syntactical as well as semantical domains. A recursively defined domain E_1, is a domain, which is defined by use of either a single equation:

$$E_1 \approx T(E_1)$$

or a set of simultaneous equations:

$$E_1 \approx T_1(E_1,\ldots,E_n)$$
$$\vdots$$
$$E_n \approx T_n(E_1,\ldots,E_n)$$

where T, $T_1,\ldots,T_n$ are domain operations.

When proving properties of specific semantics one is often only really interested in properties of elements from one of the specified domains, E_1 say. We are therefore especially interested in induction principles that will support verification of properties of the elements from any one of the domains $E_1,\ldots,E_n$ defined. We will refer to such principles as one-domain structural induction principles.

We are interested in establishing as powerful induction principles as possible. We will call an inductioin principle which characterizes a structure up to isomorphism a categorical principle. Categorical principles are the most powerful induction principles we can hope for, and they can be regarded as cornerstones of a second-order axiomatization of the least solution to the domain equations (socalled initial solution).

Another criterion for the goodness of our induction principles is how well-suited they are for being implemented in a machine system such as LCF [5]. R. Milner [7] has succeeded in doing so for a single equation, when the functor T is a disjoint summation of possibly lifted products. F. V. Jensen [1, 2] has implemented induction principles for domains specified by a single equation, where the functor is composed freely by sum, product, lifting, constant and exponentiation. Even though we won't carry out any such implementation in this paper, all the different choices we make will be highly influenced by this ultimate goal.

After the preliminary definitions and theorems in section 2 we adress the main problem which is the following: let $E_1,..,E_n$ be defined by a set of simultaneous recursive equations, let P_1 be a property of elements from E_1 and let the task be to prove (by induction) that all elements from E_1 have property P_1. Then we need a construction which provides a set $P_2,..,P_n$ of auxiliary properties of elements from $E_2,..,E_n$, such that the goal for the induction is to prove that all elements from E_i have property P_i (i=1...n). In sections 3 and 4 we present two different methods constructing these auxiliary properties. However, both methods do in the general setting construct auxiliary properties that are secondorder (i.e. involving quantifications over properties). This is unsatisfactory from a machine implementation point of view. In sections 5, 6 and 7 we transform one of the methods (Method B) such that the auxiliary properties for a large class of equations becomes first order properties. In section 8 a larger example from Denotational Semantics is given.

2. PRELIMINARY DEFINITIONS AND THEOREMS

We are interested in solving simultaneous recursive equations of the form:

$$\begin{aligned} E_1 &\approx T_1(E_1,..,E_n) \\ &\vdots \\ E_n &\approx T_n(E_1,..,E_n) \end{aligned}$$

where $E_1,..,E_n$ are domains and $T_1,..,T_n$ are domain operators. Using vector notation we can rewrite the simultaneous equation above as:

$$\mathbf{E} \approx \mathbf{T}(\mathbf{E})$$

where $\mathbf{E}=(E_1,..,E_n)$ and $\mathbf{T}=(T_1,..,T_n):\mathbf{E} \mapsto (T_1(\mathbf{E}),..,T_n(\mathbf{E}))$. Our way of solving this recursive equation is to view the category of domains as a domain itself and by restricting the functors $T_1,..,T_n$ to be in some way continuous functions on the domain of domains. By doing so we should be able to use the standard fixpoint techniques for continuous functions on domains to solve the equation. For a full treatment of the following we refer to [9].

Definition 2.1: CPO is the category of complete partial orders (called cpo's or domains) with strict continuous functions as morphisms.

In order to view CPO as a domain itself we introduce an ordering $\leq$ between domains.

Definition 2.2: Let D and E be cpo's. We write $D \leq^i_j E$ if and only if i and j are continuous functions $i:D \to E$ and $j:E \to D$ such that $j.i = id_D$ and $i.j \sqsubseteq id_E$. We call j and i a projection pair (from D to E), i an embedding and j an projection. We write $D \leq E$ iff there exists i and j such that $D \leq^i_j E$.

We now see what corresponds to increasing chains and lubs of increasing chains:

Definition 2.3: A (direct) <u>ω-chain</u> is a diagram $\Delta = \langle D_m, f_m \rangle$, where $f_m : D_m \leq D_{m+1}$. An <u>upper bound</u> of a chain $\Delta = \langle D_m, f_m \rangle$ is a <u>cone</u> $\rho : \Delta \to D$, i.e. a cpo D together with a sequence $\rho = \langle \rho_n \rangle_n$ of embeddings $\rho_n : D_n \leq D$ such that all triangles commute, i.e. for all m: $\rho_{m+1} \circ f_m = \rho_m$. As <u>least upper bound</u> of a chain $\Delta = \langle D_m, f_m \rangle$ we take the <u>initial cone</u>.

Continuing the analogy we see what corresponds to continuous functions on domains:

Definition 2.4: A covariant functor $T:CPO \to CPO$ is <u>continuous</u> iff whenever $\rho : \Delta \to D$ is an initial cone then so is $T\rho : T\Delta \to TD$.

Note that this definition implies $T(\underline{\lim}\Delta) \approx \underline{\lim}(T\Delta)$ where $\underline{\lim}\Delta$ denotes the object part of the initial cone. The above definition of continuity can of course easily be extended to n-ary functors.

Having given the above analogy we can now solve recursive domain equations by using the standard fixed-point technique. For a continuous function $f:D \to D$ the least fixpoint is given as:

$$\underline{\text{fix}}\ f = \sqcup_n f^n \bot$$

where $f^0 = Id$ and $f^{n+1} = f^n \circ f$. The analogy to this is the following:

Theorem 2.5: Let $T:CPO \to CPO$ be a continuous functor. Using the one-point domain, **1**, as an analogy to $\bot$ we consider the chain:

$$\Delta_T = \langle T^m \mathbf{1}, f_m \rangle$$

where $T^0 = Id$, $T^{m+1} = T^m \circ T$, f_0 is the unique embedding $\mathbf{1} \leq T\mathbf{1}$ and $f_{m+1} = T^m(f_0)$. Then the object part, $\underline{\lim}\Delta_T$, of the initial cone of Δ_T is indeed a solution to $TD \approx D$. We shall refer to $\underline{\lim}\Delta_T$ as the least fixed-point of T and use the notation FIX(T).

The least fixpoint of a functor **T** can equivalently be characterized as the initial object in the category of T-algebras as stated in the next definition and theorem.

Definition 2.6: Let **T** be a continuous functor $CPO^n \to CPO^n$. The <u>category of T-algebras</u> has as <u>objects</u> pairs $(\mathbf{E}, \alpha)$, where **E** is an object in CPO^n and α is an embedding $T(E) \leq E$. A <u>morphism</u> between two T-algebras $(\mathbf{E}, \alpha)$ and $(\mathbf{D}, \beta)$ is an embedding $\mathbf{j}:\mathbf{E} \leq \mathbf{D}$ such that the following diagram commutes:

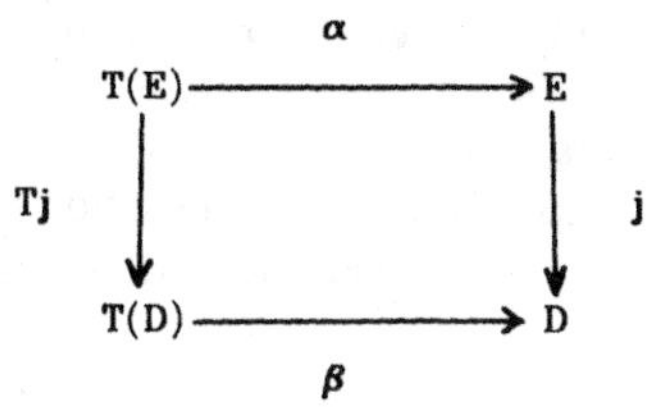

Theorem 2.7: Let T be a continuous functor $CPO^n \rightarrow CPO^n$ and let FIX(T) be the least fixpoint of T with ε:T[FIX(T)] $\rightarrow$ FIX(T) as the isomorphism. Then (FIX(T),ε) is an initial T-algebra.

We now turn to a somewhat more concrete ordering on domains; namely that of being a subdomain.

Definition 2.8: Let D be a domain and let $P \subseteq D$ for D considered as a set. Then P is a <u>subdomain</u> of D iff $\bot_D \in P$ and for any $\sqsubseteq_D$-increasing ω-chain, $x_0 \sqsubseteq_D x_1 \sqsubseteq_D x_2 \sqsubseteq_D ..$, in P, $\sqcup_D x_n \in P$ (P is ω-complete).

The following easy lemma justifies the term subdomain.

Lemma 2.9: Let D be a domain and let P be a subdomain of D. Then $(P, \sqsubseteq_D)$ is itself a domain with $\bot_P = \bot_D$ and $\sqcup_P = \sqcup_D$.

Notation 2.10: For P a subdomain of D we write $P \sqsubset D$ or sometimes $i:P \sqsubset D$, where i is the inclusion $P \subseteq D$. For any cpo D, S_D denotes all the subdomains of D.

As for $\leq$, $\sqsubset$ can be extended to a relation between n-tuples of domains in the obvious way. With this extension $(S_{\mathbf{D}}, \sqsubset)$ will be a domain for all **D** as stated in the next theorem:

Theorem 2.11: For any n-tuple of domains $\mathbf{D}=(D_1,..,D_n)$, $(S_{\mathbf{D}}, \sqsubset)$ is a domain with $1^n=(1_1,..,1_n)$ (where 1_i only contains $\bot_{Di}$) as least element. The lub of an $\sqsubset$-increasing ω-chain, $P_0 \sqsubset P_1 \sqsubset P_2 \sqsubset ..$, where $P_i=(P_i^1,..,P_i^n)$ is given as:

$$\mathbf{V}_k \mathbf{P}_k = \left[Cl_{D1}(\cup_k P_k^1),..,Cl_{Dn}(\cup_k P_k^n) \right]$$

where Cl_{Di} is the closure in D_i.

Definition 2.12: A functor $T:CPO^n \rightarrow CPO^n$ is <u>$\sqsubset$-preserving</u> iff $i:\mathbf{D} \sqsubset \mathbf{E}$ implies $T(i):T(\mathbf{D}) \sqsubset T(\mathbf{E})$. A $\sqsubset$-preserving functor $T:CPO^n \rightarrow CPO^n$ is <u>$\sqsubset$-continuous</u> iff for any **D**, if $D_0 \sqsubset D_1 \sqsubset D_2 \sqsubset ..$ is an increasing ω-chain in $S_{\mathbf{D}}$, then:

$$T(\mathbf{V}_n D_n) = \mathbf{V}_n T(D_n)$$

Theorem 2.13: Let T be a continuous and $\sqsubset$-continuous functor $CPO^n \rightarrow CPO^n$ and let $(\mathbf{D}, \boldsymbol{\alpha})$ be a T-algebra. Then the function on $S_{\mathbf{D}}$ given by:

$$\boldsymbol{\alpha}[T(-)]:\mathbf{P} \longmapsto \boldsymbol{\alpha}[T(\mathbf{P})]$$

is continuous.

Theorem 2.14: Let D be a domain and let $D_0 \sqsubset D_1 \sqsubset D_2 \sqsubset ..$ be an $\sqsubset$-increasing chain in S_D as well as an $\leq$-increasing chain, ie. $D_0 \leq D_1 \leq D_2 \leq \ldots$ Then $\bigvee_n D_n = \sqcup_n D_n$ and the inclusion $i: \bigvee_n D_n \sqsubset D$ is in fact an embedding.

Theorem 2.15: Let **T** be a continuous and $\sqsubset$-continuous functor $CPO^n \rightarrow CPO^n$ and let $(\mathbf{E},\alpha)$ be the initial **T**-algebra. Then **E** is the least fixed point of the function $\alpha(T(-))$.

Theorem 2.16: Let $E \leq_j^i D$. Then $i(E) \sqsubset D$.

Note that the opposite implication does not hold in general, ie. it is not the case that $E \sqsubset D$ implies $E \leq D$.

Theorem 2.17: Let i be an embedding $E \leq D$ and let **T** be a covariant functor $CPO^n \rightarrow CPO^n$. Then $T(iE) = Ti(TE)$.

Theorem 2.18: Let **T** be a continuous and $\sqsubset$-continuous functor $CPO^n \rightarrow CPO^n$ and let $(\mathbf{E},\alpha)$ be a **T**-algebra. Then there exists an initial **T**-algebra, (E^*,α^*), such that $E^* \sqsubset E$ and α^* is the restriction of α to $T(E^*)$.

In the rest of this paper we will restrict ourselves to look at simultaneous recursive domain equations, $\mathbf{E} \approx T(E)$, where **T** is a <u>covariant, continuous and $\sqsubset$-continuous functor</u> $CPO^n \rightarrow CPO^n$.

Fortunately these three properties hold for all our favorite functors, including <u>disjoint sum</u>, +, <u>cartesian product</u>, $\times$, <u>lifting</u>, $(-)_\uparrow$, <u>smash product</u>, $\otimes$, <u>constant</u> functors, K_D, and <u>projection</u> functors, Π_i^n. <u>Exponentiation</u>, $\rightarrow$, can be used as long as the contravariant argument is fixed, ie. we can use functors of the form $\rightarrow(K_D,I)$. Furthermore the three properties are all preserved under composition of functors.

3. STRUCTURAL INDUCTION PRINCIPLES - METHOD A

We start this section with a straightforward generalization of the structural induction principle for a single domain equation defined in [9], chapter 5. As for the single domain equation the principle turns out to be categorical as well as sound.

Theorem 3.1: Let $(\mathbf{E},\alpha)$ be a **T**-algebra. Then the following are equivalent:

(i) $(\mathbf{E},\alpha)$ is the initial **T**-algebra.

(ii) The following induction principle holds:
$\forall P \sqsubset E.\ \ \alpha[T(P)] \subseteq P \Rightarrow P=E$

In several situations one would have a predicate $P_1 \sqsubset E_1$, where E_1 is the first domain component of the least fixpoint for **T**, and the task will be to prove $P_1 = E_1$. However the induction principle in the above theorem will not be directly applicable because the predicates $P_2,\ldots,P_n$ are not described in the principle. It is therefore up to who ever is using the principle to find a set $P_2,\ldots,P_n$ of predicates such that the induction principle can be applied.

Essentially there will be two different ways of choosing the remaining predicates:

Method A: <u>Choose</u> $P_2,\ldots,P_n$ such that $\alpha_i[T_i(P)] \sqsubset P_i$ for i=2..n. Using the induction principle then amounts to <u>prove</u> $\alpha_1[T_1(P)] \sqsubset P_1$.

Method B: Choose $P_2,\ldots,P_n$ such that $\alpha_1[T_1(P)] \sqsubseteq P_1$ and then prove $\alpha_i[T_i(P)] \sqsubseteq P_i$ for i=2..n.

We are looking for a method of choosing exactly one satisfactory set $P_2,\ldots,P_n$, for a given predicate P_1. In method A we have that if $P_2,\ldots,P_n \sqsubseteq Q_2,\ldots,Q_n$ then $\alpha_1[T_1(P_1,P_2,\ldots,P_n)] \sqsubseteq \alpha_1[T_1(P_1,Q_2,\ldots,Q_n)]$ since T_1 is assumed $\sqsubseteq$-preserving. So from the point of view of proving $\alpha_1[T_1(P)] \sqsubseteq P_1$ a smallest possible set of new predicates will be the best choice.

Theorem 3.2: Let $(\mathbf{E},\boldsymbol{\alpha})$ be a T-algebra and let $P_1 \sqsubseteq E_1$ Then there exists a minimal set $P_2,\ldots,P_n$ such that $\alpha_i[T_i(P)] \sqsubseteq P_i$ for i=2..n.

Proof: By theorem 2.13 $\boldsymbol{\alpha}[\mathbf{T}(-)]$ is a continuous function on $S_\mathbf{D}$ so clearly $\boldsymbol{\alpha}[\mathbf{T}(P_1,-)]$ is a continuous function on $S_{(D2,\ldots,Dn)}$ with a least fixpoint $(P_2,\ldots,P_n)$. This least fixpoint will be the minimal set. □

Notation 3.3: Let $(\mathbf{E},\boldsymbol{\alpha})$ be a T-algebra and let $P_1 \sqsubseteq E_1$. Then $\mathbf{P}_1^{min}$ denotes the n-tuple $(P_1,P_2,\ldots,P_n)$ where $P_2,\ldots,P_n$ is the minimal set such that $\alpha_i[T_i(P)] \sqsubseteq P_i$ for i=2..n.

With this choice of $P_2,\ldots,P_n$ Method A actually becomes a both <u>sound</u> <u>and</u> <u>categorical</u> method as stated in the following:

Theorem 3.4: Let $(\mathbf{E},\boldsymbol{\alpha})$ be a T-algebra where $\mathbf{E}=(E_1,\ldots,E_n)$, $\boldsymbol{\alpha}=(\alpha_1,\ldots,\alpha_n)$ and $\mathbf{T}=(T_1,\ldots,T_n)$. Then

(i) If $(\mathbf{E},\boldsymbol{\alpha})$ is initial then
$\forall P_1 \sqsubseteq E_1.\ \alpha_1[T_1(\mathbf{P}_1^{min})] \subseteq P_1 \Rightarrow P_1 = E_1$

(ii) If the above statement holds for $(\mathbf{E},\boldsymbol{\alpha})$ then
(E_1,α_1) is the first component in an initial T-algebra.

Proof: (i) is a consequence of theorem 3.1. (ii) is obtained by putting $P_1=E^*_1$. Then $\mathbf{P}_1^{min}=\mathbf{E}^*$ and (i) yields that $E^*_1=E_1$. □

Now defining $\mathbf{P}_i^{min}$ for $P_i \sqsubseteq E_i$, to be the n-tuple $(P_1,\ldots,P_i,\ldots,P_n)$, where $(P_1,\ldots,P_{i-1},P_{i+1},\ldots,P_n)$ is the smallest set such that $\alpha_j[T_j(\mathbf{P}_i^{min})] \sqsubseteq P_j$ for j=1..i-1,i+1..n we can clearly get a categorical induction principle from theorem 3.4, by simply adding a similar induction principle for $E_2,\ldots,E_n$.

4. METHOD B - GENERAL

As seen in the previous section, Method A succeeds in giving a categorical sound and complete induction principle for simultaneous domain equations. Unfortunately the method gives rise to some problems from the point of view of implementation, since the derived predicates, $P_2,\ldots,P_n$, are second-order predicates that not in general seem to be expressible as first-order formulas. When we say first-order we mean relative to a language containing the selectors, constructors and predicates naturally derived from the domain equation. We will not go further into this language here but refer to [4] for a treatment in the case of a single domain equation.

It turns out that Method B will overcome the above problem when the functors $T_1,\ldots,T_n$ used in the equation meet certain conditions.

Definition 4.1: A functor T:CPO→CPO is <u>$\subset$-preserving</u> iff for all cpo's E and D $E \subset D$ implies $T(E) \subset T(D)$. ($\subset$ means $\subseteq$ and $\neq$).

Definition 4.2: A functor $T:CPO^n \to CPO$ <u>is dependent of its i'th argument</u> iff for all cpo's $E_1,\dots,E_{i-1},E_{i+1},\dots,E_n$ the derived functor:

$$T(E_1,\dots,E_{i-1},\_,E_{i+1},\dots,E_n):CPO \to CPO$$

is $\subset$-preserving. $DEP(T) \subseteq \{1,\dots,n\}$ denotes the set of arguments of which T depends.

Example 4.3:

$DEP(+)=DEP(\times)=\{1,2\}$	$DEP(K_D)=\phi$
$DEP(\__{\uparrow})=\{1\}$	$DEP(\Pi_i^n)=\{i\}$
$DEP(\otimes)=\phi$	$DEP(K_D \to \_)=\{1\}$

To see why for instance $1 \notin DEP(\otimes)$ observe that taking $E_2=\mathbf{1}$ makes $\_\otimes E_2 = K_1$ the constant functor always giving $\mathbf{1}$. So $\_\otimes E_2$ is not $\subset$-preserving for all E_2. Similar arguments shows that $2 \notin DEP(\otimes)$.

We will restrict ourselves to functors $\mathbf{T}:CPO^n \to CPO^n$, where $DEP(T_1)=\{1,2,\dots,n\}$. At the end of the paper we shall discuss how this restriction can be loosened.

Let us remind the reader that the idea behind Method B is - from a given <u>predicate</u> P_1 - to choose the remaining predicates $P_2,\dots,P_n$ such that $\alpha_1(T_1(P_1,P_2,\dots,P_n)) \subseteq P_1$ is known to hold. This will then leave $\alpha_j(T_j(P_1,\dots,P_n)) \subseteq P_j$ for j=2..n to be proved.

The simplest way of choosing $P_2,\dots,P_n$ is as a <u>maximal</u> (n-1)-tuple of predicates satisfying $\alpha_1(T_1(P_1,\dots,P_n)) \subseteq P_1$. Let us further remind the reader of the two basic restrictions on **T** we have introduced:

(ASSUM1)	**T** is covariant, continuous and $\sqsubset$-continuous.
(ASSUM2)	$DEP(T_1)=\{1,2,\dots,n\}$

Theorem 4.4: Let $(\mathbf{E},\boldsymbol{\alpha})$ be a **T**-algebra. Then the following holds:

(i) If $(\mathbf{E},\boldsymbol{\alpha})$ is an initial **T**-algebra then:

$$\forall P_1 \sqsubset E_1,\dots,\forall P_n \sqsubset E_n. \qquad (*)$$
$$MAXIMAL_1(P_1,\dots,P_n) \Rightarrow [\ \wedge_{j=2}^n \alpha(T_j(P_1,\dots,P_n)) \subseteq P_j \Rightarrow P_1=E_1\ ]$$

where $MAXIMAL_1(P_1,\dots,P_n)$ is true iff $(P_2,\dots,P_n) \sqsubset (E_2,\dots,E_n)$ is a maximal (n-1)-tuple st. $\alpha_1(T_1(P_1,P_2,\dots,P_n)) \subseteq P_1$ (Note that $MAXIMAL_1(P_1,P_2,\dots,P_n)$ can be formally expressed as a second-order formula in P_1).

(ii) If $(\mathbf{E},\boldsymbol{\alpha})$ satisfies (*) then (E_1,α_1) is the first component of an initial **T**-algebra.

Proof: (i) is a consequence of theorem 3.1. (ii) is proved by letting $P_1=E^*_1$ and choosing $E^*_2,\dots,E^*_n$ as auxiliary predicates. Since $\boldsymbol{\alpha}(\mathbf{T}(\mathbf{E}^*))=\mathbf{E}^*$ we can by (*) conclude, that $E^*_1=E_1$ provided $MAXIMAL_1(\mathbf{E}^*)$ is true. We therefore only have to prove the maximality of $\mathbf{E}^*$:

Let $P_2 \sqsubset E_2,\dots,P_n \sqsubset E_n$ be such that $\alpha_1(T_1(E^*_1,P_2,\dots,P_n)) \sqsubset E^*_1$ and $E^*_2 \sqsubset P_2,\dots,E^*_n \sqsubset P_n$. Then $E^*_1 = \alpha_1(T_1(\mathbf{E}^*)) \sqsubset \alpha_1(T_1(E^*_1,P_2,\dots,P_n)) \sqsubset E^*_1$. Hence $T_1(\mathbf{E}^*) = T_1(E^*_1,P_2,\dots,P_n)$, and because $DEP(T_1)=\{1,2,\dots,n\}$ this can only hold if $P_2=E^*_2,\dots,P_n=E^*_n$. □

5. METHOD B - EXPRESSIBILITY

So far we have developed Method B into a categorical induction principle where - given a prime predicate P_1 - the search for derived predicates $P_2,\ldots,P_n$ has been narrowed down to a search for maximal predicates satisfying certain conditions. However we are still far from having an <u>automatic derivation of $P_2,\ldots,P_n$</u> (there could be many maximal (n-1)-tuples, $(P_2,\ldots,P_n)$, satisfying the required conditions) and even further away from our ultimate goal: an automatic derivation of $P_2,\ldots,P_n$ as <u>first-order formulas</u> in P_1. Further restrictions on the functors seems necessary.

In the following we will suggest a new restriction and show how it helps in achieving the above goal for functors **T** for which theorem 4.4 is already known to give a categorical induction principle.

Definition 5.1: A functor $T:CPO^n \to CPO$ is said to be <u>unambiguous</u> iff for all $P_1,\ldots,P_n$ and $Q_1,\ldots,Q_n$: $T(Q_1,\ldots,Q_n) \subseteq T(P_1,\ldots,P_n)$ implies $Q_i \subseteq P_i$ for all $i \in DEP(T)$.

From the definition it follows that if T is an unambiguous functor and $T(Q_1,\ldots,Q_n)=T(P_1,\ldots,P_n)$ then $Q_i=P_i$ for $i \in DEP(T)$. This explains the term unambiguous.

Our new restriction on **T** can now be formulated:

(ASSUM3) T_1 is unambiguous.

Lemma 5.2: All functors build over $+$, $\times$, $(\_)_\dagger$, K_D and Π^n_i are unambiguous.

Lemma 5.3: Let **T** be a functor $CPO^n \to CPO^n$ satisfying (ASSUM1)-(ASSUM3) and let $(\mathbf{E},\alpha)$ be a **T**-algebra. Then $E^*_2,\ldots,E^*_n$ is the only maximal (n-1)-tuple s.t. $\alpha_1(T_1(\mathbf{E}^*)) \sqsubset E^*_1$.

Proof: Note, that $\alpha_1(T_1(\mathbf{E}^*))=E^*_1$. Now suppose $\alpha_1(T_1(E^*_1,P_2,\ldots,P_n)) \subseteq E^*_1$. Then $T_1(E^*_1,P_2,\ldots,P_n) \subseteq T_1(\mathbf{E}^*)$. The unambiguity of T_1 then yields $P_2 \subseteq E^*_2,\ldots,P_n \subseteq E^*_n$. □

The next theorem tells us what we shall look for in order to establish an automatic derivation of auxiliary predicates in such a way, that we still have a sound and categorical induction principle.

Theorem 5.4: Let **T** be a functor $CPO^n \to CPO^n$ satisfying (ASSUM1)-(ASSUM3) and let $(\mathbf{E},\alpha)$ be a **T**-algebra. Let $M_2,\ldots,M_n$ be predicate transformers:

$$M_j: \{P_1 \mid P_1 \sqsubset E_1\} \to \{P_j \mid P_j \sqsubset E_j\};\ j=2..n$$

Let COND be a condition:

$$COND: \{P_1 \mid P_1 \sqsubset E_1\} \to Bool$$

Suppose

(A) If $COND(P_1)=true$ then $(M_2(P_1),\ldots,M_n(P_n))$ is a maximal (n-1)-tuple such that $\alpha_1(T_1(P_1,M_2(P_1),\ldots,M_n(P_1))) \subseteq P_1$

(B) $COND(E^*_1)$

Then (i) If $(\mathbf{E},\alpha)$ is an initial **T**-algebra then the following induction principle holds:

$$\forall P_1 \sqsubset E_1 . \{ [\ \mathrm{COND}(P_1)\ \&\ \bigwedge_{j=2..n} \alpha_j\big(T_j(P_1, M_2(P_1),\ldots,M_n(P_1))\big) \subseteq M_j(P_1)\ ] \Rightarrow P_1 = E_1 \} \qquad (**)$$

(ii) If $(\mathbf{E},\alpha)$ satisfies (**) then (E_1,α_1) is the first component of an initial **T**-algebra.

Proof: (i) is a consequence of theorem 4.4 and (A). (ii) is proved by letting $P_1 = E^*_1$ in (**). Because of (B), (A) and lemma 5.3 we get, that $M_j(E^*_1) = E^*_j$. Thus (**) yields that $E^*_1 = E_1$. □

All we need now, is to find such predicate transformers and a condition satisfying (A) and (B), and to <u>express them as first-order formulas</u> over P_1, but independent of the actual **T**-algebra $(\mathbf{E},\alpha)$ considered.

To make the expressibility possible we restrict ourselves to functors build over the operators $+$, $\times$, $(\_)_\uparrow$, K_D and Π^n_i. We leave the precise definition of the language associated with such a composed functor to the reader (can be defined inductively on the structure of the functor).

Definition 5.5: For notational convenience we will make use of the following abbreviations.Let E, E_i i=1..n be cpo's. For $P \subseteq_\omega$ [1] $\sum_i E_i$ and j=1..n define $\amalg_j P \subseteq_\omega E_j$ as:

$$\amalg_j P = \{ \mathrm{out}_j e \mid e \in \textstyle\sum_i E_i \wedge Pe \}$$

For $P \subseteq_\omega \times_i E_i$ and j=1..n define $\prod_j P \subseteq_\omega E_j$ as:

$$\textstyle\prod_j P = \{ e_j \in E_j \mid P(<\perp,\ldots,e_j,\ldots,\perp>) \}$$

For $P \subseteq_\omega E_\uparrow$ define $\downarrow(P) \subseteq_\omega E$ as:

$$\downarrow(P) = \{ e \in E \mid P(\mathrm{up}(e)) \}$$

Lemma 5.6:

$P = \sum_j(\amalg_j P)$ and for $P \sqsubset \sum_i E_i$, $\amalg_j P \sqsubset E_j$
For $P \sqsubset \times_i E_i$, $\prod_j P \sqsubset E_j$
For $P_i \sqsubset E_i$ (i=1..n), $\prod_j(\times_i P_i) = P_j$
For $P \subseteq_\omega E_\uparrow$, $P \subseteq_\omega [\downarrow(P)]_\uparrow$
For $P \sqsubset E_\uparrow$, $P = [\downarrow(P)]_\uparrow$

6. A SIMPLE CLASS OF FUNCTORS

In order to give a soft start we restrict ourselves to functors **T**, where T_1 has the simple form:

$$\text{(F)} \qquad T_1 = \textstyle\sum_{i=1..m} S_i$$

where S_i is a product of any number of constant functors, K_D, any number of the

---

[1] $\subseteq_\omega$ means ω-complete subset

projection functor Π^n_1 and <u>at most one</u> projection functor Π^n_j with $j\neq 1$. We then define COND and $M_2,\dots,M_n$ as follows:

Definition 6.1:

$$COND(P_1) = \alpha_1\big(T_1(P_1,1,\dots,1)\big)\subseteq P_1$$

and

$$M_j(P_1)(e_j) = \bigwedge_{i=1..m}\Big[\ S_i(P_1,1,\dots,1,\{e_j\},1,\dots,1\big) \subseteq \amalg_i\big(\alpha_1^{-1}(P_1)\big)\ \Big]$$

Theorem 6.2:

(A) $COND(P_1)$=true implies
$(M_2(P_1,\dots,M_n(P_1))$ is a maximal (n-1)-tuple
such that $\alpha_1\big(T_1(P_1,M_2(P_1),\dots,M_n(P_1))\big)\subseteq P_1$

(B) $COND(E^*_1)$ = true

Proof: (B) is trivial.
For (A) suppose that $\alpha_1(T_1(P_1,1,\dots,1))\sqsubset P_1$. This means, that $S_i(P_1,1,\dots,1)\sqsubset\amalg_i(\alpha_1^{-1}(P_1))$ i=1..m. Therefore we have, that $\bot\in M_j(P_1)$ for j=2..n. We shall prove:

(1) $S_i(P_1,M_2(P_1),\dots,M_n(P_1))\subseteq\amalg_i(\alpha_1^{-1}(P_1))$ for i=1..M
(2) $(M_2(P_1),\dots,M_n(P_1))$ is a maximal tuple
for which (1) holds.

(1) holds because of the definition of $M_j(P_1)$ and the condition, that S_i contains at most one occurrence of a functor Π^n_j with $j\neq 1$. Notice that we here have used, that if $P_j\subseteq Q_j$ then $S_i(P_1,\dots,P_j,\dots,P_n)\subseteq S_i(P_1,\dots,Q_j,\dots,P_n)$. This is the reason for (2) to hold as well. Let namely $P_2\sqsubset E_2,\dots P_n\sqsubset E_n$ st. $\alpha_1(T_1(P_1,\dots,P_n))\sqsubset P_1$, then:

$$S_i(P_1,1,\dots,P_j,\dots 1) \subseteq \amalg_i(\alpha_1^{-1}(P_1))$$

for i=1..m and j=2..n. Then $e_j\in P_j$ implies:

$$S_i(P_1,1,\dots,\{e_j\},\dots,1)\sqsubset\amalg_i(\alpha_1^{-1}(P_1))\ \ (i=1..m)$$
$$\Leftrightarrow\ e_j\in M_j(P_1)$$

That is $P_j\subseteq M_j(P_1)$. Hence $M_j(P_1)$ is maximal, and (2) holds. □

The above theorem shows that the condition, COND, and the predicate transformers, $M_2,\dots,M_n$, satisfy (A) and (B). As such when they are used in (**) theorem 5.4 we will get a sound and categorical induction principle, (***), for functors satisfying the simple form condition (F).

Example 6.3: Let

$$E_1 \approx E_1{\times}E_2{\times}A$$
$$E_2 \approx E_1 + E_2$$

Then

$$COND(P_1) = \forall E_1\in P_1\ \ \forall a\in A.\alpha_1(<e_1,\bot,a>)\in P_1$$
$$M_2(P_1) = \{e_2\in E_2 \mid \forall e_1\in P_1\ \ \forall a\in A.\ \alpha_1(<e_1,e_2,a>)\in P_1\}$$

In order to prove $P_1=E_1$ using the induction principle, one would have to prove - besides that $P_1 \sqsubseteq E_1$ - that $COND(P_1)=true$, and that $\alpha_2(P_1 + M_2(P_1))) \subseteq M_2(P_1)$, that is:

(1) $\forall e_1 \in P_1\ \forall a \in A.\ \alpha_1(<e_1,\perp,a>) \in P_1$

(2) $\forall e_1, f_1 \in P_1\ \forall a \in A.\ \alpha_1(<e_1,\alpha_2(inl\ f_1),a>) \in P_1$

(3) $\forall e_2 \in E_2 \left[\forall e_1 \in P_1\ \forall a \in A.\ \alpha_1(<e_1,e_2,a>) \in P_1 \right.$
$\left. \Rightarrow \forall e_1 \in P_1\ \forall a \in A.\ \alpha_1(<e_1,\alpha_2(inr\ e_2),a>) \in P_1 \right]$.

7. FULL CLASS OF FUNCTORS

In this section we will deal with expressibility for the full class of functors build over the operators $+,\times,(\_)_\dagger$, K_D and Π_i^n and satisfying the assumption (ASSUM2) ($DEP(T_1=\{1,..,n\})$ At the end of the paper we discuss how this assumption can be removed. Again we follow the general scheme from section 5, ie. we define a condition - COND - and (n-1) predicate transformers - $M_2,..,M_n$ - such that (A) and (B) from theorem 5.4 are satisfied. We then know that (**) is a sound and categorical induction principle.

Let us start by showing why the condition and predicate transformers used for the simple class of functors considered in the previous section does not generalize to arbitrary functors over $+,\times,(\_)_\dagger$, K_D and Π_i^n. In particular we will demonstrate why the condition that a simple functor, $T=\sum_{i=1..m} S_i$, must have at <u>most</u> one projection functor Π_j^n with $j\neq 1$ in each summand, S_i, is essential. To this end consider the most simple system of equations violation this condition:

$$E_1 \approx E_2 \times E_3$$
$$E_2 \approx .....$$
$$E_3 \approx .....$$

Using the definitions from section 6 we have:

$$COND(P_1) = \alpha_1(1\times 1) \subseteq P_1$$

which is true when $P_1 \sqsubseteq E_1$.

$$M_2(P_1) = \{e_2 \in E_2 \mid \alpha_1(\{e_2\}\times 1) \subseteq P_1\} = \Pi_1(\alpha_1^{-1}(P_1))$$
$$M_3(P_1) = \{e_3 \in E_3 \mid \alpha_1(1\times\{e_3\}) \subseteq P_1\} = \Pi_2(\alpha_1^{-1}(P_1))$$

ie. $M_2(P_1)$ and $M_3(P_1)$ are maximal predicates st.:

$$\alpha_1(M_2(P_1)\times 1) \subseteq P_1 \text{ and } \alpha_1(1\times M_3(P_1)) \subseteq P_1$$

However it does not in general follow that:

$$\alpha_1(M_2(P_1)\times M_3(P_1)) \subseteq P_1$$

which is absolutely essential for (A) to hold (since $COND(P_1)$ is true). To see this let:

$$P_1 = \alpha_1(P_2\times P_3 \cup Q_2\times Q_3)$$

where $Q_2,P_2 \sqsubseteq E_2$ and $Q_3,P_3 \sqsubseteq E_3$ with $Q_2 \not\subseteq P_2, P_2 \not\subseteq Q_2$ and similar for P_3 and Q_3. Then:

$$M_2(P_1) = P_2 \cup Q_2 \text{ and } M_3(P_1) = P_3 \cup Q_3$$

but $$\alpha_1(M_2(P_1)\times M_3(P_1)) = \alpha_1((P_2\cup Q_2)\times(P_3\cup Q_3)) \not\subseteq \alpha_1(P_2\times P_3 \cup Q_2\times Q_3) = P_1$$

since - by the way P_2,Q_2,P_3 and Q_3 has been chosen -

$$(P_2\cup Q_2)\times(P_3\cup Q_3) \not\subseteq P_2\times P_3 \cup Q_2\times Q_3$$

However it is important to note that by the very structure of P_1 - essentially being a union of incompatible subdomains - P_1 cannot equal E_1. A way to repair the above example would therefore be to avoid considering predicates like P_1 at all, since they cannot equal E_1 anyhow. This can be done by making $\text{COND}(P_1)$ yield false for such predicates. More specificly we add the following requirement to $\text{COND}(P_1)$:

For all $Q_2\subseteq E_2, Q_3\subseteq E_3$
if $\alpha_1(Q_2\times 1)\subseteq P_1$ **and** $\alpha_1(1\times Q_3)\subseteq P_1$
then $\alpha_1(Q_2\times Q_3)\subseteq P_1$

or equivalently:

$$\Pi_1(\alpha_1^{-1}(P_1)) \times \Pi_2(\alpha_1^{-1}(P_1)) \subseteq \alpha_1^{-1}(P_1)$$

Note that the chosen P_1 in the example violates this requirement so (A) is no longer falsified. Also if a chosen prime predicate P_1 does not satisfy this requirement we cannot have $P_1=E_1$.

Having now given some informal indication of what a new condition, $\text{COND}(P_1)$, suitable for the full class of functors over $+,\times,(\_)_\dagger,K_D$ and Π_i^n could be we proceed with the following definition:

Definition 7.1: Let $\mathbf{E}=(E_1,\ldots,E_n)\in\text{CPO}^n$ (called the basis). Define for functors $T:\text{CPO}^n\to\text{CPO}$ (build over $+,\times,(\_)_\dagger$, K_D and Π_j^n) and predicates $P\in\text{CPO}$ the condition $\text{OK}(P,T)\in\text{Bool}$ inductively as follows:

$\text{OK}(P,T) =$
case T **of**
K_D : $D\subseteq P$
Π_i^n : $\bot\in P$
$S_\dagger$: $[\downarrow(P)]_\dagger\subseteq P \wedge \text{OK}(\downarrow(P),S)$
$\times_i T_i$: $\times_i(\prod_i P)\subseteq P \wedge \bigwedge_i \text{OK}(\prod_i P,T_i)$
$\sum_i T_i$: $\sum_i(\coprod_i P)\subseteq P \wedge \bigwedge_i \text{OK}(\coprod_i P,T_i)$
end

(Note: the condition $\sum_i(\coprod_i P)\subseteq P$ is actually trivially true and can as such be omitted. Our reasons for stating it anyway are purely aesthetic.)

Now let $(\mathbf{E},\boldsymbol{\alpha})$ be a **T**-algebra and let $P_1\sqsubseteq E_1$ be the chosen prime predicate. Then we define:

$$\text{COND}(P_1) = \text{OK}(\alpha_1^{-1}(P_1),T_1[P_1])$$

where $T_1[P_1]$ is the functor: $T_1(P_1,\_,\ldots,\_):\text{CPO}^{n-1}\to\text{CPO}$ (Note that P_1 is treated as a constant in $T_1[P_1]$). As basis is used the (n-1)-tuple $(E_2,\ldots,E_n)$.

From the definition of OK it should be clear that $COND(P_1)$ is expressible as a first-order predicate in P_1. Simply note that all the cases in OK are expressible as follows:

case	**condition**	**expression**
K_D	$D \subseteq P$	$\forall d \in D.\ P(d)$
Π^n_i	$\bot \in P$	$P(\bot)$
$[S]_\uparrow$	$[\downarrow(P)]_\uparrow \subseteq P$	$P(\bot)$
$\times_i T_i$	$\times_i(\prod_i P) \subseteq P$	$\forall e_1 \in T_1(\mathbf{E}) .. \forall e_n \in T_n(\mathbf{E}).\ [\, P(<e_1,\bot,..,\bot>) \wedge P(<\bot,e_2,..,\bot>) \wedge \vdots\ P(<\bot,..,\bot,e_n>)\,] \Rightarrow P(<e_1,..,e_n>)$
$\Sigma_i T_i$	$\Sigma_i(\coprod_i P) \subseteq P$	true

Lemma 7.2: Let $\mathbf{E}=(E_1,..,E_n) \in CPO^n$, $T: CPO^n \to CPO$ and $\mathbf{P}=(P_1,..,P_n) \sqsubset \mathbf{E}$. Then $OK(T(\mathbf{P}),T)=$true.

Using the lemma above it is easily shown that the new definition of COND satisfies the requirement (B). To see this let $(\mathbf{E}^\bullet,\boldsymbol{\alpha}^\bullet)$ be the initial T-algebra included in $(\mathbf{E},\boldsymbol{\alpha})$. Then $COND(E_1^\bullet)$ is true by the above lemma since:

$$\begin{aligned} COND(E_1^\bullet) &= OK\left(\alpha_1^{-1}(E_1^\bullet), T_1[E_1^\bullet]\right) \\ &= OK\left(T_1(E^\bullet_1,..,E^\bullet_n), T_1[E_1^\bullet]\right) \\ &= OK\left(T_1[E_1^\bullet](E^\bullet_2,..,E^\bullet_n), T_1[E_1^\bullet]\right) \end{aligned}$$

Example 7.3: Let

$$\begin{aligned} E_1 &\approx A \times E_2 \times E_2 \times E_1 + C \\ E_2 &\approx E_2 \times E_1 + C \end{aligned}$$

ie:

$$\begin{aligned} T_1 &= +\left(\times\left\langle K_A, \Pi^2_2, \Pi^2_2, \Pi^2_1 \right\rangle, K_C\right) \\ T_2 &= +\left(\times\left\langle \Pi^2_2, \Pi^2_1 \right\rangle, K_C\right) \end{aligned}$$

Then

$$\begin{aligned} & COND(P_1) = \\ & [\ \forall c \in C.\ P_1\left(\alpha_1(\mathrm{inr}\ c)\right)\ ] \wedge \\ & [\ \forall a \in A\ \forall e_2, f_2 \in E_2\ \forall e_1 \in E_1. \\ & \quad \{\ P_1\left(\alpha_1(\mathrm{inl}<a,\bot,\bot,\bot>)\right) \wedge \\ & \quad P_1\left(\alpha_1(\mathrm{inl}<\bot,e_2,\bot,\bot>)\right) \wedge \\ & \quad P_1\left(\alpha_1(\mathrm{inl}<\bot,\bot,f_2,\bot>)\right) \wedge \\ & \quad P_1\left(\alpha_1(\mathrm{inl}<\bot,\bot,\bot,e_1>)\right)\ \} \Rightarrow \\ & \qquad P_1\left(\alpha_1(\mathrm{inl}<a,e_2,f_2,e_1>)\right)\ ] \wedge \\ & [\ \forall a \in A.\ P_1\left(\alpha_1(\mathrm{inl}<a,\bot,\bot,\bot>)\right)\ ] \wedge \\ & [\ \forall e_1 \in E_1.\ P_1(e_1) \Rightarrow P_1\left(\alpha_1(\mathrm{inl}<\bot,\bot,\bot,e_1>)\right)\ ] \end{aligned}$$

Definition 7.4: let $\mathbf{E}=(E_1,..,E_n) \in CPO^n$ (called the basis). For functors $T: CPO^n \to CPO$ and predicates $P \in CPO$ define for $j=1..n$, $MAX_j(P,T) \subseteq_\omega E_j$ inductively as:

$MAX_j(P,T) =$
case T **of**
K_D : E_j
Π_j^n : $P \cap E_j$
Π_i^n : $E_j \ (i \neq j)$
$[S]_\dagger$: $MAX_j(\downarrow(P),S)$
$\times_i T_i$: $\cap_i MAX_j(\prod_i P,T_i)$
$\sum_i T_i$: $\cap_i MAX_j(\amalg_i P,T_i)$
end

Again let (E,α) be a **T**-algebra and let $P_1 \sqsubset E_1$ be the chosen predicate. Using $(E_2,...,E_n)$ as basis the n-1 transformed predicates, $M_j(P_1)$ j=2..n, of P_1 are defined as follows:

$$M_j(P_1) = MAX_{j-1}(\alpha_1^{-1}(P_1),T_1[P_1])$$

(Note that the j'th argument in T_1 is viewed as the (j-1)'th argument in $T_1[P_1]$).

From the definition of $MAX_j(P,T)$ it should be clear that M_j is expressible as a first-order formula in P_1. To see this simply note that - similar to OK(P,T) - all the cases in $MAX_j(P,T)$ are expressible.

Example 7.3 (continued): Let $P_1 \sqsubset E_1$ be the chosen predicate. Then $T_1(P_1)$:$CPO^1 \rightarrow CPO$ is given as:

$$T_1(P_1) = K_A \times \Pi_1^1 \times \Pi_1^1 \times K_{P_1} + K_C$$

Basis is the 1-tuple (E_2). Then

$$\begin{aligned} M_2(P_1) &= MAX_1\left(\alpha_1^{-1}(P_1),T_1[P_1]\right) \\ &= \Pi_2\left(\amalg_1(\alpha_1^{-1}(P_1))\right) \cap \Pi_3\left(\amalg_1(\alpha_1^{-1}(P_1))\right) \cap E_2 \end{aligned}$$

so for $e_2 \in E_2$:

$$M_2(P_1)(e_2) = P_1\left(\alpha_1(inl<\perp,e_2,\perp>)\right) \wedge P_1\left(\alpha_1(inl<\perp,\perp,e_2>)\right)$$

To achieve soundness of the resulting induction principle we must show that:

(A) $\left(M_2(P_1),...,M_n(P_1)\right)$ is a maximal (n-1)-tuple $\sqsubset (E_2,...,E_n)$ such that $\alpha_1\left(T_1(P_1,M_2(P_1),...,M_n(P_1))\right) \subseteq P_1$ <u>when</u> $COND(P_1)$ is true.

This will follow as an easy corollary of the next theorem:

Theorem 7.5: Let $E=(E_1,...,E_n) \in CPO^n$. Let $T:CPO^n \rightarrow CPO$ (build over $+,\times,(\_)_\dagger$, K_D and Π_j^n), $P \in CPO$, and let for j=1..n $P_j^M = MAX_j(P,T)$. If OK(P,T)=true then $(P_1^M,...,P_n^M)$ is a maximal n-tuple $\sqsubset$ E satisfying $T(P_1^M,...,P_n^M) \subseteq P$.

Proof: By the structure of T.

cases $T=\Pi_j^n$ and $T=K_D$: Trivial.

case $T=[S]_\uparrow$:
Then $P^M_1,\ldots,P^M_n = MAX_1(\downarrow(P),S),\ldots,MAX_n(\downarrow(P),S)$. Since $OK(P,T)=true$ we must have $OK(\downarrow(P),S)=true$. Thus by induction hypothesis $P^M_1,\ldots,P^M_n$ is a maximal n-tuple st.:

$$S(P^M_1,\ldots,P^M_n) \subseteq \downarrow(P)$$

Assume $Q_1 \sqsubset E_1,\ldots,Q_n \sqsubset E_n$ st.:

$$T(Q_1,\ldots,Q_n) = [S(Q_1,\ldots,Q_n)]_\uparrow \subseteq P$$

then since $\downarrow(\_)$ is $\subseteq$-monotonic and $\downarrow(R_\uparrow)=R$:

$$S(Q_1,\ldots,Q_n) \subseteq \downarrow(P)$$

But then $Q_1 \subseteq P^M_1,\ldots,Q_m \subseteq P^M_n$.

case $T=\times_i T_i$:
Then $P^M_1,\ldots,P^M_n = \cap_i MAX_1(\prod_i P,T_i),\ldots,\cap_i MAX_n(\prod_i P,T_i)$. $OK(P,T)=true$ implies $OK(\prod_i P,T_i)=true$ for all i, thus by the induction hypothesis for all i:

$$MAX_1(\textstyle\prod_i P,T_i),\ldots,MAX_n(\prod_i P,T_i)$$

is a maximal n-tuple st:

$$T_i\left(MAX_1(\textstyle\prod_i P,T_i),\ldots,MAX_n(\prod_i P,T_i)\right) \subseteq \Pi^n_i P$$

Now assume $Q_1 \sqsubset E_1,\ldots,Q_n \sqsubset E_n$ st:

$$T(Q_1,\ldots,Q_n) \subseteq P$$

Since $\prod_i$ is $\subseteq$-monotonic and using lemma 5.6 (iii) we have for all i:

$$T_i(Q_1,\ldots,Q_n) = \textstyle\prod_i\left(T(Q_1,\ldots,Q_n)\right) \subseteq \prod_i P$$

So for all i $Q_1 \subseteq MAX_1(\prod_i P,T_i),\ldots,Q_n \subseteq MAX_n(\prod_i P,T_i)$ and hence $Q_1 \subseteq P^M_1,\ldots,Q_n \subseteq P^M_n$.

case $T=\sum_i T_i$: Similar to previous case. □

Corollary 7.6: Let $T:CPO^n \to CPO^n$ be a functor build over +, ×, $[\_]_\uparrow$, K_D and Π^n_j. Let (E,α) be a T-algebra and let $P_1 \sqsubset E_1$. Assume $COND(P_1)$ is true then $(M_2(P_1),\ldots,M_n(P_1)) \sqsubset (E_2,\ldots,E_n)$ and $\alpha_1\left(T_1(P_1,M_2(P_1),\ldots,M_n(P_1))\right)\_\subset P_1$. Moreover $(M_2(P_1),\ldots,M_n(P_1))$ is a maximal such (n-1)-tuple.

Proof: Use theorem 7.5 on $(E_2,\ldots,E_n)$, $T_1[P_1]$ and $\alpha_1^{-1}(P_1)$. Then corollary 7.6 follows from the definition of $COND(P_1)$ and $M_j(P_1)$. □

It has now been shown that the new condition, COND, and the new predicate transformers, $M_2,\ldots,M_n$, satisfies (A) and (B). As such when they are used in (**) theorem 5.4 we will get a sound and categorical induction principle, (****).

Example 7.3 (concluded): Let $((E_1,E_2),(\alpha_1,\alpha_2))$ be the initial T-algebra. Let $f:E_1 \to E_1$ and $g:E_2 \to E_2$ satisfy:

(f1) $f(\bot) = \bot$

(f2) $\forall c{\in}C.\ f\big(\alpha_1(\text{inr } c)\big) = \alpha_1(\text{inr } c)$

(f3) $\forall a{\in}A\ \forall e_2,f_2{\in}E_2\ \forall e_1{\in}E_1.$
$f\big(\alpha_1(\text{inl}{<}a,e_2,f_2,e_1{>})\big)=\alpha_1\big(\text{inl}{<}a,g(f_1),g(e_2),f(e_1){>}\big)$

(g1) $g(\bot) = \bot$

(g2) $\forall c{\in}C.\ g\big(\alpha_2(\text{inr } c)\big) = \alpha_2(\text{inr } c)$

(g3) $\forall e_2{\in}\ \forall e_1{\in}E_1.\ \ g\big(\alpha_2(\text{inr}{<}e_2,e_1{>})\big)=\alpha_2\big(\text{inr}{<}g(e_2),f(e_1){>}\big)$

We want to show that f is its own inverse, ie. $\forall e_1{\in}E_1.\ f(f(e_1))=e_1$. Our prime predicate is therefore:

$$P_1(e_1) \Leftrightarrow f(f(e_1))=e_1$$

First it must be shown that $\text{COND}(P_1)$ holds. We deal with the comparatively harder second conjunct of $\text{COND}(P_1)$ leaving the first, third and fourth conjunct to the reader.

Assume $P_1\big(\alpha_1(\text{inl}{<}a,\bot,\bot,\bot{>})\big)$, $P_1\big(\alpha_1(\text{inl}{<}\bot,e_2,\bot,\bot{>})\big)$, $P_1\big(\alpha_1(\text{inl}{<}\bot,\bot,f_2,\bot{>})\big)$ and $P_1\big(\alpha_1(\text{inl}{<}\bot,\bot,\bot e_1{>})\big)$. Now

$$\begin{aligned}
&P_1\big(\alpha_1(\text{inl}{<}\bot,e_2,\bot,\bot{>})\big) \Leftrightarrow\\
&f(f(\alpha_1(\text{inl}{<}\bot,e_2,\bot,\bot{>})))=\alpha_1(\text{inl}{<}\bot,e_2,\bot,\bot{>}) \Leftrightarrow^{(g1,f1)}\\
&\alpha_1(\text{inl}{<}\bot,g(g(e_2)),\bot,\bot{>}))=\alpha_1(\text{inl}{<}\bot,e_2,\bot,\bot{>}) \Leftrightarrow\\
&g(g(e_2))=e_2
\end{aligned}$$

Similar:

$$\begin{aligned}
&P_1\big(\alpha_1(\text{inl}{<}\bot,\bot,f_2,\bot{>})\big) \Leftrightarrow\\
&g(g(f_2))=f_2
\end{aligned}$$

and

$$\begin{aligned}
&P_1\big(\alpha_1(\text{inl}{<}\bot,\bot,\bot,e_1{>})\big) \Leftrightarrow\\
&f(f(e_1))=e_1
\end{aligned}$$

Then:

$$\begin{aligned}
&P_1\big(\alpha_1(\text{inl}{<}a,e_2,f_2,e_1{>})\big) \Leftrightarrow\\
&f(f(\alpha_1(\text{inl}{<}a,e_2,f_2,e_1{>}))=\alpha_1(\text{inl}{<}a,e_2,f_2,e_1{>}) \Leftrightarrow^{(f3)}\\
&\alpha_1(\text{inl}{<}a,g(g(e_2)),g(g(f_2)),f(f(e_1)){>})=\alpha_1(\text{inl}{<}a,e_2,f_2,e_1{>}) \Leftrightarrow\\
&\textbf{true}\ (\textit{by assumptions})
\end{aligned}$$

This proves $\text{COND}(P_1)$. Now in order to use the induction principle (****) we must show:

$$\alpha_2(T_2(P_1,M_2(P_1))) \subseteq M_2(P_1)$$

where
$$\begin{aligned}
&M_2(P_1) \Leftrightarrow\\
&P_1\big(\alpha_1(\text{inl}{<}\bot,e_2,\bot,\bot{>})\big) \wedge P_1\big(\alpha_1(\text{inl}{<}\bot,\bot,e_2,\bot{>})\big) \Leftrightarrow\\
&g(g(e_2))=e_2
\end{aligned}$$

(Not surprisingly the derived predicate over E_2 - $M_2(P_1)$ - asserts that g also is its own inverse). Ie we must show:

$$\forall c\in C.\ M_2(\alpha_2(\mathrm{inr}\ c)) \wedge$$
$$\forall e_2\in E_2\ \forall e_1\in E_1.$$
$$\left[P_1(e_1) \wedge M_2(P_1)(e_2)\right] \Rightarrow M_2(P_1)(\alpha_2(\mathrm{inl}\langle e_2,e_1\rangle))$$

The first conjunct follows easily from (g2). For the second conjunct assume $P_1(e_1)$ and $M_2(P_1)(e_2)$, ie. $f(f(e_1))=e_1$ and $g(g(e_2))=e_2$. Then

$$M_2(P_1)(\alpha_2(\mathrm{inl}\langle e_2,e_1\rangle)) \Leftrightarrow$$
$$g(g(\alpha_2(\mathrm{inl}\langle e_2,e_1\rangle)))=\alpha_2(\mathrm{inl}\langle e_2,e_1\rangle) \Leftrightarrow^{(g3)}$$
$$\alpha_2(\mathrm{inl}\langle g(g(e_2)),f(f(e_1))\rangle)=\alpha_2(\mathrm{inl}\langle e_2,e_1\rangle) \Leftrightarrow$$
$$\mathbf{true}$$

So finally - using (****) - we can conclude that $\forall e_1\in E_1.\ f(f(e_1))=e_1$.

8. A LARGER EXAMPLE

We consider a simple programming language with two syntactic categories: commands (**C**) and expressions (**E**) given by:

c ::= c;c | i:=e | **if** e **then** c
e ::= i | e op e' | v | c:e

where $i\in \mathbf{I}$ (identifiers) and $v\in\mathbf{V}$ (values). The intended denotational semantic is the standard one, with the expression c:e introducing side-effects into expressions in order to make the example nontrivial. The intended semantic of c:e is "first execute c and then evaluate e in the resulting state".

C and **E** can also be specified as the least solution to the following simultaneous recursive domain equations:

$$\mathbf{C} \approx \mathbf{C}\times\mathbf{C} + \mathbf{I}\times\mathbf{E} + \mathbf{E}\times\mathbf{C}$$
$$\mathbf{E} \approx \mathbf{I} + \mathbf{E}\times\mathbf{E} + \mathbf{V} + \mathbf{C}\times\mathbf{E}$$

The semantic domains are given by:

$$S_{\mathbf{C}} = \mathrm{States} \to \mathrm{States}$$
$$S_{\mathbf{E}} = \mathrm{States} \to \mathrm{States}\times\mathbf{V}$$

where States = $\mathbf{I} \to \mathbf{V}$. The semantic functions $\mathfrak{C}$ and $\mathfrak{E}$ has the following functionality:

$$\mathfrak{C} : \mathbf{C} \to S_{\mathbf{C}}$$
$$\mathfrak{E} : \mathbf{E} \to S_{\mathbf{E}}$$

To make the following definitions and discussions simpler we define some syntactical (constructor-) operations:

$\_;\_$: $\mathbf{C}\times\mathbf{C} \to \mathbf{C}$
$\_:=\_$: $\mathbf{I}\times\mathbf{E} \to \mathbf{C}$
if_**then**_ : $\mathbf{E}\times\mathbf{C} \to \mathbf{C}$

and

$\ulcorner\_\urcorner$: $\mathbf{I} \to \mathbf{E}$

$$
\begin{array}{ll}
\_op\_ & : E{\times}E \rightarrow E \\
\lfloor\_\rfloor & : V \rightarrow E \\
\_:\_ & : C{\times}E \rightarrow E
\end{array}
$$

with $c_1;c_2 = \alpha_C(in_1<c_1,c_2>)$, $i:=e = \alpha_C(in_2<i,e>)$ aso.

Now $\mathbb{C}$ should satisfy the following (implicitly universally quantified) semantic equations:

$$
\begin{array}{l}
\mathbb{C}[\![\perp]\!] = \perp \\
\mathbb{C}[\![c_1;c_2]\!] = \mathbb{C}[\![c_2]\!] \,.\, \mathbb{C}[\![c_1]\!] \\
\mathbb{C}[\![i:=e]\!]s = \text{Update}\left[i,\left(\mathbf{E}[\![e]\!]s\right)_2,\left(\mathbf{E}[\![e]\!]s\right)_1\right] \\
\mathbb{C}[\![\textbf{if } e \textbf{ then } c]\!]s = \left(\mathbf{E}[\![e]\!]s\right)_2 = tt \rightarrow \mathbb{C}[\![c]\!]\left((\mathbf{E}[\![e]\!]s)_1\right) \mid s
\end{array}
$$

and $\mathbf{E}$ should satisfy:

$$
\begin{array}{l}
\mathbf{E}[\![\perp]\!] = \perp \\
\mathbf{E}[\![\lceil i \rceil]\!]s = (s,s(i)) \\
\left(\mathbf{E}[\![e_1 \text{ op } e_2]\!]s\right)_1 = \left[\mathbf{E}[\![e_2]\!](\mathbf{E}[\![e_1]\!]s)_1\right]_1 \\
\left(\mathbf{E}[\![e_1 \text{ op } e_2]\!]s\right)_2 = \left(\mathbf{E}[\![e_1]\!]s\right)_2 \text{ OP } \left(\mathbf{E}[\![e_2]\!](\mathbf{E}[\![e]\!]s)_1\right)_2 \\
\mathbf{E}[\![\lfloor v \rfloor]\!]s = (s,v) \\
\mathbf{E}[\![c:e]\!]s = \mathbf{E}[\![e]\!]\left(\mathbb{C}[\![c]\!]s\right)
\end{array}
$$

where Update:$I{\times}V{\times}$States $\rightarrow$ States is strict in all arguments and $(\_)_1$ and $(\_)_2$ indicates first and second projection.

From the above properties of $\mathbb{C}$ and $\mathbf{E}$ one would expect the following to hold:

$$\mathbb{C}[\![i := c:e]\!] = \mathbb{C}[\![c \,;\, i:=e]\!]$$

This expectation is reflected in a <u>program transformation</u> $F{:}C \rightarrow C$ with the following properties:

$$
\begin{array}{l}
F(\perp) = \perp \\
F(c_1;c_2) = Fc_1 \,;\, Fc_2 \\
F(\textbf{if } e \textbf{ then } c) = \textbf{if } e \textbf{ then } Fc \\
F(i:=j) = i:=j \\
F(i:=e \text{ op } f) = i:=e \text{ op } f \\
F(i:=v) = i:=v \\
F(i:=c:e) = Fc \,;\, F(i:=e)
\end{array}
$$

Now obviously we want to justify this program transformation, ie. we want to show:

$$\forall c \in C.\ \mathbb{C}[\![c]\!] = \mathbb{C}[\![Fc]\!]$$

We choose to do so using the induction principle (***) (ie.with COND and M_j defined as in section 6) Note that the syntactic functors in our example satisfies the simple form condition (F). So our prime predicate, $P_C \sqsubseteq C$, is:

$$P_C c \Leftrightarrow \mathbb{C}[\![c]\!] = \mathbb{C}[\![Fc]\!]$$

The condition COND(P_C) is:

$$\begin{aligned}
&\mathrm{COND}(P_C) \Leftrightarrow \\
&\alpha_C\left(P_C \times P_C + 1\times 1 + 1\times P_C\right) \subseteq P_C \Leftrightarrow \\
&\forall c,d \in \mathbf{C}.\ P_C(c) \wedge P_C(d) \Rightarrow P_C(c;d) \wedge \\
&\qquad P_C(c) \Rightarrow P_C(\mathbf{if} \perp \mathbf{then}\ c)
\end{aligned}$$

We leave the verification of $\mathrm{COND}(P_C)$ to the reader. The derived predicate $M_E(P_C) \sqsubset E$ can be formulated as:

$$\begin{aligned}
&M_E(P_C)e \Leftrightarrow \\
&\qquad\qquad \forall c \in \mathbf{C}.\ \forall i \in \mathbf{I}. \\
&(a) \ldots\ldots\ldots\ldots\ P_C(i{:=}e) \wedge \\
&(b) \ldots\ldots\ldots\ldots\ P_C(c) \Rightarrow P_C(\mathbf{if}\ e\ \mathbf{then}\ c)
\end{aligned}$$

We must prove:

$$\alpha_E\left(T_E(P_C, M_E(P_C))\right) \subseteq M_E(P_C)$$

or equivalently:

$$\begin{aligned}
&\forall i \in \mathbf{I}.\ \forall e,f \in \mathbf{E}.\ \forall v \in \mathbf{V}.\ \forall c \in \mathbf{C}. \\
&\qquad M_E(P_C)(\ulcorner i \urcorner) \wedge \\
&\qquad M_E(P_C)(e) \wedge M_E(P_C)(f) \Rightarrow M_E(P_C)(e\ \mathrm{op}\ f) \wedge \\
&\qquad M_E(P_C)(\llcorner v \lrcorner) \wedge \\
&\qquad P_C(c) \wedge M_E(P_C)(e) \Rightarrow M_E(P_C)(c{:}e).
\end{aligned}$$

Let us only prove the last conjunct. So assume $P_C(c)$ and $M_E(P_C)(e)$. To prove $M_E(P_C)(c{:}e)$ we must prove (a) and (b) for $e \equiv c{:}e$. We only prove the interesting (a), ie. $P_C(i := c{:}e)$:

$$\begin{aligned}
&P_C(i := c{:}e) \Leftrightarrow \\
&\mathbf{C}[\![i := c{:}e]\!] = \mathbf{C}[\![F(i := c{:}e)]\!]
\end{aligned}$$

now

$$\begin{aligned}
&\mathbf{C}[\![F(i := c{:}e)]\!] = \\
&\mathbf{C}[\![Fc\ ;\ F(i{:=}e)]\!] = \\
&\mathbf{C}[\![F(i{:=}e)]\!] \cdot \mathbf{C}[\![Fc]\!] = \\
&\mathbf{C}[\![i := c{:}e]\!]
\end{aligned}$$

which concludes the proof (The last equality is obtained by simply writting out the semantics of both sides).

9. DISCUSSION

The final sound and categorical induction principle (****), section 7, has been developed for functors build over $+, \times, (\_)_\tau, K_D$ and Π_i^n with the additional assumption:

$$\text{(ASSUM2)} \qquad \mathrm{DEP}(T_1) = \{1,2,\ldots,n\}$$

Thus our results do not - as they stand - hold for for example the following system:

$$\text{(S)} \qquad \begin{aligned}
E_1 &\approx E_2 \times E_1 \\
E_2 &\approx E_2 \times E_3 \\
E_3 &\approx (E_1)_\tau + A \times E_3
\end{aligned}$$

because $DEP(T_1) = \{1,2\} \neq \{1,2,3\}$.

It turns out that though (****) still yields a sound induction principle for the system it is no longer categorical. For functors **T** with $DEP(T_1) \neq \{1,2,..,n\}$ it is simply not good enough to choose the derived predicates $P_2,..,P_n$ as being a maximal (n-1)-tuple st. $\alpha_1(T_1(P_1,P_2,..,P_n)) \subseteq P_1$. A more refined method of choosing $P_2,..,P_n$ based on all the dependency sets, $DEP(T_1),..,DEP(T_n)$ is needed.

Basicly the refined method of choice will propagate the given prime predicate, P_1, in the following way: let $DEP(T_1) \setminus \{1\} = \{j_1,..,j_k\}$, then the predicates $P_{j1},..,P_{jk}$ are chosen as a maximal k-tuple making $\alpha_1(T_1(P_1,..,P_n)) \subseteq P_1$ hold. Now to determine the remaining P_i's simply recursively propagate the just chosen predicates $P_{j1},..,P_{jk}$ according to the dependency sets $DEP(T_{j1}),..,DEP(T_{jk})$ (of course at any point taking into account which predicates have already been determined) until for all j=2..n a predicate P_j has been chosen.

Formalizing the above description it is possible to extend (****) to a sound and categorical principle for general functors build over $+, \times, (\_)_{\dagger}, K_D$ and Π_i^n. However since the fundamental ideas are the same as for functors satisfying the constraint (ASSUM2) we have in this presentation chosen to restrict ourselves to this technically simple class of functors.

REFERENCES

1. Jensen, F. V. An LCF-system for Automatic Creation of Theories for 1-constructable Data Types. CSR 87-81, Department of Computer Science, University of Edinburgh, 1981.

2. Jensen, F.V. Induction Principles for Recursive Data Types. IR 82-7, Institute of Electronic Systems, Aalborg University Centre, 1982.

3. Jensen, F.V. Axiomatization and Induction for Data Types being Solutions to Simultaneous Domain Equations. IR 81-9, Institute of Electronic Systems, Aalborg University Centre, December, 1981.

4. Larsen, K. G. Specification of Data Types - extented abstract. IR-82-6, Institute of Electronic Systems, Aalborg University Centre, 1982.

5. Gordon, M, Milner, R and Wadsworth, C. P.. *LNCS*. Volume 78: *Edinburgh LCF*. Springer-Verlag, 1979.

6. Lehmann, D. and Smyth, M.B. "Algebraic Specificaiton of Data Types: A Synthetic Approach". *Math. Systems Theory* 14 (1981), 97-137.

7. Milner, R. How to derive inductions in LCF.

8. Paulson, Lawrence. *Lecture Notes in Computer Science*. Volume 173: Deriving Structural Induction in LCF. In *Semantics of Data Types, International Symposium, Sophia-Antipolis, France, Proceedings*, Springer-Verlag, 1984, pp. 197-215.

9. Plotkin, G. D. The Category of Complete Partial Orders: A Tool for Making Meanings. Lecture Notes, Pisa, 1978.

10. Plotkin, G.D and Smyth, M. "The Category Theoretic Solution of Recursive domain Equations". *SIAM* 11, 4 (nov 1982), 761-783.

11. Scott, D.S. *Lecture Notes in Mathematics*. Volume 274: Continuous Lattices, Toposes, Algebraic Geometry and Logic. In , Springer-Verlag, 1972, pp. 97-136. Proc. 1971 Dalhousie Conference, Ed. F.W. Lawvere.

12. Stoy, J.E.. *Denotational Semantics. The Scott-Strachey approach*. The MIT press, Cambridge, 1977.

13. Wadsworth, S.P. "The Relation between Computational and Denotational Properties for Scott's D_∞-models of the Lambda-Calculus". *SIAM, Jour. Comput.* 5 (1976).

Large Database Specifications from Small Views.

S. Khosla, T.S.E. Maibaum, M. Sadler

Department of Computing,
Imperial College,
London SW7 2BX.

ABSTRACT

In this paper we explore the role of specification as an aid to database construction. A modal system of logic is introduced to model databases together with a structuring technique to create larger database specifications from smaller ones. The basic theory as well as the additional modelling structure is illustrated initially by characterizing a stack data structure as a "view" of an array data structure. Later we give a more realistic example describing an airline network system. We conclude with items for further research.

1. Introduction

Two schools of thought seem to be prevalent in the area of database specifications : algebraic and logical.

The algebraic approach centers on the Abstract Data Type concept where a database is seen as an algebra whose objects are the data stored in the database and whose operations (functions) represent both the query and update operators of the database. The behavioural characteristics of the updates being given by a set of equations formulated over (in general) mixed expressions, involving functions representing both updates and queries. Similarly equalities are formulated to express structural relationships between the data in the database. However since both queries and updates are both represented as operations on an algebra it is difficult to distinguish between two very different kinds of operation. That is one used to enquire about a structure and one used to change that structure (even if we wish to model operations that do both the distinction should still be made at base level). This distinction is not formally reflected in the algebraic approach where both types of operations are treated in a uniform manner. Notable exponents in this area are Ehrig et al [EKW78] who propose a hierarchical approach, building tables and sequences, and Wirsing et al [DMW82] wherein primitives are introduced that mimic the generalisation and aggregation structures of Smith and Smith [SS76]. However, these approaches have two major shortcomings, firstly they tend to concentrate on formalising the standard data models (relational, hierarchical, etc. essentially by encapsulating the essence of these models as A.D.T.'s) introducing no new modelling concepts, and secondly, the whole approach taken is directly influenced by the A.D.T. unit of specification, which we believe is inappropriate as the major structuring unit to be focused upon whilst constructing database specifications. We think the appropriate unit is that of a view, whose definition and justification we give in section three. Due to its focus on the A.D.T. unit and its insensitivity to the distinction between updates and queries we reject the algebraic framework within which to develop database specifications.

In contrast, the logical approach seems to be more sympathetic in its treatment of distinguishing between static and dynamic issues, by (either implicitly or explicitly) introducing a concept of state/enviroment into their models. Early work both in A.I. and database modelling [Mai79],[MSF80],[Hew69],[MH69]..., simple mindedly, augmented existing techniques by explicitly introducing a state parameter with which to reason about how actions changed information. Recent work [CCF81],[AL81] has been more sutble in its approach to modelling databases, witness the use of various modal and temporal logics to describe and reason the way information changes. In this paper we would like to present a modal style of logic that describes how information changes by formulating and reasoning about the behavior of a named set of atomic actions. We shall refrain in this paper from giving action combinators to form complex actions from atomic ones, we do however deal with parameterisation and quantification on actions (we use action and update inter-changeably). We then go on to show how our formalism can be used to incorporate a modelling technique based on view integration, using this to build large database specifications from smaller ones. In the respect of having a named set of atomic actions our approach can be most likened to that of dynamic logic. In section two we introduce our logic, together with a discussion of its use. Section three introduces various formal definitions of view and how databases relate to other databases. In both sections two and three we make use of a running example, that of stacks and arrays, we chose this for its concise portrayal of the ideas we wanted to express rather than any display of a typical database specification. We give a more appropriate example of a database specification in section four where we discuss a fragment of an airline network system. Section five contains areas of further research.

2. Database Specifications

Below we present a system of modal logic that is built upon the notion of state/environment Our approach will be to tailor such a logic to the specification of particular database applications, i.e. the language of such a logic has names for, the types of data, the relationships/property names of such data and the update names, particular to a specific database. A brief intuitive account of our specification technique is given after which the formal definitions of our logic are introduced. The section concludes with a discussion of the strengths of the system as regards such issues as integrity constraints, queries and update behavior formulation, with the aid of a small example.

Traditionally, modal logic provides and reasons about a structure for a collection of possible worlds (classically, first order theories), called a reachability/accessibility relation. Such a system fits in with our view of seeing a database as a collection of database instances, and some form of control that allows only valid database transitions. We adopt the proof theoretic stance in that each database instance is a classical, many sorted, first order theory (although most logics would do e.g. equational,horn clause etc.). Queries are then theorems to be proved from a particular database instance. The control information that allows only valid database transitions is a part of each database instance. We attribute the name "schema" to this common information. The schema will contain such things as integrity constraints, rules of deduction, and rules for defining database transitions (movement between database instances). The rules for allowing database transitions are based upon a specific (finite) collection of update names, $u_0 \cdots u_n$ say, the axiomatisation of such rules effectively generating the traditional accessibility relation.

Below we present the formal details of our logical system, presenting first the language and then the axioms and rules.

The Language

a) the many sorted first order component

- a non-empty collection of sorts $S = \{s_1, s_2, \cdots\}$, each sort denoting a particular type of entity in the database.
- constant symbols: for each sort $s \in S$ there is a set (possibly empty) of constant symbols each of which is said to be of sort s.
- predicate symbols: for each $n>0$ and each n-tuple, $<s_1 \cdots s_n>$ of sorts, such that $s_1 \in S \cdots s_n \in S$, there is a set (possibly empty) of n-place predicate symbols, each of which is said to be of type $<s_1 \cdots s_n>$. Predicate names denote the properties of and relationships between the entities in the database.

- Function symbols: for each $n>0$ and each $(n+1)$-tuple $<s_1 \cdots s_n, s_{n+1}>$ of sorts, there is a set (possibly empty) of n-place function symbols, each of which is said to be of type $<s_1, \cdots s_n, s_{n+1}>$. Function names are used to denote functional relationships and other structural properties of the entities in the database.
- variables: the usual infinite collection of distinct variables for each sort $s \in S$, i.e. $V_1^s, V_2^s, V_3^s, \cdots$
- quantifiers: for each sort $s \in S$ there is a universal quantifier symbol $\forall_s$.
- existence predicates: for each sort $s \in S$ we introduce a special existence predicate IN_s to allow us to constrain the general quantifier $\forall_s$ to operate on a closed world assumption (C.W.A.) [Reit81] based on information within a particular database instance (as opposed to all potential objects over which variables actually range).
- equality symbols: for certain (possibly all) sorts $s \in S$ there may be a predicate symbol $=_s$ of sort $<s,s>$ representing equality between objects of the sort s.
- punctuation: (,) and , .
- logical connectives: $\neg, \rightarrow, \cdots$

b) the modal component

- a finite collection of typed update symbols $u_0, \cdots u_n$ each denoting a particular update operation, capable of being performed on the database being specified. The update symbols are typed in the same way as the predicate symbols above.
- the modal connectives [_] used in the formation of modal formulae.

This concludes the description of our language.

Formation Rules

a) for the many sorted logic component of our language we use the standard machinery as given by [End80]; briefly for each sort $s \in S$:

- terms:
  - any variables or constant symbols of sort s.
  - if $t_1 \cdots t_n$ are terms of sort $s_1 \cdots s_n$ respectively and f is a function symbol of type $<s_1 \cdots s_n, s_{n+1}>$ then $f\ t_1 \cdots t_n$ is a term of sort s_{n+1}.
- atomic formulae: these are sequences of the form $P\ t_1 \cdots t_n$ consisting of a predicate symbol P of type $<s_1 \cdots s_n>$ and terms $t_1 \cdots t_n$ of sorts $s_1 \cdots s_n$, respectively.
- non atomic formulae: these are then formed in the usual way using the logical connectives $\neg, \rightarrow, \wedge, \vee$, and the quantifiers $\forall_s, s \in S$.

b) given an update symbol u_m of type $<s_1 \cdots s_n>$ from the set of update symbols in our language , terms $t_1 \cdots t_n$ of sorts $s_1 \cdots s_n$, respectively and a formula ϕ then $[u_m t_1 \cdots t_n]\phi$ is also a formula.

Axioms of our system

a) the usual axioms governing $\forall$, $\rightarrow$,and $\neg$ in a classical, many sorted, first order system.

b) the following axioms governing the modal constructor $[\_]$. We use u as a metavariable over the update symbols of our language.

distribution: $[u](P \rightarrow Q) \leftrightarrow ([u]P \rightarrow [u]Q)$

negation: $[u]\neg P \rightarrow \neg[u]P$

quantification: $\forall_s\ x\ [u]P(x) \leftrightarrow [u](\forall_s\ x\ P(x))$

The negation axiom $[u]\neg P \leftrightarrow \neg[u]P$ can be asserted if all the database instances of a database are complete theories. The distribution axiom ensures that the properties of classical implication are preserved over state changes. Lastly the quantification axiom asserts that our global (see below) domains are stable (c.f. Barcan and converse formulaes).

The quantifier $\forall_s$ in the quantification axiom ranges over all values of sort s and so is global. This allows us to quantify over all potential objects of a database: local quantification, or quantification over objects within a particular database instance is achieved by the relativisation construct $\forall_s x(IN_s(x) \rightarrow \cdots)$ where IN_s is the special existence predicate introduced in our language, for the sort s of x. Such relativisation constructs make explicit the closed world assumption of [Reit80]. Note that the sort of x is left implicit, but is clear from the context. This is a practice we will follow for all symbols, leaving the context or a previous definition to determine sorts or types. This concludes the description of our logic.

We now present what a unit of database specification is within such a logic. Firstly however, we need to say that a theory within such a logic will be given as (L,A) where L is the language component of our logic (i.e. those extra-logical symbols used in the specification), and A is a collection of axioms over the language L.

Finally, a database specification unit is comprised of:

1) A schema given as a modal theory (L,A), where the language L contains all the sorts, relation names, function names, update symbols etc. needed in the specification of the database. The axioms A expressing properties such as integrity constraints and update behaviour. An example is given below detailing the contents of such a schema.

2) A collection of database instances given as a collection of modal theories $\{(L,A_i)\}$, $i\in I$ where I is an indexing set over all valid database instances. Each (L,A_i) must be an extension of the schema (L,A) and contains as subtheory the schema, i.e. $\forall i\in I\ (L,A)\subseteq(L,A_i)$ where $\subseteq$ is the subtheory relation defined as:

$$(L,A)\subseteq(L,A_i) \equiv If\ (L,A)\vdash\phi\ then\ (L,A_i)\vdash\phi$$

Each theory (L,A_i) represents a distinct database instance and so we have:

$$\forall i,j\in I,\ i\neq j\ \ implies\ \ Con(L,A_i)\neq Con(L,A_j)$$

where

$$Con(L,A_i) = \{\ \phi \mid (L,A_i)\vdash\phi\ \}$$

The set of extensions $(L,A_i)i\in I$ must also satisfiy the following coherence condition: Given any (L,A_i), if $A_i\vdash[u]\phi$, then $\exists i'\in I$ such that $A_{i'}\vdash\phi$. This coherence condition states that the properties of an update which are said to be true after the update is performed, can actually be true somewhere. The connection (given in 2 above) between the database schema and the database instances, is expressed in our logic by the following rule

$$\frac{(L,A)\vdash P}{\forall i\in I\ (L,A_i)\vdash P}$$

The rule says anything provable from the database schema is provable from any of the database instances (a kind of Necessitation Rule). Perhaps at this point it will be instructive to give an intuitive semantics for our logic. Consider the following:

1) A collection of many sorted structures $\{M_j\}$, $j\in J$ such that for each M_j

- each $s\in S$ is assigned a non empty set $|M|_s$ called the universe of sort s.
- each predicate symbol P of type $<s_1\cdots s_n>$ is assigned the relation

$$P_j\subseteq|M|_{s_1}\times\cdots\times|M|_{s_n}$$

- each constant symbol c of sort $s\in S$ is assigned a point c_j in $|M|_s$.
- each function symbol f of type $<s_1\cdots s_n,s_{n+1}>$ is assigned a function $f_j : |M|_{s_1}\times\cdots\times|M|_{s_n}\rightarrow|M|_{s_{n+1}}$.

Thus each structure M_j has the same underlying set of objects $|M|_s s\in S$. The definitions of truth and satisfaction are the standard ones given that $\forall_s$ means "for all members of the universe $|M|_s$ of sort $s\in S$". The special existence predicates IN_s distinguishes between potential and actual objects within any particular model.

2) A set of partial functions $|u_i|_M : |M|_{s_1}\times\cdots\times|M|_{s_n}\times\{M_j\}\rightarrow\{M_j\}$ one function for each update symbol u_i of type $<s_1\cdots s_n>$ given in the language (L) of our database specification.

A model for a database specification (i.e. a schema (L,A) and a collection of database instances (L,A_i) $i\in I$) is then obtained if there is an M_j for each (L,A_i) $i\in I$ such that:

$$\forall\phi\ ((L,A_i)\vdash\phi\leftrightarrow M_j^i\models\phi\ )$$

and

$$\forall j\in J\ \ (M_j\models[u_i t_1 .. t_n]\phi\leftrightarrow|u_i|_M\ (|t_1|_M,..,|t_n|_M\ )\ (M_j)\models\phi\ )$$

where $|t_k|_M(1\leq k\leq n)$ is the value of t_k in M_j as defined in the obvious way using 1) above. Thus $[u_i t_1\cdots t_n]$ is valid in M_j if and only if in the " state " or structure $|u_i t_1\cdots t_n|_M(M_j)$ obtained by performing the update on M_j , the formula ϕ is true.

We now discuss the various types of information that a schema contains and then present an example. In the example we show how our theory may by applied to a well known data structure - stacks - treating it as a simple database.

Static Integrity Constraints

These are simply expressed as first order formulae, since they deal with only the static aspects of database instances and as such this collection of constraints is used to define the collection of database instances that are valid. Examples of such constraints in English would be:

a) "If a course exists then a lecturer must teach it"

b) "All lecturers' salaries must be below 50k"

In our system these would be formulated as:

$$\forall_{course}x(In\text{-}course(x)\rightarrow\exists_{lecturer}y(In\text{-}lecturer(y)\wedge teaches(y,x))) \quad \text{(a)}$$

$$\forall_{lecturer}x(lecturer(x)\rightarrow salaryof(x)<50{,}000) \quad \text{(b)}$$

So that in (b) we are constraining all lecturers to have salaries below 50 K regardless of wheather or not we keep a record of such lecturers in our database (they might for example exist in other databases). Whereas in (a) we quantify only over information held in database being modelled. Note that in (a) we have used "$\exists x$" as shorthand for "$\neg\forall x\neg$".

Dynamic Integrity Constraints

Traditionally these have been of use in the field of database study, to constrain the manner in which database transitions may occur. The much used example of "salaries must not decrease" as a dynamic constraint, we believe, should be seen as a property to be proven from a particular specification . The specification is simply comprised of the behavioural aspects of updates and from this, properties such as "salaries must not decrease" may be deduced. This focuses the attention on specifying updates as the units which behaviourally characterise a database, these updates are then "tuned" so as to conform to constraints like "salaries don't decrease". We see the activities of update behaviour characterisation and dynamic constraint specification as essentially orthognal, but related as above.

Update Behaviour

A collection of modal formulae are used to represent both those conditions under which updates are permitted and their effects upon the states (database instances) in which they are applied. An example of such behaviour regarding updates would be "Tom can be hired as a lecturer if he is not already one". This would be formulated as:

$$\neg\, In\text{-}lecturer(TOM) \rightarrow [Hire(TOM)]In\text{-}lecturer(TOM).$$

This can be seen to be of the form $P \rightarrow [u]Q$ were P is the precondition of the update, i.e. that assertion which must be true before the update can be applied, and Q is the postcondition that asserts what is true after the update is performed. If we think of our state space as being all database instances constrained under a set of integrity constraints then pre-conditions on updates pick out all those states in which particular updates may be performed, and given the current database instance, postconditions dictate the properties of the new database instance arrived at by performing an update. The construct $[u]Q$ is to be read "after the update u 'Q' will hold", whilst the construct $P \rightarrow [u]Q$ is read as "if P holds now then after the update u is performed, then 'Q' will hold".

Work currently in progress will enable us to specify when updates can be performed not only on information that pertains to a particular database instance, but also on the "knowledge" that some information may in the future/past become/have been part of the database. This is related to the notion of hypothetical query which allows the use of modal formulae in queries. After all, a formula of the form $[u]Q$ "evaluated" in a given instance (L, A_i) is possibly true or false but says nothing about the update "u" actually being performed. Our units of specification define only the structural properties of the database . How and when updates are actually performed is then dependent on the use of some command language which tells the system to perform a particular update. Properties of such "command programs" can then be determined using the logic and the structural properties as given by the units of specification. However we shall not deal with such issues in this paper.

In the next section we introduce a structuring method, one that we believe to be the major structuring unit for databases. First we give an example of a unit of database specification.

Example

stacks (of integers) - a state based specification approach.

The usual way in which stacks are specified is within an algebraic framework by way of an equational axiomatisation, see for instance [LZ75]. However, if we think of a stack as a twofold entity viz a stack name and a stack extension (items held on the stack) then invariably the extension will change over time. This can be likened to a database in that a database's contents (extensional information) changes over time. If we see the stack in this light then the push and pop operators of a stack can be thought of as state changing updates, between all valid stack states (characterised by integrity constraints). The function top associated with a stack can then be seen to be a query operator that is evaluated within a particular (usually the current) state of the stack. We first present the language (L) and then the schema axioms (A) that specify stacks in this way.

L:

- sorts: naturals (abbreviated as nat)
- Functions

  Top: $\rightarrow$ *nat*

  Succ: nat $\rightarrow$ *nat*

- constants for nat: 0
- predicates for nat: $=_{nat}$ (nat,nat) which will normally be written in infix notation without the subscript.
- variables for nat: $n, n', n'' \cdots$
- update names:

  Pop

  Push (nat)

A:

$$\forall n\ [\text{Push(n)}]\ \text{Top}=n \tag{1}$$

$$\forall n\ \forall n'\ (\text{Top}=n \rightarrow [\text{Push(n')}][\text{Pop}]\ \text{Top}=n\ ) \tag{2}$$

$$\forall n\ \neg(0=\text{Succ(n)}) \tag{3}$$

$$\forall n\ \forall n'(\text{Succ(n)}=\text{Succ(n')} \rightarrow n=n') \tag{4}$$

We now need to define the set of extensions $(L,A_i)\ i \in I$ which stand for database instances. These extensions will all be of the following form:

$$A \cup \left\{ Top{=}n_1, [Pop]Top{=}n_2, \ldots, [Pop]^{m-1}Top{=}n_m \right\}$$

where $[Pop]^1{=}[Pop]$, $[Pop]^{j+1}{=}[Pop]^j[Pop]$ and A is the set of four axioms above. This theory is used to define the stack $<n_1, \ldots, n_m>$ with n_1 being the top and n_m being the bottom of the stack. Note that this theory is incomplete in that we could not prove that $[Pop]^m Top{=}k$ for any particular k. In other words we have no information about what happens when we pop the empty stack. A collection of extensions of the above form would then represent the collection of stack instances, each extension representing a particular instance.

The theory (L,A) together with the rule for the schema (given earlier) is the schema representing the "database" called stacks of integers. A collection of database instances (L,A_i) $i \in I$, represent the distinct states a stack can be in. A query is then a theorem to be proven from any such database instance (L,A_i). The answer to the query "Is 7 the top of stack s?" in a database state i would be "yes" if $(L,A_i) \vdash Top{=}7$, and "no" otherwise. Similarly, suppose the database is in state $i \in I$ and $(L,A_i) \vdash Top{=}5$; then if the update $Push(6)$ is performed, the database will move to state $j, j \in I$ such that $(L,A_j) \vdash Top{=}6$. We conclude this example by pointing out that this action/change centered approach best suits one's intuition when reasoning about stacks. One sees a stack as a changing object, changes being affected by the actions of pop and push.

A possible integrity constraint for such a database may be:

$$\forall_i n \ (n{=}_i 0) \vee (n{=}_i Succ(0)) \vee (n{=}_i Succ(Succ(0)))$$

which says that only the integers 0, 1, 2 are allowed on stacks . The above would be part of the schema and constrain the types of database instances that are valid.

3. Views

In the previous section we presented a system of modal logic for the specification of databases. In this section we would like to present one particular way in which database specifications relate to each other in such a system. The term (user) view (external level [ANSI]) is used in the literature to denote a conceptual description of a database which suits one user or one group of users. The idea being that different users may be interested in different and perhaps overlapping parts of a database. Most researchers in the area of views ([Web79], [PAO77]) and related issues such as the view update problem ([BS81], [BD82]), have centered their approaches around the notion of a state space. Briefly, this involves considering a database as the set of all its legal states (database instances) called a state space. A view is then something which gives rise to a partitioning of this state space. Since an invariant property of a database is its state space and a view of a database gives rise to a partitioning of this state space, we can conclude that a view agrees with the intensional characteristics of the database(under an equivalence relation on states). We note that our modal logic is built on just such a state space notion and so lends itself nicely to the notion of views and - some of the promising - research being conducted in the area of views. The algebraic approach to specifications takes a similar line in that views are regarded as (algebraic) reducts of the algebra (usually an isomorphic class of algebras) given by a database specification. A treatment of view merging is given in [Go82] using the theory of order sorted algebras [Go78]. However, such an approach still suffers from the criticisms inherent in the algebraic approach as discussed in the introduction.

We proceed now to give the definition of a view in terms of a particular kind of mapping between two database specifications. So a view can be thought of as a special kind of relation that holds between database specifications (modal theories). This definition of a view is formulated as a restricted form of logical implementation which in turn uses the mechanism of interpretations between theories. Our definition will be three tiered defining in turn what is meant by an interpretation between theories, a logical implementation and finally a view. We again emphasis that such a relation is built upon the basic unit of a database specification given in Section 2. We see the relationship of view as just one particular relationship that exists between such specification units. We comment upon other possibilities in the conclusion.

Interpretations between Theories

The theories with which we are dealing are modal in nature. An interpretation between two such modal languages $\{L\}$ and $\{L'\}$ is a function

$\Pi : L \to L'$ such that Π takes

- each sort in L to a (collection of) sort(s) in L'
- constants in L to a (collections of) constant symbol(s) in L'
- function symbols in L to (collections of) function symbol(s) in L'.
- predicate symbols in L to predicate symbols in L'.
- update symbols in L to update symbols in L'.
- each sort s in L to a special predicate R_s called the relativisation predicate in L'.
- update symbols of type $<s_1,..,s_n>$ of L to sequences of update symbols of L' where the types of the symbols appearing in the sequence are restricted to the collection $\Pi(s_i)$.

The function $\Pi : L \to L'$ is known as an interpretation between the theories (L,A) and (L',A') iff

$$\forall\phi \;\; ((L,A) \vdash \phi \to (L',A') \vdash \phi^{\pi})$$

where ϕ denotes a formula constructed in the language L, and ϕ^{π} is the formula after a language change from L to L' under Π. The definition of $\Pi : L \to L'$ leads to a straightforward inductive definition of a translation of terms over L to terms over L'. For translation of formulae over L to formulae over L' we must indicate what happens with the logical symbols:

variables of sort s	to	a (tuple of) variable(s) of sort(s) $\Pi(s)$
$\neg, \vee, \rightarrow, \cdots$	to	$\neg, \vee, \rightarrow, \cdots$ resp.
$([ut_1 \cdots t_n])^\pi$	to	$[\Pi(u)(t_1)^\pi \cdots (t_n)^\pi]$
$(\forall_s x \phi)^\pi$	to	$\forall (x)^\pi (R_s((x)^\pi) \rightarrow \phi^\pi)$

again to cope with the "legal" values which variables should be allowed to take.

A more formal account of interpretations between theories (in the first order case) can be found in [End72].

Logical Implementation

Having given a definition of what it is to be an interpretation between two modal theories (L,A) and (L',A'), we recall that a database specification consists of a schema (L,A) and a collection of database instances (L,A_i) $i \in I$. Given two databases $(L,A), (L,A_i)$ $i \in I$ and $(L',A'), (L',A'_j)$ $j \in J$ we first define the mapping SI from extensions (L,A_i) to sets of extensions (L',A'_j) by

$$(L,A_i)^{SI} = \left\{ (L',A'_j) \mid A'_j \vdash \phi^\pi \ \ if \ \ (L,A_i) \vdash \phi \right\}$$

where Π is an interpretation from L to L'.

Next we define Π (note that we use the same symbol as for the underlying interpretation between languages) from sets of extensions of (L,A) to sets of extensions of (L',A') by defining Π on singleton sets as follows:

$$\left\{ (L,A_i) \right\}^\Pi = (L,A_i)^{SI} - \cup_j (L,A_j)^{SI}$$

for (L,A_j) an extention of (L,A_i) and $j \in I$ and $\cup_j$ being a union operator on modal theories. Note that the above defines the image of the singleton (L,A_i) to be all those (L',A'_j) which preserve the properties in A_i but excludes those states which correspond to distinct states (L,A_k) which extend the information contained in (L,A_i). Thus we do not want Π to collapse states of $(L,A_i) i \in I$ and make them indistinguishable in $(L,A_j) j \in J$.

Views

Again, given two database specifications $(L,A), (L,A_i)\ i \in I$ and $(L',A'), (L',A'_j)\ j \in J$, we say the first is a view of the second iff the following conditions hold:

$$(L,A), (L,A_i)\ i \in I \text{ can be implemented in } (L',A'), (L',A'_j)\ j \in J \tag{1}$$

as above, and

$$\forall j \in J\ \exists i \in I : (L',A'_j) \in \left\{(L,A_i)\right\}^{\Pi} \tag{2}$$

The second of these properties we call the "covering" property. A database cannot move into a state which is not "visible" in a view. To conclude, any mapping that obeys the above conditions we call a view; we emphasise that it is the mapping (relationship) between two database specifications that gives rise to the fact that one database can be thought of as a view of another.

Having given the above definitions we now illustrate their purpose in the area of database construction. The interpretation mechanism is useful in that generally database specifications will not be in the same language. For example, some users would like to refer to employees by their full names whereas others may want to refer to them by national insurance numbers. Given two database specifications, $DB1$ and $DB2$, the purpose of having logical implementations is to ensure that each database instance of $DB1$ can be represented by a database instance of $DB2$ where the relation $DB1$ - logical implementation $\rightarrow DB2$ holds. There may be more than one such database instance in $DB2$; this is only to be expected as $DB2$ in general may be a "larger" database. We use "larger" in the sense of, "has the potential to contain more information", that is larger state space. So, in general the logical implementation step will take a database instance in $DB1$ say, (L,A_i), to a collection of database instances in $DB2$ $\{(L',A'_j)\}$ such that from (L,A_i) we cannot distinguish between the states $\{(L',A'_j)\}$. The extra condition introduced in the definition of view requires that for any database instance (L',A'_j) in $DB2$ there exists at least one database instance (L,A_i) in $DB1$ such that (L,A_i) represents/reflects the database instance (L',A'_j). The intuition behind this is that for any state the database DB1 may be in, there is a (collection of) state(s) the database DB2 is in, such that all the information that can be obtained (provable in our case) from the former can also be obtained from the latter.

We illustrate a view mapping between two databases, by performing just such an interpretation between schemas. We continue with our stacks example, showing how stacks are just one way to view "arrays (of integers) and pointers". We start by giving the schema for the theory of "Arrays".

L':

- Sorts: nat
- Functions:
  - val:nat → nat
  - $Succ$:nat → nat
- Constants for:
  - nat: 0
- Variables for:
  - nat: $n', n'', n''', \cdots$
- Update names:
  - Assign (nat,nat)
- Equalities: $=_{nat}$

A':

$$\forall n \forall n' \forall n'' \forall n''' (\neg n = n' \rightarrow [Assign(n',n'')][Assign(n,n''')]\phi \leftrightarrow$$

$$[Assign(n,n''')][Assign(n',n'')]\phi) \text{ for all formulae } \phi \quad (1)$$

$$\forall n \forall n' [Assign(n,n')]val(n) = n' \quad (2)$$

The above theory (L',A') is then a general theory about unbounded arrays. The extensions $(L',A'_j)j\epsilon J$ defining states of the array database are theories of the form:

$$A' \cup \left\{ val(n_1)=m_1, \ldots, val(n_k)=m_k \right\}$$

(where k is unbounded). We require that the n_i be pairwise unequal to ensure val remains a function. We can implement our previous theory about stacks using this. First, we require an extension of arrays. We introduce only the symbols and axioms needed to define the extension. Note that all the symbols introduced are derived concepts in the theory of arrays. That is, we present definitions (axioms defining properties) of the new symbols which allow us to extend any model of arrays to a model of the extended arrays.

L'':

- New constants for:
  - nat: Pointer,Top'
- New update names:
  - Incre-pointer

- Decre-pointer
- Push'(nat)
- Pop'

A'':

$$Is\text{-}nat(n) \tag{1}$$

$$Pointer=n \rightarrow [Incre\text{-}pointer]\ Pointer=Succ(n) \tag{2}$$

$$Pointer=0 \rightarrow [Decre\text{-}pointer]\ Pointer=0 \tag{3}$$

$$Pointer=n \text{ and} \neg n=0 \rightarrow [Decre\text{-}pointer]\ Succ(Pointer)=n \tag{4}$$

$$\neg\ Pointer=0 \rightarrow Top' = Val(Pointer) \tag{5}$$

$$[Push'(n)]\ Q \leftrightarrow [Incre\text{-}pointer]\ [Assign(Pointer,n)]\ Q \tag{6}$$

$$[Pop']\ Q \leftrightarrow [Decre\text{-}pointer]\ Q \tag{7}$$

This will give us the usual pointer-array representation of stacks with the pointer at array position zero representing the empty stack. Note that (1) defines the relativisation predicate for nat in stacks to be the trivial predicate Is-nat(x); i.e. all natural numbers in arrays are representatives of naturals in stacks. Axioms (2),(3) and (4) define the properties of the new updates used to manipulate pointers. Axiom (5) defines the constant Top' in terms of val and pointer. Axioms (6) and (7) define how Push and Pop are implemented in terms of pointer and array updates. Note that (6) and (7) are schematic formulae and Q is a meta variable ranging over formulae.

We now define the interpretation between the stack data base and the extended array database. Note that this is defined in terms of a language correspondence defined as follows:

	L	$L' \cup L''$
Sorts	nat	nat
Constants	0	0
Functions	Succ	Succ
	Top	Top'
Updates	Push	Push'
	Pop	Pop'
Relativisation Predicates	nat	Is-nat

We now complete the definition of the implementation of stacks via arrays and pointers by specifing the theories of arrays and pointers which are images of each stack state.

Let our stack state be defined by the axioms

$$A \cup \left\{Top=n_1,[Pop]Top=n_2,\ldots,[Pop]^{m-1}Top=n_m\right\}$$

We map this to all the theories which include

$$A' \cup A'' \cup \left\{Val(Succ(0))=n_1,\ldots,Val(Succ^m(0))=n_m,Pointer=m\right\}$$

Note that many theories of arrays and pointers represent the same stack state space. Such an implementation however is not a view as there are many theories which do not represent stacks. A simple example of a view mapping can be given in terms of the following database specification *Stack**. It is similar to *Stack* but the top of the empty stack is now defined to be error.

L^*:

- Sorts: nat^*
- Functions: $Succ^*: nat^* \rightarrow nat^*$
- Constants:
  - $0^*: \rightarrow nat^*$
  - error : $\rightarrow nat^*$

- $Top^*: \to nat^*$

- Update names: $Push^*(nat^*), Pop^*$
- Variables for nat^*: n,n',n'',...

A:*

$$\forall n[Push^*(n)]Top^*=n \tag{1}$$

$$\forall n \forall n'(Top^*=n \to [Push^*(n')][Pop^*]Top^*=n) \tag{2}$$

$$Top^*=error \to [Pop^*]Top^*=error \tag{3}$$

The extensions defining valid states are of the form A* together with:

$$\left\{\begin{matrix} Top^* = n_1,[Pop^*]Top^* = n_2, \\ [Pop^*]^{m-1}Top^* = n_m, \\ [Pop^*]^m Top^* = error, \\ [Pop^*]^{m+1}Top^* = error,.... \end{matrix}\right\}$$

The view mapping is now the obvious one where we map symbols of Stack to their corresponding asterisked versions and we map the extensions defined by

$$A \cup \left\{Top=n_1,[Pop]Top=n_2,\ldots,[Pop]^{m-1}Top=n_m\right\}$$

to the set containing only the above extension of *Stack**. Clearly this is an implementation and it has the covering property. It also illustrates the idea of a view hiding information.

Over some time we have witnessed a large growth in both the size and complexity of database systems. Databases for large multinationals and government bodies are prime examples of this. The task of specifying such information "warehouses" has equally become both lengthy and difficult, and even within the framework presented in section two, we realise that the task of specifying such large databases is less than palatable. Issues such as manageability of specifications have been addressed in the pioneering paper of [LZ76] wherein structuring techniques for program specifications are discussed.

We claim that the formation of database specifications based upon view integration has the following benefits.

- The decomposition of specifying a database into specifying a collection of database (user views) leads in general to specifications of a more manageable size.

- Since each database specification has as one component, a language, different user views may benefit from being specified using different (appropriate) languages. For example, in a "standard" employee's record database, an accountants user view may want to refer to employees via their National Insurance numbers, whereas a personnel user view may wish to refer to employees via their full names.
- Parallelism is allowed in that the specification of user views may take place concurrently

  The approach reflects not only the manner in which users or groups thereof "see" the database, but also the structural properties of how such users relate to one another via the view relationship.
- Local evolvability in that as new user views are introduced to the system their correct place can be found in the system.

We conclude by observing that our treatment of user views differs from the standard notion in the literature where, and we quote from [SPY], "A view is a database whose schema is derived from the schema of a given database". The approach taken is to think of a view as a derived object from an existing database rather than a component used in the construction of databases. We see the view mapping notion introduced above as just one particular combinator that relates database specifications.

4. Airline Example

We would now like to illustrate the use of the modal framework developed in the preceding sections, in specifing a more appropriate database application. We choose as our example a simple airline network system in which a plane is tracked as it flies between a number of cities. The function of the database is threefold

- To keep a record of where the plane is (in which city) at any time, the query function "where" given below facilitates access to this information.
- To hold information about which cities it is possible to fly to from a given city. The binary predicate "Connected" (both arguments being city) enumerates which cities it is possible to fly between using the convention flight is only possible from the first argument to the second. The query function "connectionto" facilitates access to this information.
- To take note of the fact the plane may move from city to city, and so appropriately change the city the plane is in. This is characterised by the update "Flyto" which takes as parameter the city the plane is to fly to.

We now present the example giving as before the language followed by the axioms.

L:

- Sorts: city, plane, bool
- Functions :

  where : → city
  connectionto : city → bool

- Constants for city :

  Glasgow, Manchester, London, Paris, Nice
  Frankfurt, Berlin

- Constants for plane :

  Myplane

- Constants for bool :

  true

- Predicates for city :

  Connected(city, city)
  $=_{city}$ (city, city)
  usually written infix and without subscript

- Variables for city :

  $c, c', c'' \cdots$

- Update names :

  Flyto(city)

A:

$$\left\{\begin{array}{c} Connected(Glasgow, Manchester),\ Connected(Manchester, London) \\ Connected(London, Paris),\ Connected(Paris, Nice) \\ Connected(Nice, Paris),\ Connected(Paris, Frankfurt) \\ Connected(Frankfurt, Berlin),\ Connected(Berlin, Frankfurt) \\ Connected(Frankfurt, London) \end{array}\right\} \quad (\text{:}$$

$$\forall c\ Connected(c,c) \quad (\text{:}$$

$$\forall c \forall c'\ \neg c = c' \wedge where = c \wedge Connected(c,c') \quad (\text{:}$$

$$\rightarrow [Flyto(c')] where = c'$$

$$\forall c \forall c' \; where=c \wedge Connected(c,c') \rightarrow connectionto(c')=tt \tag{4}$$

Note we do not here initilize the plane to be in any starting city. It should also be clear that once the plane flies from Manchester or Glasgow it cannot return. The intented effect of the update "Flyto" is that the location of the plane only changes after the plane has arrived at its new destination, retaining its previous location record until this is so. The extentions, $<L,A_i>i \in I$, of the above schema $<L,A>$ are of the following form

$$A \cup \left\{ where=Paris,\ connectionto(Nice)=true,\ connectionto(Frankfurt)=tt \right\}$$

where the connection to information changes depending upon what the value of the query function "where" is (i.e. the planes location). We now give another specification of an airline network database application and then discuss how it may be regarded as a view of the former. The intended meaning of the following specification should be clear from the previous example.

L':

- Sorts: airports, aircraft, bool
- Functions:

  where : → airports
  nextlink : airports → bool

- Constants for airports :

  Glasgow, London, Paris, Nice,
  Frankfurt

- Constants for aircraft :

  Jet

- Constants for bool :

  true

- Predicates for airports :

  Airlink(airports, airports)
  $=_{airports}$ (airports, airports)
  usually written infix and without subscript

- Variables for airports :

$c, c', c'' \cdots$

- Update names :

  Flyplane(airports)

A':

$$\left\{\begin{array}{c} Airlink(Glasgow, London),\ Airlink(Frankfurt, London) \\ Airlink(London, Paris),\ Airlink(Paris, Nice) \\ Airlink(Nice, Paris),\ Airlink(Paris, Frankfurt) \end{array}\right\} \quad (1)$$

$$\forall c\ Airlink(c,c) \quad (2)$$

$$\forall c \forall c'\ \neg c=c' \wedge where=c \wedge Airlink(c,c') \quad (3)$$

$$\rightarrow [Flyplane(c')]where=c'$$

$$\forall c \forall c'\ where=c \wedge Airlink(c,c') \rightarrow nextlink(c')=tt \quad (4)$$

Again the extentions $<L',A'_j>$ for this schema $<L',A'>$ are of the form

$$A' \cup \left\{where=Glasgow,\ nextlink(London)=tt\right\}$$

It is at once evident that the second specification $<L',A'>$ is very similar to the first $<L,A>$, it differs only in the fact that it does not mention knowledge about the two places Manchester and Berlin. It is clear from looking at the state spaces of our schema that, given a naive translation of the languages from L' to L (where city goes to airport, plane goes to aircraft and Flyto goes to Flyplane) $<L',A'>$ is not (in our formal sense) a view of $<L,A>$. The problems incurred by such a mapping are twofold.

a) If in the view $<L',A'>$ we wish to move the plane from Glasgow to London, the database $<L,A>$ only "knows" how to move the plane from Glasgow to Manchester and from Manchester to London. Clearly we need to translate the movement of the plane from Glasgow to London, within $<L',A'>$, as a movement from Glasgow to London via Manchester, within $<L,A>$.

b) Also since Berlin and Manchester are not represented in $<L',A'>$ it is clear that the covering property is not preserved.

To remedy both these anomalies and so represent $<L',A'>$ as a view of $<L,A>$ we need to do two things.

1) Extend the specification $<L,A>$ so that the base reacts as required when the view ($<L',A'>$) instigates plane movement from Glasgow to London. Compare this to taking

the "Push" operation on stacks to that of "Incre" and "Assign", in the stack example. The extention will be the following

- To the language L add the update name "Flyto'" and a new equality "='". Taking as argument city and (city,city) resp. We assume the usual axioms of equivalence for the predicate "='" (reflexivity, transitivity and symmetry).
- To the axioms A add the axioms

$$where{=}Glasgow \rightarrow [Flyplane'(London)]\phi$$

$$\leftrightarrow [Flyto(Manchester)][Flyto(London)]\phi$$

$$\forall c \; \neg \, where{=}Glasgow \rightarrow [Flyplane'(c)]\phi$$

$$\leftrightarrow [Flyto(c)]\phi$$

$$='(Berlin,Manchester)$$

2) Extend the specification <L',A'> so that the view (<L',A'>) state space conforms to the covering property given earlier. Compare this to the specification $stack^*$. The extention is

- To the language L' add the airport constant "Unavailable".
- Replace axiom (3) in A' by :

$$\forall c \forall c' \; \neg c{=}c' \wedge Airlink(c,c') \wedge where{=}c \wedge \neg c{=}Unavailable$$

$$\rightarrow [Flyplane(c')] \; where{=}c'$$

The following translation between the augmented languages L' and L will then ensure that <L',A'> is a view of <L,A>.

	L'	L
sorts	airports	city
	aircraft	plane
	bool	bool
constants for plane	Jet	Myplane
constants for city	Glasgow	Glasgow
	Unavailable	Manchester
	London	London
	Paris	Paris
	Nice	Nice

	Frankfurt	Frankfurt
	Unavailable	Berlin
functions	where	where
	nextlink	connectionto
predicates	Airlink	Connected
	$=_{airports}$	$='$
updates	Flyplane	Flyplane'

5. Further Research

In this paper we have described a formalism to model databases and a method to enable "larger" databases to be constructed from "smaller" ones. In this section we would like to take the oppertunity to mention some extentions under development.

An obvious addition to make would be the introduction of combinators on actions, such as sequential/parallel composition and non deterministic choice, so that more complex actions can be built from more primitive ones. It is expected that such non atomic actions will be characterised in terms of the pre and post conditions of their atomic constituents (with respect to the particular combinators used).

In section two above we said that the role of the pre condition in characterising an action was to describe states in which the application of the action transformed that state into a state of which the post condition of that action held true. We tacitly assumed however that the action could be performed in a state if it satisfied the pre condition, but we feel there is a distinction to be made between describing the behaviour of an action in a given context/state and describing the conditions under which an action can be performed. To accommodate this distinction we are developing a deontic style logic (non alethic) to enable us to specify conditions under which actions are permitted/obligatory or forbidden [Kh85]. Not only does this separation of concerns aid us in our characterisation of actions but it will also add to the kind of reasoning we are allowed to perform. For example " i can only do action 'a' if i am forbidden to do action 'b' " ,.. etc.

Another remark worth mention is that we have assumed above that users are "attached" to a particular view, we would like to extend our system to deal with users who operate across views. We have definite ideas about how such an extention can be made and this is the subject of a forth comming report [Kh85].

References

[AL81] J. F. Allen : A general model of action and time, TR97, Nov 81, Department of Computing, University of Rochester.

[ANSI] The ANSI/SPARC DBMS Model: Proc. of the Second SHARE Working Conf. on Database Management Systems, Montreal, Canada, North- Holland (1977).

[Bau81] Bauer et al: Report on a wide spectrum language for program specification and development. Report TUM-I8104, Institut fur Informatic, Technische Universitat Munchen (1981).

[BG80] R. M. Burstall, J. A. Gougen: The Semantics of Clear: A Specification Language. In Proc, Advanced Course on Abstract Software Specification (D. Bjourner (ed.)), LNCS ^S86^S (1980).

[BS81] F. Bancilhon, N. Spyratos, "Update Semantics of Relational Views," ACM-TODS, Vol. 6, No. 4, Dec. 1981.

[CCF81] M. A. Cassanova, J. M. V. Castilho, A. L. Furtado: "Properties of Conceptual and External Database Schemes". Series: Monografias em Ciencias da Computacao No. 11/81, Departmento de Informatica P.U.C do Rio de Janeiro.

[Chen76] P. Chen: The Entity-Relationship Model - Toward a Unified View of Data, ACM-TODS, Vol. 1, 1976.

[DB82] U. Dayal, P. A. Bernstein: On the Correct Translation of Update Operations on Relational Views, ACM-TODS, Vol. 8, No. 3, Sept. 1982, pp 381-416.

[DMW82] W. Dosch, G. Mascari, M. Wirsing: On the Algebraic Specification of Databases, R, 82-11 Universita di Roma, Instituto di Automatica Agosto 1982.

[EFH83] H. Ehrig, H. J. Kreowski, H. Hansen: ACT ONE, An Algebraic Specification Language with Two Levels of Semantics, Techn. Report TU Berlin, No. 83-03, 1983.

[EKW78] H. Ehrig, H. J. Kreowski, H. Weber: Algebraic Specification Schemes for Database Systems, Proc. of 4th Int. Conf. on Very large Databases, 1978.

[EmKo76] M. H. Van Emden, R. A. Kowalski: The Semantics of Predicate Logic as a Programming Language, Journal of the ACM 23(4): 733- 742, 1976.

[End72] H. B. Enderton: "A Mathematical Introduction to Logic", Academic Press (1972).

[Go78] J. A. Goguen: Order Sorted Algebra, Technical Report, UCLA Computer Science Department, 1978, Semantics and Theory of Computation, Report No. 14.

[Go82] J. A. Goguen: Merged Views, Closed Worlds and Ordered Sorts, Internal Report, SRI, 1982.

[Gol82] F. Golshani: "Growing Certainty with Null Values", Research Report DOC 82/22, Imperial College, U.K.

[GMS83] F. Golshani, T. S. E. Maibaum, M. Sadler: "A Modal System of Algebras for Database Specification and Query/Update Language Support", Ninth Int. Conf. on Very Large Databases, pp 331-339, Florence, Italy, 1983.

[GoTa79] J. A. Goguen, J. Tardo: An Introduction to OBJ: a Language for Writing and Testing Software Specifications. In "Specification of Reliable Software", pp 170-189, IEEE, 1979.

[Gut76] J. V. Guttag: Abstract Data Types and the Development of Data Structures, Supplement to Proc. Conf. on Data Abstraction, Definition and Structure, SIGPLAN Notices 8, March 1976.

[Hew69] C. Hewitt, "Planner: A language for Proving Theorems in Robots," in Proc. IJCAI, Washington DC, pp 295-301.

[Kh85] S. Khosla : A Deontic Logic to Describe Actions, Dept. of Computing Report, Imperial college, London.

[Ko81a] R. A. Kowalski: Private Communication, 1981.

[Ko81b] R. A. Kowlaski: Logic as a Database Language, Proc. of Advanced Seminar on Theoretical Issues in Databases, Cetraro, Italy, 1981.

[LZ75] B. Liskov, S. Zilles: "Specification Techniques for Data Abstractions," IEEE Transactions on Software Engineering, Vol. 1, No. 1, pp 7-19, 1975

[MH69] J. McCarthy, P. J. Hayes Some Philosophical Problems from A.I. in Machine Intelligence 4.

[NiGa78] J. M. Nicolas, H. Galliere: "Database: Theory vs Interpretation", in Logic and Databases, ed. Galliere and Minker, 1978.

[Ma81] T. S. E. Maibaum: "Database Instances, Abstract Data Types and Database Specification", To Appear in the Computing Journal of the British Computer Society.

[Mo73] J. Morriss: "Types are not Sets", Conference Record of the ACM Symposium on Principles of Programming Languages, Boston, Mass, pp 120-124, 1973.

[MSF80] T. S. E. Maibaum, C. S. dos Santos, A. L. Furtado: "A Uniform Logical Treatment of Queries and Updates", Technical Report DB018001 - Jan. 80, Department de Informatica, PUC do Rio de Janeiro.

[MSV83] T. S. E. Maibaum, M. R. Sadler, P. A. S. Veloso: Logical Implementation, Internal Report, Dept. of Computing, Imperial College, (U.K.), 1983.

[PAO77] P. Paolini, G. Pelagatti, "Formal Definition of Mappings in a Database," ACM SIGMOD conference proceedings, 1977.

[Reit78] R. Reiter: "On Closed World Databases," in Logic and Databases, ed. Galliere and Minker, 1978.

[ReBr80] N. Rescher, R. Brandom: The Logic of inconsistency, APQ Library of Philosophy, Basil Blackwell (Publishers), Oxford, 1980.

[SS76] J. M. Smith, D. C. P. Smith: Database Abstractions: Aggregation and Generalization, ACM-TODS Vol. 2, 1977.

[SanWir83] D. Sannella, M. Wirsing: A Kernal Language for Algebraic Specification and Implementation, Internal Report, CSR-131-83, University of Edinburgh, 1983.

[Web76] H. Weber: "Modularity in Data Base System Design," in Issues in Data Base Management, ed. Coiser and Wasserman, North Holland, 1979.

[Zill73] S. N. Zilles: "Algebraic Specifications of Data Types", In Project MAC progress report for 1973-74, CSG Memo 119, MIT, Cambridge, Mass. pp 1-12.

A DECISION METHOD FOR TEMPORAL LOGIC BASED ON RESOLUTION

G.VENKATESH
SSE GROUP, TIFR,
BOMBAY-400005, INDIA.

Abstract:

A decision method for linear temporal logic is presented. The given temporal formula is first converted into a normal form formula containing restricted nesting of temporal operators. The resulting formula is tested for satisfiability by using four crucial operations - Unwinding Resolution, SKIP and deletion of persistent eventual terms.

Introduction:

We present a resolution based decision method for temporal logic. Unlike in the other known resolution based procedure presented in [1], we do not extend the resolution to temporal operators. Instead, we rely on the 'unwinding' operation to separate the present and future parts of the given formula, and apply the classical resolution rule to the present part.

The given formula is first converted into another formula whcih has limited nesting of temporal operators such that it is satisfiable if and only if the original formula is satisfiable. The resulting normal form formula is analysed for satisfiability by first unwinding the temporal operators, then resolving the resulting clauses and finally identifying the critical portion of the formula which guarantees satisfaction of the whole formula.

This process turns out to be complete for formulas without eventualities. For formulas with eventualities, we isolate eventual terms that are delayed indefinitely and eliminate them from the formula. For the resulting formula without such eventual terms, the process described earlier is complete.

In section (1) we briefly define the syntax and semantics of the propositional temporal logic being considered and show how any temporal formula can be reduced to a 'normal form' formula which is satisfiably equivalent to the original, but with restricted nesting of temporal operators.

In section (2), we describe the process of unwiding, resolution and SKIP that we will be using to test the formula for satisfiability, and in section (3), we demonstrate the completeness of this procedure for formulas without eventual terms. For formulas with eventual terms we describe a method to isolate and eliminate eventualities which cannot be satisfied. Finally, in section (4), we discuss possible extensions of this work.

Section 1:

The propositional temporal formulas are built inductively from a set of propositional variables P1, P2...... as follows:

P1,P2.... are formulas.

If f,g are formulas so are f & g, ∿f, []f, Of and fUg.

Models are triples of the form $(M,S,s_0s_1\ldots.)$ where S is a set of states, M assigns to each state a subset of the propositional variables which are true in that state and $s_o s_1\ldots$ is an infinite sequence of states from S.

The relation 'satisfies', denoted by |=, is defined, inductively between models and formulas as follows:

$(M,S,s_0..)$|=P iff P ε $M(s_0)$, for the propositional variable P.

$(M,S,s_0..)$|= f & g iff $(M,S,s_0..)$ |= f and $(M,S,s_0..)$ |= g.

$(M,S,s_0..)$|= ∿f iff not $(M,S,s_0..)$ |= f.

$(M,S,s_0..)$ |= Of iff $(M,S,s_1..)$ |= f.

$(M,S,s_0..)$ |= []f iff for all i>=0 $(M,S,s_i..)$ |= f.

$(M,S,s_0..)$ |= fUg iff there exists i>=0 such that $(M,S,s_i..)$|= g
and for all j, 0<=j<i $(M,S,s_j..)$|= f.

We say that the temporal formula f can be reduced to the formula g upto satisfiability if g can be constructed from f such that f is satisfiable iff g is satisfiable.

We write f-->|= g to denote this. Clearly, -->|= is transitive.

For simplicity, we adopt the following notation:

$O^0 f=f$, $O^{i+1}(f) = O^i(Of)$, $<>f = \sim([]\sim f)$, $f\text{->}g = \sim f \vee g$, $f \equiv g = f\text{->}g \;\&\; g\text{->}f$.

A formula is said to be:

- a literal if it is either in the form P or ∼P where P is a propositional variable.
- a term if it is in one of the forms:
  $O^i L$, $O^i([]f)$, $O^i(<>f)$, $O^i(fUg)$,
  for some formulas f,g, literal L, and i>=0.
  i is called the index of the term.
- a principal term if it is in one of the forms:
  $O^i L$, $O^i([]L)$, $O^i(<>L)$, $O^i(L'UL)$,
  for some literals L,L' and i>=0.
- an eventual term if it is in the form $O^i<>L$ or $O^i L'UL$.
- a clause if it is a disjunction of principal terms.
- clause-like if it is a disjunction of terms.
- in the normal form if it is in the form $\underset{i=1}{\overset{n}{\&}} c_i \;\&\; \underset{j=1}{\overset{m}{\&}} []c'_j$, where each c_i and c'_j is a clause.

Every formula f can be reduced to a conjunction of clause-like formulas by repeatedly applying the following identities.

$\sim(g\&h) \equiv (\sim g \vee \sim h)$; $\sim(g \vee h) \equiv (\sim g \;\&\; \sim h)$;

$\sim O^i f \equiv O^i(\sim f)$; $O^i(f \vee g) \equiv O^i f \vee O^i g$; $O^i(f\&g) \equiv O^i f \;\&\; O^i g$.

$\sim[]g \equiv <>(\sim g)$; $\sim<>g \equiv [](\sim g)$; $\sim(gUh) \equiv (\sim h)U(\sim g \;\&\; \sim h) \vee [](\sim h)$.

$\sim(\sim g) \equiv g$ and $(g \vee h_1 h_2) \equiv (g \vee h_1)\&(g \vee h_2)$.

If any of the conjuncts of f is of the form []g then g can be reduced to a conjunction of clause-like formulas and the identities $[](h_1\&h_2) \equiv([]h_1\&[]h_2)$, $[]([]h)\equiv[]h$ can be applied to reduce f to the following form which we shall call the reduced form of f:

$f \equiv \overset{n}{\underset{i=1}{\&}} b_i \ \& \ \overset{m}{\underset{j=1}{\&}} []b'_j$, where the b_i and b'_j are clause-like and are not of the form []h.

The reduced form of f looks like a normal form, except that the b_i and b'_j are clause-like and not clauses.

Define d(f) as the maximum depth of nesting of temporal operators in the b_i and b'_j. More formally, define d' recursively as follows:
$d'(L)=0$, $d'(O^i g) = d'(\sim g) = d'(g)$, $d'(g\&h) = d'(gVh) = \max(d'(g),d'(h))$,
$d'(<>g) = d'([]g) = d'(g)+1$, $d'(gUh) = \max(d'(g), d'(h))+1$,
and let $d(f) = \max(\max\{b_i\}, \max\{b'_j\})$, for f with reduced form as above.

Theorem 1:

Every temporal formula is reducible upto satisfiability to a normal form formula.

Proof: By induction on d(f).

If d(f) is 0 or 1 then the reduced form is in the normal form and the theorem is obvious.

Suppose $d(f)> 1$. Let $f \equiv \overset{n}{\underset{i=1}{\&}} b_i \ \& \ \overset{m}{\underset{j=1}{\&}} []b'_j$. We can assume that f is not in normal form. We replace each non-principal term of the form $O^\ell([]g)$, $O^\ell(<>g)$ and $O^\ell(gUh)$ in b_i or b'_j by the principal terms $O^\ell([]P_g)$, $O^\ell(<>P_g)$ and $O^\ell(P_g U P_h)$ respectively, to obtain the formula f', where the P_g's so introduced are new propositional variables.

Clearly, f' is in normal form. Let $\{P_g \mid g\varepsilon G\}$ be the new propositional formulas introduced into f', where G is the set of subformulas in f that have been thus replaced by new propositional variables.

Let $f'' = f' \ \& \ \underset{g \in G}{\&} [](P_g \equiv g)$.

Lemma 1: $f \dashrightarrow|= f''$.

Proof: Let $(M,S,s_0..)|= f''$.

Then $(M,S,s_0..)|= f'$ ..(1)

and $(M,S,s_i..)|= P_g$ iff $(M,S,s_i..)|= g$ for all $i \geq 0$ and g in G. ..(2)

Since the relation $(M,S,s_0..)|= f'$ depends only on whether relations of the form $(M,S,s_i..)|= P_g$ hold or do not hold, from (2) we can replace P_g by g in f', without affecting the relation in (1).. But f', with P_g replaced by g for all g in G, is precisely f. Hence $(M,S,s_0..)|= f$.

Conversely, assume $(M,S,s_0..)|= f$. Construct $(M',T,t_0..)$ with $t_i \neq t_j$ for $i \neq j$, and let

$P \varepsilon M'(t_i)$ iff $P \varepsilon M(s_i)$, if P is a propositional variable in f. ..(3)

and $P_g \varepsilon M'(t_i)$ iff $(M,S,s_i..)|= g$ ..(4)

Note that this is well defined as $t_i \neq t_j$ for $i \neq j$.

Since the relations $(M,S,s_0..)|= f$ and $(M,S,s_i..)|= g$ depend only on the truth values assigned to the propositional variables in f, from (3) we get $(M',T,t_0..)|= f$, and $(M',T,t_i..)|= g$ iff $(M,S,s_i..)|= g$. From (4) and the above we can conclude that $(M',T,t_i..)|= g$ iff $(M',T,t_i..)|=P_g$. Hence $(M',T,t_0..)|= \underset{g \in G}{\&}[](P_g \equiv g)$. By applying an argument similar to the one used in the if-case, we can replace g by P_g in f, to obtain the relation $(M,T,t_0-.)|= f'$. Hence $(M',T,t_0..)|= f''$. Thus, f is satisfiable iff f'' is satisfiable. Thus, $f \dashrightarrow|= f''$.

It can be easily verified that $d(f'') < d(f)$.

Hence, by induction there is a normal form formula f_N such that $f'' \dashrightarrow|= f_N$

Since $f \dashrightarrow|= f''$, we obtain $f \dashrightarrow|= f_N$. QED

Example 1: For the formula (P->O∿P)&[](∿P-><>(P&[]P'))&[](P-><>∿P'), the normal form is (∿P V O∿P)&[](P V <>P")&[](∿P" V P)&[](∿P" V []P')&[](P" V ∿ P V <>∿P')&[](∿P V <>∿P').

Section 2:

For a set of clauses C, &C denotes the formula obtained by taking the conjunction of clauses in C.

Two clauses c_1 and c_2 are said to be resolvable, and c is called a resolvent of the clause c_1 and the clause c_2 if any of the following conditions hold for some literal L:

(1) $c_1 \equiv L \vee g$, $c_2 \equiv \sim L \vee h$, $c \equiv g \vee h$.

(2) $c_1 \equiv L \vee g$, $c_2 \equiv \sim L$, $c \equiv g$.

(3) $c_1 \equiv L$, $c_2 \equiv \sim L$, $c \equiv$ false.

In (3) $c \equiv$ false. We call this the empty clause.

For a set of clauses C, define its closure under resolution, C* as the smallest set of clauses containing C and satisfying:

If c is a resolvent of the clause c_1 and the clause c_2 in C* then $c \in C^*$.

Clearly, if c is a resolvent of the clauses c_1 and c_2 then $c_1 \& c_2 \rightarrow c$, and hence $c_1 \& c_2 \rightarrow c_1 \& c_2 \& c$, so that $\&C^* \equiv \&C$.

Given a set of clauses C, the set W(C) is obtained from C by the following unwinding process:

Repeatedly replace

f V <>L by f V L V O<>L.

f V []L by f V L and f V O[]L.

f V (L'UL) by f V L V L' and f V L V O(L'UL),

until the index of all non-literal terms is non-zero

Clearly, &C≡&W(C). We assume that parenthesis binds stronger than *, i.e. that W(C)* = (W(C))*.

Let c be a clause for which the index of non-literal terms is non-zero.

Let LIT(c) denote the disjunction of literals in c.

We denote by NEXT(c), the clause obtained by deleting all the literals from c, and by SKIP(c) the clause obtained by subtracting 1 from the index of all the terms in NEXT(c).

For example, if c=L V O<>L V O[]L' V L" then LIT (c)=L V L", NEXT(c) = O<>L V O[]L' and SKIP(c) = L V []L'.

Clearly, c≡LIT(c) V NEXT(c) and NEXT(c)≡O(SKIP(c)). LIT(C), SKIP(C) and NEXT(C) are the set of LIT(c), SKIP(c) and NEXT(c) respectively, for all c in C.

We say that the clause c_1 subsumes the clause c_2 if all the terms of c_1 are terms of c_2.

Define the set N(C) = {cεC | NEXT(c)=c}. i.e. N(C) consists of the clauses of C containing non-zero index terms only.

For example, if C = {∿P V O<>∿P, ∿P" V P, P V <>P"}, then W(C) ={ ∿P V O<>∿P, ∿P" V P, P V P" V O<>P"}, W(C)* = W(C) ∪ {O<>∿P V O<>P"}, N(W(C)*) = {O<>∿P V O<>P"} and SKIP(N(W(C)*))={<>∿P V <>P"}.

Let $f_N \equiv \mathop{\&}_{i=1}^{n} c_i \;\&\; \mathop{\&}_{j=1}^{m} []c'_j$, H = $\{c'_1,.., c'_m\}$ and $C_0 = \{c_1,..,c_n\} \cup H$.

Let C_{i+1} = SKIP(N(W(C_i)*)), i≥0.

Lemma 2: &C_i-->|= &N(W(C_i)*).

Proof: Since &C*≡&C and &W(C)≡&C, &W(C)*≡&C.

Hence, we need only prove that &W(C_i)* -->|= &N(W(C_i)*). To prove this we need only show that if (M,S,s_1..) =&SKIP(N(W(C_i)*)) then there is a model (M',S ∪ {s_0},$s_0 s_1$..), with $s_0 \notin$S, such that M'(s_i)=M(s_i),i>0 and (M',S ∪ {s_0},$s_0 s_1$..) =&W(C_i)*.

Let X be the subset of clauses in W(C_i)* which are satisfied by (M',S ∪ {s_0},$s_0 s_1$..) irrespective of the assignment in M(s_0). i.e. these are the clauses containing some term Of such that f is satisfied by (M,S,s_1..). Let Y = LIT(W(C_i)* - X) be the set of the literal parts of clauses remaining to be satisfied. Let $c_y \varepsilon$(W(C_i)* - X) be some clause from which yεY is obtained. Then SKIP(c_y) is not satisfied by (M,S,s_1..), for all yεY. Now, &Y is satisfiable. For if &Y=false, then by the completeness of resolution for the propositional formulas, we can obtain false from Y through resolution. In which case the same resolution process when applied to the clauses c_y will result in a clause c' consisting of only non-literal terms, each of which belongs to some NEXT(c_y). But c' belongs to N(W(C_i)*), and so SKIP(c') lies in

$SKIP(N(W(C_i)^*))$, but SKIP(c') is not satisfied by $(M,S,s_1..)$ - a contradiction. Therefore, we can find some value for $M(s_0)$ which satisfies &Y. Hence $(M,S \cup \{s_0\},s_0s_1..) = \&W(C_i)^*$.

Corr. : If false $\varepsilon W(C_i)^*$ then $f_N \equiv$ false.

Proof: From the above lemma, we can deduce that $f_N \dashrightarrow \models \&W(C_i)^* \ \& \ []\&H$, for all $i \geq 0$. If false$\varepsilon W(C_i)^*$ then $\&W(C_i)^* \equiv$false. Hence the result.

Note that the total number of distinct terms that can be generated is finite and bounded by r + s where r is the sum of the indices of distinct terms of C_0 and s is the number of literals occurring in C_0. Hence the clauses that can be generated is also finite and bounded by 2^{r+s}. Hence, for some i and j, with j<i we should have $W(C_j)^*=W(C_i)^*$.

Let $p = i-j$, and $Q_k = W(C_{k+j})^*$, $k = 0,\dots,p-1$.

Thus $Q_0,\dots,Q_{p-1}$ forms a cyclic sequence of sets of clauses (CSSC) which satisfies:

(*) $Q_i=Q_i^*$ and

(O) Q_{i+1} contains $W(SKIP(N(Q_i)))$.

Note that if a given CSSC $Q_0,\dots,Q_{p-1}$ does not satisfy either (O) or (*), then we can obtain the smallest CSSC closed under (O) and (*) and containing $Q_0,\dots,Q_{p-1}$ using the following procedure:

Step 1: If $Q_k^* = Q_k$ for $0 \leq k<p$ then stop, otherwise let $Q_k=Q_k^*$.

Step 2: Let $Q_{k+1 \bmod p} = Q_{k+1 \bmod p} \cup W(SKIP(N(Q_k)))$, $0 \leq k<p$. Go to step 1

The procedure will terminate because the total number of clauses is bounded and each Q_k increases monotonically during the procedure. Clearly closing the CSSC under (O) and (*) as above does not affect its satisfiability.

We say that a CSSC $Q_0,Q_1,\dots,Q_{p-1}$ is satisfiable if there is a model $(M,S,s_0\dots)$ such that $(M,S,s_\ell..) \models \&Q_{\ell \bmod p}$, $\ell \geq 0$.

p is called the period of the CSSC.

Lemma 3:

f_N is satisfiable iff the CSSC $Q_0,..,Q_{p-1}$ is satisfiable.
Proof: Follows from lemma 2 and its corrolary.

We devote the next section to a study of the satisfiability of CSSCs.

Section 3:

First, we restrict our attention to CSSCs whose clauses do not contain eventual terms. In this case, we see that the resolve and SKIP process described in the last section is complete. The case with eventual terms is made more complicated due to the fact that during the unwinding operation, an eventual term may be delayed indefinitely. We see how this can be tackled, by isolating persisting eventual terms and deleting them from the clauses of the CSSC.

Lemma 4:

Let $X=Q_0,..,Q_{p-1}$ be a CSSC closed under (O) and (*) such that each Q_k contains clauses with terms only of the form O^iL. Then X is satisfiable iff false $\notin Q_k$, $0 \leq k < p$.
Proof: If false $\in Q_k$, then by the corrolary to Lemma 2, X is not satisfiable.
Conversely, assume false $\notin Q_k$, $0 \leq k < p$. Then, we construct a model for X, as follows: Choose a set, T_{p-1}, of non-zero index terms, with at least one term from each clause of $N(Q_{p-1})$, such that if $O^iL \in T_{p-1}$ then $O^i{\sim}L \notin T_{p-1}$. Such a set can be found, else closure under (O) and (*) will imply that false $\in Q_k$ for some k. Extend T_{p-1} to a set U_{p-1} by choosing literal terms from the remaining clauses such that U_{p-1} does not contain ${\sim}L$ and L for any literal L. This can be done as can be seen in the proof of lemma 2. Thus $\&U_{p-1}$ is satisfiable, and since U_{p-1} contains at least one term from all clauses of Q_{p-1}, $\&U_{p-1} \rightarrow \&Q_{p-1}$, which implies that $\&Q_{p-1}$ is satisfiable.

Now, U_{p-1} determines a natural choice of non-zero index terms from clauses in $N(Q_{p-2})$, since $W(SKIP(N(Q_{p-2})))$ is a subset of Q_{p-1}. Let us denote this set of terms from Q_{p-2} by T_{p-2}. Again, we can extend this to U_{p-2}. Continuing in this manner, we obtain the set U_0.

Now, if the non-zero index terms of Q_{p-1} determined by U_0 are consistent with T_{p-1} i.e. contains T_{p-1}, then we can stop with the model $(M,S,(s_0..s_{p-1})^{\omega})$, where $(s_0..s_k)^{\omega}$ denotes the sequence $s_0..s_k$ repeated indefinitely, and $M(s_i)$ contains the literals in U_i. If the terms of Q_{p-1} determined by U_0 are not consistent with T_{p-1} then we continue as before with set T'_{p-1}. Since the sets of terms we can choose from Q_{p-1} is bounded, we should ultimately obtain a set $U_0^{(i)}$ which is consistent with $T_{p-1}^{(j)}$ for some $j<i$, whence $(M,S,s_0^{(j)}..s_{p-1}^{(j)}..(s_0^{(i)}..s_{p-1}^{(i)})^{\omega})$ with $M(s_k^{(\ell)})$ containing the non-negated literals in $U_k^{(\ell)}$, is a model for X.

Lemma 5:

Let $X= Q_0,..,Q_{p-1}$ be a CSSC closed under (*) and (O) and such that clauses in each Q_k contain only terms of the form O^iL or $O^i[]L$. Then X is satisfiable iff false $\notin Q_k$, $0 \leq k<p$.

Proof: Firstly, note that if $O^{i_1}[]L_1 \vee .. \vee O^{i_r}[]L_r$ belongs to some Q_ℓ, then $O[]L_1 \vee .. \vee O[]L_r$ belongs to all the Q_k. Further, the latter clause imples the former and so we can delete the former from Q_ℓ. Let $C=\{O[]L_{i1} \vee .. \vee O[]L_{in} \mid i=1,..,m\}$ be the set of such clauses belonging to all Q_k. We can choose a set of terms $T=\{O[]L_{1r},..,O[]L_{mr}\}$- one from each clause in the set- such that if $O[]L \in T$ then $O[]\sim L \notin T$. Such a set T can be found otherwise the set of clauses $C_L=\{L_{i1} \vee .. \vee L_{in} \mid i=1,..,m\}$, which is a subset of Q_k will satisfy $\&C_L \equiv$false, in which case false $\in Q_k$. We also assume that the set T we have chosen has the least number of terms among all such sets. Without loss of genrality, we can take $T=\{O[]L_{i1} \mid i=1,..,m\}$ after appropriately rearranging the terms of each clause in C. We delete all clauses in each Q_k which contain O^iL or $O^i[]L$ where O[]L is a term in T. Let the remaining CSSC be $X'=Q'_0,..,Q'_{p-1}$. We delete all terms of the form $O^i\sim L$ from each clause of every Q_k, where O[]L is a term in T. Also we delete all the $O^i[]L'$ terms from all clauses of each Q_k. Let the remaining CSSC be X". Intuitively, what we are trying to do, is to satisfy X by satisfying the least number of O[]L terms, and X" is the CSSC remaining to be satisfied once we have satisfied &T.

The following are evident:

(1) X" is closed under (O) and (*).

(2) No clause gets deleted from X'.

Otherwise, some Q'_k contains a clause c with terms of the form $O^i[]L'$, $O[]L' \notin T$ and $O^j\sim L$, $O[]L \in T$. Without loss of generating assume that the O[]L terms in the latter case are $\{O[]L_{i1} \mid i=1,..,r\}$. Thus $c=O^{\ell_1}[]L'_1 \vee .. \vee O^{\ell_s}[]L'_s \vee O^{j1} L_{11} \vee .. \vee O^{jr} L_{r1}$. Now, closure under (O) and (*) guarantee that the clauses of C containing $O[]L_{i1}$, i=1..r can be ultimately resolved with clauses generated from c, to get rid of the $O^{ji} L_{i1}$ terms from c. This will result in a clause $c'=O^{\ell_1}[]L'_1 \vee .. \vee O^{\ell_s}[]L'_s \vee c_h$, where $c_h = \bigvee_{i=1}^{r} (\bigvee_{j=2}^{ni} O[]L_{ij})$, and c' should belong to some Q_ℓ. Hence, $c''=O[]L'_1 \vee .. \vee O[]L'_s \vee c_h$ should belong to all Q_k and so lies in C. But then some term from c" chosen in T and this cannot be from the O[]L' and hence it should be from c_h. Let $O[]L_{ij}$ be the term chosen from c". Then, we need not have chosen $O[]L_{i1}$ from the clause $O[]L_{i1} \vee .. \vee O[]L_{in}$, and dropping $O[]L_{i1}$ from T reduces its cardinality by one - contradicting the assumption that T was the set with least number of terms.

(1) and (2) imply that X" is a CSSC as required in lemma 4, and is hence satisfiable.

For example, the formula f= (P->O∼P) & [](∼P->O(P&[]P')) & [](P->O∼P'), which is the same as in example 1, except that <>symbols have been replaced by O symbols, can be easily shown to be unsatisfiable.

We take the set of clauses obtained from the normal form of f.

W(H) consists of the following clauses:

1. $P \vee OP''$, 2. $\sim P'' \vee P$, 3. $\sim P'' \vee O[[P'$, 4. $\sim P'' \vee P'$, 5. $\sim P \vee O\sim P'$,

and $W(C_0)$ contains one additional clause:

6. $\sim P \vee O\sim P$. In the following, the clauses within each $W(C_i)^*$ is kept in a vertical column, with the clauses in $N(W(C_i)^*)$ separated from the rest by a line. We shall only generate and keep the clauses that are used to obtain false. Clauses (7) - (13) are obtained by SKIP from the N-clauses in the previous column. 1/6 before a clause denotes that the clause is obtained by resolving clauses 1 and 6.

Column 0		Column 1		Column 2		Column 3	
1.	$P \vee OP''$	3.	$\sim P'' \vee O[\,]P'$	8.	$P'' \vee P'$	11.	P'
6.	$\sim P \vee O\sim P$	7.	$\sim P \vee P''$	9.	$P'' \vee O[\,]P'$	12.	$\sim P'$
———	———	3/7.	$\sim P \vee O[\,]P'$	10.	$\sim P' \vee P''$	11/12	False
1/6	$O\sim P \vee OP''$	1.	$P \vee OP''$	4.	$\sim P'' \vee P'$		
		5.	$\sim P \vee O\sim P'$	4/8.	P'		
		———	———	5.	$\sim P \vee OP'$		
		1/3/7	$OP'' \vee O[\,]P'$	8/10	P''		
		1/5	$O\sim P' \vee OP''$	2.	$\sim P'' \vee P$		
				2/8/10	P		
				———	———		
				4/8/9	$O[\,]P'$		
				5/2/8/10	$O\sim P'$		

For CSSC $Q_0,\ldots,Q_{p-1}$, let Q_{k+} denote the set $Q_{k+1 \bmod p}$. In the following, let t represent a term of the form $O<>L$ of $OL'UL$.

A set C of clauses is said to generate clause c if $c \in C^*$, but $c \notin (C-c')^*$, for any $c' \in C$.

A CSSC $Q'_0,\ldots,Q'_{p-1}$ is said to be a t-CSSC in $Q_0,\ldots,Q_{p-1}$ and t is said to be persistent in $Q_0,\ldots,Q_{p-1}$ if the following hold:

(1) $Q'_k \subseteq Q_k$, $0 \leq k < p$.

(2) At least one clause in $N(Q'_k)$ contains t.

(3) For each clause $t \vee c \in N(Q'_k)$ there is a set $G_c \subseteq Q'_k$ which generates c.

(4) All clauses containing t in $(Q'_{k+} - N(Q'_{k+}))$ also belong to $W(SKIP(N(Q'_k)))$.

Conditions (3) and (4) imply that any clause containing t in $N(Q'_{k+})$ should have been obtained by a resolution process, which uses at least one clause in Q'_{k+} containing both L and t, which should have originated from $N(Q'_k)$. Hence, we can see that the above conditions guarantee that the term t can be unwound indefinitely in $Q'_0,..,Q'_{p-1}$ and hence cannot be satisfied. We make this more clear in the following:

Lemma 6:

Let $Q'_0,..,Q'_{p-1}$ be a t-CSSC in $Q_0,..,Q_{p-1}$, $R_k = \{t \vee c_{k\ell} \mid \ell=1,..,n_k\}$ be the clauses in $N(Q'_k)$ containing t, and $R'_k=\{c_{k\ell} \mid \ell=1,..,n_k\}$. Let $Q''_k = Q_k \cup R'_k$. Then $Q_0,..,Q_{p-1}$ is satisfiable iff $Q''_0,..Q''_{p-1}$ is satisfiable.

Proof: We first show that if the model $(M,S,s_0..)$ satisfies $Q_0,..,Q_{p-1}$ then $(M,S,s_k..) \models \& R'_{k \bmod p}$, for some $k \geq 0$.

Let if possible $(M,S,s_k..) \not\models \& R'_{k \bmod p}$, for all $k \geq 0$. Then $(M,S,s_k..) \models t$, for all $k \geq 0$. Since t is of the form $O\Diamond L$ or $OL'UL$, in either case we have $(M,S,s_0..) \models O\Diamond L$. But, since each clause $t \vee c$ in R_k is generated by some subset of clauses in Q'_k, Q'^{*}_k should contain a clause of the form $\sim L \vee c'$, where $c' \rightarrow c$. Hence $\& Q'_k \rightarrow (\sim L \vee c')$ i.e. $\& Q'_k \& \sim c' \rightarrow \sim L$, and $c \rightarrow c'$ implies that $\sim c' \rightarrow \sim c$, from which we get $\& Q'_k \& \; c \rightarrow \sim L$. Now, $(M,S,s_k..) \not\models \& R'_k$ means that $(M,S,s_k..) \models \sim c$ for some $t \vee c$ in R_k. Thus from the above we conclude that $(M,S,s_k..) \models \sim L$ for all $k \geq 0$. Hence, $(M,S,s_0..) \models O\Box\sim L$, which contradicts the fact that $(M,S,s_0..) \models O\Diamond L$. Hence, there is some $k \geq 0$ such that $(M,S,s_k..) \models \& R'_{k \bmod p}$.

Now, we show that if $(M,S,s_r..) \models \& R'_{r \bmod p}$ then $(M,S,s_{r+1}..) \models \& R'_{r+1 \bmod p}$.

Since each clause $t \vee c$ in $R_{r+1 \bmod p}$ is generated by some set of clauses in $Q'_{r+1 \bmod p}$, there should be clauses $\sim L \vee c_1$ and $L \vee t \vee c_2$ in $Q'^{*}_{r+1 \bmod p}$, such that $t \vee c_1 \vee c_2 = c$. Then using the same resolution process, c_2 can be obtained from $Q'_{r+1 \bmod p} \cup W(SKIP(R'_{r \bmod p}))$. Hence $\&Q'_{r+1 \bmod p}$ & $\&W(SKIP(R'_{r \bmod p})) \rightarrow c_2 \rightarrow c$, from which we deduce that $(M,S,s_{r+1}..) \models c$.

Thus by induction, $(M,S,s_r..) \models \&R'_{r \bmod p}$ for all $r \geq k$ and if n is the smallest integer such that $np > k$ then $(M,S,s_{np}..)$ satisfies $Q''_0,..,Q''_{p-1}$.

By repeatedly identifying t-CSSCs and deleting the persistent term from the clauses in the sequence and then closing the resulting CSSC under (O) and (*), we can reduce the CSSC to a CSSC which satisfies one of the following:

(a) false $\in Q_k$ for some $0 \leq k < p$, in which case the CSSC is unsatisfiable.

(b) $Q_0,..,Q_{p-1}$ does not contain any persistent term.

We show that in case (b) the CSSC is satisfiable, thus giving us a complete procedure for deciding the satisfiability of the formula,

Theorem:

If $Q_0,..,Q_{p-1}$ is a CSSC closed under (O) and (*), with false $\notin Q_k$, $0 \leq k < p$, and not containing any persistent eventual term, then it is satisfiable.

Proof: First, we show that if no eventual term persists then the clauses containing eventual terms can be replaced by other clauses not containing eventual terms, without affecting the satisfiability of the CSSC

Since the number of clauses containing any eventual term t is finite, and since t does not persist, t can be unwound at most finite number of times in $Q_0,..,Q_{p-1}$, say m_t times. Let m be greater than m_t for all eventual terms t. Then we can replace each clause O^i<>L V c by $O^i L \vee .. \vee O^{i+m} L \vee c$ and each clause $O^i L' U L \vee c$ by the set of clauses

$(0^iL \vee 0^iL' \vee c,..,0^i L \vee .. \vee 0^{i+m-1}L \vee 0^{i+m-1}L' \vee c,\ 0^iL \vee .. \vee 0^{i+m}L \vee c)$. Close the modified CSSC under (O) and (*) to obtain $Q'_0,..,Q'_{p-1}$. Suppose $Q'_0,..,Q'_{p-1}$ is not satisfiable, but $Q_0,..,Q_{p-1}$ is satisfiable. Then some eventual term t is required to be unwound more than m times. But this leads to a contradiction as then $m_t > m$.

If an eventual term 0^i<>L is unwound m_t times, the literal in the terms $0^{i+n}L$ for n m_t wil never be resolved upon. Hence this term can never be eliminated and hence no clause involving t can be used to generate false. In the case of terms $t=0^iL'UL$ if t is unwound m_t times then the first m_t clauses of the set replacing the clause containing t will already be generated during the unwinding process when $Q_0,..,Q_{p-1}$ is created, and the remaining clauses will not contribute to the resolution generating false. But then the only clauses used to generate false are those that do not involve any eventual terms from $Q_0,..,Q_{p-1}$ and so false should belong to some Q_k, which contradicts the assumption.

Hence false $\notin Q'_k$, $0 \leq k < p$ from which the theorem follows using lemma 5.

In general, we do not actually generate the entire CSSC $Q_0,..,Q_{p-1}$ in order to test it for satisfiability. We only produce as many clauses as are required to obtain false. To identify persistent terms, we try to force an eventual term t to be unwound as far as possible, by selecting as many clauses as are necessary to form a t-CSSC. We illustrate this in the following example.

Consider the formula (P->O∿P) & [](∿P-><>(P&[]P')) & [](P-><>∿P'), which was introduced previously in section 1. W(H) consists of the clauses:

1. P V P" V O<>P",
2. ∿P" V P,
3. ∿P" V O[]P",
4. ∿P" V P',

5. ∿P V O<>∿P' V ∿P', and $W(C_0)$ contains in addition the clause

6. ∿P V O∿P.

Column 0	Column 1	Column 2	Column 3
1. PVP"VO<>P"	7. ∿PVO<>P"VP"	8. P'	10.∿P'VO<>∿P'
2. PVO<>P"	1/2/7 P"VO<>P"	9. P"VO<>P"V∿P'VO<>∿P'	11. P'
4. ∿P"VP'	3. ∿P"VO[]P'	8/9 P"VO<>P"VO<>∿P'	-----------
5. ∿PVO<>∿P'V∿P'	--------------	--------------------	10/11 O<>∿P'
6. ∿PVO∿P	1/2/7/3 : O<>P"VO[]P'	8/9/ 2/4/5 : O<>P"VO<>∿P'	12. O[]P'
1/2 PVO<>P"	1/2/7/ 2/4/5 : O<>P"VO<>∿P'	10. O[]P'	F. false
4/5 ∿P"V∿PVO<>∿P'	A. O[]P'	B. O<>∿P'	
2/4/5 ∿P"VO<>∿P'			

1/2/6 O∿PVO<>P"			

(A) is obtained because {∿P"VO[]P', O<>P"VO[]P'}forms a O<>P"-CSSC of period 1. Similarly, for (B) we have the O<>P"-CSSC {∿P"VO<>∿P', O[]P', O<>P"VO<>∿P'} of period 1, and for (F) we have the O<>P'-CSSC{O[]P', P', O<>∿P'}, also of period 1.

Conclusions:

The other well known method of testing satisfiability of temporal formulas is the tableux method [7]. A resolution-based procedure has the following advantages over the tableux method:

1. By using various kinds of refinements [2], we can restrict the generation of unwanted clauses and thus speed up the procedure.

2. The procedure can be extended to first order temporal formulas by appropriately defining unification. The only complication arises in the handling of local variables. For this, we first unwind the clauses, then replace all the local variables in the literals of the clauses by respective skolem functions of the global variables and then proceed with resolution.

The method presented in this paper seems to work well in practice. For increasing its efficiency, we can extend the resolution operation so that O^j[]L V c can be resolved with O^i<>∿L V c' or O^iL'UL V c', for j≤i to obtain c V c'. For formulas which satisfy C_0=H, we need not SKIP to the next column, but can accumulate all the clauses in the same column, thus also simplifying the handling of eventualities. This raises the question of characterising formulas for which clauses can be accumulated in the same column. For example, for formulas with period p=1, we know that clauses can be ultimately accumulated in the same column. These and other related issues are discussed in [6].

Acknowledgements:

I would like to thank two anonymous referees for their suggestions on improving the presentation and Shri V.Mahadevan for typing a difficult manuscript.

References:

(1) Cavalli,A.R. and Del Cerro, F.L, A decision method for linear temporal logic, Proc. 7th International Conference on Automated Deduction, LNCS 170, 1984.

(2) Chang, C. and Lee, R., Symbolic logic and mechanical theorem proving, Acad. Press, New York, 1973.

(3) Manna, Z. and Pnueli, A., The verification of concurrent programs: The temporal framework. In Boyer and Moore eds., The correctness problem in computer science, pp.215-273, Acad. Press, New York, 1981.

(4) Robinson, J., A machine oriented logic based on the resolution principle, JACM 12, 1965, pp. 23-41.

(5) Sistla, A.P. and Emerson, E.A., The complexity of propositional linear time logics, Proc. 16th ACM Symposium on the theory of computing, 1982, pp. 159-168.

(6) Venkatesh, G., Resolution in temporal logic, Tech. rept. SSE-CAD-8507, SSE Group, T.I.F.R., Bombay.

(7) Wolper, P., Temporal logic can be more expressive, Information and Control, 56, 1983, pp. 72-79.

A GENERALIZATION OF THE PARIKH VECTOR FOR FINITE AND INFINITE WORDS

Rani Siromoney* and V. Rajkumar Dare**
Department of Mathematics
Madras Christian College
Tambaram, Madras 600 059

Abstract

A metric is defined on the set of all finite and infinite words based on the difference between the occurrences of different letters of the alphabet. This induces a topology which coincides with the metric topology defined by Nivat [5]. Using this metric a vector is defined which gives rise to the position vector p showing the position in the word of each letter of the alphabet. The p-vector can be regarded as a generalization of the Parikh vector [6]. While the Parikh vector of a word enumerates the number of occurrences of each letter of the alphabet, the p-vector introduced in this paper indicates the positions of each letter of the alphabet in the word. Also, the Parikh vector is defined for finite words and the p-vector gives a generalization to infite words. The p-vector has nice mathematical properties. Characterizations of regular sets, context-free languages and a few families from Lindenmayer systems are given.

0. Introduction

Infinite words and infinite languages have been studied extensively in recent years [2,5,10]. An extension has been made to infinite arrays in [4,8,9]. Nivat has pointed out that it is necessary to extend the computation domain and consider infinite words as limits of infinite successful derivation [5]. The motivation for infinite computation arises from the study of semantics of recursive programs.

---

* This work was partially supported by the Board of Research in Nuclear Science, Department of Atomic Energy.

**This work was partially supported by the University Grants Commission under the scheme 'Financial Assistance to College Teachers for Minor Projects' .

It has been found useful to introduce a metric topology in order to define the limits. Nivat has introduced a metric which measures the difference between two words when they differ at the k-th place and is insensitive to the differences occurring at any later stage. We introduce a different metric in order to measure the difference between two infinite words at later stages as well. In addition to the usefulness of the metric to study differences between two words at all stages, it enables us to define a measure associated with each word. This measure gives rise to a position vector which indicates the positions of each letter of the alphabet in a word. It has very nice mathematical properties. For example, p is a continuous mapping between any language and $\mathbb{R}^n$ where n is the cardinality of the alphabet and it is a monoid homomorphism.

We feel that the new measure introduced in this paper may be similar in scope as the parikh map while being more general than that and may have far reaching consequences. We also feel that it may have many applications. One areain which we envisage that the measure can be applied is in string matching since the measure indicates the position of each letter in the word. Another application may be to throw further light on Ehrenfeucht's conjecture on unavoidable sets [1]. In this paper we present the theoretical results associated with this new measure.

The classical parikh mapping [6](referred to as parikh vector in later usage) has played a very important and significant role in formal language theory. While parikh vector indicates the number of occurrences of each letter of the alphabet in a word, this new measure reflects their position as well. Parikh mapping is letter counting; here the position of each letter counts. For example, parikh vector of ab and ba are the same, viz., (1,1) whereas p-vector of ab is $(1/2, 1/2^2)$ while that of ba is $(1/2^2, 1/2)$. It is well-known that every context-free language is letter equivalent to a regular set. This well-known result in formal language theory is proved with the help of Parikh's theorem. Parikh vector does not distinguish between a CFL and its letter equivalent regular sets. But the p-vector introduced in this paper brings out the distinction between a CFL and its letter equivalent regular sets. For example, parikh mapping of the CFL, $\{a^n b^n | n \geq 1\}$ and the letter equivalent regular language $\{(ab)^n | n \geq 1\}$ are the same, viz., $\{(n,n) | n \geq 1\}$. But the p-vector of the former is $\{1-1/2^n, 1/2^n - 1/2^{2n} | n \geq 1\}$ and of the latter is $\{(2/3)(1-1/4^n), (1/3)(1-1/4^n) | n \geq 1\}$.

Another advantage of the p-vector is that it is possible to define the p-mapping for infinite words as well. It is not easy to extend the parikh vector to an infinite language since the number of occurrences of at least some letters of the alphabet will be infinite and will not show the distinction between several words. Whereas the p-vector of an infinite word has a nice form and reflects the distinction between the occurrences of the letters of the alphabet in different infinite words.

Many of the classical results in formal language theory regarding context-free languages and regular sets have corresponding elegant mathematical characterizations. For example, the regular expression characterization of regular sets is extended as follows: the image of a regular language under the map p is the finite union and sum of finitely generated monoids.

Bar-Hillel's theorem [3] can be rewritten in terms of the p-vector which gives a one sided characterization for every CFL. Normally this theorem is useful in establishing that certain languages are not context-free. This measure will also serve the same purpose and is likely to be easier and more useful since it is a numerical measure. One other advantage is that every component of the p-vector is a geometric series and hence can be easily computed.

1. Metric Topology on V^{∞}

Let V be a finite alphabet and V^* the free monoid generated by V. Let V^{ω} be the set of all mappings $u : N \to V$ where N is the set of all natural numbers. Elements of V^{ω} are called infinite words over V. u is denoted by $u_1u_2\ldots$ or $u(1)u(2)\ldots$. The set of all finite and infinite words is denoted by V^{∞}.

A metric is defined in Nivat [5] as follows: If $u,v \in V^{\infty}$, then

$$d^{(N)}(u,v) = 1/2^n : n = \min\{k: u_k \neq v_k\}$$
$$= 0 \quad \text{otherwise.}$$

This metric measures the difference between the two words when they differ at the n-th place and is insensitive to the differences occurring at any later stage. In order to overcome this, we define a metric which measures the difference between two words at later stages as well.

Definition 1.1

We define a function $d: V^{\infty} \times V^{\infty} \to \mathbb{R}$ such that

$$d(u,v) = \sum_{n=1}^{\min\{|u|,|v|\}} r_n + \sum_{n=\min\{|u|,|v|\}+1}^{\max\{|u|,|v|\}} r_n$$

where $r_n = 0$ if $u_n = v_n$ and $r_n = 1/2^n$ if $u_n \neq v_n$.

It is clear that

$$\text{(i)}\ d(u,v) = 0 \ \text{ iff } \ u = v$$
$$\text{(ii)}\ d(u,v) = d(v,u)$$
$$\text{(iii)}\ d(u,v) \leqslant d(u,w) + d(w,v)$$

In order to prove this let $d(u,v) = \sum k_n$, $d(u,w) = \sum p_n$ and $d(w,v) = \sum m_n$. By considering all possible values for k_n, p_n and m_n it can be shown that $k_n \leqslant p_n + m_n$ for all n. Hence $\sum k_n \leqslant \sum p_n + \sum m_n$. Thus d satisfies the requirements for a metric. Hence (V^∞, d) is a metric space.

We note that this metric is bounded and d(u,v) lies between zero and one.

We now study the nature of the open spheres in (V^∞, d). The open sphere in V^∞ of radius $1/2^k$ is denoted by $S_k(u) = \{v \in V^\infty : d(u,v) < 1/2^k\}$. Then it is clear that $S_k(u) = \{v \in V^\infty : u[k] = v[k]$ and there is at least one $n > k$ such that $u_n = v_n\}$. These open spheres form an open base at each point of (V^∞, d).

We examine the topology induced by this metric and prove that it coincides with the topology induced by Nivat's metric.

Theorem 1.1

The topology induced by the metric d coincides with the topology induced by the metric defined by Nivat.

Proof

Let $S_k^{(N)}(u) = \{v : d^{(N)}(u,v) < 1/2^k\}$ where $d^{(N)}$ is the metric defined vy Nivat. Then we have

$$S_{k+2}(u) \subset S_{k+1}^{(N)}(u) \subset S_k(u) .$$

Thus we see that both the topologies have the same open base and hence the topologies are equal.

Theorem 1.2

(V^∞, d) is a compact metric space.

Proof follows from the fact that $(V^\infty, d^{(N)})$ is compact and by Theorem 1.1.

2. Position vector of a word

The metric introduced in the last section is used to define a measure called π-vector for a word, from which we can define a position vector, which gives the position of each letter in the word. It is shown that π-vector is unique for every finite word and we also give an algorithm to evaluate it. The parikh vector of a word counts the number of occurrences of each letter of the alphabet but the position vector indicates the positions of each letter of the alphabet and may be considered as a generalization of the parikh vector.

Definition 2.1

Let $\pi : V^{\infty} \rightarrow \mathbb{R}^n$ such that $\pi(u) = (u_{a_1}, u_{a_2}, \ldots, u_{a_n})$ where $V = \{a_1, a_2, \ldots, a_n\}$. $u_{a_i} = d(u, a_i^{\omega})$ if $u \in V^{\omega}$ and $u_{a_i} = d(u, a_i^{|u|})$ if $u \in V^*$, $\pi(\lambda) = (0, 0, \ldots, 0)$. We shall call this a π-vector associated to each word.

The position vector $p(u)$ corresponding to each word u is defined as follows:

Definition 2.2

For each $u \in V^{\infty}$, let $p(u) = (p_1, p_2, \ldots, p_n)$ where $p_i = \sum_{j \in A_i} 1/2^j$ where $A_i \subset N$ and A_i gives all the positions of the letter a_i in the word u. We note that if $\pi(u) = (q_1, q_2, \ldots, q_n)$, then $p(u) = (p_1, p_2, \ldots, p_n)$ where

$$q_i = 1 - p_i \ , \ i=1,2,\ldots,n \quad \text{if } u \in V^{\omega} \text{ and}$$

$$q_i = \sum_{j=1}^{|u|} (1/2^j) - p_i \quad \text{if } u \in V^*$$

Remark

We note that in the definition of the position vector we can take any r instead of $1/2$. In the finite case r can be any positive number. But in the infinite case, in order to ensure convergence, r is assumed to be between zero and one. In the finite case we note that if $r = 1$, then the position vector counts the number of occurences of each letter of the alphabet and hence coincides with the parikh vector. The significance of the map p is that it gives the position of each letter of the word. The p-vector may be obtained directly from the word or from the π-vector which is obtained by calculating the distance between the given word and corresponding words of same length over a one letter alphabet.

From Nivat's metric $d^{(N)}(u,v)$, the relation between u and v is not known, whereas by the following theorem, given $d(u,v)$, the relation between u and v can be computed.

Theorem 2.1

Given $d(u,v)$, the relation between u and v can be computed.

Proof

Case (i) If $d(u,v) = s/2^n$, then we have

$$s/2^n = (1/2^{n_1}) + (1/2^{n_2}) + \ldots + (1/2^{n_r}) \text{ where}$$

$n_1 < n_2 < \ldots < n_r$. There are two possibilities if u and v are in V^ω viz.,

(a) $u_i \neq v_i$ for $i = n_1, n_2, \ldots, n_r$.

$u_i = v_i$ for all other i's.

(b) $u_i \neq v_i$ for $i = n_1, n_2, \ldots, n_{r-1}$ and all $i > n_r + 1$

$u_i = v_i$ otherwise.

On the other hand if $u,v \in V^*$, there is only one possibility, viz.,(a).

Case (ii) If $d(u,v) = r$ where r is not of the above form, then by using the following method we find the relation between u and v. Choose n_1 such that $(1/2^{n_1}) < r < (1/2^{n_1-1})$.

Let $r_1 = r - (1/2^{n_1})$. Now choose n_2 such that

$$(1/2^{n_2}) < r_1 < (1/2^{n_2-1})$$

Let $r_2 = r_1 - (1/2^{n_2})$. Proceeding this way we get a sequence of integers $n_1 < n_2 < \ldots$ such that

$$r = \sum_{i=1}^{\infty} (1/2^{n_i}) . \text{ Then}$$

$u_i \neq v_i$ for all $i = n_1, n_2, \ldots$

$u_i = v_i$ otherwise.

Using the theorem proved above if $\pi(u) = (q_1, q_2, \ldots, q_n)$ then from the values of q_i we can find the position in u where it is different from a_i. This gives an indirect method of obtaining $p(u)=(p_1,\ldots,p_n)$. Using the same technique we can also directly find the positions of the letters of the alphabet in the word u, when $p(u)$ is known.

We now examine the properties of p.

Theorem 2.2

The restriction of p to V^* is one to one.

Proof

Let $p(u) = p(v) = (p_1, p_2, \ldots, p_n)$ $u,v \in V^*$. Then

$p_i = (r_i/2^{n_i}) = \sum_{j \in A_i} (1/2^j)$ where A_i is a finite subset of the set of all natural numbers. Thus $(p_1, p_2, \ldots, p_n)$ uniquely fixes the positions of the letters of the alphabet in the words u and v. Hence $u = v$.

Theorem 2.3

The mapping $p : V^{\infty} \to \mathbb{R}^n$ is continuous in the usual topology in $\mathbb{R}^n$.

Proof

In $\mathbb{R}^n$ the topology induced by the Euclidean metric and the square metric coincide with the product topology.

We prove that p is continuous in the square metric on $\mathbb{R}^n$. Let $x = (x_1,\dots,x_n)$, $y = (y_1,\dots,y_n)$, then the square metric on $\mathbb{R}^n$ is $\rho(x,y) = \max_i |x_i - y_i|$. Let $\epsilon > 0$ be given. Choose k such that $1/2^k < \epsilon$. Let $u \in V^{\omega}$ and $p(u) = (p_1, p_2,\dots,p_n)$. Consider a neighborhood $S_{k+1}(u) = \{v : u[k+1] = v[k+1]\}$. Let $v \in S_{k+1}(u)$ and $p(v) = (q_1, q_2,\dots, q_n)$. Let $p_i = \sum_{j \in A_i}(1/2^j)$ and $q_i = \sum_{j \in B_i}(1/2^j)$ where A_i and B_i are subsets of N. Since $u[k+1] = v[k+1]$,

$$\left| \sum_{j \in A_i} (1/2^j) - \sum_{j \in B_i} (1/2^j) \right| < (1/2^{k+1})$$

and hence $\rho(p(u), p(v)) < \epsilon$. Thus $p(S_{k+1}(u)) \subset S_{\epsilon}(p(u))$. Similarly, we prove that p is continuous at $u \in V^*$. Hence p is continuous at each point of V^{∞}.

We now examine the relation between the coordinates of $p(u)$ and it is interesting to note that there is a well-formed linear pattern among words of the same length.

Theorem 2.4

Let $u \in V^{\infty}$ and $p(u) = (p_1,\dots,p_n)$ then

$$\text{(a)} \quad \sum_{i=1}^{n} p_i = 1 \quad \text{if} \quad u \in V^{\omega}.$$

$$\text{(b)} \quad \sum_{i=1}^{n} p_i = \sum_{j=1}^{|u|} (1/2^j) \quad \text{if} \quad u \in V^*$$

where $n = \#(V)$ and $|u|$ denotes length of u.

Proof follows easily from the definition.

Remark

It is interesting to note that by the theorem proved above, we get a nice geometrical pattern. The position vectors of the words of the same length lie on a hyper plane. For example, for a binary alphabet, we note that the p-vectors of words of the same length lie on a straight line. If we take a line through a point $p(u)$ parallel to the i-th coordinate axis, then the point $p(u\,a_i)$ lies on it. For the binary alphabet, the position vectors are illustrated by the following diagram (Figure 1).

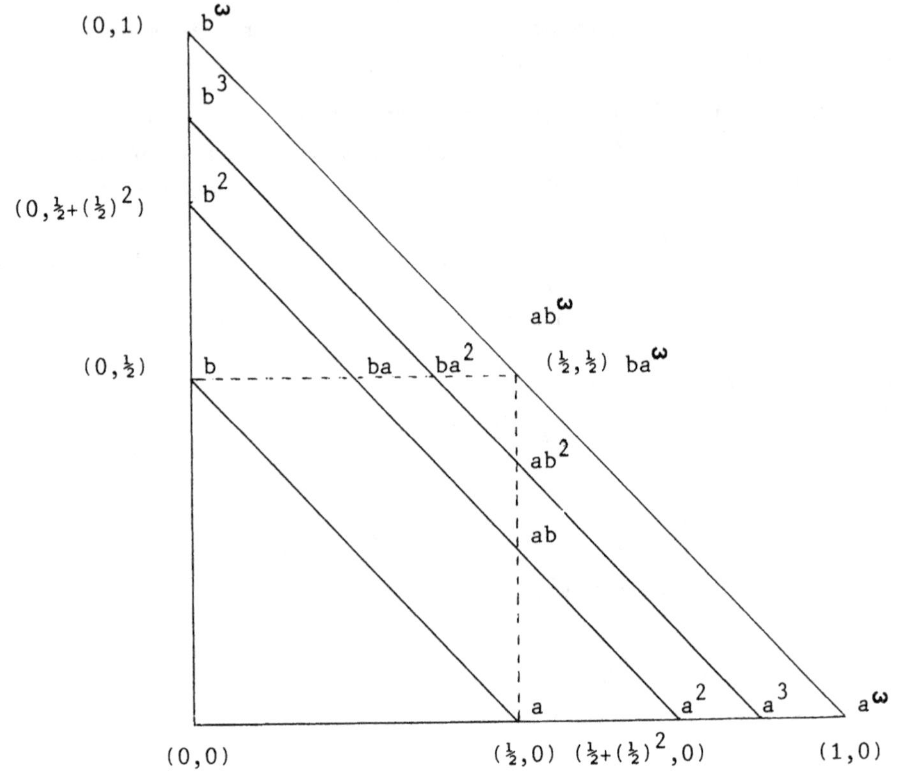

Fig. 1. Diagrammatic representation of words of a binary alphabet and position vectors.

Theorem 2.5

Let $x,y \in V^*$, then $p(xy) = p(x) + p(y)/2^{|x|}$.
This follows from the definition of p.

Theorem 2.6

If $x \in V^*$ then $p(x^n) = p(x)(1 - 1/2^{n|x|})/(1 - 1/2^{|x|})$.

Proof

Since $p(x^2) = p(x)(1 + (1/2^{|x|}))$,

$p(x^3) = p(x)(1 + (1/2^{|x|}) + (1/2^{|x|})^2)$,

by induction it follows that

$$p(x^n) = p(x)(1 + (1/2^{|x|}) + \ldots + (1/2^{n|x|})) .$$

Thus $$p(x^n) = p(x)(1 - (1/2^{n|x|}))/(1 - (1/2^{|x|})).$$

Theorem 2.7

If $x \in V^\omega$, then $p(x^\omega) = p(x)/(1 - (1/2^{|x|}))$.

This follows from the previous theorem.

3. The structure of p-vector

We shall examine the structure of $p(V^*)$. Since $p(V^*) \subset \mathbb{R}^n$, it has the topological properties of $\mathbb{R}^n$. We now define an operation on $p(V^*)$ such that it is a monoid.

Definition 3.1

$M = \{(m_1,\ldots,m_n) \in \mathbb{R}^n\} \cup \{0,\ldots,0\}$ satisfying the following conditions:

(i) each m_i is a finite sum of powers of $\frac{1}{2}$,

(ii) $\sum_{i=1}^{n} m_i = \sum_{j=1}^{k} (\frac{1}{2})^j$ where k is the maximum power of $\frac{1}{2}$ in $\{m_1,\ldots,m_n\}$.

k is defined as the order of $m = (m_1,\ldots,m_n) \in M$ and is denoted by $|m|$. We set $|(0,\ldots,0)| = 0$. We note that if $u \in V^*$ and $p(u) = m$, then $|m| = k = |u|$. Hence the notation.

We now define an operation called p-addition in M which makes M a monoid. This monoid will reflect the structure of words in V^*.

Definition 3.2

Let $p, q \in M$.

$$p \oplus q = (p_1 + (\tfrac{1}{2})^{|p|}.q_1, \ldots , p_n + (\tfrac{1}{2})^{|p|}.q_n)$$

Remark

Note that, instead of the usual vector addition, this p-addition takes care of the translation of positions needed while catenating two words.

Theorem 3.1

$(M, \oplus)$ is a monoid.

This follows from the definition of the operation on M. The identity of M is $(0, 0,\ldots,0)$.

Theorem 3.2

p is a monoid homomorphism of V^* onto M.

This follows from the fact that $p(xy) = p(x) \oplus p(y)$.

Note:

If $L_1, L_2 \subset V^*$, then $p(L_1L_2) = p(L_1) \oplus p(L_2)$.

4. Characterization of position vectors of well-known languages

We now characterize the position vectors of some of the Chomskian [3] and Lindenmayer [7] languages.

Theorem 4.1

Let $L_1, L_2 \subset V^*$, then

$$\text{(i) } p(L_1 \cup L_2) = p(L_1) \cup p(L_2)$$

$$\text{(ii) } p(L_1 . L_2) = p(L_1) \oplus p(L_2)$$

$$\text{(iii) } p(L^*) = \langle p(L) \rangle$$ where $\langle A \rangle$ is the monoid generated by A.

Proof follows easily from the properties of M.

Theorem 4.2

The position vectors of regular languages are the finite sum and union of finitely generated submonoids of M.

Proof follows from the regular expression characterization of regular sets and the previous theorem.

Theorem 4.3

Let L be any context-free language. There exist constants q and r depending on L such that if $w = x\,u\,y\,v\,z$ is in L with $|w| > q$ and $|u\,y\,v| < r$, then $p(x) \oplus k_{u,n}p(u) \oplus p(y) \oplus k_{v,n}p(v) \oplus p(z)$ is in $p(L)$ for all $n \geqslant 0$, where $k_{w,n}$ stands for $(1 - (\frac{1}{2})^{n|w|})/(1 - (\frac{1}{2})^{|w|})$.

This is Bar-Hillel's theorem, widely known as the 'pumping lemma' reformulated in terms of position vectors.

Using the concept of substitution we now characterize the context-free languages and EOL languages.

Definition 4.1

A substitution σ from V_1^* into V_2^* is a morphism from V_1^* into the power set of V_2^* such that $\sigma(a) \subset V_2^*$ for each $a \in V_1$, $\sigma(\lambda) = \lambda$, and $\sigma(uv) = \sigma(u)\sigma(v)$ for $u,v \in V_1^*$.

A substitution σ is said to be a finite substitution if $|\sigma(a)| < \infty$ for all $a \in V_1$.

Since M is a free monoid this definition holds good for M also.

Definition 4.2

Let σ be a finite substitution from M into M. Then σ_s and σ_{pa} are substitutions induced by σ defined in the following manner:

$$\sigma_s(x) = \bigcup_{i=1}^{m} \left\{ p_1 \oplus \ldots \oplus p_{i-1} \oplus \sigma(p_i) \oplus p_{i+1} \oplus \ldots \oplus p_m \right\} \text{ and}$$

$\sigma_{pa}(x) = \sigma(p_1) \oplus \ldots \oplus \sigma(p_m)$ where $x = p_1 \oplus \ldots \oplus p_m$ and p_i's are generators for M.

For a substitution σ on M, $\sigma^*(x) = \bigcup_{n=1}^{\infty} \sigma^n(x)$. We note that σ_s is the substitution introduced to reflect sequential rewriting and σ_{pa} to reflect parallel rewriting in the L-systems.

Definition 4.3

Let $G = (V_N, V_T, P, S)$ be a context-free grammar where $V_T = \{a_1, \ldots, a_n\}$ and $V_N = \{a_{n+1}, \ldots, a_m\}$. Let $M_G = p((V_N \cup V_T)^*)$ and $M_T \subset M$, be such that M_T contains points of M whose coordinates are all zeros from (n+1) to m. We now characterize the context-free languages [3] and EOL languages [7].

Theorem 4.4

For each context-free grammar G, there exists a substitution on M_G such that $p(L(G)) = \sigma_s^*(p(S)) \cap M_T$.

Proof

Let $\{p_1, \ldots, p_m\}$ be the generators for M_G. i.e. $p(a_i) = p_i$, for $a_i \in V_N \cup V_T$. The substitution σ on M_G is defined as follows:

$\sigma(p_i) = \{ p(\alpha_i) : a_i \to \alpha_i$ is in P for $n = (m+1), \ldots, n \}$

$\sigma(p_i) = p_i$ for $i = 1, \ldots, n$.

Then it is clear that $\sigma_s^*(p(S))$ gives the position vectors of the sentential forms of G. Hence $p(L(G)) = \sigma_s^*(p(S)) \cap M_T$

Theorem 4.5

For each EOL grammar G, there exists a substitution on M_G such that $\sigma_{pa}^*(p(S)) \cap M_T = p(L(G))$ where S is the start sysmbol of G.

Proof follows as in the previous theorem.

Theorem 4.6

For each finite substitution σ on $M \subset \mathbb{R}^n$, there exists OS grammars G_i such that $\sigma_s^*(p_i) = p(L(G_i))$ where G_i is a OS grammar with a_i as the start symbol, and $p(a_i) = p_i$, for $i = 1,\ldots,n$.

Proof

Let σ be a finite substitution defined on $M \subset \mathbb{R}^n$. Let $p_1,\ldots,p_n$ be the generators for M and $V = \{a_1,\ldots,a_n\}$ a finite alphabet such that $p(a_i) = p_i$, $i=1,\ldots,n$.

Let $P = \{ a_i \rightarrow \alpha_i : p(\alpha_i) \in \sigma(p_i),\ i=1,\ldots,n \}$. Let G_i be a OS grammar (V, P, a_i) where $V = \{ a_1,\ldots,a_n \}$. Then by the construction of G_i, we see that $\sigma_s^*(p_i) = p(L(G_i))$.

Theorem 4.7

For each finite substitution σ on $M \subset \mathbb{R}^n$, there exist OL grammars G_i with a_i as the axiom, $p(a_i) = p_i$, $i = 1,\ldots,n$ and $\sigma_{pa}^*(p_i) = p(L(G_i))$.

Proof follows as in the previous theorem.

In the theory of infinite languages, the concept of adherence [5] is used to derive infinite words from finite words. In the topology introduced in this paper, this coincides with the set of all limit points. Let $L \subset V^*$, then $\mathrm{Adh}(L) = \{ u \in V^\omega :$ for each $n \in N$ there exists a $v \in L$ such that $u[n] = v[n] \}$.

We now relate the position vectors with adherences.

Theorem 4.8

$p(A \cup \mathrm{Adh}(A)) = \overline{p(A)}$ where $\overline{p(A)}$ is the topological closure of $p(A)$.

Proof follows from the definition of adherence and closure.

5. Conclusion

In this paper we have introduced position vectors associated with finite and infinite words and studied their structure and mathematical properties. There are two areas in which this can be applied. Since most of the work on string pattern matching relies heavily on the position of each letter in a word, the position vector may be useful. Another interesting fact reflected by the geometrical pattern of the position vectors of finite words and infinite words shows that prefixes, suffixes and subwords follow certain pattern. This may throw further light on Ehrenfeucht's conjecture on unavoidable sets [1] and may help in the study of subword complexity of languages [7].

Acknowledgement

We wish to thank Dr Gift Siromoney for useful discussions.

References

[1] C. Choffrut and K. Culik II, On extendibility of unavoidable sets, Lecture Notes in Computer Science 166 (Springer, Berlin, 1984) 326-338.

[2] V.R. Dare and R. Siromoney, Subword topology, TR MATH 12/1985, Department of Mathematics, Madras Christian College, Madras.

[3] M. Harrison, Introduction to Formal Languages Theory, (Addison-Wesley, Reading, Mass, 1978).

[4] A. Nakamura and H. Ono, Pictures of functions and their acceptability by automata, Theoret. Comput. Sci. 23 (1983) 37-48.

[5] M. Nivat, Infinite words, infinite trees and infinite computations, Mathematical Centre Tracts 109 (1979) 1-52.

[6] R.J. Parikh, On context-free languages, Journal of the Association for Computing Machinery 13 (1966) 570-581.

[7] G. Rozenberg and A. Salomaa, The Mathematical Theory of L-systems (Academic Press, New York, 1980).

[8] R. Siromoney, V.R. Dare and K.G. Subramanian, Infinite arrays and infinite computations, Theoret. Comput. Sci. 24 (1983) 195-205.

[9] R. Siromoney, K.G. Subramanian and V.R. Dare, On infinite arrays obtained by deterministic controlled table L-array systems, Theoret. Comput. Sci. 33 (1984) 3-11.

[10] R. Siromoney and V.R. Dare, On infinite words obtained by selective substitution grammars, Theoret. Comput. Sci. 39 (1985) (in press).

THE IMPLICATION PROBLEM FOR FUNCTIONAL AND MULTIVALUED DEPENDENCIES : AN ALGEBRAIC APPROACH

V.S. Lakshmanan and C.E. Veni Madhavan
School of Automation
Indian Institute of Science
Bangalore 560 012 INDIA

Abstract

Computation of the dependency basis is the fundamental step in solving the implication problem for MVDs in relational database theory. We examine this problem from an algebraic perspective. We introduce the notion of the inference basis of a set M of MVDs and show that it contains the maximum information about the logical consequences of M. We propose the notion of an MVD-lattice and develop an algebraic characterization of the inference basis using simple notions from lattice theory. We also establish several properties of MVD-lattices related to the implication problem. Founded on our characterization, we synthesize efficient algorithms for (a) computing the inference basis of a given set M of MVDs; (b) computing the dependency basis of a given attribute set w.r.t. M; and (c) solving the implication problem for MVDs. Finally, we show that our results naturally extend to incorporate FDs also in a way that enables the solution of the implication problem for both FDs and MVDs put together.

1. Introduction

The relational model of data due to Codd [7] uses statements called data dependencies to express integrity constraints. The most important classes of dependencies are functional dependencies (FDs)[7] and multivalued dependencies (MVDs) [10,23]. Given a set M of such dependencies that a database should satisfy, there are other dependencies which follow as a logical consequence [21]. Complete axiomatizations have been proposed for FDs [1,18] and MVDs [3,6,17,20]. The implication or membership problem for MVDs is to determine whether an MVD $X \to\to Y$ is logically implied by a set M of MVDs, where $X \to\to Y$ and M are specified. Normal forms for relational databases were proposed by Codd [7,8] and Fagin [10] as a way out of update and deletion anomalies [13]. Solution to the membership problem is quite useful in designing relational database schemes in certain normal forms [21].

Given M and an MVD $X \to\to Y$, the fundamental step in solving the implication problem is to compute $DEP_M(X)$ - the dependency basis of X w.r.t. M. There have been a number of works on such problems [2,11,12,19,22].

Our principal aim in this paper is to lay down an algebraic foundation for addressing these problems. In this context, we pose the following problem. Given a set M of MVDs and m MVDs $W_1 \to\to Z_1$, ..., $W_m \to\to Z_m$, we wish to determine if each of these MVDs is logically implied by M. It is true that this problem is but an extended version of the familiar implication problem. However, its significance lies in the fact that an attempt to solve this problem very naturally prompts the introduction of the concept of an "inference basis" of M. We shall see later that the inference basis contains the maximum information about the logical consequences of M. Centered around this notion, we build an algebraic theory for MVDs that allows treatment of problems of implication among MVDs. In this connection, we introduce the notion of an "MVD-lattice" which we show to have elements corresponding to MVDs. Its merit is that inferences with MVDs can be elegantly carried out using algebraic operations on such lattices. Using MVD-lattices we obtain an algebraic characterization for the dependency basis and the inference basis. We also establish several interesting properties of MVD-lattices related to the implication problem. We use our results in synthesizing efficient algorithms for (a) computing the inference basis of M; (b) computing the dependency basis of X w.r.t. M, for a given attribute set; and (c) solving the implication problems for MVDs and FDs.

The structure of the presentation is as follows. In the next section, we review the preliminary notions of relational database theory and lattice theory. In Section 3, we introduce the notion of the inference basis and examine its significance. In Section 4, we develop our algebraic theory for MVDs and obtain characterizations for various concepts surrounding MVDs. For want of space, we have suppressed the proof details of our results, and in several cases we only give the outline of the proofs. In Section 5, we present our algorithms. We also show that our results and algorithms carry over to the implication problem for FDs and MVDs taken together. Finally, in Section 6 we present our conclusions.

2. Preliminaries

We review the fundamental notions in relational database theory and lattice theory.

2.1 Relational Databases

The relational model of data proposed by Codd [7] formats the storage of data into tables called relations. The columns in a table are called attributes. Each attribute has an associated domain of values. A row of a table is called a tuple which is really a mapping from attributes to domains.

Let $U = \{A_1, \ldots, A_n\}$ be the set of all attributes. U is called the universal relation scheme. Any subset $X \subseteq U$ is a relation scheme. Let t be a tuple over U. Then by $t[X]$ we denote the restriction of t to the attributes in X. We call $t[X]$ an X-value. A relation r over X is a finite set of X-values. We use A,B, ... with possible subscripts to denote attributes; ..., X,Y,Z with possible subscripts to denote sets of attributes. For $X \subseteq U$, $\bar{X}$ denotes the complement $U - X$ of X. The union of two attribute sets X,Y is written as XY. We shall henceforth deal with relations r over U, unless otherwise stated.

A functional dependency(FD) $X \rightarrow Y$ (read "X functionally determines Y") is a statement which holds in a relation r iff for any two tuples s,t in r, $s[X] = t[X]$ implies that $s[Y] = t[Y]$.

A multivalued dependency (MVD) is a statement of the form $X \rightarrow\rightarrow Y$. Let $Z = U - X - Y$. There are a number of ways of defining what it means for a relation r to satisfy $X \rightarrow\rightarrow Y$. One of them is to say that $X \rightarrow\rightarrow Y$ holds in r iff $\{y: \exists$ a tuple $t \in r$, s.t. $t[X] = x$, $t[Y] = y\} = \{y: \exists$ a tuple $t \in r$, s.t. $t[XZ] = xz$, $t[Y] = y\}$. Thus, $X \rightarrow\rightarrow Y$ holds in r whenever the set of Y-values associated with an X-value is independent of the values of all other attributes in the relation.

A dependency d is said to be logically implied by a set M of dependencies if d holds in any relation in which all dependencies in M hold. The implication (or membership) problem for dependencies is to determine whether a dependency d is logically implied by a given set M of dependencies. Complete axiomatizations are available for FDs and MVDs [21].

In the case of MVDs, the notion of the dependency basis plays a central role in solving the implication problem. Let M be a given set of MVDs. For $X \subseteq U$, $\bar{X}$ can be partitioned into a collection of blocks $W_1, \ldots, W_r$, s.t. if $Z \subseteq \bar{X}$ then $X \rightarrow\rightarrow Z$ is logically implied by M iff Z is the union of one or more W_i. Such a partition of $\bar{X}$ is called the dependency basis of X w.r.t. M, denoted by $DEP_M(X)$ [21]. It may be noted that MVDs not covered by the dependency basis as defined above are all trivial ones [21].

Fagin [10] has proved the existence and uniqueness of the dependency basis of any attribute set. Computation of the dependency basis is the fundamental step in solving the implication problem for MVDs. There have been a number of works on computing the dependency basis as well as solving the implication problem for MVDs [2,3,6,11,12,17,19, 20,22].

2.2 Lattices

We present here a brief review of some important notions in lattice theory. The reader may wish to consult [5]. Let $(S, \leq)$ where S is nonempty, be a poset. Then it is called a lattice if any two elements a and b in S have a greatest lower bound (glb) called meet and denoted by a.b, and a least upper bound (lub) called join and denoted by a+b.

For a nonempty set S let $\Pi(S)$ denote the set of all partitions of S. Suppose that $\Pi(S) = \{p_1, \ldots, p_r\}$. Then $(\Pi(S), \leq, \cdot, +)$ forms a lattice called the partition lattice where $\forall p_i, p_j \in \Pi(S)$

(i) $p_i \leq p_j$ if $\forall a,b \in S$, $a\ p_i\ b \Rightarrow a\ p_j\ b$;

(ii) $a\ (p_i \cdot p_j)\ b$ if $a\ p_i\ b$ and $a\ p_j\ b$; and

(iii) $a\ (p_i + p_j)\ b$ if $\exists c_o, \ldots, c_m$ where $c_o = a$, $c_m = b$, and for $k = o, \ldots, m-1$, $c_k\ p_i\ c_{k+1}$ or $c_k\ p_j\ c_{k+1}$.

Note that in the above we have used a partition p also to stand for the equivalence relation that it corresponds to. This lattice has a universal lower bound $0 = \{\{a\} : a \in S\}$, which has singleton blocks and a universal upper bound $1 = \{S\}$.

Let $L_1, \ldots, L_r$ be r lattices. The direct union of $L_1, \ldots, L_r$ is a lattice $L_1 \otimes \ldots \otimes L_r$ defined over $L_1 \times \ldots \times L_r$ as follows: for $a_i, b_i \in L_i$, $i = 1, \ldots, r$,

(1) $(a_1, \ldots, a_r) \leq (b_1, \ldots, b_r)$ if $a_i \leq b_i$, $i = 1, \ldots, r$.
(2) $(a_1, \ldots, a_r) \cdot (b_1, \ldots, b_r) = (a_1 \cdot b_1, \ldots, a_r \cdot b_r)$.
(3) $(a_1, \ldots, a_r) + (b_1, \ldots, b_r) = (a_1 + b_1, \ldots, a_r + b_r)$.

As a consequence of this definition, the universal lower bound of $L_1 \otimes \cdots \otimes L_r$ is given by $\mathbf{0} = (0_1, \ldots, 0_r)$ and the universal upper bound by $\mathbf{1} = (1_1, \ldots, 1_r)$.

3. The Inference Basis

In this section, we introduce a new notion called "inference basis" which will be shown to be useful in solving the implication problem. To begin, let us momentarily dwell on how the notion of the dependency basis assumes significance. To determine if $X \to\to Y$ is a logical consequence of a given set M of MVDs, one actually need not compute the entire dependency basis of X. Instead, only blocks W_i of the dependency basis such that $W_i \cap Y \neq \emptyset$ need be computed [19]. However, suppose that several MVDs $X \to\to Y_1, \ldots, X \to\to Y_s$ have to be tested for implication by M. Since all these have the same left-hand-side (LHS), $DEP_M(X)$ once computed can be repeatedly used for implication testing, which is much more efficient than the usual method. Thus, computation of the dependency basis may be viewed as a kind of preprocessing which pays off in implication testing of several MVDs with the same LHS.

Now, consider the more general problem of testing whether each of the MVDs $W_1 \to\to Z_1, \ldots, W_m \to\to Z_m$ is logically implied by M. This we call the generalized membership problem. In this case, in general, there might be several MVDs with the same LHS as also several with distinct LHS's. This observation tells us that precomputation of the dependency basis would improve the overall efficiency. But, since we might have to test the implication by M of MVDs with an arbitrary LHS, it appears that we need to compute the dependency basis of each $X \subseteq U$. But, this is undesirable because of its exponential complexity. Fortunately, it turns out that we need only precompute the $DEP_M(X)$ for some prespecified X's. In this context, we define the inference basis IB(M) of a set M of MVDs as follows:

$$\text{Let } LHS(M) = \{X_i : X_i \to\to Y_i \in M \text{ for some } Y_i \subseteq U\}. \text{ Then}$$
$$IB(M) = \{DEP_M(X_i) : X_i \in LHS(M)\}.$$

The significance of the inference basis defined here is that as we shall prove later, for any $X \subseteq U$, the dependency basis of X can be synthesized from the members of IB(M). Its practical attraction derives from the following. For the generalized membership problem posed above, precomputation of IB(M) improves the overall efficiency. Besides, the members of IB(M) (which are dependency bases really) can be computed using a method that is more efficient than any conventional method for computing the dependency bases in $\mathbb{B}(M)$ individually.

Before concluding this section, we describe a scheme for solving the implication problem for MVDs, using the inference basis. Fig.3.1 shows the various blocks in the scheme as well as how they interact. The preprocessor computes the inference basis of M. Let $\{d_1, \ldots, d_m\}$ be the set of MVDs whose membership is to be tested. The synthesizer generates the dependency basis of each distinct LHS. Finally, the decision element uses the appropriate dependency basis to decide whether each d_i is logically implied by M. It will be seen later that this scheme is superior (in terms of complexity) to the conventional approach. Besides, it gives rise to a nice algebraic formalism in which to treat the generalized membership problem.

4. An Algebraic Formalism For Implication Testing

Lee [15] recently developed a comprehensive theory for relational databases using partition lattices defined on the tuples of relations (called <u>relation lattices</u> in [15]). He has used that formalism to deal with various issues of FDs, MVDs, JDs (join dependencies), normal forms, and problems relating to the keys of relations. Here, we look at the static components of relations - the relation schemes. More precisely, we define lattices over partitions of relation schemes and use them in our later characterizations. It is hoped that our theory will gradually extend to uniformly treat various important issues of relational databases.

In the next subsection, we gradually develop the notion of an MVD-lattice and derive some simple properties of MVD-lattices. In Section 4.2, we present our main results which include the structural properties of MVD-lattices and algebraic characterizations for inference, and dependency, bases. Due to space constraints, we have had to suppress the details of the proofs of our results. For the most part, only the proof outline is presented. For complete details, the reader is referred to [14].

4.1 The MVD-Lattice

First, we shall introduce the notion of a "relation scheme lattice".

Definition 4.1

Let $U = \{A_1, \ldots, A_n\}$ be the universal relation scheme and let $\Pi(U)$ denote the set of all partitions on U. Then the partition lattice $(\Pi(U), \leq, \cdot, +)$ is called the <u>relation scheme lattice</u> or simply <u>scheme lattice</u>.

Notice that in this scheme lattice $0 = \{\{A_1\}, \ldots, \{A_n\}\}$ and $1 = \{U\}$. In general, one can define a scheme lattice on any relation scheme $X \subseteq U$. Computation of the meet and join of elements of a lattice has been thoroughly treated in [16]. We notice that the meet of two elements $p_1, p_2 \in \Pi(U)$ can be computed as

$$p_1 \cdot p_2 = \{Y_i \cap Z_j : Y_i \in p_1, Z_j \in p_2\} - \{\emptyset\}.$$

This is obvious from the definition of $p_1 \cdot p_2$. This observation is useful in proving a result about MVDs w.r.t. scheme lattices.

Next, we shall see how we can relate MVDs in a relational database to scheme lattices. An MVD $X \twoheadrightarrow Y$ (where $X \cap Y = \emptyset$) very naturally corresponds to the element $\{Y, Z\}$ of a scheme lattice defined on $\Pi(\bar{X})$, where $Z = U - XY$. The merit of this representation is that it easily extends to the <u>generalized multivalued dependencies</u> (GMVDs) proposed by Delobel[9]. A GMVD is a statement of the form $X \twoheadrightarrow Y_1 | \ldots | Y_r$, with $\bigcup_{i=1}^{r} Y_r = \bar{X}$. Let r be a relation over U and let $X \subseteq U$. Then the <u>projection</u> of r on X is $r[X] = \{t[X] : t \in r\}$. Let r_1 and r_2 be two relations over X and Y with $Z = X \cap Y$. Then the <u>join</u> of r_1 and r_2 is $r_1 \bowtie r_2 = \{t : t \text{ is an } XY\text{-value}, t[X] \in r_1, t[Y] \in r_2\}$. Then the GMVD $X \twoheadrightarrow Y_1 | \ldots | Y_r$ holds in a relation r if $\bowtie_{i=1}^{r} r[XY_i] = r$. Now, such a GMVD could be represented by the element $\{Y_1, \ldots, Y_r\}$ of the scheme lattice defined on $\bar{X}$. Let us denote this lattice by L_X.

Next, we want to see how relation scheme lattices could aid in solving the membership problem. For this purpose, we consider an axiom system for MVDs.

The following axiom system has been proved to be complete for MVDs [4].

<u>Complementation (MVD0)</u>: $X \twoheadrightarrow Y$ iff $X \twoheadrightarrow U - XY$.
<u>Augmentation (MVD1)</u>: If $X \twoheadrightarrow Y$ and $V \subseteq W$, then $XW \twoheadrightarrow VY$.
<u>Subset Rule (MVD2)</u>: If $X \twoheadrightarrow Y$, $W \twoheadrightarrow V$ with $W \cap Y = \emptyset$, then $X \twoheadrightarrow Y \cap V$ and $X \twoheadrightarrow Y - V$.

Suppose that $M = \{X \twoheadrightarrow Y_1, \ldots, X \twoheadrightarrow Y_m\}$. Notice that all MVDs in M have the same LHS. Each MVD in M clearly corresponds to an element of the scheme lattice $L_X = (\Pi(\bar{X}), \leq, \cdot, +)$. From the foregoing considerations, we have the following

Lemma 4.1

Let M be the set of MVDs given above. Then the dependency basis $DEP_M(X)$ corresponds to the greatest lower bound of the elements in L_X corresponding to the MVDs in M. That is,

$$DEP_M(X) = glb(\{Y_1, \bar{X} - Y_1\}, \ldots, \{Y_r, \bar{X} - Y_r\}).$$

Proof

We give an inductive proof. The basis case where $M = \{X \twoheadrightarrow Y_1\}$ is trivial. Assume the result for all M' having r-1 MVDs with LHS X. Let $M = \{X \twoheadrightarrow Y_1, \ldots, X \twoheadrightarrow Y_r\}$. Let $M' = M - \{X \twoheadrightarrow Y_r\}$. Define $p' = glb(\{Y_1, \bar{X} - Y_1\}, \ldots, \{Y_{r-1}, \bar{X} - Y_{r-1}\})$ and $p = glb(\{Y_1, \bar{X} - Y_1\}$ $\ldots, \{Y_r, \bar{X} - Y_r\})$. By the inductive hypothesis, $p' = DEP_{M'}(X)$. If $p' = \{Z_1, \ldots, Z_k\}$ then consider the set $M'' = \{X \twoheadrightarrow Z_1, \ldots, X \twoheadrightarrow Z_k, X \twoheadrightarrow Y_r\}$. Now, $p = glb(p', \{Y_r, \bar{X} - Y_r\})$. Also, $DEP_M(X) = DEP_{M''}(X)$, from the inference rules for MVDs. We need only show that $glb(p', \{Y_r, \bar{X} - Y_r\}) = DEP_{M''}(X)$. From the inference rules for MVDs, the only further inferences that we can make so that the resultant MVDs are finer, are $X \twoheadrightarrow Z_1 \cap Y_r$, $X \twoheadrightarrow Z_1 - Y_r$, $X \twoheadrightarrow Y_r - Z_1$, $\ldots$, $X \twoheadrightarrow Z_k \cap Y_r$, $X \twoheadrightarrow Z_k - Y_r$, $X \twoheadrightarrow Y_r - Z_k$. Thus, $DEP_{M''}(X) = \{Z_1 \cap Y_r, Z_1 - Y_r, Y_r - Z_1, \ldots, Z_k \cap Y_r, Z_k - Y_r, Y_r - Z_k\}$. From the operations performed above we see that they correspond to the computation of the meet of p' and $\{Y_r, \bar{X} - Y_r\}$. Thus, $DEP_{M''}(X) = glb(p', \{Y_r, \bar{X} - Y_r\})$ as required.

We have thus seen that for handling MVDs with an identical LHS, we can conveniently use an appropriate scheme lattice. Now, consider the more general case of MVDs with several distinct LHS's. Let $LHS(M) = \{X_1, \ldots, X_k\}$. For each LHS X_i, let M contain i_r MVDs with that LHS. Let $p_1, p_2, \ldots, p_{i_r}$ be the corresponding elements of the scheme lattice L_{X_i}. The partition p obtained by taking the glb of $p_1, \ldots, p_{i_r}$ is easily seen to have more information than any of these partitions, w.r.t. the logical implication of MVDs. If $p = \{Y_1, \ldots, Y_s\}$, then p corresponds to the GMVD $X_i \twoheadrightarrow Y_1 | \ldots | Y_s$. Performing the above operation w.r.t. each distinct LHS in M produces a set M* of GMVDs. We call this the <u>canonical representation</u> of M. From the inference rules for MVDs, we have the following observations. First, each GMVD in M^* is logically implied by M. Second, given an MVD d, d is logically implied by M if and only if d is logically implied by M^*. Intuitively, M^* may be regarded as some concise means of specifying the information content of M.

We next define $ALHS(M) = \{X : X \in LHS(M), \text{ or } X = X_iX_j \text{ where } X_i, X_j \in LHS(M)\}$. For each X in ALHS(M), we can have a scheme lattice $L_X = (\Pi(\bar{X}), \leq, \cdot, +)$. Let us now define a new lattice $L = \bigotimes_{(X \in ALHS(M))} (L_X)$ and call it the MVD-lattice for M. It is obtained by the direct union of several scheme lattices, identified above. Having defined this lattice, our immediate task is to identify each MVD in M (as also each GMVD in M^*) with an appropriate element of the MVD-lattice so we can bring the machinery of lattice theory to bear on the inference problem for MVDs. Before that, we make a few remarks on our notation. We use P,Q, ... with possible subscripts to denote elements of L. Let P be an element of L. Note that the elements of L are obtained by cartesian product of the elements of L_X for $X \in ALHS(M)$. So, define the X-component P_X of P to be that component of P which corresponds to a partition of $\bar{X}$. Further, for $A \in \bar{X}$, we denote the block in P_X containing A by BL(P, X, A). Finally, for $X \in LHS(M)$, define $D(P,X,A) = \{X_i \in LHS(M) : X_i \cap BL(P, X, A) = \emptyset\} - \{X\}$.

Now, an MVD $X \to\to Y$ in M corresponds to an element P of the MVD-lattice L where

(i) $P_X = \{Y, \bar{X} - Y\}$

(ii) For each W in ALHS(M)

$$P_W = \{Y - W, \bar{X} - Y - W\}, \text{ if } X \subseteq W,$$
$$= \{\bar{W}\} \qquad\qquad , \text{ otherwise.}$$

On the other hand, if one starts with the canonical representation M^* of M, then a GMVD $X \to\to Y_1 | \ \ldots \ | Y_s$ corresponds to an element P of L where

(i) $P_X = \{Y_1, \ldots, Y_s\}$.

(ii) For each W in ALHS(M)

$$P_W = \{Y_1 - W, \ldots, Y_s - W\}, \text{ if } X \subseteq W,$$
$$= \{\bar{W}\} \qquad\qquad , \text{ otherwise.}$$

In the following we assume that no X_i in LHS(M) is a subset of some other X_j in LHS(M). This assumption is made only for the convenience of treatment. Actually, our results and algorithms apply even when this assumption is violated. Consider an element $P \in L$. For $X_i, X_j \in LHS(M)$, if $P_{X_iX_j} = \{Y_1, \ldots, Y_q\}$, then it <u>induces</u> a new X_i-component $\{Z_1, \ldots, Z_r\}$ where $\{Z_1 - (X_j - X_i), \ldots, Z_r - (X_j - X_i)\}$ is any upper bound of $\{Y_1, \ldots, Y_q\}$. This induced X_i-component is <u>admitted</u> by other components if $\forall A \in X_j - X_i$, if $A \in Z_s$, for some s, $1 \leq s \leq r$, then $\exists X_{i_1}, \ldots, X_{i_u} \in LHS(M) - \{X_i, X_j\}$, such that

(i) $X_{i_t} \cap BL(P, X_i, A) = \emptyset$, $t = 1, \ldots, u$, and

(ii) $Z_s = BL(P, X_i, A) \cap (\bigcap_{t=1}^{u} BL(P, X_{i_t}, A))$

Suppose that $\{Z_1, \ldots, Z_r\}$ is an X_i-component induced by $P_{X_iX_j}$ and admitted by other components. It is then said to be the <u>principal derivative</u> of $P_{X_iX_j}$ w.r.t. P_{X_i}, denoted by $PD(P, X_iX_j, X_i)$, if it satisfies the following:

(i) $\forall A \in X_j - X_i$, if $A \in Z_s$ for some s, $1 \leq s \leq r$, then $\forall X_t \in LHS(M)$, $t \neq i,j$, either $Z_s \cap X_t \neq \emptyset$ or $Z_s \subseteq BL(P, X_t, A)$.

(ii) $\forall A \notin X_j - X_i$, if $A \in Z_s$ for some s, $1 \leq s \leq r$, then

either $Z_s = BL(P, X_i, C) \cap (\bigcap_{(X \in D(P, X_i, C))} BL(P, X, C))$ for some $C \in X_j - X_i$,

with $A \in BL(P, X_i, C)$,

or $Z_s = BL(P, X_iX_j, A)$.

Notice that if $P_{X_iX_j}$ induces at least one new X_i-component which is admitted by other components of P, then the principal derivative of $P_{X_iX_j}$ w.r.t. P_{X_i} is guaranteed to exist.

Since the definition of the principal derivative given above is nonconstructive, it is worthwhile considering its computation. It will reinforce our understanding of the notion of the principal derivative. Suppose that we want to compute $PD(P, X_iX_j, X_i)$. First, we consider each attribute $A \in X_j - X_i$. The correct block Z_s in $PD(P, X_iX_j, X_i)$ such that $A \in Z_s$, is computed as

$$Z_s = BL(P,X_i,A) \cap \Big(\bigcap_{(X \in D(P,X_i,A))} BL(P,X,A) \Big) .$$

Now, let $\tilde{Z} = \{Z_s : \exists A \in X_j - X_i, \text{ s.t. } A \in Z_s\}$, where Z_s is computed as above. Once this is over, we examine attributes which have not "already appeared" in the partition - i.e., attributes A such that $\forall Z_s \in \tilde{Z}$, $A \notin Z_s$. For each such A, the correct block Z_a in $PD(P,X_iX_j,X_i)$, with $A \in Z_a$ is simply given by $Z_a = BL(P,X_iX_j,A)$.

Now, for $P \in L$, P_{X_i} is said to be <u>saturated</u> w.r.t. $P_{X_iX_j}$ if $P_{X_i} = PD(P,X_iX_j,X_i)$. Let $P_{X_i} = \{Y_1, \ldots, Y_s\}$. We can see that P_{X_i} corresponds to the partition $\{Y_1 - X_j, \ldots, Y_s - X_j\}$ of $\overline{X_iX_j}$. This we denote by $SP(P,X_i,X_iX_j)$. P is said to be a <u>proper element</u> of L, if $\forall X_i,X_j \in LHS(M)$, $P_{X_iX_j} = glb(SP(P,X_i,X_iX_j), SP(P,X_j,X_iX_j))$. If for $P \in L$, $P_{X_iX_j}$ has the principal derivative $PD(P,X_iX_j,X_i)$, then one may obtain a new element Q from P, as follows:

(i) Replace P_{X_i} with $PD(P,X_iX_j,X_i)$.

(ii) Replace each $P_{X_iX_r}$, $\forall X_r \in LHS(M)$, $X_r \neq X_i$, with an appropriate value so that the resultant element Q (say) becomes proper. Such an element Q is said to be <u>directly generated</u> from P. It is further said to be obtained from P by an <u>X_i-refinement</u> using X_iX_j as the <u>generator</u>. Let $P_1, \ldots, P_s$, $s \geq 2$, be a sequence of elements of L such that P_{i+1} is directly generated from P_i, $i = 1, \ldots, s-1$. Then P_s is said to be <u>sequentially generated</u> from P_1.

For $A \in X_j - X_i$, we shall abbreviate

$BL(P,X_i,A) \cap \Big(\bigcap_{(X \in D(P,X_i,A))} BL(P,X,A) \Big)$ by $PDB_1^P(A,X_iX_j,X_i)$; similarly for $A \notin X_j - X_i$ such that the block in $PD(P,X_iX_j,X_i)$ containing A is given by $BL(P,X_iX_j,A)$, we denote $BL(P,X_iX_j,A)$ by $PDB_2^P(A,X_iX_j,X_i)$. Further we use $PDB^P(A,X_iX_j,X_i)$ to stand for the correct block Z_s in $PD(P,X_iX_j,X_i)$ such that $A \in Z_s$.

<u>Lemma 4.2</u>

For a proper element $P \in L$, let $PD(P,X_iX_j,X_i)$ be the principal derivative of $P_{X_iX_j}$ w.r.t. P_{X_i}. Then for each A in $\bar{X}_i$,

either $PDB^P(A,X_iX_j,X_i) = PDB_1^P(A,X_iX_j,X_i)$

or $\quad PDB^P(A,X_iX_j,X_i) = PDB_2^P(A,X_iX_j,X_i) = BL(P,X_i,A) \cap BL(P,X_j,A)$.

<u>Proof</u>

For each $A \in X_j - X_i$, the result is straightforward. If $A \notin X_j - X_i$, then either $PDB^P(A,X_iX_j,X_i) = PDB_1^P(C,X_iX_j,X_i)$ for some $C \in X_j - X_i$ such that $A \in BL(P,X_i,C)$, or $PDB^P(A,X_iX_j,X_i) = PDB_2^P(A,X_iX_j,X_i) = BL(P,X_iX_j,A)$. This follows from our remarks on how the principal derivative is computed. It only remains to show that $BL(P,X_iX_j,A) = BL(P,X_i,A) \cap BL(P,X_j,A)$. Note that $BL(P,X_iX_j,A) = (BL(P,X_i,A) - X_j) \cap (BL(P,X_j,A) - X_i)$. But, $BL(P,X_i,A) \cap X_j = BL(P,X_j,A) \cap X_i = \emptyset$. That proves the lemma.

This lemma tells us that whenever we deal with attributes appearing in $PD(P,X_iX_j,X_i)$, essentially we need only deal with two classes of attributes - (i) $A \in X_j - X_i$ and (ii) $A \notin X_j - X_i$ and $\forall C \in X_j - X_i$, $A \notin BL(P,X_i,C)$. This is because all possible values of $PDB^P(A,X_iX_j,X_i)$ are covered by just these two cases.

We say that two attributes $A,B \in \bar{X}$ are <u>separated</u> in a partition p of $\bar{X}$ if A and B belong to two distinct blocks of p. The next lemma identifies the conditions under which two attributes will be separated in a principal derivative.

<u>Lemma 4.3</u>

Let $P \in L$, $A,B \in \bar{X}_1$, $A,B \notin X_2-X_1$, where $X_1,X_2 \in LHS(M)$. Suppose that A_1 and A_2 are separated in $P_{X_1X_2}$. If for each $C \in X_2-X_1$ with $A \in BL(P,X_1,C)$, there exists an $X_3 \in D(P,X_1,A)$ such that $C \notin BL(P,X_3,A)$, then A and B will be separated in the principal derivative $PD(P,X_1X_2,X_1)$.

Proof

For each $C \in X_2 - X_1$ such that $A \in BL(P,X_1,C)$, clearly, $D(P,X_1,C) = D(P,X_1,A)$. Thus, by the hypothesis of the lemma $\exists X_3 \in D(P,X_1,C)$ with $C \notin BL(P,X_3,A)$ – that is, with $A \notin BL(P,X_3,C)$. Thus, from the definition of $PDB^P(C,X_1X_2,X_1)$ we see that $A \notin PDB^P(C,X_1X_2,X_1)$, $\forall C \in X_2 - X_1$ with $A \in BL(P,X_1,C)$. Then from the remarks on the computation of $PD(P,X_1X_2,X_1)$, we see that $PDB^P(A,X_1X_2,X_1) = BL(P,X_1X_2,A)$. But, $B \notin BL(P,X_1X_2,A)$ and the lemma immediately follows.

In the next section, we shall prove our main results.

4.2 Main Results

In this section, we prove some important properties concerning the structure of MVD-lattices. We then obtain algebraic characterizations for the inference basis IB(M) and the dependency basis $DEP_M(X)$ of an attribute set X, based on the formalism of MVD-lattices. We show in the process that the machinery for inferences with MVDs can be nicely built into the MVD-lattice structure.

Theorem 4.4

Let $P,Q,R \in L$ where Q is directly generated from P, and R is directly generated from Q by an X_a-refinement, for some $X_a \in LHS(M)$. Then there exists $R' \in L$ where R' is directly generated from P by an X_a-refinement such that two attributes are separated in R'_{X_a} if they are separated in R_{X_a}.

Proof

Since the proof is involved, we merely enumerate the various cases encountered. For a complete proof, the reader is referred to [14].

Assume that Q is obtained from P by an X_1-refinement. Further, let X_aX_b be the generator for R and X_1X_c the generator for Q. Assume that A,B are separated in R_{X_a}. The various cases that arise are

Case(a) $X_a \neq X_1$ and

Case(b) $X_a = X_1$.

Each of these cases has two subcases

(1) $A \in X_b - X_a$,

(2) $A \notin X_b - X_a$, and $\forall C \in X_b - X_a$, $A \notin BL(P,X_a,C)$.

By Lemma 4.2, it is adequate to consider just these two possibilities for $A \in \bar{X}_a$.

Further, within each of these subcases, the two analogous possibilities (i) $A \in X_c - X_1$ and (ii) $A \notin X_c - X_1$, and $\forall C \in X_c - X_1$, $A \notin BL(P,X_1,C)$, have to be taken care of.

For each of these, we identify an appropriate generator, say X_aX_i, using which we directly generate a new element R' from P, such that the attributes A and B are separated in R'_{X_a}.

Theorem 4.4 says that if we can directly generate an element R from an element Q which in turn was directly generated from P, then there exists a "corresponding" element R', directly generated from P. Let P_1 sequentially generate P_r. By an inductive extension, one can see that if P_r directly generates an element R then P_1 directly generates a corresponding element R'.

Let $P,Q \in L$, and Q_1 be directly generated from Q by an X_a-refinement. Let P_1 be obtained from P by an X_a-refinement with the same generator as used to obtain Q_1. Then P_1 is said to be obtained from P by a refinement <u>corresponding</u> to Q_1.

The next theorem establishes an interesting relationship between greatest lower bounds and the notion of directly generated elements in an MVD-lattice. This paves the way for incorporating the inference machinery for MVDs into the algebraic operations in MVD-lattices.

<u>Theorem 4.5</u>

Let $P \in L$ directly generate exactly the elements $Q_1, \ldots, Q_r$. Let $Q_{r\,1}, \ldots, Q_{r\,r-1}$ be obtained by direct generation from Q_r using refinements corresponding to $Q_1, \ldots, Q_{r-1}$ respectively. Then, $glb(Q_1, \ldots, Q_r) = glb(Q_{r\,1}, \ldots, Q_{r\,r-1})$.

Proof

It is enough to show that $Q_{r\,i} \leq Q_i$, $i = 1, \ldots, r-1$. Since we have $Q_{r\,i} \leq Q_r$, $i = 1, \ldots, r-1$, we would then get $\mathrm{glb}(Q_{r\,1}, \ldots, Q_{r\,r-1}) \leq \mathrm{glb}(Q_1, \ldots, Q_r)$. Using Theorem 4.4, equality can then be established. For details, consult [14]. □

Now, let us inductively extend the process of directly generating new elements by means of refinements corresponding to appropriate elements. Let P directly generate exactly the elements $Q_1, \ldots, Q_r$. Then obtain $Q_{r\,1}, \ldots, Q_{r\,r-1}$ by refinements corresponding to $Q_1, \ldots, Q_{r-1}$. Again, apply corresponding refinements to $Q_{r\,r-1}$ to generate $Q_{r\,r-1\,r\,1}, \ldots, Q_{r\,r-1\,r\,r-2}$. If this process is continued, it will eventually terminate upon the generation of a unique element say R which equals $\mathrm{glb}(Q_1, \ldots, Q_r)$. Thus, Theorem 4.5 establishes a relationship between the algebraic operation of meet and the sequential generation of elements of L which corresponds to performing inferences with MVDs.

Theorem 4.6

Let M be a set of MVDs and M* its canonical form. Let $P_1, \ldots, P_k$ be the elements of L corresponding to the GMVDs in M* and let $P = \mathrm{glb}(P_1, \ldots, P_k)$. If $\{Q_1, \ldots, Q_r\}$ is the set of all elements directly generated by P then $\mathrm{glb}(Q_1, \ldots, Q_r)$ is the least element of L sequentially generated by P.

Proof

We shall give an inductive proof.

Basis $r = 1$.

P directly generates only Q_1. Then, by virtue of Theorem 4.4, Q_1 is the least element of L sequentially generated by P.

Induction

Assume that for an element Q directly generating exactly $R_1, \ldots, R_{r-1}$, say, $\mathrm{glb}(R_1, \ldots, R_{r-1})$ is the least element of L sequentially generated from Q. Now, let P directly generate exactly the elements $Q_1, \ldots, Q_r$. Generate the elements $Q_{r\,1}, \ldots, Q_{r\,r-1}$ from Q_r by refinements corresponding to $Q_1, \ldots, Q_{r-1}$. It can be easily shown using Theorem 4.4 that these are the only elements directly generated from Q_r. Then by the inductive hypothesis, $glb(Q_{r\,1}, \ldots, Q_{r\,r-1})$ is the least element of L sequentially generated from Q_r. However, from the property of L, the least element of L sequentially generated by Q_r is the same as that sequentially generated by P. The result then follows by virtue of Theorem 4.5.

The next theorem concerns the algebraic characterization for the inference basis. Let P be the element of the MVD-lattice L, as identified by Theorem 4.6. Then, in simple terms, the next theorem shows that the meet of the set of all elements directly generated by P corresponds to the inference basis. We assume that LHS(M) = $\{X_1, \ldots, X_k\}$.

Theorem 4.7

Let M be a set of MVDs and M* its canonical form. Let $P_1, \ldots, P_k$ be the elements of L corresponding to the GMVDs in M*. Let $P = glb(P_1, \ldots, P_k)$. If P directly generates exactly the elements $Q_1, \ldots, Q_r$ then $Q = glb(Q_1, \ldots, Q_r)$ corresponds to the inference basis of M, i.e., $Q_{X_i} = DEP_M(X_i)$, $\forall X_i \in LHS(M)$.

Proof

We use the following criterion due to Beeri [2]. Let $\{Z_1, \ldots, Z_s\}$ be a partition of $\bar{X}$, for some $X \subseteq U$. Then it equals the dependency basis $DEP_M(X)$ if and only if for i = 1, ..., s and for each MVD $X_a \twoheadrightarrow Y_a$ in M, either $X_a \cap Z_i \neq \emptyset$, or $Y_a \cap Z_i = \emptyset$, or $Z_i \subseteq Y_a$. Our task then, is to simply show that this property holds w.r.t. the partition Q_{X_i}, $\forall X_i \in LHS(M)$.

Without loss of generality, we may prove the result w.r.t. $X_1 \in LHS(M)$. Since the proof is involved, we only give an outline. P directly generates at most the k-1 elements $Q_2, \ldots, Q_k$, with Q_i being obtained using the generator X_1X_i, $i \geq 2$. Since all possible X_1-refinements have been exhausted among $Q_2, \ldots, Q_k$ we see that $Q_{X_1} = Q'_{X_1}$ where $Q' = glb(Q_2, \ldots, Q_k)$. Now, assume that $\exists$ an MVD $X_j \twoheadrightarrow W_1$ in M, that violates Beeri's criterion - that is, for some block $Y \in Q_{X_1}$, $X_j \cap Y = \emptyset$, $Y \cap W_1 \neq \emptyset \neq Y \cap W_2$, where $W_2 = \bar{W}_1 - X_j$.

We then show [14] that such an offending MVD leads to a contradiction which implies that Q_{X_1} is the dependency basis of X_1 w.r.t. M. Similar result follows for all $X_i \in LHS(M)$.

Theorem 4.7 gives a characterization for the inference basis IB(M) based on MVD-lattices. Specifically, it proves that if $Q_1, \ldots, Q_r$ are all the elements directly generated by the element P given in the theorem, then glb($Q_1, \ldots, Q_r$) corresponds to the inference basis IB(M). From Theorem 4.6, we know that glb($Q_1, \ldots, Q_r$) is also the least element of the MVD-lattice L sequentially generated from P. As we have already seen, sequential (as also direct) generation corresponds to performing inferences with MVDs. The least element of L so generated obviously contains the maximum information about M* and hence about M. Thus, these two theorems imply that the inference mechanism for MVDs is completely built into the structure of MVD-lattices. Our next task is to prove that computation of the inference basis will deliver the goods - that is, it can be used to synthesize the dependency basis of any arbitrary attribute set. This can be accomplished by a method, rather similar in approach to the computation of the inference basis.

Given an attribute set $X \subseteq U$, where in general $X \notin LHS(M)$, define $S(X) = \{X_i \in LHS(M) : X_i \subseteq X\}$, $I(X) = \{X_j \in LHS(M) : X_j \notin S(X), X_j \cap X \neq \emptyset\}$, and $I'(X) = I(X) \cup \{X\}$. For each $X_i \in S(X)$, $DEP_M(X_i)$ may be obtained from IB(M). Notice that each such dependency basis corresponds to a GMVD with LHS X_i. If $DEP_M(X_i) = \{Y_1, \ldots, Y_s\}$ then $\{Y_1 - X, \ldots, Y_s - X\}$ corresponds to a GMVD with LHS X. Let M_X be the set of all such GMVDs (partitions of $\bar{X}$) so obtained from S(X) and IB(M). Then the glb of all these partitions produces another GMVD with LHS X which we call the X-GMVD. Again, for each X_j in I(X), $DEP_M(X_j)$ (obtained from IB(M)) corresponds to an X_j-GMVD. Define $N = \{W\text{-GMVDs} : W \in I'(X)\}$, and let $I''(X) = \{Z : Z \in I'(X)$, or $Z = W_1W_2$ where $W_1, W_2 \in I'(X)\}$. Now, we can make use of the formalism and machinery of MVD-lattices for computing the dependency basis of X. Let L_1 be the MVD-lattice for N, i.e., $L_1 = \bigotimes_{(Z \in I''(X))} (L_Z)$, where L_Z is, as before, the scheme lattice associated with Z. Let I'(X) =

$\{X_1, \ldots, X_t, X\}$ and let $P_1, \ldots, P_t, P_{t+1}$ be the elements of the MVD-lattice L_1 such that P_i corresponds to the X_i-GMVD in N, i = 1, ..., t, and P_{t+1} corresponds to the X-GMVD in N. Suppose that P is obtained as $glb(P_1, \ldots, P_{t+1})$. Now, let P directly generate exactly the elements $Q_1, \ldots, Q_r$ of L_1, and let $Q = glb(Q_1, \ldots, Q_r)$. Then we have the following

Theorem 4.8

Let P, Q be elements of the MVD-lattice L_1 as defined above. Then Q corresponds to the dependency basis of X - that is, $Q_X = DEP_M(X)$.

Proof

From the inference rules given for MVDs, one can readily see that $DEP_M(X) = DEP_N(X)$. Now, $Q_X = DEP_N(X) = DEP_M(X)$ follows immediately from Theorem 4.7.

We observe that each element directly generated from P is obtained by an X-refinement in the MVD-lattice L_1. This is because, since P_{X_i} already corresponds to $DEP_M(X_i)$, $\forall X_i \in I(X)$, it cannot be refined further. Theorem 4.8 then, proves that using the inference basis one can synthesize the dependency basis of an arbitrary attribute set, thus solving the membership problem.

An Example

In order to bring out the import of our results, let us consider an example. For simplicity, we directly begin with a set of GMVDs - that is, the canonical representation of M.

Let M* be the set of GMVDs
$\{AB \twoheadrightarrow CDE|FGH|IJKL,\ CD \twoheadrightarrow ABE|FGI|HJKL,\ I \twoheadrightarrow ABCD|EF|GJH|KL\}$.
Thus, LHS(M) = LHS(M*) = {AB,CD,I}.
The corresponding MVD-lattice would be
$L = L_{AB} \otimes L_{CD} \otimes L_I \otimes L_{ABCD} \otimes L_{ABI} \otimes L_{CDI}$,
where L_X stands for the scheme lattice corresponding to X.
The element corresponding to the AB-GMVD is
$(\{CDE,FGH,IJKL\},\{\overline{CD}\},\{\overline{I}\},\{E,FGH,IJKL\},\{CDE,FGH,JKL\},\{\overline{CDI}\})$.
Similarly, one can readily identify the elements of L corresponding

to the other GMVDs in M^*. The greatest lower bound of all the elements of M^* corresponding to the GMVDs can be easily verified to be

$$P = (\{CDE,FGH,IJKL\},\{ABE,FGI,HJKL\},\{ABCD,EF,GJH,KL\},$$
$$\{E,FG,H,I,JKL\},\{CD,E,F,GH,J,KL\},\{AB,E,F,G,JH,KL\}).$$

Next, we shall obtain an element Q_1 directly generated from P by an AB-refinement using ABCD as the generator. Using the principles described before, we have

$$Q_1 = (\{CD,E,FG,H,I,JKL\},\ P_{CD},\ P_I,\{E,FG,H,I,JKL\},$$
$$\{CD,E,F,G,H,J,KL\},\ P_{CDI}\ ).$$

Similarly, the reader can readily work out other elements directly generated from P as well as verify that the greatest lower bound of all the elements directly generated from P is given by

$$(\{CD,E,F,G,H,I,J,KL\},\{AB,E,F,G,H,I,J,KL\},\{ABCD,E,F,G,H,J,KL\},$$
$$\{E,F,G,H,I,J,KL\},\{CD,E,F,G,H,J,KL\},\{AB,E,F,G,H,J,KL\}).$$

Of course, the X-component of the above element corresponds to $DEP_M(X)$, for X = AB,CD,I.

In an analogous manner, $DEP_M(X)$ for an arbitrary $X \subseteq \{A,B, \ldots, L\}$ can be obtained from the appropriate MVD-lattice L_1 as explained earlier.

In the next section, we develop algorithms for computing the inference basis and the dependency basis and also for solving the implication problem for MVDs, using our results. The characterization given above (Theorem 4.8) for the dependency basis may be seen to be quite similar to that given earlier (Theorem 4.7) for the inference basis. Our algorithms in the next section reflect this similarity.

5. The Algorithms

In this section, we present our algorithms for the various problems. They are given here in schematic form, for brevity. For complete details regarding the implementations the reader is referred to [14].

5.1 The Inference Basis

Given a set M of MVDs, we want to compute IB(M) - the inference basis of M. Let us clarify certain conventions. An MVD in M with an

LHS X_i is called an X_i-MVD. A GMVD in M^* with an LHS X_i is called an X_i-GMVD. The new GMVD formed by shifting attributes in $X_j - X_i$ from the right-hand-side of an X_i-GMVD to the LHS is called an X_iX_j-GMVD. Note that X_iX_j-GMVDs can be formed from an X_i-GMVD as well as from an X_j-GMVD. In general, these two X_iX_j-GMVDs are distinct. An X_i-GMVD in M corresponds to P_{X_i} where $P \in L$ is the element identified in Theorems 4.6 and 4.7. Now the glb of the X_iX_j-GMVDs mentioned above gives $P_{X_iX_j}$. In the algorithm below we use notations used in connection with MVD-lattices in Section 4. For instance, $BL(P,X_i,A)$ is that block on the RHS of the X_i-GMVD to which A belongs. Similarly, the notations used have their obvious corresponding meaning for GMVDs.

<u>Algorithm 5.1</u> : <u>INFERENCEBASIS</u>

Input : A set M of MVDs
Output: The inference basis IB(M)

```
begin
  (1) for each X_i in LHS(M) do
  (2)    take the glb of all X_i-MVDs in M
      rof; / M* is generated /
  (3) for each X_i in LHS(M) do
  (4)     for each X_j in LHS(M) s.t. X_i ≠ X_j do
  (5)        form the pair of X_iX_j-GMVDs from the X_i-GMVD
             and the X_j-GMVD; take their glb;
  (6)        currentset := ∅; DEP_j(X_i) := ∅;
  (7)           for each A in X_j - X_i - currentset do
                   W := PDB_1^P(A,X_iX_j,X_i);
                   DEP_j(X_i) := DEP_j(X_i) ∪ {W};
                   currentset := currentset ∪ W
                rof;
  (8)           for each A in X̄_i - currentset do
                     DEP_j(X_i) := DEP_j(X_i) ∪ {BL(P,X_iX_j,A)};
                     currentset := currentset ∪ BL(P,X_iX_j,A)
                rof;
```

(9) $DEP(X_i) := glb(\{DEP_j(X_i) : j \neq i\})$

<u>rof</u>

<u>rof</u>

<u>end</u>;

The correctness of this algorithm immediately follows from our results in Section 4. As for the complexity, using an appropriate data structure quite similar to the SET-UNION-FIND data structure we show in [14] that Algorithm 5.1 is $O(kn + k\,\|M\|)$ where $k = |LHS(M)|$, $n = |U|$ and $\|M\|$ is the space needed to write down M. Here, generating the canonical representation M^* takes $O(kn)$ time and computing the inference basis from that takes $O(k\,\|M\|)$ time.

5.2 The Dependency Basis

As we saw in Section 4, the same principle as used to compute the inference basis can be made use of for computing the dependency basis. We present the algorithm below.

<u>Algorithm 5.2</u>: <u>DEPENDENCY-BASIS</u>

Input: A set M of MVDs and an attribute set X
/ The inference basis IB(M) is assumed to be available /
Output: $DEP_M(X)$

<u>begin</u>

(1) compute I(X) and S(X);

(2) <u>for</u> <u>each</u> X_i <u>in</u> S(X) <u>do</u>
form a new "X^i-GMVD" by shifting attributes in
$X - X_i$ to the left
<u>rof</u>;

(3) X-GMVD := $glb(\{X^i\text{-GMVD} : X_i \in S(X)\})$;

(4) <u>for</u> <u>each</u> X_j <u>in</u> I(X) <u>do</u>

(5) form the pair of XX_j-GMVDs; take their glb;

(6) currentset := $\emptyset$; $DEP_j(X) := \emptyset$;

(7) <u>for</u> <u>each</u> A <u>in</u> X_j - X - currentset <u>do</u>
$W := PDB_1^P(A, XX_j, X)$;
$DEP_j(X) := DEP_j(X) \cup \{W\}$;
currentset := currentset $\cup$ W
<u>rof</u>;

```
(8)          for each A in X̄ - currentset do
                 DEP_j(X) := DEP_j(X) ∪ {BL(P,XX_j,A)};
                 currentset := currentset ∪ BL(P,XX_j,A)
             rof;
(9)          DEP(X) := glb({DEP_j(X) : ∀X_j ∈ I(X)})
         rof
end;
```

In Algorithm 5.2, P is the element in L_1 as used in Theorem 4.8. Again, correctness immediately follows from Theorem 4.8. Using data structure similar to that used for Algorithm 5.1, [14] shows that Algorithm 5.2 takes time O(kn).

Now, consider the generalized membership problem posed earlier. We want to settle the membership of many MVDs. So, as argued in Section 3, computation of the dependency bases is bound to pay off. So, assume that we want to compute m dependency bases, m >> k. Then our approach leads to a complexity of $O(kn + k\ \|M\| + mkn)$ where $O(kn + k\ \|M\|)$ time is incurred for computing the inference basis and O(mkn) for computing m dependency bases. In [14] we prove these results rigorously and make a comparison of our approach with the conventional approach using any of the known algorithms for directly computing the dependency basis.

5.3 The Implication Problem

The algorithm for the implication problem for MVDs is obtained from simple modifications to the algorithm for computing the dependency basis, along the lines of Sagiv [19].

Algorithm 5.3 : TEST-IMPLICATION

Input : A set M of MVDs and another MVD X →→ Y.
Output : "Yes" if X →→ Y is logically implied by M and "No" otherwise.

```
begin
  (1) currentset := ∅;
  (2) for each A in Y - currentset do
          find out the block Z in DEP_M(X)
             such that A ∈ Z;
  (3)     if Z ⊈ Y then print ("No") exit
          fi
      rof;
```

```
    print ("Yes")
end;
```

An efficient implementation of this similar to the one in [19] is possible [14]. In view of the results in Beeri [2], we note that our results and algorithms extend to the implication problem for FDs and MVDs taken together.

6. Conclusions

We have developed a lattice theoretic formalism for addressing many of the important issues such as dependency basis, membership, concerning MVDs. In this connection, we introduced the concept of an MVD-lattice and showed that algebraic operations on an MVD-lattice can be used to carry out inferences with MVDs. We also introduced the concept of the inference basis of a set M of MVDs and established that it can be used to synthesize the dependency basis of an arbitrary attribute set. Based on our theory, we developed algebraic characterizations for the inference basis and the dependency basis as well as algorithms for computing these and for solving the implication problem for MVDs. It is possible to make the algorithm for synthesizing the dependency basis more efficient, by computing only the relevant portion of the inference basis. As a result, Algorithm 5.3 can be similarly modified to make it more efficient. Such possibilities are explored in [14], which also contains complete details of the proofs and algorithms. We hope that the theory developed here may be naturally extended to offer a unified treatment of several issues surrounding data dependencies.

References

1. W.W. Armstrong, "Dependency structures of database relationships", Proc. IFIP 74, North Holland, Amsterdam, 1974, pp.580-583.

2. C. Beeri, "On the membership problem for functional and multivalued dependencies in relational databases", ACM TODS 5,3 (Sept. 1980), 241-249.

3. C. Beeri, R. Fagin, and J.H. Howard, "A complete axiomatization for functional and multivalued dependencies in database relations", Proc. ACM SIGMOD Int.Conf. on Management of Data, Toronto, Aug.1977, pp.47-61.

4. C. Beeri and M.Y. Vardi, "On the properties of join dependencies", in : Advances in Database Theory Vol.I (H.Gallaire, J.Minker, and J.Nicolas, Eds.), Plenum Press, NY, 1981, pp.25-71.

5. G. Birkhoff, Lattice Theory, 3rd ed., Providence, RI : American Mathematical Society Colloquium Publ. XXV, 1967.

6. J. Biskup, "Inferences of multivalued dependencies in fixed and undetermined universes", Theor.Comput.Sci. 10, 1(Jan.1980),93-105.

7. E.F. Codd, "A relational model of data for large shared data banks", CACM 13, 6(June 1970), 377-387.

8. ________, "Further normalization of the database relational model", in: Data Base Systems (R. Rustin Ed.), Prentice Hall, Englewood Cliffs, NJ, pp.33-64.

9. C. Delobel, "Semantics of relations and decomposition process in the relational data model", ACM TODS 3,3 (Sept. 1978), 201-222.

10. R. Fagin, "Multivalued dependencies and a new normal form for relational databases", ACM TODS 2,3 (Sept.1977), 262-278.

11. Z.Galil, "An almost linear-time algorithm for computing a dependency basis in a relational database", JACM 29, 1(Jan. 1982), 96-102.

12. K. Hagihara, et al, "Decision problems for multi-valued dependencies in relational databases", SIAM J. Comput. 8,2 (May 1979), 247-264.

13. W. Kent, "A guide to the five normal forms in relational database theory", CACM 1983.

14. V.S. Lakshmanan and C.E. Veni Madhavan, "An algebraic theory of functional and multivalued dependencies in relational databases", under preparation.

15. T.T.Lee, "An algebraic theory of relational databases", The Bell Syst. Tech. Jl.62, 10 (Dec.1983), 3159-3204.

16. _____, "Order-preserving representations of the partitions on the finite set", J.Combinatorial Theory, Series A 31, No.2 (Sept.1981), 136-145.

17. A.O. Mendelzon, "On axiomatizing multivalued dependencies in relational databases", JACM 26, 1(Jan.1979), 37-44.

18. K.K. Nambiar, "A study of saturated sets and functional dependencies in relational databases using linear graphs", Proc. 1st Conf. FST and TCS, Bangalore, India, Dec.1981, pp.99-108.

19. Y.Sagiv, "An algorithm for inferring multivalued dependencies with an application to propositional logic", JACM 27,2 (April 1980), 250-262.

20. Y. Sagiv, et al, "An equivalence between relational database dependencies and a subclass of propositional logic", JACM 28,3 (July 1981), 435-453.

21. J.D. Ullman, Principles of Database Systems, Computer Science Press, Potmac, Maryland 1983.

22. M.Y.Vardi, "Inferring multivalued dependencies from functional and join dependencies", Acta Informatica,19(1983), 305-324.

23. C. Zaniolo, "Analysis and design of relational schemata for database systems", Tech.Rep.UCLA_ENG_7769, Dept. of Comp.Sci., UCLA, July 1976.

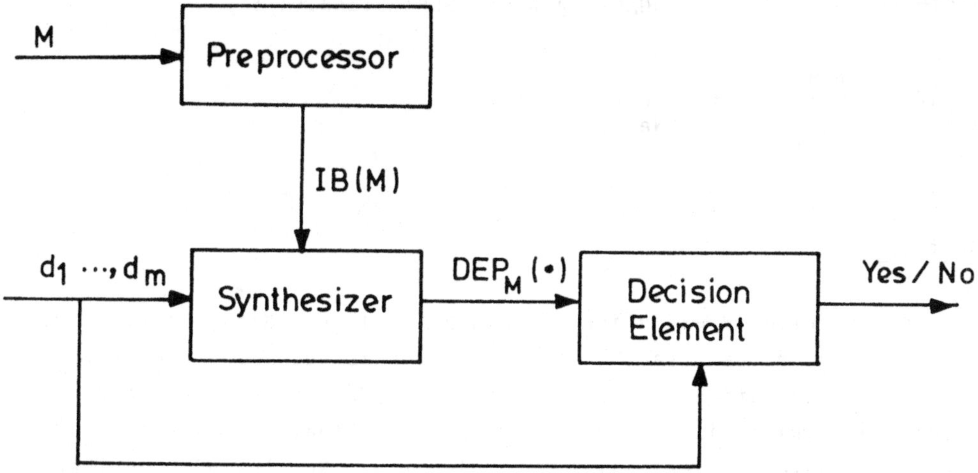

M : given set of MVDs

$d_1 \ldots, d_m$: MVDs whose implication by M has to be tested

For an explanation of how the various blocks interact consult the text.

Fig. 3.1 The role of the inference basis IB (M) in solving the implication problem for a large number of MVDs.

A SIMPLE CHARACTERIZATION OF DATABASE SERIALIZABILITY

K. Vidyasankar
Department of Computer Science
Memorial University of Newfoundland
St. John's, Nfld.
Canada A1C 5S7

Abstract

An interleaved execution of transactions in a database system is *serializable* if the effect of the execution is equivalent to that of some serial execution of the transactions. We give a simple and intuitive characterization of serializability that brings out the inherent problem of serialization explicitly. We also give another characterization which extends naturally to multiversion serializability.

The class WRW is the largest known subclass of serializable executions having polynomial membership test. We give a new characterization for this class that relates this class with the general class of serializable executions in a natural way.

1. Introduction

A database system is a collection of data items, read or written by transactions in a possibly interleaved fashion. The concurrency control mechanism ensures the correctness of the interleaved execution. A commonly accepted criterion of correctness is *serializability*, that is, the effect of the execution is equivalent to that of some serial execution of the transactions.

The theory of serializability has been extensively studied [BSW, EGLT, IKM1, P, SLR]. In this paper, we present a new characterization of serializability, using a new graph model to represent the execution. Our characterization is simple, intuitive, and it exhibits the inherent problem of serialization explicitly. We compare our characterization with the others in the literature in a later section.

We also give another characterization of serializability that extends naturally to multiversion case, where each value written by a transaction is kept as a separate version, and in a read operation one of the already created versions of a data item is read. Multiversion serializability has been studied in [BG, IK, PK].

The problem of deciding whether an execution is serializable is NP-complete. Hence serializability under some constraints have been studied [BSW, IKM1, P]. Some of these constraints give rise to subclasses of serializable executions that have polynomial membership test. The largest known polynomial class is WRW, defined in [IKM1]. We give another characterization for this class, that relates this class with the general class of serializable executions in a natural way.

In section 2, we give the basic terminology and definitions. In section 3, we define H and TP graphs, and give the main characterization. The comparison with other characterizations is given in section 4. In section 5 we give a stronger characterization of serializability and extend the result to multiversion case. The class WRW is discussed in section 6. Section 7 concludes the paper.

2. Basic Terminology and Definitions

A database system consists of a set D of data items and a set $T = \{T_0, T_1, \dots, T_n, T_f\}$ of transactions. A *transaction* is a finite partially ordered set of steps. Each *step* is either a *read step* reading (exactly) one data item, or a *write step* writing (exactly) one data item. We assume each data item is accessed by at most one read step and at most one write step in a transaction; and if both steps do occur, then the read step precedes the write step in the partial order. A transaction is a *write-only* transaction if it does not have any read steps. It is a *read-only* transaction if it does not have any write steps. The transaction T_0 is a fictitious write-only *initial transaction* which writes the initial values of all the data items, and T_f is a fictitious read-only *final transaction* that reads the values of all data items after all transactions have completed.

A read step (write step) of Transaction T_i reading (writing) the data item X is denoted $R_i[X](W_i[X])$. A set of read steps of T_i, unrelated by the partial order, reading a subset C of D and occurring together, is denoted $R_i[C]$. For example, $R_i[\{X,Y\}]$ denotes the unrelated read steps $R_i[X]$ and $R_i[Y]$ occurring together in any order; for simplicity, we write this as $R_i[X,Y]$. Similar notation is followed for the write steps. A *history* h of T is a sequence of the steps of T representing the execution of the transactions in a possibly interleaved fashion, starting with $W_0[D]$ and ending with $R_f[D]$. Note that the steps of each transaction in h must satisfy the partial order. A history is *serial* if there is no interleaving, that is once a transaction starts executing, it finishes without any other transaction executing some step in between.

A history is *correct* if it behaves like a serial history. Several correctness criteria have been proposed for different interpretations of "behaves" [B,Y]. A common notion is serializability (called *view-serializability* in [Y]), defined below.

A transaction T_j *reads* X *from* transaction T_i is a history h if $W_i[X]$ is the last write X before $R_j[X]$ in h. The *reads-from* relation rf of a history is defined as follows:

$$rf(h) = \{(T_i, X, T_j) : T_j \text{ reads } X \text{ from } T_i\}.$$

Two histories h and h' are *equivalent* [EGLT] if rf(h) = rf(h'). A history h is *serializable* (SR) if there exists a serial history h' equivalent to h.

It is known that testing whether a history is SR is NP-complete [P].

3. Main Characterization

Let h be a history of $T = \{T_0, T_1, T_2, \ldots, T_n, T_f\}$. A write X by transaction T_i is *useless* in h if no transaction reads this value, that is, there is no T_j for which (T_i, X, T_j) is in rf(h); otherwise, it is *useful*.

Definition 3.1. The *history graph* of h, denoted H(h), is a directed graph constructed as follows.

(a) The vertex set of H(h) is $T \cup T'$ where $T' = \{T'_{iX} : T_i$ has a useless write X in h$\}$. The set T' is a set of dummy transactions, one for each useless write in h.

(b) The edge set of H(h) has the following:

(i) an edge labelled X from T_i to T_j, for each (T_i, X, T_j) in rf(h);

(ii) an edge labelled X from T_i to T'_{iX} for each useless write X of T_i, for all T_i;

(iii) an unlabelled edge from each vertex in T' to T_f;

(iv) an unlabelled edge from each read-only transaction other than T_f to T_f; and

(v) an unlabelled edge from T_0 to each write-only transaction other then T_0. //

We use T_i to refer to transaction T_i and also the vertex T_i in the graph. An edge α from T_i to T_j is denoted (T_i, T_j). Here, T_i is the *positive end* $p\alpha$ of α, and T_j is the *negative end*

$n\alpha$ of α. We also refer to α as an *outdirected* edge of T_i and an *indirected* edge of T_j. A *source* is a vertex with no indirected edges, and a *sink* is a vertex with no outdirected edges. An X-*edge* refers to an edge labelled X. The labelled edges incident to T' are *useless*; all other labelled edges are *useful*.

Example 3.1. Let h be the following history.

$$W_0[X,Y]R_1[X]R_2[X]R_3[Y]W_2[Y]W_3[Y]W_4[X,Y]R_f[X,Y]$$

The history graph H(h) is given in Figure 1. The stars (*) indicate the useful edges. //

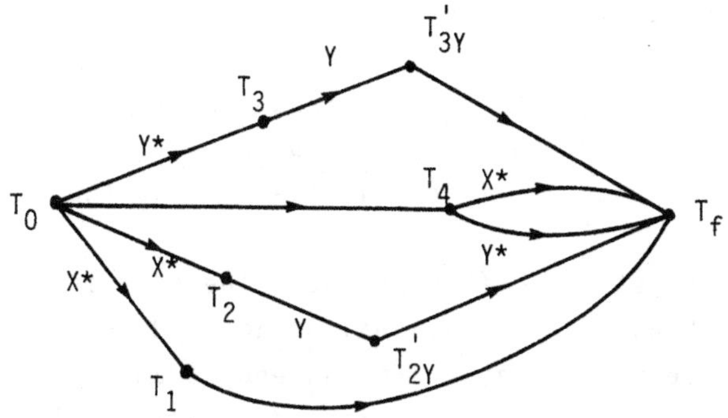

Figure 1.

PROPOSITION 3.1. A history graph has the following properties.

(a) It is a 1-source 1-sink graph.

(b) All edges between vertices in $(T - \{T_0, T_f\}) \cup T'$ are labelled.

(c) All unlabelled edges either start from T_0 or end in T_f.

(d) No two indirected edges of any vertex have the same label.

(e) If α is a useful X-edge for some X in D, then $p\alpha$ is not the positive end of any useless X-edge.

(f) A vertex that is the negative end of a useless edge is not the (negative or positive) end of any other (useful or useless) labelled edge.

(g) For every X in D, there is at least one X-edge starting from T_0.

(h) For every X in D, there is exactly one X-edge ending in T_f.

(i) No useless edge is incident to T_f. //

It is clear that two histories h and h' of T are equivalent iff H(h) = H(h').

We now introduce some more graph terminology. The *coboundary* of a subset S of the vertex set of a graph G is the set of edges each with one end in S and the other not in S. By a *coboundary* of G, we refer to a set of edges that is the coboundary of some subset of the vertex set of G. A *cutset* is a minimal non-null coboundary. (A set is *minimal* with a given property if it has the property but none of its proper subsets has the property.) A coboundary is *directed* if it can be expressed as a directed coboundary of some subset of the vertex set. A *directed cutset* is a directed coboundary that is a cutset.

We now define another graph.

Definition 3.2. A *Transaction Precedence graph* for h, denoted TP(h), is a graph having the following properties.

(a) The vertex set of TP(h) is the same as the vertex set of H(h).

(b) The edge set of TP(h) includes the edge set of H(h), and perhaps a few additional unlabelled edges. (These unlabelled edges may start and end at any vertices.

(c) *Exclusion Property*: No directed cutset in TP(h) that contains a useful X-edge α contains any other (useful or useless) X-edge β with $p\beta \neq p\alpha$, for any X in D. //

Note that TP(h) can be obtained from H(h) by repeatedly applying the following construction: if there is a directed cutset with a useful X-edge α and another X-edge β, with $p\beta$ different from $p\alpha$, then add an unlabelled edge either from $n\alpha$ to $p\beta$, or from $n\beta$ to $p\alpha$, thus making that cutset undirected. Either of these edges is an *exclusion edge* (called *exclusion arc* in [IKM1]).

Example 3.2. For the history h in Example 3.1, Figure 2 shows a TP(h) graph obtained by adding the broken lines to H(h). //

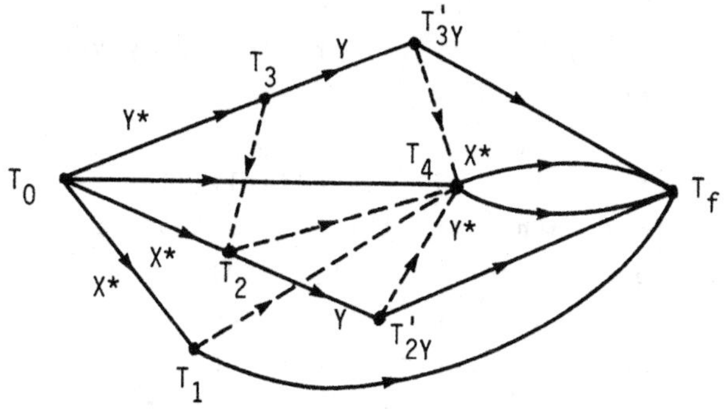

Figure 2.

We now state a simple graph property useful in the characterization of serializable histories.

THEOREM 3.2 [VY]. For any two distinct edges of a 1-source 1-sink acyclic graph, there is a directed path that contains them both iff there is no directed cutset that contains them both. //

From Theorem 3.2 and the exclusion property in Definition 3.2, we have the following property.

LEMMA 3.3. In an acyclic TP(h) of h, let α be a useful X-edge and β be any (useful or useless) X-edge such that $p\beta \neq p\alpha$. Then there is a directed path in TP(h) that contains both α and β. //

We are now ready for the characterization.

THEOREM 3.4. A history h is serializable iff there exists an acyclic TP(h).

Proof. Suppose h is serializable. Then there exists a serial history h' equivalent to h, that is, H(h) = H(h'). Without loss of generality, assume that the transaction order in h' is $(T_0, T_1, T_2, \ldots, T_n, T_f)$. We now construct a graph G by adding the following unlabelled edges to H(h):

(a) an edge from T_i to T_{i+1} for i between 1 and n-1, and

(b) an edge from T'_{iX} to T_{i+1} for each dummy vertex, for i between 0 and n-1.

We first show that G is a TP(h). Clearly, the vertex set of G is the same as that of H(h) and the edge set of G includes that of H(h). For the exclusion property, consider a directed cutset of G that contains a useful X-edge, say α. Suppose there exists another X-edge β in this cutset with $p\beta \neq p\alpha$. Let T_i be $p\alpha$, T_j be $n\alpha$, and T_k be $p\beta$. If $i < k$, then $j < k$ too, otherwise T_j will not read X from T_i in h'. Then, by the construction of G, there is a directed path in G consisting of unlabelled edges from T_j to T_k. If $i > k$, then either $n\beta$ is T_m (that is, β is useful), in which case, $i > m$ and there is a directed path consisting of unlabelled edges from T_m to T_i; or $n\beta$ is T'_{kX} (that is, β is useless), in which case, there is a directed path from T'_{kX} to T_{k+1} to T_i. Hence the cutset cannot be directed as assumed. Therefore there can be no such edge β, that is, G satisfies the exclusion property. Hence G is a TP(h).

We will now show that G is acyclic. We first note that each labelled edge is either from T_i to T_j, where $i < j$, or from T_i to T'_{iX} for some i and X. Each unlabelled edge is either from T_i to T_j where $T_i = T_0$, or $T_j = T_f$, or $j = i+1$; or from T'_{iX} to T_j, where j is either i+1 or $T_j = T_f$. Thus all edges are directed "from left to right". Hence there can be no directed cycles in G. Hence, G is an acyclic TP(h).

For the converse, suppose there exists an acyclic TP(h), say G_1. Let α be a (useful) X-edge from T_i to T_j in G_1, and β be some other X-edge with $p\beta = T_k \neq T_i$. By Lemma 3.3, there is a directed path that contains both α and β in G_1. Hence, in a topological sort, T_k will appear either after T_j or before T_i, but not in between T_i and T_j. Therefore, if h' is the serial history corresponding to the order in which the transactions in T appear in a topological sort of G_1, then rf(h') = rf(h), that is, h is serializable. //

4. Comparison with Other Characterizations

Several graph models have been used in the literature to characterize serializability of histories, for example, version-graph of [SLR], dag D of [S], TIO-graph of [IKM1] and polygraph of [P].

All these graphs contain edges, in some form, representing the reads-from relation rf(h), and a few more edges. All of them contain vertices for transactions in T. Only the TIO-graph and the (implicit) graph of [EN] have dummy vertices corresponding to useless writes. But in [EN], only one dummy vertex is used irrespective of the number of useless writes in h, whereas the TIO-graph uses one dummy vertex for each transaction that has useless writes. In contrast, history graphs use one dummy vertex for each useless write in h. Another difference is that the TIO-graph contains only labelled edges, and hence is in general a multi-source multi-sink graph. The 1-source 1-sink property of the history graphs, obtained by adding the unlabelled edges as described, has been helpful in the new characterization.

In [IKM1], serializable histories are characterized as follows. A total order << on the set of vertices of TIO(h) is a *disjoint-interval-topological-sort* (DITS, for short) if it satisfies the following two conditions:

(a) if $T_i << T_j$ then there is no directed path from T_j to T_i in TIO(h), and

(b) if $T_g << T_k$ then $T_i << T_j$, where (T_g, T_i) and (T_j, T_k) are X-edges in TIO(h) with $g \neq j$.

A history h is serializable iff TIO(h) has a DITS which orders T_0 first and T_f last.

Clearly, TIO(h) has a DITS iff there exists an acyclic TP(h). Then any topological sort of TP(h) is a disjoint-interval-topological-sort of TIO(h) (and of H(h)). Thus TP(h) embodies the disjoint-interval property.

In [IKM1] also, when a polynomial subclass c-SR of SR is discussed, a graph called TIO*[c](h) which is equivalent to TP[c](h) is introduced. (The notation c-SR and TP[c](h) are explained in section 6.) If the graph TIO*[c](h) is acyclic, then any topological sort of TIO*[c](h) is a DITS of TIO[c](h). Thus our TP-graph characterization is universal, applicable to all classes, polynomial or NP complete.

In [S], a graph called D(h) is constructed from a given history h, and h is serializable iff D(h) has a 1-pebbling. The graph D(h) is vertex-oriented, that is, it contains "a vertex for each instantaneous value taken by an item in the database", whereas the history graph is edge-oriented, containing an edge for each value. Exclusion edges are used in [S] to properly order vertices. We use them to order edges.

Our approach is similar to that of [P], which we describe now. A *polygraph* $P = (N,A,B)$ is a directed graph (N,A) together with a set B of *bipaths*, that is, pairs of edges, not necessarily in A, of the form $((v,u),(u,w))$ such that $(w,v) \in A$. A polygraph (N,A,B) can be viewed as a family $\mathcal{D}(N,A,B)$ of directed graphs. A directed graph (N,A') is in $\mathcal{D}(N,A,B)$ if $A \subseteq A'$, and for each bipath (a_1,a_2) in B, A' contains at least one of a_1,a_2. A polygraph (N,A,B) is *acyclic* if there is an acyclic graph in $\mathcal{D}(N,A,B)$.

Given a history h over T, a polygraph $P(h)$ is (T,A,B), constructed as follows: the set A contains edges from T_0 to every other transaction, and from every transaction other than T_f to T_f, and edges (T_i,T_j) for each (T_i,X,T_j) in $rf(h)$; and the set B contains the bipaths $((T_j,T_k),(T_k,T_i))$ where (T_i,X,T_j) is in $rf(h)$ and another transaction T_k writes X. Clearly the bipaths provide the exclusion edges. A history h is serializable iff $P(h)$ is acyclic, that is, there is an acyclic graph, say $A(h)$, in $\mathcal{D}(N,A,B)$.

Our (acyclic) $TP(h)$ provides the same end result as $A(h)$, namely, any topological sort of the graph gives an equivalent serial order. The main difference is that $A(h)$ does not have dummy transactions and all edges are unlabelled. The edge labels help to identify the exclusion property (of $TP(h)$) which is central to our characterization.

5. Another Characterization and Multiversion Serializability

In this section we give another characterization of serializable histories, a result stronger than Theorem 3.4. This new result extends naturally to multiversion histories also.

Let G be an acyclic $TP(h)$. As a corollary of Lemma 3.3, we have the following.

LEMMA 5.1. In graph G, for any set ψ of useful X-edges no two of which have a common end,

(a) there is a directed path that contains all the edges of ψ and

(b) for each useless X-edge β, there is a directed path that contains β and all the edges of ψ. //

While constructing $TP(h)$ from $H(h)$, at some intermediate stage, suppose some directed cutset contains a useful X-edge α and another X-edge β. If there is a directed path from p_α to p_β, then the only exclusion edge that might yield an acyclic TP(h) is (n_α, p_β), since (n_β, p_α) gives a directed cycle right away. Hence we have the following property, where a transaction is an *X-writer* if it writes X, and is a *useful (useless)* X-writer if the write X is useful (useless). Note that for some X and Y, the same transaction could be a useless X-writer but a useful Y-writer.

LEMMA 5.2. In graph G, for each X in D,

(a) there is a directed path that contains all the useful X-writers, and

(b) for each useless X-writer T_a, there is a directed path that contains all the useful X-writers and T_a. //

We now define a binary relation $\rightarrow_X$ on X-writers in G, for each X in D, as follows: $T_i \rightarrow_X T_j$ if there is a directed path in G from T_i to T_j without passing through a useful X-writer as an intermediate vertex, and either T_i is T_0 or at least one of T_i, T_j is a useful X-writer.

LEMMA 5.3. The graph corresponding to the relation $\rightarrow_X$ in G is as in Figure 3, where the transactions T_{iu} are useful X-writers, the transactions T_{ij} are useless X-writers, the write X of T_0 may or may not be useful and $T_{(k+1)u}$ is the last transaction that writes X in h. //

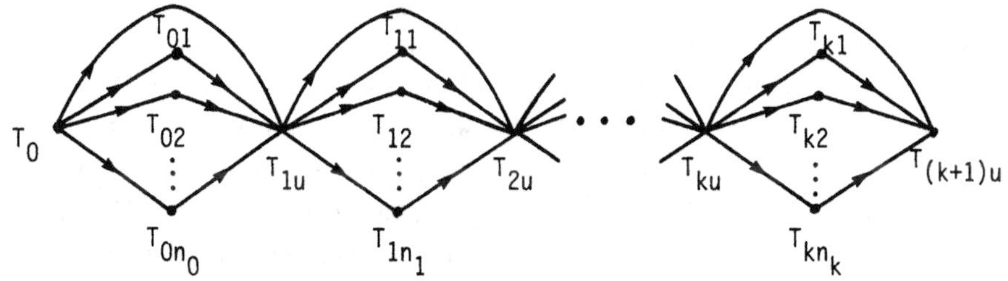

Figure 3.

Definition 5.1. A *weak order* on X-writers in h is a partial order such that

(i) it totally orders all the useful X-writers, and

(ii) for any useless X-writer T_a, it totally orders all useful X-writers and T_a.

A *weak order* in h is the union of some weak order on X-writers, for all X in D. //

Clearly the transitive closure of $\rightarrow_X$ is a weak order on X-writers. A weak order q can be represented in TP(h) by means of unlabelled edges, one for each element of q. We call the resulting graph TP[q](h).

THEOREM 5.4. A history h is serializable iff for some weak order q in h there exists an acyclic TP[q](h).

Proof: Suppose h is serializable. Then by Theorem 3.4, there exists an acyclic TP(h), say G. Now we can define a binary relation $\rightarrow_X$ on X-writers in G, for each X. The transitive closure of $\rightarrow_X$ is a weak order on X-writers. Let q be the union of these weak orders. By adding the edges corresponding to q in G, we get a TP[q](h) which is certainly acyclic. The converse is straightforward from the fact that an acyclic TP[q](h) is certainly an acyclic TP(h). //

THEOREM 5.5. For a given weak order q in h, the existence of an acyclic TP[q](h) can be checked in polynomial time.

Proof: Let G be the graph obtained by adding the edges corresponding to q in the history graph H(h) of h. Clearly G can be constructed in polynomial time. Consider an element (T_i, T_j) in q. Suppose it is an element of the weak order on X-writers. Then T_i is $p\alpha$ and T_j is $p\beta$ for some X-edges α and β in G. Add the edge $(n\alpha, p\beta)$ to G. Repeat this construction for all the elements of q. It is easy to verify that the resulting graph G' is a TP[q](h), and also G' is acyclic iff there exists an acyclic TP[q](h). Both the construction and checking acyclicity of G' can be done in polynomial time. //

Thus though checking whether a history is serializable is NP-complete, that is, checking whether there is a weak order q such that an acyclic TP[q](h) exists is NP-complete, for a given q the existence of an acyclic TP[q](h) can be checked in polynomial time. We will refer to this result in the next section when we discuss the polynomial class WRW.

We now show that Theorem 5.4 can be extended for multiversion histories also. Multiversion concurrency control schemes have been widely discussed in the literature (for example in [BG, IK, PK]). In a multiversion scheme each value written by a transaction is kept as a separate version. Calling the version of X written by T_i as X_i, the write X step of T_i will be denoted $W_i[X_i]$. In a read X step a transaction reads one of the already created versions. The read step $R_k[X_j]$ denotes that T_k reads the version of X written by T_j. A *multiversion history* is a sequence of the steps of T starting with the write steps of the initial transaction which creates the "initial" versions of all the data items, and ending with the read steps of the final transaction which reads one version of each data item. The *reads-from* relation rf of a multiversion history h can be defined as

$$rf(h) = \{(T_i, X, T_j) : R_j[X_i] \text{ is in } h\}.$$

The graphs H(h) and TP(h), and weak orders can be defined the same way as before, and it is easy to verify the following.

THEOREM 5.6. A multiversion history h is serializable iff for some weak order q in h there exists an acyclic TP[q](h). //

In multiversion histories a weak order on X-writers induces naturally a relation among the versions of X that the X-writers create. We will call this a *weak version order* on X. A *weak version order* in h is the union of some weak version order on X, for each X in D. Thus Theorem 5.6 can be considered as a characterization of multiversion histories in terms of weak version order. This contrasts with the characterization given in [BG] which is in terms of (total) version order.

6. The Polynomial Class WRW

The NP-completeness of the membership test in SR implies checking whether there exists an acyclic TP(h) for a given history h is NP-complete. With the intention of getting subclasses of SR having polynomial membership test, classes of histories which are serializable under some constraints have been studied - for example, the classes DSR, Q, 2PL and SSR in [P] and the classes of [IKM1] described below. If c specifies certain constraints, we use the notation c-SR to denote the class of histories which are equivalent to some serial history whose transaction order satisfies c. The constraints give rise to some precedence relation among transactions and are usually derived from some syntactic properties of histories. (For example, in the *strict serializable class* SSR, a transaction T_i that finishes execution before a transaction T_j starts must appear before T_j in the equivalent serial order.) This relation is added, in the form of unlabelled edges, to H(h) to get H[c](h), and we look for the existence of acyclic TP[c](h).

In this section, we study the class WRW of [IKM1], the largest known subclass of SR having a polynomial membership test. (According to our notation, we should represent the class as WRW-SR, but we use the same notation as in [IKM1]). We give another characterization of WRW which illustrates that the WRW-constraints induce a weak order on X-writers (for each X), and hence it follows from Theorem 5.5 that the membership test is polynomial. In contrast, in the well known class WW (also called DSR in [P], and CPSR in [BSW]) the WW-constraints induce a total order on these transactions irrespective of whether they have useful or useless writes.

Definition 6.1. [IKM1] Let h be a history over the set T of transactions.

(a) [*WW-constraints*] If $W_i[X]$ occurs before $W_j[X]$ for some X, then T_i must be serialized before T_j.

(b) [*WR-constraints*] If $W_i[X]$ occurs before $R_j[X]$ for some X, then T_i must be serialized before T_j.

(c) [*RW-constraints*] If $R_i[X]$ occurs before $W_j[X]$ for some X, then T_i must be serialized before T_j.

(d) [*WRW-constraints*] If $W_i[X]$ occurs before $R_j[X]$ or $R_i[X]$ occurs before $W_j[X]$, for some X, then T_i must be serialized before T_j.

A history h belongs to the classes WW, WR, RW or WRW, if h is serializable under condition (a), (b), (c) or (d) respectively. //

Definition 6.2. A WW-constraint arising due to $W_i[X]$ occuring before $W_j[X]$ in h is called

(a) ww-constraint if both $W_i[X]$ and $W_j[X]$ are useful writes,

(b) wω-constraint if $W_i[X]$ is useful and $W_j[X]$ is useless write,

(c) ωw-constraint if $W_i[X]$ is useless and $W_j[X]$ is useful write, and

(d) $\omega\omega$-constraint if both $W_i[X]$ and $W_j[X]$ are useless writes.

Furthermore, the first three are called w·w-constraint, w·ω-constraint and ω·w-constraint, respectively, if there is no useful $W_k[X]$ in between $W_i[X]$ and $W_j[X]$ in h; and the last is called $\omega\cdot\omega$-constraint if there is no (useful or useless) write $W_k[X]$ in between. //

THEOREM 6.1.

(a) WW = (ww + ωw + wω + $\omega\omega$)-SR,

(b) WR = (ww + ωw)-SR,

(c) RW = (ww + wω)-SR, and

(d) WRW = (ww + wω + ωw)-SR.

Proof: Part (a) is obvious. For the other parts, we note that for any two edges α and β, at least one of which is useful, if there is a directed path in H[c](h) from either pα or nα to either pβ or nβ, then any acyclic TP[c](h) has a directed path that contains both α and β, with α occurring before β. If α and β correspond to $W_i[X]$ and $W_j[X]$ respectively, and $W_i[X]$ occurs before $W_j[X]$ in h then the constraints in both the left and the right sides of the equalities in the theorem introduce an edge from pα or nα to pβ or nβ in different ways. For (b), β must be useful; for (c), α must be useful; and for (d), either α or β (or both) must be useful. //

THEOREM 6.2.

(a) WW = (w·w + ω·w + w·ω + $\omega\cdot\omega$)-SR,

(b) WR = (w·w + ω·w)-SR,

(c) RW = (w·w + w·ω)-SR, and

(d) WRW = (w·w + w·ω + ω·w)-SR.

Proof: The proof follows from Theorem 6.1 and the fact that (i) a ww-constraint edge, or simply ww-edge, can be replaced by a directed path consisting of several w·w-edges, (ii) a ωw-edge can be replaced by a directed path consisting of a ω·w-edge followed by several w·w-edges, (iii) a wω-edge can be replaced by a directed path consisting of several w·w-edges followed by a w·ω-edge, and (iv) a $\omega\omega$-edge can be replaced by a path consisting of several $\omega\cdot\omega$-edges and then possibly a $\omega\cdot$w-edge followed by several w$\cdot$w-edges and then a w$\cdot\omega$-edge and perhaps a few more $\omega\cdot\omega$-edges. //

THEOREM 6.3. The WRW-constraints induce a weak order in h. //

The proof of Theorem 6.3 follows from Theorem 6.1(d).

We note that when there are no useless writes in h, WRW-serializability is the same as WW-serializability. Thus for histories without useless writes, WW is still the largest known polynomial subclass. But when there are useless writes, WW-constraints impose "more constraints than necessary" among the writes. It has been shown in [IKM1] that the class WRW properly contains WW.

A history h is in WRW if there exists an acyclic TP[WRW](h). By Theorem 6.3 and 5.5, this can be done in polynomial time. We now give a simple algorithm to construct TP(h), to check WRW-serializability.

ALGORITHM 6.1. Construct a graph L(h) by adding the following unlabelled edges to H(h) (not H[WRW](h)) for each X in D.

(i) (T_i,T_j) if $R_i[X]$ is followed by $W_j[X]$ with no other *useful* $W_k[X]$ in between; here, $W_j[X]$ may be useful or useless.

(ii) (T'_{iX},T_j) if useless $W_i[X]$ is followed by useful $W_j[X]$, with no other *useful* $W_k[X]$ in between. //

LEMMA 6.4. The graph L(h) is a TP(h).

Proof. All the edges added in Algorithm 6.1 are exclusion edges between the X-edges corresponding to w$\cdot$w- and w$\cdot\omega$-constraints in (i), and $\omega\cdot$w-constraints in (ii). Hence H(h) satisfies the exclusion property. //

THEOREM 6.5. A history h is in WRW iff L(h) is acyclic.

Proof. If L(h) is acyclic, then it is an acyclic TP(h), and it is clear that any topological sort of L(h) will satisfy the WRW-constraints.

Now suppose h is in WRW, that is, there exists an acyclic TP[WRW](h), say G_1. Let α and β be the edges corresponding to the first and the second write operations, respectively, of a w·w-, w·ω- or ω·w-constraint. Then there exists a directed path in G_1 that contains both these edges with α occurring before β. That is, there is a directed path from $n\alpha$ to $p\beta$ in G_1. Add the edge $(n\alpha, p\beta)$, if this does not already exist, in G_1. Clearly, addition of this edge will not create a directed cycle. This edge is the same as specified in Algorithm 6.1.

Repeat this process for all w·w-, w·ω-, and ω·w-constraints, to get graph G_2. Now G_2 is acyclic, and it includes L(h). Hence L(h) is acyclic. //

The graph L(h) contains the edges in *H*(h), and those specified in Algorithm 6.1. Clearly L(h) can be constructed from h in polynomial time, and checking whether L(h) is acyclic can also be done in polynomial time.

7. Conclusion

We have presented a new characterization of serializable histories, and argued that it depicts the inherent problem of serialization in a transparent manner. We have given a new characterization of serializable multiversion histories also. We have also given a new characterization to the class WRW, the largest known polynomial subclass of serializable histories, and shown how this class relates to the general class in a natural way.

We have considered only one notion of serializability, namely, a serializable history h is equivalent to a serial history h' in the sense that all the transactions read the same values in both h and h', and the values of the database after the execution of h are the same as those after h'. This is called *view-serializability* in [Y], where another notion *state-serializability*, where the equivalence is only with respect to the final database values, is defined. In [B], *τ-serializability*, where the equivalence is with respect to the values read by the transactions, and not the final database values, is defined. We find that our model helps to unify these, and several other, notions of serializabilities also, in a transparent manner. This is discussed in [V].

Acknowledgement: Thanks are due to the anonymous referees whose comments improved the presentation of this paper. This research is supported in part by the Natural Sciences and Engineering Research Council of Canada Individual Operating Grant A-3182.

References

[BG] Bernstein, P.A. and Goodman, N., Multiversion Concurrency Control - Theory and Algorithms, ACM TODS 8, 4(Dec. 1983), 465-483.

[BSW] Bernstein, P.A., Shipman, D.W., and Wong, W.S., Formal Aspects of Serializability in Database Concurrency Control, IEEE Trans. Software Eng. SE-5, 3(May 1979), 203-215.

[B] Brzozowski, J.A., On Models of Transactions, Technical Report #84001, Department of Applied Mathematics and Physics, Kyoto University, Japan, April 1984.

[EGLT] Eswaran, K.P., Gray, J.N., Lorie, R.A. and Traiger, I.L., The Notions of Consistency and Predicate Locks in a Database System, CACM 19, 11(Nov. 1976), 624-633.

[EN] Ekanadham, K. and Nigam, A., On Serializability, Report RC 9257, IBM T.J. Watson Research Center, Dec. 1981.

[IK] Ibaraki, T. and Kameda, T., Multi-Version vs. Single-Version Serializability, Tech. Report LCCR TR83-1, Department of CS, Simon Fraser Univ., Dec. 1983.

[IKM1] Ibaraki, T., Kameda, T., and Minoura, T., Serializability Made Simple, Tech. Report LCCR TR82-12, Department of CS, Simon Fraser Univ., Dec. 1982.

[IKM2] Ibaraki, T., Kameda, T., and Minoura, T., Disjoint-Interval Topological Sort: A Useful Concept in Serializability Theory, Proc. 9th Int. Conf. on VLDB, Oct/Nov. 1983, 89-91.

[P] Papadimitriou, C.H., The Serializability of Concurrent Database Updates, JACM 26, 4(Oct. 1979), 631-653.

[PK] Papadimitriou, C.H. and Kanellakis, P.C., On Concurrency Control by Multiple Versions, ACM TODS 9, 1(Mar.1984), 89-99.

[S] Sethi, R., A Model of Concurrent Database Transactions, Proc. 22nd IEEE Symp. Foundation of Comp. Sci., Oct. 1981, 175-184.

[SLR] Stearns, R.E., Lewis, P.M. II, and Rosenkrantz, D.J., Concurrency Control for Database Systems, Proc. 17th IEEE Symp. Foundation of Computer Sci., Oct. 1976, 19-32.

[V] Vidyasankar, K., Generalized Theory of Serializability, Technical Report #8510, Department of Computer Science, Memorial University of Newfoundland, Canada, May 1985.

[VY] Vidyasankar, K., and Younger, D.H., A Minimax Equality Related to the Longest Directed Path in an Acyclic Graph., Can. J. Math., 27, 2(1975), 348-351.

[Y] Yannakakis, M., Serializability by Locking, JACM 31, 2(April 1984), 227-244.

Who Needs to Verify Programs if You can Test Them*

Ashok Chandra

IBM Thomas J. Watson Research Centre
York Town Heights, NY, 10598
U.S.A.

*Manuscript not received in time to include in the proceedings.

Partial correctness semantics for CP[$\downarrow$, |, &]

Vijay A. Saraswat
Computer Science Department
Carnegie-Mellon University
Pittsburgh, Pa 15213
USA

Abstract. The class of so-called *concurrent logic programming languages*, such as **Parlog** [4], **Concurrent Prolog** [18], **GHC** [23] and **CP**[$\downarrow$, |, &] [17], present an interesting new message-passing paradigm related to **CSP**, the **Actors** model of computation, and data-flow languages.

In this paper we take the first steps towards a formal understanding of this paradigm by presenting a simple, bottom-up *partial correctness* semantics for **CP**[$\downarrow$, |, &], an extension of the language **Concurrent Prolog**. In the context of Horn logic languages, a partial correctness semantics specifies, for a given program:

- the *success set*, the set of all queries which have a successful execution, together with the resulting answer substitution,
- the *finite failure set*, the set of all queries which have an execution sequence terminating in finite failure, and, if applicable,
- the *deadlock set*, the set of all queries which have an execution sequence resulting in deadlock.

The semantics that we give defines these three sets inductively, in analogy with the standard success-set semantics of pure logic programs [9]. We first give an operational semantics in the form of a transition system in the style of [14]. This semantics can be looked upon as specifying the SLD-derivations [1] for a given query that are *admissible* given the control annotations present in the program. We then invert the transition system to extract a simple inductive characterisation of the deadlock, finite failure and success sets for a given query.

This semantics is, however, not compositional. That is, it does not derive the semantics of a clause from the meaning of the atoms in its body. To get that, an *a priori* notion of the meaning of an atom is needed, a notion that is consistent with **CP**[$\downarrow$, |, &]'s annotations and control structures. As has been learnt from the semantics of data-flow languages [22], predicate letters cannot now be interpreted as predicates over the underlying Herbrand domain; more operational information is needed. Accordingly, we define the notion of *scenarios*, adapted from the semantics given in [3] for non-deterministic data-flow languages, and give the success-semantics of $\mathbf{CP}[\downarrow, |]$ based on specifying the meaning of a (possibly non-ground) atom as a set of scenarios. This semantics can be extended to a partial-correctness semantics for $\mathbf{CP}[\downarrow, |]$.

1. Introduction

The notion of Horn logic programming is predicated on the so-called procedural interpretation of universally quantified, definite sentences [1], [9]. From a programming language point of view, such a frame-work offers choice non-determinism. A Horn logic *programming language* (such as **Prolog**) is a coherent set of control features which allow the programmer to exploit this non-determinism. **Prolog**, a sequential, deterministic language, uses it to provide automatic chronological backtracking, thereby allowing the user the flexibility of programming implicit (existential) searches.

Attempts have also been made to express *concurrent* computations in this frame-work, beginning with the relational language of Clark and Gregory ([5]). This language introduced the notion of *don't care commit*('|') which is used to irrevocably chose one of many computational paths. The language **Concurrent Prolog** ([18]) futher introduced the *read-only annotation* ('?'), which provides a communication primitve in the language by dynamically labelling certain occurrences of variables as *consumer* occurrences. It led to a number of papers which showed that this language was suitable for expressing a variety of interesting programming techniques ([19], [20], [21]).

However, the proposal in [18] was *informal* and obscured a number of important semantic difficulties with the language. These had to do with the precise semantics of '?' and '|', and the very nature of a don't-care commit, which prevents the specification of implicit searches, which, it may be argued, is distinctive of Horn logic programming. These difficulties are discussed further in [16], where it is argued that much of the functionality of '?' can be obtained by a simpler *wait* annotation ('$\downarrow$') and that the '|' should be used, as far as possible, purely as a control primitive which does not affect the semantics of the program, but may lead to more efficient execution. Instead, another commit operation, the *don't know commit* '&' (with simpler logical properties) was proposed.

In [17] a complete, formal operational semantics was proposed for this new language, called $\mathbf{CP}[\downarrow, |, \&]$, which contains $\mathbf{CP}[\downarrow, |]$ as a proper subset. It was shown that given a $\mathbf{CP}[\downarrow, |]$ program P, a goal g has a successful execution sequence with the answer substitution σ iff the corresponding $\mathbf{CP}[\downarrow, \&]$ program P' (obtained by replacing all occurrences of '|' in P by '&') also has a successful execution sequence for the goal g with an answer substitution σ. This was referred to as the equivalence of the success semantics of the two languages. Furthermore, it was shown that for $\mathbf{CP}[\downarrow, \&]$ if there is an execution sequence for a goal g that ends in failure, then there is a finitely-failed SLD tree (see [1]) with g as root. This implies the *soundness* of the negation-as-failure rule with respect to the usual logical interpretation of a $\mathbf{CP}[\downarrow, \&]$ program P as a set Σ of universally quantified Horn clauses obtained from P by ignoring all occurrences of '$\downarrow$' and replacing all occurrences of '&' by ','. (Of course, completeness of the rule is not possible because of the presence of deadlocked execution sequences.)

In this paper, we examine two alternate characterisations of the partial correctness semantics of $\mathbf{CP}[\downarrow, |, \&]$ programs.

The rest of the paper is as follows. In the first part of the paper, we develop, in sequence, a semantics for the language of pure Horn clauses (**CP**), the language $\mathbf{CP}[\downarrow, |]$ (which has the 'input-only' annotation '$\downarrow$' and the don't-care commit '$|$') and the language $\mathbf{CP}[\downarrow, |, \&]$ (which has, in addition, the don't-know commit '&'). For each of these three languages we first present an informal semantics followed by a formal operational semantics using transition systems. We then invert the transition system to extract a simple inductive characterisation of the success, finite failure and (where applicable) deadlock sets for a given query.

In the second part of the paper we take the first steps towards a full denotational semantics for $\mathbf{CP}[\downarrow, |, \&]$ by introducing the notion of *scenarios*. The traditional interpretation of an atom in the fixpoint theory of [9] has been the subset of the canonical (least) Herbrand model which unifies with the atom. Because of the '$\downarrow$' annotation, we have to consider a more complex interpretation which includes more operational information. This leads, finally, to a success-set semantics for $\mathbf{CP}[\downarrow, |]$ which can be extended to a partial correctness semantics.

2. The semantics of pure Horn logic programs

2.1. Preliminaries

For any program P, let $\mathcal{L}$ be the smallest first-order language (without equality) which contains the function and predicate symbols occurring in P. (Constants will be thought of as 0-ary function symbols). Assume given a denumerable set V of *variables*. Given the signature of $\mathcal{L}$ and the set V, we assume defined as usual the notions of *terms* (built up over the function symbols and variables), *ground terms* (terms which do not contain variables), *atomic formulas* (or atoms, for short), *substitutions* (with I standing for the identity substitution), *Herbrand universe*, *Herbrand base* (denoted by B_P) and (Herbrand) *model* (subsets of B_P). See [1] or [12] for details. When the program P is clear from the context, we will drop the subscript P. We will let $a, a', a_1, \ldots$ range over atoms, $t, t', t_1, \ldots$ over terms and $\theta, \theta', \theta_1, \ldots$ over substitutions. Sometimes, specially in the context of unification, by 'term' we will mean either a term or an atomic formula. In addition, by *functional term* we mean a term that is not a variable.

We also introduce the notion of *atom systems*, which are simply multisets of atoms. They will be ranged over by $A, A', A_1, \ldots, B, B', B_1, \ldots$. An atom system denotes the conjunction of its atoms. The goal system $\emptyset$ denotes $\mathtt{true}$. If θ is a substitution, then $\theta(B)$ denotes the atom system obtained from B by applying θ to every goal in it. We let $\uplus$ denote the union operation on multisets. Sometimes, we will use multisets in contexts in which a set is expected; in such cases the set obtained from the multiset by deleting multiple occurrences of an element is intended. In the case of atom systems, two atoms are considered identical if they are syntactically identical. (Hence variable names are meaningful within an atom system.)

A *definite* clause is a clause of the form

$$a \leftarrow B.$$

where all the variables in a, B are assumed universally quantified over the whole clause. A *program* is a multi-set of definite clauses. For concreteness, we will treat a program as a *sequence*, numbering the clauses in P from 0 through $\#P - 1$, where $\#P$ is the number of clauses in P. We will let $c, c_1, c' \ldots$ range over clauses.

2.2. Informal semantics

The language of pure Horn clauses features 'don't-know nondeterminism'. Given a query $\leftarrow A$. execution proceeds by selecting some atom a in A, some clause $c_i = a' \leftarrow B$ in P such that θ is the most general unifier [1] of the head of the clause and a and then executing the query $\leftarrow \theta((A - \{a\}) \uplus B)$. Execution terminates when the query is empty. A query $\leftarrow A$. is said to *immediately fail* if there exists $a \in A$ such that there is no clause whiose head will unify with a. A query *finitely fails* if all its execution sequences terminate in an immediately failed query. A query is *infinitary* if all its execution sequences are either infinite or terminate in an immediately failed query. Note that in this language a query is either successful or finitely-failed or infinitary, where exclusive-or is intended.

For future reference we define the set of *candidate* clauses for a goal:

Definition 1: Given a program $P = \{c_0, \ldots c_{k-1}\}$ and an atom a, we define:

- $U_a^P = \{i < k \,|\, a' \leftarrow B \text{ is a variant of } c_i, \mathbf{mgu}(a, a') \text{ exists}\}$.

2.3. Operational semantics

The transition system for pure Horn logic programs follows immediately from the above description. Because we would like to extract the 'answer substitution' from the execution of a query, we define our space of configurations:

$$Conf = Subst + AtomSys \times Subst$$

where *Subst* denotes the domain of substitutions and *AtomSys* of atom systems. For the purposes of this paper we do not need to impose any structure on these domains.

Our transitions are, then:

2.3.1. Successful termination

The empty query always terminates in one step giving its associated answer substitution.

$$\langle \emptyset, \theta \rangle \longrightarrow \theta \tag{1}$$

2.3.2. Clause invocation

$$\frac{\begin{array}{c} a' \leftarrow A \texttt{ is a variant of } c_i \in P \\ \theta = \mathbf{mgu}_{\downarrow}(a, a') \end{array}}{\langle \{a\} \uplus G, \sigma \rangle \longrightarrow \langle \theta(A \uplus G), (\theta \circ \sigma) \rangle} \tag{2}$$

[1] Most treatments of pure Horn logic programs do not insist that the unifier be most general: see e.g. [1]. We do it just in order to facilitate the introduction of the '$\downarrow$' annotation.

For future reference, we define the notion of *ancestor set* via a function $\odot : 2^{AtomSys} \rightarrow 2^{AtomSys \times Subst}$. The intention is that $\odot S$ denotes the set of pairs $\langle G, \sigma \rangle$ such that $\langle G, I \rangle \xrightarrow{*} \langle G', \sigma \rangle$ for some $G' \in S$, σ a substitution. For convenience we give the definition explicitly here.

Definition 2: Given a set of atom-systems S, and a **CP** program P, $\odot S$ is the smallest set of tuples $\langle G, \sigma \rangle$, where G is a goal-system and σ a substitution, which satisfies the rules:

- If $G \in S$, then $\langle G, I \rangle \in \odot S$, where I is the identity substitution,
- Let
  - $a' \leftarrow A$ be a variant of a clause in P,
  - a be a goal such that $\theta_0 = \mathbf{mgu}(a, a')$ exists.

  Then, if $\langle \theta(A \uplus G), \sigma \rangle \in \odot S$, then $\langle \{a\} \uplus G, (\theta \circ \sigma) \rangle \in \odot S$.

2.4. Inductive semantics

We are now interested in characterising the *success* and *failure* sets for **CP** programs.

2.4.1. Success set

From the above discussion of the $\odot$ operation, it should be clear that $SS = \odot\{\emptyset\}$. The definition of $\odot$ is similar, in essence, to the trasformation T_P from Herbrand interpretations to Herbrand interpretations defined in [9].

2.4.2. Finite failure set

From the above discussion, it follows that the set of immediately failed atom-systems is

$$FF_0 = \{G \mid \exists a \in G . U_a = \emptyset\}$$

To define the set of finitely failed atoms, we simply have to note that given a configuration *each* transition from it must end in an immediately failed atom-system. Hence the following definition, which is, in essence the one given in [10].

Definition 3: $FF = \bigcup_{i \in \aleph_0} FF_i$ where $G \in FF_i$ iff for some $a \in G$ and for every clause $c_i = a' \leftarrow A$ in P such that $\theta = \mathbf{mgu}(a, a')$ exists, $\theta(A) \in FF_d$ for some $d < i$.

As should be clear from the definitions of FF and SS we have that $SS \cap FF = \emptyset$. This means that for pure Horn logic programs, the strong success set SSS(i.e. the set of all those queries for which every execution terminates in success) is the same as the success set SS. What is more, the evaluation of a does not terminate just in case $a \notin SS \cup FF$. Hence we have a complete characterisation of the semantics of pure Horn logic as a programming language.

2.5. Conclusion

Note that this simplified 'semantics' for a Horn logic program is not compositional. Indeed, a *complete* denotational semantics for pure Horn logic programs, which gives the meaning of a program in terms of the meanings of the clauses which make it up, and the meaning of clauses in terms of the meaning of atoms in it, is non-trivial. [2] This is because of the well-known problem of specifying denotationally the semantics of *don't know* search, i.e. a control structure which races multiple processes (here alternate search paths) and succeeds if any one of them does. As noted above, this does not prove to be a problem for pure Horn logic programs because an alternate characterisation of the complete semantics is available. Similarly, this is not a problem for **Prolog** because it is a sequential language, and a complete denotational semantics is worked out in [7]. In **Concurrent Prolog** and similar concurrent languages, however, this problem again crops up.

3. Semantics for CP[↓, |]

Concurrent Prolog adds two control annotations to Horn logic programs: the *don't care commit* or '|' and the *read-only annotation* or '?'.

There are a number of problems with the '?' annotation, which have been discussed in detail in [16]. We will follow the suggestions contained therein and consider **Concurrent Prolog** with the '↓' annotation instead of the '?', thereby losing some of the obscurity in **Concurrent Prolog** but retaining a substantial portion of its functionality. To emphasise this, we will call the new language **CP**[↓, |].

A **CP**[↓, |] program P is a set of definite clauses, of the form

$$a \leftarrow G \mid B.$$

where a is an atom, G, B are atom-systems, called the *guard* and the *body* respectively.

Some terms in a can be annotated with '↓', which can be thought of as a unary post-fix functor as far as the syntax of terms is concerned. We further require that if any sub-term t of a is annotated then so are all super-terms t' of t in a. By convention, the head of the clause is always annotated so that $a \leftarrow \ldots$ actually stands for $a\downarrow \leftarrow \ldots$.

Note 1: In **Concurrent Prolog**, the read-only annotation could decorate a term anywhere in the clause. In **CP**[↓, |, &], on the other hand, the '↓' annotation is used only to place restrictions on the way a clause can be used: hence the '↓' annotation can occur only in the heads of clauses.

3.1. Informal semantics

3.1.1. The ↓-annotation

The purpose of the ↓-annotation is to restrict the set of terms which can unify against an annotated term. This restriction enables a programmer to specify that when resolving a goal against a clause-head the unification should *suspend* if bindings for certain variables are not available.

Now, it is well known that two terms $f(t_1, \ldots, t_n)$ and $f(s_1, \ldots, s_n)$ $(n \geq 0)$ have a most general unifier if each of the pairs $\langle s_i, t_i \rangle$ can be shown to have consistent **mgus** *in*

[2] The 'denotational' semantics given in [10] and [11] does not deal with non-terminating computations

$$\frac{\sigma \longrightarrow \sigma' \mid \theta}{\{\sigma\} \cup \sigma_1 \longrightarrow \sigma' \cup \sigma_1 \mid \theta(\sigma_1)} \tag{3}$$

$$\{v, v'\} \longrightarrow [v \mapsto v'] \qquad \frac{v \notin \mathbf{var}(t)}{\{v, t\} \longrightarrow [v \mapsto t]} \tag{4}$$

$$\{f(t_1, \ldots t_n), f(s_1, \ldots s_n)\} \longrightarrow \{\{t_1, s_1\}, \ldots \{t_n, s_n\}\} \ (n \geq 0) \tag{5}$$

$$\{t{\downarrow}, f(s_1, \ldots, s_n)\} \longrightarrow \{t, f(s_1, \ldots, s_n)\} \tag{6}$$

We then have:

$$[t] \stackrel{\text{def}}{=} \{s | \{\{s, t\}\} \stackrel{*}{\longrightarrow} \emptyset\}$$

Table 1: Transition system defining the $\downarrow$-annotation

any order. The $\downarrow$-annotation can be thought of as placing restrictions on this order: $t_k{\downarrow}$ can unify with s_k only if s_i is a functional term and t_k unifies with s_k. If there is some scheduling of the **mgu**s of subterms of s and t which satisfies the constraints induced by the $\downarrow$-annotations, then the $\mathbf{mgu}_\downarrow$ of s and t exists, and is the same as $\mathbf{mgu}(s, t)$. Otherwise, if there is no such scheduling, but $\mathbf{mgu}(s, t)$ exists, then $\mathbf{mgu}_\downarrow(s, t)$ is said to be *input-suspended*; if $\mathbf{mgu}(s, t)$ does not exist, then $\mathbf{mgu}_\downarrow(s, t)$ does not exist (i.e. fails).

If we let $[t]$ denote $\{s | \mathbf{mgu}_\downarrow(t, s)\mathtt{exists}\}$, where t is possibly '$\downarrow$'-annotated, then the definition of $\mathbf{mgu}_\downarrow$ can be given by defining $[t]$. See Table [1] for one such definition. In this definition, σ ranges over sets of the form $\{t, t'\}$, σ', σ_1 over sets of σ, v, v' over variables, t_i, s_i over terms and f over function symbols. **var** is a function which maps a term into the set of variables occurring in it. '$\theta(\sigma_1)$' indicates the set of sets of terms obtained from σ_1 by applying the substitution θ to each term in σ_1.

Example 1: Given a program P, let

- $\mathcal{V}, \mathcal{V}_1, \ldots$ be meta-variables ranging over the set V of (language) variables,
- $\mathcal{F}, \mathcal{F}_1, \ldots$ be meta-variables ranging over the set of functional terms, and,
- $\mathcal{T}, \mathcal{T}_1, \ldots$ be meta-variables ranging over the set of terms.

Then

- $[p(a{\downarrow}, b, c{\downarrow})] = \{p(a, b, c), p(a, \mathcal{V}, c)\}$
- $[r(a{\downarrow}, X, Y, c)] = \{r(a, \mathcal{T}, \mathcal{T}_1, c), r(a, \mathcal{T}, \mathcal{T}_1, \mathcal{V})\}$
- $[f(a, Y{\downarrow})] = \{f(\mathcal{V}, \mathcal{F}), f(a, \mathcal{F}), f(\mathcal{V}\mathcal{V})\}$

Now we can define the set of clauses on which a goal may be *input-suspended.*

Definition 4: Given a program $P = \{c_0, \ldots c_{k-1}\}$ and an atom a, we define:

- $V_a^P = \{i \in U_a^P \mid a' \leftarrow B \text{ is a variant of } c_i, a \notin [a']\}$

If $U_a^P = V_a^P \neq \emptyset$, the *goal* a is said to be input-suspended.

Finally we have the notion of an *input substitution.* Given two terms a, a' (with a possibly annotated), the set of input substitutions $\mathbf{IS}(a, a')$ is the set of all those substitutions θ such that $\theta(a') \in [a]$. Note that if $a_1 \in [a]$, then $\theta(a_1) \in [a]$, for any substitution θ.

3.1.2. The commit operation

The following discussion, and the discussion in 4.1 is adapted from [16] to which the interested reader should refer for more details.

Execution of a program begins with the invocation of an atom system $\leftarrow Q$. Each goal in Q is said to be an *AND*-sibling of the others. Each goal $q \in Q$ tries to unify against the head of a clause.

Suppose that $c_k = a' \leftarrow G|B$ and $k \in U_q - V_q$ and $\theta = \mathrm{mgu}(q, a')$. Then, the atom system $\leftarrow \theta(G)$ is invoked, and is said to be a *guard system* for the goal q. At this time, θ is *not* made available to goals in $Q - \{q\}$. The guard systems for q are invoked in parallel for all *candidate clauses* c_i such that $i \in U_q - V_q$. Each guard systems is called an *OR*-sibling of the others.

There are two other situations that can arise when an atom system $\leftarrow Q$ is invoked. The first is that it may happen for some $q \in Q$ that $U_q = \emptyset$, i.e. there is no clause whose head even potentially unifies with q. In this case, the goal q is said to *fail*, and the whole invocation Q will fail.

In the second situation, *for all* goals $q \in Q$ it may happen that q is input-suspended: this corresponds to *deadlock*.

There must exist some clauses whose guards are empty: otherwise the invocation of no guard system would terminate. Assume then that the guard-system $\theta(G)$ terminates successfully (other terminology :'is solved') with answer substitution σ. (If the guard was empty, that is, $G = \emptyset$, then the answer substitution would be θ). Now the guard system is said to be ready to *commit*. If more than one guard systems are ready to commit at the same time, then they must commit in some serial order.

If the commit operator in the clause invocation is '|', and it is selected for commitment, then no further guard systems for the goal will be allowed to commit. Committing makes public the binding σ computed by the guard, that is, the binding is propogated to $q' \in Q - \{q\}$. There are a number of possibilities here, with respect to eager vs. lazy propogation of bindings, and these are discussed in [16]. We adopt the conceptually simple approach of making the bindings available to all sibling goals *atomically* , i.e. no other guard system for any goal can commit until the bindings are communicated to all the (relevant) *AND*-siblings of q. Then the body goals $(\sigma \circ \theta)(B)$ of the clause invocation whose guard committed successfully are invoked, together with the atom system $(\sigma \circ \theta)(Q - \{q\})$.

Because each of the goals a_i could be executing this process simultaneously, in general we would have a hierarchy of goals in the guard of each clause-invocation for a goal. When a guard system for a goal q commits its bindings, these bindings must be made available at all depths of this hierarchy for sibling goals of q. When this happens, there could be some goals which had generated a binding to some variable different from the one committed: such goals will be thought of as having failed immediately.

A formal, structural operational semantics for this language is given in [17]. This semantics specifies, for a given program and initial query, the set of all the transitions that can take place. Based on these transitions, the notions of *success-set*, *finite-failure* and *deadlock* sets are identified. Because of the don't care nature of '|', it turns out that a given query may belong to zero or more of those sets. It does not belong to any of these sets only in case all its transitions sequences are infinite. This is one of the reasons that **Concurrent Prolog**, which is similar to **CP**$[\downarrow, |]$, cannot be called a logic programming language: it does not distinguish refutations from failed derivations. On the other hand, as we shall see, **CP**$[\downarrow, \&]$ has a more logical semantics: the set of all queries are *partitioned* by the success, finite failure, deadlock and infinite derivation sets.

3.2. Operational semantics

The tranition system for **CP**$[\downarrow, |]$ has much in common with the transition system for **CP** given in Section 2.3. The space of configurations *Conf* remains the same. The success termination transition Transition 1 remains the same. Instead of Transition 2 we now have:

$$\frac{\begin{array}{c} a' \leftarrow A_1 \mid A_2 \ \texttt{is a variant of} \ c_i \in P \\ \mathbf{mgu}_{\downarrow}(a, a') = \theta_0 \\ \langle \theta_0(A_1), \theta_0 \rangle \xrightarrow{*} \theta \end{array}}{\langle \{a\} \uplus G, \sigma \rangle \longrightarrow \langle \theta(A_2 \uplus G), (\theta \circ \sigma) \rangle} \tag{7}$$

As before, if S is a set of atom systems, we let $\odot S$ denote the set of pairs $\langle G, \sigma \rangle$ such that there is an execution sequence of the configuration $\langle G, I \rangle$ leading to the configuration $\langle G', \sigma \rangle$ where $G' \in S$. Again, for convenience, we give the definition explicitly here.

Definition 5: Given a set of atom-systems S, and a **CP**$[\downarrow, |]$ program P, $\odot S$ is the smallest set of tuples $\langle G, \sigma \rangle$, where G is a goal-system and σ a substitution, which satisfies the rules:

- If $G \in S$, then $\langle G, I \rangle \in \odot S$, where I is the identity substitution.
- Let
  - $a' \leftarrow A_1 \mid A_2$ be a variant of a clause in P,
  - a be a goal such that $\theta_0 = \mathbf{mgu}_{\downarrow}(a, a')$ exists,
  - $\langle \theta_0(A_1), \theta_1 \rangle$ be in $\odot\{\emptyset\}$, and,
  - θ be defined as $(\theta_1 \circ \theta_0)$.

  Then, if $\langle \theta(A_2) \uplus \theta(G), \sigma \rangle \in \odot S$, then $\langle \{a\} \uplus G, (\theta \circ \sigma) \rangle \in \odot S$.

3.3. Inductive semantics

We are now interested in characterising the *success*,*failure* and *deadlock* sets for **CP**$[\downarrow, |]$programs.

3.3.1. Success set

From the above discussion of the $\odot$ operation, it should be clear that $SS = \odot\{\emptyset\}$.

3.3.2. Finite failure set

The definition of the set of immediately failed configurations remains the same as before. (See Section 2.4.2. We will now call it F_0 instead of FF_0.)

Now, a configuration $\gamma = \langle G, \sigma \rangle$ is *stuck* (i.e. no transition is possible from it) iff for each atom $a \in G$ either

- There is no candidate clause ($U_a = \emptyset$), or,
- All candidate clauses are input-suspended ($U_a = V_a$), or,
- The guard systems for all candidate clauses that are not input suspended have only infinitary, failing or deadlocked execution sequences.

We will consider a query to have failed if there is an execution sequence leading to a configuration $\gamma = \langle A, \sigma \rangle$ which is stuck and for which there is an atom $a \in A$ such that

- There is no candidate clause for a, or,
- No candidate clause for a is input-suspended ($V_a = \emptyset$); however the guard systems for all candidate clauses have only failing execution sequences.

This leads to the following inductive characterisation:

Definition 6: $F = \bigcup_{i \in \aleph_0} F_i$ where $G \in F_i$ iff for some $a \in G$ either

- there exists some substitution σ such that $\langle a, \sigma \rangle \in \odot(F_d)$, where $d < i$ or,
- $V_a = \emptyset$, and there exists some substitution σ such that $\langle \theta(G), \sigma \rangle \in \odot(F_d)$, for some $d < i$ whenever $a' \leftarrow G \mid B$ is a variant of a clause $c_j \in P$, where $j \in U_a$ and $\theta = \mathbf{mgu}_{\downarrow}(a, a')$.

And then we have:

$$FF = \{a \mid \{a\} \in F\}$$

3.3.3. Deadlock Set

Similar to the discussion in the previous section, we will consider a configuration $\gamma = \langle A, \sigma \rangle$ deadlocked iff *for each* atom $a \in A$ either

- There is at least one candidate clause that is input suspended ($V_a \neq \emptyset$) and the guard systems for all the candidate clauses that are not input suspended have execution sequences terminating in failure or deadlock, or,
- There is at least one guard system for a candidate clause that has an execution sequence terminating in deadlock, and all other guard systems for candidate clauses that are not input-suspended have execution sequences that terminate in failure or deadlock.

This leads to the following inductive characterisation of the deadlock set, where we define D_0 the set of *immediately deadlocked* atom systems to be

$$D_0 = \{G \mid \forall a \in G. U_a = V_a \neq \emptyset\}$$

Definition 7: $D = \bigcup_{i \in \aleph_0} D_i$ where $G \in D_i$ iff for all $a \in G$ either

- there exists some substitution σ such that $\langle \{a\}, \sigma \rangle \in \odot(D_d)$, where $d < i$ or,

- both of the following conditions hold:
  - whenever $j \in U_A - V_a$, and $a' \leftarrow A_1 \mid A_2$ is a variant of clause $c_j \in P$, and $\theta = \mathbf{mgu}_{\downarrow}(a, a')$, there exists some substitution σ such that $\langle\theta(A_1), \sigma\rangle \in \odot(D_d \cup F)$, for some $d < i$, and,
  - either $V_a \neq \emptyset$ or there exists $j \in U_a - V_a$ such that if A_1, θ, σ, d are as above, $\langle\theta(A_1), \sigma\rangle \in \odot(D_d)$.

Finally we have

$$DD = \{a \mid \{a\} \in D\}$$

Other definitions of deadlock are also possible.

4. Semantics for CP[$\downarrow$, |, &]

Syntactically, the language **CP**[$\downarrow$, |, &] is the same as the language **CP**[$\downarrow$, |] except that the don't know commit '&' is allowed to occur wherever the don't-care commit '|' can occur.

4.1. Informal semantics

The semantics of the input-only annotation and the don't care commit remains the same as it was in Section 3.1. We now only need to specify the semantics for '&'.

As before, assume that given a query Q, guard systems are spawned for each atom $q \in Q$. Assume further that a guard system for q terminates successfully with answer substitution σ and is ready to commit.

If the commit operator is '&', then the goals $Q - \{q\}$ are duplicated. The binding σ is made public atomically to one copy, and the body goals $(\sigma \circ \theta)(B)$ of the clause invocation whose guard committed successfully are invoked, together with the atom system $(\sigma \circ \theta)(Q - \{q\})$. On this copy '&'-commit behaves just like '|'-commit.

The other copy continues as if the committing clause-invocation had simply failed: it allows other clause-invocations for q to commit. This allows various clauses for the same atom to be explored in parallel even beyond commit-time and provides don't-know non-determinism. Here commit simply serves to synchronise AND-parallel goals: unlike '|', it does not choose between alternative committing clauses. If one of these copies succeeds with an answer substitution σ, then the original invocation would succeed with answer substitution σ. If one of the copies fails, or deadlocks, the other copy is not affected. Hence the whole system will fail (deadlock) only if *each* of the copies fails (deadlocks).

Note that if no '$\downarrow$'-annotations are used in the program, and also no '|', then the placement of '&' annotation in clauses is immaterial. The program will work as a pure logic program, i.e. all SLD-derivation sequences for any query are possible. Hence the language **CP** of pure Horn clauses discussed in Section 2.2 is the same as the language **CP**[&].

There is one additional complication that arises because we allow multiple commits. Now for a *given* clause, a guard can commit more than once, with possibly different values each time. So when it is ready to commit for the first time, we do unto the other potential solutions just what the commit operator in the clause would do unto the guard systems corresponding to *other* clauses for the same goal. So a '|' commit in the clause would kill all the other possible solutions for the guard and a '&' would continue to explore them.

4.2. Operational semantics

We now present the transition system for the full language $\mathbf{CP}[\downarrow, |, \&]$, which specifies the transitions a configuration can make, modulo non-termination of guards. This transition system is different from the one in [17] which specifies *all* the transition sequences that are possible from any configuration. As usual, we will define three kinds of *terminal* configurations, those corresponding to successful termination (SS_0), failure termination (F_0) and deadlock termination (D_0). Using the transition system in the reverse direction, we will then build up the success-, failure- and deadlock-sets for the program.

4.2.1. Configurations

The configurations we need now are substantially more complex because more information is needed. First, because of the possibility of multiple commit, we need to keep explicit track of which candidate clauses for a given goal have yet to be spawned. We do this by introducing the notion of *augmented goal*. Second, each guard-system may now produce multiple solutions. Hence, with each guard-system we now need to associate the body goals that must be executed for each successful solution. For this we introduce the notion of *partial goals*. Finally, we have to model the situation in which one guard system for a goal commits and there are other active guard systems, which must now be kept around. Hence we need a notion of *disjunction* of atomic configurations: to this end we introduce an associative, commutative, binary operator '+' on configurations. (An atomic configuration roughly corresponds to a configuration in Section 2.3).

Definition 8: An *augmented goal* is a tuple $\langle a, J\rangle$, where a is an atom and $J \subseteq U_a$. An *augmented goal system* is a multiset of augmented goals. Corresponding to each atom system A, there is an augmented goal system, denoted by $\tilde{A}$, defined as $\{\langle a, U_a\rangle | a \in A\}$. (Note: $\tilde{\emptyset} = \emptyset$). If θ is a substitution, then we define $\theta(G) \stackrel{\text{def}}{=} \{\langle \theta(a), J \cap U_{\theta(a)}\rangle | \langle a, J\rangle \in G\}$.

We will let *AugGoalSys* denote the space of augmented goal systems.

Definition 9: If γ is a finite atomic configuration, and A an atom-system, then the form '$\gamma; A$' is a *partial goal*, in which (atom-system) A represents the body of the clause which has to be executed after the partially evaluated guard system (represented by γ) terminates. If θ is a substitution, then the effect of applying θ to $\gamma; A$ is the element $\theta(\gamma); A$.

As before, with each augmented goal system, we also need to associate the *answer* substitution, which gets built up as the system makes it transitions. If the system were ever to make a transition to the empty goal system, then the corresponding substitution would be the answer substitution for the original query. A successfully terminated system would be represented by its answer substitution. Hence:

Definition 10: An *atomic configuration* is either

- a substitution θ, or,
- a tuple $\langle G, \theta \rangle$ where G (the *goal system* of the configuration) is a set of augmented or partial goals.

If θ' is a substitution, then the result of applying θ' to the atomic configuration $\langle T, \theta \rangle$ is the configuration $\langle T', (\theta' \circ \theta) \rangle$, where T' is obtained from T by applying θ' to each element in T. The result of applying a substitution θ' to an atomic configuration of the form θ is not defined.

Definition 11: A *configuration* is of the form $\sum_{i \in J} \gamma_i$ where for all $i \in J \neq \emptyset$, γ_i is an atomic configuration.

As before, we let *Conf* denote the space of confugurations.

Sometimes, we will refer to configurations of the form $\gamma' + \sum_{i \in J} \gamma_i$. This is shorthand notation for the expression $\sum_{i \in J'} \gamma_i$ where there exists $i_0 \in J'$ such that $\gamma_{i_0} = \gamma'$. Hence for such expressions, we will allow the case $J = \emptyset$, whence the expression reduce to γ'.

4.2.2. The transition system

We now define the transition system as a relation $\longrightarrow$: $Conf \times Conf$ which is the smallest relation satisfying the rules (transitions) specified below.

Transitions of configurations.

A configuration makes a transition in one step whenever any of its component atomic configurations makes a transition in one step.

$$\frac{\gamma_j \longrightarrow \sum_{i \in J'} \gamma_i}{\sum_{i \in J} \gamma_i \longrightarrow \sum_{i \in ((J - \{j\}) \uplus J')} \gamma_i} \tag{8}$$

It remains now to specify the transitions that an atomic configuration can make.

Successful termination.

This is the same as Transition 1.

The don't care commit

$$\frac{\begin{array}{c} i \in J \\ a' \leftarrow A_1 \,|\, A_2 \texttt{ is a variant of } c_i \\ \theta_0 = \mathbf{mgu}_{\downarrow}(a, a') \\ \langle \theta_0(\tilde{A}_1), \theta_0 \rangle \xrightarrow{*} \theta + \sum_{i \in K} \gamma_i \end{array}}{\langle \{\langle a, J \rangle\} \uplus G, \sigma \rangle \longrightarrow \langle \theta(\tilde{A}_2 \uplus G), (\theta \circ \sigma) \rangle} \tag{9}$$

Suppose $\langle a, J \rangle$ is an augmented goal, and there is a variant of a clause c_i against which a can reduce ($i \in J$). If the guard system has a successful execution sequence ($\langle \tilde{A}_0, \theta_0 \rangle \xrightarrow{*} \theta + \sum_{i \in K} \gamma_i$), then if the commit operator is '|', all the alternate (potential) solutions to the guard system ($\sum_{i \in K} \gamma_i$) must be pruned, as must the other guard systems for the goal a (i.e. the ones in $J - \{i\}$). All that needs to be done is to execute the body goals of the clause as siblings of the remaining elements in G, after publishing the binding θ. (Compare this with Tranisition 7).

The don't know commit.

$$\frac{\begin{array}{c} i \in J \\ a' \leftarrow A_1 \,\&\, A_2 \texttt{ is a variant of } c_i \\ \theta_0 = \mathbf{mgu}_{\downarrow}(a, a') \\ \langle \theta_0(\tilde{A_1}), \theta_0 \rangle \xrightarrow{*} \theta + \sum_{i \in K} \gamma_i \end{array}}{\langle \{\langle a, J \rangle\} \uplus G, \sigma \rangle \longrightarrow \langle \theta(\tilde{A_2} \uplus G), (\theta \circ \sigma) \rangle + \langle \{\langle a, J - \{i\} \rangle\} \uplus G, \sigma \rangle + \sum_{i \in I} \langle \{\gamma_i; A_2\} \uplus G, \sigma \rangle} \quad (10)$$

On the other hand, if the commit operator is '&', then all the alternate paths must be preserved. In the above transition, the three summands of the target configuration represent, respectively, the atomic configuration obtained by publishing the bindings θ, the clauses for the atom a which are yet to be spawned and the partial goals representing alternate partial evaluations of the guard system for clause c_i for goal a.

Partially evaluated guards.

Finally we have to specify what transition a system of the kind $\gamma; A$ can make.

$$\frac{\gamma \xrightarrow{*} \theta + \sum_{i \in I} \gamma_i}{\langle \{\gamma; A_2\} \uplus G, \sigma \rangle \longrightarrow \langle \theta(\tilde{A_2} \uplus G), (\theta \circ \sigma) \rangle + \sum_{i \in I} \langle \{\gamma_i; A_2\} \uplus G, \sigma \rangle} \quad (11)$$

If a partially evaluated guards has a successful terminating sequence, it commits its bindings but retains all the alternate branches.

4.3. Inductive semantics

As before, we proceed by identifying the terminal configurations and defining the ancestor set.

Let

$$SS_0 \stackrel{\text{def}}{=} \{\theta + \sum_{i \in I} \gamma_i \mid I \text{ finite } \}$$

We define $\odot : 2^{Conf} \longrightarrow 2^{Conf \times Conf}$ by specifying that if S is a set of configurations $\odot S$, the ancestor set of S, is the set of all the pairs $\langle \gamma, \gamma_0 \rangle$ such that $\gamma_0 \in S$ and $\gamma \xrightarrow{*} \gamma_0$.

Note 2: The conditions $\langle \tilde{A_0}, \theta_0 \rangle \xrightarrow{*} \theta + \sum_{i \in I} \gamma_i$ in Transitions [4.2.2] and [10] have to be replaced by the condition $\langle \langle \tilde{A_0}, \theta_0 \rangle, \theta + \sum_{i \in I} \gamma_i \rangle \in \odot SS_0$, but the recursion in the definition of $\odot SS_0$ is well-founded.

Note 3: This notion of ancestor set is slightly different from the previous notions. (See 3.2).

4.3.1. Success set

The success set semantics of a program P is then given by SS where

$$SS = \{\langle a, \theta \rangle \mid \langle \langle \{\langle a, U_a \rangle\}, I \rangle, \theta + \sum_{i \in I} \gamma_i \rangle \in \odot SS_0\}$$

Note that in order to simplify presentation, we assume that evaluation of a top-level query may terminate when a solution is reached for the query, even though the configuration reached may not be terminal, i.e. some transitions may still be possible from it.

4.3.2. Finite Failure set

First, we define $\bar{\ }: 2^{AugGoalSys} \rightarrow 2^{Conf}$ by specifying that if H is any set of augmented goal-systems, then $\bar{H}$ is the smallest set of configurations satisfying the rules:

1. Whenever $G \in H$, we have $\langle G, \theta\rangle \in \bar{H}$ for all substitutions θ.
2. Whenever $\gamma \in \bar{H}$, we have $\langle\{\gamma; A\}, \theta\rangle \in \bar{H}$, for all atom systems A and substitutions θ.
3. Whenever $\langle G, \theta\rangle \in \bar{H}$, we have $\langle G \uplus G', \theta\rangle \in \bar{H}$, for all goal systems G'.
4. Whenever $\forall i \in I.\, \gamma_i \in \bar{H}$ we have $\sum_{i\in I} \gamma_i \in \bar{H}$, for all configurations γ_i.

Now we can define the set of *immediately failed configurations* F_0 to be $\bar{H}$ where $H = \{\{\langle a, \emptyset\rangle\} \mid a \text{ an atom }\}$.

Now, as before, a query $\leftarrow a.$ will terminate in finite failure if $\gamma_a = \langle\{\langle a, U_a\rangle\}, I\rangle \xrightarrow{*} \gamma_0 \in F_0$. The other possibility is that there is no candidate clause that is input-suspended ($V_a = \emptyset$) and the guard systems corresponding to clause invocations in U_a *all* terminate in failure (in which case γ_a is stuck.)

Restating that formally, we have:

Definition 12: Let $F \stackrel{\text{def}}{=} \cup_{i\in\aleph_0} F_i$ where $\gamma \in F_i$ iff

- there exists γ_0 such that $\langle\gamma, \gamma_0\rangle \in \odot F_d$, for some $d < i$, or,
- $\gamma \in \bar{H}$ where H contains exactly the sets $\{\langle a, J\rangle\}$ such that $V_a = \emptyset$ and for all $j \in J$, if $c_j = a' \leftarrow A_1 \% A_2$ is a variant of a clause in P, and $\theta = \mathbf{mgu}_{\downarrow}(a, a')$, then there exists γ_0 such that $\langle\langle\theta(\tilde{A}_0), \theta\rangle, \gamma_0\rangle \in \odot F_d$, for some $d < i$.

Finally we have FF, the set of all those queries which have an execution sequence terminating in failure is given by

$$FF \stackrel{\text{def}}{=} \{a \mid \langle\{\langle a, U_a\rangle\}, I\rangle \in F\}$$

4.3.3. Deadlock set

We proceed as in the definition of FF.

We first define the operation $\bar{\ }: 2^{AugGoalSys} \times 2^{Conf}$ which converts a set of augmented goal-systems into the smallest set of configurations built up from it. The definition is the same as in the previous section, except that Rule [3] is replaced by

3′. Whenever $\langle G, \theta\rangle \in \bar{H}$ *and* $\langle G', \theta\rangle \in \bar{H}$ we have $\langle G \uplus G', \theta\rangle \in \bar{H}$, where G, G' are goal systems.

(The reason is that in a deadlocked system, each component must be deadlocked; whereas for a failed system, it is sufficient for one conjunctive system to be failed.)

Next we define D_0, the set of *immediately deadlocked configurations*, by $D_0 = \bar{H}$ where $H = \{\{\langle a, J\rangle\} \mid \emptyset \neq J \subseteq V_a, a \text{ an atom}\}$.

Now, to define the set of deadlocked configurations, we proceed as we did in Section 3.3.3.

Definition 13: Let $D \stackrel{\text{def}}{=} \bigcup_{i \in \aleph_0} D_i$ where $\gamma \in D_i$ iff

- there exists γ_0 such that $\langle \gamma, \gamma_0 \rangle \in \odot D_d$, for some $d < i$, or,
- $\gamma \in \bar{H}$, where H contains exactly the sets $\{\langle a, J \rangle\}$ such that both of the following conditions hold:
  - whenever $j \in (U_a - V_a) \cap J$, and $a' \leftarrow A_1 \,\%\, A_2$ is a variant of clause $c_j \in P$, and $\theta = \mathbf{mgu}_{\downarrow}(a, a')$, there exists some configuration γ_0 such that $\langle \langle \theta(\tilde{A}_1), \theta \rangle, \gamma_0 \rangle \in \odot(D_d \cup F)$, for some $d < i$, and,
  - $V_a \neq \emptyset$ or there exists $j \in (U_a - V_a) \cap J$ such that if θ, A_1, γ_0, d are as above, $\langle \langle \theta(\tilde{A}_1), \theta \rangle, \gamma_0 \rangle \in \odot(D_d)$.

And then we have DD, the set of all those goals which have an execution sequence terminating in deadlock, is given by

$$DD \stackrel{\text{def}}{=} \{a \mid \langle \{\langle a, U_a \rangle\}, I \rangle \in D\}$$

5. Scenarios

In the first half of the paper we have defined the partial correctness semantics for the language **CP**$[\downarrow, |, \&]$. This semantics was operational in nature: it extracted the relevant definitions from a structural operational semantics for the language.

We shall now develop the basic ideas that are needed in order to give a compositional semantics to a **Concurrent Prolog** program. In the following we will restrict our attention to the language **CP**$[\downarrow, |]$.

First, we draw a simple analogy between the execution of a **Concurrent Prolog** program and a network of dynamically reconfigurable processes communicating with each other via channels. The only way in which a process (i.e. goal) can be affected by its environment or afffect it is via the channels (i.e. variables occurring in goals) associated with it. The same channel may be shared by more than one process: the effect of complete execution of a process is to demand some (sequence of) communications on its channels and to output some (sequence of) communications on its channels.

A process can wait for a disjunction of conditions on its channels to spawn off a sub-network of processes within itself. That is, a goal can use any clause to spawn off a guard provided it satisfies the input constraints in the head of the clause. To emphasise, the only way in which this sub-network can communicate with the environment of its parent process is via the channels in the parent process which may have been passed on to it. That is, the only way that a sub-goal can influence the environment of its parent goal g is if it has an occurrence of a variable v that also occurs in the head of the clause (used by the goal to reduce to this sub-goal, possibly among other sub-goals) and all occurrences of v in the head of the clause are matched at run-time by variables in g.

When the sub-network executes successfully, the parent process also terminates. (We ignore for the moment complications arising because of the $|$ and the & annotations.)

So the net effect of execution of a process is the history of communications it leaves on its channels. That is, the effect of executing a goal successfully is to create bindings for variables in the goal.

As is well known, if the network of processes is determinate then a simple fully abstract fixpoint semantics can be given in terms of mappings on the histories of channels [8]. In the current frame-work, this means that processes can be given a simple semantics in terms of predicates (of the appropriate arity) on the underlying Herbrand universe. Such a deterministic language has been worked out in [6] but we find that approach unsatisfying. In the naturally non-determinstic framework of definite clauses, one cannot even write a simple deterministic process min/2 whose intended interpretation is $\{min(X,Y,Z) | Z = min(X,Y)\}$ using an $\leq$ operation.

However, as the merge anomaly [2] points out, for a non-deterministic network of processes the interpretation of processes as predicates is not sufficient: one also needs to carry around extra *causality* information which essentially describes what inputs are necessary for a process before it delivers its output. In his subsequent thesis, Brock [3] suggests a simple alternative using the notion of *scenarios* and here we adopt his solution to the framework of **CP**$[\downarrow, |]$.

5.1. Input-output records

Definition 14: An **input-output record** (ior) is a sequence of substitutions $\bar{\theta} = [\theta_0^{l_0}, \ldots, \theta_{k-1}^{l_{k-1}}]$ where $l_i \in \{I, O\}$ for $i < k$ are labels. The θ_i satisfy the following conditions:

- For every variable v there is at most one $i : 1 \leq i \leq k$ such that $\theta_i(v) \neq v$,
- For every variable v, for every i, $\theta_i(v)$ is either a variable or a term $f(v_1, \ldots v_n)$ where f is an n-ary function symbol, for some $v_1, \ldots v_n \in V : n \geq 0$.

If $\bar{\theta}$ is an ior, then we define the associated *answer substitution* θ to be simply the composition of all the θ_i. Because of the nature of the θ_i making up an ior, the composition is associative and commutative and hence is more easily represented by

$$\theta(v) = \begin{cases} \theta(\theta_i(v)) & \textit{if } \exists i : 1 \leq i \leq k : \theta_i(v) \neq v \\ v & \textit{otherwise} \end{cases} \tag{12}$$

We define the notion of *compacting* an ior. This will be useful when we are giving the semantics of a guard system, which does not output any bindings to its environment until commit time.

Definition 15: Given an ior $\bar{\theta} = [\theta_0^{l_0}, \ldots, \theta_{k-1}^{l_{k-1}}]$, its compaction is the ior $[\sigma_0^I, \sigma_1^O]$ where $\sigma_0 = \bigcup_{i:l_i=I} \theta_i$ and $\sigma_1 = \bigcup_{i:l_i=O} \theta_i$, where $1 \leq i \leq k$. If $\sigma_0 = \{\}$, then the compaction is $[\sigma_1^O]$.

It is also simple to define a notion of *renaming* for an ior. If $\bar{\theta}$ is an ior such that for all i, $\theta_i(v) = v$ and there is no v', i such that $v \in \mathsf{var}(\theta_i(v'))$, then the ior $\bar{\theta}[v/w]$ represents the ior obtained from $\bar{\theta}$ by replacing all occurrences of w (if any) by v. This naturally generalises to renaming in more than one variable.

Definition 16: Given an ior $\bar{\theta}$, the set of descendants of a variable v, denoted by $||v||_{\bar{\theta}}$ is defined inductively as follows:

- If for all i, $\theta_i(v) = v$, then $\|v\|_{\bar{\theta}} = \phi$.
- If $\exists i.\theta_i(v) = v', v' \neq v$, then $\bar{v} = \{v'\} \cup \|v'\|_{\bar{\theta}}$.
- If $\exists i.\theta_i(v) = f(v_1, \ldots v_n)$, then $\|v\|_{\bar{\theta}} = \{v_1, \ldots v_n\} \cup \|v_1\|_{\bar{\theta}} \ldots \cup \|v_n\|_{\bar{\theta}}$

Whenever $\bar{\theta}$ is clear from the context we will let $\|v\|$ denoted $\|v\|_{\bar{\theta}}$.

This definition naturally generalises to the notion of the set of descendants of a set of variables.

Now we can define the notion of *admissibility* of an ior with respect to a set of variables. The intuitive idea is that the ior should make input requests to the environments only in order to bind variables that are either in the given set, or are descendants of the variable via the bindings made in the ior.

Definition 17: An ior $\bar{\theta} = [\theta_0^{l_0}, \ldots, \theta_{k-1}^{l_{k-1}}]$ is **admissible** with respect to a set of variables V iff $v \in \|V\|_{\bar{\theta}}$ whenever $l_i = I$, and $\theta_i(v) \neq v$ for $i < k$.

5.2. Scenarios

A scenario is a pair that encodes the proof of a given goal as an ior:

Definition 18: **A scenario** is a pair $\langle g, \bar{\theta} \rangle$ where g is an atom, and $\bar{\theta}$ is an ior.

Renaming is defined for scenarios in a fashion similar to iors. In addition one must ensure that the variable being substituted in does not occur already in the goal.

The extra information we need to keep around with each atom g is a record of the *input* that might have been demanded from the environment in a proof of g and the output produced. Input information may be sought from the environment when attempting to unify the head of a clause against the goal, and output information is usually made available when the clause commits. We are interested also in preserving the order in which these transactions with the environment are made because this information is necessary in putting together the proofs of two goals to produce a proof of their conjunction. This is because two goals communicate with each other by instantiating shared variables and so if one of them is going to produce a binding that the other needs to input, then this establishes a temporal constraint on their order of execution: a binding must be produced before it can be consumed.

In the following examples a, b, c are constants and X, Y are variables.

Example 2: Let the program Π be the single clause

I. `p(a↓,b, c↓).`

Suppose we wish to establish a scenario for the goal $p(a, b, c)$. It is clear that this will immediately succeed without placing any demands on its environment or outputting any information to it (because there are no variables with which to communicate with the environment in the first place). Hence $s_0 = \langle p(a, b, c),\ [] \rangle$ is a possible scenario.

Now lets try for the goal $g_1 = p(X, b, c)$. Before proceeding to resolve against the head of clause **I**, it must ask its environment to supply the binding $\theta_0 = \{X \mapsto a\}$ and then it terminates successfully, without interacting any more with its environment. Hence the corresponding scenario is $s_1 = \langle g_1,\ [\theta_0^I] \rangle$.

Suppose we had the goal $g_2 = p(X, Y, c)$. As with g_0, it would input the binding θ_0, but then it would also output the binding $\theta_1 = \{Y \mapsto b\}$. So we have the scenario

$s_2 = \langle g_2, [\theta_0^I, \theta_1^O]\rangle$. This is not the only possible scenario for g_2. $s_2' = \langle g_2, [\theta_0^I, \theta_1^I]\rangle$ is also possible. But $\langle g_2, [\theta_0^O, \theta_1^O]\rangle$ is not.

The following example illustrates how to combine information from scenarios.

Example 3: Consider Σ to be:

I. `p(a↓,b,c↓).`

II. `r(a↓, X, Y, c):- p(X, b, c) | p(a, Y, c).`

Suppose we desire a scenario for $g_3 = r(A, B, b, C)$. Similar to g_1 above, the demand for $\theta_0 = \{A \mapsto a\}$ must be made to the environment. Then the output substitution made by unifying $\theta_0(g_3)$ against the head of the clause is $\theta = \{X \mapsto B, C \mapsto c, Y \mapsto b\}$. However, because of the nature of '|', we do not expect θ to be made public until $(\theta \circ \theta_0)(p(X, b, c)) = p(B, b, c)$ is solved. But we already have a scenario $\langle p(B, b, c), [\theta_1 = \{B \mapsto a\}^I]\rangle$ (obtained from s_1 above by uniformly replacing X by B. So the sequencing of interactions with the environment till now is $[\theta_0, \theta_1, \theta]$, the first two being I and the last O. To round off, we need a scenario for $(\theta \circ \theta_1 \circ \theta_0)(p(a, Y, c)) = p(a, b, c)$ which also we have (s_0). So the final scenario for g_3 that we have constructed is $s_3 = \langle g_3, [\theta_0^I, \theta_1^I, \theta^O]\rangle$.

5.3. Composition of scenarios

The examples we have seen till now have illustrated how the sequential and information hiding aspects of the commit operator may be taken care of. We now need to investigate how to combine the scenarios for a number of goals to obtain a scenario for their conjunctive (concurrent) execution.

In this section, given scenarios $s_i = \langle g_i, \bar{\theta}_i\rangle$ for $i < k$, we define an *interleaving* operation that returns possibly more than one iors, each ior representing the interactions with the environment involved in executing the goals g_i concurrently according to some specific schedule. This multiplexing operation assumes that the given scenarios are *variable-consistent*, otherwise no interleavings are defined.

Definition 19: The set of scenarios $\{s_0, \ldots, s_{k-1}\}$ where $s_i = \langle g_i, \bar{\theta}_i\rangle$ is **value-consistent** if we have $\theta_i(v) = \theta_j(v)$ whenever $i, j < k$ and $v \in \mathsf{var}(g_i) \cap \mathsf{var}(g_j)$, where θ_i indicates the answer substitution associated with the ior $\bar{\theta}_i$.

Value-consistency simply says that variables named the same get the same value in all the iors; variable-consistency also insists that if there are any intermediate variables involved, they must be named the same and have the same value as well. (Variable-consistency implies value-consistency.)

Definition 20: The set of scenarios $\{s_0, \ldots s_{k-1}\}$ where $s_i = \langle g_i, \bar{\theta}_i\rangle$ for $i < k$ is **variable-consistent** if we have $\|v\|_{\bar{\theta}_i} = \|v\|_{\bar{\theta}_j}$ and for all $v' \in \|v\|_{\bar{\theta}_i}, \theta_i(v') = \theta_j(v')$ whenever $v \in \mathsf{var}(g_i) \cap \mathsf{var}(g_j)$, where θ_i denotes the answer substitution associated with the ior $\bar{\theta}_i$

For example the scenarios

$$s_1 = \langle g(X), [\{X \mapsto f(X_1, X_4), X_4 \mapsto 4\}^I, \{X_1 \mapsto 3\}^O]\rangle$$

and

$$s_2 = \langle h(X, Y, Z), [\{X \mapsto f(X_9, X_1)\}^I, \{X_9 \mapsto 3\}^I, \{X_1 \mapsto 4, Y \mapsto a\}^O]\rangle$$

are value-consistent, but not variable-consistent. On the other hand, if we rename s_2 to get

$$s_2' = \langle h(X,Y,Z), [\{X \mapsto f(X_1,X_4)\}^I, \{X_1 \mapsto 3\}^I, \{X_4 \mapsto 4, Y \mapsto a\}^O]\rangle$$

then s_1, s_2' are both value and variable consistent.

Lemma 1: If a set of scenarios is value consistent, then it can be made variable consistent by appropriate renaming operations.

Now the multiplexing operation is easy to define.

Definition 21: Let $s_i = \langle g_i, \bar{\theta}_i\rangle$ be variable consistent scenarios for $i < k$. Let $[\sigma_0 \ldots \sigma_n]$ be some order preserving merge of $\bar{\theta}_0, \ldots, \theta_{k-1}$. Then, for all bindings that occur more than once in the sequence $[\sigma_0 \ldots \sigma_n]$ delete all occurrences except the first (counting from the left). If this causes $\sigma_j = \{\}_j^l$ for some j, delete σ_j from the sequence. The resultant sequence is a **multiplexed** ior for the scenarios s_i $(1 \leq i \leq k)$.

The reason we delete all but the first occurrence of a binding should be obvious. In an ior, we are interested in the earliest time that a request for a binding is made or a binding is output.

6. A compositional semantics.

A goal a an reduce itself by unifying against the head of a clause $c_i = a' \leftarrow A_1 \% A_2$. If $i \in V_a$, then it must make some input interactions with the environment, via an input substitution (see Section [3.1.1]). It is not necessary that it makes some minimal interaction, when we would also have insisted that if θ is an input substitution only if no subset of it is.

In the following we represent a list whose first element is a and the rest is B by $[a|B]$; therefore $[a,b|C]$ represents the list obtained by appending to the list $[a,b]$ the list C.

Definition 22: Given I_s, the scenario $s = \langle a', \bar{\rho}\rangle$ is in $S_P(I_s)$ iff the following hold:

1. There is some variant $a \leftarrow A_1 \mid A_2$ of a clause c_i in P such that a and c_i have no variables in common, $i \in U_a$.
2. If
   (a) σ_I is an input substitution for $\langle a, a'\rangle$ (i.e. $\sigma_I \in \mathbf{IS}(a,a')$),
   (b) $\sigma = \mathbf{mgu}_{\downarrow}(a', \sigma_I(a)), V = \mathbf{var}((\sigma \circ \sigma_I)(a))$,
   (c) $A_0 = (\sigma \circ \sigma_I)(A_1)$
   (d) for each $a_i \in A_0$ there is a scenario $s_i = \langle a_i, \bar{\theta}_i\rangle \in I_s$ such that they are mutually variable consistent and an ior $\bar{\theta}_g$ obtained as a multiplex of the s_i is V-admissible.
   (e) the ior $\bar{\rho}_g$ is obtained by compacting the ior $[\sigma_I^I, \sigma^O|\bar{\theta}_g]$.
   (f) $A_3 = \rho_g(A_2)$
   (g) for each $a_i \in A_3$ there is a scenario $s_i = \langle a_i, \bar{\theta}_i\rangle \in I_s$ such that they are mutually variable consistent and an ior $\bar{\rho}_b$ obtained as a multiplex of the s_i is V-admissible.

(h) there are variable consistent scenarios $s_i = \langle a_i', \bar{\theta}_i \rangle i \in B$, $s_i \in I_s$ and the ior $\bar{\rho}_b$ obtained as a multiplex of $s_i : i \in B$ is V-admissible.

then $\bar{\rho} = append(\rho_g, \rho_b)$.

Lemma 2: The transformation S_p defined above is continuous.

Monotonicity is easy to see. Continuity follows from the fact that only a finite number of scenarios are necessary to justify any scenario in $s \in S_p(I_s)$.

We then have the usual characterisation

$$\mathbf{lfp}(S_P) = \cup_{i=1}^{\infty} S_p^i(\emptyset)$$

Theorem 1: $SS = \{\langle a, \theta \rangle | \langle a, \bar{\theta} \rangle \in \mathbf{lfp}(S_p)$ is $\emptyset$-admissible$\}$

This theorem merely states that the set calculated as above is the same as the success set semantics calculated earlier using the transition system.

7. Conclusion

In this paper we have presented a partial correctness semantics for the language **CP**$[\downarrow, |, \&]$, which is a substantial generalistion of **Concurrent Prolog** in that it permits don't know as well as don't care search. From this semantics we have extracted a simplified partial correctness semantics for **CP**$[\downarrow, |]$. In addition, we have introduced the notion of scenarios, and have used it to give a compositional partial correctness semantics to **CP**$[\downarrow, |]$. Because of the equivalence of the success-semantics of **CP**$[\downarrow, |]$ and CP$[\downarrow, \&]$, this also serves as an alternate characterisation of the success-semantics of **CP**$[\downarrow, |, \&]$. We believe that the notion of scenarios can be extended to permit the development of a full denotational semantics for **CP**$[\downarrow, |]$. Such a semantics must, however, deal with the problem of fairness in the execution of guard-systems.

7.1. Acknowledgements

I would like to thank Steve Brookes and Larry Rudolph for discussions, and Roberto Minio for help with TEX.

REFERENCES

[1] Apt, K.R., van Emden, M.H., 'Contributions to the theory of logic programming', JACM, vol. 29, No.3, July 1982, pp 841-862.

[2] Brock, J.D., Ackerman, W.B., 'Scenarios: A model of non-determinate computation', *International Colloquim on Formalisation of Programming Concepts* (J Diaz, I. Ramos ed.) LNCS 107, April 1981, 252-259.

[3] Brock, J.D., 'A formal model of non-determinate dataflow computation', PhD dissertation, EECS department, MIT, August, 1983.

[4] Clark, K.L., Gregory, S., 'PARLOG: parallel programming in logic', to appear in *TOPLAS*, 1985.

[5] Clark, K.L., Gregory S., 'A relational language for parallel programming', Res report DOC 81/16, Imperial College, July 1981.

[6] van Emden, M.H., de Lucenha Filho, G.J., 'Predicate logic as a language for parallel programming', in *Logic Programming*, ed. Clark, K.L., and Tarnlund, S.-A., Academic Press, 1980.

[7] Jones, N.D., Mycroft, A., 'Stepwise development of operational and denotational semantics for Prolog', Proceedings of the 1984 International Symposium on Logic Programming, Atlantic City.

[8] Kahn, G., 'The semantics of a simple language for parallel programming', in *Information Processing 74: Proceeedings of IFIP Congress 74*, ed. Rosenfeld, J.L., August 1974, pp 471-475.

[9] Kowalski, R.A., van Emden, M.H., 'The semantics of predicate logic as a programming language', *JACM*, vol. 23, no. 4, October, 1976, pp. 733-742.

[10] Lassez, J-L., Maher, M.J. 'Closure and fairness in the semantics of programming logic', *Theoretical Computer Science* 29 (1984) 167-184.

[11] Lassez, J-L., Maher, M.J., 'The denotational semantics of Horn clauses as a production system', *Proceedings of AAAI, 1983*.

[12] Lloyd, J.W., 'Foundations of Logic Programming', Springer Verlaag, Symbolic Computation series, 1984.

[13] Mycroft, A., 'Logic programs and many valued logics', *Symposium on Theoretical Aspects of Computer Science, 1984*, LNCS 166.

[14] Plotkin, G.D., 'A structural approach to operational semantics', DAIMI FN-19, September 1981, CS Department, University of Aarhus.

[15] Plotkin, G.D., 'An operational semantics for **CSP**', In *Formal descriptions of programming concepts-II* ed. Bjørner, D., pp 199-224, North Holland, 183.

[16] Saraswat, V.A., 'Problems with **Concurrent Prolog**', forthcoming technical report, CS Department, Carnegie-Mellon University, August, 1985.

[17] Saraswat, V.A., 'An operational semantics for **CP**$[\downarrow, |, \&]$', forthcoming technical report, CS Department, Carnegie-Mellon University, August, 1985.

[18] Shapiro, E. Y., 'A subset of Concurrent Prolog and its interpreter', CS83-06, Weizmann Institute technical report.

[19] Shapiro, E. Y., 'Systems programming in Concurrent Prolog', *POPL*, 1984.

[20] Shapiro, E.Y., Takeuchi, A., 'Object oriented programming in Concurrent Prolog', *New Generation Computing*, 1 (1983) 25-48.

[21] Shapiro, E. Y., 'Systolic programming: a paradigm of parallel processing', *Proceedings of the Fifth Generation Computer Systems Conference*, 1984.

[22] Staples, J., and Nguyen, V.L., 'A fixpoint semantics for nondeterminstic data flow', *JACM* vol 32, no. 2, April 1985.

[23] Ueda, K., 'Guarded Horn Clauses', ICOT Technical report TR-103, June 1985.

A Proof Technique for Rely/Guarantee Properties

Eugene W. Stark [1]
Department of Computer Science
State University of New York at Stony Brook
Stony Brook, New York 11794-4400/USA

August 19, 1985

Abstract

A *rely/guarantee* specification for a program P is a specification of the form $R \supset G$ (R implies G), where R is a *rely condition* and G is a *guarantee condition*. A rely condition expresses the conditions that P relies on its environment to provide, and a guarantee condition expresses what P guarantees to provide in return. This paper presents a proof technique that permits us to infer that a program P satisfies a rely/guarantee specification $R \supset G$, given that we know P satisfies a finite collection of rely/guarantee specifications $R_i \supset G_i, (i \in I)$. The utility of the proof technique is illustrated by using it to derive global liveness properties of a system of concurrent processes from a collection of local liveness properties satisfied by the component processes. The use of the proof rule as a design principle is also considered.

1 Introduction

A *rely/guarantee* specification for a program P is a specification of the form $R \supset G$ (R implies G), where R is a *rely condition* and G is a *guarantee condition*. A rely condition expresses the conditions that P relies on its environment to provide, and a guarantee condition expresses what P guarantees to provide in return. This paper presents a proof technique that permits us to infer that a program P satisfies a rely/guarantee specification $R \supset G$, given that we know P satisfies a finite collection of rely/guarantee specifications $R_i \supset G_i, (i \in I)$. In a typical application, $R \supset G$ will be a global property of a large program P, whereas each $R_i \supset G_i$ will be a locally verifiable property of a smaller component P_i of P. In a top-down design methodology based on successive decomposition [Lis79] [Wir71], the proof technique can be used as a decomposition principle for

[1] This research was supported in part by ARO grant DAAG29-84-K-0058, NSF grant DCR-83-02391, and DARPA grant N00014-82-K-0125.

determining specifications $R_i \supset G_i$ for component modules, when these component modules are used to implement a "higher-level module" that must satisfy the specification $R \supset G$.

Two examples are given to illustrate the utility of the proof technique: a *distributed synchronization algorithm*, in which a collection of processes communicate in a ring-like pattern to synchronize access to critical sections, and a *distributed resource allocation algorithm*, in which processes communicate in a tree-like pattern to distribute a finite collection of resources among themselves. Although the statement of the proof technique does not depend on the choice of a particular specification or programming language, in the examples we use as a programming language a concurrent version of Dijkstra's guarded command language [Dij76], and as a specification language a version of *temporal logic* [Pnu77] [Lam80] [Lam83] [MP83].

In the examples, we are concerned with the proof of *liveness properties* of systems of concurrent processes. In particular, we are interested in deriving *global* liveness properties satisfied by a system from a collection of *local* liveness properties satisfied by the component processes. The fact that the technique applies readily to the proof of general liveness properties is interesting, since not many useful techniques for performing such proofs have been developed.

1.1 Related Work

The proof rule and examples presented in this paper are adapted from the author's thesis [Sta84].

The idea that program specifications are conveniently formulated and manipulated in the form of rely/guarantee conditions is not new. Pre/postcondition specifications for sequential programs are examples of rely/guarantee specifications, in which the precondition expresses the conditions on the program variables the program relies on when control enters it, and the postcondition expresses the conditions the program guarantees when and if control leaves it. In fact, the Floyd/Hoare techniques for proving partial correctness of sequential programs [Flo67] [Hoa69] can be viewed as a special case of the proof technique presented here (see Section 2). However, our technique extends the Floyd/Hoare approach, since the former can be applied to the proof of liveness properties, whereas the applicability of the latter (in the usual formulation) is limited to safety, or invariance properties.

For concurrent or distributed programs, a kind of rely/guarantee specification and associated proof technique was introduced in [MC81]. In that paper, a process h is specified by an assertion of the form $r|h|s$, where r and s are predicates on finite sequences (called *traces*) of *communication events*. Such an assertion is interpreted as: "The predicate s holds of the empty trace, and for all traces t that can be produced by process h, if r holds for all *proper* prefixes of t, then s holds for all prefixes (both proper and improper) of t.

Misra and Chandy's proof technique is expressed as a "Theorem of Hierarchy," which gives conditions under which specifications that are satisfied by a collection of component processes can be used to infer a specification that holds for the network formed by interconnecting the components. Their proof technique can be stated as follows: To show that the specification $R_0|H|S_0$ for the network H is a consequence of the specifications $r_i|h_i|s_i, (i \in I)$ for the components, it suffices to show that:

1. S implies S_0,

2. (R_0 and S) implies R,

where R and S denote the conjunction of the r_i and s_i, respectively. These conditions are closely related to the *cut set* conditions presented below.

In [MCS82], the techniques of [MC81] are extended to encompass a weak form of liveness specification in which an additional predicate q is used to state conditions under which a process trace is guaranteed to be extended. The Theorem of Hierarchy is augmented with additional conditions to permit its application to these more general specifications. The additional conditions do not appear to relate in a simple way to the proof technique presented here.

The use of rely and guarantee conditions has also been proposed for safety specifications by Jones [Jon81] [Jon83]. Barringer and Kuiper [BK83] (see also [BKP84]) have proposed the use of liveness specifications that are partitioned into an "environment part," which captures assumptions made about the environment, and a "component part," which captures committments made by the module being specified. Jones, as well as Barringer and Kuiper, exploit the rely/guarantee condition structure of specifications by defining inference rules for process composition.

Hailpern and Owicki [HO80] have performed some example proofs in which liveness properties (expressed in temporal logic) for network protocols are derived from more primitive liveness properties satisfied by each of the constituent processes. Although they are successful at constructing proofs for examples of reasonable complexity, it is difficult to discern much in the way of general principles that might be used to systematize the construction of proofs for different examples. In contrast, the proof rule presented here suggests a way of thinking about process interaction that can systematize and simplify the construction of correctness proofs.

2 The Proof Rule

We assume a programming language, a meaning function that assigns to each program the set of its computations, a specification language, and a binary relation $\models$ between computations and specifications, where if x is a computation and S is a specification, then $x \models S$ means that computation x *satisfies* specification S.

We assume that the specification language is closed under the formation rules for the logical connectives $\neg$ and $\supset$:

($\neg$) If S is a specification, then $\neg S$ is a specification,

($\supset$) If S_1 and S_2 are specifications, then $S_1 \supset S_2$ is a specification, and that $\neg$ and $\supset$ are endowed with their usual meanings:

($\neg$) $x \models \neg S$ iff $x \not\models S$,

($\supset$) $x \models S_1 \supset S_2$ iff $x \models S_1$ implies $x \models S_2$.

The other standard logical connectives can be treated as definitional extensions in the usual way.

We are interested in establishing statements of the form "$P \models S$," which we define to mean "$x \models S$ for all computations x of program P."

To state our proof rule we do not need to make any other assumptions about the precise form of computations or the programming or specification languages. Later, in demonstrating the application of the rule to examples, we will assume that computations are sequences of states and that specifications are sentences in a language of temporal logic. Although the proof rule is a logical truth that has nothing specific to do with the structure of programs, specifications, or computations, it derives power from the fact that the rely/guarantee paradigm is a useful way to think about interaction between program modules.

The proof rule described in this section permits us to derive a statement of the form:

$$P \models R \supset G$$

from a finite collection of statements of the form:

$$P \models R_i \supset G_i, \qquad i \in I$$

under certain conditions on the specifications R, G, R_i, and G_i.

Intuitively, $R \supset G$ should be thought of as an "abstract" or "high-level" statement that we wish to prove about the program P, and each $R_i \supset G_i$ should be thought of as a "concrete" or "low-level" statement that we have already shown to hold for P. In the examples given later on in the paper, P will be a parallel program composed of a finite set of component processes $\{P_i : i \in I\}$, and each $R_i \supset G_i$ will express a property of the component process P_i that we assume has already been shown to hold by arguments involving P_i alone.

The specification $R \supset G$ is a *rely/guarantee* specification, in which R expresses the conditions that the program P *relies on* its environment to provide, and G expresses what P *guarantees to* its environment in return. Similarly, R_i expresses the conditions that the component program P_i relies on its environment to provide, and G_i expresses what P_i guarantees to its environment in return.

The proof rule presented below is based on the following intuition: If we know, for each $i \in I$, that component program P_i guarantees condition G_i under assumption R_i, then we can prove that P guarantees condition G under assumption R by showing the existence of a set of specifications that "cuts," in a certain sense, the dependence between each pair of component programs, and between each component program and the external environment. The sense in which dependence is cut is highly analogous to the way in which a loop invariant is used to isolate reasoning about one iteration of the loop from reasoning about the preceding and succeeding iterations.

Formally, we say that the collection of specifications $\{RG_{i,j} : i,j \in I \cup \{\text{ext}\}\}$ is a *cut set* for the program P and specifications $R, G, \{R_i, G_i : i \in I\}$ if:

$$P \models R \supset (\textstyle\bigwedge_{j \in I} RG_{\text{ext},j}) \quad (1)$$

$$P \models (\textstyle\bigwedge_{i \in I} RG_{i,\text{ext}}) \supset G \quad (2)$$

$$P \models (\textstyle\bigwedge_{i \in I \cup \{\text{ext}\}} RG_{i,j}) \supset R_j, \qquad \text{for all } j \in I \quad (3)$$

$$P \models G_i \supset (\textstyle\bigwedge_{j \in I \cup \{\text{ext}\}} RG_{i,j}), \qquad \text{for all } i \in I. \quad (4)$$

Here "ext" is a special symbol that does not appear in I.

If i, j are both in I, then the specification $RG_{i,j}$ should be thought of as expressing both what component i guarantees to component j, and dually, what component j relies on component i to provide. The specification $RG_{\text{ext},j}$ expresses what the external environment of the entire program guarantees to component j, and also what component j relies on the external environment to provide. Similarly, the specification $RG_{i,\text{ext}}$ expresses what component i guarantees to the external environment, and also what the external environment relies on module i to provide. By convention, we define $RG_{\text{ext},\text{ext}} \equiv$ true. This specification is not used in the proof rule and has no particular intuitive significance. We include it merely for uniformity.

Conditions (1) and (2) above can be interpreted as stating, respectively, that the rely condition R implies what each component relies on the external environment to provide, and the guarantee condition G is implied by the conjunction of what each component guarantees to the external environment. Conditions (3) and (4) can be interpreted, respectively, as stating that component j's rely condition is implied by the conjunction of what the external environment and each component i guarantees to provide to j, and component i's guarantee condition implies the conjunction of what the external environment and each component j relies on i to provide.

The existence of a cut set is not sufficient to imply that $P \models R \supset G$ is a consequence of $\{P \models R_i \supset G_i : i \in I\}$. Intuitively, the reason is that even though the rely and guarantee conditions imply each other in the proper way, it might still be the case in a computation of P satisfying the rely condition R, that no component's rely condition R_i holds, hence no component's guarantee condition G_i need necessarily hold either, and hence the guarantee condition G need not hold. To avoid this kind of degeneracy, we introduce the additional condition that every possible cycle of mutual dependence between components is broken by at least one condition in RG that holds.

Formally, If I is a finite set, then define a *cycle* of I to be a finite set of pairs of the form $\{(i_0, i_1), (i_1, i_2), \ldots, (i_{n-1}, i_n)\}$ such that $i_n = i_0$. We say that the collection $\{RG_{i,j} : i,j \in I\}$ is *acyclic* if:

$$P \models \bigvee_{k=0}^{n-1} RG_{i_k, i_{k+1}}$$

for all cycles $\{(i_0, i_1), \ldots, (i_{n-1}, i_n)\}$ of I.

Note that acyclicity implies the "diagonal" elements $RG_{i,i}$ hold unconditionally:

$$P \models RG_{i,i} \qquad \text{for all } i \in I.$$

We now present our proof rule.

Theorem 1 *(Rely/Guarantee Proof Rule) – Suppose P is a program, I is a finite index set, and the collection $RG = \{RG_{i,j} : i,j \in I \cup \{\text{ext}\}\}$ is an acyclic cut set for program P and specifications $R, G, \{R_i, G_i : i \in I\}$. Then to prove the statement*

$$P \models R \supset G,$$

it suffices to show

$$P \models R_i \supset G_i,$$

for all $i \in I$.

Proof – Suppose $RG = \{RG_{i,j} : i,j \in I \cup \{\text{ext}\}\}$ is a cut set for program P and specifications $R, G, \{R_i, G_i : i \in I\}$. Suppose further that

$$P \models R_i \supset G_i$$

holds for each $i \in I$, but

$$P \not\models R \supset G.$$

This means that there is a computation x of P such that $x \models R$, but $x \not\models G$. We perform an inductive construction to obtain a cycle

$$\{(i_m, i_{m+1}), \ldots, (i_{n-1}, i_n)\}$$

of I such that $x \not\models \bigvee_{k=m}^{n-1} RG_{i_k,i_{k+1}}$. This implies that RG is not acyclic for P.

As the induction hypothesis at stage k of the construction, we assume that $i_0, i_2, \ldots, i_k$ have been constructed so that $x \not\models R_{i_k}$ and $x \not\models \bigvee_{j=1}^{k-1} RG_{i_j,i_{j+1}}$.

Basis: From property (1) of a cut set and the assumption that $x \models R$, we know that $x \models RG_{\text{ext},j}$ for all $j \in I$. Since $x \not\models G$, by property (2) of a cut set we know that $x \not\models RG_{i_0,\text{ext}}$ for some $i_0 \in I$. By property (4) of a cut set we know that $x \not\models G_{i_0}$, and from the assumption that $x \models R_{i_0} \supset G_{i_0}$, we conclude that $x \not\models R_{i_0}$.

Induction: Assume the induction hypothesis holds for some $k \geq 0$. By property (3) of a cut set we know that $x \not\models RG_{i_k,i_{k+1}}$ for some i_{k+1} in I. If $i_{k+1} = i_m$ for some m with $0 \leq m \leq k$, then we have obtained the desired cycle and the construction terminates. Otherwise, by property (4) of a cut set we know that $x \not\models G_{i_{k+1}}$, and from the assumption that $x \models R_{i_{k+1}} \supset G_{i_{k+1}}$, we conclude that $x \not\models R_{i_{k+1}}$. This establishes the induction hypothesis for $k+1$.

Since the set I is finite by hypothesis, we cannot extend the sequence $i_0, i_1, \ldots, i_k$ indefinitely without obtaining a cycle. ∎

In a sense, Theorem 1 can be viewed as a generalization of the Floyd/Hoare technique [Flo67] [Hoa69] for proving partial correctness of sequential programs. In the Floyd/Hoare proof technique, a program contains a collection of *control points*, which are "tagged" or "annotated" by associating with them *assertions* about the values of the program variables. The meaning of an assertion A_p associated with control point p is the invariance property: "Whenever control is at point p, assertion A_p will be true of the program variables." If we assume (which we can, without loss of generality) that to each ordered pair (S_i, S_j) of program statements there corresponds at most one control point $p_{i,j}$, representing the point at which control leaves S_i and enters S_j, then the invariance property corresponding to control point $p_{i,j}$ can be thought of both as what statement S_i guarantees to statement S_j, and as what statement S_j relies on S_i to provide. The collection of all such invariance properties therefore corresponds directly to the set RG in the proof technique presented here.

Once an annotation for a program has been selected, proving the partial correctness of the program with respect to a *precondition* R and a *postcondition* G is reduced to showing the partial correctness of each statement S_i with respect to precondition R_i and postcondition G_i, assuming a certain relationship holds between the pre- and postconditions and the annotations associated with the control points. In Floyd's original formulation, the precondition for statement S_i is required to be exactly the conjunction of the assertions associated with points at which control enters S_i, and the postcondition is required to be exactly the conjunction of the assertions associated with points at which control leaves S_i. In Hoare's version, the pre- and postconditions need not be exactly these conjunctions, as long as they imply or are implied by them in an appropriate way.

The precise relationship that must hold between the pre- and postconditions and the annotations of the control points corresponds to the "cut set" conditions defined above. Furthermore, the acyclicity condition defined above can be shown to follow from the fact that states in a computation are reachable from an initial state in a finite number of steps, plus the requirement that enough control points be tagged to cut any program loop. The problem of annotating a program with assertions can therefore be thought of as a special case of the problem of finding an acyclic cut set.

3 Parallel Programs and Temporal Specifications

To illustrate the use of the rely/guarantee proof rule in proving properties of concurrent programs, we now make some specific assumptions about the programming and specification languages.

We assume that expressions of both the specification and programming language are built from two kinds of symbols: *fixed* symbols and *variable* symbols. The set of fixed symbols includes function and relation symbols, logical connectives, and programming language constructs. The set of variable symbols comprises *logical variables* and *program variables*. Logical variables cannot appear in programs, and although both program and logical variables can appear in specifications, only logical variables are permitted to be bound by quantifiers.

We assume that the semantics of the specification and programming languages assign to fixed symbols a single interpretation that does not change during the course of a computation. An interpretation for the variable symbols is called a *state*. A *computation* is a sequence of states. We assume that all computations are infinite; this convenient assumption results in no loss of generality because finite computations can be modeled by introducing a special "halt flag" into the state, and assuming that finite computations are made infinite by repeating the final state with the halt flag set.

For our concurrent programming language, we use a self-explanatory variant of Dijkstra's guarded command language [Dij76], augmented with a parallel construct $\|$. Communication between processes is accomplished through the use of shared variables. A multiple assignment statement of the form:

$$v_1, v_2, \ldots, v_n := t_1, t_2, \ldots, t_n,$$

where the v_i are program variables and the t_i are terms, is used to read and update a collection of variables in a single atomic step. We assume that process scheduling is *fair* in the sense that no process can be forever enabled without taking a step. It is straightforward to give a formal semantics to this programming language by defining a mapping from programs to sets of computations.

We assume that our specification language is the set of all sentences in the language of first-order temporal logic whose atomic formulas are formed from variables, function symbols, and relation symbols. In addition to the usual logical connectives and quantifiers, we assume the specification language contains the temporal operators $\Box$ (henceforth) and $\Diamond$ (eventually), which are applied to formulas to yield new formulas, and $\bigcirc$ (next), which can either be applied to a formula to yield a new formula, or to a term to yield a new term. We assume that these operators are endowed with "linear time" semantics in the usual way (see [MP83]), and we write $x \models \phi$ to indicate that the computation x satisfies the temporal sentence ϕ.

It will also be convenient to introduce the derived temporal operators $\leadsto$ (leads to), $\uparrow$ (increases), and $\downarrow$ (decreases), defined by:

$$\begin{aligned} \phi \leadsto \psi &\equiv \Box(\phi \supset \Diamond\psi) \\ t\uparrow &\equiv t < \bigcirc t \\ t\downarrow &\equiv t > \bigcirc t, \end{aligned}$$

where in the latter two definitions we assume that t is an integer-valued term and the relation symbols $>$ and $<$ denote the usual ordering relations on the integers.

4 Example 1: Distributed Synchronization

In this section we consider the problem of coordinating the accesses of N *user processes* to *critical sections*, the executions of which must be mutually exclusive. The coordination should be done in such a way as to avoid the phenomenon of *starvation*, in which one process is prevented forever from entering its critical section while other processes repeatedly enter and exit their critical sections.

Program Ring in Figure 1 is a distributed algorithm that solves the mutual exclusion problem. In program Ring, each user process, represented by the code labeled User_i, has been associated with an additional *node process* Node_i. The user process User_i communicates with the associated node process Node_i through the boolean variables $\mathsf{waiting}_i$ and $\mathsf{critical}_i$. When process User_i is ready to enter its critical section, it informs process Node_i by setting the variable $\mathsf{waiting}_i$ to true. Process User_i then waits for the variable $\mathsf{critical}_i$ to become true before entering its critical section. When process User_i finishes its critical section, it sets $\mathsf{critical}_i$ to false.

The node processes communicate with each other in a ring-like pattern; that is, process Node_i communicates with processes Node_{i-1} and Node_{i+1}, where we assume the addition and subtraction to be performed *modulo N*. Mutual exclusion is obtained through the use of a single *token*, which propagates around the ring in the forward direction (i.e., 0 to 1 to 2, ...), in response to *requests*, which propagate in the reverse direction. The process Node_i permits its user process User_i to execute in its critical section only while Node_i possesses the token. The current position of the token is recorded by the variables token_i, and requests are recorded by the variables $\mathsf{request}_i$.

The main loop of process Node_i operates as follows: If Node_i does not currently have the token, and if either User_i is waiting to enter its critical section, or Node_{i+1} wants the token, then Node_i must request the token from Node_{i-1} by setting $\mathsf{request}_i$ to true. If User_i is not waiting, and Node_i doesn't want the token, then there is nothing to do. If Node_i has the token, and User_i is currently executing in its critical section, then there is also nothing to do. If Node_i has the token, and User_i is not in its critical section, then Node_i must examine the variables $\mathsf{waiting}_i$, $\mathsf{request}_{i+1}$, and sched_i to see what to do. If User_i is waiting, and Node_{i+1} doesn't want the token, then User_i is allowed into its critical section. If Node_{i+1} wants the token, and User_i is not waiting, then the token is passed to Node_{i+1}. If both User_i is waiting and Node_{i+1} wants the token, then the choice is resolved on the basis of the scheduling variable sched_i—if sched_i is true, then the token is passed to Node_{i+1}, and if sched_i is false, then User_i is allowed to enter its critical section. In either case, the variable sched_i is complemented to ensure that the opposite decision will be made next time.

Using standard concurrent program proof techniques (*e.g.*, [OG76]), we can show that the program Ring satisfies the following invariants:

$$\mathsf{Ring} \models \Box \textstyle\bigwedge_{i=0}^{N-1}(\mathsf{critical}_i \supset \mathsf{token}_i) \tag{1}$$

$$\mathsf{Ring} \models \Box \left(\textstyle\sum_{i=0}^{N-1} \mathsf{token}_i = 1\right) \tag{2}$$

where the expression $\sum_{i=0}^{N-1} \mathsf{token}_i = 1$ denotes the first order formula that states that precisely one of the variables token_i is true.[2] These invariants together imply that program Ring has the mutual exclusion property

$$\mathsf{Ring} \models \Box \textstyle\bigwedge_{i \neq j}(\mathsf{critical}_i \supset \neg\mathsf{critical}_j).$$

[2]In the sequel, we shall occasionally write expressions like this, which although not themselves first-order formulas, can be regarded as denoting equivalent first-order formulas in an obvious way.

```
Ring    ≡  boolean (token_i : 0 ≤ i ≤ N − 1) initially (if i = 0 then true else false);
           boolean (waiting_i, critical_i, request_i, sched_i : 0 ≤ i ≤ N − 1) initially false;
           ||_{i=0}^{N-1} (User_i || Node_i);

User_i  ≡  do Noncritical Section;
              waiting_i := true;
              do ¬critical_i → skip; od;
              Critical Section;
              critical_i := false;
           od;

Node_i  ≡  do ¬token_i              → if ¬request_i ∧ (waiting_i ∨ request_{i+1})   → request_i := true;
                                      □ request_i ∨ (¬waiting_i ∧ ¬request_{i+1}) → skip;
                                      fi;
           □  token_i ∧ critical_i  → skip;
           □  token_i ∧ ¬critical_i → if ¬waiting_i ∧ ¬request_{i+1} → skip;
                                      □ request_{i+1} ∧ (¬waiting_i ∨ sched_i)
                                           → token_i, token_{i+1}, request_{i+1}, sched_i
                                                := false, true, false, false;
                                      □ waiting_i ∧ (¬request_{i+1} ∨ ¬sched_i)
                                           → waiting_i, critical_i, sched_i := false, true, true;
                                      fi;
           od;
```

Figure 1: Distributed Synchronization Algorithm

Besides the above invariants, we can show (for example, by the "proof lattice" techniques of [OL82] or by the "chain principle" of [MP83]), that program Ring satisfies the following rely/guarantee specification for all i with $0 \leq i \leq N-1$:

$$\text{Ring} \models R_i \supset G_i,$$

where

$$\begin{aligned} R_i &\equiv \text{critical}_i \leadsto \neg\text{critical}_i \ \wedge\ \text{request}_i \leadsto \text{token}_i \\ G_i &\equiv \text{request}_{i+1} \leadsto \text{token}_{i+1} \ \wedge\ \text{waiting}_i \leadsto \text{critical}_i \end{aligned}$$

Of course, to prove these properties, we must make use of our fair scheduling assumption.

Our goal is to show that if critical sections always terminate, then no process waits forever to enter its critical section. That is,

$$\text{Ring} \models R \supset G$$

where

$$\begin{aligned} R &\equiv \textstyle\bigwedge_{i=1}^{N}(\text{critical}_i \leadsto \neg\text{critical}_i) \\ G &\equiv \textstyle\bigwedge_{i=1}^{N}(\text{waiting}_i \leadsto \text{critical}_i) \end{aligned}$$

Note that the property Ring $\models R_i \supset G_i$ is *local* in the sense that it is stated solely in terms of variables that are referenced by the process Node_i. In contrast, the property Ring $\models R \supset G$ is a *global* property that involves variables referenced by all processes. In general, we imagine that the proof rule presented in this paper will be most useful when it is used, as in this example, to reduce the proof of a global property to the proof of a collection of local properties.

To apply our rely/guarantee proof rule, we define the set of specifications

$$RG = \{RG_{i,j} : i,j \in \{0,1,\ldots N-1\} \cup \{\text{ext}\}\}$$

as follows:

$$RG_{i,j} \equiv \begin{cases} \text{waiting}_i \leadsto \text{critical}_i, & 0 \leq i \leq N-1, j = \text{ext} \\ \text{critical}_j \leadsto \neg\text{critical}_j, & i = \text{ext}, 0 \leq j \leq N-1 \\ \text{request}_j \leadsto \text{token}_j, & 0 \leq i,j \leq N-1, j = i+1 \\ \text{true}, & 0 \leq i,j \leq N-1, j \neq i+1. \end{cases}$$

With these definitions, the conditions required for RG to be a cut set for program Ring and specifications $R, G, \{R_i, G_i : 1 \leq i \leq N\}$, are tautological. To complete the proof that Ring $\models R \supset G$ it therefore remains only to prove that RG is acyclic for Ring.

To prove the acyclicity condition we need consider only the cycle $\{(0,1),(1,2)...,(N-1,0)\}$, since all other cycles contain links (i,j) for which $j \neq i+1$ and hence for which $RG_{i,j} \equiv$ true. We show Ring $\models \bigvee_{i=0}^{N-1} RG_{i,i+1}$ indirectly, by assuming the existence of a computation x of Ring such that $x \models \bigwedge_{i=0}^{N-1} \neg RG_{i,i+1}$, and deriving a contradiction.

Suppose $x \models \bigwedge_{i=0}^{N-1} \neg RG_{i,i+1}$. Then

$$x \models \bigwedge_{i=0}^{N-1} \neg(\mathsf{request}_i \leadsto \mathsf{token}_i).$$

Using the definition of $\leadsto$ and temporal reasoning, we have

$$x \models \bigwedge_{i=0}^{N-1} \Diamond(\mathsf{request}_i \wedge \Box(\neg\mathsf{token}_i)).$$

Since the conjunction $\bigwedge_{i=0}^{N-1}$ is finite, it is valid (in linear-time temporal logic) to interchange it and the temporal operator $\Diamond$. Since $\bigwedge_{i=0}^{N-1}$ and $\Box$ are both of universal character, it is valid to to interchange them as well, yielding

$$x \models \Diamond\Box \bigwedge_{i=0}^{N-1} \neg\mathsf{token}_i.$$

This implies that

$$x \models \Diamond\Box \left(\sum_{i=0}^{N-1} \mathsf{token}_i = 0\right),$$

which contradicts invariant (2) above.

5 Example 2: Distributed Resource Allocation

In this section we consider the problem of allocating a fixed number of *resources* in response to requests from a collection of *user processes*. An algorithm to solve this problem should have the property that as long as the total number of requests issued by users does not exceed the number of originally available resources, a resource will eventually be issued in response to each user request.

Program Tree in Figure 2 is a distributed algorithm, based on the "dynamic match" algorithm of [FLG83], that solves the problem. As in program Ring of the previous example, each user process, labeled User_i, has been associated with a node process Node_i. The user process User_i communicates with the node process Node_i through the variable $\mathsf{pending}_i$, which represents the number of user requests that have not yet been satisfied. Process User_i starts out with an initial number of requests IREQ_i, which it issues to Node_i (by incrementing $\mathsf{pending}_i$) at unpredictable times during execution of the system. Process Node_i records the number of free resources it has in the variable free_i, which is initially set to the constant IFREE_i. Process Node_i "responds" to requests from User_i by decrementing $\mathsf{pending}_i$ and free_i – a practical algorithm would also transmit a capability for a resource to the user process as well, but we ignore this here.

In contrast to the previous example, in which the communication pattern of the node processes was a ring, the communication pattern of the node processes in this example is a tree. The set T is the set of process identifiers, which we imagine to be arranged as a binary tree. For each process $i \in T$, we write $p(i), l(i), r(i)$ for the parent, left child, and right child, respectively, of process i. For uniformity, we introduce a special symbol nil, and define $p(i) = \mathsf{nil}$ when i is the root of the tree, and define $l(i) = r(i) = \mathsf{nil}$ when i is a leaf of the tree. Furthermore, we define

$$\begin{array}{lll}
\mathsf{Tree} & \equiv & \textbf{integer}\ (\mathsf{owes}_{i,j}, \mathsf{estim}_{i,j} : (j \in T \text{ and } i = p(j)) \text{ or } (i \in T \text{ and } j \in \{l(i), r(i)\})) \\
& & \quad \textbf{initially}\ (0, \sum_{k \in D(j)} \mathsf{IFREE}_k); \\
& & \textbf{integer}\ (\mathsf{pending}_i : i \in T)\ \textbf{initially}\ 0; \\
& & \|_{i \in T}\ (\mathsf{User}_i \parallel \mathsf{Node}_i);
\end{array}$$

$$\begin{array}{lll}
\mathsf{User}_i & \equiv & \textbf{integer}\ \mathsf{request}_i\ \textbf{initially}\ \mathsf{IREQ}_i; \\
& & \textbf{do}\ \ \mathsf{request}_i > 0 \rightarrow \mathsf{request}_i, \mathsf{pending}_i := \mathsf{request}_i - 1, \mathsf{pending}_i + 1; \\
& & \qquad \mathsf{request}_i \leq 0 \rightarrow \textbf{skip}; \\
& & \textbf{od};
\end{array}$$

$$\begin{array}{lll}
\mathsf{Node}_i & \equiv & \textbf{integer}\ \mathsf{free}_i\ \textbf{initially}\ \mathsf{IFREE}_i; \\
& & \textbf{do}\ \ \mathsf{pending}_i > 0 \wedge \mathsf{free}_i > 0 \qquad\qquad (\textit{issue resource to user}) \\
& & \qquad \rightarrow \mathsf{pending}_i, \mathsf{free}_i := \mathsf{pending}_i - 1, \mathsf{free}_i - 1; \\
& & \square\ \ \mathsf{owes}_{p(i),i} < 0 \wedge \mathsf{free}_i > 0 \qquad (\textit{pay resource owed to parent} - i \textit{ not root}) \\
& & \qquad \rightarrow \mathsf{owes}_{p(i),i}, \mathsf{free}_i, \mathsf{free}_{p(i)} := \mathsf{owes}_{p(i),i} + 1, \mathsf{free}_i - 1, \mathsf{free}_{p(i)} + 1; \\
& & \square\ \ \mathsf{owes}_{i,l(i)} > 0 \wedge \mathsf{free}_i > 0 \qquad (\textit{pay resource owed to left child} - i \textit{ not leaf}) \\
& & \qquad \rightarrow \mathsf{owes}_{i,l(i)}, \mathsf{free}_i, \mathsf{free}_{l(i)} := \mathsf{owes}_{i,l(i)} - 1, \mathsf{free}_i - 1, \mathsf{free}_{l(i)} + 1; \\
& & \square\ \ \mathsf{owes}_{i,r(i)} > 0 \wedge \mathsf{free}_i > 0 \qquad (\textit{pay resource owed to right child} - i \textit{ not leaf}) \\
& & \qquad \rightarrow \mathsf{owes}_{i,r(i)}, \mathsf{free}_i, \mathsf{free}_{r(i)} := \mathsf{owes}_{i,r(i)} - 1, \mathsf{free}_i - 1, \mathsf{free}_{r(i)} + 1; \\
& & \square\ \ \mathsf{DEBT}_i > 0 \wedge \mathsf{estim}_{i,l(i)} > 0 \qquad (\textit{forward request to left child}) \\
& & \qquad \rightarrow \mathsf{owes}_{i,l(i)}, \mathsf{estim}_{i,l(i)} := \mathsf{owes}_{i,l(i)} - 1, \mathsf{estim}_{i,l(i)} - 1; \\
& & \square\ \ \mathsf{DEBT}_i > 0 \wedge \mathsf{estim}_{i,r(i)} > 0 \qquad (\textit{forward request to right child}) \\
& & \qquad \rightarrow \mathsf{owes}_{i,r(i)}, \mathsf{estim}_{i,r(i)} := \mathsf{owes}_{i,r(i)} - 1, \mathsf{estim}_{i,r(i)} - 1; \\
& & \square\ \ \mathsf{DEBT}_i > 0 \wedge \mathsf{estim}_{i,l(i)} \leq 0 \wedge \mathsf{estim}_{i,r(i)} \leq 0 \qquad (\textit{reject request up to parent}) \\
& & \qquad \rightarrow \mathsf{owes}_{p(i),i}, \mathsf{estim}_{p(i),i} := \mathsf{owes}_{p(i),i} + 1, 0; \\
& & \square\ \ \mathsf{DEBT}_i \leq 0 \wedge (\mathsf{free}_i \leq 0 \vee (\mathsf{pending}_i \leq 0 \qquad (\textit{nothing to do, idle}) \\
& & \qquad\qquad \wedge\ \mathsf{owes}_{p(i),i} \geq 0 \wedge \mathsf{owes}_{i,l(i)} \leq 0 \wedge \mathsf{owes}_{i,r(i)} \leq 0)) \\
& & \qquad \rightarrow \textbf{skip}; \\
& & \textbf{od};
\end{array}$$

where

$$\mathsf{DEBT}_i = (\mathsf{pending}_i + \mathsf{owes}_{i,l(i)} + \mathsf{owes}_{i,r(i)}) - (\mathsf{free}_i + \mathsf{owes}_{p(i),i})$$

Figure 2: Distributed Resource Allocation Algorithm

$p(\mathsf{nil}) = l(\mathsf{nil}) = r(\mathsf{nil}) = \mathsf{nil}$. If $i \in T$, then let $D(i)$ represent the set of all $j \in T$ (including i itself) that are *descendants* of i.

If $i, j \in T$ and $i = p(j)$, then processes Node_i and Node_j communicate through the variables $\mathsf{owes}_{i,j}$ and $\mathsf{estim}_{i,j}$. Intuitively, the variable $\mathsf{owes}_{i,j}$ records the net number of resources that Node_i owes to Node_j. If $\mathsf{owes}_{i,j}$ is positive, then Node_i owes resources to Node_j. If $\mathsf{owes}_{i,j}$ is negative, then Node_j owes resources to Node_i. The variable $\mathsf{estim}_{i,j}$ contains an estimate of the number of free resources remaining in the subtree headed by j. It is initially set to the total number of free resources initially available in the subtree headed by j. The important invariant property of this estimate is that it is always *optimistic*; that is, $\mathsf{estim}_{i,j}$ is always greater than or equal to the number of free resources actually available in the subtree headed by j.

Intuitively, the steps of process Node_i serve either to satisfy a pending user request with a locally available resource, to pay a resource owed to a neighboring node, or to reduce a projected deficit of resources at node i. The quantity DEBT_i in the code for process Node_i represents the projected amount by which requests exceed resources at node i, once all debts have been paid. If process Node_i projects a deficit, then to reduce this deficit, it can either *forward* a request to its left or right child, or *reject* a request to its parent. Requests are forwarded to a child only in case it is estimated that there is a surplus of resources in the subtree headed by that child. Requests are rejected to the parent only if neither of the subtrees headed by the child nodes are estimated to have a surplus of resources.

Certain of the steps of process Node_i, involving the transfer of resources to a parent or child, are to be omitted from the program in case i is the root or a leaf, respectively. These branches are indicated by comments in Figure 2.

The program Tree can be shown, by standard techniques, to satisfy the following invariants:

$$\mathsf{Tree} \models \Box(\mathsf{owes}_{\mathsf{nil},\mathsf{root}} \geq 0), \tag{1}$$

$$\mathsf{Tree} \models \Box \textstyle\bigwedge_{i \in T} \left(\mathsf{owes}_{p(i),i} > 0 \supset \mathsf{owes}_{p(i),i} \leq \sum_{j \in D(i)} (\mathsf{pending}_j - \mathsf{free}_j)\right). \tag{2}$$

Invariant (2) expresses the fundamental relationship between amount owed and amount needed: If node i is owed resources by its parent, then the amount owed to i by its parent is a lower bound on the instantanous amount by which pending requests exceed available resources in the subtree headed by i.

It can also be shown that Tree satisfies the following rely/guarantee specifications for all $i \in T$:

$$\mathsf{Tree} \models R_i \supset G_i,$$

where

$$\begin{aligned} R_i \;\equiv\;& \mathsf{owes}_{p(i),i} > 0 \leadsto \mathsf{owes}_{p(i),i} \downarrow \\ & \wedge\ \mathsf{owes}_{i,l(i)} < 0 \leadsto \mathsf{owes}_{i,l(i)} \uparrow \\ & \wedge\ \mathsf{owes}_{i,r(i)} < 0 \leadsto \mathsf{owes}_{i,r(i)} \uparrow \\ G_i \;\equiv\;& \mathsf{pending}_i > 0 \leadsto \mathsf{pending}_i \downarrow \\ & \wedge\ \mathsf{owes}_{p(i),i} < 0 \leadsto \mathsf{owes}_{p(i),i} \uparrow \\ & \wedge\ \mathsf{owes}_{i,l(i)} > 0 \leadsto \mathsf{owes}_{i,l(i)} \downarrow \\ & \wedge\ \mathsf{owes}_{i,r(i)} > 0 \leadsto \mathsf{owes}_{i,r(i)} \downarrow \end{aligned}$$

The rely condition R_i states that debts owed to node i by its parent and each of its children will eventually be paid. The guarantee condition G_i states that debts owed by node i to its parent and each of its children will eventually be paid. To obtain these properties, we must assume the scheduling of the branches of the main loop in the node program is *strongly fair*, in the sense that no branch that is enabled infinitely often during the course of a computation can fail to be selected during that computation.

We are interested in establishing that, assuming the total number of user requests never exceeds the total number of resources initially available, then a resource will eventually be issued for every user request. Formally, we would like to show:

$$\mathsf{Tree} \models R \supset G,$$

where

$$\begin{aligned} R \;&\equiv\; \Box\left(\textstyle\sum_{i\in T} \mathsf{pending}_i \le \sum_{i\in T} \mathsf{free}_i\right) \\ G \;&\equiv\; \left(\textstyle\sum_{i\in T} \mathsf{pending}_i > 0\right) \leadsto \left(\textstyle\sum_{i\in T} \mathsf{pending}_i\right) \downarrow \end{aligned}$$

That this property holds is not immediately obvious. Examples of the kinds of things that might go wrong are resources being shuttled endlessly around the system without ever reaching nodes where they are needed, and nodes with surplus resources never receiving requests from nodes with deficits.

To apply our rely/guarantee proof rule, we define the set of specifications

$$RG = \{RG_{i,j} : i,j \in T \cup \{\mathsf{ext}\}\}$$

as follows:

$$RG_{i,j} \equiv \begin{cases} \Box(\mathsf{owes}_{\mathsf{nil},\mathsf{root}} = 0), & i = \mathsf{ext}, j = \mathsf{root} \\ \mathsf{true}, & i = \mathsf{ext}, j \in T - \mathsf{root} \\ \mathsf{pending}_i > 0 \leadsto \mathsf{pending}_i \downarrow, & i \in T, j = \mathsf{ext} \\ \mathsf{owes}_{i,j} > 0 \leadsto \mathsf{owes}_{i,j} \downarrow, & i,j \in T, i = p(j) \\ \mathsf{owes}_{j,i} < 0 \leadsto \mathsf{owes}_{j,i} \uparrow, & i,j \in T, j = p(i) \\ \mathsf{true}, & i,j \in T, j \ne p(i), i \ne p(j). \end{cases}$$

We must first show that RG is a cut set. To prove condition (1) in the definition of a cut set, we must show that

$$\mathsf{Tree} \models R \supset (\bigwedge_{j\in T} RG_{\mathrm{ext},j}),$$

which, applying the definitions of R and $RG_{\mathrm{ext},j}$, becomes

$$\mathsf{Tree} \models \Box\,(\textstyle\sum_{i\in T} \mathsf{pending}_i \leq \sum_{i\in T} \mathsf{free}_i) \supset \Box(\mathsf{owes}_{\mathsf{nil},\mathsf{root}} = 0).$$

Suppose x is a computation of Tree such that

$$x \models \Box\,(\textstyle\sum_{i\in T} \mathsf{pending}_i \leq \sum_{i\in T} \mathsf{free}_i).$$

Then

$$x \models \Box\,(\textstyle\sum_{i\in T} \mathsf{free}_i - \mathsf{pending}_i \geq 0). \tag{3}$$

From the fundamental invariant (2) above, and the fact that $D(\mathsf{root}) = T$, we infer that

$$x \models \Box(\mathsf{owes}_{\mathsf{nil},\mathsf{root}} > 0 \;\supset\; \mathsf{owes}_{\mathsf{nil},\mathsf{root}} \leq \textstyle\sum_{i\in T} \mathsf{pending}_i - \mathsf{free}_i).$$

From this and (3), we conclude that

$$x \models \Box(\mathsf{owes}_{\mathsf{nil},\mathsf{root}} > 0 \supset \mathsf{owes}_{\mathsf{nil},\mathsf{root}} \leq 0),$$

which, combined with the invariant (1), implies that

$$x \models \Box(\mathsf{owes}_{\mathsf{nil},\mathsf{root}} = 0),$$

as required.

To prove condition (2) in the definition of a cut set, we must show that

$$\mathsf{Tree} \models (\bigwedge_{i\in T} RG_{i,\mathrm{ext}}) \supset G,$$

that is,

$$\begin{aligned}\mathsf{Tree} \models\; & \textstyle\bigwedge_{i\in T} (\mathsf{pending}_i > 0 \leadsto \mathsf{pending}_i \downarrow) \\ & \supset ((\textstyle\sum_{i\in T} \mathsf{pending}_i > 0) \leadsto (\sum_{i\in T} \mathsf{pending}_i) \downarrow)\end{aligned}$$

This is obviously true, because at most one of the $\mathsf{pending}_i$ can change in a single step of execution.

To prove condition (3), we must show that

$$\mathsf{Tree} \models (\bigwedge_{i\in T\cup\{\mathrm{ext}\}} RG_{i,j}) \supset R_j, \quad \text{for all } j \in T.$$

We split the proof into two cases, $j = \mathsf{root}$ and $j \in T - \mathsf{root}$. In case $j = \mathsf{root}$, we must show

$$\begin{aligned}\mathsf{Tree} \models\; & (\Box(\mathsf{owes}_{\mathsf{nil},\mathsf{root}} = 0) \\ & \quad \wedge\; \mathsf{owes}_{\mathsf{root},l(\mathsf{root})} < 0 \leadsto \mathsf{owes}_{\mathsf{root},l(\mathsf{root})} \uparrow \\ & \quad \wedge\; \mathsf{owes}_{\mathsf{root},r(\mathsf{root})} < 0 \leadsto \mathsf{owes}_{\mathsf{root},r(\mathsf{root})} \uparrow) \\ & \supset \\ & (\mathsf{owes}_{\mathsf{nil},\mathsf{root}} > 0 \leadsto \mathsf{owes}_{\mathsf{nil},\mathsf{root}} \downarrow \\ & \quad \wedge\; \mathsf{owes}_{\mathsf{root},l(\mathsf{root})} < 0 \leadsto \mathsf{owes}_{\mathsf{root},l(\mathsf{root})} \uparrow \\ & \quad \wedge\; \mathsf{owes}_{\mathsf{root},r(\mathsf{root})} < 0 \leadsto \mathsf{owes}_{\mathsf{root},r(\mathsf{root})} \uparrow)\end{aligned}$$

This is obviously true.

In case $j \in T - \text{root}$, we must show

$$\begin{aligned}\text{Tree} \models\ & (\text{owes}_{p(j),j} > 0 \rightsquigarrow \text{owes}_{p(j),j} \downarrow \\ & \wedge\ \text{owes}_{j,l(j)} < 0 \rightsquigarrow \text{owes}_{j,l(j)} \uparrow \\ & \wedge\ \text{owes}_{j,r(j)} < 0 \rightsquigarrow \text{owes}_{j,r(j)} \uparrow) \\ & \supset \\ & (\text{owes}_{p(j),j} > 0 \rightsquigarrow \text{owes}_{p(j),j} \downarrow \\ & \wedge\ \text{owes}_{j,l(j)} < 0 \rightsquigarrow \text{owes}_{j,l(j)} \uparrow \\ & \wedge\ \text{owes}_{j,r(j)} < 0 \rightsquigarrow \text{owes}_{j,r(j)} \uparrow),\end{aligned}$$

which is a tautology.

To prove condition (4), we must show that

$$\text{Tree} \models G_i \supset (\textstyle\bigwedge_{j \in T \cup \{\text{ext}\}} RG_{i,j}), \qquad \text{for all } i \in T.$$

Using the definitions of R_i and $RG_{i,j}$, this becomes

$$\begin{aligned}\text{Tree} \models\ & (\text{pending}_i > 0 \rightsquigarrow \text{pending}_i \downarrow \\ & \wedge\ \text{owes}_{p(i),i} < 0 \rightsquigarrow \text{owes}_{p(i),i} \uparrow \\ & \wedge\ \text{owes}_{i,l(i)} > 0 \rightsquigarrow \text{owes}_{i,l(i)} \downarrow \\ & \wedge\ \text{owes}_{i,r(i)} > 0 \rightsquigarrow \text{owes}_{i,r(i)} \downarrow) \\ & \supset \\ & (\text{pending}_i > 0 \rightsquigarrow \text{pending}_i \downarrow \\ & \wedge\ \text{owes}_{p(i),i} < 0 \rightsquigarrow \text{owes}_{p(i),i} \uparrow \\ & \wedge\ \text{owes}_{i,l(i)} > 0 \rightsquigarrow \text{owes}_{i,l(i)} \downarrow \\ & \wedge\ \text{owes}_{i,r(i)} > 0 \rightsquigarrow \text{owes}_{i,r(i)} \downarrow),\end{aligned}$$

which is a tautology.

Finally, we must show that RG is acyclic for Tree. To do this, it suffices to show that Tree $\models$ $RG_{i,p(i)} \vee RG_{p(i),i}$ for all $i \in T - \text{root}$. This is because every cycle

$$\{(i_0, i_1), (i_1, i_2), \ldots, (i_{n-1}, i_n)\}$$

of T either contains a link (i_k, i_{k+1}) for which $RG_{i_k,i_{k+1}} = \textbf{true}$ by definition, or else contains both links $(i, p(i))$ and $(p(i), i)$ for some $i \in T - \text{root}$.

To show that Tree $\models RG_{i,p(i)} \vee RG_{p(i),i}$ for all $i \in T - \text{root}$, let i be arbitrarily fixed, and suppose, to obtain a contradiction, that x is a computation of Tree such that

$$x \models \neg RG_{i,p(i)} \wedge \neg RG_{p(i),i}. \tag{4}$$

From (4) and the definition of $RG_{i,p(i)}$ we know that

$$x \models \Diamond(\text{owes}_{p(i),i} < 0 \wedge \Box\neg\text{owes}_{p(i),i} \uparrow),$$

which implies that

$$x \models \Diamond\Box(owes_{p(i),i} < 0).$$

Similarly, from (4) and the definition of $RG_{p(i),i}$ we have that

$$x \models \Diamond\Box(owes_{p(i),i} > 0).$$

These two statements are contradictory, and we conclude that RG is acyclic.

6 Comparison With Other Techniques

To obtain perspective on the rely/guarantee proof method presented here, it is useful to compare this method with other extant methods. In this section we consider two methods: the "proof lattice" method of Owicki and Lamport [OL82], and the "well-founded set" method originally applied by Floyd [Flo67] to termination proofs for sequential programs, and later adapted by Manna, Pnueli [MP83], and others to prove eventuality properties expressed in temporal logic. Below we sketch how alternative proofs of the property Ring $\models R \supset G$ might be constructed for the distributed synchronization example. The reader is challenged to produce simple proofs, at an adequate level of rigor, along the lines sketched. The author's own inability to accomplish this is what led him to devise the rely/guarantee proof technique.

6.1 Proof Lattice Method

The proof lattice method of Lamport and Owicki is designed to permit the proof of temporal implications of the form $\phi \leadsto \psi$ from simpler implications of the same form, plus auxiliary invariance properties of the program under consideration. A proof lattice for the program $P \models \phi \leadsto \psi$ is a finite, directed, acyclic graph, whose nodes are labeled by temporal sentences, with the following properties:

1. There is a single root node, labeled by ϕ.
2. There is a single leaf node, labeled by ψ.
3. If the children of a node labeled by ρ are labeled by $\sigma_1, \sigma_2, \ldots, \sigma_n$, then

$$P \models \rho \leadsto (\sigma_1 \vee \sigma_2 \vee \ldots \vee \sigma_n).$$

A proof lattice for $P \models \phi \leadsto \psi$ represents a sufficiently rigorous proof when each node labeled ρ, with children labeled $\sigma_1, \sigma_2, \ldots, \sigma_n$, can be justified by appeal to primitive inference rules associated with the constructs of the programming language, by appeal to an auxiliary invariance property, or by appeal to a theorem of temporal logic.

To use the proof lattice technique to prove the statement Ring $\models R \supset G$, we might assume R, (that is, we consider a computation x such that $x \models \bigwedge_{i=0}^{N-1} \mathsf{critical}_i \leadsto \neg\mathsf{critical}_i$), and attempt to construct a proof lattice for $\mathsf{waiting}_i \leadsto \mathsf{critical}_i$. The informal content of the argument that would be captured formally by the proof lattice is as follows: We would show that if $\mathsf{waiting}_i$ holds, then a chain of requests is generated that propagates around the ring in the reverse direction until a node is reached that has the token. The token is then forced to propagate in the forward direction around the ring until node i is reached. Once node i is reached, then depending upon the value of sched_i, either $\mathsf{critical}_i$ will become true right away, or the token will be passed to node $i+1$. In the latter case, we have to follow another chain of requests and subsequent token passes until the token again reaches node i.

In the construction of the proof lattice, we would make use of simple eventuality properties like the following, which can be verified by local reasoning about the control flow within the process Node_i:

$$\mathsf{Ring} \models \mathsf{waiting}_i \leadsto \mathsf{critical}_i \vee \mathsf{request}_i$$
$$\mathsf{Ring} \models \mathsf{request}_i \leadsto \mathsf{token}_i \vee \mathsf{request}_{i-1}$$
$$\mathsf{Ring} \models \mathsf{token}_i \wedge \mathsf{waiting}_i \leadsto \mathsf{critical}_i \vee \neg\mathsf{sched}_i$$
$$\mathsf{Ring} \models \mathsf{waiting}_i \wedge \mathsf{token}_i \wedge \neg\mathsf{sched}_i \leadsto \mathsf{critical}_i$$

In addition, we would make use of safety properties like the following:

$$\mathsf{Ring} \models \mathsf{waiting}_i \ \textit{latches-until}\ \mathsf{critical}_i$$
$$\mathsf{Ring} \models \mathsf{request}_i \ \textit{latches-until}\ \mathsf{token}_i$$
$$\mathsf{Ring} \models \mathsf{sched}_i \ \textit{latches-until}\ \mathsf{token}_{i+1}$$
$$\mathsf{Ring} \models \neg\mathsf{sched}_i \ \textit{latches-until}\ \mathsf{critical}_i$$
$$\mathsf{Ring} \models \mathsf{token}_i \ \textit{latches-until}\ \mathsf{token}_{i+1}$$
$$\mathsf{Ring} \models \Box(\mathsf{request}_i \supset \neg\mathsf{token}_i)$$
$$\mathsf{Ring} \models \Box(\mathsf{critical}_i \supset \mathsf{token}_i),$$

where ϕ *latches-until* ψ means, intuitively, "If ϕ ever holds, then ϕ remains true from then until the next instant at which ψ holds." (See [SM81] for a formal definition of this construct.)

If one actually tries to construct a proof lattice according to the preceding informal sketch, one is quickly overwhelmed by the number of branches and cases that it is necessary to consider. Problems are also caused by the fact that the depth of the lattice is dependent upon the parameter N, which is the size of the ring. This variable parameter necessitates the use of elipses in the proof lattice.

6.2 Well-Founded Set Method

Another alternative to the rely/guarantee method is to use a method based on well-founded sets. In this approach, the proof of a statement $P \models \phi \leadsto \psi$, might proceed by contradiction as follows: Assume x is a computation of P such that $x \models \Diamond(\phi \wedge \Box\neg\psi)$. Define a ***variant function*** f that maps the program state into a well-founded set W (typically the nonnegative integers under the usual ordering), and prove the following properties:

$$P \models \Box((\phi \wedge \Box\neg\psi) \supset \Box\neg f\uparrow)$$

$$P \models \Box((\phi \wedge \Box\neg\psi) \leadsto \Box\Diamond f\downarrow)$$

The first condition states that, assuming ϕ holds at some instant, and $\neg\psi$ holds for that instant and all future instants, then the value of the variant function f does not increase from that instant on. The second condition states that, under the same assumptions, the value of f is repeatedly decreased. If $P \models \Diamond(\phi \wedge \Box\neg\psi)$, then we would have a contradiction with the well-foundedness of W. We conclude that $P \models \Box(\phi \supset \Diamond\psi)$; that is, $P \models \phi \leadsto \psi$. The power of this rule lies in the fact that it is typically easier to prove the two conditions above than to prove the original statement $P \models \phi \leadsto \psi$.

Let us consider how a well-founded set proof of $\mathsf{Ring} \models R \supset G$ might proceed. Suppose, to obtain a contradiction, that x is a computation of Ring such that $x \models R \wedge \neg G$. Then for some i with $0 \leq i \leq N-1$, we have that $x \models \Diamond(\mathsf{waiting}_i \wedge \Box\neg\mathsf{critical}_i)$. Making use of the invariant that states that there is precisely one token in the system at all times, we know that for each state in x, there is precisely one j for which token_j is true. We select a variant function f that maps each program state to a nonnegative integer according to the following intuition: The value of f on a program state measures a kind of "distance" between that state and a "desired" state (one for which $\mathsf{critical}_i$ holds). In particular, f takes into account:

1. The distance around the ring the token has to travel from j to i.

2. The distance around the ring requests have yet to propagate from i to j.

3. The values of the scheduling variables sched_k for k on the path the token must take from j to i.

A appropriate f can be defined in the form of a polynomial in N, whose coefficients depend upon the program variables token_i, $\mathsf{request}_i$, and sched_i.

Having defined f, we must prove:

$$\mathsf{Ring} \models \Box((\mathsf{waiting}_i \wedge \Box\neg\mathsf{critical}_i) \supset \Box\neg f\uparrow)$$

$$\mathsf{Ring} \models \Box((\mathsf{waiting}_i \wedge \Box\neg\mathsf{critical}_i) \leadsto \Box\Diamond f\downarrow)$$

The first condition can be proved by a case analysis on all the kinds of steps that the program Ring might take. The second condition can be proved by showing that it is invariantly the case that there is an enabled process whose steps must decrease the variant function (for example, a node that has the token and whose next step must pass it along the ring closer to node i), and therefore by the fair scheduling assumption must eventually execute.

Although it seems intuitively clear that such a proof can in principle be carried out, the problem of doing so in a sufficiently rigorous, perhaps machine-checkable fashion seems formidable.

7 Conclusion

We have examined a technique by which rely/guarantee statements of the form $P \models R \supset G$ can be inferred from a finite collection of rely/guarantee statements of the form $\{P \models R_i \supset G_i : i \in I\}$. The technique involves the discovery of a collection $RG = \{RG_{i,j} : i \in I \cup \{\text{ext}\}\}$ of specifications that "cut" the interdependence between the rely-conditions R_i and R, and the guarantee-conditions G_i and G, in a fashion analogous to the way in which a loop invariant cuts the dependence of one iteration on the preceding and succeeding iterations. An "acyclicity" condition must also be proved, to ensure that there are no computations of P for which the interdependence between the rely and guarantee conditions is degenerate. The utility of the proof technique was illustrated by two examples, in which the technique was used to infer "global" liveness properties of a system of concurrent processes from "local" liveness properties of the individual processes. We expect the inference of global properties from local ones to be the typical way in which the technique will be useful in practice. An interesting feature of the proof technique is the way in which it can be applied, with equal facility, to both ring-structured and tree-structured communication patterns.

In the examples presented in this paper, judicious selection of the local rely and guarantee conditions R_i and G_i, resulted in tautological, or nearly tautological "cut set" conditions, leaving most of the interesting content of the proof to be captured in the "acyclicity" part. This phenomenon suggests that the rely/guarantee proof technique might be valuable as a decomposition principle to be used during top-down design. This decomposition principle can be codified as follows:

> To decompose a module M, which is to satisfy the specification $R \supset G$, into a system of submodules $\{M_i : i \in I\}$, and to determine the specifications $\{R_i \supset G_i : i \in I\}$ that the submodules must satisfy, one should:
>
> 1. By considering what each module M_i relies on and guarantees to the external environment and each other module M_j, determine a collection of specifications $RG_{i,j}$ that satisfies the acyclicity condition and cut set conditions (1) and (2).
> 2. Use cut set conditions (3) and (4) as *definitions* of the rely and guarantee conditions R_i and G_i for component module i. Since the conditions R_i and G_i should be expressed in terms of information local to module i, this step can actually be used to help determine what variables need to be accessible to module i.
> 3. Verify that the resulting component module specifications $R_i \supset G_i$ are reasonable, in the sense of being "consistent" or "implementable." For example, $R_i \supset G_i$ should not be logically equivalent to false. Consistency can be checked either by completing the top-down decomposition to the level of primitive modules, or by performing checks at the abstract level [Sta84].

In general, the discovery of a cut set RG for a program will require the use of intuition about why the program works correctly. Since discovery of a collection of loop invariants in the Floyd/Hoare approach to sequential program correctness can be viewed as a special case of the problem of finding a cut set, it will be at least as difficult in general to discover cut sets as it is to discover loop invariants. We therefore consider it unlikely that the proof technique presented here can be fully automated. However, once a human verifier has discovered an appropriate cut set for a program, along with necessary global invariants, it seems quite possible that the checking of the cut set and acyclicity conditions is a task that is within the capability of an automated verification system.

Acknowledgement

The author wishes to thank Professor Nancy Lynch for her support and guidance during his thesis research. Gail Buckley, Jieh Hsiang, and Scott Smolka made helpful comments on drafts of this paper.

Bibliography

[BK83] H. Barringer, R. Kuiper, "A Temporal Logic Specification Method Supporting Hierarchical Development," Manuscript, University of Manchester Department of Computer Science, November, 1983.

[BKP84] H. Barringer, R. Kuiper, A. Pnueli, "Now You May Compose Temporal Logic Specifications," *Sixteenth ACM Symposium on Theory of Computing*, 1984.

[Dij76] E. W. Dijkstra, *A Discipline of Programming*, Prentice Hall, 1976.

[FLG83] M. J. Fischer, N. D. Griffeth, L. J. Guibas, N. A. Lynch, "Probabilistic Analysis of a Network Resource Allocation Algorithm," to appear in *Information and Control.*

[Flo67] R. W. Floyd, "Assigning Meanings to Programs," in *Mathematical Aspects of Computer Science*, American Math. Soc., 1967.

[HO80] B. T. Hailpern, S. S. Owicki, "Verifying Network Protocols Using Temporal Logic," Technical Report No. 192, Computer Systems Laboratory, Stanford University, June, 1980.

[Hoa69] C. A. R. Hoare, "An Axiomatic Basis for Computer Programming," *Comm. ACM*, Vol. 21, October, 1969.

[Jon81] C. B. Jones, "Development Methods for Computer Programs Including a Notion of Interference," Wolfson College, June, 1981.

[Jon83] C. B. Jones, "Specification and Design of (Parallel) Programs," *IFIP Conference*, 1983.

[Lam80] L. Lamport, "'Sometime' is Sometimes 'Not Never'," *Seventh ACM Conference on Principles of Programming Languages*, 1980.

[Lam83] L. Lamport, "Specifying Concurrent Program Modules," *ACM Transactions on Programming Languages and Systems*, 5, 2 (April, 1983), 190-222.

[Lis79] B. H. Liskov, "Modular Program Construction Using Abstractions," MIT Computation Structures Group Memo 184, September, 1979.

[MP83] Z. Manna, A. Pnueli, "Verification of Concurrent Programs: A Temporal Proof System," Stanford University Report No. STAN-CS-83-967, June, 1983.

[MC81] J. Misra, K. M. Chandy, "Proofs of Networks of Processes," *IEEE Trans. on Software Eng.*, SE-7, 4, (July, 1981).

[MCS82] J. Misra, K. M. Chandy, T. Smith, "Proving Safety and Liveness of Communicating Processes with Examples," *ACM Conf. on Principles of Distributed Computing*, 1982.

[OG76] S. S. Owicki, D. Gries, "Verifying Properties of Parallel Programs: An Axiomatic Approach," *Comm. ACM* 15, 5 (1976).

[OL82] S. S. Owicki, L. Lamport, "Proving Liveness Properties of Concurrent Programs," *ACM Transactions on Programming Languages and Systems*, 4, 3 (July 1982), 455-495.

[Pnu77] A. Pnueli, "The Temporal Logic of Programs," *IEEE Symposium on Foundations of Computer Science*, 1977.

[SM81] R. L. Schwartz, P. M. Melliar-Smith, "Temporal Logic Specification of Distributed Systems," *Second International Conference on Distributed Systems*, INRIA, France, April, 1981.

[Sta84] E. W. Stark, "Foundations of a Theory of Specification for Distributed Systems," M.I.T. Laboratory for Computer Science MIT/LCS/TR-342, August, 1984.

[Wir71] N. Wirth, "Program Development by Stepwise Refinement," *Comm. ACM* 14, 4 (April, 1971), 221-227.

A Complete Proof System for SCCS with Modal Assertions

Extended Abstract

by

Glynn Winskel

University of Cambridge,
Computer Laboratory,
Corn Exchange Street,
Cambridge CB2 3QG.

Introduction.

This paper presents a proof system for Robin Milner's *Synchronous Calculus of Communicating Systems* (SCCS) with modal assertions. The language of assertions is a fragment of dynamic logic, sometimes called *Hennessy–Milner logic* after they brought it to attention; while rather weak from a practical point of view, its assertions are expressive enough to characterise observation equivalence, central to the work of Milner *et al* on CCS and SCCS. The paper includes a completeness result and a proof of equivalence between an operational and denotational semantics for SCCS. Its emphasis is on the theoretical issues involved in the construction of proof systems for parallel programming languages.

The style of the proof system has been motivated by ideas from denotational semantics. The idea is to model an SCCS process as the set of assertions it satisfies in the modal language. The labelled transition systems of Milner still play a role in determining the logical relationship that exists between the modal assertions. This done, one obtains an *information system* and so a *domain*, in the sense of Dana Scott [S]. But more, the constructs in SCCS induce operations on the information system making it into an algebra. In the framework of information systems these operations are relations of entailment, and presenting proof rules is seen as specifying how to generate these relations effectively. A novelty of the proof system is the way it uses a syntax which mixes assertions from the modal language in with the syntax for SCCS, a perfectly natural thing to do given the way the domain is built–up from assertions. For example, it makes sense to take the parallel composition of two assertions because assertions correspond to finite elements of the domain on which an operation of parallel composition is defined. Recently there has been a great deal of interest in the problem of how to compose modal assertions, in order to deduce the truth of an assertion for a composition of processes from the truth of certain assertions for its components *e.g.* [BKP], [St1,2] and this paper works out those ideas in detail for SCCS with this brand of modal assertions.

This recasts the semantics of SCCS in the traditional framework of Scott–Strachey denotational semantics where one sees, for example, the translation between different semantics for Milner's *bisimulation equivalence* and Hoare's *failure-set equivalence* expressed as an *embedding–projection* pair between domains.

1. The language SCCS.

Assume a set of process variables $x \in \mathrm{Var}$. Assume a set of elementary actions $\alpha \in Act$ forming a *finite* Abelian monoid $(Act, \bullet, 1)$ with *composition* $\bullet$, and *identity* 1. Define $\alpha/\beta = \{\gamma \mid \beta \bullet \gamma = \alpha\}$, the set of β–divisors of α.

The language of SCCS consists of the following terms

$$p ::= \mathbf{O} \mid x \mid \alpha p \mid p + p \mid p \otimes p \mid p\lceil \Lambda \mid rec x.p \mid rec^n x.p \mid \Omega$$

where $x \in$ Var, $\alpha \in Act$, Λ is a subset of Act containing 1 and n is a positive integer.

For convenience we have extended SCCS to include numbered terms of the form $rec^n x.p$ and the completely undefined term Ω. Intuitively the label on such a term bounds the number of calls to the recursive definition. This will be useful later when we come to give proofs involving induction on this number. As a useful convention we shall regard $rec^0 x.p$ as being Ω, and sometimes use $rec^\infty x.p$ to mean $rec x.p$.

We say a recursive definition $rec x.p$ is *well-guarded* when p has the form αq for some term q and action $\alpha \in Act$. However we shall not assume that recursive definitions are well-guarded in general.

Write $\mathbf{P}$ for the set of SCCS terms, and $\mathbf{P}_C$ for the set *closed* of SCCS terms which we shall call *processes*. We call a numbered term a SCCS term in which *all* occurrences of *rec* are labelled by numbers, and write the set of numbered terms as $\mathbf{P}_N$ and the set of closed numbered terms as $\mathbf{P}_{CN}$.

We explain informally the behaviour of the constructs in the language SCCS. The $\mathbf{O}$ term represents the *nil* process which has stopped and refuses to perform any action. The behaviour of Ω will be the same as that of $rec x.x$ which is busily doing nothing of interest. A *guarded* process αp first performs the action α to become the process p. A *sum* $p + q$ behaves like p or q. Which branch of a sum is followed will often be determined by the context and what actions the process is restricted to; only in the case when both component processes p and q are able to perform an identity action 1 can the process $p + q$ always choose autonomously, no matter what the context, to behave like p or q. A *product* process $p \otimes q$ behaves like p and q set in parallel but in such a way that they perform their actions synchronously, in "lock-step", together performing the $\bullet$-product of their respective actions. (To avoid confusion later, we have chosen a notation different from Milner's, using $\otimes$ instead of $\times$.) The *restriction* $p\lceil\Lambda$ behaves like the process p but with its actions restricted to lie in the set Λ. Restriction is a surprisingly powerful construction; it determines what kind of communications are allowed between processes, and without it two processes in parallel would behave in a manner completely independent of eachother. We present the formal definition of behaviour in the next section.

Write FV(p) for the set of free variables of a term p.

A *substitution* is a map σ : Var $\rightarrow \mathbf{P}$ assigning SCCS terms to variables. Given an SCCS term p and a substitution σ the term $p[\sigma]$ is the result of substituting $\sigma[\![x]\!]$ for each free occurrence of x in p—we assume changes are made in the naming of bound variables to avoid the binding of free variables in the substituted terms. We use $[p_0/x_1, \cdots, p_m/x_m, \cdots]$ as an abbreviation for the substitution which replaces free occurrences of the variables x_m by the terms p_m while leaving the other free variables the same.

Let p be a term. A *valuation* is a substitution ϑ : Var $\rightarrow \mathbf{P}_C$ which assigns a *closed* SCCS term to each variable. So, of course, $p[\vartheta]$ is a closed SCCS term.

2. The behaviour of SCCS.

Following Milner [M1,2,3], the behaviour of a process is represented as a labelled transition system. Its states are processes and so the transition system can be given in a syntax-directed way by defining inductively those transitions which are possible from each process term.

2.1 Definition.

Define the labelled transition relations $\xrightarrow{\alpha}$, for $\alpha \in Act$, between closed SCCS terms to be the least relation closed under the following rules:

$$\alpha p \xrightarrow{\alpha} p$$

$$\frac{p \xrightarrow{\alpha} p'}{p+q \xrightarrow{\alpha} p'} \qquad \frac{q \xrightarrow{\alpha} q'}{p+q \xrightarrow{\alpha} q'}$$

$$\frac{p \xrightarrow{\alpha} p' \quad q \xrightarrow{\beta} q'}{p \otimes q \xrightarrow{\alpha \bullet \beta} p' \otimes q'}$$

$$\frac{p \xrightarrow{\lambda} q}{p\lceil \Lambda \xrightarrow{\lambda} q\lceil \Lambda} \quad \text{if } \lambda \in \Lambda$$

$$\frac{p[recx.p/x] \xrightarrow{\alpha} q}{recx.p \xrightarrow{\alpha} q} \qquad \frac{p[rec^n x.p/x] \xrightarrow{\alpha} q}{rec^{n+1} x.p \xrightarrow{\alpha} q}$$

Notice there are no rules for $\mathbf{O}$ or Ω because we do not wish there to be any transitions from such terms. Because the relations $\xrightarrow{\alpha}$, $\alpha \in Act$, are defined to be the least relations given by the rules it follows that *e.g.*

$$p \otimes q \xrightarrow{\alpha} r \Leftrightarrow \exists p', q', \beta, \gamma.\ \beta \bullet \gamma = \alpha \ \ \& \ \ r = p' \otimes q' \ \ \& \ \ p \xrightarrow{\beta} p' \ \ \& \ \ q \xrightarrow{\gamma} q' \quad \text{and}$$
$$recx.p \xrightarrow{\alpha} r \Leftrightarrow p[recx.p/x] \xrightarrow{\alpha} r.$$

A process *diverges* if it can be forever busy performing internal events. In the case of SCCS this can only arise through a process unwinding its recursive definition continually. A diverging process has an unsettled status. In the absence of communication with the environment, it never settles down into a stable state, or settles on the full set of actions it is prepared to do. Viewed behaviourally, from the outside so to speak, it continues to "click and whir" and it never becomes clear whether an action refused now will necessarily be refused later. Mathematically it is the complementary notion of *convergence* which has the more basic definition, by induction.

2.2 Definition. Define the predicates $\downarrow$ on $\mathbf{P}_C$ to be the least predicate such that

$$\mathbf{O}\downarrow, \quad \alpha p\downarrow,$$
$$p\downarrow \ \& \ q\downarrow \Rightarrow (p+q)\downarrow,$$
$$p\downarrow \ \& \ q\downarrow \Rightarrow (p\otimes q)\downarrow,$$
$$p\downarrow \Rightarrow (p\lceil \Lambda)\downarrow,$$
$$(p[recx.p/x])\downarrow \Rightarrow (recx.p)\downarrow,$$
$$(p[rec^l x.p/x])\downarrow \Rightarrow (rec^{l+1} x.p)\downarrow.$$

where p and q are closed SCCS terms and l is an non-negative integer.

Say a closed SCCS term p is *convergent* iff $p\downarrow$.

Say a closed term p *diverges*, and write $p\uparrow$, when p does not converge.

Intuitively a divergent term is one whose transitions are not completely specified by a finite stage in the recursion. If all recursions were assumed to be well-guarded then all closed terms but Ω would be convergent. Note $\alpha\Omega$ converges and so does $recx.1x$.

Thus an SCCS process p determines a labelled transition system, $(S, p, \{\xrightarrow{\alpha}\}_{\alpha \in Act}, \uparrow)$, with states S those processes reachable from the initial state p, and in which some states are distinguished as being divergent. For example, the process

$$p = recx.\alpha(\beta x + \gamma\Omega)$$

describes the transition system:

$$\text{initial state} \rightarrow p \downarrow \xrightarrow{\alpha} (\beta p + \gamma \Omega) \downarrow \xrightarrow{\gamma} \Omega \uparrow$$

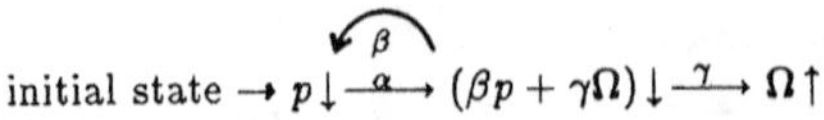

In fact, it is not hard to see that any finite labelled transition system like this, with labels from the set *Act* and some states distinguished as divergent, can be described by an SCCS process. For example, the transition system

$$\text{initial state} \rightarrow x \downarrow$$

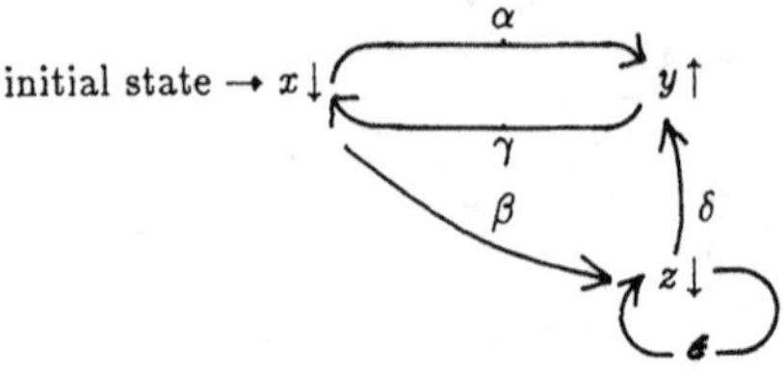

is described by the process

$$rec x. \ (\alpha\, rec y. \ [\Omega + \gamma x] + \beta\, rec z. \ [\delta\, rec y. \ [\Omega + \gamma x] + \epsilon z]),$$

obtained by successively eliminating variables in favour of the recursive definitions they satisfy, making states divergent by summing them with Ω. (We have taken the liberty of using state names as variables). More generally, along these lines one can show:

2.3 Lemma. *Any finite transition system, $(S, p, \{\xrightarrow{\alpha}\}_{\alpha \in Act}, \uparrow)$, can be described by an SCCS process* p.

The number attached to occurrences of *rec* specifies how many times the recursive definition can be unwound when determining the transition system associated with a term. Roughly, the larger the numbers the larger the transition system associated with the term. There corresponds an approximation order between terms which we write as $\leq$.

2.4 Definition. Define $\leq$ to be the least binary relation on $\mathbf{P}_C$ such that

$$\Omega \leq p, \qquad p \leq p$$
$$p \leq q \Rightarrow \alpha p \leq \alpha q$$
$$p \leq p' \ \& \ q \leq q' \Rightarrow p + q \leq p' + q'$$
$$p \leq p' \ \& \ q \leq q' \Rightarrow p \otimes q \leq p' \otimes q'$$
$$p \leq q \Rightarrow p\lceil \Lambda \leq q\lceil \Lambda$$
$$p \leq q \ \& \ m \leq n \Rightarrow rec^m x.p \ \leq \ rec^n x.q$$
$$p \leq q \Rightarrow rec^n x.p \ \leq \ rec x.q.$$

The order $\leq$ on terms $\mathbf{P}_C$ respects the language of SCCS, as expressed in the following lemma.

2.5 Lemma. *Let ϑ and ϑ' be valuations in the relation $\vartheta \leq \vartheta' \Leftrightarrow_{def} \forall x \in Var. \ \vartheta[\![x]\!] \leq \vartheta'[\![x]\!]$. Let p, q be terms in the relation $p \leq q$. Then $p[\vartheta] \leq q[\vartheta']$.*

Proof. By structural induction. ∎

3. The assertion language.

Hennessy and Milner defined an equivalence relation between processes called *observational equivalence* in [HM, M1]. For our language of SCCS, two processes are observationally equivalent iff whenever one can do an action to become a process then so can the other do the same action to become an equivalent process. They found an alternative characterisation so that processes were observationally equivalent iff they satisfied the same assertions in a simple language of modal assertions [HM]. However there are inadequacies in this treatment of processes because it does not take proper account of divergence. So Milner, in [M2], generalised the definition of observational equivalence and the definition of a process satisfying a modal assertion in order to cope with divergence. (See [HP] for a closely related but different extension of observational equivalence to diverging processes.) In this way Milner extended the result he had obtained with Hennessy, so that in SCCS, for example, two processes are observationally equivalent iff they satisfy the same assertions in the modal language of Hennessy and Milner. In future, in this paper, "observational equivalence" shall refer to the more refined equivalence of [M2]. Following [P, St1,2] we have simplified the modal language of Hennessy and Milner a little.

3.1 Definition.

The *assertion language* consists of simple modal expressions built up according to:

$$A ::= true \mid false \mid \bigwedge_{i\in I} A_i \mid \bigvee_{i\in I} A_i \mid \langle\alpha\rangle A \mid [\alpha]A$$

where I is a finite indexing set and $\alpha \in Act$.

We shall call elements of this language *assertions*, and write the set of assertions as **Assn**.

By convention we understand $\bigwedge_{i\in I} A_i$ to be *true* and $\bigvee_{i\in I} A_i$ to be *false* when the indexing set I is null. When the indexing set is $I = \{0,1\}$ we can write $\bigwedge_{i\in I} A_i$ as $A_0 \wedge A_1$, and $\bigvee_{i\in I} A_i$ as $A_0 \vee A_1$.

The meaning of an assertions is given by specifying the subset $\Pi[\![A]\!]$ of SCCS processes $\mathbf{P}_C$ which satisfy A:

3.2 Definition. Define

$$\begin{aligned}
\Pi[\![true]\!] &= \mathbf{P}_C\\
\Pi[\![false]\!] &= \emptyset\\
\Pi[\![\bigwedge_{i\in I} A_i]\!] &= \bigcap_{i\in I} \Pi[\![A_i]\!]\\
\Pi[\![\bigvee_{i\in I} A_i]\!] &= \bigcup_{i\in I} \Pi[\![A_i]\!]\\
\Pi[\![\langle\alpha\rangle A]\!] &= \{p \in \mathbf{P}_C \mid \exists q.p \xrightarrow{\alpha} q \ \&\ q \in \Pi[\![A]\!]\}\\
\Pi[\![[\alpha]A]\!] &= \{p \in \mathbf{P}_C \mid p\downarrow \ \&\ \forall q.p \xrightarrow{\alpha} q \Rightarrow q \in \Pi[\![A]\!]\}
\end{aligned}$$

Write $p \models A \Leftrightarrow_{def} p \in \Pi[\![A]\!]$, where p is a SCCS process and A is an assertion, and say *p satisfies A*.

Remark. Let $T = (S, p, \{\xrightarrow{\alpha}\}_{\alpha\in Act}, \uparrow)$ be a transition system as described in section 1. It is obvious how to define a satisfaction relation $T \models A$, between transition system T and modal assertions A, in such a way that a process satisfies an assertion iff its associated transition system does.

Clearly $p \models \langle\alpha\rangle A$ means the process p can do an α–action to become a process satisfying A, and $p \models [\alpha]false$ means the process p refuses to do an α–action. The latter kind of properties are important for detecting deadlock. Notice that $\Omega \not\models [\alpha]true$ and $\Omega \not\models [\alpha]false$ because we insist diverging processes, like Ω, cannot satisfy any assertion of the form $[\alpha]A$.

3.3 Proposition. *Let $p \in \mathbf{P}_C$. Then $p\downarrow \Leftrightarrow p \models [\alpha]true$, for any action α.*

Because we insist that a process satisfying a modal assertion $[\alpha]A$ must converge, satisfaction will be effective; if a process p in $\mathbf{P}_C$ satisfies an assertion A then it can be approximated by a numbered version p' which also satisfies the assertion. To show this we must first see how the transition system associated with a term $p' \leq p$ approximates, and simulates, the transition system associated with p.

3.4 Lemma. *For SCCS processes*

(i) For $p, p', q' \in \mathbf{P}_C$
$$p' \xrightarrow{\alpha} q' \ \& \ p' \leq p \Rightarrow \exists q.\ q' \leq q \ \& \ p \xrightarrow{\alpha} q.$$

(ii) For $p, q \in \mathbf{P}_C, q_0 \in \mathbf{P}_{CN}$
$$p \xrightarrow{\alpha} q \ \& \ q_0 \leq q \Rightarrow \exists p', q' \in \mathbf{P}_{CN}.\ p' \leq p \ \& \ p' \xrightarrow{\alpha} q' \ \& \ q_0 \leq q'.$$

(iii) For $p, p' \in \mathbf{P}_C$
$$p'\downarrow \ \& \ p' \leq p \Rightarrow p\downarrow \ \& \ (\forall q.\ p \xrightarrow{\alpha} q \Rightarrow \exists q' \leq q.\ p' \xrightarrow{\alpha} q').$$

(iv) For $p \in \mathbf{P}_C, Y \subseteq \mathbf{P}_{CN}$
$$\begin{aligned} & p\downarrow \ \& \ (\forall q.\ p \xrightarrow{\alpha} q \Rightarrow \exists q_0 \in Y.\ q_0 \leq q) \\ \Rightarrow & \ \exists p' \in \mathbf{P}_{CN}.\ p' \leq p \ \& \\ & p'\downarrow \ \& \ (\forall q.\ p' \xrightarrow{\alpha} q \Rightarrow \exists q_0 \in Y.\ q_0 \leq q). \end{aligned}$$

Proof. The proofs follow by induction on the inductive definitions of $\{\xrightarrow{\alpha}\}_{\alpha \in Act}$ and $\downarrow$. ∎

Note that part (iv) above specialises to the result

$$p\downarrow \Rightarrow \exists p' \in \mathbf{P}_{CN}.\ p' \leq p \ \& \ p'\downarrow$$

when we take $Y = \{\Omega\}$. Using parts (i) and (ii) for the modalities $\langle\alpha\rangle$ and (iii) and (iv) for the modality $[\alpha]$ one can prove:

3.5 Theorem. *Let* $p \in \mathbf{P}_C$. *Then*

$$p \models A \Leftrightarrow \exists p' \in \mathbf{P}_{CN}.\ p' \leq p \ \& \ p' \models A.$$

We can see the results above in topological terms. There is a natural topology on processes which is the Scott-topology.

3.6 Proposition. *The family of sets of the form* $\{p \in \mathbf{P}_C \mid q \leq p\}$ *for* q *a closed numbered term are the basis of a topology on* $\mathbf{P}_C$. *So the open sets have the form*

$$U = \{p \in \mathbf{P}_C \mid \exists p_0 \in X.\ p_0 \leq p\}$$

for a subset X *of closed numbered terms.*

The open sets of $\mathbf{P}_C$ *are those subsets* $U \subseteq \mathbf{P}_C$ *which are*

(i) $\forall p, q.\ p \geq q \in U \Rightarrow p \in U$,
(ii) $\forall$ *directed* $S \subseteq \mathbf{P}_C.\ \bigsqcup S \in U \Rightarrow \exists p \in S.\ p \in U$.

Then theorem 3.5 says each assertion determines an open set of $\mathbf{P}_C$ *i.e.* $\Pi[\![A]\!]$ is open for each assertion A. In fact 3.5 can be generalised, important were we to extend our present language of assertions.

3.7 Theorem. *Let $\alpha \in Act$. If U is an open set in the topology on processes then so are the sets*

$$\langle\alpha\rangle U =_{def} \{p \in \mathbf{P}_C \mid \exists q \in U.\, q \xrightarrow{\alpha} p\} \quad \text{and}$$
$$[\alpha]U =_{def} \{p \in \mathbf{P}_C \mid \ p\downarrow \ \& \ \forall q.\, p \xrightarrow{\alpha} q \Rightarrow q \in U\}.$$

This topological view is in line with Dana Scott's development of the theory of domains from neighbourhood systems [S1] and with the ideas of Mike Smyth in [Sm], where it is proposed that computational properties of a topological space be identified with effective open sets. In the approach to domains using neighbourhood systems, to know more information about a process is to know a smaller neighbourhood in which it is contained. These topological ideas have been applied by Gordon Plotkin in [P] to extend the language of assertions and its interpretation to cover intuitionistic negation and implication; their interpretation are those standard for topological models of intuitionistic logic, so in this extension of **Assn** one takes $\Pi[\![A \supset B]\!] = ((\mathbf{P}_C \setminus \Pi[\![A]\!]) \cup \Pi[\![B]\!])^o$ where X^o is the topological interior of the set X (Plotkin's topology is not that here however). One advantage of intuitionistic logic over classical logic is that satisfaction is still effective even for this extended set of assertions. We shall say more on denotational semantics in section 5.

4. The decomposition of assertions.

We are interested in how the goal of proving an assertion holds of a process reduces to the subgoals of proving assertions about its subprocesses, and in the converse problem, of how assertions about subprocesses combine to yield assertions about the compound process. It is clear for example that an assertion $\langle\alpha\rangle A$ holds of a process αp iff A holds of p. Similarly $[\alpha]A$ holds of a process $p + q$ iff $[\alpha]A$ holds of both components p and q. However $p + q \models \langle\alpha\rangle A$ iff $p \models \langle\alpha\rangle A$ or $q \models \langle\alpha\rangle A$; there is not a unique subgoal. Similarly there are many possible ways in which $p \otimes q \models \langle\alpha\rangle \mathit{true}$; this holds whenever $p \models \langle\beta\rangle \mathit{true}$ and $q \models \langle\gamma\rangle \mathit{true}$ with $\beta \bullet \gamma = \alpha$.

For each unary operation *op* of SCCS we show how for an assertion A there is an assertion $\mathcal{D}_{op}[\![A]\!]$ so that

$$op\,(p) \models A \Leftrightarrow p \models \mathcal{D}_{op}[\![A]\!].$$

For each binary operation *op* of SCCS we show how for an assertion A there is a finite set of pairs of assertions $\mathcal{D}_{op}[\![A]\!]$ so that

$$p \ op \ q \models A \quad \text{iff} \quad \exists (B, C) \in \mathcal{D}_{op}[\![A]\!].\ p \models B \ \ \& \ \ q \models C.$$

Thus we see how, with respect to each operation *op* in SCCS, every assertion has a *decomposition* which reduces the problem of proving the assertion holds of a compound process built-up using *op* to proving assertions about its components. These results provide the foundations of our proof system for SCCS with assertions **Assn**. All the proofs of this section are by structural induction.

The guarded–decomposition of assertions:

4.1 Definition. Let $\alpha \in Act$. Define the assertion $\mathcal{D}_\alpha[\![A]\!]$, for an assertion A, by the structural induction:

$$\mathcal{D}_\alpha[\![\mathit{true}]\!] = \mathit{true}$$
$$\mathcal{D}_\alpha[\![\mathit{false}]\!] = \mathit{false}$$
$$\mathcal{D}_\alpha[\![\bigwedge_{i \in I} A_i]\!] = \bigwedge_{i \in I} \mathcal{D}_\alpha[\![A_i]\!]$$

$$\mathcal{D}_\alpha[\![\bigvee_{i\in I} A_i]\!] = \bigvee_{i\in I} \mathcal{D}_\alpha[\![A_i]\!]$$

$$\mathcal{D}_\alpha[\![\langle\beta\rangle A]\!] = \begin{cases} A & \text{if } \beta = \alpha \\ \mathit{false} & \text{if } \beta \neq \alpha \end{cases}$$

$$\mathcal{D}_\alpha[\![[\beta]A]\!] = \begin{cases} A & \text{if } \beta = \alpha \\ \mathit{true} & \text{if } \beta \neq \alpha. \end{cases}$$

4.2 Theorem. *Let $\alpha \in Act$. Let A be an assertion.*

$$\forall p \in \mathbf{P}_C.\ \alpha p \models A \Leftrightarrow p \models \mathcal{D}_\alpha[\![A]\!].$$

The sum–decomposition of assertions:

4.3 Definition. Define $\mathcal{D}_+[\![A]\!]$ by structural induction on the assertion A:

$$\begin{aligned}
\mathcal{D}_+[\![\mathit{true}]\!] &= \{(\mathit{true}, \mathit{true})\} \\
\mathcal{D}_+[\![\mathit{false}]\!] &= \{(\mathit{true}, \mathit{false}), (\mathit{false}, \mathit{true})\} \\
\mathcal{D}_+[\![\bigwedge_{i\in I} A_i]\!] &= \{(\bigwedge_{i\in I} A_{i0}, \bigwedge_{i\in I} A_{i1}) \mid \forall i \in I.(A_{i0}, A_{i1}) \in \mathcal{D}_+[\![A_i]\!])\} \\
\mathcal{D}_+[\![\bigvee_{i\in I} A_i]\!] &= \bigcup_{i\in I} \mathcal{D}_+[\![A_i]\!] \\
\mathcal{D}_+[\![\langle\alpha\rangle A]\!] &= \{(\langle\alpha\rangle A, \mathit{true}), (\mathit{true}, \langle\alpha\rangle A)\} \\
\mathcal{D}_+[\![[\alpha]A]\!] &= \{([\alpha]A, [\alpha]A)\}.
\end{aligned}$$

4.4 Theorem. *For all p and q in $\mathbf{P}_C$*

$$p + q \models A \Leftrightarrow \exists (B, C) \in \mathcal{D}_+[\![A]\!].\ p \models B\ \&\ q \models C.$$

The parallel–decomposition of assertions:

The problem of decomposition for $\otimes$ is a little more difficult.

4.5 Definition. Define $\mathcal{D}_\otimes[\![A]\!]$ by structural induction on the assertion A:

$$\begin{aligned}
\mathcal{D}_\otimes[\![\mathit{true}]\!] &= \{(\mathit{true}, \mathit{true})\} \\
\mathcal{D}_\otimes[\![\mathit{false}]\!] &= \{(\mathit{true}, \mathit{false}), (\mathit{false}, \mathit{true})\} \\
\mathcal{D}_\otimes[\![\bigwedge_{i\in I} A_i]\!] &= \{(\bigwedge_{i\in I} A_{i0}, \bigwedge_{i\in I} A_{i1}) \mid \forall i \in I.(A_{i0}, A_{i1}) \in \mathcal{D}_\otimes[\![A_i]\!])\} \\
\mathcal{D}_\otimes[\![\bigvee_{i\in I} A_i]\!] &= \bigcup_{i\in I} \mathcal{D}_\otimes[\![A_i]\!] \\
\mathcal{D}_\otimes[\![\langle\alpha\rangle A]\!] &= \{(\langle\beta\rangle B, \langle\gamma\rangle C) \mid \beta \bullet \gamma = \alpha\ \&\ (B, C) \in \mathcal{D}_\otimes[\![A]\!]\} \\
\mathcal{D}_\otimes[\![[\alpha]A]\!] &= \quad \text{the set of pairs}
\end{aligned}$$

$$\Big(\bigwedge_{\beta\in Act} [\beta] \bigvee_{i\in I_\beta} \bigwedge_{\gamma\in\alpha/\beta} \bigwedge_{j\in J_\gamma} B_{ij}^{\beta\gamma},\quad \bigwedge_{\gamma\in Act} [\gamma] \bigvee_{j\in J_\gamma} \bigwedge_{\beta\in\alpha/\gamma} \bigwedge_{i\in I_\beta} C_{ij}^{\beta\gamma}\Big)$$

such that

$$\beta \bullet \gamma = \alpha \Rightarrow (B_{ij}^{\beta\gamma}, C_{ij}^{\beta\gamma}) \in \mathcal{D}_{\otimes}[\![A]\!].$$

4.6 Theorem. *For all p and q in $\mathbf{P}_C$*

$$p \otimes q \models A \Leftrightarrow \exists (B, C) \in \mathcal{D}_{\otimes}[\![A]\!].\ p \models B \ \& \ q \models C.$$

The restriction–decomposition of assertions:

We can associate with any assertion A an *assertion* $\mathcal{D}_{\lceil \Lambda}[\![A]\!]$ so that A is satisfied by $p\lceil \Lambda$ iff $\mathcal{D}_{\lceil \Lambda}[\![A]\!]$ is satisfied by p.

4.7 Definition. Let Λ be a subset of *Act* containing 1. Define $\mathcal{D}_{\lceil \Lambda}[\![A]\!]$, for an assertion A, by the structural induction:

$$\mathcal{D}_{\lceil \Lambda}[\![\mathit{true}]\!] = \mathit{true}$$
$$\mathcal{D}_{\lceil \Lambda}[\![\mathit{false}]\!] = \mathit{false}$$
$$\mathcal{D}_{\lceil \Lambda}[\![\bigwedge_{i \in I} A_i]\!] = \bigwedge_{i \in I} \mathcal{D}_{\lceil \Lambda}[\![A_i]\!]$$
$$\mathcal{D}_{\lceil \Lambda}[\![\bigvee_{i \in I} A_i]\!] = \bigvee_{i \in I} \mathcal{D}_{\lceil \Lambda}[\![A_i]\!]$$
$$\mathcal{D}_{\lceil \Lambda}[\![\langle\alpha\rangle A]\!] = \begin{cases} \langle\alpha\rangle \mathcal{D}_{\lceil \Lambda}[\![A]\!] & \text{if } \alpha \in \Lambda \\ \mathit{false} & \text{if } \alpha \notin \Lambda \end{cases}$$
$$\mathcal{D}_{\lceil \Lambda}[\![[\alpha]A]\!] = \begin{cases} [\alpha]\mathcal{D}_{\lceil \Lambda}[\![A]\!] & \text{if } \alpha \in \Lambda \\ [\alpha]\mathit{true} & \text{if } \alpha \notin \Lambda. \end{cases}$$

One clause of the above definition may be puzzling. Why do we take $\mathcal{D}_{\lceil \Lambda}[\![[\alpha]A]\!] = [\alpha]\mathit{true}$ if $\alpha \notin \Lambda$ rather than taking it to be simply the assertion *true*? The answer: because of divergence. For example, because Ω diverges, $\Omega\lceil\Lambda \not\models [\alpha]A$ while $\Omega \models \mathit{true}$.

4.8 Theorem. *Let $p \in \mathbf{P}_C$ and A be an assertion. Then*

$$p\lceil\Lambda \models A \Leftrightarrow p \models \mathcal{D}_{\lceil \Lambda}[\![A]\!].$$

5. From a denotational point of view.

So far our presentation has been based on the operational semantics of SCCS processes. To summarise, we have modelled each SCCS process as a labelled transition system in which some nodes are distinguished as being convergent. Treating the transition system as a Kripke model we defined the satisfaction relation between processes in $\mathbf{P}_C$ and modal assertions **Assn**.

If the language of modal assertions captures all the nature of a process that is of interest to us then it is natural to regard two processes as equivalent iff they satisfy exactly the same assertions. We write

$$p \approx q \quad \text{iff} \quad \forall A \in \mathbf{Assn}.\ p \models A \Leftrightarrow q \models A$$

for closed SCCS terms p and q. Because we assume the set of actions *Act* is finite, it follows from Milner's result in [M2] that $\approx$ coincides with his extended notion of *observational equivalence* and that of *bisimulation equivalence* due to Park [M3, Pa], again extended to cope with divergence. In fact for the language SCCS this equivalence is a congruence too.

We can go further and take the more radical view that a process can be identified with the set of assertions it satisfies, so a process p is identified with the set

$$\mathcal{A}[\![p]\!] = \{A \in \mathbf{Assn} \mid p \models A\}.$$

This step takes us into the realm of denotational semantics, with its own approach and techniques.

To see this first notice the obvious relation of entailment between (open) sets of processes, thought of as *properties*. One property $U \subseteq \mathbf{P}_C$ entails another $V \subseteq \mathbf{P}_C$ iff $U \subseteq V$. Spelt out, $U \subseteq V$ simply says that every process which satisfies U also satisfies V. This induces an entailment relation between assertions.

5.1 Definition. Let $\gg$ be the binary relation between assertions given by:

$$A \gg B \Leftrightarrow_{def} \Pi[\![A]\!] \subseteq \Pi[\![B]\!].$$

Now as is well known from *e.g.* the work on *information systems* [S, LW], and the specific applications in *e.g.* [Gol], there is a *domain* associated with this entailment on modal assertions. Its elements, like $\mathcal{A}[\![p]\!]$, are sets of assertions which are consistent and closed under entailment. Ordered by inclusion these form a Scott domain of information in which more information corresponds to more assertions being true. For our purposes it is more natural to allow sets of assertions inconsistent assertions which entail *false*.

5.2 Definition. Define the partial order $\mathbf{D}$ to consist of the following elements ordered by inclusion. The *elements* of $\mathbf{D}$ are those subsets $a \subseteq \mathbf{Assn}$ which are $\gg$*-closed:*

$$\forall B \forall X \subseteq a.\ \bigwedge X \gg B \Rightarrow B \in a.$$

5.3 Proposition. *The set* $\mathbf{D}$ *ordered by inclusion forms an* ω*–algebraic complete lattice. Its finite elements are precisely those elements of the form* $\overline{A} =_{def} \{B \in \mathbf{Assn} \mid A \gg B\}$ *for some assertion* A*. The least element* $\perp$ *is* $\overline{true}$ *and the greatest element is* $\top = \overline{false}$*.*

Let p *be an SCCS process. The set* $\{A \mid p \models A\}$ *is an element of* $\mathbf{D}$*.*

Of course the method by which we have obtained the *denotation* $\mathcal{A}[\![p]\!] = \{A \in \mathbf{Assn} \mid p \models A\}$ of a process p is rather roundabout, in contrast to the usual direct way of giving denotational semantics. Generally in denotational semantics one reflects the constructs in the language as operations on a complete partial order and uses least fixed points to give a meaning to recursive definitions. To follow this more traditional route we must first define operations on the elements $\mathbf{D}$ to correspond to the syntactic operations of guarding, sum, product and restriction. The operations are determined by further relations of entailment between properties which we define first.

5.4 Definition. For U and V be open sets in the topology on processes, and $\alpha \in Act$ and $\Lambda \subseteq Act$ with $1 \in \Lambda$, define

$$\alpha U = \{\alpha p \mid p \in U\}$$
$$U + V = \{p + q \mid p \in U \ \& \ q \in V\}$$
$$U \otimes V = \{p \otimes q \mid p \in U \ \& \ q \in V\}$$
$$U \lceil \Lambda = \{p \lceil \Lambda \mid p \in U\}.$$

From the definition of $\leq$ and the topology on processes we see the above are indeed well-defined operations on open sets. In section 5 we have seen how the truth of an assertion in a compound process reduces to certain assertions holding of the component processes. For example $p \otimes q \models A$ iff $p \models B$ and $q \models C$ for some $(B, C) \in \mathcal{D}_{\otimes}[\![A]\!]$. Thus in particular if B is true of process p and C is true of process q then A is true of $p \otimes q$. Clearly this relation can be expressed as $\Pi[\![B]\!] \otimes \Pi[\![C]\!] \subseteq \Pi[\![A]\!]$, which we can write as $B \otimes C \gg A$. Following this style we define relations between assertions. (They correspond to *approximable mappings* on the information system of assertions. And then these induce continuous operations on the domain of elements **D**, making it into a continuous algebra.)

5.5 Definition. Let A, B, C range over **Assn**. Let $\alpha \in Act$ and let $\Lambda \subseteq Act$ be such that $1 \in \Lambda$.
(i)Define a unary relation on assertions by $\mathbf{O} \gg A \Leftrightarrow_{def} \mathbf{O} \models A$.
(ii)Define a binary relation on assertions by $\alpha B \gg A \Leftrightarrow_{def} \alpha\Pi[\![B]\!] \subseteq \Pi[\![A]\!]$.
(iii)Define a ternary relation on assertions by $B + C \gg A \Leftrightarrow_{def} \Pi[\![B]\!] + \Pi[\![C]\!] \subseteq \Pi[\![A]\!]$.
(iv)Define a ternary relation on assertions by $B \otimes C \gg A \Leftrightarrow_{def} \Pi[\![B]\!] \otimes \Pi[\![C]\!] \subseteq \Pi[\![A]\!]$.
(v)Define a binary relation on assertions by $B\lceil\Lambda \gg A \Leftrightarrow_{def} \Pi[\![B]\!]\lceil\Lambda \subseteq \Pi[\![A]\!]$.

The domain **D** consists of sets of assertions. Once we extend the relations to continuous operations on **D**, we can give a denotation to each term of **P** with respect to an environment in the standard way. However note that we have an added freedom. Not only do processes sit naturally in **D**, so too of course do assertions; any assertion A can be identified with the element $\overline{A} =_{def} \{B \mid A \gg B\}$. Consequently we can make sense in **D** of syntax like $A \otimes B$ where A and B are assertions, or even more free mixes of the assertion language and the programming language like, for example, $recx.\ (x \otimes \langle\alpha\rangle[\beta]true + \gamma true)$. Note in the latter example assertions only occur at the roots of the syntax tree. Here we shall not take the more liberal step of having a complete mix of program syntax and assertion language syntax. But this should not be taken to indicate any deep prejudice against such things, or as far as I can see any real difficulties—it's easy to extend the modal operators to elements of **D**, *e.g.* take $[\alpha]a = \{B \mid \exists A \in a.\ [\alpha]A \gg B\}$. The work of the next section only requires the following enrichment of SCCS by assertions **Assn**.

5.6 Definition. Define the language of SCCS *with assertions* by

$$p ::= A \mid \mathbf{O} \mid x \mid \alpha p \mid p + p \mid p \otimes p \mid p\lceil\Lambda \mid recx.p \mid rec^n x.p \mid \Omega$$

where $A \in$ **Assn**, and $x \in$ Var, $\alpha \in Act$, Λ is a subset of Act containing 1 and n is a positive integer.
Write **AP** for the language of SCCS with assertions.

5.7 Definition. *Denotational semantics of SCCS with assertions:*
Define an *environment* to be a function $\rho : \text{Var} \to \mathbf{D}$. Write $\rho[a/x]$, where ρ is an environment, $x \in$ Var and $a \in \mathbf{D}$, for the environment which results by replacing ρ's value on x by a.

Define $\mathcal{A}[\![p]\!]\rho$ for a term $p \in \mathbf{AP}$ and any environment ρ by the structural induction:

$$\begin{aligned}
&\mathcal{A}[\![A]\!]\rho = \{B \mid A \gg B\} \quad \text{where } A \in \mathbf{Assn}\\
&\mathcal{A}[\![\mathbf{O}]\!]\rho = \{A \mid \mathbf{O} \gg A\}\\
&\mathcal{A}[\![x]\!]\rho = \rho[\![x]\!]\\
&\mathcal{A}[\![\alpha p]\!]\rho = \{A \mid \exists B \in \mathcal{A}[\![p]\!]\rho.\ \alpha B \gg A\} \quad \text{where } \alpha \in Act\\
&\mathcal{A}[\![p+q]\!]\rho = \{A \mid \exists B \in \mathcal{A}[\![p]\!]\rho, C \in \mathcal{A}[\![q]\!]\rho.\ B + C \gg A\}\\
&\mathcal{A}[\![p \otimes q]\!]\rho = \{A \mid \exists B \in \mathcal{A}[\![p]\!]\rho, C \in \mathcal{A}[\![q]\!]\rho.\ B \otimes C \gg A\}\\
&\mathcal{A}[\![p\lceil\Lambda]\!]\rho = \{A \mid \exists B \in \mathcal{A}[\![p]\!]\rho.\ B\lceil\Lambda \gg A\} \quad \text{where } 1 \in \Lambda \subseteq Act\\
&\mathcal{A}[\![\Omega]\!]\rho = \bot\\
&\mathcal{A}[\![rec^n x.p]\!]\rho = \Gamma^n(\bot)\\
&\mathcal{A}[\![rec x.p]\!]\rho = \text{fix } \Gamma
\end{aligned}$$

where $\bot = \{A \mid true \gg A\}$ and $\Gamma : \mathbf{D} \to \mathbf{D}$ is given by $\Gamma(a) = \mathcal{A}[\![p]\!]\rho[a/x]$ and fix is the least fixed point operator fix $\Gamma = \bigcup_{i \in \omega} \Gamma^i(\bot)$.

Note how the numbered term $rec^n x.p$ is the syntactic counterpart of the nth iteration of the functional in the construction of the least fixed point of $a \mapsto \mathcal{A}[\![p]\!]\rho[a/x]$. Of course the above denotational semantics specialises to one for pure SCCS by just ignoring the clause for assertions.

5.8 Proposition. *(The denotational semantics is well-defined)*
We have $\mathcal{A}[\![p]\!]\rho \in \mathbf{D}$ for all $p \in \mathbf{P}$ and any environment ρ.
The function $\Gamma : \mathbf{D} \to \mathbf{D}$ in the above definition is continuous, so fix Γ is the least fixed point of Γ.

It becomes vital to check that the denotational semantics agrees with the operational semantics we have given earlier. The decomposition results of section 4 play a key role, as does theorem 3.5 saying a process satisfies an assertion iff there is some numbered term approximating it which satisfies it too.

5.9 Theorem. *Let ϑ be a valuation. Let $\hat{\vartheta}$ be the associated environment*

$$\hat{\vartheta}[\![x]\!] = \{A \mid \vartheta[\![x]\!] \models A\}.$$

Then for $p \in \mathbf{P}$,

$$\mathcal{A}[\![p]\!]\hat{\vartheta} = \{A \mid p[\vartheta] \models A\}.$$

In particular if p is a closed term then

$$\mathcal{A}[\![p]\!]\rho = \{A \mid p \models A\}$$

for an arbitrary environment ρ.

Proof. By structural induction on p, with an inner induction on n in the case where p has the form $rec^n x.q$, and by invoking 3.5 when p has the form $rec x.q$. ∎

The decomposition results of section 4 play a vital role in the above proof. They can be seen as ensuring the language of assertions meets an *expressiveness criterion*; that there are enough assertions so that any differences in those assertions satisfied by the composition of processes is detected as differences in the assertions satisfied by the components (a property whose failure for CCS led Stirling to introduce another modality which he wrote as ◯ [St2]).

Thus the denotational semantics is in perfect agreement with the work of the previous sections. Of course the entailment relation and operations on the information system of assertions have been derived from the satisfaction relation between processes and one would like an independent construction of them. But this is the job of a proof theory and is tackled in the next section.

We can generalise the satisfaction relation to elements of **AP** , assured it is consistent with our previous use.

5.10 Definition. Let $p \in \mathbf{AP}$. Let $A \in \mathbf{Assn}$. Define

$$p \models A \Leftrightarrow \forall \text{ environments } \rho.\ A \in \mathcal{A}[\![p]\!]\rho.$$

Of course one can take issue with the view that the assertions **Assn** capture all those basic properties of importance that can be noted about a process. The work of Milner et al, *e.g.* [M1,3], shows how much can be done with the observational and bisimulation equivalence induced by the assertions. This argues that the assertions are sufficiently rich to capture a great many of the properties of interest. This should not seem so surprising. Remember a process denotes the set of assertions it satisfies so is essentially modelled as an (infinite) conjunction of these assertions; only for a finite process could a single assertion in **Assn** capture its full behaviour.

Although the assertions may make it possible to distinguish all the processes one could wish, this is not to say the logic is as expressive as one would like from all points of view. Clearly it is rather primitive. For example one would like the ability to specify infinite behaviours by finite assertions.

Quite possibly there are other properties of interest to which the language of assertions is blind. However it is interesting that two other well-known notions of equivalence can be induced by taking fragments of the assertion language **Assn**. They are *trace equivalence* and *failure–set equivalence*. Strictly speaking the failure–set equivalence has not been defined on SCCS but the definition that follows has been based on the work of [HBR] modified to take proper account of divergence. The use of traces and their associated equivalence is widespread, see *e.g.* [H] and [HdeN]. As far as these two equivalences are concerned **Assn** is certainly expressive enough. It is a pleasing fact that the domains of assertions for these two equivalences are related to the domain **D** and to each other by the classical notion of embedding–projection pairs. This is because the embedding–projection pairs between domains are associated with restriction in their representation as information systems (see [LW]). We define the corresponding fragments of **Assn**. Define $\mathbf{Assn}_T$, *the trace assertions,* to consist of all those assertions of the form

$$\langle\alpha_0\rangle\langle\alpha_1\rangle\cdots\langle\alpha_{j-1}\rangle true.$$

Define $\mathbf{Assn}_{FS}$, *the failure–set assertions,* to consist of all those assertions of the form

$$\langle\alpha_0\rangle\langle\alpha_1\rangle\cdots\langle\alpha_{j-1}\rangle(\bigwedge_{\beta\in I}[\beta]false).$$

6. A proof system for SCCS with modal assertions.

In this section we take advantage of the observation we made in the last section that we can make perfectly good sense of terms which mix the syntax of assertions in with the syntax of the programming language. We use terms in **AP** to define a proof system.

First we define a proof system for the entailment relation $\gg$ between assertions. I am grateful to Colin Stirling for sending [St3] which showed me how to do the completeness proof for the assertion language, without SCCS operators.

6.1 Definition. In the following let $A, B, \cdots$ stand for assertions, and $X, Y, \cdots$ for a finite subset of assertions. Let $\vdash_A \subseteq$ Fin (**Assn**) $\times$ **Assn** be the least relation between finite sets of assertions and assertions closed under the following rules:

Structural rules:

refl. rule $\quad X \vdash_A A \quad$ if $A \in X$

tran. rule $\quad \dfrac{X \vdash_A \bigwedge Y \quad Y \vdash_A A}{X \vdash_A A}$

Logical rules:

true r. rule $\quad \vdash_A \mathit{true}$

false l. rule $\quad \mathit{false} \vdash_A A$

$\bigwedge r.$ rule $\quad \{A_i \mid i \in I\} \vdash_A \bigwedge_{i \in I} A_i$

$\bigwedge l.$ rule $\quad \bigwedge_{i \in I} A_i \vdash_A A_i$

$\bigvee r.$ rule $\quad A_i \vdash_A \bigvee_{i \in I} A_i$

$\bigvee l.$ rule $\quad \dfrac{\{X, A_i \vdash_A B \mid i \in I\}}{X, \bigvee_{i \in I} A_i \vdash_A B}$

Modal rules:

$$\frac{A \vdash_A B}{\langle\alpha\rangle A \vdash_A \langle\alpha\rangle B}$$

$$\langle\alpha\rangle \bigvee_{i \in I} A_i \vdash_A \bigvee_{i \in I} \langle\alpha\rangle A_i$$

$$\frac{A \vdash_A B}{[\alpha]A \vdash_A [\alpha]B}$$

$$\bigwedge_{i \in I} [\alpha]A_i \vdash_A [\alpha]\bigwedge_{i \in I} A_i \quad \text{where } I \neq \emptyset$$

$$\langle\alpha\rangle \mathit{false} \vdash_A \mathit{false}$$

$$[\alpha]A \wedge \langle\alpha\rangle B \vdash_A \langle\alpha\rangle(A \wedge B)$$

Convergence rules $[\alpha]true \vdash_A [\beta]true$

$[\alpha]true \vdash_A \langle\beta\rangle true \vee [\beta]false.$

The first convergence rule simply expresses the fact that a process converges iff it satisfies any assertion of the form $[\alpha]true$. The second convergence rule says that a convergent process either can perform an action α or refuses to perform an action α. The other rules are fairly intuitive. Note we must insist the indexing set I is nonempty in the rule expressing how conjunctions interact with $[\alpha]$ because $[\alpha]true$ is not always satisfied.

6.2 Theorem. *(Soundness and completeness)*

$$X \vdash_A A \Leftrightarrow \bigwedge X \geqslant A.$$

Proof. The proof of soundness is routine. The proof of completeness follows the following scheme: If $A \nvdash_A B$ then a labelled transition system $H = (S, s_0, \{\xrightarrow{\alpha}\}_{\alpha \in Act}, \uparrow)$ is built from the proof system, such that $H \models A$ and $H \not\models B$. The construction of this Henkin model is closely based on that of Stirling [St3]. Then the technique of filtration, using the set of subformulae of A and B together with $[\alpha]true$ (for the convergence structure), reduces this model to a finite transition system which satisfies A but does not satisfy B. By lemma 2.3 this can be described by an SCCS process p. Hence $p \models A$ and $p \not\models B$ so $A \not\models B$. Thus $A \models B \Rightarrow A \vdash B$, so completeness follows directly. ∎

Now we define the proof rules to generate a relation $p \vdash_{AP} A$, meaning $p \models A$, *i.e.* $A \in \mathcal{A}[\![p]\!]\rho$ for p a term in **AP**—and so a mix of SCCS and **Assn**—and A an assertion, and ρ an arbitrary environment.

6.3 Definition. In the following let $A, B, C, \cdots$ stand for assertions, X for a finite subset of assertions and p, q terms in **AP**. Define $\vdash_{AP}$ to be the least relation between elements of **AP** and assertions **Assn** given by the rules:

Structural rules:

$$\frac{A \vdash_A B}{A \vdash_{AP} B}$$

$$\frac{p \vdash_{AP} A, C[A] \vdash_{AP} B}{C[p] \vdash_{AP} B} \quad \text{where } C[\;] \text{ is any context in } \mathbf{AP}\,.$$

$$\frac{\{p \vdash_{AP} A \mid A \in X\}, X \vdash_A B}{p \vdash_{AP} B}$$

$$\frac{\{C[A] \vdash_{AP} B \mid A \in X\}}{C[\bigvee X] \vdash_{AP} B} \quad \text{where } C[\;] \text{ is any proper context in } \mathbf{AP}\,.$$

(Note because $\bigvee \emptyset = false$, this includes the rule *op* (*false*) $\vdash_{AP} A$ where *op* is any derived unary operator.)

Correctness rules:

O-$[\alpha]$ rule $\quad \mathbf{O} \vdash_{AP} [\alpha]A$

α–$\langle\alpha\rangle$ rule $\qquad \alpha A \vdash_{AP} \langle\alpha\rangle A$

α–$[\alpha]$ rule $\qquad \alpha A \vdash_{AP} [\alpha]A$

α–$[\beta]$ rule $\qquad \alpha A \vdash_{AP} [\beta]B \quad \text{if } \beta \neq \alpha$

$+$–$\langle\alpha\rangle$ rule $\qquad \langle\alpha\rangle A + B \vdash_{AP} \langle\alpha\rangle A \quad \text{and} \quad B + \langle\alpha\rangle A \vdash_{AP} \langle\alpha\rangle A$

$+$–$[\alpha]$ rule $\qquad [\alpha]A + [\alpha]A \vdash_{AP} [\alpha]A$

$\otimes$–$\langle\alpha\rangle$ rule $\qquad \dfrac{B \otimes C \vdash_{AP} A}{\langle\beta\rangle B \otimes \langle\gamma\rangle C \vdash_{AP} \langle\beta \bullet \gamma\rangle A}$

$\otimes$–$[\alpha]$ rule $\qquad \dfrac{\{B_\beta \otimes C_\gamma \vdash_{AP} A \mid \beta \bullet \gamma = \alpha\}}{(\bigwedge_\beta [\beta]B_\beta) \otimes (\bigwedge_\gamma [\gamma]C_\gamma) \vdash_{AP} [\alpha]A}$

$\lceil\Lambda$–$\langle\lambda\rangle$ rule $\qquad \dfrac{A\lceil\Lambda \vdash_{AP} B}{(\langle\lambda\rangle A)\lceil\Lambda \vdash_{AP} \langle\lambda\rangle B} \quad \text{if } \lambda \in \Lambda$

$\lceil\Lambda$–$[\lambda]$ rule $\qquad \dfrac{A\lceil\Lambda \vdash_{AP} B}{([\lambda]A)\lceil\Lambda \vdash_{AP} [\lambda]B} \quad \text{if } \lambda \in \Lambda$

$\lceil\Lambda$–$[\mu]$ rule $\qquad ([\alpha]\mathit{true})\lceil\Lambda \vdash_{AP} [\mu]B \quad \text{if } \mu \notin \Lambda$

rec. rule $\qquad \dfrac{p[\mathit{rec}x.p/x] \vdash_{AP} A}{\mathit{rec}x.p \vdash_{AP} A}$

$$\frac{p[\mathit{rec}^n x.p/x] \vdash_{AP} A}{\mathit{rec}^{n+1}x.p \vdash_{AP} A} \quad \text{for } n \in \omega$$

Remark. The requirement above that $C[\,]$ is a proper context (*i.e.* a context with a real "hole") is mad for one of the structural rules above so that $C[\mathit{false}] \models \mathit{false}$. This is clearly not the case for a non-prop context like $C[\,] = \mathit{true}$. For the latter context, with X empty, the rule is clearly invalid.

The proof of completeness depends on the following lemma which shows how the decomposition rul of section 4 are captured in the proof system.

6.4 Lemma. *For assertions A, B, C*

(i) $\alpha\mathcal{D}_\alpha[\![A]\!] \vdash_{AP} A$,

(ii) $B + C \vdash_{AP} A$ *if* $(B, C) \in \mathcal{D}_+[\![A]\!]$,

(iii) $B \otimes C \vdash_{AP} A$ *if* $(B, C) \in \mathcal{D}_\otimes[\![A]\!]$,

(iv) $\mathcal{D}_{\lceil\Lambda}[\![A]\!]\lceil\Lambda \vdash_{AP} A$.

Proof. By structural induction on the assertion which is decomposed. ∎

Using this lemma we can show that the entailment relations $A \gg B$, $A \otimes B \gg C$ *etc.* on the domai **D** are all provable.

6.5 Lemma. *For assertions A, B, C*

(i) $\alpha A \gg B \Rightarrow \alpha A \vdash_{AP} B$,
(ii) $B + C \gg A \Rightarrow B + C \vdash_{AP} A$,
(iii) $B \otimes C \gg A \Rightarrow B \otimes C \vdash_{AP} A$,
(iv) $A\lceil\Lambda \gg B \Rightarrow A\lceil\Lambda \vdash_{AP} B$.

Proof. All the proofs follow a similar line. We show (iii). Suppose $E \otimes F \gg A$. Let $p \in \Pi[\![E]\!]$ and $q \in \Pi[\![F]\!]$. Then there is $(B_{p,q}, C_{p,q}) \in \mathcal{D}_{\otimes}[\![A]\!]$ such that $p \models B_{p,q}$ and $q \models C_{p,q}$. Thus $p \models \bigwedge_{q \in \Pi[\![F]\!]} B_{p,q}$ and $q \models \bigwedge_{p \in \Pi[\![E]\!]} C_{p,q}$, where both are conjunctions of finite sets as $\mathcal{D}_{\otimes}[\![A]\!]$ is finite. Hence $E \models \bigvee_{p \in \Pi[\![E]\!]} \bigwedge_{q \in \Pi[\![F]\!]} B_{p,q}$, where the disjunction is of a finite set. Thus

$$E \vdash_A \bigvee_{p \in \Pi[\![E]\!]} \bigwedge_{q \in \Pi[\![F]\!]} B_{p,q}, \text{ and similarly } F \vdash_A \bigvee_{q \in \Pi[\![F]\!]} \bigwedge_{p \in \Pi[\![E]\!]} C_{p,q}.$$

By lemma 6.4 each $B_{p,q} \otimes C_{p,q} \vdash_{AP} A$, so by the structural rules we obtain $E \otimes F \vdash_{AP} A$. ∎

6.6 Theorem. *Let $p \in$ **AP** and $A \in$ **Assn**. Then $p \models A$ iff $p \vdash_{AP} A$.*

Proof. The proof of soundness is routine. To show completeness use structural induction on p and induction on iterates in the case of a recursive definition to show

$$\forall A.\ p \models A \Rightarrow p \vdash_{AP} A.$$

The cases of the structural induction use the above lemma. ∎

7. Related work.

Colin Stirling has produced a related proof system for SCCS but without restriction and in the case where recursive definitions are well-guarded. His proof system captures the concept of *relative satisfaction*, so he has proof rules which generate the relation $p \models^{St}{}_B A$ with this interpretation: if a process q satisfies B then $p \otimes q$ satisfies A; so relative satisfaction takes account of the environment. Clearly we can translate relative satisfaction into our notation by noting that $p \models^{St}{}_B A$ iff $p \otimes B \models A$.

There is some overlap in the work of this paper and that in [W] which presented the decomposition results of section 4 though in the more restricted case where the monoid of actions is a group. The proof system in [W] was unsatisfactory in several respects: it did not achieve strong completeness and relied on process variables in a somewhat *ad hoc* way.

The use of mixed assertions, mixing program syntax with assertions, makes the proof system and proofs about it much smoother. This realisation seems to have occurred independently to a number of people, though it was present some time ago in the paper [OH] by Olderog and Hoare. It is central in the work Graf and Sifakis [GS], which does not treat parallel composition however, and in the work of Brookes [B] which uses assertions built from synchronisation trees to survey a range of proof systems.

Acknowledgements

I have been strongly influenced by the work of Colin Stirling. I owe the proof system $\vdash_A$ and a large part of its proof of completeness to Colin's work.

References

[Ac] Aczel, P., An introduction to inductive definitions. In the handbook of Mathematical Logic, Ed. Barwise, J., North-Holland (1983).

[B] Brookes, S. D., On the axiomatic treatment of concurrency. In the proceedings of the joint US–UK seminar on the semantics of concurrency, July 1984, Carnegie–Mellon University, Pittsburgh, Springer–Verlag Lecture Notes in Comp. Sc. 197 (1984).

[BKP] Barringer H., Kuiper R. and Pnueli A., Now you may compose temporal logic specifications. In the proceedings of STOC 84 (1984).

[deNH] de Nicola, R. and Hennessy, M.C.B., Testing Equivalences for Processes, Lecture Notes in Comp. Sc. vol. 154 (1983) and in Theoretical Computer Science (1984).

[Gol] Golson, W. G., Denotational models based on synchronously communicating processes: refusal, acceptance, safety. In the proceedings of the joint US–UK seminar on the semantics of concurrency, July 1984, Carnegie–Mellon University, Pittsburgh, Springer–Verlag Lecture Notes in Comp. Sc. 197 (1984).

[GS] Graf, S., and Sifakis, J., A logic for the specification and proof of controllable processes of CCS. Advanced Seminar on logics and models for verification and specification of concurrent systems, La Colle–sur–Loup, France, to appear in Springer–Verlag Lecture Notes in Comp. Sc. (1984).

[H] Hoare, C.A.R., A model for communicating sequential processes. Monograph of the Programming Research Group, Oxford University (1981).

[HBR] Hoare, C.A.R., Brookes, S.D., and Roscoe, A.W., A Theory of Communicating Processes, Technical Report PRG-16, Programming Research Group, University of Oxford (1981); appears also in JACM (1984).

[HM] Hennessy, M.C.B. and Milner, R., On observing nondeterminism and concurrency, Springer LNCS Vol. 85. (1979).

[HP][HM] Hennessy, M.C.B. and Plotkin, G.D., A term model for CCS. Springer Lecture Notes in Comp. Sc., vol. 88 (1980).

[LW] Larsen, K. and Winskel, G., Using Information Systems to solve Recursive Domain Equations Effectively. Springer Lecture Notes in Comp. Sc., vol. 173 (1984). A full version appears as report No 51 of the Computer Laboratory, University of Cambridge.

[M1] Milner, R., A Calculus of Communicating Systems. Springer Lecture Notes in Comp. Sc. vol. 92 (1980).

[M2] Milner, R., A modal characterisation of observable machine–behaviour. Springer Lecture Notes in Comp. Sc. vol. 112 (1981).

[M3] Milner, R., Calculi for synchrony and asynchrony, Theoretical Computer Science, pp.267–310 (1983).

[OH] Olderog, E., and Hoare, C.A.R., Specification–oriented semantics for communicating processes. ICALP 83, Springer Lecture Notes in Comp. Sc. vol. 154 (1983).

[P] Plotkin, G. D., Some comments on Robin's "A modal characterisation of observable machine–behaviour". Handwritten notes, Comp. Sc. Dept., University of Edinburgh (1983).

[Pa] Park, D., Concurrency and automata on infinite sequences. Springer Lecture Notes in Comp. Sc. vol. 104 (1981).

[S] Scott, D. S., Domains for Denotational Semantics. ICALP 1982.

[S1] Scott, D. S., Lectures on a mathematical theory of computation. Oxford University Computing Laboratory Technical Monograph PRG–19 (1981).

[Sm] Smyth, M.B., Power domains and predicate transformers: a topological view. Proc. of ICALP 83, Springer Lecture Notes in Comp. Sc. vol. 154 (1983).

[St1] Stirling, C., A complete modal proof system for a subset of SCCS. Research report, Dept. of Comp. Sci., Edinburgh University (1984).

[St2] Stirling, C., A proof theoretic characterisation of observational equivalence. Research report, Dept. of Comp. Sci., Edinburgh University, CSR–132–83 (1983). A version also appears in the proceedings of the Bangalore conference, India (1983) and is to appear in Theoretical Computer Science.

[St3] Stirling, C., A Complete Intuitionistic Hennessy–Milner Logic. Handwritten note, Comp. Sc. Dept, University of Edinburgh (Sep. 84).

[W] Winskel, G., On the composition and decomposition of assertions. In the proceedings of the joint US–UK seminar on the semantics of concurrency, July 1984, Carnegie–Mellon University, Pittsburgh, Springer–Verlag Lecture Notes in Comp. Sc. 197, and appears as a report of the Computer Laboratory University of Cambridge (1984).

Demand-Driven Evaluation on Dataflow Machine*

Arvind

Laboratory for Computer Science
Massachusetts Institute of Technology
Cambridge, Massachusetts, 02139
U.S.A.

Abstract

G. Kahn in his IFIP's 1974 paper gave a straightforward denotational semantics of dataflow graphs by treating the history of an arc as a stream value, and a dataflow operator as a monotonic and continuous function from streams to streams. Operationally, a data-driven evaluation of dataflow graphs does not, in general, compute the total history of output arcs. We describe a program transformation technique whereby a data-driven evaluation of the transformed graph will perform exactly the same computation as a demand-driven evaluation of the original program. More importantly, the transformation technique suggests a simple denotational characterization for demand-driven evaluation. We hope this characterizationwill prove to be useful in designingefficient "lazy" interpreters.

*Manuscript not received in time for inclusion in the proceedings.

Design and Implementation of a Procedural VLSI Layout System

Jose M. Mata

Departamento de Ciencia da Computacao
Universidade Federal de Minas Gerais
Caixa Postal 702
30000 - Belo Horizonte, Minas Gerais
Brasil

Gopalakrishnan Vijayan

School of Information and Computer Science
Georgia Institute of Technology
Atlanta, Georgia 30332
U. S. A.

ABSTRACT

This paper describes the main features of a Integrated Circuit Layout system called ALI2. The system is based on a procedural layout language which allows the designer to specify layouts at a conceputal level. The system attempts to make layout design similar to software design. The language has a cell mechanism that is hierarchical and parametric, and allows the user to design truly generic cells whose instances are dependent on the environments in which the cell is invoked. Several layouts have been successfully designed and fabricated using the system. Initial versions of the system were designed and implemented when the authors were at Princeton University, and later versions were developed when the first author was still at Princeton and the second author was at Georgia Institute of Technology.

1. Introduction:

In this paper we describe the main features, usage, and implementation of a language designed at Princeton to automate the layout of VLSI circuits. The language is called ALI2 and has been operational for some months at Princeton. The language ALI1, also developed at Princeton was a forerunner to ALI2. The main concepts in both the languages are the same, and the reader is referred to the papers ([LN1], [LN2]) for descriptions of ALI1. We refer the reader to Mead and Conway [MC] for VLSI terminology that we use in this paper.

The main thesis in the ALI project is that VLSI design can be profitably thought of as a *programming task*, as opposed to a geometric editing task. We believe that making layout design similar to software design has many advantages and that much is to be gained by consciously attempting to apply our knowledge about programming to this new activity. We have thus tried to create tools for the VLSI designer that incorporate many useful features of the software development tools that we are familiar with.

The main feature of ALI2 as a layout language is that it allows its user to design layouts at a *conceptual* level, in which only the topological relations between the layout components can be specified. Absolute positions of the layout components cannot be specified.

The majority of current layout tools are graphics editors, such as STICKS[Wi] and CAESAR[Ou]. There are also some procedural or descriptive tools, such as LAVA[MNE], PLATES[SK], HILL[LM], and ALI1[LN2]. The difference between ALI2 and other layout languages is in the way the layouts are described, the kind of intermediate description generated (these are usually linear constraints), and also the form of implementation of the system.

2. An Overview of ALI2 Layout Language:

The ALI2 layout system [KV,KVV,Vi] was developed at Princeton, and has been used successfully, with many layout designs completed and chips fabricated.

ALI2 is a superset of Pascal. The objects manipulated by ALI2 programs can be classified naturally into two categories: those that a normal Pascal program can manipulate (which are called Pascal objects) and those that are specific to ALI2 (called ALI2 objects). There are three ALI2 objects: *cells, boxes,* and *wires.* ALI2 programs can also manipulate aggregates of wires, just as Pascal programs can manipulate aggregates of variables using structured types. Although ALI2 programs will typically manipulate all three kinds of objects, the final product of an ALI2 program is a layout composed entirely of wires. Cells and boxes are simply used as ways to express the relations between groups of wires in a structured and systematic way.

A *cell* is a prototype for a rectangular piece of a layout. In a cell definition, the user describes a prototype, and in a cell creation, also called instantiation, the user requests the insertion of a cell in a given environment. Multiple instances of a prototype can be created. It is possible to define a cell whose content and structure depends on the values of parameters which will be supplied at run-time. The sizes and shapes of actual instances of a given cell will then vary according to the 'actual parameters' provided when the instance is created. Thus, ALI2 cells are very much like the familiar parametrized procedures and functions.

Each cell instance is enclosed in a *cell bounding box*, cells are thus restricted to have rectangular shape. Cell boundaries may not overlap, nor may they be crossed by wires which are not parameters to the cell. Cell boundaries therefore impose a strict hierarchy on the arrangement of wires in a layout. Wires are rectilinear objects which lie on a specific *layer*, have a given *width*, and carry a specified *signal*. Wires are used primarily to interconnect cells and must have both of their endpoints lying on cells boundaries. The entire layout generated by an ALI2 program is itself actually an instance of a single cell.

An ALI2 program produces a set of linear inequalities and equalities involving the coordinates of the endpoints of the wires and boxes in the layout. These equalities and inequalities are then solved to generate the positions and sizes of the layout elements. The objective function which is minimized is the total area of the final layout. The algorithm used for solving the simple linear constraints is based on topological sort of a directed acyclic graph [Kn], and has running time proportional to the number of variables and constraints. The algorithm is described in detail in [Vi].

Fig. 1 shows a simple ALI2 program and the layout it produces. The various statements and constructs in the program in Fig. 1 will be explained in the next few sections.

3. Main Features of ALI2:

This section describes how ALI2 appears to its user. Its four subsections deal, in turn, with the *type structure*, the *cell mechanism*, the *primitive cells*, and the *placement statments* of the language. ALI2 has been built on top of Pascal and has inherited most of its features. In the interest of shortening this section we have assumed a certain familiarity with the general features of Pascal [JW]. A complete documentation of the ALI2 language is given in [KV]. We describe only the salient features of the language.

3.1. Type Structure:

As the example of Fig. 1 shows, the wires manipulated by ALI2 are declared by stating their *name* and their *type*. Wires can be of a *simple type* (a single wire) or of a *structured type* (a group of wires).

ALI2 is a strongly typed language. The ALI2 compiler will perform type checking just as compilers for conventional languages do. Type checking can be effective in catching certain errors very early during the design phase. For example, cells can be designed to accept only certain types of wires, and any violation will be reported during compilation time even before the layout is actually produced.

Wire types in ALI2 are parametric types. These are modeled after the parametric types for Pascal proposed in [HE]. Parametric types are designed to make type checking more selective or weaker as the user wishes. It works particularly well as a way to permit the user to regulate the extent of type checking that is to be performed during procedure or function calls (cell calls in the case of ALI2).

In ALI2 there is just one predefined wire type called *wire*. This parametric type has three parameters corresponding to the three attributes of a wire:

wire (l: wirelayer; w: integer; s: signal)

The types *wirelayer* and *signal* are predefined scalar types, which enumerate the possible layers and signals of the technology. The user is allowed to redefine the *signal* type. The parameter *w* stands for the width of the wire.

Other parametric types can be defined by pseudo-calls to the type *wire* . For instance, the following type definition

polywire (w: integer) = wire (poly, w, nullsignal)

creates a new parametric type *polywire*. All wires of this new type will have *poly* as their layer and *nullsignal* as their signal. The following wirevar declaration

*mywire: polywire (2*lambda)*

creates a *poly* wire with width *2*lambda*.

The values used as actual parameters can be arbitrary expressions of the appropriate type. These expressions will be evaluated at run time. Thus if *k* is a variable of type integer defined in the current scope, the following would have been a legal type declaration:

*localpoly = polywire ((2*k - 1)*lambda)*

Thus the actual parameters of the parametric types of ALI2 are *bound* at run time. This allows for a great deal of flexibility and permits the construction of dynamic types within a cell.

There are three composite wire types in ALI2: *bus, bundle* and *list*. The types *bus* and *bundle* are roughly analogous to the *record* and *array* types of Pascal, and represent,

```
wiretype
        polywire = wire ( poly, 2*lambda, nullsignal );
        diffwire = wire ( diff, 2*lambda, nullsignal );
        metalwire = wire ( metal, 4*lambda, nullsignal );
        fivewires ( lr: layer ) = bus
                                    w1: polywire;
                                    w2: metalwire;
                                    w3: wire ( lr, minwidth(lr), nullsignal );
                                    w4: metalwire;
                                    w5: polywire;
                              end;

wirevar ll, rr: fivewires ( poly );

cell shift ( left ll: fivewires; right rr: fivewires ); rigid ('shift.rc');

cell shiftregister ( left inbus: fivewires; right outbus: fivewires ) ( length: integer );
        wirevar temp: fivewires ( poly );
        begin
                if length = 1 then
                        create shift ( inbus, outbus )
                else begin
                                create shift ( inbus, temp );
                                create shiftregister ( temp, outbus ) ( length-1 )
                        end;
        end;

create shiftregister ( ll, rr ) ( 3 )
end.
```

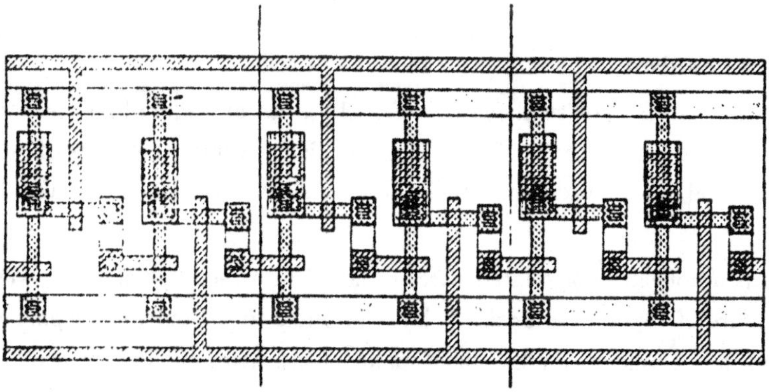

Fig. 1 - **An ALI2 Program and Layout**

respectively aggregates of wires of the same type and aggregates of wires of different types. Below are some sample definitions of composite types.

data1 (low, high, width: integer) =
bundle *[low .. high] of polywire(width);*

*data2 = bundle[1..100] of wire (metal, 10*lambda, nullsignal);*
foo1 (w1, w2: integer; l: layer; s: signal) = **bus**
f1: polywire (w1);
f2: wire (l, w2, s)
end;

The type *fivewires* in Fig. 1 is another example of a definition of a bus type.

The type *bundle* is a parametric type in its own right, since the number of wire it contains and the values used to access them may be parameters of the type (as in *data1* above). Thus the type *bundle* is actually a dynamic type, because these parameters can be bound within a cell during run time. The type *bus* is parametric only because the types of its components may be parametric (as in *foo1* above).

The type *list* is peculiar to ALI2. A list is either the *nulllist* or an aggregate of one or more wires, each of any type whatsoever. This type is intended to facilitate the writing of general-purpose cells which accept a variable number of wire parameters.

The accessing of the elements of bundles and buses is done as in Pascal. Thus if x is of type *data1*, $x[i]$ refers to the ith element of x, and if y is of type *fivewires*, *y.ph1* refers to the first component of *fivewires*. Accessing of lists is similar to that of bundles. ALI2 also provides the user with a number of predefined functions that take composite or simple wires as parameters and return various interesting attributes of the wires like layer, width, number of elements etc.

3.2. Cell Mechanism:

Perhaps the most powerful feature of ALI2 is its procedure-like mechanism for the definition and creation of *cells*. The cell mechanism permits the users of ALI2 to introduce hierarchical information into their programs, and therefore into the layouts they describe.

A cell is a collection of related wires enclosed in a rectangular area. Wires that are inside a cell are of two types: *local* which are invisible to the outside, or *parameters* which can interact in a simple and well defined manner with wires outside the cell.

A cell is *defined* by specifying its local objects, its formal parameters and the relations among all of them. Once a cell has been defined, it can be *instantiated* as many times as desired by specifying the actual parameters for the instance, much the same way as one invokes a procedure or function in a procedural language. The result of instantiating a cell is to create a brand new copy of the prototype described in the cell definition with the formal parameters connected to the actual parameters.

A cell definition is made up of a *header*, in which the formal parameters are described, a set of *local wire declarations* and a *body* in which the relationship between the parameters and the local wires, as well as those among local wires, are specified.

The cell header describes the names and types of the parameters and the side of the bounding rectangle through which they come into contact with the inside of the cell. The header can also include non-wire parameters for use in the body of the cell. In the program of Fig. 1, *inbus* is a left wire parameter, outbus is a right wire parameter to the cell *shiftregister*, while *length* is a non-wire parameter.

Cells may have any number of wire parameters on each of their four sides. The order in which they are listed in the cell header gives the order in which they should appear in the layout. Horizontal parameters (i.e., those touching the cell on the left or right) are assumed to be listed in top to bottom order and vertical parameters in left to right order. In the case of composite wire parameters the order of separation is determined by recursively applying the following rules: bundle elements are separated ordered by their indices, and bus elements are separated in the order in which they are listed in the bus declaration. In the program of Fig. 1, the five components *w1,w2,w3,w4,w5* of the composite wire *inbus* which is a left parameter to the cell *shiftregister* are separated from top to bottom in that order.

The body of a cell will contain Pascal and ALI2 statements. Cells can be defined to be 'external' cells and separately compiled. Cells can also be 'rigid' cells to indicate that the cell definition is not given textually as part of the ALI2 program but instead the actual layout produced by a previous instantiation of the cell is to be used. In the example of Fig. 1, the cell shift is defined to be a rigid cell, and the cell shiftregister is built recursively using the shift cell. Note that the 'main' program is just a single *create* statement, which creates a copy of the *shiftregister* cell with *ll* and *rr* as the actual wire parameters, and *length* parameter being 3.

There are two important ways in which the cell mechanism helps in the automatic generation of constraints between objects. When an object of a structured type is passed as a parameter to a cell, its component wires are separated as described earlier. Thus, in the example of Fig. 1, the components of parameter *inbus* would be separated from top to bottom. The second mechanism involves the automatic separation of cells that share a parameter; thus in the example of Fig. 1, the individual instances of *shift* are separated automatically, since adjacent instances share parameter wires.

By declaring a formal wire parameter to be of parametric type, the user deems as acceptable actual parameters that are of a type *derived* from the type of the formal parameter. These parameters will become bound(i.e., values for the formal parameters in their type definition will be assigned) at run time by inheriting the characteristics (layer, width and signal) of the actual parameters assigned to them at cell instantiation. Note that actual wire parameters have to be declared in the wirevar section of the program and thus are completely bound.

The type checking used as described above allows for a great deal of flexibility. Only certain properties, selected by the user, of the parameters are checked when a wire parameter is passed. All others are inherited by the formal parameter from the actual parameter. This allows the user to write cells that are truly generic; cells whose instances can be radically different from one another depending on the attributes of the parameter wires.

The cell mechanism gives the ALI2 user the ability to describe layouts in a truly hierarchical manner. A proper ALI2 design, very much like a well structured program, will consist of a hierarchy of cell instances with only a small amount of information at a given level (the parameters of the cell instances at that level) being visible from the immediately higher level. Cells can be written and debugged separately and then put together with the least effort to obtain more complicated cells.

3.3. Primitive Cells:

The primitive cells in ALI2 are the predefined cells. These are the cells that appear at the leaves of the hierarchy of cells. In fact, the whole layout can be viewed as a collection of primitive cells joined together by straight line wires. The higher level cells are just rectangular regions enclosing subsets of these primitive cells.

The primitive cells in ALI2 are called *systransistor*, *syscontact* and *syspullup*. These are quite general cells that implement the transistor, contact, and pullup of nMOS. Each of these primitive cells have four parameters: four lists of wires, one for each side of the cell. The contents of an instance of a primitive cell will depend on the attributes of the actual parameter wires used in that instance. So, these cells are 'smart' cells which do a large amount of processing internally.

There are also some non-wire parameters to these cells, which also contribute to the contents of an individual instance. The systransistor cell has a boolean parameter which determines whether the transistor is implanted or not. The pullup ratio is a parameter to the syspullup cell. The syscontact cell has a boolean parameter which determines whether all the wires are to be electrically connected at the contact, or only the wires on independent layers are to be connected to each other. For the actual syntax and semantics of these cells the reader is again referred to the language overview document[KV].

The reason for making these primitive cells general and thus having fewer number of these cells, is to keep the number of technology dependent features of the language small. However, the user can define simpler versions of these cells to facilitate their repeated invocation. As mentioned earlier, all the technology dependent features of ALI2 are hidden inside the design rules table, the primitive cells, and a few reserved identifiers. Even in the design rules table only the separation and width rules are stored, because the other design rules are enforced inside the primitive cells. ALI2 currently supports only nMOS primitive cells. Design of cells for other technologies is currently under investigation.

3.4. Relative Placement:

There are two placement statements in ALI2: the *ordered* statement and the *separate* statement. These statements are used to relatively place the various objects (wires and bounding boxes) in the layout.

The *ordered* statement is given a direction of separation, and a list of creations of objects, and effect is to place the created objects in the order in which they are created. An example of an ordered statement and the arrangement of objects it generates is given in Fig. 2.

The actual objects that are ordered within an ordered statement are really bounding boxes. Each ordered statement or cell create statement is associated with a rectangular bounding box. The bounding box created for an ordered statement will enclose the bounding boxes created for the statements within its scope, and in addition these bounding boxes will be separated in the given direction.

Since ALI2 is an extension of Pascal, repetition statements of Pascal can be used within an ordered statement to create a succession of objects that are separated as specified. Also, as shown in Fig. 2 ordered statements can be nested within one another.

The ordered statement matches quite well with the notion of floor-plans of layouts. Once the ALI2 user has a rough sketch of the floor-plan of his layout, he can quickly translate the sketch into a series of nested ordered statements. He can then refine each of his regions in the floor-plan in a similar manner.

Both the cell structure and the ordered statement contribute to the hierarchy in the layout description. However, there is a fundamental difference in the hierarchies created

```
ordered ltor do
    begin
        < bounding box 1 >
        < bounding box 2 >
        ordered ttob do
            begin
                < bounding box 3 >
                < bounding box 4 >
            end;
        < bounding box 5 >
    end
```

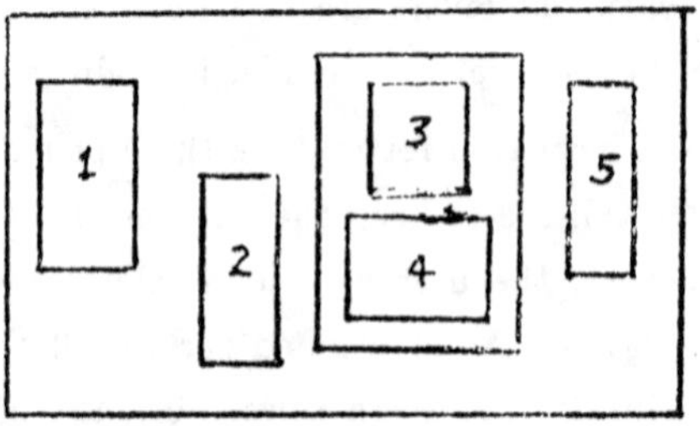

Fig. 2 - **Ordered Statement**

by the cells and the ordered statement: wires cannot straddle the bounding box of a cell, but the same is not true for an ordered statement. Thus, wires are subject only to the hierarchy defined by the cell boundaries. The combination of strict hierarchy of the cell structure and the lenient hierarchy of the ordered statement seems to give the ALI2 user the right mixture of rigidity and flexibility that he needs.

The other placement statement -- the *separate* statement -- is used to separate a given list of bounding boxes and wires in a given direction of separation. The statement

separate ltor box1, wire1, wire2;

will force *box1* to the left of *wire1* and *wire1* to the left of *wire2.* The separation distances enforced will depend on the layers of the wires, and are extracted from the design rules table. The user can override the default minimum separation by specifying the required separation distance as in the following:

*separate ltor box1, wire1, wire2 by 4*lambda;*

Unlike the ordered statement, the separate statement is not a structured statement. It can be used to separate objects within different hierarchies of ordered statements. This can cause difficulty in debugging ALI2 programs. An ALI2 program can be written without using the separate statement, but it may be used to make small local changes in the layout to avoid rewriting major portions of the ALI2 program.

4. Layout Issues Addressed in ALI2:

A sample of the main issues that we tried to address with ALI2 are the following:

1. The creation of an *open ended tool.* Most layout design tools require the specification of absolute sizes and positions, thus making the creation of a general purpose library of cells a hard task, since information about the sizes and positions of the cell elements that can interact with the outside world has to be apparent to the user of the library. The absence of absolute sizes and positions makes this problem much less severe in ALI2. ALI2 has been built on top of Pascal, and is a full-fledged programming language having all the powers of Pascal, thereby making it easily extensible. The generation of tools to automate the layout process, such as simple routers or PLA generators, involves writing Pascal routines to solve some abstract version of the problem and having done so invoke ALI2 cells to generate the layouts.
2. Facilitating the *division of labor.* Large layouts have to be produced by more than one designer. If the piece produced by each designer is specified in absolute positions, serious problems are likely to arise when the different pieces are put together. ALI2 allows the partitioning of tasks in such a way that the designer of a piece of the layout does not need to know anything about the positions or sizes of other pieces of the complete layout.
3. Facilitating *hierarchical design.* In ALI2, the information about a given level of the hierarchy needed at the level immediately above is reduced by the absence of absolute sizes and positions, to topological relations among the layout elements of the lower level visible to the higher one.
4. Facilitating easy *update of layouts.* Successful designs seem to be more or less continuously updated as improved processes become available during their lifetime. Therefore, layout tools must be easily amenable to changes in the technology or design rules. The technology dependent part of ALI2 is confined to a few design

rules tables and primitive cells and only these have to be rewritten in order to update ALI2 to a new technology. Future versions of ALI2 will give its user the flexibility of writing one ALI2 program to describe a layout, and then producing different layouts for different processes by just setting certain appropriate flags when invoking the ALI2 system.

5. Allowing *parametric design.* Having a layout design which produces different layouts for different values of a set of parameters is extremely useful. This is especially true for cell designs which are used repeatedly. These parameters will allow decisions about the detailed characteristics of the cell in a layout to be delayed until later in the design phase. In ALI2, the cell mechanism has been designed so that the number as well as the attributes of the wires connecting to a cell can be parameters of the cell. In addition, the cells can have other parameters that affect the insides of the cell. ALI2 offers all the wealth of a full-fledged programming language, such as do-loops, conditional statements etc., which can be used to exploit the availability of these parameters.

6. To allow *easy modification of layouts.* The fact that absolute sizes and positions are absent in an ALI2 specification makes modification of a layout a very simple task. Such modifications are actually being made to a program, which is a much easier task compared to making changes in the final layout.

5. The ALI2 System and its Implementation:

The ALI2 system comprises of a compiler for the ALI2 layout language and other useful utilities. A block diagram of the system is presented in Fig. 3. The document [KVV] describes the system in more detail.

The ALI2 compiler will take as input an ALI2 program, precompiled cells as well as descriptions of rigid cells. Rigid cells, such as cell shift in Fig. 1, are described in a language slightly different from CIF (California Intermediate Format, [MC]). In addition to the positions and sizes of various wires inside the cell, a rigid cell description has to include information about the wires that are parameters to the cell. A precompiled cell is like an external procedure. These cells are flexible and are just like cells in an ALI2 program, except that they are compiled separately.

The final output created by the compiler is in CIF. The ALI2 compiler can also precompile cells or produce rigid versions of cells, that can be stored in a library and used in various ALI2 programs.

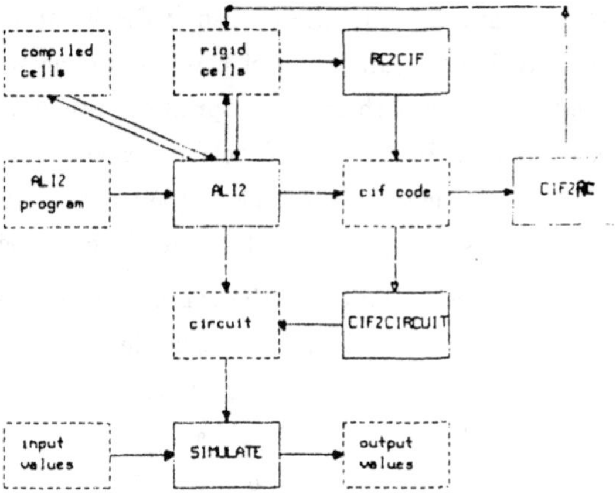

Fig. 3 - **The ALI2 System**

There are programs (RC2CIF and CIF2RC) that can translate rigid cell descriptions into CIF and vice versa. Thus a cell that is generated by some other tool, for example one of the Berkeley VLSI tools [Ma], can be translated to a rigid cell and used in any ALI2 program.

The ALI2 compiler also generates a switch-level description of the circuit described in the ALI2 program. The ALI2 system includes a switch-level simulator for simulating such descriptions produced by the ALI2 compiler. The ALI2 system guarantees that the layout it produces will match the switch-level description, thus avoiding the need to extract the circuit from the layout.

The ALI2 system also includes tools such as PLA generators [Ma1], and Weinberger array generators [Ma2], which are actually ALI2 programs themselves, and thus can be invoked from any ALI2 program.

The system is implemented under Berkeley Unix. There are six steps in going from the text of an ALI2 program into a layout in CIF. The first step is the translation of the ALI2 program into standard Pascal. This translator [Ka,VV] was written using YACC

[Jo], and does all the syntax and semantic checks of Pascal and ALI2. The most interesting part of the translator is the translation of the parametric wire types. These types are translated into Pascal functions with the appropriate parameters. Declaration of a wire is translated into a call to the corresponding function. Every composite wire type is implemented as a *list* of its components. Hence the wiretypes in a cell header are replaced by the list type. The cells themselves are translated into Pascal procedures.

The second step is the compilation of the Pascal program produced by the previous step. This is done using the Berkeley Pascal compiler. The third step is to load the object file generated with other precompiled modules into an executable file. The fourth step is the execution of this file, which produces a set of linear constraints, as well as connectivity information for the simulator. The fifth step is the solving of the linear constraints [Vi], using an efficient (linear time) algorithm, thus producing the final layout in terms of a rigid cell description. The sixth step is to translate this rigid cell description into CIF.

6. Conclusions:

The ALI2 system has been used by students in VLSI courses taught at Princeton and at Georgia Tech., and has been found to be a valuable learning tool. Several small designs have been successfully fabricated. We are currently extending the system for CMOS and related technologies.

A main drawback of the ALI2 system is its requirement that all wires in the layout have to be given names and declared as either variables or parameters. Another disadvantage concerns proper use of relative placement. The designer must guess the approximate sizes of the various cells in the layout in order to place them relative to each other in an appropriate manner for producing an area efficient final layout. The designer must also guess the lengths of long wires in the layout in order to create proper drivers for these wires. Note that the actual sizes of the cells and the lengths of the wires is in the control of the layout system. The designer may have to try a few alternate relative placements (using appropriate 'ordered' statements) before a satisfactory layout is obtained. This problem may be alleviated by fixing some of the cells as 'rigid' cells, so that the designer knows the precise sizes of these cells. Note that a problem with 'rigid' cells is that they cannot be parametrized.

A third drawback arises in the solving of the linear constraints. Although the designer describes layouts hierarchically, there is no hierarchy at the constraint level. For large layouts the number of linear constraints to be solved can be large enough to cause memory thrashing in the solver program. Again this problem can be alleviated by use of 'rigid' cells. These cells are pre-solved and generate only a few constraints that are needed to connect these cells to the outside.

Some of these problems have been eliminated in a new layout system called ALLENDE, designed and implemented at Princeton by one of the authors [Ma3].

Acknowledgements:

Several people have made contributions to the design and implementation of the ALI2 system. Lipton and Valdes participated actively in the design of the language and the system. Kalin and North were helpful to us in the implementation of the system. We also thank Andrea LaPaugh for her valuable criticisms and for using ALI2 in her VLSI course at Princeton.

References:

[HE] Hennessy, J., Elmquist, H., "The Design and Implementation of Parametric Types in Pascal", *Software -- Practice and Experience*, vol. 12, 1982.

[JW] Jensen, K., Wirth, N., *Pascal User Manual and Report*, 2nd ed., Springer-Verlag.

[Jo3] Johnson, S. C., "YACC: Yet Another Compiler-Compiler", *Unix Programmer's Manual*, January 1979.

[Ka] Kalin, R. L., "Design and Implementation of the Parser/Translator", *ALI2 Documentation and Implementation Guide*, Department of EECS, Princeton University.

[KV] Kalin, R. L., Valdes, J., "Language Overview", *ALI2 Documentation and Implementation Guide*, Department of EECS, Princeton University.

[KVV] Kalin, R. L., Valdes, J., Vijayan, G., "System Overview and User's Notes", *ALI2 Implementation and Documentation Guide*, Department of EECS, Princeton University.

[Kn] Knuth, D. E., *The Art of Computer Programming*, vol. 1, *Fundamental Algorithms*, Addison-Wesley, 1971.

[LM] Lengauer, T., Mehlhorn, K., "The HILL System: A Design Environment for the Hierarchical Specification, Compaction, and Simulation of Integrated Circuit Layouts", 1984 Conference on Advanced Research in VLSI, MIT, Jan. 1984.

[LN1] Lipton, R. J., North, S. C., Sedgewick, R., Valdes, J., Vijayan, G., "ALI: a Procedural Language to Describe VLSI Layouts", *Proc. of the 19th Design Automation Conference*, June 1982.

[LN2] Lipton, R. J., North, S. C., Sedgewick, R., Valdes, J., Vijayan, G., "VLSI Layout as Programming", *ACM Trans. of Programming Languages and Systems*, July 1983.

[Ma] Mayo, R., et. al., "1983 VLSI Tools", Report No. UCB/CSD 83/115, University of California, Berkeley, March 1983.

[Ma1] Mata, J. M., "PLA Generator", *ALI2 Documentation and Implementation Guide*, Department of EECS, Princeton University.

[Ma2] Mata, J. M., "An Array Generator in ALI2", *ALI2 Documentation and Implementation Guide*, Department of EECS, Princeton University.

[Ma3] Mata, J. M., "A Methodology for VLSI Design and A Constraint-Based Layout Language", *Ph.D. Thesis*, Department of EECS, Princeton University, October 1984.

[MNE] Mathews, R., Newkirk, J., Eichenberger, P., "A Target Language for Silicon Compilers", COMPCON 1982, Feb. 1982.

[MC] Mead, C., Conway, L., *Introduction to VLSI Systems*, Addison-Wesley Publ. Co. , 1980.

[Ou] Ousterhout, J., "CAESAR: An Interactive Editor for VLSI Layouts", VLSI Design, Fourth Quarter, 1981.

[SK] Sastry, S., Klein, S., "PLATES: A Metric Free VLSI Layout Language", 1982 Conference on Advanced Research in VLSI, MIT, January 1982.

[VV] Valdes, J., Vijayan, G., "The Translation of ALI2 into Pascal and the ALI2 Runtime system", *ALI2 Documentation and Implementation Guide*, Department of EECS, Princeton University.

[Vi] Vijayan, G., "Design Implementaion and Theory of a VLSI Layout Language", *Ph.D. Thesis*, Department of EECS, Princeton University, August 1983.

[Wi] Williams, J. D., 'STICKS - A Graphical Compiler for High Level LSI Design", Proceedings of the 1978 National Computer Conference, June 1978.

VLSI Systems For Matrix Multiplication*

Kam Hoi Cheng and Sartaj Sahni
University of Minnesota

ABSTRACT
We examine several VLSI architectures and compare these for their suitability for various forms of the matrix multiplication problem. The following architectures are considered: chain, broadcast chain, mesh, broadcast mesh and hexagonally connected. The forms of the matrix multiplication problem that are considered are: matrix $\times$ vector, band matrix $\times$ vector, matrix $\times$ matrix and band matrix $\times$ band matrix.

Keywords and Phrases
VLSI systems, systolic systems, matrix multiplication

1. Introduction

Several authors have considered VLSI architectures for matrix multiplication. Cannon [CANN69], Van Scoy [VANS76], and Flynn and Kosaraju [FLYN76] have proposed an array architecture for this problem. More recently, Kung [KUNG79] has proposed chain and hexagonal processor array architectures for matrix multiplication. [KUNG79] spawned considerable further work in the development of VLSI systems for specific problems. A bibliography of over 150 research papers dealing with this subject appears in [KUNG83a]. [HORO79], [HUAN82], [PRIE81] and [LEIS83] are additional references that deal specifically with some form of the matrix multiplication problem.

In this paper, we reconsider the following forms of the matrix multiplication problem: matrix $\times$ vector, band matrix $\times$ vector, matrix $\times$ matrix and band matrix $\times$ band matrix. For each of these forms, we consider how the multiplication problem can be solved in VLSI. For this, we consider various VLSI architectures. The major architectures considered are:

a. **Chain** --- This architecture consists of some number of processing elements (PEs) connected together as in Figure 1.1(a). PEs may directly communicate with neighboring PEs only. Input/Output may be performed through some subset of the PEs.

b. **Broadcast Chain** --- A broadcast line is drawn as a continuous line through all the PEs that are to receive broadcast data. Figure 1.1(b) shows a broadcast chain with one broadcast line. Data put onto the broadcast line is assumed to reach all PEs on the line in one time unit.

c. **Mesh** --- A mesh is a two dimensional arrangement of PEs with nearest neighbor connections (see Figure 1.1(c)). Input/output can be performed only through some subset of the boundary PEs.

d. **Broadcast Mesh** --- This is a mesh with broadcast lines added. The broadcast lines may span rows or columns as in Figure 1.1(d).

e. **Hexagonal Processor Array** --- This is a two dimensional PE arrangement in which each PE has 6 nearest neighbors and connections to each (Figure 1.1(e)). Once again, input/output can be performed only via the PEs at the boundary.

In addition to these six architectures, variations of some are also considered. We make the assumption that the VLSI system for matrix multiplication will be connected to the bus of the host computer as a peripheral (Figure 1.2).

---

*This research was supported in part by the National Science Foundation under grant MCS-83-05567.
Professor Kam Hoi Cheng is presently with the Computer Science Department, University of Houston, Houston, TX.

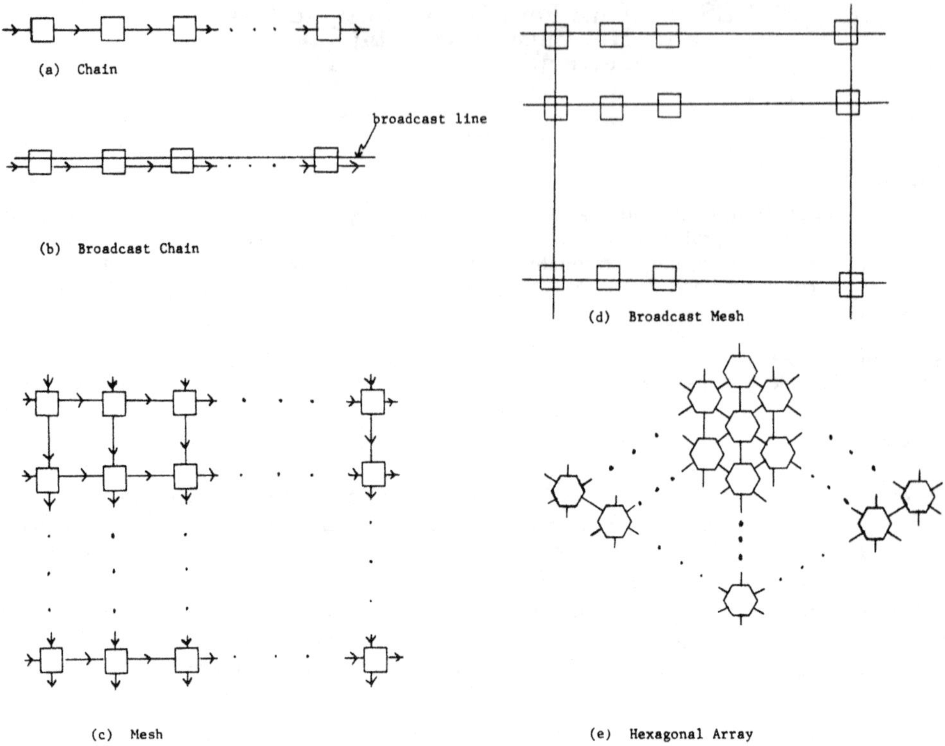

Figure 1.1

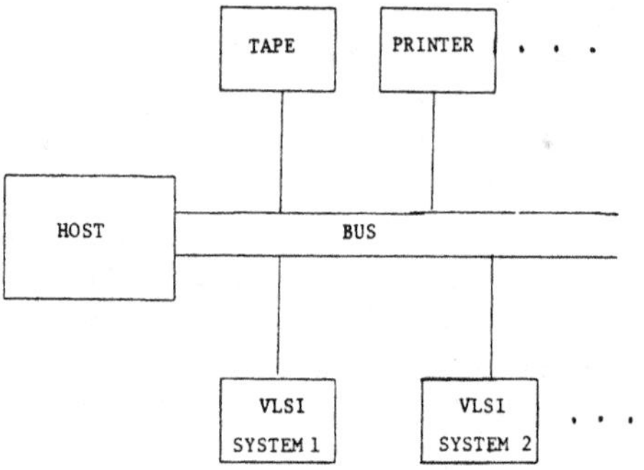

Figure 1.2

The design of a VLSI system should take the following into account:

1. Bus bandwidth --- how much data is to be transmitted between the host and the VLSI system in any cycle? This figure is denoted by B.
2. Speed --- how much time does the VLSI system need to complete its task? This time may be decomposed into the times T_C (time for computations) and T_D (time for data transmissions both within the VLSI system and between the host and the VLSI system).

One may expect that by using a very high bandwidth B and a large number of processors P, we can make T_C and T_D quite small. So, T_C and T_D are not in themselves a very good measure of the effectiveness with which the resources B and P have been used. Let D denote the total amount of data that needs to be transmitted between the host and VLSI system for a particular matrix product problem. The ratio

$$R_D = B * T_D / D$$

measures the effectiveness with which the bandwidth B has been used. Clearly, $R_D \geq 1$ for every VLSI design. As an example, consider the multiplication of two $n \times n$ matrices. The host needs to send $2n^2$ elements to the VLSI system and receive n^2 elements back. So, $D = 3n^2$. With a bandwidth of n, T_D must be at least $3n$. T_D will exceed $3n$ if the bandwidth is not used to capacity at all times.

Let C denote the time spent for computation by a single processor algorithm. The ratio

$$R_C = P * T_C / C$$

measures the effectiveness of processor utilization. Once again, we see that $R_C \geq 1$ for every VLSI design. Consider the problem of multiplying two $n \times n$ matrices A and B to get C. Each element of C is the sum of n products. We shall count one multiplication and addition as one arithmetic (or computation) step. Hence, $C = n^3$. (We shall consider VLSI algorithms based on the classical $O(n^3)$ matrix multiplication algorithm only.) If $P = n$, then $T_C \geq n^2$. Note that C is being used to denote both the matrix product and the number of computations. This dual use of the symbol C should not cause any confusion as the context of use makes clear what C denotes.

In evaluating a VLSI design, we shall be concerned with T_C and T_D and also with R_C and R_D. We would like R_C and R_D to be close to 1. Finally, we may combine the two efficiency ratios R_C and R_D into the single ratio $R = R_C * R_D$. A design that makes effective use of the available bandwidth and processors will have R close to 1.

Huang and Abraham [HUAN82] have proposed an efficiency measure that is identical to R when $T_D = T_C$. They do not, however, decompose their measure into the constituent components R_C and R_D.

For each of the designs considered in this paper, we compute R_C, R_D and R. In several cases, our designs have improved efficiency ratios than all earlier designs using the same model. In comparing different architectures for the same problem, one must be wary about over emphasizing the importance of R_C, R_D and R. Clearly, using $P = 1$ and $B = 1$, we can get $R_C = R_D = R = 1$ and no speed up at all. So, we are really interested in minimizing T_C and T_D while keeping R close to 1.

An important feature of this paper is the inclusion of correctness proofs. These proofs are provided for selected designs and illustrate how VLSI designs may be proved correct. Remaining proofs are easily obtained. We use neither the s-transform notation developed in [JOHN81a and b], [WEIS81] and [KUNG83b] nor the formal model developed in [MELH84]. It is our contention that VLSI designs of the type developed here can be proved correct using traditional mathematical methods.

2. Matrix $\times$ Vector Multiplication

2.1. The Problem

Input: An $n \times n$ matrix A and a column vector b.

Output: A column vector c such that $c = Ab$.

Parameters: $C = n^2$, $D = n^2 + 2n$.

2.2. Chain with $O(n)$ Bandwidth

Kung and Leiserson [KUNG78] and Kung [KUNG79] have proposed a $2n+1$ bandwidth chain for matrix $\times$ vector multiplication. This is shown in Figure 2.1(a). The c_is generated at the left end are all zero. This initialization of the c_is is not regarded as input to the VLSI system. Consequently, the bandwidth is just $2n+1$ ($2n$ inputs from top and bottom; one output from right end). At each time instance, each PE computes $c \leftarrow c + a\,b$. For this design, we have $P = n$, $B = 2n + 1$, $T_C = 2n - 1$, $T_D = 2n$, $R_C = n * (2n - 1)/n^2 \sim 2$, $R_D = (2n + 1) * 2n/(n^2 + 2n) \sim 4$, $R \sim 8$.

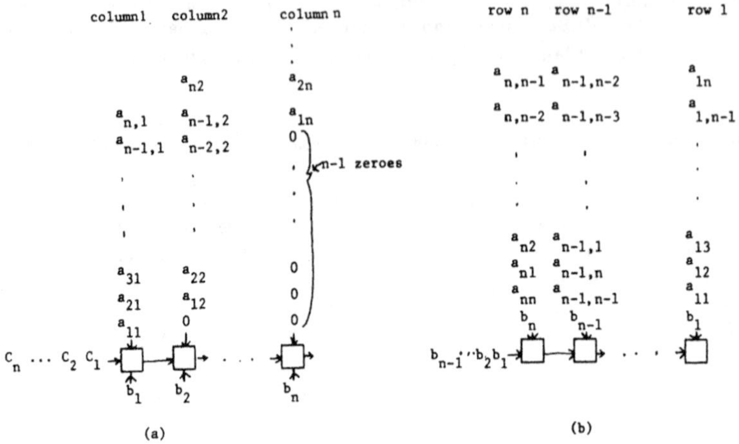

Figure 2.1

The bandwidth of Kung's array is easily reduced to $n + 1$ by entering all the b values once at the beginning and then continuing with the cs and as. This increases T_D by 1 but reduces R_D and R to 2 and 4, respectively. The R value can further be reduced to 1 by structuring the computation as shown in Figure 2.1(b). The ith PE computes c_i. Algorithm 2.1 describes the working of the system. Each PE reads in a b and an A value from above and stores the product in its c register. This step is followed by $n - 1$ cycles in which the bs shift right by one PE (the leftmost PE inputs the next b value), each PE reads an A value from above and the product is added to c. Finally, the computed c values are output from the top.

input the row of bs from the top;
input the first row of as from the top;
$c \leftarrow a * b$;
for $i \leftarrow 2$ **to** n **do**
    input next row of as from top;
    input a b from the left shifting all other bs right by one;
    $c \leftarrow c + a\,b$;
end
output the n cs from the top;

Algorithm 2.1

Correctness

The correctness of the scheme of Figure 2.1(b) may be established in the following way. Let $a(i,t)$ and $b(i,t)$ denote the tth a and b values to enter PE i. Then the value c_i computed by PE i is $\sum_{t=1}^{n} a(i,t) * b(i,t)$. From Figure 2.1(b), we see that $a(i,t) = a_{i,(i+t-2) \bmod n + 1}$ and $b(i,t) = b_{(i+t-2) \bmod n + 1}$. Hence, c_i is computed correctly.

Performance

We see that $P = n$, $B = n + 1$, $T_C = n$, $T_D = n + 2$, $R_C = 1$, $R_D = 1 + 1/n \sim 1$ and $R \sim 1$. In computing T_D, it is assumed that input from the top and left are done in parallel using the available $n + 1$ bandwidth.

2.3. Chain with O(1) Bandwidth

n processors are chained together as in Figure 2.2. The input consists of b_1; followed by column 1 of A; followed by b_2; followed by column 2 of A; ...; followed by b_n; followed by column n of A. The operation of the n processor chain is described by Algorithm 2.2. Observe that while the interface between the chain and the outside world need be just one word wide, that between adjacent PEs needs to be two words wide.

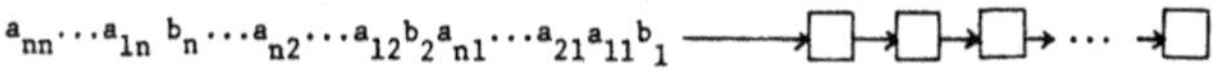

Figure 2.2

$c \leftarrow 0$; {each PE sets its c register to 0}
for $j \leftarrow 1$ **to** n **do**
    leftmost PE inputs b_j and a_{1j};
    for $i \leftarrow 1$ **to** $n - 1$ **do**
        all PEs except the leftmost one receive an a
        and a b value from the PE on their left;
        the leftmost PE inputs an a value;
    end
    $c \leftarrow c + a\,b$; {each PE multiplies and adds}
end
for $i \leftarrow 1$ **to** n **do**
    shift c leftwards outputting one at a time;
end

Algorithm 2.2

The initialization of c to 0 can be accomplished by means of a global initialization signal. Alternatively, b_1 can be preceded by a 0 in the input and the 0 propagated to the right. The array can be used in pipeline mode if we extract the output from the right end rather than from the left. This increases the bandwidth to 2 but permits us to start the next matrix vector product while the results of the previous one are being removed from the array.

The bandwidth of the interface between adjacent PEs can be reduced to one word and a bit. The additional bit is used to distinguish between an a value and a b value. The algorithm executed by each PE is shown in Algorithm 2.3

$c \leftarrow 0$;
for $j \leftarrow 1$ **to** n **do**
    for $i \leftarrow 1$ **to** $n + 1$ **do**
        input (bit,x) from left;
        if bit $= 1$ **then** $b \leftarrow x$; {bit=1 iff x is a b value}
    end
    $c \leftarrow c + b\,x$;
end
for $i \leftarrow 1$ **to** n **do**
    shift c leftwards outputting one at a time;
end

Algorithm 2.3

Performance

We readily see that $P = n$, $B = 1$, $T_C = n$, $T_D = n^2 + 2n$, $R_C = P * T_C / C = 1$, $R_D = B * T_D / D = 1$, $R = 1$.

2.4. Broadcast Chain

Huang and Abraham [HUAN82] develop a broadcast chain for matrix × vector products that has n PEs, $P = n$, $B = n + 1$, $T_C = 2n - 1$, $T_D = 2n$, $R_C \sim 2$, $R_D \sim 2$ and $R \sim 4$. The R value can be reduced to 1 by using the broadcast chain as in Figure 2.3(a). The system begins by initializing the c register of each PE to 0. In the ith time instance, b_i is broadcast to the n PEs. Also, the ith column is input by the n PEs and the computation $c \leftarrow c + a\,b$ performed. Clearly, after n such steps, the ith PE has computed c_i. The n c_i values may be extracted in one time unit.

Performance

$P = n$, $B = n + 1$, $T_C = n$, $T_D = n + 1$, $R_C = 1$, $R_D \sim 1$ and $R \sim 1$.

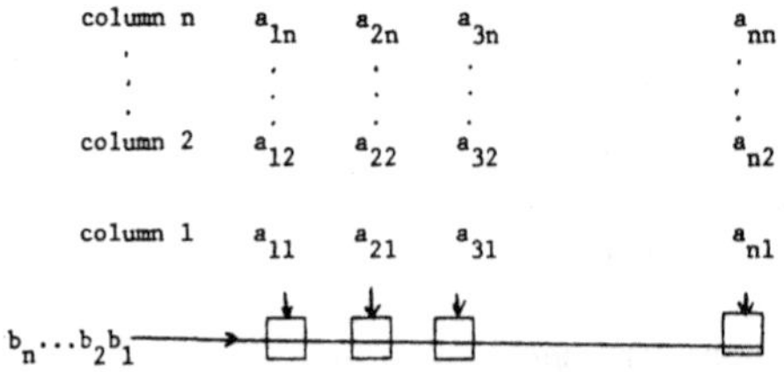

Figure 2.3(a)

Note that in the absence of a broadcast capability, the data pattern of Figure 2.3(a) can be used to achieve an R of 2 using a bandwidth of $2n$ as in Figure 2.3(b). Here, we simply use the n processors independently.

2.5. Mesh with Two Rows

Horowitz [HORO79] has proposed a two row architecture to compute matrix × vector products. This is shown in Figure 2.4. Each row contains n processors.

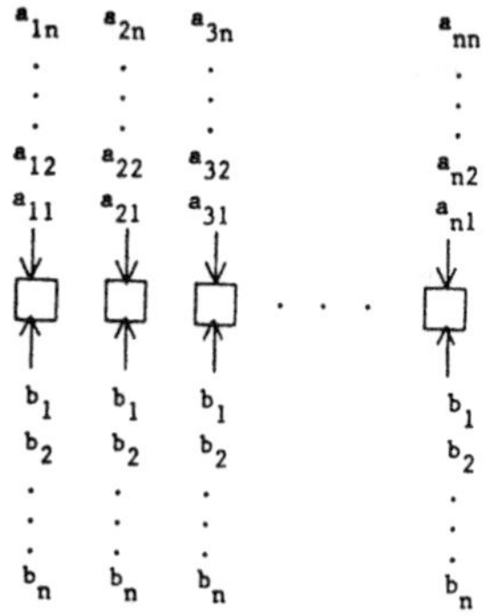

Figure 2.3(b)

The system initializes the c registers of the row 2 PEs to zero. The product Ab is computed in n cycles. Each cycle is itself comprised of $n + 2$ time steps. At the start of the ith cycle, b_i is entered into the leftmost row 1 processor. In the next $n - 1$ steps, this value is propagated to the remaining row 1 processors. During these same n steps, the ith column of A is entered into the row 2 processors. Now the row 1 processors transmit the b values to the row 2 processors. At this time, the jth row 2 processor contains a_{ji} and b_i. The computation $c \leftarrow c + a\,b$ completes the ith cycle. After n such cycles, the product vector c has been computed and it is extracted from the right end of row 2.

Performance

$P = 2n$, $B = 2$, $T_C = n$, $T_D = n^2 + 2n$, $R_C = 2$, $R_D = 2$ and $R = 4$.

The similarity between Horowitz's two row design and our broadcast chain of the previous section should be evident. The row 1 processors are really unnecessary as they perform no computation.

2.6. $n \times n$ Mesh With $O(n)$ Bandwidth

The architecture for a matrix $\times$ vector product is shown in Figure 2.5. The as and bs are input into the $n \times n$ mesh in n time units. Following this, the PE at position (i,j) contains a_{ij} and b_j. Each PE computes $a * b$ and then sends the result to the leftmost PE in the row. This PE sums the

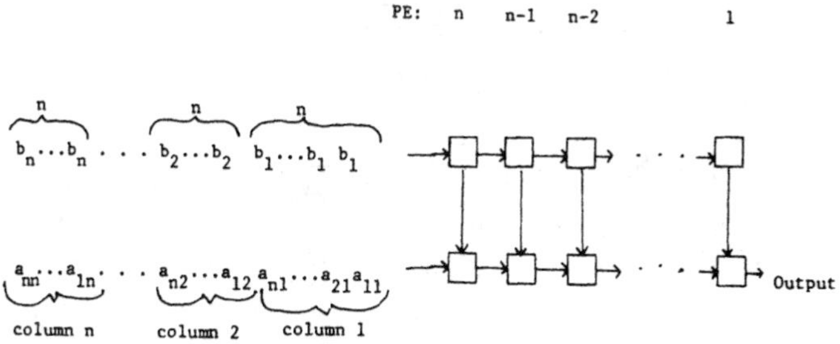

Figure 2.4

products. Following $n - 1$ such steps, the PE at position $(i,1)$ has computed c_i and the results are extracted from the mesh.

Performance

For this design, we see that $P = n^2$, $B = 2n$, $T_C = n$, $T_D = 2n$, $R_C = n$, $R_D \sim 4$ and $R \sim 4n$.

One should note that the n computation steps comprising T_C consist of 1 multiply and $n - 1$ additions. In our earlier examples, each computation step consists of 1 multiply and 1 addition.

2.7. $n \times n$ Mesh With $O(1)$ Bandwidth

This is quite similar to the $O(n)$ bandwidth case except that all the input is provided through the PE at position (1,1) (see Figure 2.6). During the input phase, a row of as is read into the row 1 PEs and the bs are read into the column 1 PE. The rows of as are shifted down and the columns of bs shifted right. This is done concurrently. Following n iterations of this, the PE at position (i,j) contains a_{ij} and b_j. Each PE performs a product and sends the result to the leftmost column where the products are summed. The results are extracted from the PE at position (1,1) or (n,n).

Performance

For this design, we have $P = n^2$, $B = 2$, $T_C = n$, $T_D = n^2 + 2n - 1$, $R_C = n$, $R_D \sim 2$ and $R \sim 2n$.

2.8. Summary

The performance of the VLSI architectures for the matrix $\times$ vector product problem is summarized in Table 2.1. As can be seen, we have improved upon earlier designs for chains with and without broadcast capability when the bandwidth is $O(n)$. The performance of the $n \times n$ mesh is not very good for this problem.

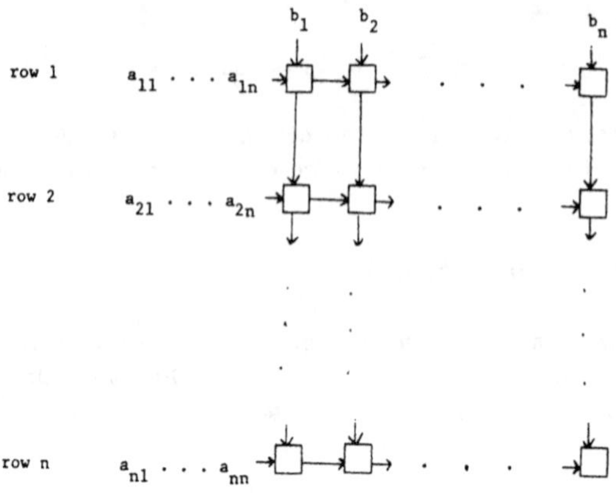

Figure 2.5

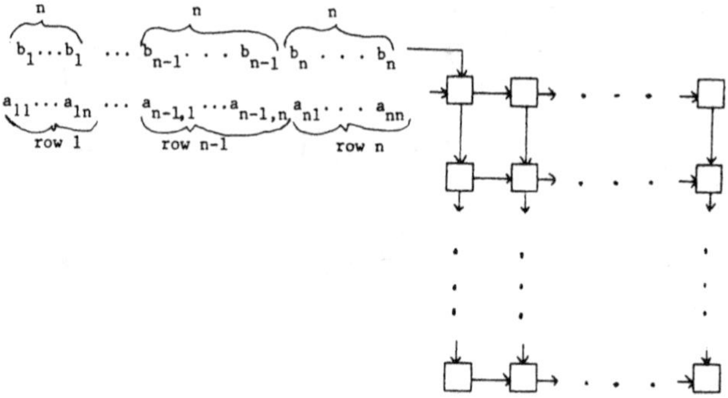

Figure 2.6

3. Band Matrix $\times$ Vector Multiplication

3.1. The problem

Input: An $n \times n$ matrix A with bandwidth w ($w << n$) and a column vector b.

Output: A column vector c such that $c = Ab$.

Parameters: $C \sim w\,n$, $D \sim (w+2)\,n$.

3.2. Chain With O(n) Bandwidth

The architecture and input structure are shown in Figure 3.1. PE i computes c_i. w_1 and w_2 are, respectively, the number of diagonals below and above the main diagonal. As can be seen, the as are input by diagonals starting with the lowermost one. Algorithm 2.1 describes the working of the PEs.

Correctness

To establish the correctness of Figure 3.1, we use the same notation as in our proof of Section 2.2. $a(i,t) = a_{i,i-w_1+t-1}$ and $b(i,t) = b_{i-w_1+t-1}$, $1 \le i \le n$, $1 \le t \le w$ (the defined a_{ij}s and b_js are extended so that $a_{ij} = b_j = 0$ whenever $j \le 0$ or $j > n$). As t ranges from 1 to w, the w diagonals of A enter the VLSI system (from lowermost to uppermost). The computed c_i is $\sum_{t=1}^{w} a_{i,i-w_1+t-1} * b_{i-w_1+t-1}$, which is readily seen as being correct.

Performance	Architecture: Chain With O(n) Bandwidth [KUNG79]	Chain With O(n) Bandwidth Our	Chain With O(1) Bandwidth	Broadcast Chain With O(n) Bandwidth [HUAN82]	Broadcast Chain With O(n) Bandwidth Our
P	n	n	n	n	n
B	$2n+1$	$n+1$	1	$n+1$	$n+1$
T_C	$2n-1$	n	n	$2n-1$	n
T_D	$2n$	$n+2$	n^2+2n	$2n$	$n+1$
R_C	2	1	1	2	1
R_D	4	1	1	2	1
R	8	1	1	4	1

Performance	Architecture: n Independent Processors	Two Rows Mesh With O(1) Bandwidth [HORO79]	$n \times n$ Mesh With O(n) Bandwidth	$n \times n$ Mesh With O(1) Bandwidth
P	n	$2n$	n^2	n^2
B	$2n$	2	$2n$	2
T_C	n	n	n	n
T_D	$n+1$	n^2+2n	$2n$	n^2+2n-1
R_C	1	2	n	n
R_D	2	2	4	2
R	2	4	$4n$	$2n$

$C = n^2$, $D = n^2 + 2n$

Table 2.1

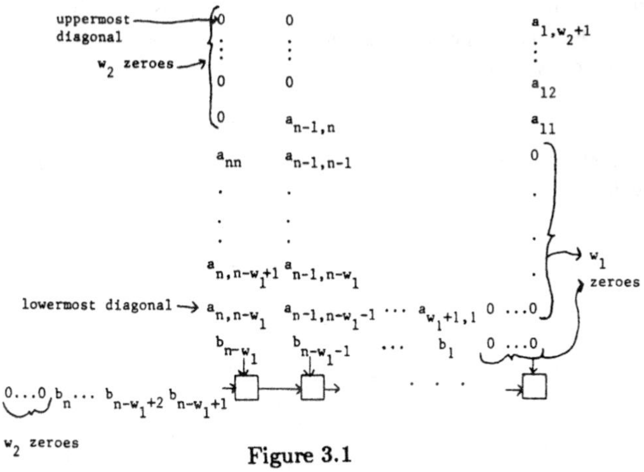

Figure 3.1

Performance

We see that $P = n$, $B = n + 1$, $T_C = w$, $T_D = w + 2$, $R_C \sim 1$, $R_D \sim 1 + 1/n \sim 1$, $R = 1 + 1/n \sim 1$ (when n is large).

3.3. Chain With O(1) Bandwidth

The architecture is the same as that shown in Figure 2.2. The data is input in the order needed by the design of Section 3.2. The row of bs and the lowermost diagonal of A are entered first. Next, b_{n-w_1+1} and the next diagonal of A are entered, and so on.

Performance

For this new scheme, $P = n$, $B = 1$, $T_C = w$, $T_D = (w+2)n$, $R_C \sim 1$, $R_D \sim 1$, $R \sim 1$.

3.4. Bidirectional Chain With O(w) Bandwidth

Kung [KUNG79] and Leiserson [LEIS83] have proposed the bidirectional chain architecture of Figure 3.2(a). The performance figures for this design are $P = w$, $B = (w/2+1)$, $T_C \sim 2n + w$, $T_D \sim 2n + w$, $R_C \sim 2$, $R_D \sim 1$ and $R \sim 2$. Leiserson [LEIS83] points out that pairs of processors can be combined into 1 as only half the processors are active at any time instance. When this is done, R_C and R become 1.

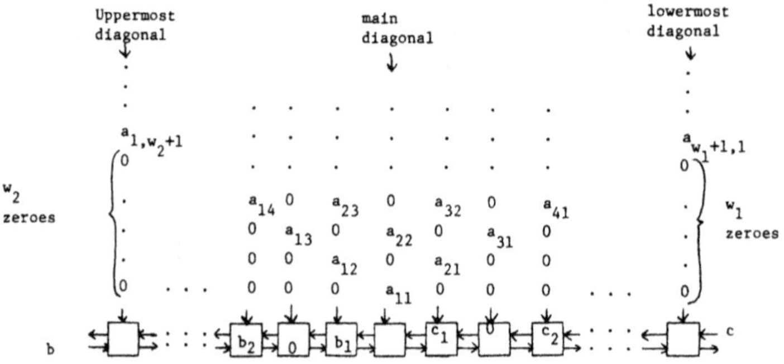

Figure 3.2(a)

It is interesting to note that similar performance can be obtained by a unidirectional chain with O(w) bandwidth. The system computes c in $m = \lceil n/w \rceil$ cycles. In cycle q, PE(i) computes $c_{i+(q-1)w}$, $1 \le q \le m$. Example input for the case $w = 4$, $w_1 = 2$, $w_2 = 1$ is shown in Figure 3.2(b). Algorithm 3.1 describes how the system works.

Performance

For the unidirectional chain, we have $P = w$, $B = w + 2$, $T_C = mw \sim n$, $T_D = mw + 1 \sim n + 1$, $R_C \sim 1$, $R_D \sim 1$, and $R \sim 1$.

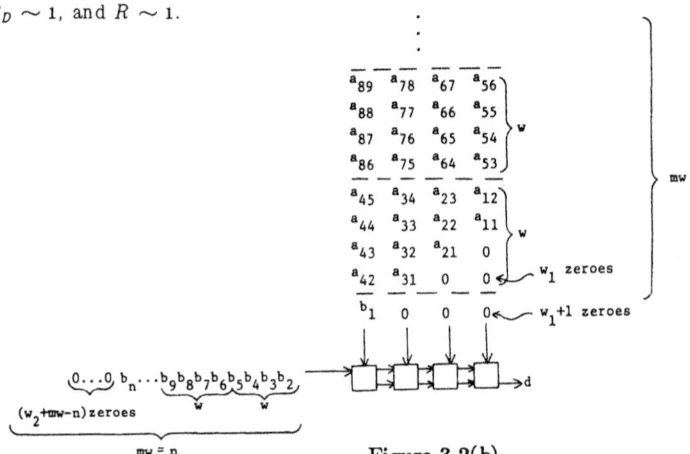

Figure 3.2(b)

```
input row of bs from above;
for q ←1 to m do
    d ← c;
    c ← 0;
    for k ←1 to w do
        input row of as from top;
        input a b from left and shift bs right;
        output and shift ds right;
        c ← c + a b;
    end
end
output the last w cs from top;
```

Algorithm 3.1

3.5. Broadcast Chain With O(w) Bandwidth

Huang and Abraham [HUAN82] have proposed the broadcast chain architecture of Figure 3.3. The number of PEs used is w, the as are entered by columns and the bs broadcast in the order $b_1, b_2, \ldots$. Each processor computes $c \leftarrow c + a\,b$ and then sends the c value to the left. Clearly, $P = w$, $B = w + 1$, $T_C = n$, $T_D \sim n + w$, $R_C \sim 1$, $R_D \sim 1 + w/n \sim 1$, $R \sim 1 + w/n \sim 1$. In light of our unidirectional chain design of Section 3.4, there is little advantage to having a broadcast capability for chains for the band matrix $\times$ vector problem.

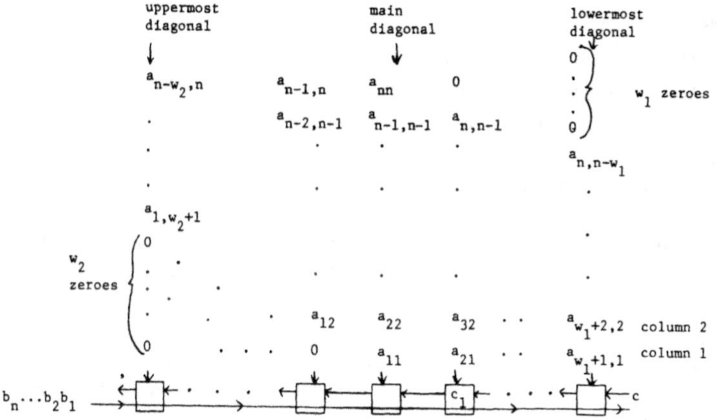

Figure 3.3

3.6. $n \times n$ Mesh

The $n \times n$ mesh architectures presented in Section 2.6 and 2.7 for the matrix $\times$ vector product problem are quite inefficient. Those for the band matrix $\times$ vector product problem are no more efficient than before and we shall not present these.

3.7. Summary

The performance of the VLSI architectures for the band matrix $\times$ vector product problem are summarized in Table 3.1. This appears to be the first time that O(n) and O(1) bandwidth chain designs have been developed for this problem. Earlier work has been restricted to O(w) bandwidth chains. In one case, a bidirectional chain was used and, in the other, a broadcast capability. We have shown that neither of these capabilities is needed. Equally good performance is obtainable by a unidirectional chain with $O(w)$ bandwidth.

Performance	Architecture				
	Chain With $O(n)$ Bandwidth	Chain With $O(1)$ Bandwidth	Bidirectional Chain With $O(w)$ Bandwidth [LEIS83]	Chain With $O(w)$ Bandwidth	Broadcast Chain With $O(w)$ Bandwidth [HUAN82]
P	n	n	$w/2$	w	w
B	$n+1$	1	$w/2+1$	$w+2$	$w+1$
T_C	w	w	$2n+w$	n	n
T_D	$w+2$	$(w+2)n$	$2n+w$	$n+1$	$n+w$
R_C	1	1	1	1	1
R_D	1	1	1	1	1
R	1	1	1	1	1

$C \sim wn$, $D \sim (w+2)n$

Table 3.1

4. Matrix $\times$ Matrix Product

4.1. The Problem

Input: Two $n \times n$ matrices A and B.

Output: An $n \times n$ matrix C such that $C = AB$.

Parameters: $C = n^3$, $D = 3n^2$.

4.2. Chain With $O(n)$ Bandwidth

The product matrix C can be formed by performing n matrix $\times$ vector products involving the matrix A and the columns of B. This is done using the architecture of Figure 2.1(b).

Performance

We get $P = n$, $B = n+1$, $T_C = n^2$, $T_D = n^2 + 2n$, $R_C = 1$, $R_D \sim n/3$, $R \sim n/3$. R_D and R can be reduced to 1 by providing each PE with enough memory to store a row of A, a column of B and an element of C and by making the inter PE bandwidth n. We shall not go into the details of this here. Some of the necessary ideas are developed in Section 4.3.

4.3. Chain With $O(1)$ Bandwidth

Once again, we may use the matrix $\times$ vector multiplication algorithm n times. The result matrix may be extracted from the right end.

Performance

We see that $P = n$, $B = 2$, $T_C = n^2$, $T_D = n^3 + n^2 + n$, $R_C = 1$, $R_D \sim 2n/3$, $R \sim 2n/3$,

System performance may be improved by providing each PE with enough memory to hold a row of A and a column of each of B and C. The B values are first input in column major order. Following this, PE(i) contains column i of B. Next, A is input in row major order. Following this, PE(i) contains column i of B and row i of A. PE(i) computes column i of C using the procedure of Algorithm 4.1. Finally, the results are extracted from one end of the chain.

for $q \leftarrow 1$ **to** n **do**
PE(i) computes $c_{(i+q-2) \bmod n+1, i}$, $1 \le i \le n$
using the A and B values it already has;
if $q < n$ **then**
[all PEs (except the rightmost) send their row of A to the PE on the right and the leftmost PE, PE(n), inputs row q of A];
end

Algorithm 4.1

Performance

It is not too difficult to see that $P = n$, $B = 1$, $T_C = n^2$, $T_D = 4n^2 - n$, $R_C = 1$, $R_D \sim 4/3$, $R \sim 4/3$. Note that the additional input of $n - 1$ rows of A can be avoided by providing an end around connection that connects PEs 1 and n. In this case, the **if** statement of Algorithm 4.1 simply becomes:

if $q < n$ **then**
[all PEs send their row of A to the PE on the right];

This change does not affect any of our performance measures. Further, the memory requirements of the PEs can be reduced by extracting the Cs as they are computed. When this is done, each PE needs only $2n + 1$ words of memory. The performance figures are unaffected. While even this memory requirement may seem excessive, it should be observed that programmable systolic computers that are currently being developed, [KUNG83c], will have this much memory.

4.4. Broadcast Chain

The broadcast chain of Section 2.4 may be used n times to multiply two matrices.

Performance

The performance values are $P = n$, $B = n + 1$, $T_C = n^2$, $T_D = n^2 + n$, $R_C = 1$, $R_D \sim n/3$, $R \sim n/3$.

4.5. $n \times n$ Mesh With O(n) Bandwidth

The architecture is shown in Figure 4.1. The A and B elements enter the mesh from the left and top respectively. Row i of the mesh receives $2n - 1$ elements from row i of A while column j receives $2n - 1$ elements from column j of B. Clearly, some elements enter the mesh more than once. Let a_{ij} be an element that enters row i of the mesh. The next element from A to enter this row is a_{ik} where

$$k = \begin{cases} j - 1 & \text{if } j \neq 1 \\ n & \text{if } j = 1 \end{cases}$$

Let b_{jp} be an element that enters column p of the mesh. The next element from B to enter this column is b_{kp} where k is as above. The first column of A values being input is the main diagonal a_{11}, a_{22}, ..., a_{nn} and the first row of B values being input is again the main diagonal b_{11}, b_{22}, b_{33}, ..., b_{nn}. Figure 4.1 shows the input sequence.

We begin by initializing the c register of each PE to zero. Next, n rows of B values and n columns of A values are read into the mesh. Following this, the PE at position (i,j) has $a_{i,(i+j-1) \bmod n+1}$ in its a register and $b_{(i+j-1) \bmod n+1, j}$ in its b register. Each PE multiplies the contents of its a and b registers and adds the result to its c register. This is followed by $n - 1$ cycles of reading in a row of bs from above, a column of as from the left, multiply and add to c. Note that each time a row of bs is input, all bs are shifted down one row. Similarly, each time a column of as is input, all as are shifted right one column.

This algorithm is quite similar to that proposed for a mesh connected computer [DEKE81]. The result matrix can be extracted either from the left or the top.

Correctness

Let $a(i,j,t)$, $b(i,j,t)$ and $c(i,j,t)$ denote respectively the a, b and c values in PE(i,j) just after the tth multiplication and addition is performed. As remarked above, $a(i,j,1) = a_{i,(i+j-1) \bmod n + 1}$ and $b(i,j,1) = b_{(i+j-1) \bmod n + 1, j}$. From the input data pattern of Figure 4.1 and the data flow, it follows that $a(i,j,t) = a_{i,(i+j-t) \bmod n + 1}$ and $b(i,j,t) = b_{(i+j-t) \bmod n + 1, j}$. Hence,

$$c(i,j,n) = \sum_{t=1}^{n} a(i,j,t) * b(i,j,t)$$

$$= \sum_{t=1}^{n} a_{i,(i+j-t) \bmod n + 1} * b_{(i+j-t) \bmod n + 1, j}$$

$$= \sum_{t=1}^{n} a_{it} * b_{tj}$$

$$= c_{ij}$$

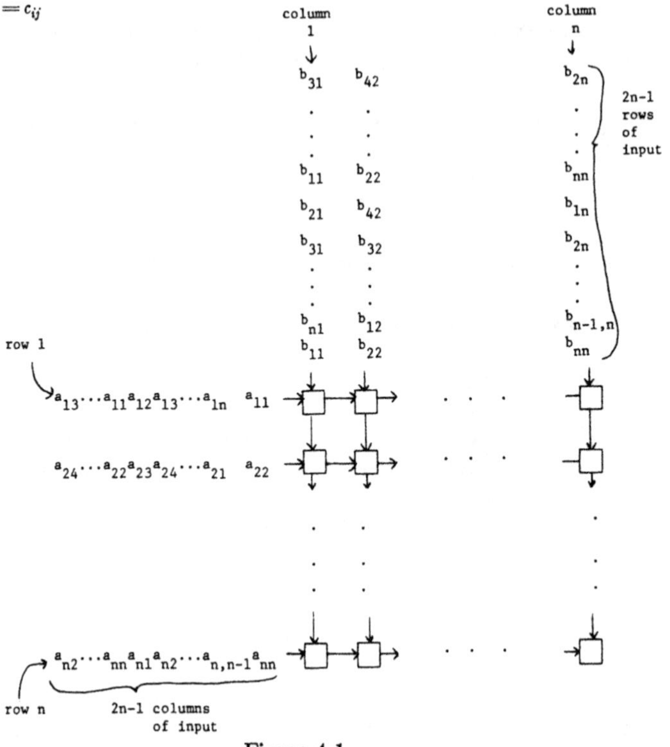

Figure 4.1

Performance

We see that $P = n^2$, $B = 2n$, $T_C = n$, $T_D = 3n - 1$, $R_C = 1$, $R_D = 2 - 2/(3n) \sim 2$, $R \sim 2$.

4.6. Broadcast Mesh With O(n) Bandwidth

Huang and Abraham [HUAN82] present an O(n) bandwidth mesh architecture which has a broadcast capability only along the rows of the mesh. This architecture has $P = n^2$, $B = 2n$, $T_C = 2n - 1$, $T_D = 3n - 1$, $R_C \sim 2$, $R_D \sim 2$, $R \sim 4$. These performance figures can be improved by providing a broadcast capability along both the rows and columns of the mesh. The architecture is as in Figure 4.2. The B matrix enters the mesh by rows and the A matrix by columns. The PE at position (i,j) computes c_{ij}. In the kth step, this PE computes $a_{ik} * b_{kj}$ and adds the result to its c register.

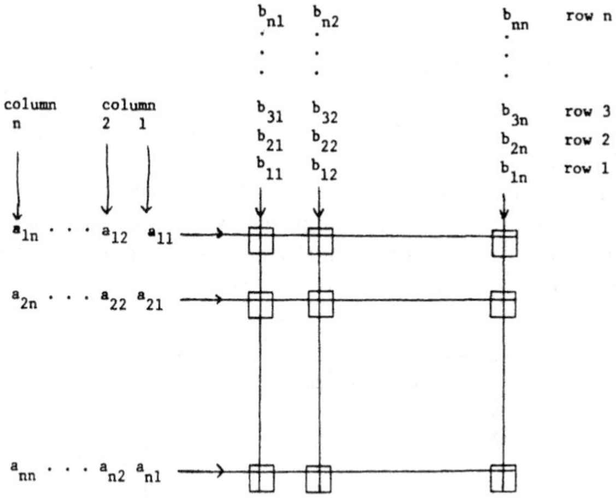

Figure 4.2

Performance

For this architecture, we have $P = n^2$, $B = 2n$, $T_C = n$, $T_D = 2n$, $R_C = 1$, $R_D = 4/3$, $R = 4/3$.

4.7. $n \times n$ Mesh With O(1) Bandwidth

The architecture is shown in Figure 4.3. This works in a manner quite similar to the case when the bandwidth is $2n$. The essential difference is that the input comes only through the PE at position (1,1). Consequently, it takes n input steps to simulate 1 input step of the O(n) bandwidth architecture.

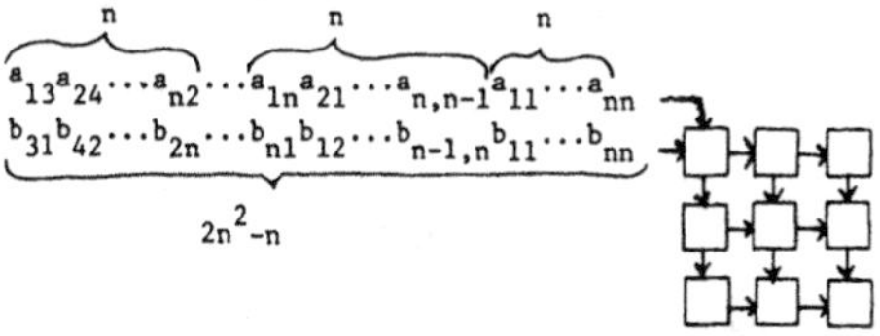

Figure 4.3

Performance

The performance figures are $P = n^2$, $B = 2$, $T_C = n$, $T_D = 3n^2 - n$, $R_C = 1$, $R_D = 2 - 2/(3n) \sim 2$, $R \sim 2$.

4.8. $n \times n$ Broadcast Mesh With O(1) Bandwidth

The architecture is shown in Figure 4.4. It is somewhat simpler than that used for the O(n) bandwidth case as the broadcast capability is now needed only for the row 1 and column 1 PEs.

Performance

It is easily seen that $P = n^2$, $B = 2$, $T_C = n$, $T_D = 2n^2$, $R_C = 1$, $R_D = 4/3$, $R = 4/3$.

4.9. Hexagonally Connected PEs

The hexagonally connected architecture together with the data flow proposed by Kung [KUNG79] has an R value of 50. Huang and Abraham [HUAN82] have proposed an alternate data flow which results in $R = 8$. The architecture proposed in both [KUNG79] and [HUAN82] use n^2 PEs. It is interesting to note that the hexagonal architecture actually contains all the connections in a mesh arrangement (and more). A mesh interpretation for a hexagonal architecture is shown in Figure 4.5. Hence, we may use the algorithm and data flow of Section 4.5 and ignore the two additional connections per PE that are available. The resulting scheme has an R of 2.

It is an interesting exercise to see how well one can perform on a hexagonally connected processor array under the assumptions of [KUNG79] and [HUAN82] that the a, b, and c values must move in each cycle and that all cycles must be identical. We can improve on the R value by using the data pattern shown in Figure 4.6. This data pattern is most easily defined by labeling the inputs as in Figure 4.7. Note that the c values are initialized to zero at the input PEs. This is not regarded as input to the system and so does not affect the bandwidth.

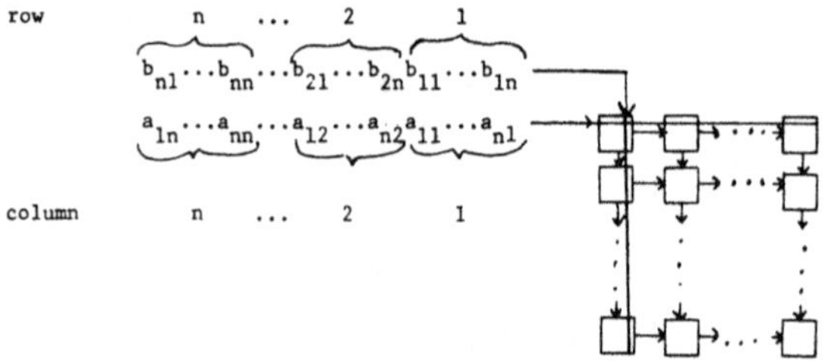

Figure 4.4

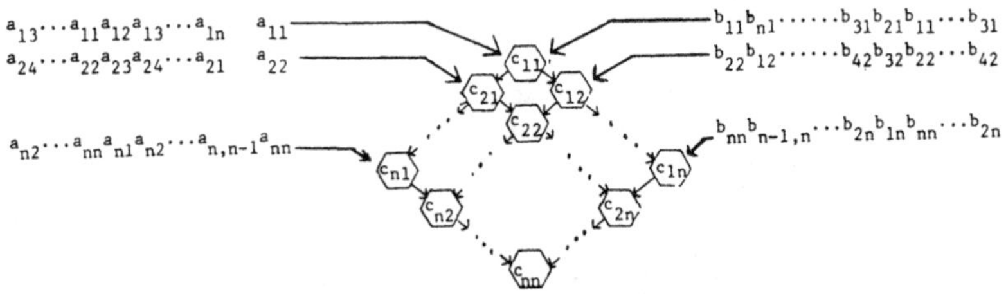

Figure 4.5

The input and the output data patterns are defined as:

$$A(i,j) = a_{i,(i+j-1) \bmod n + 1}, \qquad 1 \le i \le n,\ 1 \le j < 2n$$

$$B(i,j) = b_{(i-j) \bmod n + 1,\ (j-1) \bmod n + 1}, \qquad 1 \le i \le 3n-2,\ 1 \le j < 2n$$

$$C(i,j) = c_{i,(i+j-2) \bmod n + 1}, \qquad 1 \le i \le n,\ 1 \le j \le n$$

In each cycle, the as, bs and cs move along their respective connections with the PEs on the three upper boundaries inputting new as, bs and cs. Each PE multiplies the new a and b value received, adds it to the input c value and passes the a, b and new c out.

From the data flow, it follows that the terms accumulated in $C(i,j)$ are

$$A(i, n-j+1) * B(2i-1, i+j-1)$$
$$A(i, n-j+2) * B(2i, i+j-1)$$
$$A(i, n-j+3) * B(2i+1, i+j-1)$$
$$\vdots$$
$$A(i, 2n-j) \quad * B(2i+n-2, i+j-1)$$

Hence the final value of $C(i,j)$ is

$$\sum_{k=1}^{n} A(i, n-j+k) * B(2i-2+k, i+j-1)$$

$$= \sum_{k=1}^{n} a_{i,(i-j+k-1) \bmod n+1} * b_{(i-j+k-1) \bmod n+1, (i+j-2) \bmod n+1}$$

$$= c_{i,(i+j-2) \bmod n+1}$$

For the system of Figure 4.7, we see that $P = n^2$, $B = 5n - 3$ (note that the cs begin to exit after n steps. From this time on, the number of As input on each cycle is $\leq n$ and the number of Bs $\leq 3n - 3$.), $T_C = 2n - 1$, $T_D = 2n$, $R_C = 2$, $R_D = 10/3$, $R = 20/3$.

The R value can further be improved to 5 by using a VLSI system that has two types of cycles. In the first type of cycle, only data moves take place and there is no computation. The second cycle type is identical to that employed in the design of Figure 4.7. Cycles of the first type are used to load all the PEs with a suitable pair of A and B values and also to extract the results. After the PEs have been loaded with a suitable pair of A and B values, cycles of the second type are used to compute C. The input data pattern for 3×3 matrices is shown in Figure 4.8(a). Three type 1 cycles are used to get the As, Bs and Cs into the right PEs. Following this, we have the configuration of Figure 4.8(b). Now, we have three cycles of multiply, add and shift. During the shift, the values of A, B and C move. The C values that exit the system are fed back into the system as shown in the figure. Finally, the results are extracted using three type 1 cycles.

The data pattern for the general $n \times n$ matrix multiplication is given by the formulae below. The labeling scheme of Figure 4.9 is used.

$$A(i,j) = a_{(j-i) \bmod n+1, (j-1) \bmod n+1}, \qquad 1 \leq i \leq n, 1 \leq j < 2n$$
$$B(i,j) = b_{(i-1) \bmod n+1, (j-1) \bmod n+1}, \qquad 1 \leq i < 2n, 1 \leq j \leq n$$
$$C(i,j) = c_{(i-j) \bmod n+1, (i-1) \bmod n+1}, \qquad 1 \leq i \leq n, 1 \leq j \leq n$$

The n terms accumulated by each $C(i,j)$, $1 \leq i \leq n$, $1 \leq j \leq n$ are:

$$A((n-i) \bmod n+1, n-j+1) \quad * B(n-j+1, i)$$
$$A((n-i+1) \bmod n+1, n-j+2) * B(n-j+2, i)$$
$$A((n-i+2) \bmod n+1, n-j+3) * B(n-j+3, i)$$
$$\vdots$$
$$A((2n-i-1) \bmod n+1, 2n-j) \quad * B(2n-j, i)$$

Therefore,

$$C(i,j)$$
$$= \sum_{k=1}^{n} A((n-i+k-1) \bmod n+1, n-j+k) * B(n-j+k, i)$$

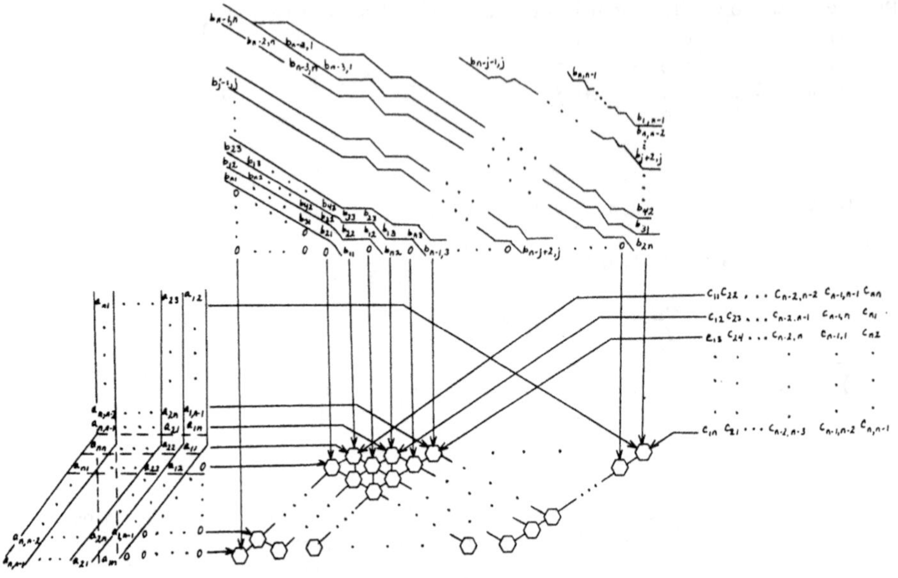

Figure 4.6

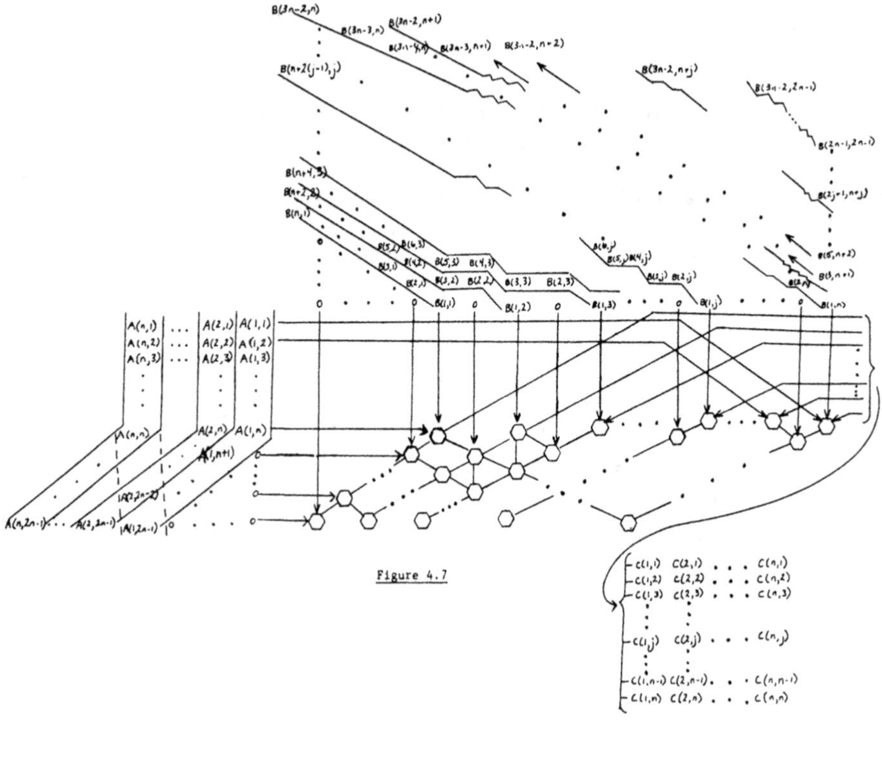

Figure 4.7

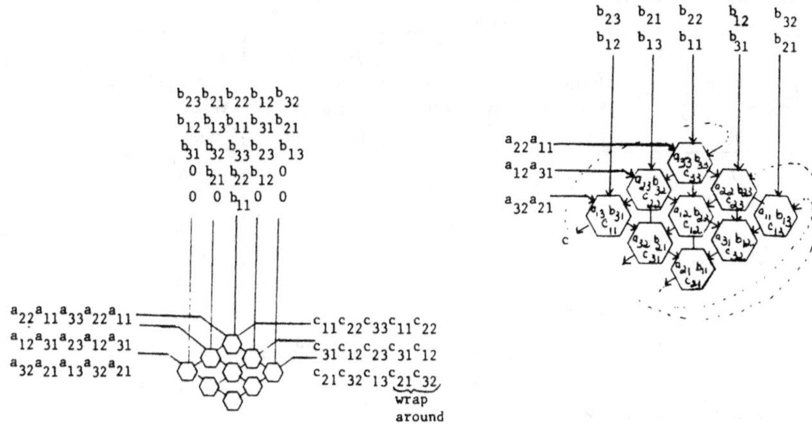

(a) (b)

Figure 4.8

$$= \sum_{k=1}^{n} a_{(i-j) \bmod n+1,\,(n-j+k-1) \bmod n+1} * b_{(n-j+k-1) \bmod n+1,\,(i-1) \bmod n+1}$$

$$= c_{(i-j) \bmod n+1,\,(i-1) \bmod n+1}$$

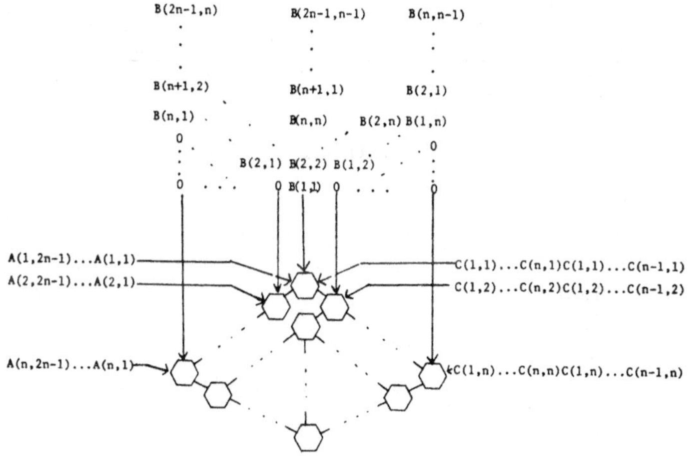

Figure 4.9

Performance

From Figure 4.9, we see that $P = n^2$, $B = 5n - 1$, $T_C = n$, $T_D = 3n - 1$, $R_C = 1$, $R_D = 5$ and $R = 5$.

4.10. Summary

The performance of the various architectures for the matrix $\times$ matrix product problem is summarized in Table 4.1. Our designs reflect an improvement over earlier ones for the case of broadcast meshes and hexagonal processor arrays. The improvement for a broadcast mesh is obtained at the expense of increased broadcast requirements.

Performance	Architecture				
	Chain With O(n) Bandwidth	Chain With O(1) Bandwidth	Chain With O(n) Memory	Broadcast Chain With O(n) Bandwidth	$n \times n$ Mesh With O(n) Bandwidth
P	n	n	n	n	n^2
B	$n+1$	2	1	$n+1$	$2n$
T_C	n^2	n^2	n^2	n^2	n
T_D	n^2+2n	n^3+n^2+n	$4n^2-n$	n^2+n	$3n-1$
R_C	1	1	1	1	1
R_D	$n/3$	$2n/3$	$4/3$	$n/3$	2
R	$n/3$	$2n/3$	$4/3$	$n/3$	2

Performance	Architecture			
	Broadcast Mesh With O(n) Bandwidth	$n \times n$ Mesh With O(1) Bandwidth	Broadcast Mesh With O(1) Bandwidth	Hexagonal With O(n) Bandwidth
P	n^2	n^2	n^2	n^2
B	$2n$	2	2	$5n-1$
T_C	n	n	n	n
T_D	$2n$	$3n^2-n$	$2n^2$	$3n-1$
R_C	1	1	1	1
R_D	$4/3$	2	$4/3$	5
R	$4/3$	2	$4/3$	5

$C = n^3$, $D = 3n^2$

Table 4.1

5. Band Matrix Multiplication

5.1. The Problem

Input: Two $n \times n$ band matrices A and B. The bandwidth of A is w_A and that of B is w_B.

Output: An $n \times n$ band matrix C that is the product of A and B. The bandwidth of C is at most $w_A + w_B - 1$.

Parameters: $m = \min\{w_A, w_B\}$, $M = \max\{w_A, w_B\}$, $S = \min\{n, w_A + w_B - 1\}$, $w = w_A + w_B$, $C \sim w_A w_B n$, $D \sim 2(w_A + w_B)n$.

5.2. Chain With O(w) Bandwidth

The product matrix can be computed one column at a time using the architecture of Figure 3.1. Only S processors are needed as there are at most this many non-zero terms in a column. Computing each column of C requires us to compute the product of an $S \times w_B$ band matrix with bandwidth w_A and a $w_B \times 1$ vector. This is done n times to get all the columns of C.

Performance

We see that $P = S$, $B = w$, $T_C = w_A n$, $T_D = (w_A + 2)n$, $R_C \sim 1 + w_A/w_B$, $R_D \sim 1 + w_A/2$, $R \sim (1 + w_A/w_B)(1 + w_A/2)$. If $w_A > w_B$, the computation may be rearranged so that $R_C \sim 1 + w_B/w_A$, $R_D \sim 1 + w_B/2$, $R \sim (1 + w_B/w_A)(1 + w_B/2)$. So, $T_C = mn$, $T_D = (m+2)n$,

$R_C \sim 1 + m/M \sim 2$, $R_D \sim 1 + m/2$, $R \sim (1 + m/M)(1 + m/2) \sim 2 + m$.

When each PE has $2w_A + 2w_B - 1$ words of memory, system performance may be improved by using the PEs in a manner similar to that of Section 4.3. A chain with n PEs is employed. When $w_A \leq w_B$, PE(i) is used to compute column i of C. When $w_A > w_B$, PE(i) computes row i of C. We describe the process only for the case $w_A \leq w_B$.

The band of B is input in column major order and that of A by rows. Following this, PE(i) contains column i of the band of B and row $i - \min\{u_1 + u_2, n - 1\}$ of the band of A. If $i \leq \min\{u_1 + u_2, n - 1\}$, then the A elements are zero. u_1 and u_2 are, respectively, the upper bandwidths of A and B. Each PE is now ready to compute the uppermost diagonal of C. The computation of the band of C proceeds as in Algorithm 5.1.

```
for q ←1 to w_A + w_B - 1 do
    PE(i) computes the element (if any) in column i of
    the q^th diagonal of the band of C (Diagonals are
    numbered from the top);
    if q < w_A + w_B - 1 then
        [each PE except the rightmost shifts its row of A
         to the right and the leftmost PE inputs row
         n + q - min{u_1 + u_2, n - 1} of the band
         of A (if this is > n, then zeros are input)];
end
```

Algorithm 5.1

Performance

For this design, we have $P = n$, $B = 1$, $T_C = w_A w_B$, $T_D \sim (2n + m) w$, $R_C \sim 1$, $R_D \sim 1 + w_A/(2n) \sim 1$ and $R \sim 1$.

5.3. Chain With O(n) Bandwidth

The n processors are used to compute the $w_A + w_B - 1$ diagonals of C in $w_A + w_B - 1$ steps. In the ith phase, the jth processor from the left computes the jth element in the ith diagonal from the bottom. The position of a diagonal element is determined by extending the band of C in the natural way so that each diagonal has exactly n elements in it (see Figure 5.1). The ith element in a diagonal is on row i. The appropriate A and B data needed for the computation of the diagonal elements is input into the system for each C element to be computed. As the processors do not share data, no interconnection between the PEs is needed. So, they might as well be independent PEs. Let l_1 and u_1 be, respectively, the number of diagonals below and above the main diagonal of A. Let l_2 and u_2 be the corresponding figures for B. An example input data for the case $n = 5$, $l_1 = 2$, $u_1 = 1$, $l_2 = 1$, $u_2 = 1$ is shown in Figure 5.1.

Performance

As can be seen, $P = n$, $B = 2n$, $T_C = w_A w_B$, $T_D = 2 + \sum_{i=1}^{m} i + [w_A + w_B - 2m - 1] m + w_A + w_B - 1 = w_A w_B + w_A + w_B - 1$, $R_C \sim 1$, $R_D \sim 1 + (w_A w_B)/w$ and $R = 1 + (w_A w_B)/w$.

5.4. Chain With O(1) Bandwidth

Two algorithms can be devised from the multiple input chain. The first algorithm works like the chain with $O(w)$ bandwidth except that all input enters from the leftmost PE and the results are extracted from the right. For this algorithm, $P = S$, $B = 2$, $T_C = m\,n$, $T_D = ((m+1)n+1)S$, $R_C \sim 1 + m/M \sim 2$, $R_D \sim 1 + m$ and $R \sim 2(1+m)$.

The second algorithm works essentially as the n independent PE computation described in Section 5.3. However, this time the PE to PE interconnection is used. The performance figures for this design are $P = n$, $B = 2$, $T_C = w_A\, w_B$, $T_D = n(w_A\, w_B + w - 1)$, $R_C \sim 1$, $R_D \sim 1 + (w_A\, w_B)/w$ and $R \sim 1 + (w_A\, w_B)/w$.

5.5. Mesh with O(n) Bandwidth

The result matrix consists of $w_A + w_B - 1$ diagonals. The mesh architecture contains one PE for each element on these diagonals. Hence, the configuration depends on the precise $w_A + w_B - 1$ diagonals of the product matrix C that contain non-zero elements. Figure 5.2 shows the architecture for the same case as Figure 5.1, i.e. when the bandwidth of C is 6 and there are two diagonals above and three below the main diagonal. The PE at position (i,j) computes c_{ij}.

The PEs are initially loaded so that they contain multipliable pairs. I.e., PE(i,j) contains a_{ik} and b_{kj} for some k, or one or both of the A and B registers are zero. In addition, the bs in each column and the as in each row repeat with a period M. The configuration for an example A and B is shown in Figure 5.2. S data moves are required to obtain this configuration. Now a multiplication takes place. This is followed by $M - 1$ cycles in which the as move right, the bs down and a multiply-add is performed. Finally, the results are extracted in S units of time.

More specifically, let $A(i,j)$ and $B(i,j)$ be respectively the A and B values in the PE at position (i,j) (we extend the PE configuration by $w_A - 1$ PEs to the left of each row and above each column from those pictured in Figure 5.2). Let l_1 and u_1 be, respectively, the number of diagonals below and above the main diagonal of A. Let l_2 and u_2 be the corresponding figures for B. We consider the case $w_A \geq w_B$ only. The case $w_A < w_B$ is similar. First define the A and B values to be: (for $k = 0, 1, 2, \ldots$)

$$A(i,j) = \begin{cases} a_{i,\,i+j+w_A k - n} & j \in [\,n - w_A k - l_1,\, n - w_A k\,] \\ a_{i,\,i+j+w_A(k+1)-n} & j \in [\,n - w_A(k+1) + 1,\, n - w_A k - l_1) \end{cases}$$

$$B(i,j) = \begin{cases} b_{i+j+w_A k - n,\,j} & i \in [\,n - w_A k - u_2,\, n - w_A k\,] \\ 0 & i \in (\,n - w_A(k+1) + l_2,\, n - w_A k - u_2) \\ b_{i+j+w_A(k+1)-n,\,j} & i \in (\,n - w_A(k+1),\, n - w_A(k+1) + l_2\,] \end{cases}$$

This gives us a preliminary data pattern with period w_A. If an index above exceeds n or is less than 1, the corresponding value is set to 0.

Now, some of the As and Bs defined above need to be changed to zero. In the computation of c_{ij}, only the terms in the sum: $\sum_{q=\max\{i-l_1,\, j-u_2\}}^{\min\{i+u_1,\, j+l_2\}} a_{iq}\, b_{qj}$ are needed. Suppose that a_{is} and b_{rj} are the A and B values assigned to the PE at position (i,j). For a_{is} to be useful, s must be in the range

$$[\min_{0 \leq t < w_A} \{\max\{i - l_1,\, j - u_2 + t\}\},\ \max_{0 \leq t < w_A} \{\min\{i + u_1,\, j + l_2 + t\}\}]$$
$$= [\max\{i - l_1,\, j - u_2\},\, \min\{i + u_1,\, j + l_2 + w_A - 1\}]$$

If s is not in this range, then $A(i,j)$ is set to zero. Similarly, for b_{rj} to be useful, r must be in the range:

$$\left[\min_{0 \le t < w_A} \{\max\{i - l_1 + t,\ j - u_2\}\},\ \max_{0 \le t < w_A} \{\min\{i + u_1 + t,\ j + l_2\}\}\right]$$

$$= [\max\{i - l_1,\ j - u_2\},\ \min\{i + u_1 + w_A - 1,\ j + l_2\}]$$

If r is not in this range, then we may set $B(i,j)$ to zero. We now have the final data pattern to be used.

Correctness A correctness proof may be found in [CHENG84].

$$\begin{bmatrix} a_{11} & a_{12} & & & \\ a_{21} & a_{22} & a_{23} & & \\ a_{31} & a_{32} & a_{33} & a_{34} & \\ & a_{42} & a_{43} & a_{44} & a_{45} \\ & & a_{53} & a_{54} & a_{55} \end{bmatrix} \begin{bmatrix} b_{11} & b_{12} & & & \\ b_{21} & b_{22} & b_{23} & & \\ & b_{32} & b_{33} & b_{34} & \\ & & b_{43} & b_{44} & b_{45} \\ & & & b_{54} & b_{55} \end{bmatrix} = \begin{matrix} 0\ 0\ 0 \\ 0\ 0 \\ 0 \\ \\ \\ \end{matrix} \begin{bmatrix} c_{11} & c_{12} & c_{13} & & \\ c_{21} & c_{22} & c_{23} & c_{24} & \\ c_{31} & c_{32} & c_{33} & c_{34} & c_{35} \\ c_{41} & c_{42} & c_{43} & c_{44} & c_{45} \\ & c_{52} & c_{53} & c_{54} & c_{55} \end{bmatrix} \begin{matrix} \\ \\ \\ 0 \\ 0\ 0 \end{matrix}$$

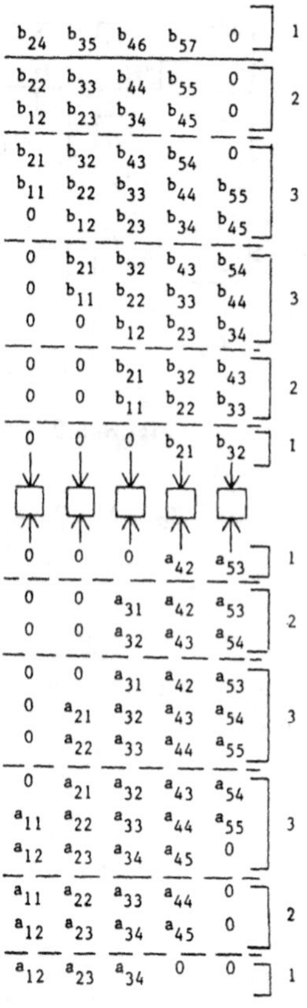

Figure 5.1

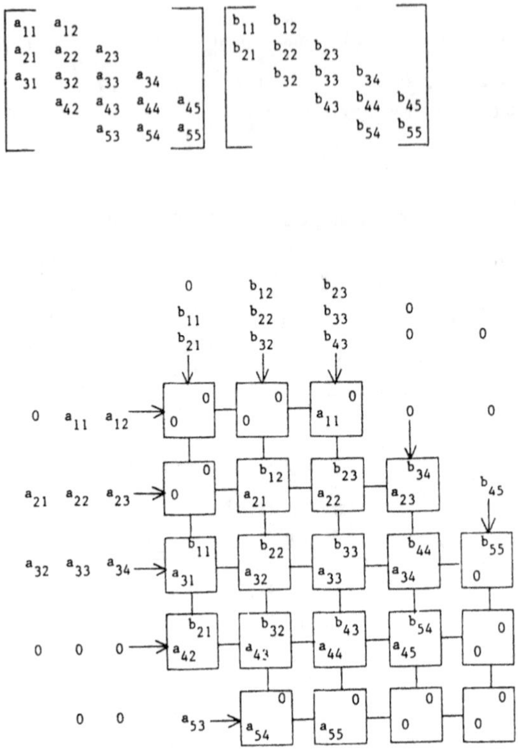

Figure 5.2

Performance

For this scheme, we have $P \sim S n$, $B = 2n$, $T_C = M$, $T_D = 2S + M - 1$, $R_C \sim M$, $R_D \sim 3$ and $R \sim 3M$.

5.6. Mesh With O(1) Bandwidth

This is very similar to the mesh with $O(n)$ bandwidth. An interconnect along the lowermost and uppermost diagonals is added (Figure 5.3) to facilitate easy input and output to and from the system.

Performance

For this architecture, we have $P = m\,n$, $B = 2$, $T_C = M$, $T_D = 2\,m\,n + M - 1$, $R_C \sim M$, $R_D \sim 3$ and $R \sim 3M$.

5.7. Broadcast Mesh With O(n) Bandwidth

A broadcast mesh architecture suitable for the multiplication of band matrices is shown in Figure 5.4. Here, we assume that $w_A + w_B - 1 \leq n$ and $w_B \leq w_A$ (the case when $w_A < w_B$ is symmetric). The broadcast capability is used only for matrix B. The bs are broadcast into the systolic array by diagonals while the as are input as exactly $\min\{n + u_2, w_A + w_B - 1\}$ columns. Row i of the systolic array inputs row i of matrix A (i.e. the part of this row in the band with a suitable shift; the elements enter right to left). Figure 5.4(a) shows the input pattern for the matrices of Figure

5.1. Figure 5.4(b) shows the input pattern for two 6×6 matrices A and B with $w_A = w_B = 2$. A has one diagonal below the main diagonal while B has one above. Figure 5.4(c) shows the input sequence for the case where $w_A = 3$, $w_B = 2$ and neither have any diagonals below the main diagonal. The architecture and input pattern for $n \times n$ matrices with bandwidth w_A and w_B are shown in Figure 5.5. Let l_1, u_1, l_2 and u_2 be as in Section 5.5.

The system begins by initializing the A, B and C registers of all PEs to zero. Then, $\min\{n - u_1, w_A\} - 1$ columns of A input are accepted, shifting each to the right one unit. This is followed by w_B cycles of input and shift As right, broadcast Bs, multiply and add to C. Finally, S left shifts suffice to extract the results. The correctness of the systolic scheme described above follows from the observation that the elements on the uppermost diagonal of C have just one $a_{ik}\, b_{kj}$

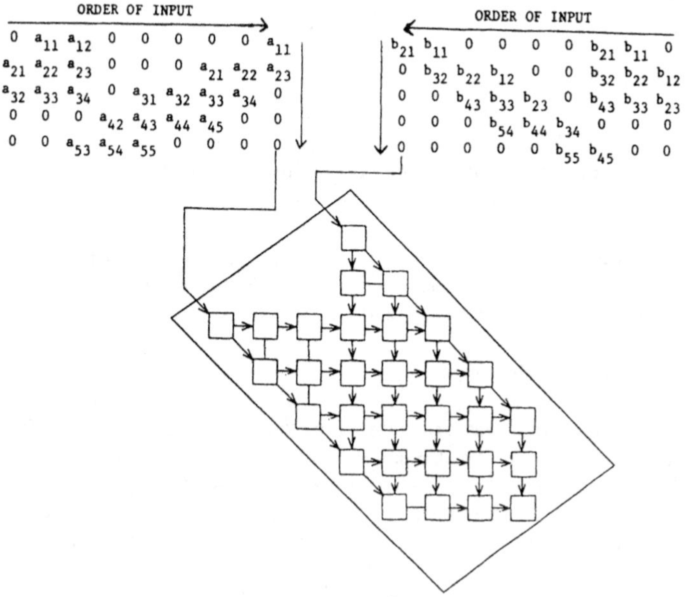

Figure 5.3

term, those on the next have 2, and so on. So, it is sufficient to load only the first $\min\{n - u_1, w_A\}$ diagonals of C before the first product is performed. The input patterns for A and B ensure that PE(i,j) computes only the terms in the product of c_{ij}.

Correctness

To establish the correctness of Figure 5.5 ($w_B \le w_A$), let $a(i,j,t)$, $b(i,j,t)$ and $c(i,j,t)$ be, respectively, the a, b and c values in PE(i,j) just after the tth multiplication and addition is performed. It is easy to see that,

$$a(i,j,t) = a_{i,\, j + l_2 - t + 1}$$

$$b(i,j,t) = b_{j + l_2 - t + 1,\, j}.$$

(The defined a_{ij}s and b_{ij}s are extended so that $a_{ij} = b_{ij} = 0$ whenever $j \le 0$ or $j > n$.)
Now, the value c_{ij} can be seen to be

$$C(i,j,w_B) = \sum_{t=1}^{w_B} a(i,j,t) * b(i,j,t)$$

$$= \sum_{t=1}^{w_B} a_{i,\, j + l_2 - t + 1} * b_{j + l_2 - t + 1,\, j}.$$

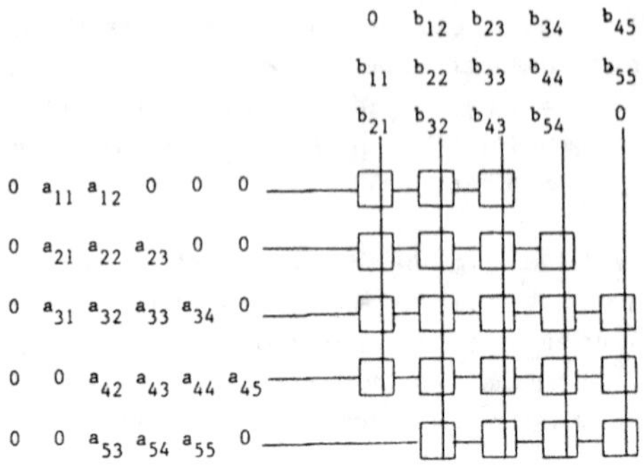

Figure 5.4(a)

This is readily seen as being correct.

Performance

The working of the algorithm can be divided into the following two cases:

1. $w_A \leq n - u_1$, $w_A + w_B - 1 \leq n$
2. $w_A > n - u_1$, $w_A + w_B - 1 \leq n$

For each case, T_D can be shown to be $\leq 2(w_A + w_B - 1)$. Hence, the performance figures are $P \sim S\,n$, $B = 2\,n$, $T_C = m$, $T_D \leq 2(w_A + w_B - 1)$, $R_C \sim S\,m\,n\,/(n\,w_A\,w_B)$. If $w_A + w_B - 1 \leq n$, $R_C \sim (w_A + w_B - 1)\,m\,/(w_A\,w_B) \leq 2$, $R_D \sim 2$ and $R \leq 4$.

5.8. Hexagonally Connected Processor Array

The hexagonal connection was originally employed by Kung [KUNG79] for the band matrix product problem. His original design has an R value of 3. This has been improved to 1 by Huang and Abraham [HUAN82]. The design of [HUAN82] is shown in Figure 5.6 with the input pattern for the matrices of Figure 5.1. The essential difference between this and the design of [KUNG79] is that in Kung's design, the Cs flow from bottom to top rather than from top to bottom. This

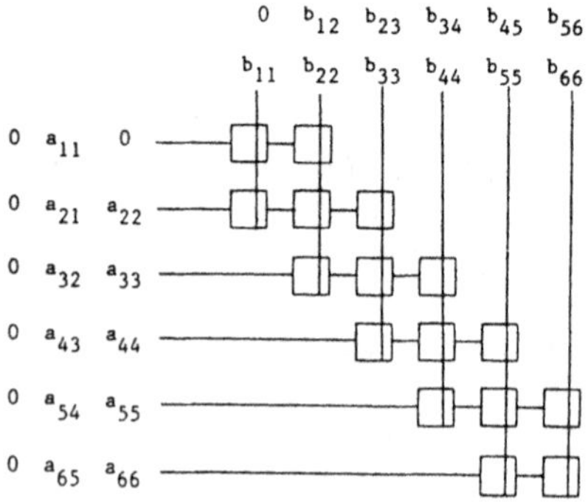

Figure 5.4(b)

difference in the direction of flow requires a separation in time between successive elements of A, B and C.

Performance

From Figure 5.6, we see that $P = w_A\,w_B$, $B = 2\,w$, $T_C = n + m - 1$, $T_D = n + m$, $R_D = R_C \sim 1$ and $R \sim 1$ (when $n >> m$).

5.9. Summary

The performance of the VLSI architectures for the band matrix multiplication problem is summarized in Table 5.1. The use of chains and meshes for the band matrix × band matrix problem has not been explored earlier. Despite the complexity of several of our designs, we have been unable to achieve R values close to 1 except for some instances. It remains to be seen whether an R of 1 can be achieved.

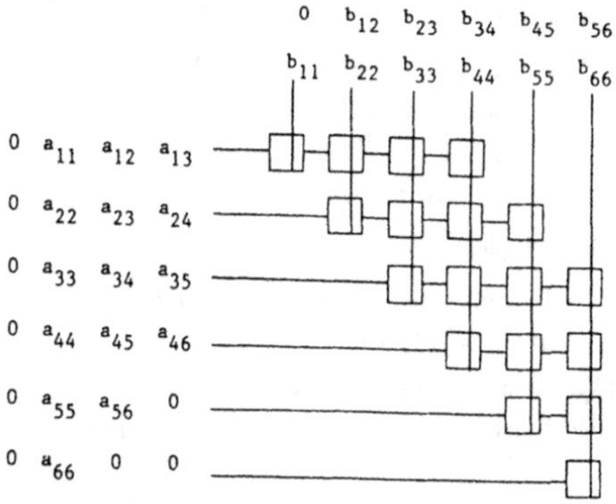

Figure 5.4(c)

6. Conclusions

This paper has examined VLSI systems for the matrix product problem. Most of the commonly proposed VLSI architectures have been considered. In many cases, we have been able to improve upon earlier work. We have show that the correctness of even complex VLSI designs for the matrix product problem can be established using traditional mathematical tools. While in some instances, the proof obtained is itself quite intricate, it appears unlikely that the design or proof could have been obtained any easier (if at all) using the s-transform method.

Unlike earlier designs, many of our designs use a single PE to compute an individual element of C. Consequently, error diagnosis is easier than for designs in which each C value results from computations in several PEs.

7. References

[CANN69] L. Cannon, *A cellular computer to implement the Kalman filter algorithm*, PhD Thesis, Montana State University, 1969.

[CHENG84] K. Cheng and S. Sahni, VLSI architectures for matrix multiplication, University of Minnesota, Technical Report, 1984.

[DEKE81] E. Dekel, D. Nassimi and S. Sahni, *Parallel matrix and graph algorithms,* SICOMP **1981,** 10, 4, pp. 657-675.

[FLYN76] M. Flynn and R. Kosaraju, *Processes and their interactions,* Kybernetics, 5, 1976, pp. 159-163.

[HORO79] E. Horowitz, *VLSI architectures for matrix computations,* IEEE International Conference On Parallel Processing, **1979,** pp. 124-127.

[HUAN82] K.H. Huang and J.A. Abraham, *Efficient parallel algorithms for processor arrays,* IEEE International Conference On Parallel Processing, **1982,** pp. 271-279.

[JOHN81a] L. Johnsson and D. Cohen, *A mathematical approach to modeling the flow of data and control in computational networks,* in VLSI Systems and Computations, Kung et al. editors, Computer Science Press, **1981,** pp. 213-225.

[JOHN81b] L. Johnsson, D. Cohen, U. Weiser and A. Davis, *Towards a formal treatment of VLSI arrays,* CALTECH Conference on VLSI, **1981,** pp. 375-398.

[KUNG78] H.T. Kung and C.E. Leiserson, *Systolic arrays for VLSI,* Department of Computer Science, Carnegie-Mellon University, **April 1978.**

[KUNG79] H.T. Kung, *Let's design algorithms for VLSI systems,* Proceedings CALTECH Conference on VLSI, **Jan. 1979,** pp. 65-90.

[KUNG83a] H.T. Kung, *A Listing of Systolic Papers,* Department of Computer Science, Carnegie-Mellon University, **May 1984.**

[KUNG83b] H.T. Kung and W.T. Lin, *An algebra for VLSI algorithm design,* Carnegie-Mellon University, Technical report, **April 1983.**

[KUNG83c] H.T. Kung, A. Nowatzyk, M. Ravisharkar, *The Universal Host: Architectures and System configuration,* Carnegie-Mellon University, Technical report, **October 1983.**

[LEIS83] C.E. Leiserson, *Area-Efficient VLSI Computation,* MIT Press, **1983.**

[MELH84] R. Melhem and W. Rheinboldt, *A mathematical model for the verification of systolic networks,* SIAM J. Comput., **1984,** 13, 3, pp. 541-565.

[PRIE81] R.W. Priester, H.J. Whitehouse, K. Bromley and J.B. Clary, *Signal Processing With Systolic Arrays,* IEEE International Conference on Parallel Processing, **1981,** pp. 207-215.

[VANS76] F. Van Scoy, *Parallel algorithms in cellular spaces,* PhD thesis, University of Virginia, 1976.

[WEIS81] U. Weiser and Al Davis, *A Wavefront notation tool for VLSI array design,* in VLSI Systems and Computations, Kung et al. editors, Computer Science Press, **1981,** pp. 226-234.

Performance	Architecture			
	Chain With O(w) Bandwidth	Chain With O(w) Memory	Chain With O(n) Bandwidth	Chain With O(1) Bandwidth
P	S	n	n	n
B	w	1	$2n$	2
T_C	$m\,n$	$w_A\,w_B$	$w_A\,w_B$	$w_A\,w_B$
T_D	$(m+2)\,n$	$(2n+m)\,w$	$w_A\,w_B + w$	$n\,(w_A\,w_B + w)$
R_C	2	1	1	1
R_D	$1 + m/2$	1	$1 + (w_A\,w_B)/w$	$1 + (w_A\,w_B)/w$
R	$2 + m$	1	$1 + (w_A\,w_B)/w$	$1 + (w_A\,w_B)/w$

Performance	Architecture			
	Mesh With O(n) Bandwidth	Mesh With O(1) Bandwidth	Broadcast Mesh With O(n) Bandwidth	Hexagonal With O(w) Bandwidth [HUAN82]
P	$S\,n$	$S\,n$	$S\,n$	$w_A\,w_B$
B	$2n$	2	$2n$	$2w$
T_C	M	M	m	$n + m - 1$
T_D	$2S + M$	$2nS + M$	$2w$	$n + m$
R_C	M	M	2	1
R_D	3	3	2	1
R	$3M$	$3M$	4	1

$m = \min\{w_A, w_B\}$, $M = \max\{w_A, w_B\}$, $S = \min\{n, w_A + w_B - 1\}$
$w = w_A + w_B$, $C \sim w_A\,w_B\,n$, $D \sim 2(w_A + w_B)\,n$

Table 5.1

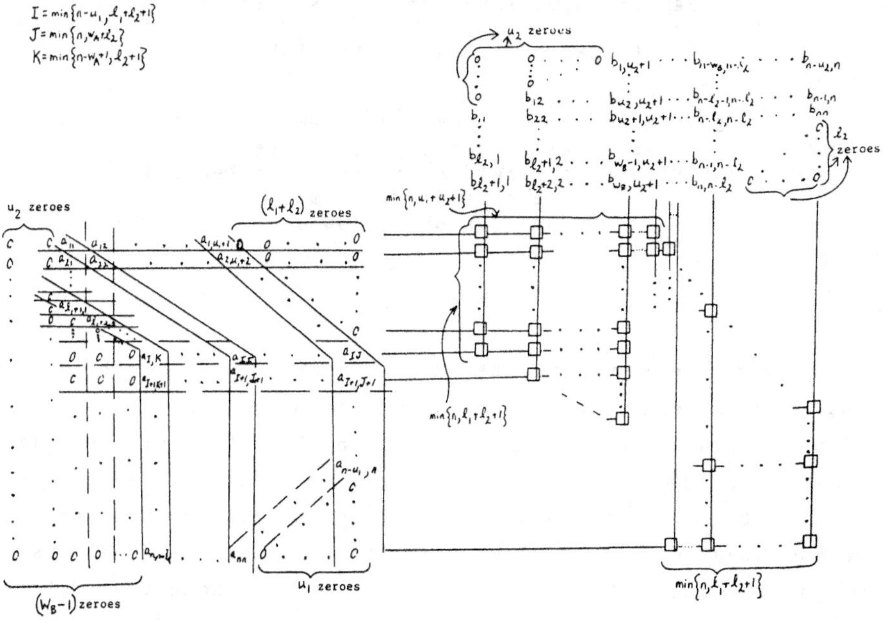

Figure 5.5

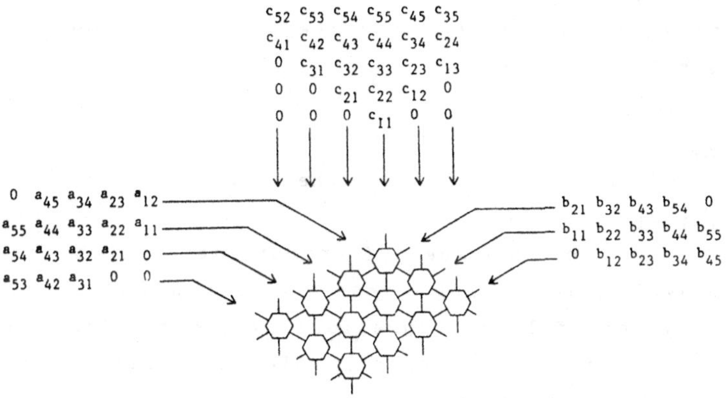

Figure 5.6

PARALLEL ALGORITHMS FOR SOLVING CERTAIN CLASSES OF LINEAR RECURRENCES

S. Lakshmivarahan and Sudarshan K. Dhall
Parallel Processing Institute
School of Electrical Engineering and Computer Science
University of Oklahoma
Norman, Oklahoma 73019

ABSTRACT

This paper presents two new time and/or processor bounds for solving certain classes of linear recurrences. The first result provides a parallel algorithm for solving $X_i=a_iX_{i-1}+d_i$ for $1\le i\le n$ in 2logn units of time using only 3/4n processors. The second results relate to solving $X_i=X_{i-1}+X_{i-2}+d_i$ for $1\le i\le n$. It is shown that X_i's can be computed in at most 3logn units of time using 5/4n processors. In the special case when $d_i=0$ for all i, it is shown that X_i's (the first n-Fibonacci numbers) can be computed in parallel in 2logn-1 units of time using only n/2 processors. These time and processor bounds compare very favourably with the previously known results for these problems.

1. Introduction

Solution of linear recurrence of the type

$$X_i=a_iX_{i-1}+d_i \qquad 1\le i\le n \tag{1.1}$$

lies at the heart of a number of computational problems such as polynomial evaluation using Horner's method [3], solution of tridiagonal system of linear equations [7], carry look-ahead adder [10] etc. Recognizing this central role, a number of authors have developed parallel algorithms for solving (1.1). The methods of cyclic reduction [1,7,16] and recursive doubling [7,8] are the earliest of the parallel methods known for the solution of (1.1). These two methods solve for X_i, $1\le i\le n$ in 3logn units of time using n processors (all logarithms are to the base 2). These methods have been extensively analyzed in the context of solution of tridiagonal system of linear equations [6,7,9]. Later Chen and Kuck [12,13] among other things, proposed a method for the solution of (1.1). This

---

Research reported in this paper was supported in part by the grant from the Energy Resource Institute, University of Oklahoma

latter method solves for all the X_i's, $1\leq i\leq n$ in only 2logn units of time using n-1 processors. For a detailed discussion of these and other related methods refer to the survey paper by Don Heller [4] and the book by Kuck [2].

In this paper, using a shared memory model called PRAM, which allows simultaneous read but only single write in the same memory location [15] we describe a new class of algorithms for solving X_i, $1\leq i\leq n$. More specifically, it is shown that X_i's can be computed in (n/p) [2+logp] units of time using only 3/2p processors where $p=2^K$ for some $K\geq 1$ and n=2mp for some $m\geq 1$. It is shown that when p=n/2, our algorithm computes all the X_i's in (2logn+1) units of time using only 3/4n processors. Thus, this new algorithm has 100% more processor efficiency compared to the cyclic reduction and recursive doubling and is 50% more processor efficient compared to the method of Chen and Kuck [12].

If $a_i=1$ for all i in (1.1), then the recurrence reduces to the problem of finding the cascade sums [1]. It will be shown that our algorithm, when specialized to this latter problem, can compute the cascade sums in (n/2p)[2+logp] units of time using only $p(=2^K)$ processors where n=mp for some $m\geq 1$. When p=n/2, it will be shown that our method computes the cascade sums in logn time. This result again compares favorably with the algorithm in [5] which computes the cascade sums in 2logn units of time using n processors as well as the one given in [1] which takes logn units of time using n processors. This problem of computation of cascade sums is a special case of the prefix computation problems. The papers by Snir [10] and Fich [11] and the references contained therein deal with the time-size trade-off studies in prefix computation. In fact, it is shown in [10] that the cascade sums can also be computed in logn units of time using circuits with a maximum width (same as maximum degree of parallelism) of n/2.

Our second result relates to the solution of second order recurrences of the type

$$F_i=F_{i-1}+F_{i-2} \quad \text{for } i\geq 2 \qquad (1.2)$$

where $F_0=F_1=1$ and

$$X_i=X_{i-1}+X_{i-2}+d_i \quad \text{for } i\geq 2 \qquad (1.3)$$

where $X_0=0$ and $X_1=d_1$. The recurrence (1.2) is the defining relation for the well known Fibonacci sequence and (1.3) has an additional driving term. Don Heller [4] and Chen and Kuck[12] have extensively studied higher order linear recurrences of which (1.2) and (1.3) are special cases. In [12] Chen and Kuck present a parallel algorithm for solving (1.3) in (3logn-1) units of time using (3n-8) processors. In his dissertation Chen [13] presents another variation of the above algorithm for solving (1.3) in (5logn-3) units of time using 5/4n processors. Since (1.2) is a special case of (1.3) in which all d_i's are zero, in [2] it is observed that the first n Fibonacci numbers can also be generated in (5logn-3) units of time using only 5/4n processors.

In this paper we present parallel time and processor bounds for solving (1.2) and (1.3) both of which are improvements over the existing results. In particular, it is shown that the first n Fibonacci numbers can be generated in parallel in 2logn-1 units of time using only n/2 processors. Using an extension of this algorithm it is shown that X_i, $1 \leq i \leq n$ defined in (1.3) can also be computed in at most 3logn units of time using only 5/4n processors. It should be interesting to note that the algorithms on the PRAM model such as the ones described in this paper can be easily implemented on the Heterogeneous Element Processor [17].

In section 2, the new parallel algorithm for solving (1.1) is presented. Section 3 develops parallel algorithms for the solution of (1.2) and (1.3). Concluding observations are given in section 4.

2. Parallel Algorithm for Solving the First-Order Linear Recurrence

The solution to the linear first-order recurrence (1.1) in closed form is given by

$$X_i = \sum_{j=0}^{i} \left[\prod_{s=j+1}^{i} a_s \right] d_j \tag{2.1}$$

In this section we present a new parallel algorithm for computing (2.1). To this end, we introduce two functions A[u,v] and Y[s,t] of a_i's and a_i's and d_i's respectively.

Let

$$A[u,v] = \prod_{r=u+1}^{v} a_r \tag{2.2}$$

where vacuous products are taken to be unity and let

$$Y[s,t]=\sum_{j=s}^{t} A[j,t]d_j, \quad \text{for } t\geq s \tag{2.3}$$

A number of useful properties of the functions $A[\cdot,\cdot]$ and $Y[\cdot,\cdot]$ are developed in the following lemmas.

Lemma 2.1: The function $A[u,v]$ satisfies the following:

(a) $A[u,v]=1$ for all $u\geq v$

(b) $A[u,v+m]=A[u,v]\cdot A[v,v+m]$ for any integer $m>0$

The proof of this lemma is straightforward.

Lemma 2.2: The function $Y[s,\cdot]$ also satisfies the recurrence of the type (1.1), that is,

$$Y[s,t]=a_t Y[s,t-1]+d_t \tag{2.4}$$

Proof: Rewriting (2.3) we readily obtain

$$Y[s,t]=\sum_{j=s}^{t-1} A[j,t]d_j+A[t,t]d_t$$

Since $A[t,t]=1$ and $A[j,t]=a_t A[j,t-1]$, the lemma follows.

Lemma 2.3:

$$X_t=Y[1,t] \text{ for all } 1\leq t\leq n.$$

The proof follows from the definitions.

The following lemma which is a generalization of the Lemma 2.2 provides the basis for our algorithm.

Lemma 2.4: If $t\geq s$ then for $i>0$

$$Y[s,t+i]=A[t,t+i]Y[s,t]+Y[t+1,t+i] \tag{2.5}$$

Proof: From equation (2.3) it follows that

$$Y[s,t+i]$$

$$=\sum_{j=s}^{t+i} A[j,t+i]d_j$$

$$=\sum_{j=s}^{t} A[j,t+i]d_j+\sum_{j=t+1}^{t+i} A[j,t+i]d_j \tag{2.6}$$

It is readily seen from equation (2.3) that the second term is in fact $Y[t+1,t+i]$. From Lemma 2.1

$$A[j,t+i]=A[j,t]A[t,t+i] \tag{2.7}$$

Substituting (2.7) in the first term of (2.6), the lemma follows.

Let $n=2mp$, $p=2^K$ where $m\geq 1$ and $K\geq 1$. In the following a functon of p will denote the number of processors. Let $1\leq s\leq K$ and $0\leq g\leq 2^{K-s}-1$. Our algorithm for solving (1.1) consists of two parts: (1) a parallel Algorithm A for computing $A[u,v]$ and (2) a parallel Algorithm Y for computing $Y[s,t]$. In fact Algorithm A computes all those $A[u,v]$ which are needed in the computation of [s,t]. Since these two algorithms are working in parallel, the total number of processors is equal to the sum of the processors used in both the algorithms but the time is maximum of the time needed by the two algorithms. The Algorithm Y uses p processors $P_0, P_1 \ldots P_{p-1}$ and Algorithm A uses q processors $Q_0, Q_1 \ldots Q_{q-1}$ where q=p/2.

Algorithm A:

Stage 1: Each processor Q_j $0 \leq j \leq q-1$ computes the following:

```
FOR i=1 to 2m
Compute A[2m(1+2j), 2m(1+2j)+i]
END.
```

In this stage totally 2qm number of the A(·,·) functions are updated using q processors. Each update involves one multiplication. This stage takes n/p units of time.

Stage 2: Each processor $Q_j, 0 \leq j \leq q-2$, computes the following:

```
FOR i=1 to 2m
Compute A [4m(1+j), 4m(1+j)+i]
END
```

In this stage totally 2m(q-1) number of A[·,·] functions are updated using (q-1) processors. This stage also takes (n/p) units of time.

Stage 3:

```
FOR s=1 to K-1
   FOR j=0 to 2^(K-s)-2
      Let h_j=6m2^(s-1)+2^(s+1)mj
         FOR i=1 to 2ms
         Compute A[h_j-2ms, h_j+i]
         END
   END
END
```

In any step s, there are $2^{K-s}-1$ groups of computations and within each group 2ms number of A[·,·] functions are updated. Since $2ms(2^{K-s}-1) \leq 2m(q-1)$, using not more than (q-1) processors, each of the above steps can be finished in not more than (n/p) units of time. Thus the entire Algorithm using q processors does not take more than (n/p)[1+log p] units of time.

Algorithm Y:

Stage 1: Each processor $P_i, 0 \le i \le p-1$, computes the following:

```
FOR j=0 to m-1,
    Y[2im+1,2im+1+j]=a_{2im+1+j}Y[2im+1,2im+j]+d_{2im+1+j}
END.
```

Stage 2: Each of the processors P_i, $0 \le i \le p-1$, computes the following:

```
FOR j=0 to m-1,
  Y[2im+1,(2i+1)m+1+j]=a_{(2i+1)m+1+j}Y[2im+1),(2i+1)m+j]
                          +d_{(2i+1)m+1+j}
END.
```

In each of the stages 1 and 2, totally n/2 of the Y[·,·] functions are updated using p processors. Since each update requires two operations (a multiplication and an addition) each of the above stages takes (n/p) units of time.

Stage 3:

```
FOR s=1 to K
    FOR g=0 to 2^{K-s}-1
        FOR i=1 to m2^s
        Y[2^{s+1}mg+1, 2^s m(1+2g)+i]
        =A[2^s m(1+2g),2^s m(1+2g)+i]Y[2^{s+1}mg+1,2^s m(1+2g)]
            +Y[2^s m(1+2g)+1,2^s m(1+2g)+i]
        END
    END
END.
```

It is readily seen that at any step s in stage 3, the algorithm identifies 2^{K-s} groups indexed by g and within each group there are 2^s processors working in parallel. Thus within each group $2^s m$ number of Y[·,·] functions are updated. It readily follows that computations in each group take the same amount of time equal to (n/p) units. Thus the entire stage 3 takes (n/p)logp units of time.

For the correct functioning of the Algorithm Y, the values of $A[2^s m(1+2g), 2^s m(1+2g)+i]$ for $0 \le g \le 2^{K-s}$ and $1 \le i \le K$ must be made available for each $1 \le s \le K$. In fact, these functions are generated in parallel by the Algorithm A. A close scrutiny reveals that all the values of the A[·,·] functions that are needed in stage 3 of Algorithm Y are in fact generated by Algorithm A at least one step ahead of time. Thus the overall time for solving for X_i's in (1.1) is decided by the running time of the Algorithm Y.

Before stating our main result of this section, we illustrate the Algorithms Y and A through an example.

Example 2.1: Let p=8, q=4, K=3, m=4, n=64. The various stages of the Algorithm Y are shown in Figure 2.1. In Figure 2.2 further details of the computations in Stage 3 of Algorithm Y are illustrated. Figure 2.3 illustrates various stages of Algorithm A. Comparing Figures 2.2 and 2.3, it is readily seen that the values of the A[·,·] function are made available at least one step ahead of the time they are needed in Algorithm Y.

We now state the main result of this section as the following theorem:

Theorem 2.5: Using a total of 3/2 p processors, Algorithms Y and A compute Y[1,t] for $1 \leq t \leq n$ in (n/p)[2+logp] units of time.

Proof: At the end of stage 1 of Algorithm Y, Y[1,t] for $1 \leq t \leq m$ and at the end of stage 2, Y[1,t] for $1 \leq t \leq 2m$ are computed. In stage 3, at the end of each step s=i, Y[1,t] for $1 \leq t \leq 2^{i+1}m$ are computed. Thus the entire sequence of Y[1,t] for $1 \leq t \leq n$ is available at the end of stage 3. This proves the correctness of the Algorithm Y.

Of the 3/2 p processors, Algorithm Y uses p and Algorithm A uses p/2. Further, since Algorithms A and Y are acting in parallel and Algorithm Y takes longer time compared to Algorithm A, the total time is that of Algorithm Y. It is readily seen from the description of the algorithms, that this latter algorithm takes (n/p)[2+logp] units of time and the theorem follows.

For the purposes of comparison, consider the case when p=n/2 (same as m=1). In this case, it is seen that stage 1 does not require any arithmetic computaton and the Algorithm Y needs only 2logn units of time. In other words, using only 3/4n processors Algorithms A and Y compute the results in 2logn units of time. The best previous result due to Chen and Kuck solves (1.1) in 2logn time using n processors. Thus compared to this latter result our Algorithm has 33% more processor efficiency. It is well known that the method of cyclic reduction [1,7,16] solves (1.1) in 3logn time using n processors. Again compared to this method our algorithm has 100% more processor efficiency.

STAGE 1 $0 \le j \le 3$	STAGE 2 $0 \le j \le 3$	STAGE 3 $s = 1$ $1 \le i \le 8$	 $s = 2$ $1 \le i \le 16$	 $s = 3$ $1 \le i \le 32$
P_0: Y[1,1+j]				
	P_0: Y[1,5+j]			
P_1: Y[9,9+j]		$P_0 - P_1$ Y[1,8+i]		
	P_1: Y[9,13+j]			
P_2: Y[17,17+j]				
	P_2: Y[17,21+j]		$P_0 - P_3$ Y[1,16+i]	
P_3: Y[25,25+j]		$P_2 - P_3$ Y[17,24+i]		
	P_3: Y[25,29+j]			
P_4: Y[33,33+j]				
	P_4: Y[33,37+j]			$P_0 - P_7$ Y[1,32+i]
P_5: Y[41,41+j]		$P_4 - P_5$ Y[33,40+i]		
	P_5: Y[41,45+j]			
P_6: Y[49,49+j]				
	P_6: Y[49,53+j]		$P_4 - P_7$ Y[33,48+i]	
P_7: Y[57,57+j]		$P_6 - P_7$ Y[49,56+i]		
	P_7: [57,61+j]			

Figure 2.1: Various Stages of Algorithm Y when $n = 64$, $p = 8$, $m = 4$.

s = 1, 1 ≤ i ≤ 8

g = 0: Y[1,8+i] = A[8,8+i]Y[1,8] + Y[9,8+i]

g = 1: Y[17,24+i] = A[24,24+i]Y[17,24] + Y[25,24+i]

g = 2: Y[33,40+i] = A[40,40+i]Y[33,40] + Y[41,40+i]

g = 3: Y[49,56+i] = A[56,56+i]Y[49,56] + Y[57,56+i]

s =2, 1 ≤ i ≤ 16

g = 0: Y[1,16+i] = A[16,16+i]Y[1,16] + Y[17,16+i]

g = 1: Y[33,48+i] = A[48,48+i]Y[33,48] + Y[49,48+i]

s = 3, 1 ≤ i ≤ 32

g = 0: Y[1,32+i] = A[32,32+i]Y[1,32] + Y[33,32+i]

Figure 2.2: Details of the Stage 3 Computation for Algorithm Y when n = 64, p = 8 and m = 4.

STAGE 1	STAGE 2	STAGE 3	
		$s = 1$	$s = 2$
$1 \leq i \leq 8$	$1 \leq i \leq 8$	$1 \leq i \leq 8$	$1 \leq i \leq 16$
Q_0: A[8,8+i]			
	Q_0: A[16,16+i]		
Q_1: A[24,24+i]		Q_0: A[16,24+i]	
	Q_1: A[32,32+i]		
Q_2: A[40,40+i]		Q_1: A[32,40+i]	
	Q_2: A[48,48+i]		$Q_0 - Q_1$ A[32,48+i]
Q_3: A[56,56+i]		Q_2: A[48,56+i]	

Figure 2.3: Various Stages of the Algorithm A when $n = 64$, $m = 4$ and $p = 8$.

Another special case which is of intrinsic interest in itself is when all the a_j's in (1.1) are unity. In this case X_i's are given by the cascade sum of the d_j's [1], that is

$$X_i = \sum_{j=1}^{i} d_j \qquad (2.8)$$

Define

$$C[s,t] = \sum_{j=s}^{t} d_j$$

Then, clearly

$C[s,t]=0$ for $s>t$

$C[s,s]=d_s$

$C[s,t+i]=C[s,t]+C[t+1,t+i]$, for $i \geq 0$ and

$C[1,t]=X_t$ for $1 \leq t \leq n$

In the following, a parallel algorithm for computing C[1,t]'s is given. Let $n=mp$, $p=2^K$, $m \geq 1$ and $K \geq 1$. Let $P_0, P_1, \ldots P_{p-1}$ be the p processors.

Algorithm CS:

Stage 1: Each processor P_i, $0 \leq i \leq p-1$, computes the following

```
FOR j= 0 to m-1
Compute C[im+1, im+1+j]
END
```

Using p-1 processors, this step can be completed in (n/p) units of time.

Stage 2:

```
FOR s=1 to K
   FOR g=0 to 2^(K-s)-1
      FOR j=1 to m2^(s-1)
         Compute C[2^s mg+1, m2^(s-1)(1+2g)+j]
      END
   END
END.
```

For each value of s, using p processors, all the computations indexed by g and j can be computed in parallel in (n/2p) units of time. The following theorem summarizes the properties of the Algorithm CS.

Theorem 2.6: Using p processors, the Algorithm CS computes C[1,t] for $1 \leq t \leq n$ in

$$(n/2p)[2+\log p]$$

units of time.

The proof of this theorem is quite straightforward and is omitted. The following example illustrates the mechanics of the above algorithm.

Example 2.2: Let $p=4$, $m=4$, $n=16$. Various stages of the Algorithm CS are shown in Figure 2.4.

When $p=n/2$, it is readily seen that this algorithm takes $\log n+1$ units of time which is optimal. This result compares favorably with the bound given in [5]. Further, Snir [10] arrived at a bound of $\log n$ units of time for the above problem in the context of depth-size trade-off for parallel prefix circuits with a maximum width of $n/2$.

3. Parallel Algorithm for Solving Second-Order Linear Recurrence with Unit Coefficients

The general form of the second-order linear recurrence is given by

$$X_i = a_{i,i-2}X_{i-2} + a_{i,i-1}X_{i-1} + d_i \qquad (3.1)$$

for $2 \leq i \leq n$ where X_0 and X_1 are taken to be the initial conditions. Let $n=2^K$ for some $K \geq 1$. In this section, we first consider the special case when all the a_{ij}'s in (3.1) are unity and all the d_i's are zero. Since this special case corresponds to the well known recurrence for the generation of Fibonacci sequence, we rewrite the resulting recurrence as

$$F_i = F_{i-1} + F_{i-2} \quad 2 \leq i \leq n \qquad (3.2)$$

with $F_0 = F_1 = 1$.

The following lemma plays a key role in the design of our parallel algorithm for the generation of the first n Fibonacci numbers.

Lemma 3.1: If $n=2^K$, then for $1 \leq i \leq 2^{K-1}$, F_i defined by (3.2) also satisfies the following recurrence:

$$F_{2^{m-1}+1} = F_{2^{m-1}}F_i + F_{2^{m-1}-1}F_{i-1} \qquad (3.3)$$

where $F_0 = F_1 = 1$.

<table>
<tr><th rowspan="2">STAGE 1
$0 \leq j \leq 3$</th><th colspan="2">STAGE 2</th></tr>
<tr><th>s = 1
$1 \leq j \leq 4$</th><th>s = 2
$1 \leq j \leq 8$</th></tr>
<tr><td>P_0: C[1,1+j]</td><td></td><td rowspan="2"></td></tr>
<tr><td>P_1: C[5,5+j]</td><td>$P_0 - P_1$
C[1,4+j]</td></tr>
<tr><td>P_2: C[9,9+j]</td><td></td><td rowspan="2">$P_0 - P_3$
C[1,8+j]</td></tr>
<tr><td>P_3: C[13,13+j]</td><td>$P_2 - P_3$
C[9,12+j]</td></tr>
</table>

Figure 2.4: An Illustration of the Algorithm CS for n = 16, m = 4 and p = 4.

Proof: The proof is by induction on i. For i=1 the above relation is trivially true. Assume that (3.3) is true for all $1 \le i \le s$. Now consider $F_{2^{m-1}+s+1}$. From (3.2) we obtain

$$F_{2^{m-1}+s+1} = F_{2^{m-1}+s} + F_{2^{m-1}+s-1}$$
$$= F_{2^{m-1}}[F_s + F_{s-1}] + F_{2^{m-1}-1}[F_{s-1} + F_{s-2}]$$
(by induction hypothesis)
$$= F_{2^{m-1}}F_{s+1} + F_{2^{m-1}-1}F_s \quad \text{(by 3.2)}$$

Hence the lemma.

A parallel algorithm for the generation of the Fibonacci numbers may be stated as follows:

Algorithm F: $n=2^K$, $K \ge 1$.

This stage does not involve any arithmetic.

Stage 1: Initialization.

$F_0=F_1=1$ and $F_2=2$

Stage 2: For s=2 to K,

FOR i=1 to 2^{s-1}, Compute

$F_{2^{s-1}+1} = F_{2^{s-1}}F_i + F_{2^{s-1}-1}F_{i-1}$

The basic computation scheme of this algorithm is illustrated in Figure 3.1 for the case when n=16. The following theorem summarizes the properties of the above algorithm.

Theorem 3.2: For $n=2^K$, Algorithm F generates the first n Fibonacci numbers in $2(\log n-q-1)+3(2^q-1)$ units of time using only 2^{K-q} processors for $1 \le q \le K-2$.

Proof: The proof of correctness of the Algorithm F follows from Lemma 3.1. At any step s all of $F_{2^{s-1}+i}$ for $1 \le i \le 2^{s-1}$ are computable in parallel and maximum parallelism is available at s=K. Further, each computation of $F_{2^{s-1}+i}$ involves two multiplications and one addition. Thus, using 2^{K-q} processors, computations in steps s=2 through K-q can be completed in $2[\log n-q-1]$ units of time. Likewise, computations at any step K-q+j for $1 \le j \le q$, using 2^{K-q} processors, can be completed in $3 \times 2^{j-1}$ units of time. Hence, the entire stage 2 can be finished in $2(\log n-q-1)+3(2^q-1)$ units of time. Further, for a meaningful speed-up of Algorithm F, it is necessary that $q \le K-2$.

When q=1, Algorithm F takes 2logn-1 units of time using only n/2 processors.

The best previous results [2] due to Chen and Kuck [12] describes a parallel algorithm for the generation of F_i $1 \le i \le n$ in (3logn-1) units of time using (3n-8) processors. Another version of this parallel

STAGE 1	STAGE 2		
	s = 2	s = 3	s = 4
$F_0 = 1$ $F_1 = 1$ $F_2 = 2$			
	$F_3 = F_2F_1 + F_1F_0 = 3$ $F_4 = F_2F_2 + F_1F_1 = 5$		
		$F_5 = F_4F_1 + F_3F_0 = 8$ $F_6 = F_4F_2 + F_3F_1 = 13$ $F_7 = F_4F_3 + F_3F_2 = 21$ $F_8 = F_4F_4 + F_3F_3 = 34$	
			$F_9 = F_8F_1 + F_7F_0 = 55$ $F_{10} = F_8F_2 + F_7F_1 = 89$ $F_{11} = F_8F_3 + F_7F_2 = 144$ $F_{12} = F_8F_4 + F_7F_3 = 233$ $F_{13} = F_8F_5 + F_7F_4 = 377$ $F_{14} = F_8F_6 + F_7F_5 = 610$ $F_{15} = F_8F_7 + F_7F_6 = 987$ $F_{16} = F_8F_8 + F_7F_7 = 1597$

Figure 3.1: An Illustration of Algorithm F for n = 16.

algorithm due to Chen [13] generates the same numbers in (5logn-3) units of time using 5/4n processors. Thus our algorithm provides improvement over the existing time and processor bounds.

We now consider the following recurrence

$$X_i = X_{i-1} + X_{i-2} + d_i \qquad (3.4)$$

for $2 \leq i \leq n = 2^K$ and $X_0 = 0$ and $X_1 = d_1$.

The following lemma is immediate.

Lemma 3.3: The solution X_t of the above recurrence (3.4) is given by

$$X_t = \sum_{i=0}^{t-1} F_i d_{t-i} \qquad 1 \leq t \leq n \qquad (3.5)$$

where F_i is th i^{th} Fibonacci number.

Proof: The proof is by induction. For t=1, since $X_1 = F_0 d_1 = d_1$, (3.5) is true. Assume it is true for $1 \leq t \leq s$. Consider X_{s+1}. From (3.4) it follows that

$$X_{s+1} = X_s + X_{s-1} + d_{s+1}$$

$$= \sum_{i=0}^{s-1} F_i d_{s-i} + \sum_{i=0}^{s-2} F_i d_{s-1-i} + d_{s+1}$$

(by induction hypothesis)

$$= F_0 d_s + \sum_{i=1}^{s-1} (F_i + F_{i-1}) d_{s-i} + d_{s+1}$$

$$= \sum_{j=0}^{s} F_j d_{s+1-j} \quad (\text{since } F_0 = F_1 = 1)$$

Hence the lemma.

Analogous to the development in section 2 we now define a function Z[s,t] as

$$Z[s,t] = \sum_{j=0}^{t-s} F_j d_{t-j} \qquad (3.6)$$

where F_j's are the Fibonacci numbers. The properties of this function proved in Lemma 3.4 are crucial to our development.

Lemma 3.4: (a) $Z[s,t]=0$ for $t<s$

(b) $Z[s,s] = F_0 d_s = d_s$

(c) $Z[s,s+1] = F_0 d_{s+1} + F_1 d_s = d_{s+1} + d_s$

(d) $Z[1,t] = X_t$ for all $1 \leq t \leq n$

and for $t>s$ and $i \geq 0$

(e) $Z[s,t+i] = Z[t+1,t+i] + F_i Z[s,t] + F_{i-1} Z[s,t-1]$ (3.7)

Proof: (a), (b), (c) and (d) immediately follow from the definitions and we only prove (e) in the following. Consider the right-hand side of (e): Using (3.6) we obtain

$$Z[t+1,t+i]+F_i Z[s,t]+F_{i-1} Z[s,t-1]$$

$$= \sum_{j=0}^{i-1} F_j d_{t+i-j} + F_i \sum_{j=0}^{t-s} F_j d_{t-j} + F_{i-1} \sum_{j=0}^{t-s-1} F_j d_{t-j-1}$$

$$= \sum_{j=0}^{i-1} F_j d_{t+i-j} + \sum_{j=0}^{t-s} (F_i F_j + F_{i-1} F_{j-1}) d_{t-j}$$

Since

$$F_j = 0 \text{ for } j<0$$

and

$$F_{i+j} = F_i F_j + F_{i-1} F_{j-1}$$

the above sum after some algebraic manipulations is equal to

$$\sum_{j=0}^{i-1} F_j d_{t+i-j} + \sum_{j=i}^{t-s+i} F_j d_{t+i-j}$$

$$= \sum_{j=0}^{t-s+i} F_j d_{t-i-j} = Z[s,t+i]$$

and the lemma is proved.

The parallel algorithm for computing the X_i's defined by (3.4) may be stated as follows:

<u>Algorithm Z</u>: $n=2^K$

<u>Stage 1</u>: For $i=1$ to 2^{K-1} compute

$Z[2i-1,2i-1]$ and

$Z[2i-1,2i]$

END.

<u>Stage 2</u>: For $s=2$ to K

For $g=0$ to $2^{K-s}-1$

For $i=1$ to 2^{s-1}

Compute $Z[2^s g+1, 2^{s-1}(1+2g)+i]$ using (3.7)

END

END

END.

The values of F_i, $1 \leq i \leq 2^{s-1}$ needed in the computation of (3.7) are generated in parallel using Algorithm F.

The example in Figure 3.2 illustrates the mechanics of this algorithm for $n=8$.

The following Theorem 3.5 summarizes the time and processor bounds for the Algorithm Z.

STAGE 1	STAGE 2	
	s=2	s = 3
$Z[1,1] = d_1$ $Z[1,2] = d_2 + d_1$		
$Z[3,3] = d_3$ $Z[3,4] = d_4 + d_3$	$Z[1,3] = Z[3,3] + F_1Z[1,2] + F_0Z[1,1]$ $Z[1,4] = Z[3,4] + F_2Z[1,2] + F_1Z[1,1]$	
$Z[5,5] = d_5$ $Z[5,6] = d_6 + d_5$		$Z[1,5] = Z[5,5] + F_1Z[1,4] + F_0Z[1,3]$ $Z[1,6] = Z[5,6] + F_2Z[1,4] + F_1Z[1,3]$ $Z[1,7] = Z[5,7] + F_3Z[1,4] + F_2Z[1,3]$ $Z[1,8] = Z[5,8] + F_4Z[1,4] + F_3Z[1,3]$
$Z[7,7] = d_7$ $Z[7,8] = d_8 + d_7$	$Z[5,7] = Z[7,7] + F_1Z[5,6] + F_0Z[5,5]$ $Z[5,8] = Z[7,8] + F_2Z[5,6] + F_1Z[5,5]$	

Figure 3.2: An Example of the Computation Scheme for Algorithm Z when n = 8.

Theorem 3.5: Algorithm Z computes $Z[1,t]$ for all $1<t\leq n=2^K$ in at most $3\log n$ units of time using only $5/4n$ processors.

Proof: The proof of correctness of Algorithm Z follows from lemma 3.4. From (3.7) it follows that if F_i and F_{i-1} are available, then $Z[2^s g+1, 2^{s-1}(1+2g)+i]$ can be computed using two multiplications and two additions. By alloting two processors, this computation can be done in 3 units of time. Notice that the maximum parallelism of n/2 is available at s=K. Hence, using only n processors, stages 1 and 2 can be completed in not more than 3 logn units.

The above time and processor bound is true only if F_i for $1\leq i\leq 2^{s-1}$ are available at step s in stage 2 of Algorithm Z. Since not more than the first n/2 Fibonacci numbers are needed, we generate them using Algorithm F with n/4 processors. Thus, by letting Algorithms F and Z to work in parallel using n/4 and n processors respectively, it is readily seen that Algorithm F generates all F_i's just on time for use in the Algorithm Z. Thus, the theorem is proved.

Again our results compare very favorably with the best known previous bounds which are (3logn-1) units of time using (3n-8) processors in Chen and Kuck [12,2] and (5logn-3) units of time using 5/4n processors in Chen [13,2].

4. Conclusions

In this paper we described a new class of parallel algorithms for finding the cascade sums, solving linear first-order recurrence and linear second-order recurrence with unit coefficients. The parallel time and processor bounds for our algorithms are improvements over the existing results. These algorithms are easily implementable on HEP-like MIMD machines. Extension of these algorithms to higher order linear recurrences must prove interesting.

Acknowledgement: The authors wish to thank C.P. Kruskal of University of Illinois for informing us of the existence of the reference [10].

References

1. R.W. Hockney and C.R. Jesshope, Parallel Computers, Adam and Hilger Ltd., Bristol 1981, Chapter 5, Section 5.2.

2. D.J. Kuck, The Structure of Computers and Computations, Vol. 1, Addison-Wesley, 1980, Chapter 2, Section 2.3.

3. L. Hyafil and H.T. Kung, "The Complexity of Parallel Evaluation of Linear Recurrences," Journal of ACM, Vol. 24, 1977, pp. 513-521.

4. D. Heller, "A Survey of Parallel Algorithms in Numerical Algebra," SIAM Review, Vol. 20, 1978, pp. 740-777.

5. J.T. Schwartz, "Ultracomputers," ACM Transactions on Programming Languages and Systems, Vol. 2, 1980, pp. 484-521.

6. J.L. Lambiotte, Jr. and R.G. Voigt, "The Solution of Tridiagonal Linear Systems on CDC STAR 100 Computer," ACM Transactions on Mathematical Software, Vol. 1, 1975, pp. 308-329.

7. H.S. Stone, "An Efficient Parallel Algorithm for the Solution of a Tridiagonal Linear System of Equations," Journal of ACM, Vol. 20, 1973, pp. 27-38.

8. H.S. Stone, "Parallel Tridiagonal Equation Sovers," ACM Transactions on Mathematical Software, Vol. 1, 1975, pp. 289-307.

9. A.H. Sameh and R.P. Brent, "Solving Triangular Systems on a Parallel Computer," SIAM Journal of Numerical Analysis, Vol. 14, 1977, pp. 1101-1113.

10. M. Snir, "Depth-Size Trade-Offs for Parallel Prefix Computation," Technical Report, Hebrew University of Jerusalem, 1983.

11. F.E. Fich, "New Bounds for Parallel Prefix Circuits," Proceedings of the 15th Annual ACM Symposium on Theory of Computing, 1983, pp. 100-109.

12. S.C. Chen and D.J. Kuck, "Time and Parallel Processor Bounds for Linear Recurrence Systems," IEEE Transactions on Computers, Vol. 24, 1975, pp. 701-707.

13. S.C. Chen, "Speedup of Iterative Programs in Multiprocessing Systems," Ph.D. Dissertation, Computer Science, University of Illinois, Urbana, 1975.

14. R.W. Hockney, "A Fast Direct Solution of Poisson's Equation Using Fourrier Analysis," Journal of ACM, Vol. 12, 1965, pp. 95-113.

15. S. Fortune and J. Wylie, "Parallelism in Random Access Machines," Proceedings of the 10th Annual ACM Symposium on Theory of Computing, 1978, pp. 114-118.

16. B.L. Buzbee, G.H. Golub and C.W. Nelson, "On Direct Methods for Solving Poisson's Equations," SIAM Journal on Numerical Analysis, Vol. 7, 1970, pp. 627-656.

17. H.F. Jordan, "Experience with Pipelined Multiple Instruction Streams," IEEE Proceedings, 1984, pp. 113-123.

O(1) Parallel Time Incremental Graph Algorithms

Deepak D. Sherlekar †
Shaunak Pawagi ‡
I.V. Ramakrishnan ††

Department of Computer Science
University of Maryland
College Park, MD 20742

Abstract Fast parallel algorithms are presented for updating minimum spanning trees, connected components and bridges of an undirected graph when a minor change is made to the graph such as addition or deletion of a vertex or an edge. The machine model used is a parallel random access machine that allows simultaneous reads as well as simultaneous writes into the same memory location. In the latter case one processor succeeds but we do not know which. The algorithms described in this paper require O(1) time and are efficient when compared to previously known O(logn) time algorithms for initial computation of the above mentioned graph properties on this model. An important feature of our algorithms is their versatility, that is, they can be adapted to run efficiently on all variations of this model with very little modification.

1. Introduction

Incremental graph algorithms deal with recomputing properties of a graph after a "minor" modification is made to it. These modifications are as follows. First, an edge joining two vertices may be added to the graph. Second, an edge may be deleted from it. Finally, a vertex along with edges incident with other vertices in the graph may be added or deleted. If the edges have weights associated with them, then we also permit increase or decrease in their weights. These cases subsume the cases of edge insertion and deletion if nonexistent edges are assumed to have infinite edge weights. For such "minor" modifications it should be possible to construct efficient algorithms to recompute the properties of the graph when compared to start-over algorithms [C76] that do not use any of the previous information.

We can characterize incremental algorithms in terms of stages. The first stage is to determine what part of the solution is unaffected by the graph change. This is important as substantial gains can be made by avoiding the recomputation of the unaffected part of the solution. The second stage is the actual recomputation of that part of the solution which is affected by the graph change. This stage can be implemented efficiently by using the previous solution and possibly some auxiliary information that is generated during the initial computation of the solution. This in turn leads us to a third stage which consists of updating the auxiliary information. The efficiency of an incremental algorithm depends on the

---

† Research supported by AFOSR grant AFOSR-82-0303 and NSF grant MCS-83-05992.
‡ Research supproted by AFOSR grant F-49620-83-C-0082.
†† Research supported by ONR grant N00014-84-K-0530 and NSF grant ECS-84-04399. Author's present address: Dept. of Computer Science, SUNY, Stony Brook, NY 11794.

complexity of these three stages and our objective is to design incremental algorithms that are efficient when compared to start-over algorithms.

Incremental algorithms for sequential machine models have received some attention in the past. In particular Spira and Pan [SP75], Chin and Houck [CH78] and Frederickson [F83] have investigated the update problem for minimum spanning tree (MST) of an undirected graph. Cheston [C76] and Spira and Pan [SP75] describe algorithms for shortest path update. Even and Shiloach [ES82] have investigated the update of connected components under the operation of edge deletion. Ibaraki and Katoh [IK83] examine incremental algorithms for the transitive closure of directed graph.

Several researchers have investigated the design of efficient algorithms for graph problems on a model of synchronized parallel computation in which all processors have access to a common memory. Such a model is referred to as PRAM (parallel random access machine) in the literature. There are three versions of PRAMs -- CRCW (Concurrent Read, Concurrent Write), CREW (Concurrent Read, Exclusive Write), and EREW (Exclusive Read, Exclusive Write).

Kucera [K82] describes algorithms for computing the connected components and minimum spanning trees on a CRCW-PRAM. In this model all processors can simultaneously read from the same location. They can also simultaneously write into the same location as long as they are writing the same value. His algorithms require O(log n) time and $O(n^4)$ and $O(n^5)$ processors for the above mentioned problems respectively. Shiloach and Vishkin [SV82] have developed algorithms for computing the connected components of an undirected graph on a slight variation of the CRCW-PRAM model in which processors can simultaneously write different values into the same location. In the latter case only one succeeds but we do not know which. Their algorithms require O(log n) time and use O(n+m) processors, where m is the number of edges in the graph.

Tsin and Chin [TC84] and Savage and Ja'Ja' [SJ81] describe algorithms for these graph problems on the weaker CREW-PRAM model. In such a model processors are not permitted to write simultaneously into the same location. Their algorithms require $O(\log^2 n)$ time and use $O(n^2)$ processors.

Finally, Nath and Maheshwari [NM82] describe algorithms for the connected component and minimum spanning tree problems on the EREW-PRAM model. This model differs from the CREW-PRAM in disallowing simultaneous read from the same memory location. Their algorithms also require $O(\log^2 n)$ time and use $O(n^2)$ processors.

Incremental graph algorithms on a model of parallel computation have not been studied until recently. Pawagi and Ramakrishnan [PR85] first examined incremental algorithms for minimum spanning trees, connected components, bridges and bridge-connected components on a CREW-PRAM. Their algorithms require O(logn) time and use $O(n^2)$ processors. Thus their algorithms are efficient when compared to the start-over algorithms of Savage and Ja'Ja' and also of Tsin and Chin for the same model.

In this paper we describe algorithms for incremental computation of the above graph properties on the CRCW-PRAM model used in [SV82]. We consider all the minor modifications mentioned earlier except vertex deletion. All our algorithms require O(1) time (that is, constant time). We use $O(n^4)$, $O(n^2)$ and $O(n^3)$ processors to recompute the minimum spanning tree, connected components and bridges respectively. An important feature of our algorithms is their *versatility*, that is, they can be adapted to run efficiently on CREW and EREW PRAM models with only minor modifications. On both these models our algorithms require O(logn) time and use $O(n^2)$ processors. The O(logn) factor arises due to the minimum finding operations used by our algorithm. Computing the minimum of n numbers on both these models requires Θ(logn) time ([CD82]).

The rest of this paper is organized as follows. In Section 2 we introduce some notations and procedures that will be used to describe our algorithms for incremental computation of Minimal Spanning Trees, connected components and bridges respectively. Sections 3,4,5 and 6 deal with incremental algorithms for minimal spanning trees, connected components, cycle basis, and bridges and bridge connected components respectively. Concluding remarks appear in Section 7.

2. Preliminaries

We shall need the following graph theoretic preliminaries to describe our algorithms.

2.1. Definitions

Let G=(V,E) denote a *graph* where V is a finite set of vertices (nodes) and E is a set of pairs of vertices called edges. If the edges are unordered pairs then G is *undirected* else it is *directed.* Throughout this paper we assume that V consists of the set of vertices {1,2,...,n} and |E|=m. We denote an undirected edge between u and v by (u,v) and a directed edge between them by <u,v>. An adjacency matrix A of G is an n$\times$n Boolean matrix such that A[u,v]=1 if and only if (u,v) ϵ E. A path in G joining two vertices i_0 and i_k is defined as a sequence of vertices $(i_0,i_1,i_2,..i_k)$ such that all of them are distinct and for each $0 \leq p < k$, (i_p,i_{p+1}) is an edge of G. If $i_0 = i_k$ then the path is called a cycle. We denote an undirected path from vertex u to vertex v by [u-v] and a directed path by [u$\rightarrow$v]. We say that an undirected graph G is *connected* if for every pair of vertices u and v in V, there is a path [u-v] in G. Each connected maximal subgraph of G is called a *component* of G. An edge in G is a *bridge* if its removal increases the number of components of G. Let B be the set of bridges in G. The *bridge-connected components* of G are the components of the graph obtained by removing all the edges in B from G. A rooted *tree* T is a connected undirected acyclic graph with a distinguished vertex called root. We say that vertex u is an *ancestor* of vertex v if u is on the path from v to the root of the tree. A *descendant* of a vertex is defined similarly. The *lowest common ancestor* of vertices x and y in T is the vertex z such that z is a common ancestor of x and y, and any other common ancestor of x and y in T is also an ancestor of z in T.

Let w:E→R denote a function that associates a positive weight with the edges of G. Let these weights be stored in a matrix W called the weight matrix such that W[i,j] is the weight of the edge (i,j). W[i,j] is ∞ if there is no such edge. All graphs are assumed to have no self loops and no multiple edges joining two distinct vertices. A minimum spanning tree (MST) of G is a spanning tree of G such that sum of the weights of the edges in the tree is minimum over all spanning trees for G.

The algorithms presented in this paper assume that the trees are represented as a set of paths. We now proceed to define this data structure and some auxiliary procedures that modify it.

2.2. Data Structures and Auxiliary Procedures

An important aspect of incremental algorithms is the design of data structures to store the previous solution as well as some auxiliary information that may be generated during the initial computation of the solution. Such data structures should provide rapid access to the necessary information for efficient update of the solution.

Our incremental algorithms assume that a spanning tree (forest) of a graph G is stored as rooted tree(s) in an n × n array called PATH. The ith row contains the path [i-r], where r is the root of the tree to which i belongs. An array L of size n contains the lengths of these paths for every vertex. For any row i in PATH, the entries beyond the column L(i) are assumed to be invalid. While modifying PATH, if we want to explicitly invalidate an entry, we store a zero in it. Both PATH and L for a spanning forest of G can be computed in O(log n) time using $O(n^2)$ processors using a technique due to Savage [S77] that is described in [TC84]. When the graph undergoes a change our algorithms recompute the properties of the modified graph and also update the contents of PATH and L.

The data structure used by the incremental algorithms in [PR85] is an inverted tree (a rooted tree where a node points to its parent). These algorithms use the inverted tree for computing the paths between pairs of vertices and identifying the vertices in the two components that are created by deletion of an edge from the tree. These computations require O(log n) time on the CREW and CRCW PRAM models, and $O(\log^2 n)$ time on EREW-PRAMs. However, the start-over algorithms for computing minimum spanning trees, connected components and bridges also require O(log n) time on a CRCW-PRAM and $O(\log^2 n)$ time on the EREW-PRAM. Therefore, the inverted tree data structure does not appear appropriate for for designing efficient incremental algorithms on CRCW or EREW PRAMs for the above graph problems.

In this paper we avoid such computations by explicitly storing the paths from every vertex to the root. We will show later that such a representation enables us to develop incremental graph algorithms running in O(1) time on CRCW-PRAMs and O(logn) time on EREW-PRAMs.

We now describe a set of routines that extract information from PATH and L and perform elementary operations to update them. We assume that these routines operate on a tree T rooted at r. They are used by the algorithms in subsequent sections.

The first function, LCA(i,j), returns indices into the ith and j^{th} row of PATH that correspond to the lowest common ancestor of vertices i and j.

function LCA(i,j)

/* Let i be closer than j to the root r of the tree containing them. */

for each k, $0 \leq k < L(i)$ /* assign a processor to each vertex in the path [r-i] */

compare the kth and the $(k+1)^{th}$ descendant of r on the path [r-i] with the corresponding descendants of r on the path [r-j].

if the first test succeeds and the second fails

/* The vertex assigned to the processor is a common ancestor of i and j but its child is not. Note that exactly one processor succeeds this test. */

Return the indices corresponding to k into the ith and j^{th} rows of PATH.

end

The following lemma gives the time and processor complexity of the function LCA.

Lemma 2.1: The lowest common ancestor of a pair of vertices i and j in a rooted tree represented by PATH and L can be found in O(1) time using O(n) processors.

Proof: Each step in the function LCA takes O(1) time. Since there can be at most n vertices on any path, the function uses at most n processors. ●

To find the maximum weight edge on any path [i-j] in T we use the function MAX(i,j) described below. This path passes through the lowest common ancestor of i and j.

function MAX(i,j)

1. Compute the lowest common ancestor u of i and j using LCA(i,j).
2. Construct the paths [i-u] and [j-u] from PATH.
3. Determine the maximum weight edge from among the edges on the above paths.

end

The time and processor complexity of finding the maximum weight edge on any path in T can be expressed by the following lemma.

Lemma 2.2: The maximum weight edge on the path [i-j] in T can be determined in O(1) time using $O(n^2)$ processors.

Proof: Steps (1) and (2) use O(n) processors and require O(1) time. Step (3) can be performed using the implementation in ([SV81]) of Valiant's algorithm [V75]. This computes the maximum of n elements in O(1) time using $O(n^2)$ processors. ●

If an edge (i,j) is deleted from the spanning forest of G stored in PATH, the tree T containing (i,j) is split into two trees. Procedure DELETE updates PATH and L after the edge (i,j) has been deleted from the forest. If j is the parent of i in T, then deletion of (i,j) splits T into two trees, one rooted at i and the other rooted at r. This procedure replaces T by these new trees.

procedure DELETE(i,j)

/* Assume that j is a parent of i. Note that any vertex k is a descendant of i if i is closer to the root than k and PATH(k,L(k)-L(i)) = i */

for each descendant k of i

$L(k) \leftarrow L(k) - L(i)$. /* make i the root of the tree to which k belongs */

end

An analysis of DELETE gives us the following lemma.

Lemma 2.3: Updating PATH and L following deletion of an edge (i,j) from the forest takes O(1) time using O(n) processors.

Proof: Each vertex is assigned a processor to detect whether it is a descendant of i. All steps in DELETE take O(1) time. Therefore DELETE takes O(1) time using O(n) processors. ●

The incremental algorithms in this paper often need to merge two trees by an edge. PATH and L then have to be updated to reflect this change. Let (i,j) be an edge joining two trees T_i and T_j. The procedure described below updates PATH and L after (i,j) merges T_i and T_j into one tree. The new tree thus constructed replaces T_i and T_j in the forest.

procedure INSERT(i,j)

/* Assume without loss of generality that r_j is the root of the new tree. The paths from the vertices in T_i to r_j are constructed as given below. L is also assumed to be modified along with PATH in steps (1), (2) and (3) */

1. the ith row of PATH ← i followed by the the path $[j-r_j]$.
2. for each ancestor k of i in T_i
   the kth row of PATH ← the reverse of the path [i-k] in T_i followed by the new path of i.
3. for each node k in T_i not processed in steps (1) and (2)
   Compute the lowest common ancestor u of i and k in T_i using LCA(i,k).
   the kth row of PATH ← the path [k-u] followed by the new path $[u-r_j]$.

end

An analysis of INSERT follows.

Lemma 2.4: Procedure INSERT takes O(1) time using $O(n^2)$ processors.

Proof: Each step in INSERT takes O(1) time. In the worst case, at most O(n) vertices must change their paths. Every such path is at most O(n) long. Therefore we need $O(n^2)$ processors. ●

The incremental algorithms for minimal spanning trees and bridge-connected components need to update PATH and L following removal of multiple tree edges from the spanning tree/forest of G. The procedure MULTIDELETE below is an algorithm for doing this.

procedure MULTIDELETE($(i_1,j_1),(i_2,j_2),\ldots,(i_k,j_k)$)

/* Assume that i_p is the child of j_p, $1 \le p \le k$. Let *root* be a boolean array of size n which indicates whether or not a vertex becomes the root of a tree upon deletion of the above tree edges */

1. for each (i,j) in $\{(i_1,j_1),\ldots,(i_k,j_k)\}$ do

    root(i) ← TRUE. /* i becomes the root of a new tree */

2. for each vertex v do

    for each ancestor w of v /* including v itself */

    if *root*(w) then

    for each l, $L(w)+1 \le l \le L(v)$, do PATH(v,l) ←0

    /* remove all ancestors of v beyond w by invalidating the corresponding entries in row v of PATH. */

3. for each vertex v

    Check every element and its right neighbor in row v of PATH by assigning a processor to each element. There is exactly one processor that finds its element to be valid and the element to its right invalid. This processor gives the last valid entry in row v. This then is the root of the of the tree to which v belongs.

    The column index to the above element gives the length of the path from v to the new root of its tree.

end

The above algorithm runs in O(1) time using $O(n^3)$ processors. Its analysis is described in the following lemma.

Lemma 2.5: Computing the changes in PATH and L following removal of at most n-1 edges from the forest requires O(1) time and $O(n^3)$ processors.

Proof: Step 1 of MULTIDELETE needs O(n) processors, since at most O(n) edges can be deleted from the spanning forest. Step 2 needs $O(n^3)$ processors, while step 3 needs $O(n^2)$ processors. All steps in the procedure take O(1) time. Thus MULTIDELETE takes O(1) time using $O(n^3)$ processors. ●

3. Incremental Algorithms for MST

The problem of updating an MST involves reconstructing the new MST from the current MST when the weight of an edge has changed or a vertex along with all its incident edges is inserted or deleted from the underlying graph. We refer to these two subproblems as the edge update and the vertex update problem respectively.

Savage and Ja'Ja' [SJ81] have described an $O(\log^2 n)$ time algorithm for constructing an MST on a CREW-PRAM. For this problem Kucera [K82] has described an O(log n) time algorithm that runs on a CRCW-PRAM. Pawagi and Ramakrishnan [PR85] have described O(log n) time algorithms for the above mentioned update problems which run on a CREW-

PRAM. Our algorithms for the edge update problem require constant time on a CRCW-PRAM. Using an approach described in [PR85] we also solve the vertex insertion problem in constant time.

The MST is represented as a rooted tree in the data structure PATH, with an arbitrary vertex as the root. After an update, the algorithms ensure that the reconstructed MST is also represented as a rooted tree. Using the technique of Tsin and Chin [TC84], the parallel algorithm for constructing the MST in [SJ81] can be easily modified to compute the set of paths required by our algorithm without affecting the time complexity of the start over algorithm.

The edge update problem is concerned with reconstructing the new MST when the weight of an edge in the underlying graph changes. There are several cases to be handled in edge update. The weight of an edge may either increase or decrease and this edge may currently be either in the tree or not in the tree. If the weight of a tree edge decreases, or the weight of a non-tree edge increases, then the old MST will not undergo any change. On the other hand, it may undergo changes when the weight of a tree edge increases or the weight of a non-tree edge decreases. However, in both cases, at most one edge will enter the tree and another edge will leave it.

If the weight of a tree edge (x,y) increases then the new MST is recomputed using the following algorithm MSTED.

procedure MSTED(i,j)

1. if (i,j) is not in the current MST then return.

/* Let j be the parent of i in the MST rooted at r */

2. call DELETE(i,j) to remove (i,j). This splits the MST into two trees, one of which is rooted at r and the other at i.
3. Compute the minimum weight edge (x,y) connecting the above two trees.
4. call INSERT(x,y) to construct the new MST from these two trees.

end

If the weight of a non-tree edge (i,j) decreases, then we proceed to recompute the new MST as given in the procedure below.

procedure MSTEI(i,j)

/* Let r be the root of the current MST and i be closer to root than j */

1 call MAX(i,j) to find the maximum weight edge (u,v) on the path [i,j] in the MST.

2. if $w(u,v) \leq w(i,j)$ then return else
   call DELETE(u,v) to remove (u,v) from the tree
   call INSERT(i,j) to obtain the new MST.

end

Lemma 3.1: The above algorithms take O(1) time and require $O(n^3)$ processors.

Proof: All the steps in our algorithms can be done in O(1) time. Calls to DELETE require O(n) processors. Calls to INSERT and MAX require $O(n^2)$ processors. Selection of the edge (x,y) in step 3 of MSTED requires $O(n^3)$ processors. This involves the following two steps. First, for each vertex i find the minimum weight edge (i,j) such that i and j are not in the same tree. This can be done in constant time by assigning n^2 processors to each vertex of G ([SV81]). Since there are n vertices we need $O(n^3)$ processors. Second, select a minimum cost edge among the edges selected in the first step. This selection can be done in constant time using $O(n^2)$ processors. ●

Note that edge insertion and edge deletion can be easily handled by our algorithms. Assign large positive weights ($+\infty$) to edges not in the underlying graph. Then inserting a new edge into the graph is equivalent to decreasing the weight of a non-tree edge. Similarly edge deletion is equivalent to increasing the weight of the deleted edge to $+\infty$.

The vertex update problem involves reconstructing the new MST when a vertex is either inserted or deleted from the underlying graph. We only consider the problem when a new node is inserted into the underlying graph. The other case of reconstructing the MST when a vertex is deleted from the graph appears difficult to handle. For instance, if the MST is in the form of a "star" (that is, there exists a vertex on which all the edges in the MST are incident), the deletion of such a vertex deletes all the edges in the tree. Updating the MST then requires reconstructing it all over again (that is, by examining all the remaining edges in the graph).

Spira and Pan [SP75] update the MST in O(n) time when a vertex is inserted in the graph. Their algorithm constructs the MST all over again by examining the n-1 edges in the old MST and the new edges (there can be at most n of them) brought in by the inserted vertex. The O(n) time complexity obtained by Spira and Pan to update the MST is primarily due to the smaller number of edges that need to be examined. However, parallel algorithms to construct an MST by just examining the edges in the old MST and the new edges brought in by the inserted vertex still requires O(logn) time. Chin and Houck [CH78] also describe a sequential algorithm of time complexity O(n) for the vertex update problem. However, their algorithm is inherently sequential.

Our solution to this problem is essentially based on a novel way of examining the old tree edges and the new edges brought in by the inserted vertex ([PR]). Every pair of edges incident on the new vertex induces a cycle in the old MST. At most n such edges are incident on the inserted vertex thereby creating $\binom{n}{2}$ (number of unordered pairs of n elements), that is $O(n^2)$ cycles. We break all these cycles *simultaneously* by *removing* the *maximum-weight* edge on each cycle. This is an interesting situation because $O(n^2)$ cycles are broken, but instead of $O(n^2)$ edges only (n-1) edges get deleted. Proof that the resulting graph is indeed an MST appears in [PR]. The details of our algorithm are given in the procedure MSTVI below.

procedure MSTVI($z,i_1,i_2,..i_k$)

/* Let z be the new vertex inserted in the graph with edges incident with vertices $i_1,i_2,..i_k$ */

1. for all distinct pairs (u,v) where u,v is in $i_1,i_2,..i_k$
   call MAX(u,v).
2. Determine the maximum weight edge on the cycle formed by the edge (z,u), the path [u-v] and the edge (v,z) by selecting the maximum weight edge among the edges (z,u), (v,z) and MAX(u,v).
3. call MULTIDELETE to delete the maximum weight edges selected in step (2).
4. for all new edges (i_p,z) $1 \leq p \leq k$ retained in step (2)
   call INSERT(i_p,z).

end

Lemma 3.2: Updating the MST after a vertex has been inserted into the graph requires O(1) time and uses $O(n^4)$ processors.

Proof: It is easy to see that all steps can be done in O(1) time. Each cycle contains at most n edges. Hence computing the maximum weight edge on the $O(n^2)$ cycles requires $O(n^4)$ processors. By Lemma 2.5, MULTIDELETE uses $O(n^3)$ processors. The deletion of edges in step (3) fragments the old MST into multiple trees. Since procedure INSERT affects only those entries in PATH that correspond to the trees being merged, it is possible to perform INSERT simultaneously for all the new edges. Moreover, the total number of nodes in all these trees put together is at most n, and the tree into which they are merged has only one vertex. Hence it can be shown that the processor complexity of step (4) is $O(n^2)$. ●

4. Connected Components

In this section we describe incremental algorithms to recompute the connected components of G following an edge or vertex insertion, or an edge deletion.

A sequential algorithm for the edge deletion problem is discussed in [ES82]. A survey of incremental sequential algorithms for the problem appears in [C76]. The start-over parallel algorithm in [SV82] requires O(logn) time on a CRCW-PRAM and uses O(n+m) processors. The incremental parallel algorithms in [PR85] handle the three cases in O(logn) time using $O(n^2)$ processors on a CREW-PRAM. The algorithms presented in this section take O(1) time using $O(n^2)$ processors on a CRCW-PRAM.

We shall label the connected component by a representative vertex in that component. For every vertex in G the algorithm outputs the label of the component to which it belongs. This convention is also followed by the start-over and incremental parallel algorithms mentioned above. For every tree in the spanning forest of G the root of the tree represents the corresponding component of G.

Our algorithms assume the existence of PATH and L for G prior to its change. An algorithm in [TV84] computes a spanning forest of G in O(log n) time using O(m+n) processors by modifying the start over algorithm in [SV82]. PATH and L can be obtained from this spanning forest in O(log n) time using $O(n^2)$ processors ([TC84]).

If i and j belong to different components then insertion of the edge (i,j) merges the two components. Otherwise the connected components and the data structures remain unaltered. The details appear in procedure CCEI below.

procedure CCEI(i,j)

if i and j belong to different components then

call INSERT(i,j) to merge the two components.

end

To handle edge deletion we proceed as follows. If (i,j) is a non-tree edge, there is no change in either the connected components or the data structures; otherwise we split the tree containing (i,j) into two trees by deleting (i,j) from it. The two trees are merged back into one if there is an edge joining them. The details appear in the following procedure.

procedure CCED(i,j)

1. if (i,j) is not a tree edge then return;
   /* Let j be the parent of i and r, the root of the tree containing (i,j). */
2. call DELETE(i,j) to split the tree into trees T_i and T_j rooted at i and r.
3. for each non-tree edge (u,v)
   if u is in T_i and v is in T_j then *selected* ← (u,v).
4. if *selected* $\neq$ NULL and *selected* = (x,y) then
   call INSERT(x,y) to join the two trees back.

end

We next define a procedure CCVI to handle vertex insertion. If the new vertex v has edges incident with vertices $i_1,\ldots,i_k$ of G, then components containing these vertices are merged into one. The corresponding tree, rooted at v, replaces the trees corresponding to the components that got merged in the process.

procedure CCVI($i_1,i_2,\ldots,i_k$)

1. for each tree with root r do
   for each i in $i_1, \ldots, i_k$ do
   if i belongs to the tree rooted at r then *selected* (r) ← i.
2. Add a row to PATH corresponding to v, with v as a root of a one node tree.
3. for each vertex r that is a root of some tree do
   if *selected* (r) = i then merge the trees rooted at r and v using INSERT(i,v).

end

Step 1 selects an edge from every component to add to the new tree. This selection is done using concurrent write. Step 3 merges these components into a component with representative v. Since INSERT affects only the entries in PATH that correspond to the components being merged into a component with representative v, it is possible to perform INSERT simultaneously on all components.

The time and processor complexity of the incremental algorithm for connected components is determined by the routines CCEI, CCED and CCVI. Its analysis appears in the following lemma.

Lemma 4.1 Our incremental algorithm for connected components runs in O(1) time using $O(n^2)$ processors.

Proof: The time bounds for all three cases can be verified easily. The same holds for the processor requirements for edge insertion and deletion. The processor complexity follows from the analysis in Lemma 3.2. ●

5. Cycle Basis

The set of fundamental cycles corresponding to any spanning forest of G provides a cycle basis for G. This cycle basis can be computed in O(1) time using $O(n^3)$ processors by finding the fundamental cycles corresponding to each of the non-tree edges. The cycles are stored in an array CYCLE. Every row of CYCLE corresponds to an edge in G, and holds the fundamental cycle (if any) corresponding to that edge. The computation is done using the procedure FC below, which computes the fundamental cycle for a given non-tree edge in O(1) time using O(n) processors and stores it in CYCLE.

procedure FC(i,j)

/* Let i and j belong to a tree T with root r. Let i be closer to r than j. */

1. Call LCA(i,j) to find the lowest common ancestor w of i and j.
2. CYCLE((i,j)) ← the cycle formed by i, followed by the paths [j-w] and [w-i] in T.

end

In many cases however, it is possible to obtain the same time complexity using fewer processors. The only case that needs to compute all cycles is that of deleting a tree edge which is not a bridge. The procedure CBED below is the algorithm to handle edge deletion.

procedure CBED(i,j)

1. if (i,j) is a non-tree edge then return
2. call CCED(i,j) to update the data structures and connected components
3. if i and j belong to different components then return
4. for each non-tree edge (p,q) do
   call FC(p,q) to find the fundamental cycle induced by (p,q)

end

When an edge (i,j) is inserted to merge two connected components, the cycle basis does not change. Only the data structures must be updated to reflect the change, which can be done using the edge insertion procedure CCEI for connected components. If the inserted edge joins the vertices in the same component then the corresponding cycle is added to the cycle basis. In the next routine, CBEI, we outline the algorithm to handle edge insertion.

procedure CBEI(i,j)

if i and j belong to same connected component then

call FC(i,j) to find the cycle induced by the inserted edge (i,j).

else

call CCEI(i,j) to update the data structures PATH and L.

end

When a new vertex v with edges incident to $i_1, i_2, \ldots, i_k$ is inserted into G, the connected components and spanning forest of G are updated using CCVI. After v has been inserted some of the edges incident on v become new non-tree edges. The new cycle basis is then formed by adding the cycles induced by the new non-tree edges to the old cycle basis. This is possible because the vertex insertion algorithm for connected components merges them without affecting any of the previous fundamental cycles. This idea is summarized in the routine CBVI below.

procedure CBVI($v, i_1, i_2, \ldots, i_k$)

1. call CCVI($v, i_1, i_2, \ldots, i_k$) to get a new spanning forest for G.
2. for each non-tree edge (j,v) call FC(j,v)

end

The time complexity of the incremental algorithms for cycle basis is O(1) in all cases. However, as expressed in the next lemma, the processor complexity depends on the changes in the underlying graph.

Lemma 5.1: The incremental algorithms for cycle basis run in O(1) time using $O(n^2)$ processors for edge and vertex insertion, and $O(n^3)$ processors for edge deletion.

Proof: Follows readily from an analysis of procedures CBEI, CBED, and CBVI above. Note that the only case where edge deletion needs $O(n^3)$ processors is when the deleted edge is in the forest, but is not a bridge.

6. Bridges and Bridge-Connected Components

Using the data structures PATH and L it is possible to compute all the bridges of G in O(1) time using the following lemma.

Lemma 6.1 An edge e in G is a bridge iff e does not lie on any fundamental cycle of G.

Proof: See [H69].

The algorithm FINDBRIDGES below returns a boolean array BRIDGE of size $O(n^2)$, which for every edge e indicates whether e is a bridge. It computes the bridges by finding all the fundamental cycles using procedure FC.

procedure FINDBRIDGES

for each non-tree edge (i,j) do

call FC(i,j) to find the fundamental cycle for (i,j).

for each tree edge (u,v) in the cycle for (i,j), BRIDGE(u,v) ← FALSE.

end

Edge deletion is handled as follows. If the deleted edge is not a bridge then use FINDBRIDGES to recompute the bridges. On the other hand, if it is a bridge then all the other bridges remain unaffected. The details appear in procedure BED below.

procedure BED(i,j)

1. call CCED(i,j) to update the data structures
2. if BRIDGE((i,j)) then BRIDGE((i,j)) ← FALSE
   else call FINDBRIDGES

end

Vertex and edge insertion are handled in procedures BEI and BVI respectively.

procedure BEI(i,j)

/* (i,j) is the edge being inserted */

if i and j belong to different trees then

BRIDGE((i,j)) ← TRUE.

call CCEI(i,j) to update the spanning forest and data structures.

else

call FC to find the cycle C induced by the edge (i,j).

for each edge e in C, BRIDGE(e) ← FALSE.

end

procedure BVI($v,i_1,i_2,\ldots,i_k$)

/* v is the new vertex to which $i_1,i_2,\ldots,i_k$ are adjacent */

1. call CCVI($v,i_1,i_2,\ldots,i_k$) to update the data structures.
2. for each i in $i_1,i_2,\ldots,i_k$ do
   if (i,v) is a non-tree edge then
   call FC(i,v) to find the fundamental cycle C induced by the edge (i,v).
   for each edge e in C, BRIDGE(e) ← FALSE.

end

The processor complexities of our incremental algorithms for bridges depend on the change being handled and their analysis is as follows.

Lemma 6.2: The incremental algorithms for bridges run in O(1) time using $O(n^2)$ processors for edge and vertex insertion and $O(n^3)$ processors for edge deletion.

Proof: The time complexity for each case is evident from inspection of the respective procedures. The edge deletion case uses FINDBRIDGES which requires $O(n^3)$ processors in the worst case. The processor complexity for edge insertion can be determined easily from the above procedures, using previous analysis of CCEI, CCVI and FC.

The representation of bridge-connected components is similar to that of connected components. Foe every node, the representative vertex of the bridge-connected component to which it belongs is maintained in an array BCC. The bridge-connected components of G can be found in O(1) time using its spanning forest stored in PATH and L. This is done by using the procedure MULTIDELETE (see Section 2) to simultaneously delete all bridges from the spanning forest. Each tree in the resulting forest corresponds to a bridge-connected component. We require $O(n^3)$ processors to identify bridge-connected components in O(1) time.

Again, it is possible to achieve the same time complexity using fewer processors for edge and vertex insertion. The edge deletion case needs to compute all bridge-connected components from scratch unless the deleted edge is a bridge. Sc in the worst case, edge deletion still needs $O(n^3)$ processors.

When a new vertex v is inserted, all bridge-connected components that lie on a cycle containing v get merged into one large bridge connected component with representative vertex v. Procedure BCCVI below handles vertex insertion.

procedure BCCVI($v, i_1, i_2, \ldots, i_k$)

1. call CCVI($v, i_1, i_2, \ldots, i_k$) to find the new PATH and L.
2. newrep(v) ← v. /* newrep holds the new representatives of the BCCs of G */
3. for each vertex w in G do
   if BCC(w) = w then newrep(w) ← w. /* unless the BCC merges with others its representative remains the same. */
4. for each non-tree edge (i,v) do
   call FC(i,v) to find the fundamental cycle for (i,v).
   for each vertex w in the fundamental cycle for (i,v) do
      newrep(BCC(w)) ← v. /* the new rep. of the BCC containing w is v */.
5. for each vertex w do
   newrep(w) ← newrep(BCC(w)) /* reflect the change in the BCC rep. (if any) for every vertex. */
6. BCC ← newrep.

end

Our strategy for edge insertion is similar to that of vertex insertion. The only difference is that we need to merge only the bridge-connected components which lie on the cycle (if any) induced by the inserted edge. The details appear in procedure BCCEI.

procedure BCCEI(i,j)

1. if i and j are in different components then call CCEI(i,j) and return.
2. call FC(i,j) to find the cycle for (i,j).

3. newrep ← BCC(i). /* the rep of all merged BCCs is the rep. of i's BCC*/

4. for each vertex w in the cycle for (i,j) do

   change(BCC(w))← TRUE. /* change keeps track of all BCCs that are threaded by the cycle and get merged in step 5 */

5. for each vertex w do

   if change(BCC(w)) then BCC(w) ← newrep. /* merge marked components */.

end

The processor and time complexities of our algorithms for bridge-connected components are as follows.

Lemma 6.3: The incremental algorithms for bridge-connected components run in O(1) time using $O(n^2)$ processors for edge and vertex insertion and $O(n^3)$ for edge deletion.

Proof: The time complexity for edge and vertex insertion can be determined easily by inspection of the above procedures. The processor complexity follows from that of CCVI, CCEI, and FC. The time and processor complexity for edge deletion is analysed in the discussion preceding BCCEI and BCCVI.

7. Concluding Remarks

In this paper we developed incremental algorithms for updating minimum spanning trees, connected components, bridges and bridge-connected components on a CRCW-PRAM. The central idea was to represent the graph by its rooted spanning tree (forest for a graph with more than one component). By explicitly storing the paths from all vertices to the root we were able to develop O(1) time incremental algorithms.

An important feature of our algorithms is their versatility, that is, they can be run on both CREW and EREW PRAMs with little or no modification. A straightforward transformation of our algorithms using the technique discussed in [V83] will result in algorithms of time complexity O(logn) on CREW-PRAMs and $O(\log^2 n)$ on EREW-PRAMs. However, it is possible to achieve O(logn) time complexity on the EREW-PRAM. The details are as follows.

Observe that the concurrent-write feature is used in a few steps in our algorithms. These write conflicts can be resolved (without generating read conflicts) by imposing a linear ordering on the competing processors and use this ordering to select the lowest ranked processor for writing. Such a selection can be done in O(logn) time among n competing processors. For instance, in procedure CCVI we are required to select a representative edge from multiple edges that are incident on the same component. This selection is done in O(1) time using the concurrent-write feature on our model. To do the same step on a CREW-PRAM we resolve the write conflict by imposing a linear order on the contending processors based on the lexicographic ordering of the edges which are incident on that component. The resulting algorithms run in O(logn) time on a CREW-PRAM.

The read conflicts in our algorithms can be resolved using a well-known technique of making multiple copies of data. This technique requires O(logn) time to resolve read conflicts among n competing processors. Applying this transformation to the CREW-PRAM algorithms obtained above yields O(logn) time algorithms for EREW-PRAMs.

Finally, the processor complexity of all our algorithms can be reduced to $O(n^2)$ on CREW-PRAMs by appropriately modifying procedures MAX, LCA, MULTIDELETE and MSTVI (section 2). Computing the minimum and maximum of n elements on these models can be done in O(logn) time using O(n) processors. The technique in [TC84] reduces the processor complexity of LCA to O(1). The $O(n^2)$ max finding operations for vertex insertion in MSTs can be done in $O(n^2)$ processors as in [PR85]. The modifications required for procedure MULTIDELETE appear in [SPR85].

Our incremental algorithms can therefore be adapted to run on CREW and EREW PRAMs in O(logn) time. Thus our algorithms are faster by a factor of O(logn) over corresponding start-over algorithms on all the three PRAM models. Previous work on incremental parallel algorithms which addresses the same problems as this paper appears in [PR85], which deals only with algorithms on CREW-PRAMs. The CREW-PRAM versions of the algorithms in this paper have the same processor complexity as those in [PR85] for all problems. The time complexity is also the same in all cases except edge insertion for connected components, cycle basis, and bridges, where our algorithms run faster by a factor of O(logn). Unlike previously published start-over or incremental parallel algorithms, our algorithms can be adapted to run efficiently on all three PRAM models with only minor changes.

References

[C76]

G. Cheston, "Incremental Algorithms in Graph Theory", TR 91 (1976), Dept. of Computer Science, Univ. of Toronto, Toronto.

[CH78]

F. Chin and D. Houck, "Algorithms for Updating Minimum Spanning Trees", *Journal of Computer and System Sciences*, 16 (1978), pp. 333-344.

[CD82]

S. Cook and C. Dwork, "Bounds on the Time for Parallel RAMs to Compute Simple Functions", *Proc. 14th ACM Symposium on Theory of Computing*, 1982, pp. 231-233.

[ES82]

S. Even and Y. Shiloach, "An On-line Edge Deletion Problem", Journal of ACM, 28 (1982), pp. 1-4.

[F83]

G. Frederickson, "Data Structures for On-line Updating of Minimum Spanning Trees", *Proc. 15th ACM Symposium on Theory of Computing* (1983), pp. 252-257.

[H69]

F. Harary, **Graph Theory** , Addison-Wesley, Reading, Mass., 1969.

[IK83]

T. Ibaraki and N. Katoh, "On-line Computation of Transitive Closure of Graphs", *Information Processing Letters*, 16 (1983), pp 95-97.

[K82]

L. Kucera, "Parallel Computation and Conflicts in Memory Access", *Information Processing Letters*, 14 (1982), pp. 93-96.

[NM82]

D. Nath and S.N. Maheshwari, "Parallel Algorithms for the Connected Components and Minimal Spanning Tree Problems", *Information Processing Letters*, 14 (1982), pp. 7-10.

[PR]

S. Pawagi and I.V. Ramakrishnan, "An O(logn) Algorithm for Parallel Updates of Minimum Spanning Trees", *Information Processing Letters*, (to appear).

[PR85]

S. Pawagi and I.V. Ramakrishnan, "Parallel Updates of Graph Properties in Logarithmic Time", *Proc. 14th International Conference on Parallel Processing* (1985), St. Charles, Illinois.

[S77]

C. Savage, "Parallel Algorithms for Some Graph Problems", TR-784 (1977), Dept. of Mathematics, Univ. of Illinois, Urbana.

[SJ81]

C. Savage and J. Ja'Ja', "Fast Efficient Parallel Algorithms for Some Graph Problems", *SIAM Journal on Computing*, 10 (1981), pp. 682-691.

[SP75]

P. Spira and A. Pan, "On Finding and Updating Spanning Trees and Shortest Paths", *SIAM Journal on Computing*, 4 (1975), pp. 375-380.

[SPR85]

D.D. Sherlekar, S. Pawagi and I.V. Ramakrishnan, "Fast Incremental Parallel Algorithms for Graph Problems on PRAMs", Technical Report, U. of Maryland, 1985 (in preparation).

[SV81]

Y. Shiloach and U. Vishkin, "Finding the Maximum, Merging and Sorting in a Parallel Computation Model", *Journal of Algorithms*, 2 (1981), pp. 88-102.

[SV82]

Y. Shiloach and U. Vishkin, "An O(logn) Parallel Connectivity Algorithm", *Journal of Algorithms*, 3 (1982), 57-63.

[TV84]

R.E. Tarjan and U. Vishkin, "Finding Biconnected Components and Computing Tree Functions in Logarithmic Parallel Time", *Proc. 23rd Annual Symp. on Foundations of Computer Science* (1984), pp. 12-20.

[TC84]

Y. Tsin and F. Chin, "Efficient Parallel Algorithms for a Class of Graph Theoretic Problems", *SIAM Journal on Computing*, 14 (1984), pp. 580-599.

[V75]

L.G. Valiant, "Parallelism in Comparison Problems", *SIAM Journal on Computing*, 4 (1975), pp. 348-355.

[V83]

U. Vishkin, "Implementation of simultaneous Memory Access in Models That Forbid it", *Journal of Algorithms*, 4 (1983), pp. 45-50.

NC Algorithms for Comparability Graphs, Interval Graphs, and Testing for Unique Perfect Matching

Dexter Kozen[1]
Cornell University

Umesh V. Vazirani[2]
University of California, Berkeley

Vijay V. Vazirani[3]
Cornell University

ABSTRACT

Laszlo Lovasz recently posed the following problem: "Is there an *NC* algorithm for testing if a given graph has a unique perfect matching." We present such an *NC* algorithm. The ideas developed may be a step towards obtaining an *NC* algorithm for determining if a graph has a perfect matching. We also give *NC* algorithms for obtaining a transitive orientation for a comparability graph, anad an interval representation for an interval graph. These enable us to obtain an *NC* algorithm for finding a maximum matching in incomparability graphs.

1. Introduction

One of the most important results in parallel computation was obtained by Karp, Upfal and Wigderson [KUW], showing that the maximum matching problem is in Random *NC*. An important open problem remaining is whether there is an *NC* algorithm (deterministic) for this problem. The first step would be to obtain an *NC* algorithm for testing if a graph has a perfect matching. The known parallel algorithm, based on a method of Lovasz [Lo], involves randomization (see [BGH]). Rabin and Vazirani [RV] give an *NC* algorithm for obtaining perfect matchings in graphs having unique perfect matching. In this paper we give an *NC* algorithm for the following problem posed by Lovasz: "Does the given graph G have a unique perfect matching?" Our solution may be a step towards answering the above stated open problem.

---

[2]Supported by NSF Grant MCS 82-04506, and an IBM Graduate Fellowship.
[3]Supported by NSF Grant BCR 85-03611, and an IBM Faculty Development Award.

We also give NC algorithms for obtaining a transitive orientation for a comparability graph, and an interval representation for an interval graph. The first sequential algorithms for these problems were obtained by Gilmore and Hoffman [GH]. More efficient algorithms are obtained by Even, Pnueli, and Lempel [EPL, PLE], Ghouila-Houri [Gh] and Golumbic [Go]. The NC interval graph algorithm, together with the Random NC Two-Processor Scheduling algorithm of Vazirani and Vazirani [VV] gives us a Random NC algorithm for obtaining maximum matchings in interval graphs. This result was subsumed by [KUW]. The NC comparability graph algorithm, together with the recent NC Two-Processor Scheduling algorithm of Helmbold and Mayr [HM] gives us an NC algorithm for maximum matching on incomparability graphs. This may be suggesting that the maximum matching problem is in NC.

2. Testing for Unique Perfect Matching

We will first consider the case of bipartite graphs:

Input: A bipartite graph $G(X,Y,E)$.
Question: Does G have a unique perfect matching?

Let $|X| = |Y| = n$, and A be the $n \times n$ adjacency matrix for G, i.e. $A(i,j) = 1$ if (x_i, y_j) $memberE$, and is 0 otherwise. For permutation σ on $\{1,2, \ldots n\}$, define

$$value(\sigma) = \prod_{i=1}^{n} A(i, \sigma(i)).$$

Permutation σ corresponds to a perfect matching in G iff $value(\sigma) = 1$. Now,

$$|A| = \sum_{\sigma} sign(\sigma) \cdot value(\sigma).$$

If G has a unique perfect matching, there is a simple NC algorithm [RV] for obtaining this. Firstly, notice that $|A| = \pm 1$. If edge (x_i, y_j) is in the perfect matching, then $G - \{x_i, y_j\}$ has a unique perfect matching, and the minor $|A_{ij}| = \pm 1$. Else $|A_{ij}| = 0$. Hence by inverting A, we can obtain the perfect matching. Moreover this can be accomplished in NC. Let M be this matching. Let us renumber the vertices in Y so that the matched edges are $M = \{(x_1, y_1) \ldots (x_n, y_n)\}$.

If G has no perfect matchings, $|A| = 0$, and we will detect this. However, G may have more than one perfect matching, and yet the above algorithm may succeed. To check that G has a unique perfect matching, we must check $\forall i$, $1 \le i \le n$, $G - (x_i, y_i)$ has no perfect matching.

This seems to require a test for perfect matching. We will circumvent this as follows: we will obtain matrix B from A by replacing the diagonal entries (which correspond to M), by the indeterminate x. We will show

Lemma 1: $|B| = x^n$ iff G has a unique perfect matching.

Proof: Clearly, if G has a unique perfect matching, $|B| = x^n$. Else, G must have a *cycle*, i.e. a set of edges of the form $\{(x_{i_1}, y_{i_2}), (x_{i_2}, y_{i_3}) \ldots, (x_{i_l}, y_{i_1})\}$.

Any non-vanishing permutation (i.e. perfect matching) must choose such cycles, and the remaining edges from M. Let k be the length of the shortest such cycle. Any non-vanishing permutation that chooses $n-k$ edges from M must choose such a k cycle, since k is the length of the shortest cycle. Its sign must be $(-1)^{k-1}$. Hence the term containing x^{n-k} must appear in $|B|$.

The following result enables us to evaluate $|B|$ in NC:

Theorem (Borodin, Cook, and Pippinger [BCP]: The determinant of an $n \times n$ matrix of polynomials with a constant number of variables and degree of each matrix element bounded by n can be computed in $0(\log^2 n)$ steps using $0(n^{4.5})$ processors. We now turn to general graphs:

Input: Graph $G(V,E)$.
Question: Does G have a unique perfect matching?

The algorithm is similar to the bipartite case. Let $|V| = n$, and A be the $n \times n$ adjacency matrix for G, i.e. $A(i,j) = 1$ if $(v_i, v_j) member E$, 0 otherwise. Notice that A is symmetric. The Tutte Matrix [Tu] of G is obtained as follows: if $A(i,j) = A(j,i) = 1$, replace these entries by x_{ij} and $-x_{ij}$, so that the entries above the diagonal appear with a positive sign. Retain the zero entries. The resulting matrix, T, will be skew-symmetric.

If A has a unique perfect matching, substituting $x_{ij} = 1$ for each of the indeterminates we will get $|T| = 1$. Once again, inverting T will give us the perfect matching, M [RV]. Now, corresponding to each matched edge (v_i, v_j), we will substitute $x_{ij} = x$, and $1's$ for the remaining indeterminates. Let B be the resulting matrix. Once again, $|B| = x^n$ *iff* G has a unique perfect matching. The proof is similar to that of Lemma 1. Graph G will contain another perfect matching *iff* it contains an alternating cycle, i.e. a cycle consisting alternately of edges in M and not in M. Let k be the length of the shortest such cycle. As in Lemma 1, the term containing x^{n-k} will survive in $|B|$. Hence we get:

Theorem 1: There is an NC algorithm for testing if the given graph has a unique perfect matching.

3. Comparability Graphs

An undirected graph $G(V,E)$ is called a *comparability* graph if we can direct its edges to obtain a transitively closed acyclic digraph H. We give an NC algorithm for the following problem:

Instance: An undirected graph $G(V,E)$.

Output: Check if G is a comparability graph. If so, obtain a transitive orientation of the edges.

The first polynomial time algorithm for this problem was given by Gilmore and Hoffman [GH]. They also prove:

Theorem [GH]: Graph G is a comparability graph *iff* each odd cycle has at least one triangular chord.

It is easy to get an NC algorithm for checking this condition. Our parallel algorithm for transitive orientation is based on the sequential algorithm of Golumbic [Go]. We will give the details of Theorem 2 in the final paper.

Theorem 2: There is an NC algorithm for checking if the given graph $G(V,E)$ is a comparability graph, and if so, for obtaining a transitive orientation of its edges

4. Interval Graphs

We give an NC algorithm for:

Input: An undirected graph $G(V,E)$.

Output: Check if G is an interval graph. If so, obtain an interval representation for it.

Definition [GH]: Let σ be a linearly ordered finite set. An *interval* α of σ is any set of contiguous elements of σ. Two intervals intersect *iff* they have an element in common. Let I be a set of intervals on σ. Then (σ,I) is an *interval representation* for graph $G(V,E)$ if there exists a bijection $f: V \rightarrow I$ *s.t.* $(u,v) member E$ *iff* the intervals $f(u)$ and $f(v)$ intersect. Graph $G(V,E)$ is an *interval graph* *iff* there exist σ and I such that (σ, I) is an interval representation for G.

The following characterization immediately gives us an NC algorithm for checking if $G(V,E)$ is an interval graph:

Theorem [GH]: Graph G is an interval graph *iff* G^c is a comparability graph, and every quadrilateral in G has a diagonal.

By G^c we mean the *complementary graph* of G, i.e. it has the same set of vertices as G, and $\forall u, v member V$ *s.t.* $u \neq v$, $(u,v) member G^c$ *iff* $(u,v) \notin G$.

Our NC algorithm for getting an interval representation for G is essentially a parallelization of the sequential algorithm of Gilmore and Hoffman [GH]. We give below this sequential algorithm:

1). Transitively orient the edges of G^c.

2). Let σ be a set of maximal cliques for G, s.t. every vertex and every edge is in at least one such clique. For each pair of cliques C_1, C_2, *member* σ, there is an edge of G^c connecting some vertex in C_1 to some vertex in C_2. Gillmore and Hoffman prove that under the orientation assigned in step 1, either all such edges are directed from C_1 to C_2, or else all are directed from C_2 to C_1.

3). Form a diagraph $\vec{G}$ whose vertices are cliques in σ, and whose edges are directed in accordance with the orientation of G^c. This will assign a linear order to the vertices of G^c [GH], i.e. to the maximal cliques in σ.

4). For any vertex $v member G$, let $\alpha(v)$ be the set of maximal cliques to which v belongs. These cliques will be contiguous, i.e. they will form an interval of σ [GH]. Let I be the set of all the intervals corresponding to the vertices of G. Then (σ, I) is an interval representation for $G(V,E)$.

We will now parallelize this algorithm:

1). Transitively orient G^c using Theorem 2.

2). For each vertex $v_i member G$, do in parallel:
Find a maximal clique C_{v_i} containing v_i.

3). For each pair $v_i, v_j member G$, $i < j$, do in parallel:
if $C_{v_i} = C_{v_j}$, remove C_{v_j} from the list of cliques. Let σ be the list of cliques remaining.

4). For each pair C_i, $C_j member \sigma$, do in parallel:
In parallel, examine all pairs of vertices $\{u,v\}$, $u member C_i$, $v member C_j$, to order C_i, C_j in accordance with the orientation of G^c.
This will linearly order σ.

5). For each vertex $v member G$, do in parallel:
Obtain the interval $\alpha(v)$, for v.
This will yield the set of intervals I.

To accomplish Step 2, we can use the parallel maximal clique algorithm of Karp and Wigderson [KW], or the more efficient algorithm of Luby [Lu]. We thus obtain:

Theorem 3: There is an NC algorithm which checks if the given graph $G(V,E)$ is an interval graph, and if so obtains an interval representation for it.

5. Parallel Matching Algorithms

We will use Theorems 2 and 3 to obtain parallel maximum matching algorithms for special classes of graphs. For this, we will use parallel algorithms for the two-processor scheduling problem. This problem can be stated as follows:

Instance: A directed, acyclic graph $G(V,E)$ whose vertices represent unit time jobs, and edges specify precedence constraints among the jobs.

Output: An optimal schedule for the jobs on two identical processors, satisfying all the precedence constraints.

Two jobs which are scheduled in the same time unit on the two processors are said to be *paired*. The connection of this problem with the maximum matching problem is established by the following theorem:

Theorem (Fujii, Kasami, and Ninomiya [FKN]): Let $G(V,E)$ be a directed, acyclic graph, and let $\overline{G}^*$ be the complement of its transitive closure. Then the paired jobs in an *optimal schedule* for G form a *maximum matching* in $\overline{G}^*$.

This theorem enabled [FKN] to obtain an algorithm for two-processor scheduling, using a maximum matching algorithm as a subroutine. We will do the reverse.

Theorem 4: There is a Random NC algorithm, which given an interval graph $G(V,E)$ obtains a maximum matching in it.

Proof: We will use the following scheme:

1). Obtain an interval representation for $G(V,E)$, (σ,I).

2). Use this to direct the edges of G^c. If (u,v) *member* G^c, $\alpha(u)$ and $\alpha(v)$ do not overlap. Suppose $\alpha(u)$ is before $\alpha(v)$ in the linear ordering σ. Then direct (u,v) form u to v. This gives a transitively closed, acyclic digraph, $\vec{G^c}$.

3). Compute the optimal two-processor schedule for $\vec{G^c}$, and output the list of paired jobs.

By [FKN], the list of paired jobs for $\vec{G^c}$ will form a maximum matching for G. Vazirani and Vazirani [VV] give a Random NC algorithm for the two-processor scheduling problem. They use the Random NC matching algorithm of Karp, Upfal, and Wigderson [KUW] as a subroutine.

However, in the case of interval graphs, when the interval representation is given, their algorithm for two-processor scheduling becomes simpler and does not require the Random *NC* matching algorithm. It is interesting to note that this algorithm was obtained before the parallel matching algorithm was discovered. Theorem 4 gives the first non-trivial class of graphs for which maximum matchings could be obtained fast in parallel. It was subsumed by [KUW], who solve the entire matching problem.

More recently, Helmbold and Mayr [HM] have obtained an *NC* algorithm for the two-processor scheduling problem. This enables us to extend the scheme of Theorem 4 to incomparability graphs. The complement of a comparability graph is called an *incomparability graph*. Incomparability graphs form a proper superset of interval graphs. Moreover, we are also able to dispense with randomization.

Theorem 5: There is an *NC* algorithm which given an incomparability graph $G(V,E)$, obtains a maximum matching in it.

Proof: The scheme is similar to that of Theorem 4.

1). Transitively orient G^c, to obtain $\vec{G^c}$.

2). Compute the optimal two-processor schedule for $\vec{G^c}$, and output the list of paired jobs.

The claim follows from Theorem 2, [HM], and [FKN].

Acknowledgements: We are grateful to Ashok Chandra and Alan Hoffman for several inspiring and informative discussions.

References

[BCP] A. Borodin, S.A. Cook, and N. Pippenger. "Parallel computation for well-endowed rings and space bounded probabilistic machines." *Information and Control 58 1-3* (1983) 113-136.

[BGH] A. Borodin, J. von zur Gathen, and J. Hopcroft, "Fast parallel matrix and GCD computations. *Prod. 23d STOC* (1982) pp. 65-71.

[EPL] S. Even, A. Pnueli, and A. Lempel, "Permutation graphs and transitive graphs," J. Assoc. *Comput. Mach. 19* (1972), 400-410.

[FKN] Fujii, M., Kasami, T., and Ninomiya K. "Optimal Sequencing of Two Equivalent Processors," *SIAM J. of Computing*

[GH] Gilmore, P.C., and Hoffman, A.J. "A Characterization of Comparability Graphs and of Interval Graphs," *Canad. J. Math. 16* (1964), 539-548.

[Gh] A. Ghouila-Houri, Caracterisation des graphes nonorientes dont on peut orienter les aretes de maniere a obtenir le graphe d'une relation d'ordre," *C.R. Acad. Sci. Paris 254* (1962), 1370-1371.

[Go] M.C. Golumbic, "Comparability Graphs and a New Matroid," *J. Combinatorial Theory*, Feb. 1977, Vol. 22, No.1, 68-90.

[HM] D. Helmbold and E. Mayr, "Two Processor Scheduling is in *NC*," to appear.

[KUW] Karp, R.M., Upfal, E., and Wigderson, A. "Finding a Maximum Matching is in Random *NC*," *STOC* (1985), 22-32.

[KW] R.M. Karp and A. Wigderson, "A Fast Parallel Algorithm for the Maximal Independent Set Problem," *STOC* (1984), 266-272.

[Lo] Lovasz, L. "On Determinants, Matchings, and Random Algorithms," To appear.

[Lu] M. Luby, "A Simple Parallel Algorithm for the Maximal Independent Set Problem," *STOC* (1985), 1-10.

[PLE] A. Pnueli, A. Lempel, and S. Even, "Transitive orientation of graphs and identification of permutation graphs," *Canad. J. Math. 23* (1971), 160-175.

[RV] Rabin, M.O., and Vazirani, V.V. "Maximum Matchings in General Graphs through Randomization," Report No. TR15-84, Center for Research in Computing Technology, Harvard University, Cambridge, Massachusetts (1984).

[Tu] W.T. Tutte. "The factors of graphs." *Canad. J. Math. 4* (1952) pp.314-328.

[VV] U.V. Vazirani and V.V. Vazirani, "The Two-Processor Scheduling Problem is in Random *NC*," *STOC* (1985), 11-21.

Fast and Efficient Parallel Algorithms for the Exact Inversion of Integer Matrices

Victor Pan
Computer Science Department
State University of New York at Albany
Albany, New York
(Supported by NSF Grants MCS 8203232 and DCR 8507573.)

Abstract

Let $A = (a_{ij})$ be a nonsingular $n \times n$ integer matrix such that $\log ||A|| \leq n^{O(1)}$, $\max_{i,j} | a_{ij} | \leq ||A|| \leq n \max_{i,j} | a_{ij} |$. Then adj A, A^{-1} and all the coefficients of the characteristic polynomial of A including det A can be exactly evaluated on arithmetic circuits using $O(\log^2 n)$ parallel steps and M(n) processors where M(n) is the minimum number of processors required in order to multiply two $n \times n$ matrices in O(log n) steps, $M(n) = o(n^{2.5})$. This substantially improves the processor bound $\sqrt{n}\, M(n)$ of [Preparata and Sarwate, 78] and extends the recent results of [Pan and Reif, 85], where the same complexity estimates were obtained for the approximate evaluation of A^{-1} and under the additional assumption that A is a well-conditioned or strongly diagonally dominant matrix. All arithmetic operations can be performed with the precision of $\leq d$ bits so the total cost of computation is only $O(\log(dn))^2$ steps, $o(n^{2.496} d \log d \log\log d)$ processors under the Boolean circuit model of parallel computation. Here d is $O(n^2 \log(n||A||))$ in the worst case; d is $O(n \log(n||A||))$ with probability $1-O(1/(n^{h-1}\, ||A||^h))$ for arbitrary constant h. This extends our $\sqrt{n}$-improvement of the efficiency of the previously known algorithms to the case of the Boolean circuit model and consequently increases the efficiency of the known parallel algorithms for several related algebraic and combinatorial problems.

Key Words. Parallel algorithms, computational complexity, matrix inversion, systems of linear equations, determinant, characteristic polynomial of a matrix.

1. Introduction

1.1 The Problems and a New Progress.

The competition in efficiency between direct and iterative methods for solving a system of linear equations has a rather long history, see [Golub and van Loan, 83], [Wilkinson, 65]. Recently that competition took a new ground in the area of the design of polylogarithmic time parallel algorithms for such systems and for some related computations in linear algebra. Until recently, only *direct* parallel algorithms running in polylogarithmic time were known for matrix inversion, for the evaluation of the determinant and the characteristic polynomial of a matrix A and for solving a system of linear equations $Ax = b$. The record efficiency of such algorithms (over rational constants) was attained in [Preparata and Sarwate, 78], where the above problems defined by an $n \times n$ input matrix A (and by a vector b of length n in the case of linear systems $Ax = b$) were solved on arithmetic circuits using $O(\log^2 n)$ parallel arithmetic steps and $\sqrt{n}\, M(n)$ processors; $M(n)$ denotes the minimum number of processors required in order to multiply two $n \times n$ matrices in $O(\log n)$ steps; $M(n) = o(n^{2.496})$, see [Pan and Reif, 85], Appendix A. Here and hereafter we assume that the number of processors is defined within a constant factor for we may always decrease that number h times increasing the number of steps $O(h)$ times. The above processor bound $\sqrt{n}\, M(n) = o(n^{2.996})$ is about $\sqrt{n}$ times larger than the number of arithmetic operations in the best sequential algorithms for the same problems; this is a rather high price for parallelism.

First time the desired improvement to $O(\log^2 n)$ time and $M(n)$ processors was obtained in [Pan and Reif, 85] in the form of *iterative* algorithms for computing the inverse matrix A^{-1} with the relative precision 2^{-n^d} for an arbitrary positive constant d provided that the given $n \times n$ matrix A was well-conditioned or strongly diagonally dominant, see Definition 2.1 below. (Note that matrix multiplication can be reduced to matrix inversion, [Borodin and Munro, 75], [Pan, 84], so the product of the number of steps times the number of processors required for matrix inversion cannot be decreased to $o(M(n))$.) In many applications only strongly diagonally dominant and/or well-conditioned matrices need to be inverted and usually the above precision is acceptable. One of such applications (to solving sparse systems of linear equations) is presented already in [Pan and Reif, 85]. On the other hand, for such problems as testing matrices for singularity and matrix rank computation, the algorithms of [Pan and Reif, 85] may turn out to be of no help because in those cases one frequently deals with singular or ill-conditioned matrices. Also it is important (at least for the computational complexity theory) to extend the results of [Pan and Reif, 85] to the exact evaluation of the inverse, the determinant and all the coefficients of the characteristic polynomial of a matrix. This would immediately imply the improvement of the efficiency of the known algorithms for several computational problems (some of them are listed at the end of Section 1.3).

Thus we arrive at the two following questions, i) whether the results of [Pan and Reif, 85] can be extended to the case of ill-conditioned matrices A that are not strongly diagonally dominant and ii) whether A^{-1}, det A and the coefficients of the characteristic polynomial of A can be computed *exactly* using $O(\log^2 n)$ steps, $M(n)$ processors.

In this paper we will positively answer the two latter questions in the case of integer matrices A. Note that rational matrices can be turned into integer matrices by scaling, (see Remark 2.2, where we also comment on the extension to the inversion of real matrices and of matrix polynomials). Furthermore we first present our algorithms and estimate their cost under the arithmetic circuit model but then we modify them so that the exact values of all the outputs are obtained even where all the arithmetic operations are performed with a reasonable (that is, not extremely high) precision. Thus the algorithms remain efficient under the Boolean circuit model of parallel computation. Previously some sequential case estimates for the Boolean complexity of the considered problems have been supplied in [Pan, 84] and [Pan, 84a]. Technically the present paper [Pan and Reif, 85] is little related to [Pan and Reif, 85]. We borrow Newton's iteration for the inversion of strongly diagonally dominant matrices from [Pan and Reif, 85] but this is a minor and not novel part of [Pan and Reif, 85]. The matrix inversion algorithms of [Pan and Reif, 85] belong to the class of the algorithms of numerical linear algebra while the zest of the present paper is the application of several discrete and finite techniques (old and new) in a way quite unusual for numerical linear algebra.

1.2. The Main Result and the Outline of Its Proof under the Arithmetic Circuit Model of Parallel Computation.

In this subsection, as in [Pan and Reif, 85], (as well as in [Csanky, 76], [Preparata and Sarwate, 78] and [Berkowitz, 84]), we will assume the arithmetic parallel machine model of [Borodin, von zur Gathen and Hopcroft, 82], where on each step each processor can perform a single addition, subtraction, multiplication, or division over real or rational numbers. In addition we will also allow a processor to perform such operations over integers modulo a fixed integer, to compare the values of two given real numbers and to round a real number to the nearest integer. (We consider this a reasonable extension of the model of [Borodin, von zur Gathen and Hopcroft, 82], compare some other extensions in [Eberly, 84], [Bini and Pan, to appear]. Furthermore we were able to extend our resulting estimates from our arithmetic model to the more realistic Boolean circuit model, in Sections 1.3 and 4. We measure the cost of our parallel algorithms in terms of the numbers of parallel steps and processors used. That cost can be also expressed in terms of the depth and the size of arithmetic (or Boolean) circuits, compare [Borodin, Cook and Pippenger, 83].) Using our model of parallel computation, we will prove the following result.

Theorem 1.1. $O(\log^2 n)$ *parallel steps and* $M(n) = o(n^{2.496})$ *processors suffice for the exact evaluation of* A^{-1}, adj A, $A^{-1}b$ *and all the coefficients* c_k *of the characteristic polynomial of* A,

$$\det(\lambda I - A) = \lambda^n - c_1\lambda^{n-1} - \ldots - c_{n-1}\lambda - c_n, \quad c_n = \det A, \tag{1.1}$$

provided that $A = (a_{ij})$ *is a given* $n \times n$ *integer matrix,* b *is a given integer vector of length* n, *and*

$$\log ||A|| \le n^{O(1)}. \quad (1.2)$$

Here and hereafter it is assumed that $n \rightarrow \infty$, *logarithms are to the base 2, and* $||A||$ *is the 2-norm of a matrix* A *associated with the Euclidean norm* $||v||$ *of a vector* $v = (v_1,...,v_n)^T$ *(see* [Golub and van Loan, 83]) *such that*

$$||A|| = \max_{v \neq 0} \frac{||Av||}{||v||},\ \max_{i,j} |a_{ij}| \le ||A|| \le n \max_{i,j} |a_{ij}|,\ ||v||^2 = \sum_{i=1}^{n} v_i^2. \quad (1.3)$$

Remark 1.1. *We may extend this result and similarly all other results of this paper using any of two other customary matrix norms,*

$$||A||_1 = \max_j \sum_i |a_{ij}|,\ ||A||_\infty = \max_i \sum_j |a_{ij}|, \quad (1.4)$$

as well as using $\max_{i,j} |a_{ij}|$, *on the place of the 2-norm; all the three norms may differ from each other and from* $\max_{i,j} |a_{ij}|$ *at most by the factor n,* [Wilkinson, 65], [Golub and van Loan, 83].

For comparison, here is the corresponding result from [Pan and Reif, 85], which will be used in the proof of Theorem 1.1.

Theorem 1.2. *Let* d *be a positive constant,* A *be an* $n \times n$ *matrix that is well-conditioned and/or strongly diagonally dominant, see Definition 2.1 below. Then* $O(\log^2 n)$ *steps,* $M(n)$ *processors suffice to evaluate a matrix* $\tilde{A}^{-1}$ *such that*

$$||A^{-1} - \tilde{A}^{-1}|| \,/\, ||A^{-1}|| \le 2^{-n^d}.$$

Next we will outline our proof of Theorem 1.1.

Step 1. Recall that the vector $A^n v$ and the *Krylov matrix,*

$$K = K(A,v) = (v, Av, A^2v, A^3v, ..., A^{n-1}v), \quad (1.5)$$

(defined by a given $n \times n$ matrix A and by a given vector v of length n), can be computed using $O(\log^2 n)$ steps, $M(n)$ processors.

Step 2. The Cayley-Hamilton theorem,

$$A^n - c_1 A^{n-1} - ... - c_n = 0, \quad (1.6)$$

where $c_1, c_2, ..., c_n$ are defined by (1.1), implies that the coefficient vector

$$c = c(A) = (c_n, c_{n-1}, ..., c_1)^T \quad (1.7)$$

of the characteristic polynomial (1.1) always satisfies the n following linear equations,

$$K(A,v)c = A^n v; \quad (1.8)$$

the vector c can be defined as the unique solution to (1.8) if the matrix K(A,v) is nonsingular. (In (1.7) and hereafter u^T denotes the transpose of u.)

Step 3. The vector c can be computed with the relative precision 2^{-n^d} via solving the system (1.8). This gives the coefficients c_k with the absolute precision $< 1/2$. By Theorem 1.2, $O(\log^2 n)$ steps, M(n) processors suffice in this step provided that K(A,v) is a well-conditioned or diagonally dominant matrix.

Step 4. If all the entries of A are integers, then all the entries c_k of c are also integers, so rounding the above approximations to the nearest integers we obtain the exact values of c_k.

Step 5. If A is a well-conditioned and/or strongly diagonally dominant matrix, then A^{-1} can be computed (within the relative precision $\leq 2^{-n^d}$ for any positive constant d) using $O(\log^2 n)$ steps, M(n) processors, Theorem 1.2.

Step 6. If det A is available, then the approximation to A^{-1} computed at Step 5 can be used in order to compute $\text{adj } A = A^{-1} \det A$ within the absolute error norm $< 1/2$. This gives the exact values of all the entries of adj A if A is an integer matrix for in that case adj A is also an integer matrix. Dividing adj A by det A gives A^{-1}.

Steps 1-6 prove Theorem 1.1 provided that A and K(A,v) are well-conditioned and/or strongly diagonally dominant integer matrices. The next three steps extend this proof to the case of arbitrary matrix A.

Step 7. Reduce the evaluation of the coefficient vector c(A), (see (1.7)), of the characteristic polynomial of an integer matrix A to the evaluation of such a coefficient vector c(W) modulo a natural q for an integer matrix W such that $q > 2\|c\|$, $A - W = 0 \bmod q$, and K(W,v) is a strongly diagonally dominant matrix for an appropriate vector v. Compute c(W) using Steps 1-4, then obtain $c(W) \bmod q = c(A) \bmod q$ and find c(A).

Step 8. Reduce the evaluation of adj A to the evaluation of adj V modulo a natural p where $p > 2\|\text{adj } A\|$, $A - V = 0 \bmod p$, and V is a strongly diagonally dominant integer matrix. Replace A by V on Steps 5,6 and 7; compute det V using Step 7, then compute $\text{adj } V = V^{-1} \det V$ using Steps 5 and 6, finally compute $\text{adj } A \bmod p = \text{adj } V \bmod p$ and recover adj A from adj A mod p.

Step 9. Compute det A using Step 7 and adj A using Step 8. Then compute $A^{-1} = \text{adj } A / \det A$.

In Sections 2 and 3 we will elaborate and substantiate the above outline of the proof of Theorem 1.1. In Section 4 we will efficiently extend it to the case of the Boolean circuit model. Furthermore we will see that the extension is possible even under the choice of p and q having $O(\log(n\|A\|))$ bits and being $\leq (n\|A\|)^{O(1)}$ in Steps 7 and 8; this refinement of Steps 7 and 8 will give us favorable Boolean circuit complexity estimates.

1.3. Extension to the Boolean Circuit Model.

In Section 4 we will extend the resulting algorithm to the case where the Boolean circuit model of parallel computation has been applied, such that on every step each processor may perform at most one Boolean operation. We will give a *constructive proof* of the following result.

Theorem 1.3. *For an integer matrix A satisfying (1.2), the matrix* adj A *and the vector* c *of the coefficients of the characteristic polynomial of A, see (1.1), can be evaluated by a parallel randomized algorithm that uses* $O(\log^2(dn))$ *parallel steps and* $O(d \log d \log\log d\, M^*(n))$ *processors under the Boolean circuit model of computation. Here* $M^*(n)$ *is the minimum number of processors required in order to multiply two* $n \times n$ *matrices on arithmetic circuits using one multiplication step and* $O(\log n)$ *addition/subtraction steps,* $M^*(n) = o(n^{2.496})$; $d = O(n \log(n||A||))$ *with probability* $1-O(1/(n^{h-1}||A||^h))$ *for arbitrary* h *and* $d = (O(n^2 \log(n||A||))$ *in the worst case.*

Remark 1.2. Compare the definitions of M(n) and $M^*(n)$. Note that the constraint on the number of multiplication steps (see the definition of $M^*(n)$) enables us to derive a favorable upper bound on the number of Boolean steps, see Lemma 4.1 below. (This idea is due to Zvi Galil.) Applying the parallelization of bilinear algorithms for $n \times n$ matrix multiplication presented in Appendix A of [Pan and Reif, 85], we note that $M^*(n) = o(n^\omega)$ for any $\omega > 2$ such that two $n \times n$ matrices can be multiplied in $O(n^\omega)$ arithmetic operations by a bilinear algorithm that uses only integer constants. The latter restriction on the constants is satisfied in particular in the bilinear algorithms of [Coppersmith and Winograd, 82] , which involve only the constants 0,1 and -1 and give the bound $\omega < 2.496$, so $M^*(n) = o(n^{2.496})$.

To prove Theorem 1.3, then again we apply Steps 1-9 of the proof of Theorem 1.1 with a small modification of Step 8. Specifically we choose some special orthogonal matrix H and let $V=W = A+pH$ where p is a random prime in the interval $n<p\leq n^{O(1)}$. Under this choice, the matrix V is not strongly diagonally dominant but K(W,v) and VH^{-1} are. Therefore at Step 8 we invert the matrix VH^{-1} and then recover $V^{-1} = H^{-1}(VH^{-1})^{-1}$ for the matrix H^{-1} is available, $(H^{-1} = H^T)$. This choice of p, (unlike the choice of p and q in our initial version of Steps 7 and 8 of Section 1.2), keeps the precision sufficiently low (consistent with Theorem 1.3). We then compute $c(A) \bmod p = c(W) \bmod p$ and adj A mod p, which gives us $A^{-1} \bmod p$ if $\det A \bmod p \neq 0$. (The probability that $\det A = 0$ is small, [Schwartz, 80].) Applying Newton's-Hensel's lifting, ([Moenck and Carter, 79], p. 67), we obtain $A^{-1} \bmod p^{2^k}$ and choose k being of the order log n. This result is already sufficient in such applications as the polynomial gcd computation over the integers modulo a large prime but we seek for even a more general result of Theorem 1.3. So we apply a similar approach, choose p as before and in addition choose $p^* = hp$ in a rather delicate way, see (4.7). (Specifically we need to invert the matrix $K^* = K(A,v) \bmod p$ at that stage of our algorithm. We use the auxiliary matrix $W = K^* + p^*H$. Here p^* must be sufficiently large in order to assure the strong diagonal dominance of WH^{-1} and K(W,v). For instance, the choice $p^* = p$ would not work. On the other hand, it turns out that the choice (4.7) suffices even though this requires only moderately large p^*.) Then we compute the matrix $K^{-1}(W,v) \bmod p^*$, reduce this matrix to $K^{-1}(W,v) \bmod p = K^{-1}(A,v) \bmod p$, lift it to $K^{-1}(A,v) \bmod p^{2^k}$ and finally obtain $K^{-1}(A,v)\, A^n v \bmod p^{2^k} = c(A) \bmod p^{2^k} = c(A)$. In particular the algorithm gives us the exact value of det A; this enables us to compute $\operatorname{adj} A \bmod p^n = \operatorname{adj} A$. Thus we prove Theorem 1.3 for at all steps we are able to comply with the prescribed restrictions on the precision of

the operands of the arithmetic operations.

It remains an open problem if it is possible to reduce the number of processors to, say $O(M(n)\log p)$ in the case where det A and adj A are sought only modulo $p \leq n^{O(1)}$. Otherwise Theorem 1.3 settles the problem (at least over the class of randomized algorithms) and also clears the result from the assumption (1.2). It is known that several other computations, such as computing the greatest common divisors and the least common multiples of two and several polynomials, computing all entries of the extended Euclidean scheme of two polynomials, testing a matrix for singularity, matrix rank computation and so on, are reduced to the inversion of integer matrices and/or solving systems of linear equations, [Borodin, von zur Gathen and Hopcroft, 82], [Gathen, von zur, 84]. [Galil and Pan, 85] exploit similar reduction for several matching problems. Thus Theorem 1.3 implies the improvement of the efficiency of all of those computations.

1.4. Extension to a Special Computational Model.

In the short concluding Section 5 we recall the model of Section 40 of [Pan, 84], which extends an approach from [Pan, 80]. In that model we allow to represent an integer matrix by a single long integer and to segment such an integer back to form a matrix; we charge no cost for these transformations and count an arithmetic operation with long integers as a single step that requires only one processor. Then we need only $O(\log n)$ steps and one processor to evaluate all the coefficients of the characteristic polynomial of A, and also adj A and (adj A)b. It only remains to divide adj A and (adj A)b by the computed value of det A in order to obtain A^{-1} and $A^{-1}b$.

2. Algorithms in the Cases Where the Krylov Matrices Are Well-Conditioned and/or Strongly Diagonally Dominant

In this section we will complete Steps 1-6 of the proof of Theorem 1.1. We will use the following definition, [Pan and Reif, 85].

Definition 2.1. Let $A = (a_{ij})$ be an $n \times n$ matrix, $n > 1$. If A is singular, then $\text{cond}\, A = \infty$, otherwise $\text{cond}\, A = ||A|| \cdot ||A^{-1}||$, $\text{cond}_h A = ||A||_h \cdot ||A^{-1}||_h$ for $h=1$ and $h = \infty$, see (1.4). A is *well-conditioned* if

$$\text{cond}\, A \leq n^{O(1)}. \tag{2.1}$$

A is *ill-conditioned* otherwise. A is *strongly diagonally dominant* (with respect to a constant C) if

$$||I-D^{-1}(A)A||_1 < 1-1/n^C \tag{2.2}$$

or

$$||I-A\, D^{-1}(A)||_\infty < 1-1/n^C \tag{2.3}$$

where $D(A) = \text{diag}(a_{11}, a_{22}, \ldots, a_{nn})$, C is a constant, $C \neq \infty$. (2.2) and (2.3) can be equivalently rewritten as $(2-1/n^C)\ |a_{ii}| > \sum_j |a_{ij}|$ for all i and $(2-1/n^C)\ |a_{jj}| > \sum_i |a_{ij}|$ for all j, respectively, see (1.4). If (2.2) holds, A is *strongly row-diagonally dominant;* if (2.3) holds, A is *strongly column-diagonally dominant.* (Actually A is nonsingular if it is well-conditioned or strongly diagonally dominant. Many well-conditioned matrices are not strongly diagonally dominant while such strongly diagonally dominant matrices as $\text{diag}(1,p,p^2,\ldots,p^{n-1})$ are ill-conditioned for $p > 1$. Note, however, that any strongly diagonally dominant matrix A becomes well-conditioned in the result of its pre- or postmultiplication by appropriate diagonal matrices D or D^* such that $||DA||_1 = 1$ if (2.3) holds or $||AD^*||_\infty = 1$ if (2.2) holds, respectively, see (1.3).)

We note that $A^{-1}D(A) = \sum_{i=0}^{\infty}(I-D^{-1}(A)A)^i$ if (2.2) holds, $D(A)A^{-1} = \sum_{i=0}^{\infty}(I-AD^{-1}(A))^i$ if (2.3) holds. This implies

Proposition 2.1. $||A^{-1}D(A)||_1 < n^C$ *if (2.2) holds,* $||D(A)A^{-1}||_\infty < n^C$ *if (2.3) holds where* $D(A) = \text{diag}(a_{11}, a_{22}, \ldots, a_{nn})$.

Theorem 2.1. *Given a positive constant* d, *an* $n \times n$ *matrix* A *and a vector* v *of length* n *such that the Krylov matrix* $K = K(A,v)$, *see* (1.5), *is well-conditioned or strongly diagonally dominant, then* $O(\log^2 n)$ *parallel steps and* $M(n)$ *processors suffice in order to evaluate a vector* $\tilde{c}$ *such that at least one of the three next inequalities holds,*

$$||c - \tilde{c}|| \,/\, ||c|| \leq 2^{-n^d} \text{cond } K, \quad ||c - \tilde{c}||_h \,/\, ||c||_h \leq 2^{-n^d} \text{cond } K, \ h=1, h=\infty. \tag{2.4}$$

Here $c=c(A)$ *is the coefficient vector of the characteristic polynomial of* A, *(1.1).*

Proof. At first compute K(A,v) and $A^n v$ following [Borodin and Munro, 75], p. 128, and [Keller, 82]. Specifically, choose the integer h such that $2^h \leq n < 2^{h+1}$ and successively compute $A^2, A^4, \ldots, A^{2^h}$,

$$\begin{gathered} v = v, \\ A\,v = A\,v, \\ (A^3v, A^2v) = A^2(A\,v, v), \\ (A^7v, A^6v, A^5v, A^4v) = A^4(A^3v, A^2v, Av, v), \\ \cdots\cdots\cdots\cdots\cdots\cdots \\ (A^{2 \cdot 2^h - 1}v, \ldots, A^{2^h}v) = A^{2^h}(A^{2^h - 1}v, \ldots, v). \end{gathered} \tag{2.5}$$

This covers Step 1 of the proof of Theorem 1.1.

First assume that K is well-conditioned. Then apply the iterative algorithms of [Pan and Reif, 85] to compute an approximation $\tilde{K}^{-1}$ to K^{-1} such that

$$||K^{-1} - \tilde{K}^{-1}|| \,/\, ||K^{-1}|| \leq 2^{-n^d}, \tag{2.6}$$

compare (1.4). Finally evaluate the vector $\tilde{c} = \tilde{K}^{-1}u$, which approximates the vector $c = K^{-1}u$. Here and hereafter $u = A^n v$; the equation $c = K^{-1}u$ holds by the virtue of (1.8).

It can be immediately verified that the above computation of $\tilde{c}$ uses a total of $O(\log^2 n)$ steps, $M(n)$ processors, so it remains to prove (2.4).

Note that

$$c - \tilde{c} = (K^{-1} - \tilde{K}^{-1})u, c = K^{-1}u,$$

so

$$||c|| \geq ||u|| \;/\; ||K||, \; ||c - \tilde{c}|| \leq ||K^{-1} - \tilde{K}^{-1}|| \cdot ||u||.$$

Combine these estimates with (2.6) and derive (2.4).

If K is strongly diagonally dominant, then use one of the norms (1.4) in place of the 2-norm (1.3); otherwise proceed similarly to the case of well-conditioned K. Q.E.D.

Lemma 2.1. *Let (1.2) hold, let* $\log||v|| \leq n^{O(1)}$ *and let (2.4) hold for a sufficiently large* d. *Then*

$$||c - \tilde{c}|| < 1/2. \tag{2.7}$$

Proof. (1.1) implies that

$$|\, c_k \,| \leq (n! \;/\; k!(n-k)!)\; D_k(A) \tag{2.8}$$

where $D_k(A)$ denotes the maximum absolute value of all the $k \times k$ minors of A, (that is, of the determinants of all the $k \times k$ submatrices of A), $k=1,2,...,n$, and $0! = 1$. Combine (2.8) with the Hadamard inequality,

$$|\det W\,| \leq ||W||^k, \tag{2.9}$$

which holds for every $k \times k$ matrix W, ([Marcus and Minc, 64]), and note that $||A|| \geq ||\hat{A}||$ for every submatrix $\hat{A}$ of A, compare the proof of Lemma 4.4 in [Pan and Reif, 85]. Therefore

$$|\, c_k \,| \leq (n! \;/\; k!(n-k)!)\; ||A||^k \text{ for } k=1,2,...,n. \tag{2.10}$$

(1.2),(2.4) and (2.10) immediately imply (2.7). (Note that (1.2) implies that $\log||K|| \leq n^{O(1)}$ and recall Remark 1.1.) Q.E.D.

Thus Steps 1-3 of the proof of Theorem 1.1 have been completed.

Hereafter we assume that A is an integer matrix satisfying (1.2). Then Step 4 is immediate.

We also deduce from (1.6) that

$$(\text{adj } A)b = c_n A^{-1} b = A^{n-1} b - c_1 A^{n-2} b - ... - c_{n-1} b$$

for arbitrary vector b.

Since we may apply the algorithm defined by (2.5) for $v=b$ in order to evaluate Ab, $A^2 b, ..., A^{n-1} b$, we arrive at

Corollary 2.1. *Let the assumptions of Theorem 2.1 hold and let* A *be an integer matrix satisfying (1.2). Then* $O(\log^2 n)$ *steps and* $M(n)$ *processors suffice in order to evaluate* $(\text{adj } A)b$ *and the coefficients of the characteristic polynomial of* A, *which also gives the solution* $(\text{adj } A)b/\det A = A^{-1}b$, *to the system of linear equations* $Ax=b$ *for an arbitrary vector* b *provided that* $\det A \neq 0$.

Steps 5 and 6 of the proof of Theorem 1.1 do not cause any troubles (the bound $||\text{adj } A - \text{adj } \tilde{A}|| < 1/2$ is deduced similarly to Lemma 2.1). We arrive at

Theorem 2.2. *Let a matrix* A *satisfy the assumptions of Corollary 2.1 and let at least one of (2.1), (2.2) and (2.3) hold. Then* $O(\log^2 n)$ *steps and* $M(n)$ *processors suffice for the exact evaluation of* A^{-1}.

Remark 2.1. Corollary 2.1 may seem redundant for we may immediately compute $A^{-1}b$ if we know A^{-1}. However, the assumption of Corollary 2.1 that $K(A,v)$ is well-conditioned or strongly diagonally dominant does not imply yet that at least one of (2.1), (2.2) and (2.3) holds. For instance, $K(A,v)=I$ is well-conditioned and strongly diagonally dominant for each of the next two choices of A and v,

$$A = H^-,\ v = (1,0,\ldots,0)^T, \quad \text{and } A = H^+,\ v = (0,0,\ldots,0,1)^T,$$

$$\text{where } H^- = \begin{pmatrix} 0 & \cdots & \cdots & 0 \\ 1 & & & \cdot \\ & \cdot & \cdot & \cdot \\ & \cdots & \cdots & \cdot \\ \cdot & \cdot & \cdot & \cdot \\ 0 & \cdots & 1 & 0 \end{pmatrix}, \quad H^+ = \begin{pmatrix} 0 & 1 & \cdots & 0 \\ & \cdot & \cdot & \cdot \\ \cdot & & \cdot & \cdot \\ \cdot & & \cdots & \cdot \\ \cdot & & & 1 \\ 0 & \cdots & \cdots & 0 \end{pmatrix},$$

$H^- = (h_{ij}^-)$, $h_{ij}^- = 1$ if $j=i-1$, $h_{ij}^- = 0$ otherwise, $H^+ = (h_{ij}^+)$, $h_{ij}^+ = 1$ if $j=i+1$, $h_{ij}^+ = 0$ otherwise. However, in both of those two cases A is singular, so none of (2.1), (2.2) and (2.3) holds. (Note that, conversely, for $A=I$ (2.1), (2.2) and (2.3) hold but $K(A,v) = (v,v,\ldots,v)$ is a singular matrix for any vector v if $n>1$.) Similarly $K(A,v)$ is strongly diagonally dominant but neither of (2.1),(2.2) and (2.3) holds if $A = MH^- + W$ and if a positive M is much larger than $||W||$. In such cases we may apply Corollary 2.1 but not Theorem 2.2.

Remark 2.2. Let a matrix W be filled with finite binary integers and let it be required to compute $\det W$, $\text{adj } W$, W^{-1}. Then it is sufficient to compute $\det A$, $\text{adj } A$, A^{-1} for an integer matrix A where $A = 2^k W$ or, more generally, $A = D W \tilde{D}$, k is an integer, D and $\tilde{D}$ are diagonal matrices whose all diagonal entries are equal to the powers of 2. (Indeed, $\det W = \det A / (\det D \det \tilde{D})$, $W^{-1} = \tilde{D}A^{-1}D$.) $\det A$, $\text{adj } A$ and A^{-1} can be computed using Steps 1-6 of the proof of Theorem 1.1 provided that A satisfies the assumptions of Corollary 2.1 and/or Theorem 2.2. If A is a real matrix, we may represent its entries as binary numbers, chop their fractions to sufficiently many digits, invert the resulting matrix as above and obtain an approximation to A^{-1}. That approximation can be further refined by Newton's iteration, [Pan and Reif, 85]. If A is a matrix polynomial or, equivalently, is a matrix whose entries are (univariate) polynomials of degrees $\leq m$ in a variable v, (so $\det A$ and the entries of $\text{adj } A$ are polynomials of degrees $\leq mn$), then we may apply our algorithms in order to evaluate $\det A$

and adj A at mn+1 distinct Fourier points $v_k = \omega^k$, k=0,1,...,m, ω being a primitive (mn+1)-th root of 1, ($\omega^{mn+1} = 1$, $\omega^s \neq 1$ for $0 < s \leq mn$), and then interpolate using FFT at mn+1 points. This does not change the number of steps and increases the number of processors only mn+1 times.

Remark 2.3. It is an interesting problem to find out how restrictive is the assumption of Theorem 2.1 that the matrix K(A,v) is well-conditioned and/or strongly diagonally dominant provided, say that $||A||_1 = 1$ (the latter equation can be assured by scaling the matrix A). We will avoid that problem in the next sections but here is an approach to its study. Suppose that A is symmetric. (Note that we may replace A by A^TA as long as our problem is to evaluate A^{-1} and $|\det A|$ for $A^{-1} = (A^TA)^{-1}A^T$, $|\det A|^2 = \det(A^TA)$.) Then A has n pairwise orthogonal unit eigenvectors $\gamma_1, \gamma_2, \ldots, \gamma_n$. W.l.o.g. assume that $\gamma_1, \gamma_2, \ldots, \gamma_n$ are unit coordinate vectors (this amounts to an orthonormal transformation of coordinates). Let $v = \sum_{i=1}^{n} v_i \gamma_i$. Then

$$K(A,v) = \begin{pmatrix} v_1 & \lambda_1 v_1 & \cdots & \lambda_1^{n-1} v_1 \\ v_2 & \lambda_2 v_2 & \cdots & \lambda_2^{n-1} v_2 \\ \cdot & \cdot & \cdots & \cdots \\ \cdot & \cdot & \cdots & \cdots \\ \cdot & \cdot & \cdots & \cdots \\ v_n & \lambda_n v_n & \cdots & \lambda_n^{n-1} v_n \end{pmatrix}$$

where $\lambda_1, \lambda_2, \ldots, \lambda_n$ are the eigenvalues of A. The matrix K(A,v) is a Vandermonde matrix (within a row scaling transformation). It is easy to recognize that such matrices are closely related to the interpolation to (n-1)-th degree polynomials at the points $\lambda_1, \lambda_2, \ldots, \lambda_n$, [Golub and van Loan, 83], p. 119. This correlation might give some insight into estimating cond K(A,v).

3. Computation for Arbitrary Integer Input Matrices of Bounded Norms

In this section we will complete the remaining Steps 7,8 and 9 of the proof of Theorem 1.1. We only need to choose natural p and q such that

$$q > 2|c_k| \text{ for } k=1,2,\ldots,n, \text{ see (1.1); } p > 2|(\text{adj } A)_{ij}| \text{ for all pairs } i,j \tag{3.1}$$

and to choose appropriate matrices W and V on Steps 7 and 8. Here $(\text{adj } A)_{ij}$ denotes the entry i,j of the matrix adj A.

It is easily verified that (3.1) is certainly satisfied if

$$p > 2||A||^{n-1}, \; q > 2^{n+1} ||A||^n, \tag{3.2}$$

see (2.9) and (2.10). Then the values c_k and $(\text{adj } A)_{ij}$ can be immediately recovered from c_k mod p and $(\text{adj } A)_{ij}$ for all i,j,k. Indeed for any s such that $-p < 2s < p$, either $s = s \bmod p$ if $s \bmod p < p/2$ or $s = (s \bmod p) - p$ if $s \bmod p > p/2$. Similarly an integer s can be recovered from s mod q if $-q < 2s < q$. On Step 8 we choose

$$V = A + p \text{ diag } (d_1,d_2,...,d_n)$$

such that $d_1,d_2,...,d_n$ are integers, $pd_i > 2 \sum_j |a_{ij}|$ for all i, compare (2.2), so V is strongly diagonally dominant. On Step 7 we choose

$$W = A + q H^-, \; v = (1,0,...,0)^T, \tag{3.3}$$

where H^- is defined in Remark 2.1. Let us show that K(W,v) is strongly diagonally dominant under (3.2) and (3.3). We expand

$$W^s v = (A + q H^-)^s v \text{ for } s=1,2,...,n-1 \tag{3.4}$$

and note that the term $(p H^-)^s v$ contributes only to the (s,s) diagonal entry of the matrix K(W,v) where it contributes exactly q^s. Next we compare the expansion of (3.4) with the expansion of

$$(||A|| E + q H^-)^s v$$

where $E = (e_{ij})$ is the matrix filled with ones, so $e_{ij} = 1$ for all i,j. We delete the term $(q H^-)^s v$ from both of these expansions, sum the absolute values of all remaining terms of each expansion and note that such sum for (3.4) does not exceed the sum of the remaining terms of $(||A||E + q H^-)^s v$. On the other hand, it is easy to verify that the latter sum does not exceed

$$\sum_{i=1}^{s} q^{s-i} ||A||^i s! / ((s-i)!i!) < sq^{s-1} < (1/2) q^s, \tag{3.5}$$

for s=1,2,...,n-1, see (3.2). It follows that K(W,v) is strongly diagonally dominant (compare (2.3) where K(W,v) plays the role of A; note that the first column of K(W,v) is $v=(1,0,...,0)^T$). This completes the substantiation of Steps 7-9 of the proof of Theorem 1.1. Q.E.D.

Remark 3.1. It is possible to unify the choice of the natural p and q and of the matrices V and W by setting

$$p = q > 2^{n+1} ||A||^n, \tag{3.6}$$

$$V = W = A + pH, \; v = (1,0,...,0)^T \tag{3.7}$$

where the matrix H is obtained from H^- by changing the right upper entry h^-_{1n} of H^- from 0 into 1. The proof of the strong diagonal dominance of K(W,v) remains the same as above except that H should replace H^- throughout. In that case the matrix V is not strongly diagonally dominant but the matrix VH^{-1} is, so its inverse, $(VH^{-1})^{-1}$ can be exactly computed if $|\det(VH^{-1})| = |\det V|$ is known. When $(VH^{-1})^{-1} = HV^{-1}$ is known, $V^{-1} = H^{-1}(HV^{-1})$ is easily recovered for the matrix $H^{-1} = H^T$ is available. Finally we note that (3.5) implies that K(W,v) remains strongly column-diagonally dominant even if we only require that $p = q > 2n||A||$. We have imposed the larger lower bound on p=q in (3.6) above in order to assure that adj W mod p = adj A mod p and c(W) mod p = c(A) mod p.

4. The Complexity Estimates Under the Boolean Circuit Computational Model

In this section we will prove Theorem 1.3, that is, we will extend the estimates of Theorem 1.1 for the complexity of our algorithms (devised at Steps 1-9 of our proof of Theorem 1.1) to the case of the computation on Boolean circuits, where at every step every processor performs at most one Boolean operation. (So far we have been assuming the arithmetic circuits model of parallel computation.)

We note that our algorithms require at most two division steps (one division step per matrix inversion or solving a system of linear equations, which is reduced to matrix inversion) and $O(\log n)$ matrix multiplications and matrix-vector multiplications. Now Theorem 1.3 follows from Remark 1.2, from the well-known estimates for the complexity of arithmetic operations, listed in the next lemma, ([Savage, 76], [Knuth, 81]), and from the bit-precision bounds that support our computation to be supplied in the remainder of this section.

Lemma 4.1. *Addition of two integers modulo* 2^d *requires* $O(1)$ *steps and* $O(d)$ *processors. Multiplication of two integers modulo* 2^d *requires* $O(\log d)$ *steps and* $O(d \log d \log\log d)$ *processors. Evaluation of the quotient and the remainder of the division of two integers lying between* 0 *and* 2^d *requires* $O(\log^2 d)$ *steps and* $O(d \log d \log\log d)$ *processors.*

Finally we will estimate the bit-precision d required in our algorithms. It can be verified that our algorithms need to involve at most d^*-bit binary numbers where $d^* = O(n^2 \log(n||A||))$; this implies the worst case bound of Theorem 1.3. Let us deduce the probabilistic bound of Theorem 1.3 on the bit-precision d.

We note that the final output can be represented by the vector c(A) and by the matrix adj A filled with integers of the order of magnitude at most $(2||A||)^n$ and $||A||^{n-1}$, respectively, see (2.9), (2.10). This suggests trying to compute the exact values of c(A) and adj A operating only with g-bit numbers where $g = O(n \log||A||)$ or at least

$$g = O(n \log(n\, ||A||)). \tag{4.1}$$

In that case Theorem 1.3 would follow.

At first we will assume that h is a constant, $h > 2$, and $p=q$ is a prime in the interval

$$2n||A|| < p = q < 2(n||A||)^h \tag{4.2}$$

such that

$$\det A \bmod p \neq 0. \tag{4.3}$$

We will prove the following auxiliary result.

Lemma 4.2. *Let* A *be an* $n \times n$ *integer matrix;* p *be defined by (4.2); (4.3) hold;* k *be a natural number. Then the matrix* $A^{-1} \bmod p^{2^k}$ *can be computed using* $O(\log^2 d(n,p,k))$ *steps,* $O(d(n,p,k) \log d(n,p,k) \log\log d(n,p,k)\, M(n))$ *processors under the Boolean circuit model, where*

$$d(n,p,k) = O(n \log(n||A||) + 2^k \log p). \tag{4.4}$$

Proof. We will proceed as in Remark 3.1 but will assume that the new p and q of (4.2) should replace the previous values of p and q defined by (3.6). Note that (3.7) and (4.2) assure that K(W,v) is a strongly column diagonally dominant matrix, see the end of Remark 3.1. Since the postmultiplication by a diagonal matrix preserves (2.3), the matrix $\hat{K}(W,v) = K(W,v)\,\mathrm{diag}(1,p^{-1},p^{-2},\ldots,p^{1-n})$ is strongly diagonally dominant; furthermore, it becomes well-conditioned due to such a postmultiplication, (see (3.5) and recall Proposition 2.1 and Remark 1.1); so cond $\hat{K}(W,v) = n^{O(1)}$. It follows that for the evaluation of $K^{-1}(W,v)$ with the relative precision 2^{-Cn} (for any given constant C) it is sufficient to apply the algorithms of Sections 2 and 3 operating with O(n log p)-bit numbers. This way we arrive at the approximations to the vector c(W) and to the matrix adj W with the absolute error norms less than 1/2, then we recover the exact values of c(W) and of adj W and finally of c(A)mod p = c(W) mod p and of adj A mod p = adj W mod p.

Next we will recall that (4.3) holds and will compute the matrix

$$B(0) = A^{-1} \bmod p = (\mathrm{adj}\, A \bmod p)\ /\ (\det A \bmod p) \bmod p. \tag{4.5}$$

(The division is possible due to (4.3).) Then we will compute $A^{-1} \bmod p^{2^k}$ for a natural k using Newton's iteration in the form of Hensel's lifting, [Moenck and Carter, 79], p. 67. Specifically, we will successively compute the matrices

$$E(i) = I - AB(i-1) \bmod p^{2^i},$$

$$B(i) = B(i-1)(I + E(i)),\ i=1,2,\ldots,k,$$

where B(0) is defined by (4.5). It is easily verified that

$$AB(i) = I \bmod p^{2^i} \text{ for all } i,$$

([Moenck and Carter, 79], p. 67), which means that

$$B(k) = A^{-1} \bmod p^{2^k}.$$

Finally note that throughout the whole computation we need to operate only with d(n,p,k)-bit precision numbers where d(n,p,k) is defined by (4.4). Q.E.D.

Hereafter let p denote a random prime in the interval (4.2). (O(log(n||A||)) binary bits suffice in order to represent p.) Then we may couple Lemma 4.2 with the next lemma.

Lemma 4.3 [Schwartz, 80]). *(4.3) holds with the probability* $1-O(\log(n\|A\|))\ /\ (n^{h-1}\|A\|^h)$ *as* $n \to \infty$.

(Note that the probability of the occurrence of (4.3) increases as h grows.)

Proof. det A may have at most n distinct factors greater than n||A||, (so (4.3) does not hold for at most n distinct values of p satisfying (4.2)). On the other hand, it is well known, ([Ireland and Rosen, 82], p. 2), that there exist more than $Cn^h\|A\|^h\ /\ \log(n\|A\|)$ distinct primes p satisfying (4.2) where C is a positive constant. Q.E.D.

Remark 4.1. Even if we choose p nonprime, we may apply our construction above as long as we can invert det A mod p. The latter inversion is possible if and only if det A and p are relatively prime (which in particular would follow if p is prime and does not divide det A). If in the process of computing we obtain that det A mod p = 0, we may simply repeat the computation trying new random p.

We have already obtained fast and efficient algorithm for several computations that can be reduced to finding $A^{-1} \bmod p^{2^k}$ for sufficiently large k. (For instance, computing the greatest common divisor of two polynomials over the field of integers modulo a prime can be reduced to that problem, [Borodin, von zur Gathen and Hopcroft, 82], [Yun, 76], p. 155.) We will not be satisfied at this point, however, but will continue our proof of Theorem 1.3.

We will keep assuming that p is a random prime in the interval (4.2) and additionally assume that $h > 3$. Next we will invert modulo p the matrix $K^* = K(A,v) \bmod p$ unless $\det K^* \bmod p = \det K(A,v) \bmod p = 0$. Note that the latter equation holds only with the small probability $O(\log(np) / n^{h-1}p^h)$, (indeed, repeat the proof of Lemma 4.3 where K(A,v) replaces A, note that $\det K(A,v) \leq ||A||^{n^2}$ and recall that $h>3$). We will use the construction of the proof of Lemma 4.2 where K^* replaces A and where

$$p^* = ph \tag{4.6}$$

replaces p in the definition of W by (3.7) and (4.2). We choose h in (4.7) being the minimum integer such that

$$p^* > 2n\ ||K^*||. \tag{4.7}$$

This makes $p^* > p$ unless $p > 2n||K^*||$ but, on the other hand, p and p^* are represented with the same number of bits within a constant factor. Then (3.7) and (4.7) imply that the resulting matrices $W\,H^{-1}$ and K(W,v) are strongly diagonally dominant, so we may, indeed, apply the construction of the proof of Lemma 4.2 in order to compute det W and adj W. The reduction mod p^* would give us $\det K^* \bmod p^*$ and $\operatorname{adj} K^* \bmod p^*$; however, we reduce modulo p and arrive at the equations $\det K(A,v) \bmod p = (\det K^* \bmod p^*) \bmod p$ and $\operatorname{adj} K(A,v) \bmod p = (\operatorname{adj} K^* \bmod p^*) \bmod p$, see (4.6). This immediately gives us the desired matrix $K^{-1}(A,v) \bmod p$ unless (with a small probability) $\det K(A,v) = 0 \bmod p$.

Finally we use Newton's-Hensel's lifting to compute $K^{-1}(A,v)\, u \bmod p^{2^k}$ where $u = A^n v$ and

$$2^{k-1} < 2n \leq 2^k. \tag{4.8}$$

This defines the characteristic vector $c(A) \bmod p^{2^k}$.

The $O(n \log(n||A||) + 2^k \log p)$ -bit precision that we need in that computation, (see 4.4)), turns out to be the g-bit precision of (4.1) under (4.8), so the algorithm keeps us within the bounds prescribed by Theorem 1.3. Since $p^{2^k} \geq p^n > 2\,|\,c_j\,|$ for all j, we may recover the exact value of all the coefficients c_j of the characteristic polynomial of A. (4.8) and Lemma 4.2 imply that the subsequent evaluation of the matrix $B(k) = A^{-1} \bmod p^{2^k}$ does not increase the total parallel complexity. Multiplying the resulting matrix B(k) by c_n = det A and reducing the latter results mod p^n, we will obtain the matrix adj A mod p^n. From that matrix, we will easily recover adj A. It is immediately verified that these latter steps also keep us within the complexity bounds prescribed by Theorem 1.3. Q.E.D.

5. Solution Using O(log n) Steps and One Processor under a Special Computational Model

The complexity of the whole computation of det A and adj A is dominated by the complexity of O(log n) matrix multiplications (including here some matrix-vector multiplications). If the input matrix A is filled with integers, then all the operands of those multiplications are either nonnegative integer matrices or can be represented in the form (s/q)(U-W) where s and q are integers and U and W are nonnegative integer matrices. If we keep representing all the operands-matrices in this form while performing the computation, then all matrix multiplications (and additions) are reduced to the same operations with integer matrices. Using the special model of computation of Section 40 of [Pan, 84], compare also [Pan, 80], p. 12, (in that model nonnegative integer matrices can be cost-free represented by long integers and such long integers can be cost-free segmented to form matrices) we may reduce every nonnegative integer matrix multiplication/addition to a single multiplication/addition of two long integers. If we consider such an operation as one step performed on a single processor, then the whole evaluation of det A and adj A by our algorithms would require only O(log n) steps and one processor for arbitrary integer matrix A satisfying (1.2).

Acknowledgements. My old interest in computing the exact inverse of integer matrices via computing their approximate values (see [Pan 84,84a]) was revived due to my discussions with John Reif and then with Zvi Galil. Zvi Galil pointed out Lemma 4.3 of J. Schwartz and suggested the idea of the improvement from the straightforward time bound O(log d log(dn) log n) to O($\log^2$(dn)), see Remark 1.2. John Reif and then Erich Kaltofen pointed out the reference [Moenck and Carter, 79]. Zvi Galil, John Reif and a reviewer suggested several improvements of the original text.

References

Berkowitz, S., "On Computing the Determinant in Small Parallel Time Using a Small Number of Processors", *Information Processing Letters* 18, 147-150 (1984).

Bini, D., and V. Pan, "Fast Parallel Polynomial Division via Reduction to Triangular Toeplitz Matrix Inversion and to Polynomial Inversion Modulo a Power," to appear in *Information Processing Letters.*

Borodin, A., S. Cook and N. Pippenger, "Parallel Computation for Well-Endowed Rings and Space-Bounded Probabilistic Machines," *Information and Control* 58, 113-136 (1983).

Borodin, A., J. von zur Gathen, and J. Hopcroft, "Fast Parallel Matrix and GCD Computations", *Proc. 23-rd Ann. ACM FOCS,* 65-71 (1982) and *Information and Control* 53,5 241-256 (1982).

Borodin, A. and I. Munro, *The Computational Complexity of Algebraic and Numeric Problems,* American Elsevier, New York (1975).

Coppersmith, D. and S. Winograd, "On the Asymptotic Complexity of Matrix Multiplication", *SIAM J. on Computing* 11(3), 472-492 (1982).

Csanky, L., "Fast Parallel Matrix Inversion Algorithms", *SIAM J. on Computing* 5(4), 618-623 (1976).

Eberly, W., "Very Fast Parallel Matrix and Polynomial Arithmetic," *Proc. 25-th Ann. IEEE Symp. FOCS,* 21-30 (1984).

Galil, Z. and V. Pan, "Fast and Efficient Parallel Computation of Perfect Matching," Tech. Report , *Columbia University,* N.Y. (March 1985).

Gathen, I. von zur, "Parallel Algorithms for Algebraic Problems", *SIAM J. on Computing* 13, 4, 802-824 (1984).

Golub, G.H. and C.F. van Loan, *Matrix Computation,* The Johns Hopkins University Press, Baltimore (1983).

Ireland, K. and M. Rosen, *A Classical Introduction to Modern Number Theory,* Springer-Verlag (1982).

Keller, W., Fast Algorithms for the Characteristic Polynomial, Master's Thesis, *Institüt für Angewandte Mathematik, Univ. Zürich* (1982).

Knuth, D.E., *The Art of Computer Programming: Seminumerical Algorithms,* v.2, Addison-Wesley (1981).

Marcus, M. and H. Minc, *A Survey of Matrix Theory and Matrix Inequalities,* Allyn and Bacon, Boston (1964).

Moenck, R.T., and J.H. Carter, "Approximate Algorithms to Derive Exact Solutions to Systems of Linear Equations", *Proc. EUROSAM 1979,* Lecture Notes in Computer Science 72, 63-73, Springer (1979).

Pan, V., The Bit-Complexity of the Convolution of Vectors and of the DFT, Tech. Report TR-80-6, *Computer Science Dept., SUNY Albany,* New York, (May 1980).

Pan, V., *How to Multiply Matrices Faster,* Lecture Notes in Computer Science 179, Springer-Verlag, Berlin (1984).

Pan, V., "The Bit Complexity of Matrix Multiplication and of Related Computational Problems in Linear Algebra. The Segmented λ Algorithms", Nota Interna, *Dept. of Informatica, University of Pisa,* Italy (August 1984), to appear in *Computers and Mathematics (with Applications)* (1984a).

Pan, V., and J. Reif, Fast and Efficient Parallel Solution of Linear Systems, Tech. Report TR-02-85, *Center for Research in Computer Technology, Aiken Computation Laboratory, Harvard University* (1985), (Short version in *Proc. 17-th Ann. ACM Symp. on Theory of Computing,* 143-152, Providence, R.I. (1985)).

Preparata, F.P. and D.V. Sarwate, "An Improved Parallel Processor Bound in Fast Matrix Inversion", *Information Processing Letters* 7(3), 148-149 (1978).

Savage, J.E., *The Complexity of Computing,* John Wiley and Sons, N.Y. (1976).

Schwartz, J.T., "Fast Probabilistic Algorithms for Verification of Polynomial Identities," *J. of ACM* 27(4), 701-717 (1980).

Wilkinson, J.H., *The Algebraic Eigenvalue Problem,* Clarendon Press, Oxford (1965).

Yun, D.Y.Y., "Algebraic Algorithms Using p-adic Constructions", *Proc. 1976 ACM Symp. Symbolic and Algebraic Computation,* 248-259 (1976).

INDEX OF AUTHORS

Vol. 167: International Symposium on Programming. Proceedings, 1984. Edited by C. Girault and M. Paul. VI, 262 pages. 1984.

Vol. 168: Methods and Tools for Computer Integrated Manufacturing. Edited by R. Dillmann and U. Rembold. XVI, 528 pages. 1984.

Vol. 169: Ch. Ronse, Feedback Shift Registers. II, 1–2, 145 pages. 1984.

Vol. 171: Logic and Machines: Decision Problems and Complexity. Proceedings, 1983. Edited by E. Börger, G. Hasenjaeger and D. Rödding. VI, 456 pages. 1984.

Vol. 172: Automata, Languages and Programming. Proceedings, 1984. Edited by J. Paredaens. VIII, 527 pages. 1984.

Vol. 173: Semantics of Data Types. Proceedings, 1984. Edited by G. Kahn, D.B. MacQueen and G. Plotkin. VI, 391 pages. 1984.

Vol. 174: EUROSAM 84. Proceedings. 1984. Edited by J. Fitch. XI, 396 pages. 1984.

Vol. 175: A. Thayse, P-Functions and Boolean Matrix Factorization, VII, 248 pages. 1984.

Vol. 176: Mathematical Foundations of Computer Science 1984. Proceedings, 1984. Edited by M.P. Chytil and V. Koubek. XI, 581 pages. 1984.

Vol. 177: Programming Languages and Their Definition. Edited by C.B. Jones. XXXII, 254 pages. 1984.

Vol. 178: Readings on Cognitive Ergonomics – Mind and Computers. Proceedings, 1984. Edited by G.C. van der Veer, M.J. Tauber, T.R.G. Green and P. Gorny. VI, 269 pages. 1984.

Vol. 179: V. Pan, How to Multiply Matrices Faster. XI, 212 pages. 1984.

Vol. 180: Ada Software Tools Interfaces. Proceedings, 1983. Edited by P.J.L. Wallis. III, 164 pages. 1984.

Vol. 181: Foundations of Software Technology and Theoretical Computer Science. Proceedings, 1984. Edited by M. Joseph and R. Shyamasundar. VIII, 468 pages. 1984.

Vol. 182: STACS 85. 2nd Annual Symposium on Theoretical Aspects of Computer Science. Proceedings, 1985. Edited by K. Mehlhorn. VII, 374 pages. 1985.

Vol. 183: The Munich Project CIP. Volume I: The Wide Spectrum Language CIP-L. By the CIP Language Group. XI, 275 pages. 1985.

Vol. 184: Local Area Networks: An Advanced Course. Proceedings, 1983. Edited by D. Hutchison, J. Mariani and D. Shepherd. VIII, 497 pages. 1985.

Vol. 185: Mathematical Foundations of Software Development. Proceedings, 1985. Volume 1: Colloquium on Trees in Algebra and Programming (CAAP'85). Edited by H. Ehrig, C. Floyd, M. Nivat and J. Thatcher. XIV, 418 pages. 1985.

Vol. 186: Formal Methods and Software Development. Proceedings, 1985. Volume 2: Colloquium on Software Engineering (CSE). Edited by H. Ehrig, C. Floyd, M. Nivat and J. Thatcher. XIV, 455 pages. 1985.

Vol. 187: F.S. Chaghaghi, Time Series Package (TSPACK). III, 305 pages. 1985.

Vol. 188: Advances in Petri Nets 1984. Edited by G. Rozenberg with the cooperation of H. Genrich and G. Roucairol. VII, 467 pages. 1985.

Vol. 189: M.S. Sherman, Paragon. XI, 376 pages. 1985.

ı. 190: M.W. Alford, J.P. Ansart, G. Hommel, L. Lamport, B. Liskov, Mullery and F.B. Schneider, Distributed Systems. Edited by nd H.J. Siegert. VI, 573 pages. 1985.

ringer, A Survey of Verification Techniques for Parallel pages. 1985.

Infinite Words. Proceedings, 1984. Edited by 216 pages. 1985.

Proceedings, 1985. Edited by R. Parikh.

Vol. 194: Automata, Languages and Programming. Proceedings, 1985. Edited by W. Brauer. IX, 520 pages. 1985.

Vol. 195: H.J. Stüttgen, A Hierarchical Associative Processing System. XII, 273 pages. 1985.

Vol. 196: Advances in Cryptology: Proceedings 1984. Edited by G.R. Blakley and D. Chaum. IX, 491 pages. 1985.

Vol. 197: Seminar on Concurrency. Proceedings, 1984. Edited by S.D. Brookes, A.W. Roscoe and G. Winskel. X, 523 pages. 1985.

Vol. 198: A. Businger, PORTAL Language Description. VIII, 186 pages. 1985.

Vol. 199: Fundamentals of Computation Theory. Proceedings, 1985. Edited by L. Budach. XII, 533 pages. 1985.

Vol. 200: J.L.A. van de Snepscheut, Trace Theory and VLSI Design. VI, 0–140 pages. 1985.

Vol. 201: Functional Programming Languages and Computer Architecture. Proceedings, 1985. Edited by J.-P. Jouannaud. VI, 413 pages. 1985.

Vol. 202: Rewriting Techniques and Applications. Edited by J.-P. Jouannaud. VI, 441 pages. 1985.

Vol. 203: EUROCAL '85. Proceedings Vol. 1, 1985. Edited by B. Buchberger. V, 233 pages. 1985.

Vol. 204: EUROCAL '85. Proceedings Vol. 2, 1985. Edited by B.F. Caviness. XVI, 650 pages. 1985.

Vol. 205: P. Klint, A Study in String Processing Languages. VIII, 165 pages. 1985.

Vol. 206: Foundations of Software Technology and Theoretical Computer Science. Proceedings, 1985. Edited by S.N. Maheshwari. IX, 522 pages. 1985.